The Lonely Way
Volume 1

—◌◌◌—

As Luther once went *the lonely way* between Rome and
Spiritualism, so the Lutheran Church today stands
alone between the world powers of Roman Catholicism on the one hand and modern Protestantism on
the other. Her doctrine which teaches that the Spirit is
bound to the means of grace is as inconceivable to
modern people in the twentieth century as it was to
their predecessors in the sixteenth.

"The Lutheran Doctrine of the Office of the Ministry," 1943

THE LONELY WAY

SELECTED ESSAYS AND LETTERS

BY
HERMANN SASSE
VOLUME 1 (1927–1939)

Translated by Matthew C. Harrison,
together with Robert G. Bugbee, Lowell C. Green,
Gerald S. Krispin, Maurice E. Schild, and John R. Stephenson

With historical introductions and a biographical sketch
by Ronald R. Feuerhahn

SAINT LOUIS

This book was made possible by a generous grant
from the Marvin M. Schwan Charitable Foundation.

Wolfgang Sasse, son of Hermann Sasse, has graciously given permission to publish translations of his father's essays and letters for which he holds the copyright.

Permission to publish the translation "Where Christ Is, There Is the Church" was granted by *Internationale Kirchliche Zeitschrift*, Bern, Switzerland.

The translations of "The Confession of the Church" and "The Church and the Word of God" first appeared in *Logia*. They are reprinted by permission of *Logia: A Journal of Theology*, 15825 373rd Ave., Northville, SD 57465.

"Luther and the Teaching of the Reformation" © Geoffrey Bles, London. Used by permission.

Unless otherwise indicated, quotations from Scripture and the Lutheran Confessions are translations of the author's original.

Scripture quotations marked RSV are from the Revised Standard Version of the Bible, copyrighted 1946, 1952, © 1971, 1973. Used by permission.

Quotations marked KJV are from the King James or Authorized Version of the Bible.

Scripture quotations marked NKJV are taken from the New King James Version. Copyright © 1979, 1980, 1982 by Thomas Nelson, Inc. Used by permission. All rights reserved.

Quotations marked NIV are taken from the HOLY BIBLE, NEW INTERNATIONAL VERSION.® NIV.® Copyright © 1973, 1978, 1984 by International Bible Society. Used by permission of Zondervan Publishing House. All rights reserved.

Quotations from the Lutheran Confessions so indicated are from *The Book of Concord*, trans. and ed. Theodore G. Tappert, Philadelphia: Fortress Press, 1959.

The Symbol Greek and Hebraica fonts used to print this work are available from Linguist's Software, Inc., PO Box 580, Edmonds, WA 98020-0580; USA telephone (206) 775-1130.

Copyright © 2001 Concordia Publishing House
3558 S. Jefferson Avenue, St. Louis, MO 63118-3968
Manufactured in the United States of America

Library of Congress Cataloging-in-Publication Data

Sasse, Hermann, 1895–1976
    [Selections. English. 2002]
    The lonely way : selected essays and letters / by Hermann Sasse ; translated by Matthew C. Harrison ... [et al.] ; with historical introductions and a biographical sketch by Ronald R. Feuerhahn.
    p. cm.
    ISBN 0-570-01640-1
    1. Theology. 2. Lutheran Church—Doctrines. 3. Christian union—Lutheran Church.
4. Sasse, Hermann, 1895–1976.—Correspondence. I. Feuerhahn, Ronald R., 1937–   . II. Title.
    BX8080.S18 A25 2002
    230'.41—dc21   2001006197

---

1   2   3   4   5   6   7   8   9   10   10   09   08   07   06   05   04   03   02   01

CONTENTS

—⟋∾∾⟍—

Volume 2 (1941–1976) partial list of essays:

—⟋∾∾⟍—

Principal Abbreviations
and Works Cited

AC	Augsburg Confession
Ap	Apology of the Augsburg Confession
AThR	*Anglican Theological Review*
BC	*The Book of Concord: The Confessions of the Evangelical Lutheran Church*. Edited by T. G. Tappert. Philadelphia: Fortress, 1959
BS	*Die Bekenntnisschriften der evangelisch-lutherischen Kirche*. 6th ed. Göttingen: Vandenhoeck & Ruprecht, 1967
ChrCent	*Christian Century*
CTM	*Concordia Theological Monthly*
EA	Erlangen Ausgabe ("edition") of Luther's works. *Dr. Martin Luther's Sämmtliche Werke*. 67 vols. Erlangen: C. Heyder, 1826–1857
Enders/Enders-Kawerau	Ernst Ludwig Enders, followed by Peter Gustav Kawerau, ed., *Dr. Martin Luther's Briefwechsel*
Ep	Epitome of the Formula of Concord
ET	English translation
FC	Formula of Concord
Hopf number	Bibliographical number assigned to Sasse's writings by Friedrich Wilhelm Hopf in *ISC*. The Hopf and Huss numbers are given for the essays in this volume to aid in identification and because the titles of some of Sasse's works are very similar to each other
Huss Collection	The archive materials from Hermann Sasse's own collection held by Pfarrer Hans-Siegfried Huss of Würzburg, Germany
Huss number	Bibliographical number assigned to Sasse's writings by Ronald R. Feuerhahn in *Hermann Sasse: A Bibliography*. Lanham, Md.: Scarecrow, 1995
ISC	*In Statu Confessionis: Gesammelte Aufsätze von Hermann Sasse*. Edited by Friedrich Wilhelm Hopf. 2 vols. Berlin, 1966, 1975–1976
KJV	King James Version of the Bible
LC	Large Catechism of Martin Luther
Lutheran Cyclopedia	*Lutheran Cyclopedia*. Edited by Erwin L. Lueker. Rev. ed. St. Louis: Concordia, 1975
Lutheran Worship	*Lutheran Worship*. St. Louis: Concordia, 1982
LW	*Luther's Works*. American ed. 55 vols. St. Louis: Concordia; Philadelphia: Fortress, 1955–1986
New Schaff-Herzog	*The New Schaff-Herzog Encyclopedia of Religious Knowledge*. Edited by S. M. Jackson. 12 vols. New York: Funk & Wagnalls, 1911
NIV	New International Version of the Bible
NKJV	New King James Version of the Bible

NT	New Testament
ODCC	*The Oxford Dictionary of the Christian Church.* Edited by F. L. Cross and E. A. Livingstone. 3d ed. Oxford: Oxford University Press, 1997
OT	Old Testament
RGG¹	*Die Religion in Geschichte und Gegenwart.* 1st ed. 5 vols. Tübingen: Mohr, 1909–1913
RGG²	*Die Religion in Geschichte und Gegenwart.* 2d ed. 6 vols. Tübingen: Mohr, 1927–1932
RSV	Revised Standard Version of the Bible
RTR	*Reformed Theological Review*
SA	Smalcald Articles
SC	Small Catechism of Martin Luther
SD	Solid Declaration of the Formula of Concord
St. Louis ed.	St. Louis ed. of Luther's works. *Dr. Martin Luthers Sämmtliche Schriften.* Edited by J. G. Walch. 23 vols. in 24. St. Louis: Concordia, 1881–1910
Str-B	Strack, H. L., and P. Billerbeck. *Kommentar zum Neuen Testament aus Talmud und Midrasch.* 6 vols. Munich: C. H. Beck, 1922–1961
The Lutheran Hymnal	*The Lutheran Hymnal.* St. Louis: Concordia, 1941
Treatise	Treatise on the Power and Primacy of the Pope
Triglotta	*Concordia Triglotta: The Symbolic Books of the Evangelical Lutheran Church.* St. Louis: Concordia, 1921
WA	Weimar Ausgabe ("edition") of Luther's works. *Luthers Werke: Kritische Gesamtausgabe. [Schriften.]* 65 vols. Weimar: H. Böhlau, 1883–1993
WA Br	Weimar Ausgabe Briefwechsel ("correspondence"). *Luthers Werke: Kritische Gesamtausgabe. Briefwechsel.* 18 vols. Weimar: H. Böhlau, 1930–1985
WA TR	Weimar Ausgabe Tischreden ("table talk"). *Luthers Werke: Kritische Gesamtausgabe. Tischreden.* 6 vols. Weimar: H. Böhlau, 1912–1921
ZNW	*Zeitschrift für die neutestamentliche Wissenschaft und die Kunde der älteren Kirche*

The following initials are used with the footnotes to indicate who wrote them. Initials are used also on the contents page to indicate translators of the essays.

HS	Hermann Sasse
MH	Matthew Harrison
RF	Ronald Feuerhahn
RB	Robert Bugbee
LG	Lowell Green
GK	Gerald Krispin
MS	Maurice Schild
JS	John Stephenson

TRANSLATOR'S PREFACE

As much as he criticized Rome, Hermann Sasse envied the Roman Catholic Church's sense of time. On a trip to Rome he stopped to visit Augustin Cardinal Bea. Sasse was apologetic for taking the cardinal's time with such a visit. Bea responded, "I always have time, only no time to waste."

It seemed to Sasse that the Lutheran churches of the world were always rushing matters, establishing dogma without proper historical and exegetical deliberation. And Sasse was witness to more than a few such decisions, such as the Barmen Declaration, which ultimately compromised the confession of the church. On the other hand, it was the corrective of a broad perspective of dogma through the ages which Sasse, throughout his career, strove to give the church. His message was always urgent but never faithless, for he was convinced that the church has a future because Jesus Christ has a future.

Sasse's perspective is needed in the church today. It certainly was helpful to me as a pastor. As a young and eager seminary graduate, I headed off to my first parish, St. Peter's Lutheran, Westgate, Iowa. In my own struggles to bridge the gap between zealous orthodoxy and wise pastoral practice, Sasse became a godsend, the single most influential literary resource for the molding of my own pastoral practice. Sasse helped me move from talking about the Gospel to delivering it. Sasse taught me that there is no contradiction between confessional Lutheran fidelity and true ecumenicity. Sasse made it all so profoundly simple, concrete, and practical.

At the seminary my dear father in Christ, Professor Kurt Marquart, had introduced many of us to Sasse, who had been his own colleague, father in Christ, and confessional Lutheran mentor during Marquart's Australian years. I then spent a year studying at Sasse's seminary (years after his death) and read every bit of Sasse I could get hold of. In my STM studies at Concordia Theological Seminary in Fort Wayne, I delved into Sasse's German. So I developed the habit of translating several pages of Sasse's work nearly every day over the course of a four-year pastorate in a little Iowa farming village. This I continued, albeit less regularly, as I continued my pastoral ministry at Zion Lutheran Church, Fort Wayne.

Through all of these studies and pastorates, Sasse provided perspective. His sweeping historical-dogmatic treatises, at once utterly orthodox and truly ecumenical, gave me doctrinal confidence, confessional depth, and historical sensibility as I dealt not only with my own people, but also with the clergy and laity of other denominations. All of what I was reading in Sasse, like the Lutheran Confessions themselves, emphasized the point of all orthodox dogma and practice as loving pastoral care. Sasse's breadth helped provide a very young and inexperienced pastor with what he sorely needed to be a true pastor of Christ's people: confessional fidelity and patience.

There is a long history to the church's dogma and practice. Where that dogma and practice have gone awry, only patient teaching and loving practice can possibly right it again, and this only as God grants by his grace. Entire eras have their movements and weaknesses and inabilities to perceive the truth of this or that reality of NT and confessional Lutheran Christianity. In such eras the faithful pastor must have the biblical and historical tools to be able to recognize the circumstances in which he finds himself, to diagnose the malady, and then patiently to meet the challenge, leaving the results to Christ.

The Sasse essays included in this first volume were profoundly influential to me in all the aspects I have mentioned. Many of these papers were written in the white-hot heat of the *Kirchenkampf*—the struggle of the church under Nazism. And if Sasse could maintain such confessional fidelity, evident ecumenical spirit, and faithful confidence in the Lord of the church, even under Hitler, then I could patiently meet the challenge of lovingly standing firm in the comparatively meager challenges I faced in the parish.

In June of 2000 I visited the grave of Sasse on the south side of the city of Adelaide, South Australia. The stone bears this epitaph: *Tuis fidelibus Domine, vita non tollitur, sed mutatur* ("For your faithful, O Lord, life is not taken away, it is changed"). He had chosen the words himself. Hermann Otto Eric Sasse was taken to be with Christ in 1976. We rejoice now that far from being taken away from the church which he so loved, Sasse's voice now continues to live, even if changed by translation through this publication. And it just may be that Sasse's voice will be heard today for the cause of confessional Lutheranism to a far greater extent than ever before. Such posthumous service is all the more meaningful and appreciated in light of what was for him most often a very "lonely way."

My heartfelt appreciation to the many that have in many different ways made this project a reality. Ron Feuerhahn has for over a decade now been a dear friend, mentor, and *Amtsbruder*. He has provided us all with an invaluable wealth of information on Sasse, and happily, he kindly consented to continue to do so for this volume. Sincere thanks also to Dr. Norman Nagel for his decades of interest in Sasse and for his constant encouragement. I am deeply thankful to and for my dear brother in Christ Paul McCain, whose enthusiasm for reading fresh translations of Sasse has never flagged. He made time to edit some of the essays of this work and approached the Marvin M. Schwan Charitable Foundation for a grant. My sincere thanks to the Schwan Foundation for enabling us to produce, at reasonable cost to the reader, this volume and the second which will soon follow. And here too I must thank our sainted President A. L. Barry for his support for the project. May his legacy of confessional fidelity endure like Sasse's. I heartily thank the others who gladly provided translations for this volume: Maurice Schild, Lowell Green, Gerald Krispin, Robert Bugbee, and John Stephenson. The capable staff at CPH has been a pure pleasure to work with, especially Fritz Baue, who has guided this project through the long process of publication, and Julene Dumit, who meticulously copyedited the manuscript. I should be remiss were I to fail to mention the constant companionship and strength I receive from one Kathy Harrison, the greatest single First Article gift of my life. Though the many essays of this book look toward the past, they do so with the intent of building a bridge to the future of a confessional Lutheran Church, and that for the sake of my dear sons, Matthew M. L. and Mark M. C. Harrison, as well as generations to come.

Translating is challenging business. Thankfully, Sasse's German is straightforward. Others have checked the translation here and there, but I shall not mention their names so that responsibility for any deficiencies, and I am sure there are plenty, falls squarely in my lap. Those who actually knew and heard Sasse will find my translations less than true to Sasse's own unique literary and oral style. I plead the indulgence of such brothers. I never knew or heard the man. That stated, I should like to dedicate this volume of translations to the Reverends Bruce Adams, John Kleinig, Andrew Pfeiffer, Avito DaCosta, David Buck, and Mark Hampel (all beloved brothers in Christ) and to the entire ministerium of the Lutheran Church of Australia. The way may be lonely, but *ne desperemus!* The Lord still prays for his church.

Matthew C. Harrison
Lent IV, 2001

HERMANN SASSE (1895–1976)
A BIOGRAPHICAL SKETCH

Hermann Sasse has captured our attention for several good reasons. First, we are drawn to his mastery of history and the breadth of his knowledge. His synthesis of disciplines and powers of analysis give his work authority. As he described one of his own teachers, so his students might have said of him that he was a great *polyhistor*—a man of great and varied learning. This learning is expressed in writing that is lucid, in contrast to much theological literature of his day. For depth of insight and clarity of expression, Sasse is like Luther and Walther.

The second and more important reason is that we appreciate the forthrightness of his confession. Like one of his ancestors, Valentin Löscher (Timotheus Verinius),[1] he opposed unionism and Pietism. He had a sense of church and churchmanship which, after his early liberal training at the University of Berlin, grew into a conscious and confident assertion of the confessions of the Evangelical Lutheran Church. In this lonely vocation he gave encouragement to many others, often telling students that they must reclaim these confessions in their own lives.

Sasse was a good student. He attended several *Gymnasia* before matriculating at the University of Berlin in the summer semester, 1913.[2] There he was inscribed in two faculties simultaneously—theology and classical philology.[3] Berlin was at the height of its powers then, and young Sasse relished the experience. The faculty included some of the greats of modern theology: Adolf von Harnack, Karl Holl, Reinhold Seeberg, Julius Kaftan and, of course, Adolf Deissmann, who

---

[1] Valentin Ernst Löscher (1673–1749) studied at Wittenberg and Jena. He was the last great orthodox opponent of Pietism, syncretism, and unionism before these swamped what had been an orthodox Lutheran Church in Germany. While superintendent at Dresden, he wrote a powerful critique of Pietism under the pseudonym Timotheus Verinus: *Vollständiger Timotheus Verinus, oder, Darlegung der Wahrheit und des Friedens in denen bitzherigen Pietistischen Streitigkeiten* (*The Complete Timotheus Verinus, or, a Statement of the Truth and a Call for Peace in the Present Pietistic Controversy*; part 1, 1718; part 2, 1721; ET: *The Complete Timotheus Verinus* [trans. James L. Langebartels and Robert J. Koester; Milwaukee: Northwestern, 1998]).

There is a rather detailed genealogy tracing the Sasse family link in the collection of documents of Wolfgang Sasse, Hermann Sasse's elder son.

[2] *The Bond* (Immanuel Seminary, Adelaide) 3 (July 1949): 9.

[3] "Reminiscences of an Elderly Student," *Tangara* (Luther Seminary, Adelaide) 9 (1976): 4–5; Biographical Note, File of the Dean of Faculty, Archives of the Theological Faculty, University of Erlangen.

would later become Sasse's *Doktorvater*. Many years later Sasse described his work under Deissmann:

> Thus my studies, mainly centered in New Testament and Patristics, were divided between two loyalties. My main work I did with Adolf Deissmann. From him I learned not only the love for the language of the New Testament and for the Greek speaking church, but also a deep appreciation of the Septuagint as well as the mission of the Synagogue which preceded the mission of the Church in East and West. My main teachers in Church history were Harnack and Holl.[4] Old Testament I did with Baudissin, Gressmann (who later as dean conferred my first academic degree on me) and Eissfeld. . . . My great teacher in Systematic Theology was Heinrich Scholz, who later, as colleague and friend of Karl Barth in Münster, taught Philosophy, and helped, as one of the great *polyhistors* of our time, to lay the philosophical foundations of modern mathematics and physics.[5]

Sasse then recalled, perhaps whimsically: "The gaps in Practical Theology were later filled at the *Kriegsschule* ("officers training school") and in the first years in the ministry."[6] His military service came between the two important exams of his education. Again, with some wit he recalled: "Since the army, in the beginning of the war, had committed the great blunder to believe that a world war could be won (or lost) without my participation, I had been able to reach just the minimum of time required."[7]

He entered the army in October 1916 and was assigned to an infantry regiment. In just over a month he saw battle.[8] As a sergeant, he led his men into what was arguably the bloodiest battle of World War I. He later recalled:

> And then we went up to Passchendaele. We were a hundred and fifty men, fully equipped and a full company. On the sixth we came back and six men reported. The others were killed or had disappeared in the fire, the water, and the gas of one of the worst battles of the First World War.[9]

---

[4] Sasse had Adolf von Harnack for early church history and Karl Holl for nineteenth-century theology. Sasse once said, "It is easier to live by Harnack's theology than to die by it" (Heino O. Kadai, "Professor D. Hermann Sasse: Congratulations for a Septuagenerian [*sic*]," *The Springfielder* 29.2 [Spring 1965]: 5).

[5] "Reminiscences of an Elderly Student." In addition to Harnack and Holl, Sasse mentions Adolf Deissmann, NT exegesis; Wolf Wilhelm Graf von Baudissin, OT exegesis; Hugo Gressmann, OT exegesis; Otto Eissfeldt, OT theology; Heinrich Scholz, systematic theology. For a full list of the faculty, see *Kirchliches Jahrbuch für die evangelischen Landeskirchen Deutschlands 1916* (ed. J. Schneider; Gütersloh: C. Bertelsmann, 1916), 583.

[6] "Reminiscences of an Elderly Student" (parenthesis in original). Since Sasse was not an officer, "military academy," a translation for *Kriegsschule* found in some dictionaries, might be more accurate here.

[7] "Reminiscences of an Elderly Student."

[8] Biographical Note, File of Dean of Faculty, Archives of the Theological Faculty, University of Erlangen. The German expression used, *im Felde*, indicates combat.

[9] "The Impact of Bultmannism on American Lutheranism, with Special Reference to His Demythologization of the New Testament," *Lutheran Synod Quarterly* 5.4 (June 1965): 4.

After being discharged, Sasse returned to the University of Berlin to pursue graduate work in NT under Adolf Deissmann, receiving his doctorate in 1923. During that time he was ordained in the Church of the Old Prussian Union in 1920 and served as assistant pastor to parishes in Berlin. His first full pastorate was at Oranienburg bei Berlin, 1921–1928. There he met his wife, Charlotte; they were married in 1924.[10] From 1928 to 1933 he was the social pastor connected to the noted St. Marienkirche in Berlin.[11]

During the academic year of 1925–1926, he was an exchange student at Hartford Theological Seminary, Hartford, Connecticut. He later observed that it was during this period, through his contact with the United Lutheran Church in America, that he became a conscious Lutheran. Here he began reading the works of the leaders of the nineteenth-century confessional renewal, such as Löhe, Vilmar, and Walther.

From 1927 on Sasse was involved in the Ecumenical Movement. He participated in the First World Conference on Faith and Order in Lausanne in 1927 and soon became a member not only of its Continuation Committee but also its Executive Committee. His ecumenical commitment was quite different from most, however. He later wrote to a colleague, "I believed strongly that the future of Christianity in Germany and in the world depended on those churches which still dared to confess their dogma."[12]

In September 1932, as editor of a noted yearbook for all Protestant pastors in Germany, he published an essay on the church situation of the previous year.[13] In that essay he directly criticized the National Socialist party. That was nearly half a year before Hitler became chancellor of Germany. From that time on Sasse was marked as an enemy of the Nazis, who tried at various times to limit his advancement.

The following year was momentous for Germany and for Sasse as well. Hitler was made chancellor at the end of January. By July the German Evangelical Church (*Deutsche Evangelische Kirche*) was formed. That was the attempt by the new government to form a united Protestant church throughout all Germany. Meanwhile Sasse had been called to the University of Erlangen as professor. The minister of education for the new regime had threatened to halt the move but let it go through with a warning to Sasse.

Early in August 1933, Pastor Friedrich von Bodelschwingh, director of the famous institutions at Bethel in Bielefeld, Westphalia, received two independent

---

[10] They had three children. The eldest, Wolfgang, lives in Melbourne. Maria died on the day of her birth in December 1930, and Hans, the youngest, died at Eastertide 1982.

[11] Concerns for social ministry are reflected, for example, in the essay "The Social Doctrine of the Augsburg Confession and Its Significance for the Present," 1930, found in this collection.

[12] Klaas Runia, "Dr. Hermann Sasse 'In Statu Confessionis,'" *RTR* 27.1 (January/April 1968): 1.

[13] "Die Kirche und die politischen Mächte der Zeit," part 2 of "Kirchliche Zeitlage," in *Kirchliches Jahrbuch* (ed. Hermann Sasse; Gütersloh: C. Bertelsmann, 1932), especially 65–66.

appeals from Berlin—one from a "circle of young theologians," the other from a "circle of younger Berlin theology students." Both called for a confession to address the crisis of the time. Both asked Bodelschwingh to arrange this venture. Both appeals requested the same men for the task of writing such a new confession: Dietrich Bonhoeffer of Berlin and Sasse, now of Erlangen.[14] The selection of these men (and Pastor Jacobi of Berlin who was requested in one of the letters) was perhaps natural: they "were personally associated with one another and they had all spoken out against the introduction of the Aryan Paragraph in the church."[15]

While the working circle was to be enlarged, it was Bonhoeffer and Sasse who would be the chief authors of the confession—at least of its draft edition and the subsequent August Confession.[16] The basic approach reported by Bodelschwingh was to "take a position on the contemporary questions from the evidence of the Lutheran Confessions."[17] Both men were noted for their loyalty to the Lutheran Confessions. In the case of Sasse it was said that he combined a deeply held confessional Lutheranism with a passion for Christian unity.[18] The venture was described by Sasse as "the work of a happy collaboration"[19]—a sentiment echoed by Bonhoeffer in a letter from Bethel to his grandmother on August 20. There followed two weeks of intense work so that the draft copy and a revised August Confession were completed by the end of the month. This assessment of the August Confession has been offered by Klaus Scholder:

> The original version of the Bethel confession remains a brilliant, sharp and impressive witness to what theological effort was still capable of achieving in the summer of 1933—indeed specifically because of the great German Christian upsurge in German theology at this time. Ponderous though it was and loaded with numerous passages from the Bible, from Luther, and above all from confessional texts, this confession was nevertheless theologically and politically clearer and more exact in some passages than the famous Barmen declaration of May, 1934.[20]

It is interesting to note Karl Barth's reaction to the Bethel document. When Bodelschwingh invited him to comment on the August Confession, Barth questioned "whether a Lutheran confession was enough for the present, or whether it

---

[14] Guy C. Carter, *Confession at Bethel, August 1933—Enduring Witness: The Formation, Revision and Significance of the First Full Theological Confession of the Evangelical Church Struggle in Nazi Germany* (Ph.D. diss., Marquette University, 1987), 61–62.

[15] Carter, *Confession at Bethel*, 66.

[16] Carter, *Confession at Bethel*, 74.

[17] Carter, *Confession at Bethel*, 71.

[18] Carter, *Confession at Bethel*, 78.

[19] Eberhard Bethge, *Dietrich Bonhoeffer: Man of Vision, Man of Courage* (New York: Harper & Row, 1970; Fountain Edition, 1977), 232.

[20] Klaus Scholder, *The Churches and the Third Reich* (Philadelphia: Fortress, 1987), 1:456.

was not rather necessary 'to work through the draft together so that it . . . could appear before the public as an Evangelical confession of faith.' "[21] Barth—who enjoyed enormous influence in theological circles—eventually got his wish. Bethel prepared the way for Barmen.

Doubtless one of the most famous and significant documents to come out of the *Kirchenkampf* ("church struggle") during the Third Reich was the Barmen Declaration/Confession of 1934. While the final document was chiefly the work of Karl Barth, Sasse had been involved right up to the end. It was Sasse's bishop, Hans Meiser, territorial bishop of Bavaria, who requested Sasse to become involved. The bishop was concerned to safeguard the Lutheran character of the planned declaration. The document to be presented to the meeting at Barmen at the end of May 1934 was therefore passed back and forth between Barth for the Reformed and Sasse for the Lutherans.

In the end, the failure of the Lutheran leadership at Barmen secured the triumph of Barth's position. The Reformed had demanded that the statement of the synod be a common confession of all—Union, Reformed, and Lutheran—insisting that it was a time when all Christians must be seen to stand together. Barth's slogan was "the act of confessing is more important than the content." For Sasse, however, this was impossible: "These clauses could under no condition be adopted by the synod as a whole, because with this resolution the synod lays claim to the teaching office of the Lutheran and Reformed congregations."[22]

When Sasse saw what was planned for the final plenary meeting of the synod, he asked—and received from his bishop—permission to leave. For Sasse this event represented the collapse of Lutheranism in Germany. Between Barmen in 1934 and the formation of the *Evangelische Kirche in Deutschland* ("Evangelical Church in Germany"; EkiD) in 1948, confessional Lutheranism ceased in the German territorial churches.[23] In a tribute to Sasse, Hermann Dietzfelbinger, successor to Meiser as bishop of the Bavarian Territorial Church, writes:

> The EKiD, according to Sasse's opinion, meant the end of the Lutheran *Landeskirchen* ["territorial churches"] in Germany, and with that a considerable weakening of the Lutheran Church in the whole world. . . . Today, therefore, one reads Sasse with new eyes in this regard as well as in regard to his passionate attacks against not only a few of us.[24]

Sasse's critique was directed particularly at Karl Barth, whose mistaken assumption that the church can preserve its confession and also embrace the

---

[21]   Scholder, *The Churches and the Third Reich*, 1:458.

[22]   "Das Bekenntnis der lutherischen Kirche und die Barmer Theologische Erklärung," *ISC*, 1:281.

[23]   Sasse gives one of the most explicit accounts of Barmen and his role there in the essay "Union and Confession" of 1936, found in this collection.

[24]   Hermann Dietzfelbinger, "Aus Treue zum Bekenntnis Hermann Sasses Vermächtnis," *Lutherisches Monatsheft* 6.1 (1977): 7 (trans. Kathryn Feuerhahn).

Prussian Union is the same error as that of Frederick William III in 1834. Considering the way in which the Barmen Declaration came about, it is *Schwärmerei* ("Enthusiasm, Fanaticism") insofar as it makes the Union to be a work of God rather than a work of people.[25]

Within two years, certainly by 1935, the so-called "Confessing Movement" within the German churches was split between Lutherans and Barthians. The title *Bekennende Bewegung* ("Confessing Movement") or *Bekennende Kirche* ("Confessing Church") was chosen to reflect the Barthian "act of confessing" principle. The Lutherans would have preferred *Bekenntnis Kirche* ("Confessional Church"), giving emphasis to the role of the historic confessional writings. Nevertheless, for a period even the Lutheran group continued to use the title themselves. From 1936–1938 Sasse was coeditor of a series of publications under the title Bekennende Kirche.[26]

It was the growing influence of Barth which, for the Erlangen theologians, threatened Lutheranism as much as anything during that time. Sasse's essays reflected that concern more and more. For the English translation of his book *Was heißt lutherisch*, he prepared a new chapter called "Lutheran Doctrine and the Modern Reformed Theology of Karl Barth."[27] However, the Barthian model for the German church would carry the day following the war. As Clifford Nelson observes:

> Lutherans in Germany and other countries resisted giving the Barmen Declaration status equal to the confessional statements of the sixteenth century. Whether Barmen was a "significant historic event" (Lutheran) or a churchly "confessional" statement (Confessing Church) was the subject of debate which caused a rift in Evangelical churches during the remainder of the Nazi regime and which extended into the era of postwar reorganization of German church life.[28]

The postwar years were almost more traumatic for Sasse and his family than the years under the Nazis. There were of course real and daily hardships facing

[25] In August 1936 Sasse published two essays with this critique, "Wider die Schwarmgeisterei" ("Against Fanaticism"; found in this volume) and "Wider das Schwärmertum," *Allgemeine Evangelisch-Lutherische Kirchenzeitung* 69.33 (August 14, 1936): 773–81.

[26] Sasse was coeditor in association with Georg Merz and Christian Stoll of Bekennende Kirche, volumes 41/42 to 59/60 (1936–1938), published by Chr. Kaiser in Munich. Four essays from that series are reprinted in this volume: "The Lutheran Confessions and the *Volk*" (1933); "Church Government and Secular Authority according to Lutheran Doctrine" (1935); "Union and Confession" (1936); and "Church and Lord's Supper: An Essay on the Understanding of the Sacrament of the Altar" (1938).

[27] *Here We Stand: Nature and Character of the Lutheran Faith* (trans. Theodore G. Tappert; New York: Harper & Bros., 1938), 153–70; (2d ed.; Minneapolis: Augsburg, 1946), 153–70; (3d ed.; Adelaide: Lutheran Publishing House, 1987), 161–78. The book has also been translated into Norwegian and Japanese; a Chinese translation was never published.

[28] E. Clifford Nelson, *The Rise of World Lutheranism: An American Perspective* (Philadelphia: Fortress, 1982), 329.

them—starvation and freezing winters without coal. On the other hand, things appeared to have improved dramatically with regard to Sasse's career. Not only was he made full professor—a position he was supposed to have when he arrived in 1933 but which was denied him by the Nazi authorities—but he was also appointed prorector of the university. This came at the insistence of the occupying American military government. Sasse, having taken a clear anti-Nazi stand, was deemed to be a safe choice. He was called upon by the occupation authorities to offer an opinion on the political stance of his colleagues in the theological faculty. This was supposed to be a confidential memo, but nevertheless it became public. "What Sasse wrote concerning his colleagues conforms with the facts," observed one of his fellow professors.[29] Sasse's comments cost no one his position. Nevertheless this process of de-Nazification created a painful barrier between him and his colleagues.

But while that personal burden—along with the hardships of poor health and the lack of heating and food in the grim postwar days—was great, perhaps even greater pain was caused for Sasse by the course of church affairs. He had hoped that the crisis of the war would give opportunity for Lutheran renewal. Instead, the formation of the *Evangelische Kirche in Deutschland* was a great disappointment for him. In his view it suffered the same misconception as Barmen: it was the triumph of unconfessional Barthian ecclesiology.

The Erlangen professor finally withdrew, resigning his post as *Ordinarius* (full professor) and his membership of the Bavarian Church. He joined the *Evangelisch-lutherische (altlutherische) Kirche*, an independent or "free" church which had formed in reaction to the Prussian Union. A day (literally hours) before receiving a call to Concordia Seminary, St. Louis, he accepted the call of the United Evangelical Lutheran Church of Australia (UELCA) to be professor of church history at its Immanuel Seminary (later renamed Luther Seminary), North Adelaide, Australia. He was installed in this new office on October 12, 1949.

In his correspondence in later years he frequently spoke of the great limitations in this new setting, especially in the area of library resources. He was forced to end his research on further articles for the Kittel *Wörterbuch* (*Theological Dictionary of the New Testament*). But the new situation provided new challenges, chief of which was the union of the two Lutheran churches in Australia. He related to his American friend Herman Preus that this was one of the main reasons he had gone to Australia. As a UELCA member of the Intersynodical Committee, he

[29] Walther von Loewenich, *Erlebte Theologie: Begegnungen, Erfahrungen, Erwägungen* (Munich, 1979), 134. This conflict was to be waged even in the United States. See the charges of Sasse's colleague Hermann Strathmann and others in *The Lutheran* (Philadelphia) 28.48 (August 28, 1946): 13–14, 37, and *ChrCent* 63.39 (September 25, 1946): 1152–53, and the defense offered by Sasse, *The Lutheran* 29.16 (January 15, 1947): 35, and others, *The Lutheran* 29.1 (marked as 28.53; October 2, 1946): 32; *ChrCent* 64.7 (February 12, 1947): 209; *CTM* 18.4 (April 1947): 301–2.

was instrumental in preparing for the merger—achieved in 1966—with the Evangelical Lutheran Church of Australia, forming the Lutheran Church of Australia. From this outpost of the Christian world, Sasse also commenced his *Briefe an lutherische Pastoren* ("Letters to Lutheran Pastors"), a series of essays published by his disciple and friend in Germany Friedrich Wilhelm Hopf.[30]

Professor Sasse's own words briefly summarize his estimation of the transitional period of his life. Describing in 1948 the situation of what it was like for a confessionally minded pastor in the Bavarian Church, he explains his resignation and planned move to Australia:

> All the men who cannot give up the Formula of Concord—which is among the official confessions of the Church of Bavaria—must either go or subscribe to the new church laws with a broken conscience. This is the reason why I accepted the first call which came to me, and that was the call from Australia. . . . You know—and your friends know it also—that I am not a fanatic. I spent more than twenty years in the Ecumenical Movement. I gave more time to it than any other theologian in this country. But since this movement has become a means to further the political plans of Geneva I cannot take part in it any longer. During the Third Reich the party and the *Kirchliches Aussenamt* ["Church's Foreign Office"] prevented me from attending ecumenical conferences. Since 1945, Niemöller and Barth have been doing the same. Can you understand that I am longing for a country in which the Lutheran Church is still free? I shall go—if my plans can be carried out— to one of the smallest and poorest Lutheran churches. My Bavarian government is trying to keep me here. They are prepared to pay me the highest salary a German professor can get. But if I see the distress of my students I must go, and I hope that God will show me the way. *Weg hast du allerwegen, an Mitteln fehlt dir's nicht,* ["Thy hand is never shortened, All things must serve Thy might"],[31] as we sing with Paul Gerhardt.[32]

From Australia Sasse's influence as a teacher of the church was perhaps even greater than it had been in Germany. Through the *Briefe* and other essays, published in journals of growing diversity, he was teaching an expanding number of pastors and church leaders. While he was no longer associated with the Faith and Order Movement after 1950, he was now involved in an even more ecumenical scene. In Australia, more of his essays were published in Reformed journals than in Lutheran. Most of the earlier *Briefe* were translated into English within months of appearing. Some were translated into Norwegian and Swedish.

---

[30] Hopf had also left the Bavarian Church to join the *Evangelisch-lutherische (altlutherische) Kirche*. He published *Lutherische Blätter* chiefly as a vehicle for the *Briefe* and for reprints of earlier essays by Sasse. The *Briefe* began appearing in 1948, before Sasse left Germany. Letters 1–40 are to be published in English translation by the Lutheran Heritage Association.

[31] Translation from *The Lutheran Hymnal* 520, stanza 4.

[32] Letter to Herman Preus, November 27, 1948, American Lutheran Church Archives, St. Paul, Minn.

Once Sasse moved to the English-speaking world, he discovered a lacuna in his theological work—the doctrine of the sacred Scriptures.[33] He devoted himself to that study more and more in this period. It would prove to be one of—if not *the*—most controversial subjects in his work. It became a work in process. *Brief* number 14, "On the Doctrine *de Scriptura Sacra*" (August 1950) was so controversial that it was the only writing which Sasse withdrew.

His personal correspondence was voluminous. He wrote church presidents (e.g., John W. Behnken of The Lutheran Church—Missouri Synod), university professors (e.g., Leiv Aalen, Oslo), seminary professors (e.g., F. E. Mayer, St. Louis), pastors, and students. One of the most remarkable exchanges was that with a young pastor and graduate student in Sweden, Tom Hardt. Between the first exchange in 1958 until Sasse's death in 1976 Sasse wrote almost weekly.

Sasse developed friendships with many churchmen in Australia and became honorary president of the Inter-Varsity Christian Fellowship. He was a member of the committee in dialog with the Roman Catholic Church in Australia and was invited to the Vatican by Augustin Cardinal Bea. An extensive correspondence followed, especially with Bea's secretary, Father Schmidt. Some have conjectured that Sasse's intense interest in the Roman Church was due to the fact that his younger son, Hans, converted to Roman Catholicism in Adelaide. In addition, Sasse maintained close contact with The Lutheran Church—Missouri Synod, especially with its Springfield (now Fort Wayne) seminary, which awarded him an honorary doctorate on January 20, 1967. The following sentence from the citation on that occasion gives a good summary of his life: "Dr. Sasse is recognized as one of the outstanding leaders of confessional Lutheranism in the modern Ecumenical Movement."

Most of those who encountered this man were never quite comfortable unless they were willing and able to hear his call of repentance to the church: for conservative Lutherans as well as liberal Protestants, Hermann Sasse was a voice of catholic Christianity. He had a particular talent for "opening up new perspectives and offering penetrating insight."[34]

Ronald R. Feuerhahn

---

[33] For an excellent treatment of Sasse's study, see the essay by Jeffrey J. Kloha, "Hermann Sasse Confesses the Doctrine *de Scriptura Sacra*," an appendix in *Scripture and the Church: Selected Essays of Hermann Sasse* (ed. Jeffrey J. Kloha and Ronald R. Feuerhahn; Concordia Seminary Monograph Series 2; St. Louis: Concordia Seminary, 1995), 337–423.

[34] Dietzfelbinger, "Aus Treue zum Bekenntnis Hermann Sasses Vermächtnis," 7.

1927

AMERICAN CHRISTIANITY
AND THE CHURCH[1]

An American Lutheran churchman described this essay as "a fair and frank estimate of American church life. The author feels that the American church is destined to play a conspicuous part in the future development of western Christianity. . . . These lectures were intended for a German audience, but we Americans shall do well to listen in a bit on the presentations."[2] Abdel Ross Wentz, the noted historian of American Lutheranism, wrote Sasse shortly after its publication, saying that he had appreciated it so much that he and his wife had translated it.[3] The translation was never published but was used as the basis for the review article by Paul Hoh.

Sasse wrote this essay on the basis of his visit to the United States in 1925–1926 (see the biographical sketch in the front of this book). In the foreword to his book *Here We Stand*, he described the importance of this visit:

> Personally I must confess that it was in America that I first learned fully to appreciate what it means to be loyal to the Lutheran Confessions; but for what I learned from the Lutheran theologians and church bodies in the United States, I probably could never have written this book.[4]

Later he wrote: "I had learned in America, where I spent a year at Hartford (1925/1926), what undogmatic Christianity is and where it ends."[5]

Dietrich Bonhoeffer read Sasse's book before his own study at Union Theological Seminary, New York.[6]

---

[1] This essay originally appeared under the title *Amerikanisches Kirchentum* (Berlin-Dahlem: Wichern-Verlag, 1927). MH

[2] Paul J. Hoh, "The American Church," *The Lutheran Church Review* 46.2 (April 1927): 162. Hoh's article is essentially a summary of Sasse's essay. RF

[3] Wentz to Sasse (November 18, 1933; Huss Collection). RF

[4] Hermann Sasse, "Foreword to the American Edition," *Here We Stand: Nature and Character of the Lutheran Faith* (trans. Theodore G. Tappert; New York: Harper & Bros., 1938), x–xi. RF

[5] Letter from Sasse to Klaas Runia, cited in Runia, "Dr. Hermann Sasse 'In Statu Confessionis,' " *RTR* 27.1 (January/April 1968): 1. RF

[6] Eberhard Bethge, *Dietrich Bonhoeffer: Man of Vision, Man of Courage* (New York: Harper & Row, 1970;

This essay by Sasse fits into a genre of works about American life by European visitors, each of which made similar observations about the religious life of the country. Not unlike Alexis de Tocqueville's book *Of Democracy in America* (1835), this essay by Sasse offers a keen and well-informed analysis of American Christianity, almost a century later. In the same year as Sasse's publication was one by André Siegfried, *America Comes of Age: A French Analysis* (1927).

Sasse states his thesis in the following way: "The development of the social forms of the church always deeply correspond with the general process of societal formation."

Huss number 009
Hopf number 008

OUTLINE

Preface
Introduction
1. Church and Civilization
2. The Concept of the Church
Conclusion: The Ecumenical Question

PREFACE

This publication contains two lectures (in somewhat expanded form) which were delivered at the Theological Week at Frankfurt an der Oder in August of 1926. The content of these lectures is based upon studies and observations made while the author spent a year of study at Hartford Theological Seminary, at Hartford, Connecticut.[7] Since he is presenting these lectures to the public, it is necessary for him to thank those who made possible this trip for study purposes and who smoothed his way in America, especially Professor Dr. Julius Richter in Berlin;[8] the president of the [Hartford] seminary, Dr. W. Douglas Mackenzie;[9] the theo-

---

Fountain Edition, 1977), 105 (British title: *Dietrich Bonhoeffer: Theologian, Christian, Contemporary*). RF

[7] September 1925–May 1926. RF

[8] Sasse's time in America had been arranged by the German Evangelical Church Committee (*Deutscher Evangelischer Kirchenausschuß*) under an initiative by Dr. Julius Richter. Six theologians from each country were part of the exchange. In addition to Sasse, Peter Brunner and Wilhelm Pauck were among the Germans (*Verhandlungen des zweiten Deutschen Evangelischen Kirchentages 1927*, Königsberg, Prussia, June 17–21, 1927, published by Deutscher Evangelischer Kirchenausschuß; Berlin-Steglitz: Evangelischen Preßverband für Deutschland, [1928?], 59). RF

[9] Mackenzie was president and professor of Christian theology (1903–1930). RF

logical faculty at Hartford; and friends in the United Lutheran Church.[10]

Oranienburg near Berlin, October 1926

The Author

INTRODUCTION

Through the Universal Christian Conference on Life and Work in Stockholm,[11] American Christianity [*amerikanische Kirchentum*] has gained the interest of widening circles of German Protestantism. A discussion of its forms of life and its ideas has begun. And this discussion not only possesses the highest practical significance for the life and work of the German Evangelical Church, but it also has already deeply influenced our religious and theological thought. Indeed, it is forcing us to seriously evaluate ourselves and to reconsider the rudiments of our religious life. The uniqueness of the intellectual situation in which we find ourselves is that all the individual questions and tasks with which we wrestle broaden into larger questions of fundamental principle. Basic questions of worldview lie behind contemporary problems regarding politics, legislation, and pedagogics and make the proposing and completion of practical tasks of the present so unendingly difficult. And the problems of modern-day ecclesiastical life, too, ever again wend their way back to the basic questions of the Reformation. This is especially true of the problems which American Protestantism places before us.

What significance did American Christianity have for us twenty years ago? It was a very interesting phenomenon for the church historian or one who studies the psychology of religion. The German Protestant shook his head in confusion when he compared his church with the chaos of American sects. It amounted to a sum total of hypocrisy, ridiculousness, and nonsense for a reader of the newspaper, who read easy anecdotes about the land of unbridled possibility.

What is American Christianity today? It is the greatest mission force on earth, in control of two-thirds of all Protestant mission work. America is a world power, whose social forms and ideas are beginning to force their way into Europe. No less than Oswald Spengler[12] has declared that American religious life will be the future form of Protestant Christianity.

---

[10] Sasse was very grateful for his contact with and the support of the United Lutheran Church in America and its president, Frederick Hermann Knubel. For details on this American visit, see Ronald R. Feuerhahn, "Hermann Sasse and North American Lutheranism," *Logia* 4.4 (October 1995): especially 11–12. RF

[11] This conference in 1925, under the leadership of Nathan Söderblom, archbishop of Uppsala, was one of the foundational events of the modern Ecumenical Movement. RF

[12] Oswald Spengler (1880–1936) was a German freelance writer in history and philosophy. Here is probably a reference to Spengler's *Der Untergang des Abendlandes Umrisse einer Morphologie der Weltgeschichte* (2 vols.; Munich: Oskar Beck, 1918, 1924); in English *The Decline of the West: Form and Actuality* (trans. Charles Francis Atkinson; New York: Knopf, 1939). This was making quite a stir at the time. Spengler was influenced by Nietzsche; *The Decline of the West* was a philosophy of history and political predictions

This changed situation corresponds to the altered position of America over against the European states. That Good Friday of 1917 when Woodrow Wilson declared war on the German Reich in the name of America ("God help him, it cannot be otherwise," reads the conclusion to the famous address to Congress) signified the greatest turning point in the history of the United States. On this day the meaning of American history changed. Up to this point the States were a world unto themselves; a better, happier world than Europe, unburdened by the conventions of an old culture and the traditions of a thousand years of history. America for Americans—that was the meaning of the Declaration of Independence and the Monroe Doctrine.[13]

Now this idea was given up. One could say, *cum grano salis* ["with a grain of salt"], "The Declaration of Independence was taken back." When America decisively entered into the World War (for America conquered us and in doing so defined history for the coming century), it bound its fate together with that of Europe for all time. If people's quintessential question in American politics today is whether it is still possible, and to what extent it is necessary, to withdraw from dealings with the old world, then they forget that the decision has already been irretrievably rendered.

The fatefulness of this change in the history of the United States was temporarily veiled by its incomparable ascent in the wake of the successful war. The years of prosperity which the United States has experienced since the war are unparalleled in economic history. Entire cities have sprung up. The people are seized with a sense of good fortune. It is evident—so it appears to them—that God has spoken. The religious feeling which enlivens the Americans, who see the ascent of their land, can only be expressed by these words: what a critical outcome brought about by divine intervention! Led to the head of humanity, Americans today are the leading people on earth. The prospects are bright for a glorious future, and they deeply believe that God has called upon them to ensure the security of all humanity. America has been summoned to nurse to health the suffering, shattered, and helpless world. The prophetic remark once made by Platen[14] at the time of Napoleon is beginning to be fulfilled: "The history of the world flies westward." The political and domestic center of gravity of the Western world is moving across the Atlantic Ocean.

Under the weight of this new and strange political and domestic situation in the world, not only is the European state system breaking up, but also perhaps even the European national state itself. Apparently no state can maintain its eminence over against the effect which the Americans are having worldwide. We

---

(*Lutheran Cyclopedia*, 730). See references in Sasse's earlier essay "Der Paraklet im Johannesevangelium," *ZNW* 24.2 (1925): 260–77. RF

[13] The Monroe Doctrine (1823) declared an end to colonization of the New World by European nations. Any such intervention would be considered a threat to the United States. RF

[14] Metropolitan of Moscow, 1737–1812. MH

must view the change of American Christianity, and its altered position over against the European churches, against this world-political backdrop. While American influence upon the religious domain up to now has been exercised, shall we say, by unofficial forms of propaganda for individual sects, the World Conference at Stockholm means that for the first time in the history of the church, American Protestantism stood before the churches of the old world, not to receive, but to give. And it did so convinced it was bringing deliverance to a European Protestantism in danger of disintegration. And this "deliverance" came in the form of a new understanding of the Gospel, the "Social Gospel," and a new conception of the church, unknown up to this point in time. This new understanding of the Gospel is intent on answering the question regarding the relationship of Christianity and secular culture. This concept of the church intends to make possible the unification of the church. It deals with the fundamental ideas of Stockholm. As we trace these ideas in American Christianity, we will attempt to come to an understanding of its unique character.

1. CHURCH AND CIVILIZATION

An American advertising company, which erects colorful, illuminated billboards (familiar to every American), published an advertisement for a number of churches. It appeared in the newspaper of the Federal Council of the Churches of Christ, the great Protestant church federation.[15] The ad was officially commissioned by the same. In the advertisement a city is portrayed against the light of daybreak. There are houses, factory smokestacks, a harbor, and a railway. Above these, in the morning overcast, appears the silhouette of a church depicted in tasteless Gothic. An inscription explains the image: "Out of the dusk comes the dawn and out of the church comes civilization." This image helps very much to explain the essence of modern American church life. The American does not perceive that this image can be misconstrued. The logical conclusion is really this: as the light replaces the darkness, so civilization steps into the place of the church. He sees here only an expression of the conviction that, behind all civilization, the church stands as the source of all creative powers, and that it is the task of the church to create civilization. This faith is finally the secret of American Christianity.

The greater portion of the religious life on the other side of the Atlantic is explained by this close connection between church and civilization. This is one of the first impressions made upon the German theologian in America, when he sees the completely unbroken churchliness, the general interest in religious matters, and the high value placed upon religious institutions. In America the fearful divide between religion and culture, between church and secular civilization, which has rent the people of Europe, is absent.

---

[15] Formed in 1908, the Federal Council of the Churches of Christ merged into the National Council of the Churches in 1950. RF

There is in America, to be sure, a strong atheistic movement, and large masses of completely unchurched people. Of the 115 million residents of the United States, only 48 million are registered church members. Even if many of the unchurched are in some way loosely connected with the churches, still many millions remain who have never had any ecclesiastical influence. But public opinion is not determined by such people. The skepticism over against the church, the gnawing criticism which disintegrates it and which the "cultured" European man[16] has customarily leveled at the church, is not present like it is in Europe. A person is not behind the times if he belongs to the church. The businessman and the official, the successful worker and the proletarian immigrant are not ashamed to belong to a church. Indeed, it is a mark of social standing to be a member of a congregation.

When Calvin Coolidge became president,[17] he joined the Congregational Church, the church of the Pilgrim fathers. On high festival days he dons a top hat and passes photographers, camera men, and reporters as he goes to church. When the Congregationalists held their great synod in Washington, he was given the place of honor as *membrum praecipuum* ["distinguished member"], and he delivered an address on the significance of religion for the maintenance of good government. He happily expresses in his speeches the desire that religion be preserved among his people and culture [*Volk*]—naturally not precisely at the festive banquet of the Chamber of Commerce of New York, where he spoke on the prosperity of the country, but, for instance, before the farmers of Iowa. This all is as sincere and well meant as in the case of other government leaders and is taken quite seriously by the public. "We are a God-fearing people"—this statement from the message of the president last Thanksgiving Day—is the confession of the American. It comes out of the hearts of the people, and it holds true as much or little as any such assertion made by a people [*Volk*]. If it is understood in this way: "We are churchly people," then it is by all means true.

A glance at the newspapers demonstrates this. Since the war they have been filled with religious news. Individual events and people are subjected to criticism, but never the church. It is demonstrated by the high view of the pastoral office. It is demonstrated by full churches. It is one of the most impressive experiences which a German pastor can have, who commonly, Sunday after Sunday, preaches in an empty church, to see these small congregations (the average has scarcely more than five hundred adult members) with their impressive church attendance, their willingness to give, their active cooperation with other members of the congregation.

It is clear that this is in no way only a result of the performance of the clergy. For one sees full churches where the pastor, perhaps an unstudied man or a

---

[16] Is this perhaps a reference to the "cultured despisers of religion" for whom Friedrich Schleiermacher wrote his famous *Reden* in 1799? RF

[17] Coolidge became president in 1923 upon the death of Harding; in 1924 he was elected president and served a full term. RF

completely immature student, preaches twice every Sunday in a manner which, among us, would satisfy no congregation. Since colonial times there has been a strong churchly tradition in America, an unbroken, naive churchliness. Religion is part of life, part of the existence of the nation, of the civilization. A peace between church and secular culture rules undisturbed.

This churchliness of life has a down side to be sure: the secularization of the church. You can sense the old religious tradition of earliest American history when you travel about through the historic colonial states, through the Puritan cities of New England, the Philadelphia of William Penn and the Lutheran fathers, and the Mennonite towns of Pennsylvania. But this tradition has definitely been modified. In the old Puritan cities many shops are open on Sunday. The churches have only maintained their position in the life of the culture by retreating step by step in the face of the demands of modern life. They have opened their doors in part to modern civilization, which has endangered the purity and the depth of the faith. Here is the reason for that superficiality of American church life which repulses us Germans.

There are advertisements which seek to bait the public. Why should colorful billboards and psychologically designed newspaper advertisements not serve the church? There are all the organizations which are part of the modern American church, from the kitchen to the bowling alley. Why should the church not offer what a secular club offers? And these things progressively force their way into religious life itself. Worship [*Gottesdienst*] has been, as we say, "developed." There must always be something new, and everything must be effective: lighting effect, musical effect, an effective liturgy.

I remember a large new Baptist church. The room had only artificial lighting, for around and throughout the entire structure were built rooms for the offices, societies, and religious instruction. Next to the sanctuary there was a special control room from which the lighting was adjusted. As soon as the preacher knelt to pray, the attendant rotated the great lever on the control board. Darkness filled the church. The desired feelings were literally "switched on."

Then there is the congregational bulletin. It has to be very interesting if it is to be read, and it is especially interesting when the reader finds his own name in it. "Wouldn't it be nice if your name were to appear here, and if possible a donation of $5 or $10 after it?" Thus read the congregational bulletin of one Catholic cathedral. The youth, of course, must be wooed. Naturally they come to Bible class, but only if sports are included. Why shouldn't the church have a flashy football club? The confession of faith of one of the most popular authors[18] reads, "A football player with religion is a better football player than one without religion."

The most difficult, and for us the most objectionable, question is of course that of money. What a force the dollar is in the church! To be sure, one must realize that for the American, money is something different than what it is for us. One German complained to me that he considered it blasphemy to present to God a

---

18 Edward A. Guess, "What My Religion Means to Me," *The American Magazine* (1925). HS

plate full of dollar bills on the altar during worship and to pray over it. But this is
the German speaking. The quiet aversion which we idealistic Germans have to
money, especially when we do not possess it, the feeling that mammon is something devilish, is unknown to the American. Old Calvinism already quite happily
noted that God had made Abraham very rich. Money is the blessing of God in
crystallized form, and a bank account is proof of [the presence of] the Spirit and
power.

One must see for himself how the American handles money, and how generous he is in giving it away. And this includes not only the wealthy man, who parts
with a million more easily than a wealthy German a hundred marks, but also the
simple worker who gives a week's pay for a college of his church. And I saw this
in the case of the Lutherans. Americans really do deal with money quite differently. But money also creates great dangers, to be sure. It is a particularly crass
case when Rockefeller with his millions stands behind the liberal wing of the
Northern Baptist Church. And synodical decisions are rendered in view of his
person.[19] A fruitful form of private patronage indeed!

But beyond these matters, the selling of influence in the church through the
blandishments of technical civilization shall not be further mentioned here. Our
knowledge of American Christianity and our interest in it has often enough been
limited to these matters. In so doing we forget that we too are in a similar process
of development, and we overlook the plank in our own eye. Among us too the
question of money is playing an ever greater role in ecclesiastical life. Acquiring
a pay raise is appearing to become one of the chief tasks of the pastor. And among
us too the great word "organization" and organizations themselves are being
viewed in an ever-more American fashion.

Perhaps this is necessary. If there is no longer any congregation, there is
nothing left but to found one club after another. Already today what we have of
real ecclesiastical life is, to a large degree, the result of a giant system of associations. There are great para-ecclesiastical and para-congregational organizations,
youth federations, federations for the elderly, the Evangelical Federation, and
women's societies, and whatever other names they go by (and every one of them
is of course indispensable). But for anyone who seriously reflects upon the nature
of the church, the role they play presents much for consideration.

The great J. H. Wichern[20] is in part responsible for this development. When
he organized the Inner Mission in the form of a free society, he introduced a form
of social life into the church which did not originate from within the church and
has nothing to do with it. Consider, furthermore, all the attempts at reinvigorat-

---

[19]   This situation came to be discussed in a dramatic way at the synod of the Northern Baptist Church in
       1926, when a woman accused "a certain rich Baptist" of the sin of the rich man in Nathan's parable. He
       wanted the church to rescind her Baptism [er wolle der Kirche ihre Taufe nehmen]. HS

[20]   Johann Hinrich Wichern (1808–1881) was founder of Inner Mission and other para-church associations,
       homes for children, and so on (Lutheran Cyclopedia, 816). RF

ing dead congregations. What proposals and experiments are made today in order to develop "artistic" unity in the Divine Service where possible! What an absurd idea it is to make the Word of God, which has become ineffective, now effective by showing a film about Christ in the church! The holy spectacle of the Roman Mass would be preferable. Along with the movie about Christ is of course the Luther film. It is self-evident that people again grasp the meaning of justification by faith when a slick performer portrays for them the struggles of the soul of a great man. When we criticize the superficiality of American ecclesiastical life, we should always consider these similar phenomena of our own ecclesiastical life. An earnest Eastern or Russian Christian would perhaps barely note the difference between the American and ourselves in this regard.

The secularization process stretches not only over the forms of ecclesiastical life, but it also goes deep into religious convictions and theology. A Christianity open and welcoming to the world is in part a reaction against the austere piety of strict Calvinism and the old Methodist religion of conversion. Insight into the shape of *popular religion* [*Volksreligion*] is provided by a book which is among the most popular of the day. *The Man Nobody Knows*, by Bruce Barton, is an investigation of Jesus. The book bears the subtitle "Do you not know that I must be about my Father's *business?*" And it celebrates Jesus as the founder of *modern business.*

One must note here that "business" in English in no way has the contemptuous meaning that we attribute to the word *Geschäft*, which Schleiermacher, as everyone knows, used to describe the work of Christ. Did not Christ found the greatest organization on earth? Did he not, in his Sermon on the Mount, give the eternal instructions for a successful life? How then have the greatest men of American business achieved their success, if not by following these commands? They have achieved success in self-sacrificing hard work, without considering their own needs. And even if they themselves no longer had any personal needs, they continued to work selflessly to see to the needs of their fellow man through the production and distribution of goods. Ford wanted his neighbor and everyone else to have an automobile.

Other chapters show Jesus as the master salesman or sportsman. What substantial accomplishments took place in his "outdoor life" (life in the open country, which is an American ideal), in his independence while suffering on the cross. If Jesus were living today he would, in principle, affirm American civilization. The basic idea behind this piety is that Christianity is something which belongs in this world, and in this American culture. There is a pre-established harmony between Christianity and civilization. If they do not coincide then we are still incomplete Christians in an unfulfilled civilization. But both have the same goal: the perfection of the church coincides with the perfection of civilization. The kingdom of God, the goal of the church, cannot be considered, unless it is simultaneously thought of as the final goal of all of human culture.

This basic concept of modern American piety has been expressed in *theology*, if one can call it a theology, by the doctrine of the "Social Gospel." And I repeat, *if* it can be called a theology. Theology is doctrine, so far as it is a theory. But a theory is something quite different for the American than it is for us. For the German a theory is a view of reality. For the American, it is a plan for action. He is not born to observe, but to create. And for him the doing is the source of joy, not the observation. Thus the theology of the Social Gospel is a plan for action.

It is not correct to translate "Social Gospel" literally, simply with the words *soziales Evangelium*. For the word "social" (a foreign word in the German language, but not in English, that fortunate tongue in which there are no foreign words, because half of it consists of foreign words) has for us a very narrow meaning. The doctrine of the Social Gospel is the doctrine of the perfection of society through the Gospel. The presupposition for this doctrine is the fact that the idea of society in all Western nations plays an entirely different role than it does among us. The goal of culture, in the German sense, is man. The goal of civilization in the West European/American sense is society. This is a well-known fact, but we must always remember it. The importance of this idea of society was made clear to me when I heard an American theologian of Scottish descent develop the doctrine of the Trinity as the doctrine of society [*Gesellschaft*] occurring within the Godhead. The goal of civilization is the perfection of society. But this perfection is only possible through the Gospel, which up to now has been treated much too one-sidedly as the perfection of the individual soul.

But the American, like all the peoples of the West, has a very definite idea of society: the idea of democracy. As various as the doctrines of society of the French, English, and Americans may be, for us, who do not belong to the West, they form a unity. This idea of democracy rules Western men with the power of a high ideal. And without it they could not live. They entered the World War for this ideal, and this war was finally to destroy a Germany which would not acknowledge this ideal and thus excluded itself from the family of Western nations.

The power of this ideal is explained by the fact that it is deeply rooted in religion, namely Calvinism, as Emanuel Hirsch has shown in his study *The Kingdom of God Concept in More Recent European Thought*.[21] It is the reflection of a religious faith, an idea of the kingdom of God, secularized during the age of the Enlightenment. We Germans may smirk at the fanatical belief in freedom, equality, and brotherhood. (The English language has two words for *Freiheit*—freedom and liberty—and their use is sharply defined. One is Germanic, the other Roman, and they correspond to the old-Germanic and ancient Southern concepts of freedom.) But the peoples of the West live by them.

One should not think that our criticism of this doctrine of society has had no impact upon them. Never have I found a more blunt criticism of democracy than

---

[21] *Die Reichsgottesbegriffe des neueren europäischen Denkens* (Göttingen, 1919). HS

in the circles of the brightest young Americans, who have direct experience with its dark side. But W. A. Brown[22] expressed the faith of his people when he said: "Even if all its mistakes are granted, it is still true that the hope of the world lies in democracy."[23] And Brown is quite happy to note his agreement with Dean Inge,[24] the well-known English theologian. Our political commentators who happily busy themselves with the refutation of democracy and yet are continually amazed that it survives overestimate the power of arguments. There are things which no argument can refute because they are convictions of faith and they are the manifestation of prevailing thought forms. "Certainly our democracy is weak and immature"—that is granted by every thinking American. "So now we have the task of creating an even better one. After all, what could possibly replace democracy?"

Thus the truth of the democratic doctrine of society is self-evident to the American. The truth of the Gospel is likewise evident to him. And so the task of theology is to combine both and bring them into harmony. The great theological question for William A. Brown is about what democracy has to give Christianity, and vice versa.

There are three types of religion within Christendom: imperialistic, individualistic, and democratic religion. The imperialistic form is represented by Roman Catholicism, the individualistic by Lutheranism, the democratic by early Christianity and American Protestantism. The decisive criterion for rendering a judgment on every religion is the position it takes over against democracy. Islam is false, according to Samuel Zwemer,[25] and incapable of creating real culture, because its autocratic doctrine of God (God as absolute sovereign power) cannot be reconciled with democracy. Whoever would view this theology as insufficient would do well to consider that in America a theology is a plan for action, a hypothesis providing rationale for work [*Arbeitshypothese*]. It is not of primary importance whether it is correct or false. The decisive question is whether or not the world can be bettered by it.

Thus we have the basis for the practical church program of the American: the realization of democratic society through the work of the church. Everything which serves to this end has been assumed into the church's program, from the elimination of war through international understanding and mandatory arbitra-

---

[22] William Adams Brown (1865–1943) was educated at Yale and Union Theological Seminary, New York, and studied in Germany, Scotland, and England. He taught at Union as an ordained Presbyterian. He was a liberal and a proponent of ecumenicity (*Lutheran Cyclopedia*, 113). Sasse would later have much contact with Brown in meetings of the Faith and Order Movement. MH

[23] W. A. Brown, *The Church in America* (New York, 1922), 354. HS

[24] William Ralph Inge (1860–1954) was the Anglican dean of St. Paul's Cathedral, London. RF

[25] Samuel Marinus Zwemer (1867–1952) was educated at New Brunswick Theological Seminary. He helped found a mission to Islamic peoples and was a missionary to Arabia (1890–1912), then professor of theology at Cairo Study Center, Cairo, Egypt. He founded the periodical *The Moslem World* and was professor of religion and missions at Princeton Theological Seminary from 1929 until 1938 (*Lutheran Cyclopedia*, 844). MH

tion, to the legalization of birth control. This last point plays a significant role. For if the human race increases its numbers at the present rate, new military conflicts will of course be inevitable.

The clear words of the NT demonstrate that all these things are practical Christianity. Did not Jesus promise his disciples peace and send them out into the world as messengers of peace? Did he not proclaim the new righteousness of the kingdom of God, which includes social justice? That birth control accords with the mind of Jesus is proved by the words of Jesus himself.[26] He came "that they might have life and have it more abundantly" [John 10:10], that is, as every American understands it, that they should have sufficient means to live. And so an entire theology is born (its founder is a deceased professor at the Baptist Seminary in Rochester, Walter Rauschenbusch[27]). This theology explicates the NT in the following manner. The Greek word εἰρήνη ["peace"] is the peace which obtains between peoples; ἀγάπη ["love"] is the consciousness of the solidarity of the human race; ζωή ["life"] is human existence. But the theologians of the Social Gospel do not understand that "peace" in the NT, also in the sense of a condition of human society, is more than an eternal treaty. And "love" in the Christian religion is more than a consciousness of solidarity. "Life" in the Johannine writings is more than mere existence, and precisely in this "more" lies the essential uniqueness of this biblical idea.

One explanation of the Sermon on the Mount[28] begins its glorification of peacemakers with the remark that the general strike is the best means to create peace in an industrial civilization (i.e., to prevent war). And then the author ventures to state that the flag of the kingdom of God is red, embodying the common blood of human brotherhood.[29] Certainly this last sentence is an exaggeration, with which only a few Americans would agree. But this exaggeration precisely shows the tendency of this theology, which is the identification of the democratic, and in part also the socialistic societal ideal, with the idea of the Gospel. When the church brings about this democratic-evangelical ideal, the kingdom of God comes on earth. The consummation of the church coincides with the consummation of civilization.

These are the ideas of modern American church life. They have not been accepted by all churches. The Fundamentalist, or conservative-biblicistic, stream which flows through many churches has rejected the Social Gospel as much as

---

[26] "We believe that these recommendations are in accord with the spirit of Jesus, who came that we might have abundant life, which means the possibility of everyone living up to the best and fullest of his powers, and not a flooding of the country with numbers of uneducated and underfed children" ("Resolution of the Student Conference of Evanston," *ChrCent* [1926]: 61). HS

[27] Walter Rauschenbusch (1861–1918), Baptist cleric, was pastor at Louisville, Kentucky, and New York City, where he worked among German immigrants. He was a professor of church history at Rochester Theological Seminary (1902–1918) and an exponent of the Social Gospel. He identified the kingdom of God with social evolution (*Lutheran Cyclopedia*, 661). MH

[28] H. S. Brewster, *The Simple Gospel* (New York, 1922), 23. HS

[29] Brewster, *Simple Gospel*, 18. HS

Lutheranism has. But neither Fundamentalism nor the Lutheran churches have thus far been prepared to counter the new doctrine with something of equal stature. They actually represent the spirit of modern American Protestantism. One realizes how great this doctrine is, not by treating it as an abstract theory, but by coming to know men whose confession of faith it is.

What a serious consideration of social questions and tasks lies behind the doctrine of the Social Gospel![30] How seriously the question is posed whether Christianity will leave the world to itself or penetrate the world with its spirit! We may not be satisfied with the answer, but it is to the credit of the Americans that they seriously and energetically pose the question regarding the relationship between Christianity and culture. What high idealism, what faith, unshaken by any disappointment, is expressed in the pacifism of these men! The religious power which lives in these men must finally be experienced first hand. This power may not be evident in their books on theory. And the German does not notice it at once in American addresses and sermons. But one learns to recognize this unique religiosity when one has lived among the Americans for a considerable time. Moreover, it has found a wonderful expression in the more recent poetry of their hymnody.

If we are to understand this close connection between church and civilization, we must consider that this modern American Protestantism is of Calvinistic origin. And Calvinism, early on, forged a positive relationship to the economic questions and tasks of modern culture, in a way quite different from Lutheranism. The modern world economy arose alongside colonial politics in the Calvinistic nations of Western Europe. The parallels of religious and economic interest which we encounter so often in English history, and find so astounding, are in America a heritage of colonial times. This immeasurably rich land, in which the first task of the immigrant was to unlock its treasures, was bound to become a civilization of powerfully expanding economic forces. There was little time left for other tasks. Thus the American needed a religion which allowed him to be a businessman. America needed a Christianity which essentially affirmed an economic civilization.

And on the other hand, this civilization had a positive relationship with religion. The tragic separation between culture and religion which has become ever more unbearable in Europe and is crying out for reparation does not exist here. There is no hatred of the church. In Europe all of modern culture developed through a struggle against the Middle Ages. All spheres of life have finally freed themselves from the "dark" Middle Ages, and this in the course of intense struggle against ecclesiastical connections. This conscious or unconscious opposition to the past, which was ruled by the church, has in recent centuries given European culture a purely secular, unchurchly or anti-church stamp. If today the judgment on the Middle Ages has changed, if the most recent manifestation of Romanticism

---

[30] Note, for instance, the treatment of the strike by Passaic in *ChrCent* (1926): 964 ff. HS

seeks connections to Catholicism, if today within Protestantism the idea of the church has been born anew, these are signs that within our culture a great transformation is in the offing.

America has never known this opposition between church and culture, because it has never had a Middle Ages which had to be overcome. In America the church never has been an obstacle for civilization, an enemy of advancement, or whatever other form the accusations may take. But similar to early medieval Europe, the church has been an institution without which this civilization could not have come to exist. Even the Enlightenment, the ideas of which have exercised decisive influence on the formation of American civilization, changed nothing of this valuing of the church. The Enlightenment took hold deep in the life of the church but did not tear the bond between religion and civilization.

Here we have alluded to a point which very profoundly differentiates American intellectual life from its European counterpart. America has a completely different relationship to history. We ever live under the control of a long and rich history. For America history begins with the Pilgrim fathers and William Penn. And this is not history as knowledge of what once was, accumulated in books. It is a living and effective past, alive in the soul. At the edge of the American's historical horizon stand the silhouettes of the Reformers, but they are fading fast. Calvin is hardly read by the average theologian. Luther still lives on in the Lutheran Church through his catechism. The Middle Ages and antiquity (despite all the pronouncements of death) are still living among us. For America, they are dead. The great figures of the past which in Europe again and again experience resurrections, such as Plato and Augustine, no longer arise in America. There are things which cannot be brought over the ocean. These varying connections to history make the European peoples so old, the Americans so young. For us everything has existed before. For the Americans everything is still on the way.

As a consequence of this difference of experience, there is a difference of worldview. For worldview is determined by life experience. Our view of history is the result of a long and successive history. The American view is the result of the experience of the incomparable rise of a new world, from a colony to the greatest power on earth in the course of a few centuries. In Europe this faith in advancement has been overturned by the facts. In America it has been confirmed by the facts. There has never been a truly great thinker in Germany who has believed in advancement in the American sense. And even the best of American philosophers cannot view the world in any other way. Therefore throughout our history we have had the great critics of culture, from Goethe[31] to Nietzsche,[32] to say nothing

---

[31] Johann Wolfgang von Goethe (1749–1832) was a German poet, novelist, and scientist, a Romanticist who tended toward Pantheism. MH

[32] Friedrich Wilhelm Nietzsche (1844–1900) was born in Saxony and trained for the ministry at Bonn and Leipzig. He abandoned the ministry and accepted a professorship at Basle, where he became a friend of Wagner (whom he later turned against). He developed an individualistic, antidemocratic, and bitterly

of Dostoevski.[33] America has not yet experienced these men. It believes, with the complete self-confidence of youth, in the value and the future of its civilization. The Europeans look over the ruins of their culture which is laden with history, philosophizing about history and culture (thus the Americans view us). And we are like Lot's wife who turned into a pillar of stone, looking back at Sodom. But the Americans are like Lot himself, unencumbered by what lies behind, sight fixed forward to the future.

This is the American Christianity which stepped before the churches of the old world at Stockholm[34] and there collided with its German counterpart. It was a tragic encounter. The Germans came with the most serious question of how the fearful cleft between modern culture and the Gospel, which has destroyed us, could be overcome. The Americans came with a ready answer: the doctrine of the Social Gospel. But the question and the answer do not coincide. For the presupposition of the answer, the fundamental unity of church and civilization, is false for us. They absolutely did not understand the question.

How will things develop? No doubt one day in America the doctrine of the Social Gospel will be shattered. And it will be refuted not by argument, but by fate. And what will happen then? What will happen, for instance, when Pacifism proves to be utopian? Will American Protestant Christianity also be refuted? Doubt is already stirring regarding the new movement. Among American youth, that is, among the brightest youth of the country, a perceptible criticism of culture is awaking. Nietzsche and Spengler are making their way through America. The apocalyptic teachings are not dying out and ever and again find haven among simple people. What a fearful catastrophe will finally have to befall Protestantism, when fate itself speaks, when God's judgment comes upon that country, as it has come upon Europe!

And we Germans? What do we have other than a purely negative criticism to pose over against American Christianity, with its doctrine of culture? So far, nothing! Will it be like Marxism, which we have refuted a thousand times over but still lives on simply because an error is never set aside merely because it has been refuted? An error must rather be replaced with a truth. Is it sufficient for the church to make a few social demands and begin a bit of social work here and there?[35] Is it sufficient for us to formulate a few sentimental religio-social theories, in which socialistic and Christian thoughts are combined and interchanged?

---

anti-Christian atheistic philosophy. Its fundamental idea is the "will to power." Christianity is regarded as a blot on the history of mankind (*Lutheran Cyclopedia*, 577). MH

[33] Fyodor Mikhailovich Dostoevski (1821–1881), born in Moscow of Orthodox or Uniat priestly ancestry, was a well-known Russian novelist. The center of his religious experience was "the consciousness of salvation as the free gift of God to the weak and miserable and the refusal to admit any cooperation between God and man. . . . The result is the complete absence from religion of reason and will" (*ODCC*, 503). RF

[34] The conference had as one of its chief aims to encourage Christian cooperation in treating social ills (*Lutheran Cyclopedia*, 256–57). See also the discussion of this conference (including the note on it) at the beginning of the introduction to this essay. RF

[35] Sasse himself would be called as a *Socialpfarrer*, "social pastor," in Berlin, 1928–1933. RF

No, the task which stands before us in this century is the construction of a theology (and as everybody knows, a theology always has to be something more than a theory) in which the problems of modern culture are thought through in a manner consistent with the two pillars of our religious thought: justification by faith and the Lutheran definition of the church. In the experiences of a long and very difficult history, we Germans have seen the limits of human desire and action. Our philosophy has produced a distinction between culture and civilization which is foreign to the peoples of the West. And yet this is essential for the construction of a Christian doctrine of culture. Thus we have the presuppositions for a different Social Gospel, in which the truth clearly recognized by the Americans—that we have to work in the world as long as it is day—is bound together with another truth—that our doing does not perfect the world and humanity. This happens by the grace of God.

2. THE CONCEPT OF THE CHURCH

There is a deep and innate connection between the form of the church and the form of the state. This is a fact which until now has not been given serious enough consideration by theology, or by the church as it carries out its practical work. The ancient church of the empire corresponded to the ancient empire [*imperium*]. The Roman Papal Church corresponded to the medieval kingdom of the emperor. The national and territorial churches of modern times correspond to the national state. And the striving of peoples of the Western world in our day for political formations which transcend the national state has its parallel in the church in the Ecumenical Movement.

If we are to understand American Christianity we must proceed from these facts. There is a moralizing treatment of church history which explains the fact that the church takes on forms dependent upon the forms of the state and society in which it finds itself. It presumes a fall into sin on the part of the church from time to time in the transition from one phase to the other, for instance, at the time of Constantine the Great[36] and at the time of the little Constantines of the era of the Reformation. This manner of proceeding has its relative legitimacy, if it means to deal with the question of the conscious subordination of the church to the state. But it alone does not suffice. And this is proven by American ecclesiastical formations, which came about essentially independent from the state and which still demonstrate the same parallels to secular societal forms.

For sociologists, there can be no more interesting object of study than the United States. Emigration to America in the course of the past three centuries is the classic example of a migration of peoples. It has taken place in full view, under the brightest lights of the stage of history. And its significance for general politi-

---

[36] Constantine I (ca. 280–337) was Roman emperor from 306 until 337. RF

cal and sociological studies has been realized only because we are accustomed to learn of such matters merely from books. The history of the emigration which began in the seventeenth century; the formation of the state, which began with the Declaration of Independence; and the formation of a nation, which began with the Civil War, has meant the rejection of all theories which base the essence of the nation and the state upon race.

An enormous flood of immigrants has flowed into America during the course of the centuries, and this flood, checked by immigration laws and directed in ordered paths, still continues to flow. To see the mix of languages, nations, and races today in the centers of immigration is to sense that this is a world completely different from Europe. And life in America must be something different as well. It cannot be measured with our calibrations. If you wish to understand Rome at the time of the Caesars, travel though the immigrant quarters of New York and see the blacks, Chinese, Poles and Jews, Russians, Italians, and Irishmen.

In this country there now lives an unconscious passion for unity within all people. In earlier centuries this country was a free state for all who sought a new home. All who desired to cultivate their faith, their customs, their language and manner of life in freedom could do so without difficulty, in this incredibly spacious land. But since the Civil War, and particularly since the World War, the United States has become a nation which consciously strives to rise together into a real inner unity. All of life hinges on this point. It is completely wrong-headed to condemn it. If you think yourself into the soul of this people you will understand that it cannot be otherwise. The Americans themselves rightly note that the old era of the freedom [to pursue one's individual culture in isolation] has passed. It has passed because this country can no longer supply the luxury of individuality. Thus all manner of life is becoming unified.

There is one definite form of dress, one style of shirt collar. Fashion provides a uniform. Houses are built the same way everywhere. Whether a man is in San Francisco or New York, he is in the same restaurant and buys his cigars in the same shop. The formation of trusts in industry, the great companies with countless affiliates across the country, the standardization of all industrial production (things which are now happening in Germany), all of it coincides. One enters the same theater and sees the same movies. The old settler ideal is roused when the "Wild West" film is shown, where people can shoot and ride so well. One sheds tears of emotion over the Methodistic conversion film, where a lawbreaker is converted into a solid member of society by the love of a noble woman. One feels like an American while watching the inevitable film set in Europe, depicting an American marrying a princess. Everything is alike. The newspapers exercise uniform influence; just how much influence, we saw to our horror during the war.

The school system likewise serves the movement for unity. Education is one of the great catchwords of the day. There is always money for education. Teaching in public schools is done in large part by young women, and with bewildering success. The person who has passed through eight years of this education is an American. Every morning instruction begins with the Pledge of Allegiance to the flag, which hangs in every school room (and for that matter, in most churches): "I pledge allegiance to the flag." He who has seen the effect of this education on German families, indeed, on very good families, where the children have been completely Americanized knows the psychological power of this system.

There are, of course, also confessional or denominational schools in America. And no one is required to attend the public school if there is a denominational school present. What remains of things German in America today is due to the German church school. But these only exist among the strict Lutherans of the West. The Catholics, of course, have their separate schools, but they are often as American as the public schools. They pass on ecclesiastical traditions, but no longer old national traditions. And not only children are the subject of this education.

Night schools attract the adults. The children of the immigrants train their parents to become Americans. That is often an accentuated part of the education process. The tendency toward uniformity also reigns in the area of higher education, in the high school, the college, and in the higher seminaries and faculties. The surprising similarity of theological views of even the most capable professors is striking to the German theologian, who is observing American scholarship for the first time. Among us, almost every theologian has his own theology (individualism extends so far that everyone not only has his own system, but also a unique method, and more recently, a unique terminology, which must first be explained to other scholars in the same field). In America there is a theological consensus, or rather two consensuses, one conservative and one modern. If a half-dozen books on the same subject appear, they all have the very same content.

But we must not overlook the fact that a reaction against this tendency toward uniformity has begun. Among a few independent and solitary thinkers, in the elite literary criticism of the best American journals, and among the modern, skeptical, anti-Methodistic, and, in part, atheistic youth, one finds a sharp criticism of this striving for uniformity which kills individual freedom and produces a dreary mediocrity.

We would depict this striving for uniformity very poorly if we failed to describe yet one more thing: the social talent of the American. Here we mean his congeniality with other people in the common discourse of life, which developed in this process of the formation of a unified nation. His politeness, willingness to help, and hospitality to the stranger are something wonderful to behold. Friendship is an important matter. Even if a person is met once, he is a friend, and this isn't just put on. When I got to America, there was a picture of a man in the newspaper who belonged to some ninety societies and lodges, and his friends numbered in the thousands. He returned from a European vacation, and his friends chartered a ship to meet him.

To be sure, these are not exactly the friends for which Friedrich Nietzsche cried in the agony of his loneliness—but still, American friendship means something. This phenomenon too is a symptom of a "becoming" nation, of a society growing together into an inner unity. I have intentionally and expressly depicted this melting process, because it is important if we are to understand things American. The political theories of the Americans are much more profoundly understood from this vantage. Americans can only think of the history of humanity in terms of such a process of unification, because American life is a unification process of a mass of humanity, thrown together from every nation of the old world. And Americans can think nationally and internationally at the same time, without contradicting themselves (and this too is very essential), because in America the formation of a nation has meant the unification of various national elements.

There is finally one thing which explains the state of affairs I have depicted. It is the doctrine of the equality of all men. The concept that all men are brothers rules in American Christianity. In sermons it is proved by the words of Acts 17:26, that God created all the human race on earth from *one* blood. And many times I heard this thought corroborated by the argument that chemistry proves that all human blood is equal. Samuel Zwemer himself does not reject this argument. It is characteristic to stop at this passage of Acts (which accords with Stoic philosophy), and not at the words of Jesus in which he proclaims the brotherhood of those who do God's will. But one must understand the significance of this thought for the Americans. The general brotherhood of all men is the great hypothesis for action which forms the foundation for the melting process. It is an *articulus stantis et cadentis nationis* ["an article by which the nation stands or falls"]. Thus the religious devotion to this concept. Because the life of the nation would lose its meaning without this faith, its agreement with Christianity is asserted, and its denial is regarded as blasphemy.

The ecclesiastical development must be viewed against this background in order to be understood. Here we remind you of the thesis with which we began. The development of the social forms of the church always deeply corresponds with the general process of societal formation. This thesis is proven true at this point. The greatest movement for union in the history of the church corresponds to the great melting process, brought about by the migration of peoples across the ocean. Once the churches in America were the focal point of unique national traditions. In part they still are today. The Germans, Scandinavians, Irishmen, Poles, Russians, French, and Italians all have their churches. But the national character of these churches is receding more and more. Taken as a whole, American Christianity has stepped into the melting process and is playing a significant role therein. The beginnings of this movement were in earlier times.

The decisive turning point came in the first decade of this century. The war quickly brought this development full circle. The declaration of war presupposed the formation of a unified national will and a unified conviction regarding the legitimacy of this war. This moral mobilization could not happen through the press alone. It required the cooperation of the churches. The decisive question for the American churches, which boasted that they were free from any dependence upon the state, was how they were to respond to the demands of the state. With few exceptions they bowed to the state. They gave to Caesar what he demanded, and this gift was not given for nothing. The rise of power of American Christianity, won in the wake of the war, dates from this capitulation. Even if today an honorable, bitter shame has befallen the most sincere American Christians regarding what they did to those who proclaimed an ardent pacifism in the church,[37] and even if the intention to do better next time (this is the American form of repentance) is entirely sincere, American Protestantism will still never be able to undo what has been done. And in the history which lies ahead, this decisive deed-bowing to Caesar will always come into play.

The mobilization of the church,[38] the erecting of a sort of state church in the United States during the war, the civil installation of a military chaplaincy, the funds issued to the church, the connections between the secretary of war and the clergy—all of these necessitated in America what did not exist: one unified church. Thus a war organization was created as part of the Federal Council of the Churches of Christ, which had existed since 1908. This organization is an umbrella organization over the Protestant churches, something along the lines of the German Evangelical Committee.[39] Under the influence of the mood of war and enthusiasm [Begeisterung], which (as happened among us) for the first time allowed the antagonisms of the confessions and theological schools to fade, a mood of brotherly love arose, a spirit of brotherly cooperation, and mutual, self-sacrificing tolerance. It was one of the most beautiful things the American churches have ever experienced. Next to all the bad which was produced in the war propaganda, the most exemplary of the Americans, convinced of the rightness of their cause, experienced something of what we experienced in 1914. They look back on those days with sorrowful longing. And among the greatest things they experienced was the rise of a new and great ideal for the church, which up to this point lie quietly and unconsciously within their souls: the ideal of the *one* American church.

The American church situation looks like chaos to the European. There are more than two hundred official religions and denominations. The immigrants have come from all countries of Europe and brought with them the faith of their

---

[37] It is to the merit of the *Christian Century*, the most influential ecclesiastical weekly in America, that it raised the question of guilt regarding the war in a completely honorable fashion by means of the article by H. E. Barnes. HS

[38] Compare the depiction by W. A. Brown, *The Church in America*, 92 ff. RF

[39] *Deutscher Evangelischer Kirchenausschuß*, under whose auspices Sasse had studied in America. RF

homeland. Roman and Eastern Catholic churches exist alongside Anglican and Calvinistic churches, Lutherans alongside the sects which arose at the time of the Reformation. And not only do these religions which in Europe are separated by the borders of countries exist next to each other in the same city, even in the same house, but also even the various centuries are advocated! There are Lutherans today for whom the fathers of the sixteenth and seventeenth centuries yet have canonical authority, and among whom Ihmels[40] is completely distrusted. There are others who have already reached the nineteenth century and have an understanding of Erlangen theology. The Prussian Union too is in America in a small and therefore fairly insignificant church, The Evangelical Synod, which appears to be irretrievably lost in Calvinism. One sees how complicated the situation is when he considers that all these, and the many new fellowships which have come to existence in the country itself, dwell next to each other as individual congregations scattered over the same area. And further complicating matters is the fact that the populace of America is not stationary, but in the throes of steady migration. Thus the old Puritan cities, like Boston for instance, have become major cities for Catholicism.

The consequence of this, along with the concurrent leveling effect of American life, is an elimination of confessional antitheses. It is clear that it was finally unbearable when the congregations of a small city of ten thousand (at least six or seven in such cities) were in standing competition, each condemning the others for false doctrine and seeking their members. It was often purely accidental that one belonged to this or that confession, and very easy to switch. Interdenominational organizations, such as the Young Men's Christian Association, have existed for a long time. A common type of Methodistic piety was cultivated in revival meetings and has spread from church to church through its very singable songs. And there is the inborn and nurtured American sense for tolerance, and the influence of Freemasonry, which is quite powerful throughout America, but especially in the Calvinistic churches. All this has created a common religious atmosphere, in which the confessional lines are blurred. Thus fighting has been replaced by cooperation, one of the great American catchwords.

The Federal Council of the Churches of Christ is the great advocate of this work. The following is an example of how this movement takes form in concrete situations of ecclesiastical life. People invite each other to services at their respective churches, even to common celebrations of the Supper. There are common pastoral conferences for the clergy of the various churches. Laymen and even pastors move quite easily from one church to another. Joint evangelization of the

---

[40] Ludwig Heinrich Ihmels (1858–1933) taught systematic theology at Erlangen and Leipzig and tended toward orthodox Lutheranism. Pieper, for example, criticizes Ihmels' "subjectivism" and his understanding of the inspiration of Scripture, justification, the vicarious satisfaction, and many other points. See Francis Pieper, *Christian Dogmatics* (St. Louis: Concordia, 1950), 1:124 et passim. MH

unchurched takes place, and everyone is free to join the church of his liking. The Federal Council of Hartford, for instance, organized a visitation mission. The messengers go from house to house and ask the residents whether they belong to a church and propagandize not only for *one* church, but also for *the* churches. There are common lecture halls for free religious instruction. Common curricula are handed out, and even joint education takes place. Indeed, there are already churches which no longer belong to any confession—"Community Churches"[41]—in which "free" Christian or general religious services are held. And even Jews often belong to these [organizations]. More and more such churches are being started, not only in the large cities, but also in other areas.

And Judaism too, which in the American mix of peoples is not a foreign nation, but a religious fellowship, has been drawn into this movement. The synagogue, in common American parlance, is one of the "churches." When a new church is dedicated, the local rabbi brings his best wishes along with the other clergy of the area. In Baltimore this summer Christian services were held in a synagogue.[42] The question of how far Jesus of Nazareth can be acknowledged moves liberal Judaism very much. In any case, liberal Judaism has already appropriated the Social Gospel with its message of the kingdom of God and thus belief in a personal Messiah has been given up. The idea behind all this is called the "catholic mind," the catholic, universal-churchly spirit, in contrast to the "sectarian mind," the sectarian spirit of the old confessions, in particular, Roman Catholicism and Lutheranism. This great movement is making its way through the people, who are completely unfamiliar with theological differences. But it is also permeating theological circles; indeed, it is beginning to rule theology.

The theological faculties, for the most part, do still serve the various individual denominations, but the large and most significant institutions of the East are nearly all already interdenominational. Theologians from twenty-five churches studied at the seminary at Hartford, where I was a guest for a year. They all leave the institution with the same theology. Which church they will serve depends completely upon happenstance. I know of Quakers, unbaptized at that, who went to serve as pastors in Congregationalist churches. There they will baptize adults and children by immersion or sprinkling, whichever is desired. They will administer the Supper to anyone who may request it. This is the visible expression of the great desire for unity. The ideal of the *one* American church is like a dream in the souls of the Americans. The people and the theologians, the youth[43] who are

---

[41] Sasse writes this in English in the original. MH

[42] The synagogue was placed at the disposal of a homeless Christian congregation on Sundays, but only after a spirited struggle within the leadership of the synagogue regarding the question whether or not a house dedicated to the service of the one God may be allowed to be used by preachers of the Trinity. The idea of tolerance won the day. HS

[43] The student conference at Evanston demanded "that one united Church be substituted for denominational organizations" (*ChrCent* [1926]: 59). HS

impetuous and demanding that the last denominational fences be torn down, and the older men, such as Dr. Cadman,[44] the president of the Federal Council (who is naturally very circumspect and convinced that this goal will not be accomplished in the immediate future)—they all hope for the day when *one* American church will encompass the *one* American nation. To us Germans this development appears to be shining justification of the European idea of one church for one people [*Volkskirche*]. The great-grandchildren of those who once forsook the churches of the old world in order to find freedom of faith in the sects long for the church. A very clear picture emerges when we note the positive position of the state over against the churches. It learned to understand and value its significance during the war. We consider the remarks of the leading politicians who constantly emphasize that the problems of educating the people cannot be solved without the effective cooperation of the church. We furthermore consider the movement for the introduction of religious instruction in the public schools (which surely cannot achieve its goal). There is a powerful movement toward the church running through the American people. The age of the sect is past, and an age of the church is beginning.

How will this movement run its course? Will it lead to a great union movement? There are unions in process, but there will be no great, general union. The great organizations of the existing churches will not be dissolved. An organizational unification has been impossible and will remain so. A doctrinal or liturgical unification is even less possible. Thus the way of American church union will be something else. It is the way of the service organization [*Arbeitsgemeinschaft*]. Each standing church may keep its organizational forms, its confession, its liturgy. These things are all finally unessential. The nature of Christianity, so say the Americans, is service, *Dienst*, deed. What each one believes, what Christology he has, how he prays to his God, and what doctrine of the Sacraments he has—these are all matters of indifference.[45] Christianity is service, the church is a service organization [*Arbeitsgemeinschaft*]. What was formerly a confession of faith is today a program for deeds of service, and this program is the Social Gospel. This is the new concept of the church in America. She came to Stockholm with this concept of the church and with it pointed to the way of unity for all of Christianity on the earth.

---

44 Samuel Parkes Cadman (1864–1936) was a Congregationalist clergyman, pastor at various churches in New York City, President of the FCCCA and radio preacher (*Lutheran Cyclopedia*, 123). Sasse heard Cadman preach at his church in Brooklyn on December 20, 1925. Letter to Canon Leonard Hodgson, December 23, 1935 (Geneva: WCC Archives, Faith & Order Files). MH/RF

45 "Why should things like Baptism divide?" says the well-known Dr. Fosdick, currently pastor of a Baptist church in New York. HS

Harry Emerson Fosdick (1878–1969) was the minister of Park Avenue Baptist Church from 1925 until his retirement in 1946. This church, under his leadership, became the well-known interdenominational Riverside Church (J. D. Douglas, *New 20th-Century Encyclopedia of Religious Knowledge* [2d ed.; Grand Rapids: Baker, 1991], 337). RF

He who has understood and grasped this idea of the church, and why circumstances in America necessarily lead to it, has perceived the essence of modern American Christianity. So many of the phenomena in the ecclesiastical life of America (think of the blurring of the confessional boundaries and the practical exercise of tolerance) remind us Germans of our own ecclesiastical history of the eighteenth century. And we see the ideas of the Enlightenment clearly repeated in this concept of the church and this view of Christianity. Spinoza's[46] definition of belief and unbelief in the fourteenth chapter of the *Theological and Political Tractate*, Lessing's conception of Christianity as the implementation of the command to love,[47] all the classic thoughts of the Enlightenment on the replacement of dogmatic religion by a religion of "sentiment and deed"—all these are alive and well in the churches of the Social Gospel. The great prophecy about the future of Protestantism which Goethe expressed in his last dialogue with Eckermann,[48] which summarized the ideas of the Enlightenment, appears to have been fulfilled:

> And the unfortunate Protestant propensity toward the sect will cease to be as well. . . . Then as soon as the pure teaching and love of Christ is grasped and inculcated as it really is, one will feel like a man, great and free. And he will place very little value in the trifling matters of external worship [*Kultus*]. And we will all, more and more, move from a Christianity of the Word and faith ever more to a Christianity of sentiment and deed.

Will this be the future of Protestantism? Or perhaps its end? We who have seen the fulfillment of Goethe's prophecy in the modern American concept of church find a much different assertion ringing in our souls, a very old and unmodern assertion: "Est autem ecclesia congregatio sanctorum et vere credentium in qua evangelium recte docetur et recte administrantur sacramenta" ["And the church is the gathering of the saints and those who truly believe, among whom the Gospel is rightly taught and the Sacraments are rightly administered"].[49] Is

---

[46] Benedict or Baruch Spinoza (1632–1677) was born in Amsterdam of Jewish parents. He became skeptical of the past and discarded both Judaism and Christianity. He was expelled from the synagogue at Amsterdam.

> In the *Theologico-politicus* Spinoza argues for religious freedom so long as the interest of the State in good works is satisfied. He maintains that theology and philosophy have nothing in common, and repudiates the authority demanded by the former over the latter on the ground that theology deals with the anthropomorphic attributes and relations of God, and philosophy with clear notions. (*New Schaff-Herzog*, 9:49) MH

[47] Gotthold Ephraim Lessing (1729–1781) was a rationalist. Lessing contrasted Christianity with the Christian Religion and the Gospel of John with the simple Testament of John, devoid of all dogmas. John's message then was reduced to these "simple and short" words: "Little children, love one anther" ("The Testament of John," *Lessing's Theological Writings* [trans. Henry Chadwick; Stanford: Stanford University Press, 1957], 58). RF

[48] Johann Peter Eckermann (1792–1854) was a German writer and a "friend and literary assistant to Goethe" (*Webster's Biographical Dictionary* [Springfield, Mass.: G. & C. Merriam, 1964], 463). MH

[49] This reading of the Latin text of AC VII 1 is the same as the one found in the *Triglotta* (p. 46) with the addition of the words *et vere credentium*, "and those who truly believe." The text found in the *BS* (p. 61) has *pure docetur* in place of *recte docetur*. MH

this concept of the church antiquated? And if it is not, why has it not made the trip to America? It has not because it poses with inexorable seriousness the question which for our religious thought is final and most important: the question of truth.

The American concept of the church basically avoids this question. It surrenders dogma and liturgy as something unessential—"trifling matters" as Goethe put it. For us, however, both of these belong to the essence of the church: the Word and the Sacrament, confession and liturgy. We understand the protest against an ossified orthodoxy and a dreary ritualism, and we agree with this protest. But we believe that the church possesses in the *Verbum Dei* ["Word of God"] the eternal truth, over against all the relativism of human knowledge. And we believe that in the evangelically understood Sacraments of Baptism and the Lord's Supper, that in the liturgical life of the church which is grounded on these things, the powers are present which are able to establish a new and real human fellowship, even in an age in which all human fellowships are unraveling.

Just as one cannot conceive of the concept of truth without granting the possibility of error, so our concept of church cannot be conceived of without simultaneously considering the concepts of apostasy and heresy. It is interesting to note how, in the new American hymnals, verses of hymns which lament the division of the church or heresy have been expunged or changed—and this not merely for esthetic reasons. The American church which is the Federal Council finally stands ready to accept any sect that wishes to join it, whether the sacramental-less Quakers, the most absurd Adventism, or the Baptists. It would also accept Roman Catholicism with open arms. It is a church which has renounced the idea that it is possible to possess the truth and the requirements necessitated by that truth for carrying out its work.

This development is deeply connected with the entire intellectual situation in America. Just as the question of truth in American philosophy has, since the time of William James,[50] been replaced by the question of utility, so also pragmatism has forced its way into theology. The necessary consequences of this are clear to anyone who has noted how steadily the question has arisen that if Christianity is finally service, whether faith in a personal God is of the essence of Christianity. When a program for service [*Arbeitsprogramm*] replaces the confession of the faith, then this is only a short step to take. The eternal truths of the faith become theories to justify our work [*Arbeitshypothesen*]. The living God becomes the theory to justify our work of perfecting civilization. The cross of Christ becomes the theory to justify the work of missions among the Islamic peoples. The living Christ becomes the theory to justify missions in India. To be sure, this final step

---

50 William James (1842–1910), pragmatist, was a professor of psychology and philosophy at Harvard University. "He held that we have a 'right to believe in' the existence of God (because it makes us 'better off'), but [we have] no scientific certainty of the validity of that belief" (*ODCC*, 861). RF

is not taken consciously. But is this not the consequence of this concept of the church?

If we Germans criticize this programmatic concept of the church from the viewpoint of our own presuppositions, we must never forget the fact that pragmatism contains a deep truth. It is the worldview of people whose greatness has been revealed not in the realm of philosophical speculation, but in practical dealings. Such people have a keen ability to recognize the correspondence between theoretical truth and practical life. They have the correct conviction that the great theoretical questions are at the same time practical questions, and that there are truths which are discovered not at a desk, but in the struggles of life. It is the thought which expresses the Johannine concept that he who does God's will will know whether the teaching of Jesus is from God. American theology highly values this concept (just as Ritschl[51] once did). The question of the absolute nature of Christianity is, for instance, not merely a theoretical but a practical problem. And it will only be decided by wrestling with the religions of the world.

The mistake of the American thought, however, is the one-sided emphasis on the connection between truth and life. And a concept's significance for life, or the outcome in life, has been made the criterion for truth. What does the thousand-year rule of Islam over the lands of ancient Christianity prove in respect to the truth of one or both of these religions? Is the Catholic veneration of Mary proof of its truth content? Are there not errors which have the highest practical significance for life? This is the point at which every philosophy of value [Wertphilosophie] fails, and pragmatism is a philosophy of value. There is no bridge leading from value to truth. Judgments of value never allow themselves to be transformed into [absolute] judgments of being.

A church may be ever so valuable for the education of the human race.[52] It may perform many practical tasks in service of its culture. But it cannot base its claim to the truth upon such things. The foundation of truth must be found by going down a different path. This is what we criticize in the modern American concept of church, not its emphasis upon the significance of the church for life. We too know that Christianity is a matter of life, that its greatest powers and its deepest essence are revealed in the work of life, in the struggles of the world. We too hear the "This do, and you will live," which Jesus leveled at the scribe who was stuck in his theories (Luke 10:28). But the question is not merely about the fact *that* we are called to act in the world, but rather *how* we are to act. To be sure, the church and the individual Christian are called to serve humanity. But not every human action

---

[51] Albrecht Ritschl (1822–1889) was a German Protestant theologian who had an immense influence through the turn of the twentieth century. He was the founder of the so-called "Ritschlian School." His system, with its emphasis on ethics, has been called the "Theology of Moral Value." It had two foci, reconciliation and especially the kingdom of God, neither of which resembled the confessional statements of Lutheranism. RF

[52] Perhaps this is a reference to Lessing's essay "The Education of the Human Race," in Chadwick, *Lessing's Theological Writings*, 82–98. RF

is Christian, even if it springs from the most noble motives of a purely human ethic. The Gospel desires not only to be the impulse to action, but it also wants to provide a great content to our doing. And this while it establishes eternal norms, which in opposition to the relative worth of a purely human ethic lay claim to absolute validity. This is the point at which ethics and dogmatics are inseparably connected. It is the point at which the church's program for service meets its confession of faith. At this point it becomes clear that the effect of the church on the world depends upon its possession of the eternal, absolute truth.

But even as we level this criticism, we are convinced that this applies not only to the Americans, but also in large measure to our own theological thought. We will not point out individual examples here of how among us the concept of the church has also so often been mollified, that the claim to truth has disappeared or threatens to do so. In our theology the relativism of historical thought has had an effect which is shown most clearly by the theology of Ernst Troeltsch.[53] His concept of the church (here we think of his well-known definitions of church and sect) consciously excludes the question of truth. The doctrine of the church, among other things, is given up, said Troeltsch,[54] with that "propensity to over-formulate the living connection of Jesus to life into an absolute, . . . dogmatic truth, which alone saves." Then he continues, "In view of all this, one could perhaps find [the use of] the word 'church' to designate the form of religious reality among us to be generally objectionable." And when he then seriously proposes "to generally renounce the word 'church,' " he unwillingly confirms that the claim to truth is of the essence of the church.

The example of this great and honest scholar, who consistently carries modern relativism to its end, shows that the situation in all of Protestantism on both sides of the ocean is the same. A powerful desire for the church is today moving through the Protestantism of all countries. But it lacks a great concept of the church, which truly comprehends its nature. The tasks of the future are arising from this situation.

Thus the concept of the church will also be at the center of the crisis in American Christianity. The confessionalism which has been condemned and rejected as a "sectarian mind" lives and will rise up in a mighty counterattack. It is apparent that it will not be renewed in those churches and sects of Calvinistic origin. The destruction of the confessional inheritance, even in churches such as the Presbyterian,[55] shows that it is doubtful whether there will be a rebirth of dogmatic Calvinism. It appears as though the churches of the Federal Council, which

---

[53] Ernst Peter Wilhelm Troeltsch (1865–1923) was a leader of the *Religionsgeschichtliche Schule* ("History of Religions School"). He was "among the first seriously to consider the claims to truth of other world religions alongside Christianity. . . . This position led him into increasing relativism" (*ODCC*, 1643). He was a professor of the history of philosophy and civilization at Berlin (1915–1923) when Sasse was a student there. RF

[54] *RGG*[1] 3:1154–55. HS

[55] This is most clearly seen in the disappearance of the doctrine of predestination. HS

is of Calvinistic background, may be the future form of American Calvinistic Christianity. The conservative wing in these churches, the Fundamentalists, sharply criticize the cultural Protestantism of the Federal Council from a strongly biblicistic standpoint. But this Fundamentalism has no connection to the idea of the church of the Reformation. Fundamentalism[56] is a powerful movement of great religious force, but it knows, in a way similar to our "Christianity of Fellowship" [*Gemeinschafts-christentum*],[57] only of the concept of the religious fellowship, not that of the church. And therefore it is incapable of real church formation and exerting creative influence on the culture. Above all its naive eschatology, its expectation of the immediate end of the world, limits the horizon of its disciples to the present living generation.

Three real churches, however, each of which possess an independent and unique concept of the church, preserve the confessional inheritance of the past and will in the coming religious struggles wrestle for the soul of America: the Anglican (called "Protestant Episcopal" in America), the Roman Catholic, and the Lutheran churches.

AMERICAN ANGLICANISM

Among these the Episcopal Church is small in number but has great influence, and the greatest prospects in the struggle for the American soul.[58] The liturgical movement which is beginning also in America has its center here. This church possesses what the Calvinistic churches have given up, and which they, in spite of all their attempts to "shape" the Divine Service, could never restore. It has a real liturgy with all the "irrational value" which resided in the historically transmitted cultus. Thus it exercises a powerful force of attraction upon people who are tiring of the dispassionate "enlightenment" of the average Divine Service of modern America and long for a religion with more depth. One differentiates in America between liturgical and nonliturgical churches. A victory of the liturgical churches over the others, which would be demonstrated by a quick and strong growth of these churches, is completely in the realm of possibility. Such an event would benefit the Episcopal Church most of all. This church, furthermore, has a unique concept of church and is at the center of an ecclesiastical movement for unification which runs parallel to the Federal Council effort. While modern American Calvinism sees Christianity's bond of unity, as we have seen, in practical work (Life and Work), the Anglicans advocate a program for unification on the

---

[56]   This movement began after the war, called forth according to W. A. Brown by the apocalyptic currents consequent to the disillusionment which the war brought to the belief in advancement (*The Church in America*, 145). Its basic doctrines are the verbal inspiration of the Bible, the virgin birth of Jesus, the sacrificial death of Jesus, the return to judgment. HS (Also the resurrection and deity of Christ. RF)

[57]   Perhaps a reference to Schleiermacher's concept of the church as above all "a fellowship," a *Gemeinschaft* (*Glaubenslehre*, § 2.2). RF

[58]   This church has approximately one and a quarter million members. HS

basis of the symbols of the ancient church and an episcopal system of church government (Faith and Order).[59] The Anglicans have treated the work of the Federal Council only as the first step in the realization of their own program.

This church also possesses a concept of the church different from that of the Federal Council, to which it does not belong and is only connected by a loose cooperation in practical matters. According to the view of the Episcopal Church, confession and church order [Verfassung] are of the essence of the church. But the confession meant here accords neither with the content nor the meaning of that of the Reformation. It is the ancient church's confession, a portion of the ancient ecclesiastical tradition, more a matter of liturgy and canon law than dogmatics.If we can describe the church which is the Federal Council as a fellowship for service [Arbeitsgemeinschaft], then this church is a fellowship for worship [Kultusgemeinschaft]. It is like every church without dogmatics. Every dogmatics finds a haven within it, from a Catholicism independent from Rome to the most liberal Protestantism. The great issues of the Reformation, such as the doctrine of justification, have been shoved aside in its program for unification. The uncertainty of this church regarding dogmatic questions is revealed again and again in the minutes of its synodical meetings where questions of doctrine and worship [Kultus] are dealt with. Here we do not find the decisive question "Is it true?" but rather, "What is ecumenical?" In this concept of the church the question of truth is avoided.

But precisely here lies the reason for the great prospects for the Episcopal Church. Here is the reason for its affinity with the Federal Council, in spite of all its particular differences. And here is the possibility that it may finally be successor to the Federal Council. This point of view regarding dogmatic questions corresponds to the intellectual situation described above, to that "catholic mind," that absolute tolerance which maintains that it is un-Christian to pose the question of truth and falsehood in religion. It would be a good thing for all those in Germany interested in the Anglican movement for unity, and the coming deliberations in Lausanne regarding it, to consider that this concept of the church will destroy the movement. For it is a concept of the church concerned not with the one fellowship of faith, but with the one fellowship of worship [Kultus]. And its concern with the question of the ancient symbols is not so much for the sake of their dogmatic validity, as for their liturgical [kultische] and legal validity.

With its program for unification, the Episcopal Church will, in all likelihood, have a great significance for the religious future of America. Its concept of the church possesses much more religious depth than that of the Federal Council. But it breaks down at a crucial point. In the final and decisive struggle between

---

[59] Sasse was very involved in this movement. He attended the First World Conference on Faith and Order in Lausanne, Switzerland, in 1927; he edited the official German report of that conference. The First Universal Christian Conference on Life and Work was in Stockholm in 1925 (see above; see also the reference to Lausanne below.) RF

Catholic and Protestant Christianity taking place in the West (in Europe as much as in America), it has nothing to say. Standing between Catholicism and Protestantism[60] and as interested in unification with Rome as with the Evangelical churches, the Episcopal Church naively believes that these two great forms of Christianity can be united into a higher synthesis, a third confession, which can help lead Protestantism toward Rome. But the decisive question in this discussion between the confessions is whether or not the Reformation was right or not. If it was incorrect, then we Protestants must return to Rome. If it was correct, then the Roman Church must be transformed by the Reformation. There is no third option, no *via media* in which Cardinal Newman believed during his later Anglican period.[61] There is no third option, at least not for people who still know what truth and falsehood are.

Thus the shadow of Rome looms behind the Episcopal Church. The discussion with Roman Catholicism is moving nearer and nearer. This will have a profound effect upon the Protestant churches in America and perhaps lead to very difficult confessional struggles. For the rise of the Catholic Church, which now is already significantly stronger than any individual Protestant church,[62] its entrance into the political arena, its confidence of victory, its not-always circumspect demeanor—all seriously jeopardize the peace which exists between the denominations. Already now there is, especially in Freemasonry, a strong and partially fanatical anti-Catholic movement. Up to now traditional American tolerance, the basic American principle of the freedom of faith, protected the Catholic Church and made possible its advancement. Perhaps Rome's confidence of victory and its conviction that it will outlast Protestantism are justified nowhere as well as in the United States, where it stands over a teeming chaos of Protestant Christianity. And perhaps nowhere is the world politics of the Vatican, which thinks in terms of continents and centuries, seen more clearly than in the United States.

AMERICAN CATHOLICISM

American Catholicism, to be sure, requires Rome's diligent attention. On the one hand, the means of American civilization are used in service of the church, and unique characteristics of the American situation have been calculated with great psychological adroitness. But on the other hand, the strength and purity of

---

[60] "I believe that the Episcopal Church in America will cease to be, when it ceases to be Protestant; and 2. it will cease to be, should it ever become merely Protestant" (Henry Davies, "The Future of the Episcopal Church in America," *AThR* [July 1926]). Compare also the article "What Is Disturbing the Episcopalians?" *ChrCent* (1926): 861 ff. HS

[61] John Henry Newman (1801–1890) was a priest of the Church of England and a leader of the Oxford Movement. He and other Anglicans used the term *via media* to describe Anglicanism as "the middle way" between the Papacy and Protestantism. In 1845 he was received into the Roman Catholic Church and in 1879 was made cardinal (*ODCC*, 1141–42, 1691). RF

[62] In America, Rome numbers some fourteen to sixteen million members. The numbers aren't entirely certain. HS

Catholicism is threatened by the all-leveling effect of American life. The decline of the contemplative life as the ideal of piety, the influence of the laity in the life of the congregation, the often very weak character of confessional consciousness, the frequent apostasy of individuals and entire congregations, the American sense of tolerance and characteristic patriotism—all these phenomena are dangers to the faithfulness of American Catholicism to Rome. If the most difficult conflict which Rome's politics can evoke in the human soul, and which could exist for American Catholics were to arise, namely, the conflict between faithfulness to nation and faithfulness to Pope, it is doubtful how the issue would be decided. Often in their circles one hears it expressed that American Catholicism ought to represent a higher, purer form of Catholicism than that of Europe. And many a Catholic feels a closer kinship to high church Anglicans than to his own fellow Catholics in Europe, especially those in officially Roman Catholic countries. To guard the American Catholics from the heresy of "Americanism"[63] and apostasy remains a difficult task. And the church is attempting to do this by educating higher level American clergy in Europe.

Wherein does the attractive force of this church lie? It is found, as with every church, in the uniqueness and strength of its concept of the church. The Catholic Church is not only a fellowship for work and worship, but it is also a fellowship of faith in the strictest dogmatic sense. It possesses not only a complete approach to the problem of culture [*Kulturprogramm*], and indeed one which has been much more thoroughly thought through than that of the Federal Council, it possesses not only a worship [*Kultus*] which satisfies religious sensibilities, as does the Episcopal Church, but it also gives, in its dogma, the answer to the question of truth. "It is for this reason so difficult to say why I am a Catholic, because there are ten-thousand reasons which are all encompassed in one reason: Catholicism is true. . . . It alone speaks as though it possesses the truth."[64] Thus one intellectually significant convert spoke for himself, and many others, as he gave the reason for his conversion to Rome. Thus the great time of Catholicism in America will come when the question of truth finally becomes the burning question of life. There are times when this question is silent, because other questions are the order for the day. America is passing through such a time today, an entirely undogmatic age, in which the question of what is "effective" rules life and thought.

We Germans too are passing through such an era, but at least it is nearing its end in theology. For the theological thought of the future will again become strongly dogmatic. The mark of the intellectual situation in Europe and America is the disintegration of the eternal norms of thought and action, which in earlier

---

[63] "Americanism" was an ill-defined movement in American Catholicism, associated with efforts to adapt Catholicism to American culture, condemned by Pope Leo XIII in *Testem Benevolentiae* in 1899 (Gerald P. Fogarty, *The HarperCollins Encyclopedia of Catholicism* [ed. Richard P. McBrien; San Francisco: Harper, 1995], 40–42). RF

[64] "Why I Am a Catholic," *Forum* (1925). HS

times were provided people by their belief in revelation. The Enlightenment stripped these norms of their character as revelation and declared them a product and result of the human mind, but sought to maintain their absolute validity. In the course of the nineteenth century this validity was lost as well. Absolute norms became relative values. What has become of the idea of the good in the ethical systems of modern philosophy? One need only compare the ethics of Kant[65] and Paulsen[66] in order to know why today most of humanity no longer knows the difference between good and evil. Or one need only compare the doctrine of truth in Nietzsche, Spengler, and Troeltsch in order to grasp the tragedy of the philosophy which has dug its own grave by discovering that there finally is no truth.

This disintegration of eternal norms, which are based upon the revelation of the living God and not upon the human mind, is the most profound cause for the decline of modern culture. This explains the chaos of our intellectual and especially of our religious life. This explains the desire for a reparation of what has been lost. Here lies the power for attraction of all sects and churches which claim to possess the absolute truth. They may be strict biblicists, or claim some newly revealed meaning of the Bible, or be a fellowship in which an allegedly halo-clad prophet claims to be able to produce new revelations, or be a theosophy with claims of revelation, or be the Catholic Church with its dogma. There is certainly no doubt that Catholicism will always have the greatest prospects among these various phenomena. This is the situation in Germany and other European countries. These things will certainly likewise appear in America. The Catholics see them coming and are waiting for the day when erring people, hungering and thirsting for the truth, will bow before Catholic dogma. And this dogma, according to a well-known expression, recognizes only two confessions in America: Roman Catholicism and unbelievers.

AMERICAN LUTHERANISM

Whenever Protestantism encounters Catholicism in a decisive discussion, it is necessary for it to remember its religious uniqueness and to grasp once again the basic thoughts of the Reformation. Protestantism lives from and has its superiority over the Catholic Church in the religious ideas of the Reformation, not in the Enlightenment's ideas of a churchless cultural Protestantism. One church can always and only be overcome by another. Thus the discussion with Catholicism must give rise among the Protestant churches to a consideration of their Reformation heritage.

But where is this heritage? In its purest form it has been preserved in the Lutheran churches. And here is their significance for the religious future of the

---

[65] Immanuel Kant (1724–1804) denied the metaphysical and considered morality to be the chief content of Christianity. MH

[66] Friedrich Paulsen (1846–1908), educator, philosopher, and ethicist, taught at the University of Berlin from 1871 to the end of his life. MH

United States. It is quite in vogue in Germany to undervalue American Lutheranism. The reason for this is that the Lutheran churches have far fewer members than do the churches of Calvinistic origin.[67] And the Lutherans are not united, leading an isolated life, having little influence on the intellectual life of the nation. But they are living and growing churches. If the movement toward unity (the first great consequence of which was the formation of the United Lutheran Church in 1918[68]) continues and leads to the unification of all Lutherans into one church, it will be one of the most significant churches in America. The life of these churches dispels the foolish notion that Lutheranism's doctrine of justification necessarily leads to quietism. There is in America perhaps no more active church than the Missouri Synod, which is the most dogmatically rigorous Lutheran Church in the country. The history of the organization of this church demonstrates that Lutheranism can exist in forms other than a state church or a church dependent upon the state (as we hear happily repeated time and again in Europe). Lutheranism is never more vibrant than where it is free from all guardianship by a secular authority.

Furthermore, American Lutheranism dispels the prejudice that Lutheranism is only a national expression of the Christian faith. Certainly, it was brought by the German and Scandinavian immigrants to America. But by setting aside its mother tongues and becoming an American, English-speaking Lutheranism, it is making an attempt—very significant for the history of the church—to show that the greatest thing which the German people have brought to a developing American culture is the heritage of the German Reformation. And the Reformation is a matter which transcends nations. To be sure, the dangers of the process of Americanization are great. The Lutheran churches will only be able to overcome them if they become a great intellectual force in the country. They must, by means of a great theology, which must be more than a defense and repetition of old Protestant Orthodoxy, engage the other churches in discussion and compel these churches to seriously consider the basic ideas of the Reformation.

And not only the fate of these Lutheran churches depends upon whether or not this happens, but also this is the decisive question for the religious future of all of America. For a strong and intellectually powerful church—one which rests on the concept of the church of the *Confessio Augustana* [Augsburg Confession] and thus is not merely a society for work and worship, but a real fellowship of faith in the Evangelical sense—will of necessity have a leading role in the history of the church to come in America. It alone is prepared to do that which neither the churches of the Federal Council nor Anglicanism can do. *Only Lutheranism*

---

[67] The Lutherans number about as many as the Presbyterians, about two and a half million, while the Methodists and the Baptists count more than eight million members. The Congregationalists list nine hundred thousand. HS

[68] The United Lutheran Church in America (ULCA) was formed by the merger of the General Synod (1820), the United Synod South (1863), and the General Council (1867). RF

can pose the question of truth over against the Roman Catholic Church [emphasis added]. For it belongs to the essence of Lutheranism to raise the claim to truth, not for a human authority, for an infallible teaching office, rather for the *Verbum Dei* ["Word of God"], which it possesses. It acknowledges that every church possesses the truth in so far as the Word of God is present. The greatness and uniqueness of the Lutheran concept of the church is in this connection between its view of the church and its view of the Word of God.

The difference, however, over against the Fundamentalist fellowship is in the view of the Word of God. The Fundamentalists too pose the question of truth over against all churches on the basis of their strict biblicism. But what a difference there is between their view of the Bible, which elevates the letter of the Bible to law for human thought and dealings,[69] and the Lutheran doctrine of the Word of God! Over against the mechanism and clandestine materialism of that way of explaining the Bible stands genuine Lutheran theology as something completely different. Lutheranism conceives of the Word of God as something more living, because it considers it first as the spoken and incarnate Word, and only secondly as the written Word.

These are the confessional forces which stand over against the Federal Council in America. Each of these confessional churches has its own concept of the church and its own ecumenical program. The Lutherans too possess their own unity movement in the Lutheran World Convention.[70] Thus the Federal Council of the Churches of Christ, with its program for church unification, does not represent, as its name asserts, "the churches of Christ." It represents only the churches of Calvinistic background and fellowship. Alongside modern Calvinism, which is embodied in this great organization, stand the other great confessions of Western Christianity: Catholicism, Anglicanism, and Lutheranism. The old confessional distinctions are not antiquated. They continue to exist in their stark contrast. They will not allow themselves to be extinguished. For in these distinctions the questions posed by the Reformation continue to live. And questions are never resolved by being ignored, but only by being answered. The great American movement for union necessarily shatters on this fact. The religious future of the United States does not lie in the gradual, peaceful, and joint rise of the Christian churches into a higher unity. It lies rather in the intense struggles of the old confessions for the soul of the American people.

CONCLUSION: THE ECUMENICAL QUESTION

We have attempted in what has preceded to depict a few characteristic features of modern American Christianity, especially those which are most significant for our

---

[69] Think of the fight over the teaching of evolution and the "Ape Lawsuit" [Monkey Trial] at Dayton! HS

[70] Formed in 1923 at a conference in Eisenach, it was the predecessor to the Lutheran World Federation (1947). MH/RF

discussion with America. In conclusion, we would like to present a few remarks on the tasks of this discussion, and with this a fundamental thought on the ecumenical question.

A deep longing for the unity of the church of Christ is passing through the Christian world today. It is one of the most gripping testimonies of a coming rebirth of religion. In the days of the World War the idea of the *una sancta* ["one holy (church)"] awoke anew in the souls of people separated by an abyss of hatred. And since then the question of how a Christianity, divided by national and confessional differences, can be united has been raised everywhere. But here we must always make the fundamental distinction between national and confessional questions. For the real religious problem lies in the confessional divisions. We will only be able to grasp the nature of the ecumenical question, in its full seriousness and entire range, if we have genuinely perceived the unfathomable tragedy of this division of Christianity into various confessions, even within Protestantism. This tragedy lies in the fact that the confessional differences have to do not only with unessential and unimportant matters, but they also have to do precisely with Christ and the doctrine of God. It is common to denote the opposition between our piety and that which stands behind the Social Gospel of the Americans as an opposition between two different views of the kingdom of God. This is certainly correct. But this assertion will not suffice.

Modern Calvinism awaits the kingdom of God as the product of a development which in large measure is brought about by man's cooperation and his "good will." It rejects—in a way similar to the theory of catastrophe in Darwinistic evolution—real eschatology, because it attempts to conceive of the kingdom of God without its correlate, the last judgment. It can think in this way because the concept of judgment has simultaneously vanished from the doctrine of God. The severe characteristics of God which are contrary to reason, and which for us are of the essence of the living God, are not found in the modern American theologian's doctrine of God. How different are the doctrine of the universal "fatherhood of God" and the Lutheran doctrine of the sinner justified by grace! This is how foundational the differences are between the great forms of Protestant Christianity! These differences go to the very heart of the faith! Only a theological dilettantism, which never advances from talk to fact, can overlook this difference or declare it unessential.

We cannot, in the face of all this enthusiasm over the *una sancta*, and in the admiration of the many great characteristics of American Protestantism (e.g., its enormous power for action), ignore these great contradictions in faith and thought. Nor can we blur or give up the uniqueness of our faith. The secret of all individuality is that within all the particularities which distinguish one phenomenon from all others, life itself is concealed. So also we religious people live from that which is our most unique possession of faith. No matter what we can learn from the Americans (and these are important things, e.g., a view for the task of the church in modern society), the German churches cannot accept the American concept of God and its idea of the kingdom of God and thereby the Social Gospel. If our churches do so, they will be destroyed.

As true as it is, however, that our religious life depends upon the unique characteristic of the faith [*fides quae*] which we possess, still, we may not overlook another truth. We cannot separate ourselves from the other churches without becoming torpid in this isolation. We as a nation must give up the naive belief which every people has regarding itself, namely, that we are the focal point of world history. And likewise, as a church we must get used to the idea that we are not Protestantism. The religious and ecclesiastical decisions rendered in Germany may be ever so great. The events in the history of the church unfolding in America may be still more significant for the fate of all of Protestantism. Perhaps the decisive battle between Catholicism and Protestantism for the intellectual leadership of the West will be waged on American soil.

And in this connection we must also consider missions. Because we take part in the religious movements and theological discussions in present-day Germany, we see in them the advance of the history of the church. It may be that in the future, church historians will treat them as purely provincial events compared to the decisions of world historical dimension which in our century are being rendered on the mission fields. Here we think of the discussions of Christianity with the great religions of Asia or the struggles for the religious future of primitive peoples. These mighty tasks lie, so far as Protestantism is concerned, predominately in the hands of the American and English churches. Our participation in them may be limited to a more or less modest cooperation.

Even if we do take very seriously the differences of the faith which divide the Protestant churches (and we have to do this for the sake of the truth), still another fact remains. These churches stand together in a great fellowship of common fate. We must view our relationship to the American churches in view of this common fate. They cannot live without us, nor we without them. In this situation which our church faces, within the context of all of Protestantism (just as every denomination finds itself in the context of all of Christendom), is repeated the eternal tension between individuality and fellowship, freedom and constraint. This tension rules all of life and its dissolution would mean the end of life itself. Therefore the ecumenical problem is an eternal task, for which there is no final solution. The unity of the church of Christ will only be revealed at the end of the history of the church.

Therefore it is not our task to invent some utopian church ideal, in which the hard realities of the world are done away with, and which can only be realized upon the presupposition that error and sin no longer exist. Rather our practical tasks must be formulated on the basis of the current ecclesiastical situation. The most important task is the mutual understanding of churches. With terrifying clarity the events since the outbreak of the World War have made us all realize that not only peoples, but also churches as well, have lived side by side without knowing each other. And it is one of the most felicitous signs of our times that an earnest desire for mutual understanding has arisen and that a great self-encounter has begun between churches. This understanding is not easy, to be sure. Hasty contacts will not suffice for this. On all sides there must be a long, penetrating encounter with the uniqueness of an ecclesiastical culture, foreign to one's own, and this encounter must be born of deep love. For us this means, for instance, not only getting to know the American churches or viewing them as they are, but we also have to ask why their development necessarily has made them what they are today. If this question is seriously put, real understanding will result, and not that *tout comprendre* which ends in a characterless *tout pardonner*.[71] It must be that deep understanding which may always end at that point where further understanding is impossible. At that point the advocate of his point of view can only say, "Here I stand. I cannot do otherwise."[72]

We Germans—who perhaps possess, through the uniqueness of our historical thought, the gift of sympathy for a foreign piety [*Seelenleben*] in special measure—perhaps have the greater capability for such understanding. But the Americans perhaps have the stronger will for it. As a rule such discussion does not happen at conferences or in public discussions which separate people (which is one of the most ineffective means to create fellowship). It occurs rather in the course of personal encounter, in one-on-one contact. Anyone who has lived together with people of a different ecclesiastical culture remembers the unforgettable times when the discussion turned to the fundamental questions and revealed the deepest differences of faith and thought. Over such times lay the mystery of love, not the feeble feeling of sympathy which flows from belief in man, but the strong love of the NT, born of faith in God, which is only present where complete truthfulness rules, because love and truth are inseparable.

This understanding is the presupposition for the cooperative work of the church. Cooperation is one of the greatest concepts of American life. Its presupposition is the conviction that where more people of various characteristics work together, their power is not simply added, but multiplied exponentially. Here we individualistic Germans have something to learn from the Americans, even if we must reject the consequences of this thought for our understanding of the church. Already the striving for mutual understanding presupposes cooperation. There is something which belongs to the tasks of theology and which is theological work, though indeed it does not belong at the root of theology. It is rather an effect of theology and it transcends the boundaries of churches. How much has German theology meant for America! How much of Ritschl's thought, for instance, is found in the theology of the Social Gospel! And on the other hand, how have William James and the American psychology of religion affected us Germans! This cooperation in theology will, in the future, be organized according to plan and will concentrate particularly upon the socio-ethical problems.

---

[71] *Tout comprendre, c'est tout pardonner* ("To understand all is to forgive all"). RF

[72] As Luther at Worms. RF

In addition to the theological tasks, there are the practical matters. Each individual church cannot solve these on its own. Above all there are the great tasks of world missions, in which churches have begun to learn to work together. Missions are like no other ecclesiastical work. Nothing else causes churches to deal more closely with the NT, and this requires each denomination ever and again to measure its possession of the faith according to the Word of God. Thus missions cause a church to pose the question of truth to itself and others with inexorable seriousness. And there is no other sphere of ecclesiastical life in which the fearful tragedy of confessional splintering is so felt and the belief in one, holy, universal church—not as a human ideal, but as a divine reality—has become so living as here. In humble love and in inflexible truthfulness, the way of cooperation has to be found in each individual circumstance. It is the conscious decisions of people which point this way, and not laws and rules.

The only answer we have to the ecumenical question is for the churches to learn to understand each other, and work together at common tasks. There is no program for unification of the church. Man cannot organize the *una sancta*. For the church is more than a human organization. No attempt at union can ever bring about the goal. All such programs of the past and present make the same mistake. They circumvent the truth question. Unions have a purpose if they seek to heal divisions which have not arisen for dogmatic reasons or if they desire to unite churches whose faith life is essentially the same. But they can never unite the great types of Christianity as they have found form in the historic confessions. Therefore, the way to the unity of the church of Christ is never the way of the union. Finally, there simply is no way which people know or can manifest. Only God knows the way.

1928

KYRIOS[1]

In 1928, Sasse's name appeared for the first time as a participant in a series of conferences of British and German theologians; this, the second, was held at the Wartburg, near Eisenach, August 11–18, 1928. The conferences, which grew out of a suggestion at the Universal Christian Conference on Life and Work, Stockholm, 1925, were organized by George Bell, Bishop of Chichester, and Dr. Adolf Deissmann of the University of Berlin, Sasse's *Doktorvater*. This essay was presented at the Eisenach conference.

Following the third conference in Chichester, which Deissmann was unable to attend, Bishop Bell wrote his German collaborator "a brief account."

> I think that the person who made the greatest contribution to the Conference, or at any rate was outstanding and in advance of his previous work at previous Conferences, was Dr. Sasse. He was excellent and most constructive and suggestive.[2]

Such a remark must be considered in view of the very impressive company of scholars that he was honored to join: General Superintendent Otto Dibelius and Wilhelm Stählin among the Germans and from England J. M. Creed; C. H. Dodd; Sir Edwyn Hoskyns; J. K. Mozley; E. G. Selwyn.

Huss number 015-II
Hopf number 013

———◁◦◦◦▷———

All Christological expressions are, like all true theological propositions, confessions of faith. We can never say who Christ is without using expressions which imply the adoption of a personal attitude toward him.

The church's Christology begins in the NT with two great confessions of faith. The first is that of St. Peter: σὺ εἶ ὁ χριστός ("You are the Messiah," Mark 8:29). The second is the anonymous confession of the original Christian commu-

---

[1] This essay was published in English as "ΚΥΡΙΟΣ" in *Theology* 17.100 (October 1928): 223–29. It was published simultaneously in German in *Theologische Blätter* 7.10 (October 1928): 261–65. The translation given here is a reprint of that published in the journal *Theology*. The translator was A. E. J. Rawlinson. RF

[2] March 30, 1931; Lambeth Palace Library, Bell Papers, vol. 63, p. 177. RF

nities: Κύριος Ἰησοῦς ("Jesus is Lord," Rom 10:9; 1 Cor 12:3; Phil 2:11; cf. 2 Cor 4:5; Col 2:6). There is an inner connection between the two, but there are characteristic differences also. The first looks to the past. "You are the Messiah"—that is, the end, the fulfillment, of the history, a thousand years long, of the prophetic religion. "Jesus is Lord"—with the formulation of this sentence Christian faith begins to leave the Jewish homeland and to run its course through the peoples and religions of the world. The second confession represents an advance upon the first. The apostolic experience, the knowledge of the resurrection of Jesus, lies between. Beyond these two confessions, to which the other Christological expressions of the NT are subordinate, nothing more that is essential is said about Christ. There are no discoveries in Christology. The Christology of subsequent ages has no further task beyond the task of understanding more and more deeply the implications of these two confessions.

Kyrios is the name above all other names which Jesus bears in the Hellenistic communities of primitive Christianity. As the bearer of this name he stands on the side of God, inasmuch as Kyrios is God's holy name in the LXX. He stands at the same time as a rival, over against all other bearers of the name Kyrios. The name gives expression to his divine rank and majesty. He is invoked as Kyrios in prayer. He has become Kyrios as the result of his resurrection and exaltation. He bears the name as being the living and present "Lord," towards whom believers stand in that profound life relationship which is expressed by the formula ἐν Χριστῷ ["in Christ"]. His κυριότης ["lordship"] stands in a specific relation to the life of his ἐκκλησία ["church"], more especially as that life finds expression in worship. It is a relationship which is experienced more particularly in the κοινωνία ["fellowship"] which Christians have with him in the δεῖπνον κυριακόν ["Lord's Supper"]. The primitive church thus expresses by means of the name Kyrios the ultimate depths of its Christian faith, and at the same time distinguishes itself sharply in contrast with all other religions.

The *origin of this confession* of Jesus as Kyrios is one of the most important of the historical problems presented by the study of primitive Christianity. St. Paul found it already in existence before his conversion. Does it go back to Palestinian Christianity? Had the title Kyrios an Aramaic antecedent? Or are its origins Hellenistic?

In Hellenistic linguistic usage Kyrios is employed as a title of rulers, especially for the Roman Caesars, for numerous cult deities, and in the LXX as a substitute for the Jewish divine name. Behind the Greek word lurks an Oriental idea—the thought of an inner connection between godhead and kingship. The epithets applied to gods and kings are interchangeable all through the East. Jahve [Yahweh] in ancient Israel is called "King," and in later Judaism "King of kings." The replacement of the name Jahve by *Adonai* [אֲדֹנָי, "Lord"] belongs to the same context of ideas. In Aramaic the same process of linguistic development may be followed in the history of the word *mare* [מָרֵא, "lord"], which occurs twice in the book of Daniel as a title of the Babylonian world ruler (Dan 4:16, 21 [ET 4:19, 24]), and as a designation of God in the form "Lord of all kings" (Dan 2:47) and "Lord of heaven" (Dan 5:23). A similar use of the Aramaic *mare* may be illustrated also from Egypt and Syria. It is a forerunner—if not *the* forerunner—of the Hellenistic Κύριος in the Aramaic language. In Judaism the use of *mare* in the religious sense, despite the beginnings of such usage in Daniel and the fact that it occurs apparently already in the book of Job (36:22),[3] did not become generally prevalent, though it is found occasionally in the Talmud. The Hebrew *adonai* is not displaced by *mare*. The Kyrios idea, then (as it becomes generally evident, wherever we meet with it), is of Oriental origin. Hellenism, by supplying a Greek word which could take the place of a number of different Semitic words (*adon, mare, baal*), contributed merely a new and mighty expression to it. Especially characteristic is the use of the title Kyrios for the numerous cult deities of the period. From Asia Minor, through Syria, and as far as Egypt, there stretches an unbroken chain of evidence for the designation of cult deities as κύριοι ["lords"]. From the East the title was disseminated westward in the course of the dissemination of the cults. But it was not only these cult deities who were called κύριοι. It was not in the capacity of cult heroes that the title was borne either by Caesar or by Jahve.

The facts being so, we return to our question whether the primitive Christian Kyrios title, and the type of piety bound up with it, is to be understood from the point of view of the Hellenistic Kyrios cults. Our answer runs this way: the Kyrios title, as used in the NT, can no more be explained from the point of view of the Hellenistic mystery cults than it can be explained from the LXX or the cult of the Caesars. Nevertheless a relationship exists toward these other forms of "kyrios" faith. Just as the fact that the title assigned to Jesus was the same as the divine name of the LXX contributed to an essential modification of emphasis in the Christian faith in the Christ, so the fact that Jesus bore the same title as the Caesars who were venerated as divine and as the cult deities of Hellenism was not without influence on Christology.

In favor of a derivation of the primitive Christian Kyrios conception from Hellenism, it is urged that it is a question of a parallelism which extends not merely to the terminology but to the facts. With the title Kyrios there came into Christianity (it is urged) a type of piety of a kind foreign to Palestinian Christianity and peculiarly characteristic of Hellenistic cults. It was under Hellenistic influences, then, that the original Christian religion assumed the form of a Christ cult and of a Christ mysticism. Such a method of treatment, however, underestimates the difference between primitive Christianity as a whole and

---

[3]   The Masoretic Text of Job 36:22 has מוֹרֶה, which usually is understood to be the Hiphil participle of יָרָה (used as a noun) and to mean "teacher." RF

Hellenistic religion, and overestimates the difference between primitive Hellenistic and primitive Palestinian Christianity.

To describe primitive Christianity as a "Christ cult" conveys very good sense, if by the statement is meant (with Deissmann) that it is a living type of piety (*Frömmigkeit*) which finds expression in a church's worship, and not merely a system of doctrine. So again the term may, of course, also be used with the object of bringing clearly before the mind the parallels which actually exist between Christianity and heathenism upon Hellenistic soil, both in the sphere of religious terminology and in the forms of religious social organization, and which point unquestionably to the exercise of an influence upon the new religion by its environment. A "Christ cult," however, in the same sense as that in which there was an Isis cult or an Asklepios cult, never existed. Christ never became a "cult deity" or "cult hero." Beside him and over him there was always God the Father. The phrase ἀββᾶ ὁ πατήρ ["Abba, Father"] does not admit of elimination from the worship of the primitive church. Wherever St. Paul speaks of the Kyrios, he is speaking also, explicitly or implicitly, of the God and Father who has exalted Jesus to the position of Kyrios. The worship of the primitive church, moreover, never became what the liturgies of the mystery cults are, namely, a drama. Rom 6:1 ff. is not a description, but a figurative interpretation, of Baptism. A further element which the "Christ cult" lacks is the element of "myth." Why did the ancient world, which gave otherwise so ready a welcome to all forms of Oriental mythology, reject the message of Christ? Surely for the reason that it realized that this message, notwithstanding its mythological traits, this message with its historical core, did not belong to the realm of myth. It is no "necessary truth of reason," but a "contingent truth of history," and for that very reason (from the point of view of antiquity) not truth at all.

The same is true as regards mysticism. The discovery of the NT "Christ mysticism," the interpretation by Deissmann of the formula ἐν Χριστῷ ["in Christ"], represented an achievement which at the time exercised a liberating effect upon NT theology. According to the terminology then current, and, indeed, still very commonly used today, the description of the type of piety in question as "mysticism" was, moreover, correct. This conception of mysticism cannot, however, be maintained. Mysticism is not a particular side of religion, it is a great religion in itself. It depends on the tenet, held by all the great mystics, of the identity of the human soul, in its deepest nature, with the divine. Atman is Brahman, σὺ γὰρ εἶ ἐγὼ καὶ ἐγὼ σύ ["for you are I and I you"],[4] *bonus homo est unigenitus filius dei*[5] ["the good man is the only-begotten son of God"]. This same tenet constitutes also the presupposition of the Hellenistic mystery cults. It is incapable of being combined with primitive Christianity, in which (notwithstanding the "Christ in

---

[4]   Reitzenstein, *Poimandres*, 17. HS

[5]   Bernhart, *Deutsche Mystiker* (Meister Eckhardt), 3:198. HS

me" and the "we in Christ") the bounds between the divine and the human are strongly maintained. That is the reason why everyone who attempts (as Bousset[6] has done) to explain primitive Christianity as a cult mysticism has to explain away such central ideas of the NT as the conceptions of sin, justification, and faith. The misunderstanding is to be explained by the fact that Christianity knows something analogous to mysticism, the truth which appears in mysticism distorted— the reality of the Holy Spirit.

The difference between primitive Christianity and Hellenistic mysticism is the difference between two religions, of which the one can only regard the other as the delusive work of the demons, or as folly. An opposition of this kind does not exclude the possibility of influence, as the history of Israelite religion sufficiently shows, but it renders a priori improbable that the central conception of Christology, the Kyrios idea, is Hellenistic in origin.

The Kyrios idea, as a matter of actual fact, admits perfectly well of being traced back to the Aramaic period of Christianity. *Maranatha* is an erratic block from that forgotten period which cannot by any theory be set aside. The phrase is evidence that already in Aramaic the word *mare* (a forerunner in other cases also of the Greek κύριος) was used in application to Jesus. In what sense it was used, and in what precise linguistic forms, it is impossible any longer to be sure. It cannot be determined whether the actual confession "Jesus is Lord" had been formulated already in Aramaic. We do know, however, that Jesus was not merely recognized as the future Messiah, but that he was known also as the present and living "Lord," and that he was invoked as "Lord" in prayer. The idea of the presence of Christ in his community is clearly evidenced by the saying "Where two or three are gathered together in my name, there am I in the midst of them" [Matt 18:20 KJV]—a saying which goes back to the Aramaic-speaking, and in all probability, therefore, to the Palestinian, community.[7] It involves no "Hellenistic mysticism." It is a saying, moreover, which proves that the formula "in the name of Jesus" is to be understood on the basis of Jewish presuppositions. The Palestinian church knew already of prophetic utterances, exorcism, and miracles "in the name of Jesus," and it is not accidental that in the Sermon on the Mount these evidences of the power of Christ in his church are brought into connection, just as in the Pauline Epistles, with the address to him as Κύριε (Matt 7:22; cf. 1 Cor 12:4 ff.).

This Matthean passage, then, is fully intelligible on the basis of Palestinian relationships to Jesus. Let it once be assumed that—as the NT evidence suggests—the original church of Jerusalem was, like the Hellenistic, a "pneumatic" church, and the cleavage which we theologians have introduced between them on the ground of our theories about Hellenism disappears at the most important

---

[6] Johann H. Wilhelm Bousset (1865–1920) was a NT scholar and a professor at Giessen. This is probably a reference to his study *Kyrios Christos* (1913; ET 1970). See *ODCC*, 229. RF

[7] Compare the Jewish saying "Where two sit together and the words of the Torah are between them, the Shekinah too is among them" (*'Abot* 3:2, quoted by Str-B 1:94). HS

point. No doubt further developments, actual influences from the side of Hellenistic religions, took place: the essential thing, the idea of the living Lord who was present in his church and who wrought by the power of the Spirit, was there from the beginning. The Eucharist, for example, as it appears in St. Paul, has clearly undergone development, but the experience of fellowship with the living Lord—as witness the story of the disciples at Emmaus [Luke 24:30]—was already involved in the primitive "breaking of the bread" [e.g., Acts 2:46].

As to the time at which this earliest faith in Jesus the Lord—of which the scanty notices which have come down to us from the original Aramaic period of Christianity afford only a faint, though a still discernible, picture—originated, the NT as a whole bears unanimous witness: it arose out of the deep spiritual experiences of the Easter days. That Jesus was risen and that he was *therefore* the Lord—that was the content of what, after the analogy of the (confessedly quite different in character) "prophetic" experience, may be described as the "apostolic" experience. To reach a new understanding of the nature and content of this experience is one of the greatest tasks of NT theology.

Out of the apostolic experience arose the apostolic testimony: Jesus is Lord. That was already the church confession when Christianity moved out into the arena of Greek-speaking civilization. It was Hellenism, however, which, with the Greek word Κύριος, first contributed to this confession a form of expression which was of historical significance for the world. What was concealed in germ in *Maranatha* was now unfolded. Now for the first time Christ came into competition with the great powers of the period. *Kyrios Jesus:* such was the war cry of the *ecclesia militans* ["church militant"], to the Jews a blasphemy against the "one only God," to the Greeks a piece of folly, to the Romans a *crimen laesae majestatis* ["crime of offending the divine majesty"],[8] for the church itself the epitome of its message, its eternal confession of faith.

For ourselves the task is set of understanding afresh this confession of faith in its ultimate depths. As regards this dogmatic task a brief word alone can be said here. The Kyrios problem is the problem of the Godhead of Christ. That there is a living Christ, not merely in some vague metaphorical sense, but in the full meaning of the words, a Christ to whom his church prays, and who is in the church's midst; that this Christ is not an intermediate being, but *vere deus* ["truly God"], of the same essence with God, and yet a person over against the Father and that the unity of God is in no wise affected thereby—these paradoxical positions are implicit in the simple confession of the original church, directed to Jesus the Lord. The road to the understanding of what the original church meant by it is never opened out to us so long as in our dogmatic thinking we take as our starting point either the nature of God or the person of Christ. The starting point of our thought must be rather the nature of the Holy Ghost. It is not an accident

---

[8] See Pieper, *Christian Dogmatics*, 1:563. RF

that the Kyrios faith in St. Paul leads on directly to the beginnings of the doctrine of the Trinity (cf. 1 Cor 12:4 ff.), and that it was only in the form of the doctrine of the Trinity that the ancient church found itself able to express its Christology. The question of the Holy Ghost is the true problem of the theology of today, even in dealing with the Christological question. Only when the nature of the Holy Spirit in the NT has been clearly discerned, only then shall we escape from the cloud of "religious historical" hypotheses and be able to reach a general insight into primitive Christianity as a whole, a new understanding of the resurrection, and so also a new Christology. This is the way of Christian *thought* corresponding to the way of Christian *faith* which is indicated by St. Paul in his saying "No man can call Jesus Lord save in the Holy Ghost" (1 Cor 12:3), a way which the church understood, since in the Veni, Creator Spiritus she sings: *Per Te sciamus da Patrem, Noscamus atque Filium* ["Oh, make to us the Father known; Teach us the eternal Son to own"].[9]

---

[9] As in *Lutheran Worship* 156, stanza 6. RF

1929

WHERE CHRIST IS, THERE IS THE CHURCH[1]

The official minutes of the Continuation Committee of the World Conference on Faith and Order, meeting at Maloja, Switzerland, note for August 29, 1929, that "at 9:30 a.m. Pastor Sasse led the devotions." This is the sermon for that occasion, based on Matt 28:20.

Huss number 036
Hopf number 024

———✦✦✦———

"And behold, I am with you always, even to the end of the age" (Matt 28:20).

At the other end of the lake whose shore lies before us, by the Sils Maria, there is an inscription carved into a mighty stone on a forested peninsula. The inscription reads "Friedrich Nietzsche,"[2] and above is the song of deep midnight from Zarathustra who once originated in Sils Maria. Year after year Nietzsche had fled from the hustle of the world to the loneliness of this mountain vale,[3] upon which at that time lay the deep stillness of natural isolation. Before the green mirror of the lake, to the right and to the left the steep cliffs, and in the distance the desolate ice and snow of the high mountain peaks, far from people and their boisterous bustle, there he sat and wrote his great works. Among the poems which he created here are some of the greatest written in the German language. The deep isolation, the most desperate lostness of the soul, has perhaps never found such expression as in them. There is one which describes how, in the terrifying loneliness of the mountain heights, he cries out for people who understand him: "The

---

[1] This essay was originally published as "Ansprache zur Eröffnung der Fortsetzungsausschuss der Weltkonferenz für Glauben und Kirchenverfassung am 29. August 1929 in Maloja. Text: Matth. 28,20" in *Internationale Kirchliche Zeitschrift* [Bern] 37 NF 19.3 (July–September 1929): 152–56. It was later republished as an essay in *Lutherische Blätter* 16.81 (May 1964): 37–40, and in *ISC*, 2:19–21. MH/RF

[2] Friedrich Nietzsche (1844–1900) was a German philosopher and the son of a Lutheran pastor from Saxony. RF

[3] Sasse's reference is to the village of Sils Maria at the opposite end of the Lake of Sils from Maloja. Here Friedrich Nietzsche spent the summers of 1881 and then 1883–1888 at a modest boarding house. It was here that he completed part 2 of his famous book *Also Sprach Zarathustra*. "The most important single clue to *Zarathustra* is that it is the work of an utterly lonely man" ("Introduction" and "Editor's Preface," *The Portable Nietzsche* [ed. and trans. Walter Kaufmann; London: Penguin, 1968], 21, 103). RF

friend remains, ready day and night." But no one comes who understands him. And finally his screams subside, the cry of an endless desire: "The song is over, the desire of a sweet cry dies in the mouth. . . . Now the world laughs, the terrifying curtain is torn, the wedding came for light and darkness." He just passes into the night of insanity.[4]

Why do I recount this? Not merely because it is a gripping episode from the intellectual history of our German people, but for another reason. There are men whose lives embody the fate of an entire epoch, and Nietzsche is such a man. His desperate destitution and loneliness is the loneliness of the modern man. To be sure, there still burns in his soul the desire for God. Indeed, he cries as Friedrich Nietzsche for the unknown God, and he consecrates to him solemn altars in the deepest depths of his heart. But the voice of the living God he no longer hears. At best he sees the apparitions like the dark form of Nietzsche's Zarathustra. He no longer knows Christ the Lord. In his destitution he cries out for fellowship with other souls. But he no longer finds the brethren.

All this signifies the destruction of people, the destruction of the soul. And it is the great fateful question of Western humanity today, whether it will go the dark road of self-destruction without God, without Christ, without brotherhood, which the Lord has established in his church. If a new day of Jesus Christ does not dawn upon it, it will go into the night in which Friedrich Nietzsche met his end.

Do we not see here the great task of the church? We are gathered here at the other shore of the Lake of Sils. Do we hear the cry coming across the water from the other shore? Do we hear the cry to the unknown God? Do we hear voices of longing for the reestablishment of a human fellowship destroyed? And do we also hear the other voice which comes over from there, the complaint which Friedrich Nietzsche once raised against us, against Christianity?[5] Today in a new form in a thousand languages it rings out through every portion of the earth:

> You must sing me a better song so that I learn to believe in your Redeemer: Why are his disciples so joyless in their salvation? We don't need your Christ. We desire God, but you have only pious talk about God. We desire the Redeemer, but you only recount old history to us. Your theologians are not in agreement on what redemption is—and you want to preach redemption to us? We desire the deepest fellowship, we long for true brotherhood, and you give us only pious societies, which are in conflict with each other. Be done with your pious talk—it does not interest us. We desire to hear God, not you. Your subjectivity, your beautiful mystical experiences, keep to yourself. We are dying, we are doubting, we have no time for it!

---

4   In early January 1889, Nietzsche became insane. RF

5   Nietzsche developed a bitterly anti-Christian atheistic philosophy, accusing Christianity of a "slave morality," which makes a virtue of humility and tends to weakness in contrast to his ideal *Übermensch* ("superman") view of humanity. (*Lutheran Cyclopedia*, 577) RF

Brothers! Do we hear these voices? Do we hear the cry of a humanity which is wrestling with death? Woe to us if we were not to hear it! God hears it. He who hears the groans of the distressed understands this cry. And the Lord who once came to call sinners and not the righteous to repentance will perhaps regard these accusations in a way completely different than we are accustomed to "on that great day when he comes to judge the living and the living dead."

How should we respond to these voices? What can we say? There is only one thing we can say: *Kyrie eleison!* ["Lord, have mercy"]. We can only do one thing: we can repent. Here indeed lies one of the greatest mysteries of the church of Jesus Christ. It continues to live in spite of all the indictments leveled at it through the course of nineteen centuries, for it lives from repentance. No criticism of the church, including the criticism of Nietzsche, has so unsparingly, so truthfully revealed all the wrongs of the church as the repentance which the great saints of Christianity, which the disciples of the Lord in all centuries have done. We live only from repentance. Only as we continuously repent can we live. Just as Christianity once began as a powerful repentance movement, all great epochs of the church have begun with the call to repent.

If God the Lord will graciously grant his church today a new great day in her history—and it is our prayer that he will do so—then this day will also begin with repentance. A world which wrestles with death, a humanity that threatens to be drowned in the night of insanity cries out for deliverance. And we stand powerless over against it. We do not know what we should do. There is no program to solve this problem. Evangelization of the world, mission work among the masses, the restoration of destroyed fellowship, unification of Christianity—will we bring all this about? No, we must recognize that we can do none of it. Only if we first recognize our complete powerlessness and helplessness, only if we first acknowledge before the face of him who is holy and true that we in our sins can indeed in no way encounter the world with the claim that it should hear us, only if we first acknowledge that our lips are impure and our hands are stained, only if we first can say nothing other than *Kyrie eleison*—only then can we learn to grasp the mystery of the church of Christ.

If our mouths are dumb, then he speaks. If we with our wisdom and our power are at an end, then he speaks his great Word to us: "Behold, I am with you always, until the end of the age!" With these words he once sent his apostles into the world, to tasks which humanly speaking were impossible, to destinations which they knew not. And they joyously went the unknown way. They knew that his forgiveness, his peace, his power were with them. "Behold, I am with you always"—this is the mystery of the church. For upon what does the church rest? No not our faith, not on the holiness of our lives—then it would have long since dwindled out of history—but solely on Christ the Lord. *Ubi Christus, ibi ecclesia* ["where Christ is, there is the church"[6]]—with these words every definition of the church must begin. Because there is one *Kyrios*, there is therefore one church.

---

[6] Ignatius, *Epistle to the Smyrnaeans* 8:2. MH

Have we not all too often forgotten this? That there is one living Christ, that God raised the Crucified One and made him Lord, and that this Lord really and personally is with us always—these are not parables or pictures, rather realities of which we know in faith. Where his Gospel is plainly and purely preached, where his Sacraments are rightly administered, there he is really and personally present.

Only this faith in the living Lord poises us properly for our tasks. He guards us from the two great sins of the Christianity of our times. The terrible sin of pessimism doubts the possibility that the church can accomplish anything, because it no longer takes seriously the confession of the present Christ. Such pessimism does not take it seriously that to Christ also today all power is given in heaven and on earth, and he is just as near to us as to Christianity of the beginning. He guards us too from the terrible sin of optimism, which overlooks the fearful reality of sin in the world and knows nothing of the fact that the power of evil works most wretchedly where it destroys the community [Gemeinde] of Jesus. Pessimism and optimism are human emotions. Where they rule, faith is falsified. For faith has nothing to do with emotions. It is the unshakable trust in the unbreakable promises of God.

In humble repentance let us all turn ourselves to him. That we all, though belonging to entirely different communions, turn ourselves to him, the one [Redeemer], therein lies the essence of the ecclesia universalis ["universal church"] which we seek. If we all with empty hands and with contrite hearts come to him, then he will place us before our tasks, just as he once sent his first disciples into the world, with the great promise which we hear today in faith: "Lo, I am with you always, even to the end of the age."

CHURCH AND CHURCHES

CONCERNING THE DOCTRINE OF THE UNITY OF THE CHURCH[1]

This essay was dedicated to Wilhelm Zoellner (1860–1937), a German Lutheran theologian, general superintendent of the Church of Westphalia (Prussian Union) from 1905, and chairman of the German Federation of Churches from 1935. Sasse was greatly appreciated by Zoellner for his support of the German efforts in the Ecumenical Movement. By 1935 however, Sasse became disillusioned by this mentor as Zoellner came more and more under the influence of National Socialist church leaders.

This essay reflects Sasse's involvement in and knowledge of the Ecumenical Movement. It manifests his historical perspective on unity and church fellowship. Here also he offers a critique of the church in the modern era.

Huss number 042b
Hopf number 027

It was a favorite thought of Vilmar[2] that the history of the church passes through a series of epochs, each of which has the task of experiencing and presenting a particular part of the truth of the Christian faith. In the day in which he lived, he saw the beginning of a great epoch of church history in which the question of the church became the reigning central point of the faith and life of Christianity that would inform theology and ecclesiastical work. Over and again he emphasized in his writings that the doctrine of the church is something not yet concluded, that neither Catholicism nor the Reformation has fulfilled it, that moreover, what the church is must still be lived, experienced, and that this experience would provide the content of church history for the coming generation, indeed, perhaps the next century.

---

[1] This essay was originally published as "Kirche und Kirchen: Über den Glaubenssatz von der Einheit der Kirche" in *Credo Ecclesiam: Festgabe zum siebenzigsten Geburtstage des hochwürdigsten Herrn Generalsuperintendenten der evangelischen Kirche in Westfalen am 30. Januar 1930, D. Wilhelm Zoellner* (Gütersloh: C. Bertelsmann, 1930), 295–317. It was reprinted in *ISC*, 1:155–67. MH
[2] August Friedrich Christian Vilmar (1800–1868) was a confessional Lutheran churchman and a professor at Marburg. His works had a great influence on Sasse. RF

What the great theologian of Lutheranism foresaw with prophetic insight appears to be fulfilled in our day. The movement toward the "church" which in the second third of the last century was found here and there in Christianity has today become a world movement. In those years Löhe could begin his *Three Books about the Church* with these words: "Everyone speaks of the church today. Every one has an inkling that 'church' is no mere name."[3] It was the time in which the Christendom of the English-speaking world, especially Anglicanism, experienced its great rise to world prominence. In those decades lies the root of the Ecumenical Movement, like the course of a subterranean river flowing through the history of the church of the nineteenth century and which now, after the catastrophe of the World War, quickly burst forth into the light of day with unabated power. In the drums of the Roman government, Augustine discovered "the millennium of the church" as the meaning of that history of which he was an eyewitness. In view of the world history which we experience we begin again to have an inkling that the meaning of all history is not to be sought in the *Volk*, in the "state," or in "humanity," not in "culture," nor even in "Christian culture," not in "personality," rather only in the church of God. As the church as historical reality once obtained immeasurable meaning for life during the demise of ancient culture, so in this day and age of disintegration, in which all human communities are affected and in which all orders of life threaten to go under, the church appears to be winning an entirely new meaning for all of our lives.

What is the demise of ancient culture—a historical experience limited to a small area—in comparison to the revolutionary changes which find consummation in our day? Entire culture worlds are toppled together. Struggles [*Geisteskampf*] break out, the likes of which history has never experienced, for the theater of this struggle is the entire world. This is only a reminder of the problem which is today customarily comprehended by the word "secularism." In view of this world situation Christianity awoke from its comfortable church sleep of religious individualism. It came to realize that God did not send his Son into the world that we might have beautiful religious experiences, but rather "that the world be redeemed by him" [John 3:17]. Those who for a century had lived in the narrow boundaries of national church fellowships and in the limited horizon of solidly defined confessions began to understand anew the universality of the church. With new eyes they read the great Word of the NT concerning the church, which is the body of Christ, the struggling multitude of God in this world (Eph 6:10 ff.), and with new faith they spoke at their altars the old confession which is inseparably bound to the confession of faith in the Triune God: *Credo unam, sanctam, catholicam et apostolicam ecclesiam* ["I believe in one holy catholic and apostolic church"].

But what does this article of the old confession mean? How varied are its interpretations! How varied are the pictures which stand before the spiritual eyes of Christians when the phrase *una sancta ecclesia* resounds! The Roman Catholic

---

[3]   *Three Books about the Church* (seminar editions; trans. and ed. James L. Schaaf; Philadelphia: Fortress, 1969); see the opening sentences of the foreword, p. 43. RF

Christian understands by the one church something entirely different than the Eastern Orthodox Christian, the Lutheran something other than the Congregationalist, the Anglican something other than the Methodist or Baptist. The entire tragedy of the divisions of the church thus become manifest in that the individual confessions never stand farther apart than when they confess "I believe in one holy church," for each understands something different by "church" and "unity of the church." But is it perhaps the case that we all know only incompletely what the church is? At any rate, the task is posed for the theology of all confessions to think through and give basis anew for the article of faith of the *one* church, to answer this question: What is the church, which we define with the adjective "one," and in what relation does this "church" stand to the "churches" of Christendom?

PART 1

A look at the Christianity in which we live shows us the great difficulty of the problem. Hundreds of confessions and denominations stand next to one another, diverse in their piety, in their doctrine, and in their ecclesiastical structures. The problem is difficult enough when we consider only the main types of the Christian faith and life, as they have worked themselves out in the great confessions of Christendom. What binds these images, so entirely different, often standing in the deepest opposition to one another, into one unity? If this question is to be answered, it must be kept in mind that the present condition of Christianity— as with all the "present"—is only a gate of passage, a fleeting look at a historical process. This condition is the result of a historical process of nineteen centuries, and this history in its entirety must be kept in mind if the question is to be answered whether and in which sense we need to speak of the unity of the church. Might there be in fact one last, deepest unity of all the various forms of the Christian faith and life? If so, this unity cannot be found if people take a quick look at a period of Christian history and isolate it from the events which surround it. Countless attempts to define the concept of church founder on this mistake. The result is always a lifeless, static, completely abstract concept of the church, a pale mental construct, but never a living view of reality.

We are accustomed to describe the vast, complicated events of Christian history of the nineteen centuries as *church history*, that is, as the history of the church. According to this old manner of speaking, the church is the subject or the object of those events. Modern theology has in part consciously, in part unconsciously, in part openly, in part silently, replaced the concept of "church of the Christian religion" by the concept "Christendom." The church historian[4] wanted to show how the religion whose origin is demonstrated in the NT has developed, how it spread over humanity, how the various peoples and ages accepted it and what they did with it. He depicted the expansion and differentiation process which gave

---

[4]   In this part Sasse may be referring to Adolf von Harnack (1851–1930), one of his teachers at Berlin, who sought to define the "essence of Christianity" and the development of its dogma. RF

birth to the various churches, confessions, and types of piety. That which holds together these many forms of the Christian religion he found in a common principle which he called the essence of Christianity [*Wesen des Christentums*] and which he even defined according to his personal faith conviction and worldview. The theme of church history is accordingly the development of the Christian religion, a segment of religious history in general which is in turn a part of general world history.

The modern church historian is also a specialist among the historians. He indeed possesses an intimate understanding of this side of history—an understanding which proceeds from the principle of the practical division of labor and is conditioned by his personal faith. He treats a distinct area of history just as the art historian and political or economic historian do their own areas. The writing of church history during the last few generations was ruled by these principles. The result was, on the one hand, an immeasurable expansion of our knowledge of the past. There came forth an abundance of discoveries of the most important historical connections and a grand overview of the development of Christianity—all knowledge which cannot be valued highly enough and which form the presupposition for all theological work of the future. On the other hand, for theology it was a catastrophe in that there was not a church history in the strict sense of a history of the church of Jesus Christ. This consequence was in general not expressly intended, but it was unavoidable. In the writing of church history the words "church" and "church history" are indeed still used, because they are traditional. But it is done with reservation or with a bad conscience, and it is no accident that such great and discerning scholars as Harnack and Troeltsch had quite happily done away with "the misleading colloquial word 'church.' "[5] Thus modern historical theology has lost the concept of "church" and replaced it with the concept "Christendom." This is a consequence of its principles which appear to be irreconcilable with a dogmatic viewpoint; the concept of *church* belongs to dogmatics.

We will understand the consequences this has when we consider the picture of the development of Christendom which we all bear in place of a real view of church history. From early Christianity the river of this development flows through the centuries. We see how the Christian faith advanced in the world of late antiquity and how the old Catholic Church was formed on the soil of the Roman government and Hellenic Roman culture. The entire development of Christendom in piety, dogma, and polity was from this point on defined by the influences of the surrounding world. It was thrown into the torrent of world events and was now driven by this torrent. The formation of its piety was defined by the psychologies of peoples and cultures to which it came. There is a Roman and a Byzantine, an early Germanic and a medieval, a northern Protestant, an American, a Russian Christianity, as the various types of Christianity are labeled. The transformations of dogma were defined by the philosophical development of

---

[5]   On A. von Harnack and the so-called *Consensus quinque-saecularis* as the basis for the reunification of the church, see *Die Eiche* XIII (1925), 287 ff., especially p. 296. On the position of Troeltsch, compare his article "Kirche" in *RGG*[1] 3:1147 ff. HS

humanity. The social forms of Christianity are dependent upon the forms of contemporary society. To the old undivided *Imperium Romanum* ["Roman Empire"] corresponded the "old undivided church" of early Catholicism. The separation of the *Imperium* into a East Roman and a West Roman kingdom resulted in the division of this church into the Hellenic Byzantine Church of the East and the Latin Church of the West. The political fates of both halves of the kingdom were played out in the developments of both parts of Christianity. Here consider the Monophysite, Nestorian, and Arian churches. These parallels may be followed through all of history, through the Middle Ages and modern era into the present, where the Ecumenical Movement of the church corresponds to great international attempts at political unity. The shape of the church always runs parallel to the great configurations of social life.[6] Thus the development of Christendom appears to be nothing other than a part of world history in general, nothing other than a part of European culture, insolubly interlaced with it and fully dependent upon it. The determinative impetus for every new stage of development comes from without, not from within, Christianity itself. This is the construct which lives within us all, in place of a living comprehension of the history of the church of Christ. The crass vacuousness and superficiality of this image is tempered by a fact which lays down an insurmountable barrier for every superficial treatment of history. This is the completely irrational fact of the great personalities of church history. The rise of great men like Augustine and Luther always appears as something inconceivable, and wherever it happens it presents the church historian with a peculiarity which reminds him that the history of the church is independent from all world history. And in an event such as the Reformation it has ever and again become clear, at least to the Protestants, that the history of the church possesses its own logic, its own causality and finality.

But the view of history as a whole was not thereby essentially influenced, for the attention on the personalities of the great epoch-making men remained affixed to the treatment of world history in general. At best one saw these individuals and noted how in each "Christendom" had found form. But they could not be arranged in a history of the church. It could not be seen that in Irenaeus and Athanasius, in Augustine and Luther, Christendom not only attained a new level, but also that in these men arose not only personalities which had significance as religious geniuses or as theological thinkers for generations and centuries, but rather that in them the *church* experienced history (a history of a completely different form than that which a nation or a culture experiences in its great men). One studied "Christian history of religion" but not the history of the church. One saw "Christendom" but not the church.

Over against all this we strongly insist that there is a church history, which is something completely different than the history of religion applied to Christianity. Furthermore, we maintain that the countless events of those nineteen centuries in general only obtain meaning if the history of the church, the *one*

---

[6] A similar idea was the thesis of "American Christianity and the Church" in this collection. RF

church of Jesus Christ, is seen in them. It is all but impossible to understand the manifold, logically disunified forms of faith and life of Christianity, which stand in deepest contradiction to one another, as a unified whole if one seeks to conceive of them as various manifestations of the essence of Christianity [*Wesen des Christentums*]. Indeed, they may all stand in living relation to the reality [*Tatsache*] of the church which lives her history within them. If Christianity is treated according to the history of religions[7] approach—and we do not question the correctness of this way of proceeding, we only deny that it is the only possible way of proceeding and that it fully exhausts the topic—then the following, very serious question is raised: Are the differences between the great forms of the Christian faith and life finally not that great? Can these different forms of Christianity be treated as nothing more than variants of one and the same religion, or are they rather distinctive forms of religion, even different religions? Is not Luther's faith a different religion than that of Meister Eckhardt?[8] What does the religion of Calvin have in common with the popular religion of the Spanish peasant? What does modern American Protestantism have to do with orthodox Christianity at the time of Chalcedon? To be sure, Christ and his Gospel in some way stand before the souls of all Christians. But are not the conceptions of Christ and the comprehensions of the Gospel entirely different? To be sure, all Christianity prays to God the Father. Are there not variations even in the very concept of God? And certainly no theologian will venture to declare that these variations are trifling theological differences! If the categories of the history of religions are taken seriously, it is impossible to find one unified religion in the various forms of Christianity.[9]

Every attempt to define the "essence" of Christianity ends—aside from the fact that hitherto no definition has found universal assent—with a bland, lifeless abstraction. This is not only because of the general difficulty in defining a complicated state of affairs—finally even the concept of the church is undefinable—but especially because of this: the Christian faith, as the NT and the various confessions testify, does not primarily understand itself as another new religion, but rather as something completely different. And this historical reality that entered world history in Jesus Christ conceives of itself in the concept of the *ecclesia*, the church. For the Christian faith the reality which is the basis of the history of Christianity is not "Christendom," but rather the church, the very same church which our church historians declare an unreality, a fiction, because there are only churches, temporally conditioned, and varying forms of the Christian religion, over which the concept of "the church" only sweeps as a mental construct. Can a

---

[7]   Sasse refers to the so-called History of Religions School (*Religionsgeschichtliche Schule*), which formed in the latter part of the nineteenth century. RF

[8]   Johannes Eckhart (ca. 1260–ca. 1327) was the founder of German mysticism (*Lutheran Cyclopedia*, 255). RF

[9]   "There is no general Christendom which forms the basis of the various confessions" (E. Seeberg, *Ideen zur Theologie der Geschichte des Christentums* [1929], 32). HS

conception of church history be correct which simply shoves aside the concept by which the Christian faith has expressed its essence from the beginning on?

No. To understand church history is to acknowledge the *reality of the one* church in the events of the history of Christianity, to see the connections between the countless churches and confessions of Christianity and this church. We also know that the history of the church is rejected in the disciplines of the history of religions and world history. But we maintain that next to the causality which the study of the history of religions reveals there is another causality. We maintain that in the history of the church a teleology is firmly planted which no history of religions can understand because it knows nothing of the τέλος [*telos*, "end, goal"] of the church, nothing of the return of Christ. When we assert this, it is not our intention to replace the scientific treatment of church history with a devotional treatment which perhaps looks for miracles in history. Rather we propose a *theological* treatment which understands events such as the establishment of the Roman Church in the demise of the Roman *Imperium* ["Empire"], the Christianization of the German peoples, the Reformation, the world mission efforts of the last century, the Ecumenical Movement of the present, as events in which the church of Christ certainly finds her history interwoven with world history, but yet delimited from world history. It is not the case that in the person of Christ Christianity at one time entered the world and is at the hands of fate among the various peoples of the world. It is rather the case that the church, prepared in the history of revelation, became a reality on earth through Christ, not as something complete and accomplished, rather as something becoming. The church *comes* into the world; that is her history. In war and peace, in work and rest, in triumph and defeat, in ascendancy or stagnation, in serious decline (in which she comes close even to the point of death), in being brought up again (in which she experiences something like a resurrection), she travels through the centuries to meet the returning Christ. This is not a new realization. It is something that was known by the great theologians of every century. It is an understanding which has temporarily been darkened in the study of theology by the incursion of a manner of thought foreign to the Christian faith. But it has been darkened only to be the more brightly illumined in the future against the backdrop of a knowledge of the historical facts immeasurably broadened by modern investigation.

PART 2

So what is the church, the existence of which we perceive in the history of Christianity, in the chaotic, apparently meaningless events of nineteen hundred years? If we ask this question of the various churches, if we search the great confessional writings of all ages, we note, much to our amazement, that all of Christianity confesses a belief in one holy church. But the nature of this church is defined only very rarely and never with complete dogmatic clarity. This is a fact of the history of dogma which is all too often overlooked. The church fathers said only very little about the church. They only gave deeper consideration to the nature of the church at those times when the unity of the church was threatened and these times necessitated a reconsideration of what the church is. Thus Cyprian and Augustine gave the classic definition of the doctrine of the church. In contrast to the Latin West, the Eastern church never produced a fully developed doctrine of the church. There was indeed a definite consensus among the theologians of orthodoxy in the explication of the four adjectives of the Nicene Creed regarding the church (one, holy, catholic, apostolic). But no doctrine concerning this definition of the church was ever made confessionally binding. The church of the Middle Ages in the West demonstrates a remarkable silence on the doctrine of the church. A locus on the church is sought in vain in the great systems of the scholastic theologians. It was only at the beginning of the fourteenth century that there again appeared a writing concerning [the doctrine of] the church. It appeared at the very same time as the bull *Unam Sanctam*,[10] in which Boniface VIII elevated the claim of papal primacy and simultaneously renewed the "early catholic" [*frühkatholische*] doctrine of the church and her unity immediately before the collapse of the medieval Papal Church. But this did not provide a dogmatic fixation of the doctrine of the church.

The first confessional exposition of the concept of the church—the first to be set down at all in the history of the church—is found in the relevant articles of the Augsburg Confession. This is of great significance. The entire effort of doctrinal formation of Christendom began with this fundamental confession of Lutheranism. Its effects on the Protestant world are well known. It is very significant that the confession of the Church of England, the Thirty-nine Articles [1571], takes its Article XIX word for word from Augustana Article VII (with the significant change of "visible church" in place of "church") and that this Article XIX still today nominally forms the Anglican doctrine of the church, though Anglicanism's actual concept of the church today, which has after all never been confessionally defined, is something completely different. The Roman Church did not deal with the doctrine of the church at the Council of Trent. It was the *Catechismus Romanus* [1566] which developed the Roman concept of church in opposition to the Reformation. Still, the catechism is not dogma in the strict sense of Roman dogmatics. The Roman Catholic doctrine of the church should have finally been established at the Vatican Council.[11] But this council did not complete its task. It completed only the doctrine of the papacy, which since the Middle Ages was the most important part of the doctrine of the church for Roman Catholicism. The final formalization of the concept of church thus yet remains incomplete in the Roman Catholic Church. As far as Lutheranism is concerned, it is evident that in spite of the Augustana, the problem of the church is still an open question even in its doc-

---

[10] This famous papal bull of 1302 declared that there was "One Holy Catholic and Apostolic Church" outside of which there was "neither salvation nor remission of sins" (*ODCC*, 1655). RF

[11] The First Vatican Council (December 8, 1869–October 20, 1870). RF

trine. For the doctrine of the church is not systematically treated in the Augustana. It is dealt with in several articles and cannot be taken only from Articles VII and VIII. As history demonstrates, Lutheranism itself has not yet come to a consensus on the relationships of church, congregation, office, congregation of believers, and communion of saints to each other. Thus we stand in the face of the remarkable fact that no part [*Teilkirche*] of Christendom has thus far presented a fully developed doctrine of the church.

But this fact does not relieve us of the obligation to answer this question: What church do we mean when we speak of the one church of Christ? It is self-evident that we can only give an answer from the standpoint of our confession. No theologian can ignore the experiences of his church, for no theologian lives in a vacuum. Neither can we simply gather the statements of the NT on the church, for such passages are simply understood in light of Christian experience. It is self-evident that we shall not provide a solution to the problem of church here, rather we shall only develop a few thoughts which appear to have significance in the present for the posing of the great question of the church.

Most attempts to define the church, or rather, to describe the church, conceive of the church as a *societas*, a visible community of people, and such attempts ask, Who belongs to the church? What qualities are the basis for the membership of individual people or human communities in the one church of Christ? What are the characteristics of the *societas* church, and how is the community of the church distinguished from other communities? Because it has been taken out of its context, the definition of the church in Article VII of the Augustana ("Est autem ecclesia congregatio sanctorum, in qua evangelium recte docetur et recte administrantur sacramenta" ["The Church is the congregation of saints, in which the Gospel is rightly taught and the Sacraments are rightly administered"])[12] has also often misled theologians to take this direction. But this path has never led to an understanding of the church. For the church is indeed a *societas*, but it is still something else. No treatment of the church which begins with people, with human communities, with the faith of people, ever leads to that other aspect of the church which the NT describes with the words "body of Christ." Here lies the particular mystery, the final difference (*ultima differentia*) of the church [as distinct from all other communities]. Here is the reason that no science of religions and no sociology can ever understand the essence of the church. There is no analogy for the church. The forms of the ancient Christian *ecclesia* ("church") may be compared to the cultic communities of Hellenism, the church of "early Catholicism" may be compared with the *Volk* of Islam, all conceivable parallels may be drawn between the social development of Christianity and the great world religions (e.g., Buddhism), yet in the face of striking parallels there will always remain a certain residual dissimilarity. The sociologist does not understand this

---

[12] This reading of the Latin text is the same as the one found in the *Triglotta;* the English translation is also that of the *Triglotta* (pp. 46–47). MH

dissimilarity. He sees in it the mystery of individuality which indwells every historical phenomenon. But the theologian knows that precisely in this dissimilarity which defies historical significance lies that which makes the church the church. He will assert that to understand the church one must begin with Christology and never sociology. *Because there is one living Christ, there is only one church. Ubi Christus, ibi ecclesia* ("where Christ is, there is the church"[13]): every description of the church must begin with this proposition. The church is there were the living Christ is. Only when one takes with absolute seriousness what the NT says concerning Jesus Christ as the present Lord of the church can he understand the church. Thus her essence can only be comprehended from the vantage point of faith. It can be explained to a person who does not believe in Christ as little as Baptism can be explained to him. For the world, the church is a riddle and everything which we have to say concerning it is an inconceivable folly.

It is a promising sign of our times that in the present Ecumenical Movement the great thought of the NT on the church as the body of Christ has begun to occupy the center of theological thought concerning the church. Here is presented a common starting point for opening discussion on the question of church in the various confessions, and this must proceed to a thorough discussion between the various churches. How are we to understand the statements of Paul, especially in the Letter to the Ephesians, concerning the body of Christ and its unity? To say that Protestant theology of the last generations did not fully come to grips with the problems which lie before us is to do it no injustice. The more earnestly one reflects on the question of the *corpus Christi* ["body of Christ"] in the NT, the more will he avoid another error which has been made over and again by those who have attempted to describe the church—remember what was said above about the history of the church—that the church is thought of only as a static, known quantity. The picture of "body" points to the fact that the church is a living, growing organism. *The church of the NT stands not in "being" but in "becoming."* It is significant that in passages such as Eph 2:20 ff. and 1 Peter 2:5, the static picture of the church as the house of God immediately proceeds to the picture of the church as a living organism. The house of God grows; the body of Christ is built. The church "becomes," as the "becoming" church she proceeds toward a state of completion; Christ, "the Savior of his body," leads her toward completion.

If this is the case, if the church is the body of Christ, if the church as body of Christ comes in history, then the proposition of the unity of the church needs no further foundation. If the church were constituted by our faith, then a series of churches would be conceivable, because there are varying views regarding Christ. Luther's faith in Christ is something different than that of the modern American Protestant. But if Christ, the present Lord, constitutes the church, then there can be only one church, because there is only one Christ. Then this question is imme-

---

[13] Ignatius, *Epistle to the Smyrnaeans* 8:2. MH

diately raised: Where does this one church become visible? Where is it knowable for us as a historical reality? And this does not mean for us, Where do we find the people who belong to this church? but rather, Where do we find Christ?

But to this question we can give only one answer: Christ is present for us humans only in the Word and Sacrament. "Nam per verbum et sacramenta tamquam per instrumenta donatur Spiritus Sanctus, qui fidem efficit, ubi et quando visum est Deo, in iis, qui audiunt evangelium." Thus Article V of the Augustana speaks against the churchless mysticism of *Schwärmertum*. "Through the Word and Sacraments God gives the Holy Ghost where and when he will to them that hear the Gospel" [AC V 2]. In the Word and Sacrament Christ the Lord truly comes to us. In them he is actually present; they are not mere symbols which remind us of a faraway Christ of the past. Thus the *media salutis* are at the same time the *notae ecclesiae*, the means of grace are the marks of the church. There are no other marks of the true church than the Word and the Sacrament, and indeed both exist in their inseparable unity. For there is only one grace—no particular sacramental grace, no particular grace of the Word—only one Holy Spirit, only one Christ. The Word and Sacraments are present before faith because they first awaken it. Where they are present there is the church. The Word and Sacrament are, however, concrete realities. The Word is preached and heard, the Sacraments dispensed and received by living people in this empirical world. Wherever in Christendom the Gospel is preached and the Sacraments understood in light of the Gospel are administered, there the church is an empirical reality in this world.

Where the Word and Sacraments are, there people are called to salvation, there faith is awakened. Where the *evocatio*, or calling, has happened, there is *ecclesia*, or church. It is in this sense that Article VII of the Augustana calls the church the people of God, the *congregatio sanctorum*, "the assembly of all believers." The church is a concrete, empirical *societas*, comprising concrete, living people, not an idea or an invisible reality. Thus through the apostolic mission the congregations of the NT came to exist, "the church of God" at Philippi, Corinth, Rome, or wherever it may be. Every one of these congregations knew that it was the "church of God," the communion of saints, though it was made up of sinful people. They knew this by faith in the one who justifies the sinner. Wherever on earth today a congregation has been called by the Gospel, there this congregation may in justifying faith call itself a "congregation of saints"; there is the church of Christ. This character of the congregation called by the Word and Sacrament is not lost because it is weak in faith, because some in it are beginners in the faith, or even "false Christians and hypocrites" (Augustana VIII), so long as it yet possesses the pure Word and the pure Sacraments. All the baptized, the children, those growing in the faith, those who have been called and have not yet come to the full faith, even the fallen belong (the *lapsi* of Augustana XII). The church cannot be the *congregatio vere credentium*, the assembly of those who truly believe, as long as it is a church in the becoming. Only in the state of completeness which we humans cannot bring about will the church be "glorious, without spot or wrinkle" [Eph 5:27]. Thus the one church of Christ is not constituted by our faith, not by the holiness of our life, rather by Christ, who through his Word and his Sacrament calls people to repentance and faith. And this church is present wherever in Christendom, in all congregations and all denominations, where the Gospel is not so obscured and the Sacraments are not so disfigured that Christ the Lord is no longer present in them.

Within this *congregatio sanctorum*, the assembly of all believers, which comes into existence where the Word and the Sacraments are, there is present that which the Creed calls the *communio sanctorum*, the communion of saints. In the Large Catechism Luther translated the Latin word *communio* with the German *Gemeinde* and explained "the communion of saints" as an "interpretation or explanation by which someone meant to explain what the Christian church is" [LC, Creed, Third Article, 49]. He was fully correct in doing this because he saw in the "communion" [*Gemeinschaft*] which the members of the church have with each other and with their head the consummate [reality] of the church. But linguistically and logically there is a distinction between church and communion of saints. *Communio* does not mean *Gemeinde* (*congregatio*, "congregation"), rather communion in the sense of a relationship of mutual participation [*Verhältnisses wechselseitigen Teilhabens*], as Luther himself understood it.[14] The word corresponds to the NT word κοινωνία [*koinonia*] and must be understood on the basis of this word. The main passage in the NT is 1 John 1:3: "What we have seen and heard, this we have preached unto you, in order that you might have communion with us; and our communion is with the Father and with his Son, Jesus Christ." This communion cannot be identified with the church; it is a fact within the church.

But what does this communion mean? How is this different from what we humans are otherwise accustomed to call community [*Gemeinschaft*], which otherwise obtains between people of the same religion or worldview?[15] Its essence finds classic description in the NT in John 17:21–23:

> That they all may be one, as You, Father, are in Me, and I in You; that they also may be one in Us, that the world may believe that You sent Me. And the glory which You gave Me I have given them, that they may be one just as We are one: I in them, and You in Me; that they may be made perfect in one, and that the world may know that You have sent Me, and have loved them as You have loved Me. [NKJV]

---

14 On this matter, compare Paul Althaus, *Communio Sanctorum: Die Gemeinde im lutherischen Kirchengedanken, I, Luther* (1929). HS

15 The translation of this section is somewhat complicated by the fact that the German word *Gemeinschaft* may mean "communion" in ecclesiastical contexts and also "community" in more secular contexts. I have translated accordingly. MH

"I in them"—that is the mystery of the *communio sanctorum*.[16] Again we see how important it is in everything we say about the church that we do not proceed from man, from his faith and his qualities, rather from Christ, from that which he is and does. In this fact of the *communio sanctorum* the church finds its fulfillment as *societas*, and here it becomes clear why this *societas* is at the same time the body of Christ. "That Christ dwell in your hearts through faith" (Eph 3:17)—therein the church finds its completion. Everything which God does to us through the means of grace in vocation, enlightenment, awakening, in repentance, justification, and sanctification culminates in this, that Christ takes form in our hearts. Christ's indwelling of our hearts is hidden, just as his presence in the Word and in the Sacrament is hidden. This is the truth in the erroneous proposition of the invisible church. But the church itself, the one church of Christ, is not hidden, it is recognizable in the world in all denominations in the preaching of the pure Gospel, in Baptism and the Holy Supper. And in these this church yet coming to be anticipates something of the glory of the consummate church and in faith becomes certain of the *communio sanctorum*, while longing for the second coming, the visible revelation of the glory of her Lord.

To very briefly extract the consequences from everything we have said here concerning the one church for the Ecumenical Movement of the present we must mention the following.

The church of Christ, the one church, is not an ideal, a Platonic city [*civitas platonica*], but rather a reality of faith. Were the unity of the church a human ideal and the ecumenical task an attempt to realize it by churches joining the one church like states join a national union, then we would be pursuing a phantom. Then we would have to do with Christian religious societies which join an international [society], but not the church of Christ. Christianity is certainly guilty of this erroneous idea, as also are wide circles of the Ecumenical Movement. Because the church and her unity was no longer understood as a reality of faith, it was treated as an ideal and fell into an idealism which has nothing to do with faith. One saw in [this idea of] unity either a lost paradise or a future ideal yet to be realized. One looked back to the Middle Ages with Romantic sadness, as many German Catholics do; or to the ecumenical councils as is the case in the Orthodox churches or with many Anglicans; or to the church in the age of the NT, the Romantic ideal of all the sects. But these Romantic dreams have been mercilessly destroyed by historical investigation. The bull *Unam Sanctam* shows how it was with the church in the Middle Ages. Anyone who knows his history knows how it was with the ecumenicity of the old synods. Even if one took no account of the great churches which did not participate in the ecumenical councils [*grossen Nebenkirchen des Altertums*], which from time to time were composed of a great

---

[16] This Johannine expression, which agrees throughout with the thought of Paul, is not duly considered by Paul Althaus (*Communio Sanctorum: Die Gemeinde im lutherischen Kirchengedanken, I, Luther* [1929]). On that which is said here compare A. F. C. Vilmar, *Dogmatik*, § 61. HS

portion of Christianity, the picture of these synods suffices to show that their ecumenicity was a fiction to a great extent. The "ancient undivided church" never existed, not even, as many Protestants think, in the age of the apostles.

In our treatment of church history we must finally free ourselves from the idol of a "classical time" [of the church]. The NT is for us not the record of "the classical time of Christianity," rather it is the record of the Word of God, and that is something different. The church of the NT was as much a church of sinners as the church of the twentieth century, and Christ the Lord is as near to his church today as he was nineteen hundred years ago. The first council of the church—the apostolic council—was already a council of unification. Like this Romantic ideal of a unified church of the past, we must absolutely refuse the ideal of a future reunited church, which we can create or at least bring to a fuller reality through diplomatic negotiations, through agreement on mutual recognition of offices, through unification on a minimum of confession and a maximum of tolerance. All these ideals only darken the essence of the church and her unity.

The unity of the church, the fact of the one church, is a reality which we know by faith. The one church is present as truly as Jesus is with us every day until the end of the world. It is not identical with one of the denominations nor with the sum total of the same. It is within them as a reality. It is present everywhere the pure Word of God and the pure Sacraments are present. "For the true unity of the church the agreement in the doctrine of the Gospel and the administration of the Sacraments suffices" (Augustana VII). Because the Gospel is not purely taught, because it is darkened and falsified, the unity of the church is hidden. This obfuscation of the Gospel is found not only in this or that church, rather it is the continuing danger to all of all ecclesiastical proclamation. A church can have the most beautiful confessional writings, in which the Gospel is presented in the purest conceivable form, and yet stand in danger of losing the Gospel. No church can say, "I possess the pure Gospel." For the Gospel cannot be possessed by people like they possess a book. Thus "the call to unity," that is, to the one church of God, is the call to repentance, the call to Christ and his Gospel. The more earnestly this call is heard, the more earnestly the Christians of all confessions wrestle for the one truth of the Gospel, so much more will the hidden unity of the church of Christ come into view. Thus the concern of the Ecumenical Movement—the World Conference on Faith and Order has ever and again emphasized this—is for the truth! Some are caught in the modern error of relativism, according to which there is no objective "truth," but rather only subjective "truths." Others view the message of the NT not as the redeeming truth of divine revelation, but as beautiful religious experience, pious sentiment, and useful ethics. Such persons will not understand this quest for the one truth. But he who believes in the One who is the truth and whose Holy Spirit shall lead the church into all truth will see in the events of our time a portion of the history which the Lord has allowed his church to experience so that she who is "becoming" might be prepared for completion.

One last comment on the practical tasks which the present situation of Christianity places before us. We humans cannot bring the church to its completion. There is another who does this. But there is one thing we can do. We can summon Christendom to the NT message of the church of God. It is remarkable that the word "church" again reverberates through the Christian world in our time. Not long ago Troeltsch had said the word "is only tolerated by our contemporaries with difficulty" and would have happily seen the word done away with. At a time when the forces of anti-Christendom stand over against us, we can also prepare the way for a new ordering of the relationships between the confessions. This new ordering will come. In the lands of immigration and on the mission fields, it is a vital question of the Christian faith. It will also soon be a vital question for the European churches. When one thinks about how completely the mutual interaction of the churches which have taken part in the Ecumenical Movement has changed in only a few years, it is not impossible to conceive of a new sort of interaction taking the place of the isolation and the open or latent state of war, and that the necessary intellectual discussions between the confessions may be carried out in forms other than those which have hitherto obtained. But the final thing is this, that we, furnished with the faith experience of our churches, enter into the great discussion which will occupy the coming decades of church history which will be a great struggle for a new understanding of the church of Christ. It will be a struggle for the final truth of the Christian faith. All the great questions of our faith will be posed in new form. But the final decisions in this intellectual struggle will not be fought out in the books of theologians, rather there where in the midst of a world estranged from God, in our midst, the *ecclesia Christi* ["church of Christ"] appears as a reality in this age.

1930

THE SOCIAL DOCTRINE OF THE AUGSBURG CONFESSION AND ITS SIGNIFICANCE FOR THE PRESENT[1]

In this essay Sasse describes the theology of the "two regimens" (more commonly called "two kingdoms") of the state and the church. His essay reveals an area of Sasse's ministry of which many are unaware. In April 1928 he was called to be pastor at St. Marienkirche, Berlin, and *Sozialpfarrer in Innere-mission* ("social pastor in inner mission"). Note therefore his reference to those involved in the "social work of the church." He held this position until he left to be assistant professor at Erlangen in 1933. This essay was originally published in the *Kirchlich-soziale Blätter* in 1930. It was reprinted in the same year as a brochure by the Wichern Press, named after the "father of inner missions," Johann Hinrich Wichern (1808–1881).

Sasse addresses the widespread misunderstanding of the kingdom of God. He speaks of attempts to "ecclesiasticize" or "Christianize" the world which would eventually result in the "secularization" of Christendom. Later social scientists and historians would describe this as the "politicization" of Christianity.[2]

Huss number 053b
Hopf number 028

———— ❧ ————

In view of the many Reformation anniversaries which we have celebrated since the four hundredth anniversary of the Reformation, commemorated during the war in 1917, and which find their consummation this summer [1930] with the commemoration of the Augsburg Confession, one might well ask whether we have now had enough of looking back to the past, whether we have heard enough speeches and read enough anniversary articles. But we must not forget that all

———————————

[1] This essay is a translation of "Die Soziallehren der Augsburgischen Konfession und ihre Bedeutung für die Gegenwart," which appeared in two parts in *Kirchlich-soziale Blätter* 33.5/6 (May/June 1930): 65–69, and 33.9/10 (September/October 1930): 105–9. RF

[2] Edward Norman, *Christianity and the World Order* (The B.B.C. Reith Lectures, 1978; Oxford: Oxford University Press, 1979), 2. RF

these celebrations are more than a mere look into the past. Perhaps one day the beginning of a new epoch in the history of German Protestantism will be dated from the cry "Back to Luther! Back to the Reformation!" which rang through the last decade.[3] Every new epoch in the spiritual history of the West has begun with the cry "Back to . . ." The greatest example of this is the Reformation itself. In the form of a "return" we people of a historically distinct culture experience ever and again the dawn of a new age. "Back to the Reformation" is not meant as a romantic attempt to repeat the unrepeatable, but as a great self-examination [Selbstbesinnung] for the Evangelical Church, according to her deepest essence and her special task. It is a self-examination which we all hope will mean for her the dawning of a new day.

The reconsideration of the Reformation is necessary for no one more than those who wrestle with modern questions having to do with the social work of the church. How much uncertainty, how much lack of clarity rules in our ranks regarding what is properly the task of the church in view of the social problems of our day! There can be absolutely no doubt that this uncertainty is the reason the voice of our church is so little heard today. Terrible neglect in the past is avenging itself now. But here it must not be forgotten that this is the fate of all Christian churches of our time. The great ecumenical conferences of recent years, especially the world conference at Stockholm,[4] have proven this to be the case. This applies also to the Roman Catholic Church, in which there is clarity regarding socio-ethical principles, but in which the greatest diversity rules regarding the present application of those principles.

In what follows we desire to briefly present the great, fundamental concepts of the sixteenth ["Civil Government"] and twenty-eighth ["The Power of Bishops"] articles of the Augsburg Confession and the corresponding passages of the Apology regarding state and society. And we will make a few comments about the significance of this old social doctrine for the present, as far as is possible in the space permitted.[5]

---

[3]   This is a reference to the so-called "Luther Renaissance," which was prominent in the 1920s. RF

[4]   The 1925 Universal Christian Conference on Life and Work determined to set forth "the Christian way of life as the world's greatest need." Under the slogan "doctrine divides, service unites," it endeavored to avoid issues of doctrine and address social and political issues instead. RF

[5]   We cannot here enter into the present theological discussion regarding the problem before us. The reader is directed to the writings of Althaus, Brunstäd, Gogarten, Hirsch, Holl, Joachimsen, von Tilling, Troeltsch, and Wünsch. Of the older literature, particularly noteworthy are the collected essays of A. F. C. Vilmar in "Kirche und Welt," vol. 1, 1873. A particularly noteworthy contribution to our theme is the writing by Paul Althaus, just now appearing, "Der Geist der Lutherische Ethick im Augsburgischen Bekenntnis." HS

PART 1

The Augustana was composed at a time when the modern notion of the state did not yet exist. The Latin word *status*, which originally meant "station" (it was used in this sense by Thomas Aquinas) and from which later the German word *Staat* was derived, is used occasionally by the Apology (e.g., *leges de statu civili*, "laws in the realm of civil government").[6] The Augustana speaks once of the *forma rei publicae* [sic],[7] "the form of the notion of the state," which the German text renders *weltliche Händel*.[8] Otherwise the Latin expressions *res publica*[9] and *civitas*[10] (which ecclesiastical language borrowed from Cicero and Augustine), which we are accustomed to call "state," are not used. Our confession speaks much more of *res civiles*[11] ["the civil realm"], *ordinationes civiles*[12] ["civil orders"], *magistratus*[13] ["magistrate"]; in the German text, [it speaks] of *Polizei*[14] ["authorities"], *weltlichem Regiment*[15] ["secular government"], *weltlicher Gewalt*[16] ["secular power"], *Obrigkeit*[17] ["governing authority"]. The teaching of the Augustana regarding the state is the doctrine of the governing authority [*Obrigkeit*] and the civil orders [*bürgerlichen Ordnungen*][18] established with the governing authority and maintained by it.

The governing authority [*Obrigkeit*] and the orders established with it (e.g., the stations [*Stände*]) are, according to Articles XVI and XXVIII, good works and gifts from God. They are willed by God and given to his creation. The task of the governing authority is described as the protection of people against injustice and power, and the maintenance of justice and peace. Thus the power of the sword is given to the governing authority: "The governing authority protects the body and external possessions against open injustice and rules men with the sword and with corporal punishment in order to guard civil righteousness and peace."[19]

---

[6] Ap XVI 3 (55), 6 (58); *BS*, 308.3 (55) and 308.6 (58); *Triglotta*, 330.55 and 330.58; see Tappert, *BC*, 223.3 ("laws about the civil estate") and 223.6. Note on the numbering of the paragraphs: In the original, Article XVI was a continuation of Article XV. Paragraph 1 of Article XVI is numbered 53 in the original. The paragraph numbers in the *BS* and *Triglotta* reflect this. RF

[7] Here and elsewhere there are slight discrepancies between the text Sasse quotes (perhaps from memory) and the *BS* and/or *Triglotta*. RF

[8] AC XXVIII 13. RF

[9] See, for example, LC, Eighth Commandment, 258. RF

[10] Ap VI 69; *Triglotta*, 302.69. RF

[11] AC XVI 1. RF

[12] Ap XVI 1 (53). RF

[13] Ap XVI 1 (53), 7 (59), and 12 (64). RF

[14] AC XVI 1. RF

[15] AC XVI 1. RF

[16] AC XXVIII 13. RF

[17] AC XVI 1, 2, 6, and 7, and XXVIII 13. RF

[18] Cf. LC, Lord's Prayer, Fourth Petition, 73. RF

[19] Cf. AC XXVIII 11. RF

It has claim to respect and obedience. The requirement to be obedient to its commands and laws ceases when it commands something which can only be done with sin. Then the apostolic word applies: "One must obey God rather than men" [Acts 5:29].

The Augustana presupposes the existence of ordered governing authorities and does not directly answer the question of who is to be acknowledged as the proper authority in dubious cases. Is every political power which "has authority over us" to be viewed as a "governing authority"? The Reformers would sharply contradict this explanation of Romans 13 so widespread today. Paul speaks in that passage of the "superordinated power," that is, of the legal authorities. The Augustana introduces this concept of the *legitima ordinatio* [AC XVI 1] in order to distinguish the governing authority from unordered powers. Just what the marks of the *legitimae ordinationes*, the "legal orders," are—which according to Article XVI alone must be acknowledged as good gifts of God—our confession gives no direct answer. We will treat this omission momentarily.

The office of the governing authority exists not only within Christendom. It belongs to God's created order, that is, to the order which God gave his fallen creation, and it stands independent from the religious confession of men who exercise it. No matter which peoples Christians live among, they must acknowledge the current legal authorities, "be they pagan or Christian," as governing authorities established by God, and be obedient to the applicable laws (Apology XVI 2–3 [54–55]). Also in the non-Christian world—the Reformers had in view the example of the Turks—there is a legal order [*Rechtordnung*], in which the original knowledge of all people lives on as an eternal norm for what is just. Everywhere on earth there are stations in which people live according to some legal order. Everywhere there is—even if sin has blunted it—a consciousness of right and wrong. If this "natural understanding of the just" (in which form it may appear alongside of the "positive right" [*positiven Recht*]) did not exist, then humanity would not last long. In the Apology these orders are compared to the order of nature by which the world is maintained, such as the exchange of winter and summer [Ap XVI 6 (58)].

This acknowledgment of the governing authority as a universal created order reflects exactly the doctrine of the NT. The church at the time of the apostles had acknowledged the Roman government as the governing authority established by God, insofar as it fulfilled the functions of a governing authority, insofar as it was the shield of justice and peace. The church rendered it obedience so far as it could do so without sin and as long as the pagan authorities remained within their proper legal sphere. But when the governing authority transgressed its lawful limits, as happened in the cult of Caesar, and demanded not only rule over the body, but also over the soul, there the saying applied: "One must obey God rather than men" [Acts 5:29]. Thus the struggle between Christ and Caesar broke out, as reflected in the Revelation of St. John. It is not Caesar who was the enemy of Christ, but Caesar the god [*Divus caesar*], who placed himself in the throne of

God. The doctrine of our confession directly reflects these thoughts of Holy Scripture.

But if the governing authority, remaining within its limits, is part of God's order of creation, if the state also essentially belongs to the order of creation and not to the order of salvation, *then there can be no Christian state.* Indeed, the bearers of the governing office may be Christian. From them may be demanded a special consciousness of the nature of their office and a special measure of performance of duty, but their duties are the same which all governing authorities on earth have. There is as little possibility of a Christian state as there is of Christian agriculture and Christian technology. The harsh *"we condemn"* [*damnant*] of the Augustana would strike the later Lutheran advocates of the doctrine of the Christian state as much as Roman Christianity and the *Schwärmer* if it could have foreseen this later falsification of Evangelical doctrine. God's Word provides no state law. In the Apology Karlstadt[20] is called "dumb and foolish" because he taught "that one should establish city and territorial government according to the law of Moses" (Ap XVI 3 [55]). And it is expressly stated that the Gospel offers no new law for secular government (*leges de statu civili*) [Ap XVI 3 and 6 (55 and 58)] and that Christ did not command his apostles to change the civil order (*mutare statum civilium*) [Ap XVI 7 (59)]. There is no Christian order for society, for that would be an attempt to make sin disappear from the world, that love would take the place of law, in other words, that the kingdom of God would have come in glory. But as the order of nature—one half of the created order—will cease to exist in God's new creation in the new heaven and the new earth ("there will be no more death," Rev 21:4; "there will be no more night," Rev 21:25), so the secular order of law [*Rechts*]—the other half of the created order—will cease to exist at the last judgment, to which all legal order [*Rechtsordnung*] aims. Therefore, in the Augustana the article on secular government is immediately followed by the article on the return of Christ to judgment, a correspondence which is elucidated by the fourteenth Schwabach article:[21]

> Thus (in the meantime), until the Lord comes for judgment and all power and rule cease to be, secular government [*weltliche Obrigkeit*] and rule are to be honored and obeyed as a station [*Stand*] ordered by God, to protect the godly and punish the evil.

---

[20] Andreas Bodenstein von Karlstadt (ca. 1480–1541) was a colleague of Luther at the University of Wittenberg. He at first embraced the Reformation but soon "forced the issue." For instance he rejected Baptism and the Lord's Supper as sacraments (*Lutheran Cyclopedia*, 439). RF

[21] The seventeen articles were written by Luther between July 25 and September 14, 1529, and were presented at Schwabach on October 16. They were to be considered in the discussion about a political federation with the Swiss. This document is considered to be one of sources for the Augsburg Confession. An English translation can be found in M. Reu, *The Augsburg Confession: A Collection of Sources with an Historical Introduction* (Chicago: Wartburg, 1930), part 2, pp. 40–44. RF

The "glorious, great office" of governing authority has never, in the history of Christianity, been so described as in "this high, necessary article" of the Augustana (Apology XVI [13] 65). Now next to the office of secular government is placed the spiritual office, next to the state, the church, and each is alike delimited from the other. "We make a distinction between both these forms of regiment and official authority and call them both the highest gifts of God on earth [to be held] in honor" [AC XXVIII 18].

Everything depends on the proper distinctions:

> Thus the two governments [*Regimente*], the spiritual and the secular, should not be confused and mixed together. For the spiritual power has its command to preach the Gospel and administer the Sacraments. It should not become an office foreign and contrary to its nature. It should not enthrone and remove kings, should not do away with secular law and obedience, should not prescribe laws for secular power and secular affairs (*non praescribat leges magistratibus de forma rei publicae*), as Christ said: "My kingdom is not of this world." [AC XXVIII 12–14, quoting John 18:36]

While the secular authority has been given the power of the sword, the spiritual authority has no other power than that of the Gospel. While the secular authority insures justice and peace and so is concerned about temporal life and temporal goods, [the Augustana] says of the church: "The authority of the church or bishops gives eternal goods and is exercised alone through the preaching office" [AC XXVIII 10]. The preaching office here also includes the special preaching of the Gospel in absolution and the administration of the Sacraments, and by "eternal goods" is meant "the eternal righteousness of the heart," "the Holy Spirit," and "eternal life."

The separation of the secular and the spiritual, of the state and the church, which is expressed here, serves "for the consolation of consciences" [AC XXVIII 4]. Christians can with good conscience "bear civil office, sit as judges, judge matters by the imperial and other existing laws, award just punishments, engage in just wars, serve as soldiers, make legal contracts, hold property, make oaths when required by the magistrates, marry a wife" [AC XVI 2].[22]

Condemned then are "the Anabaptists who forbid these civil offices (*civilia officia*) to Christians" and "those who do not place evangelical perfection in the fear of God and in faith, but in forsaking civil offices" [AC XVI 3–4].[23] They are condemned because they have a false understanding of the Gospel. For the Gospel "does not destroy the state or the family (*politicam aut oeconomiam*), but very much requires that they be preserved (*conservare*) as ordinances of God, and that charity be practiced in such ordinances" [AC XVI 4–5].[24]

---

[22] The English translation is based on that found in the *Triglotta* (p. 51). MH

[23] The English translation is that of the *Triglotta* (p. 51). MH

[24] The English translation is that of the *Triglotta* (p. 51). MH

Christ's command to love remains in full effect. Every act of private revenge and violence is thus forbidden.

"Public redress (*vindicta publica*), which is made through the office of the magistrate, is not advised against, but is commanded, and is a work of God, according to Paul [Rom 13:1 ff.]. Now the different kinds of public redress are legal decisions, capital punishment, wars, military service" [Ap XVI 7 (59)].[25]

It is precisely for the sake of love that the Christian must also carry out these duties within the bounds of his office, "and in such offices demonstrate Christian love and justice, good works, each according to his calling" [AC XVI 5, German text]. In so far as he performs his duty within the orders of creation he serves the kingdom of Christ. For the secular and the spiritual are indeed to be clearly distinguished and must not be mixed one with the other, but as good gifts of God, as true orders given by God, they belong together, just as creation and redemption belong together as works of God. The orders of nature and law, through which God maintains his fallen world, are the presupposition for redemption and the order of redemption for the church and the kingdom of God.

PART 2

Four centuries separate us from the memorable day on which the great Reformation confession was read before the Imperial Diet at Augsburg [June 25, 1530]. Four centuries of secular and ecclesiastical history! State and societal circumstances are completely different in our day. None of the government authorities which took part in that Imperial Diet exist yet today. The legal system [*Recht*] of that time belongs as much to the past as the social structure and domestic arrangements of Germany then. Under these circumstances, what significance can the social doctrine of the Augustana still have today? Can the modern man, who is accustomed to think of social questions in entirely different categories, still understand at all what the Augustana has to say regarding these questions without some sort of intense study? Here consider the four hundred years of rich and magnificent ecclesiastical history which have dissolved into the past since the Reformation. Today Christendom looks back on experiences which were not yet in view at the time of Luther. In light of this experience can the old Lutheran social doctrine still be maintained? Furthermore, this ecclesiastical history has led to a remarkable result. Precisely that social doctrine which the Augustana condemned because it represented a falsification of the Gospel—the doctrine of Roman Catholicism and fanaticism—has today won an enormous power over souls. Indeed, in the judgment of many, it has snatched the victory from the Lutheran doctrine. Still, we assert that the social doctrine of the Augustana possesses great significance for the present, and indeed, not only for the Evangelical

---

[25]   The English translation is that of the *Triglotta* (p. 331). MH

Lutheran Church of Germany and for Lutheranism in general, but it is our view that it still has something to say to all of Christendom.

The basic concept of the Lutheran social doctrine is the clear *separation of the world and the kingdom of God* in the sense of Christ's words: "My kingdom is not of this world" [John 18:36]. Thus Lutheranism is opposed to any attempt to draw the kingdom of God into this world,[26] be it the attempt of the Roman Church *to ecclesiasticize the world* or the attempt of fanaticism and Protestantism influenced by fanaticism *to Christianize the world.* The Roman Church too knows of the difference between the world and the kingdom of God, and in its doctrine of natural law it speaks of state and government authority very often in a manner similar to old Lutheranism, which to a great extent took over Roman ecclesiastical traditions. But because the Roman Church asserted the lordship of Christ—and that means for it the lordship of the Papal Church—over all areas of life, because it subordinated the state to the church, the apparent ecclesiasticizing of the world became, in reality, a secularization of the church. That is the great doctrine of medieval Europe. If at some time the Roman Church faces a situation when it once again makes the gigantic attempt at a world led by the church, the result would likely be more successful than was the case at the close of the Middle Ages. It should never be forgotten that the terrible secularization of modern culture, this shocking spectacle of a humanity determined to strip off the last bonds of an eternal norm, is *not* a consequence of the Reformation—otherwise this phenomenon would be limited to the Protestant world. It is rather a reaction against the Middle Ages. In asserting this, we do not desire to absolve Protestantism of the deep guilt it bears in this regard. For the attempts of fanaticism—and the influence of fanaticism stretches through all Protestant churches—to Christianize the world lead to precisely the same result with a *secularization of Christendom.* Here one need only consider the consequences of the heresy of the Christian state in Germany, or the heresy of the "Social Gospel" in the Anglican world. There the Sermon on the Mount, and consequently the Gospel, becomes the basic law of social life of humanity whereby "the world is changed into the kingdom of God." But in truth, the kingdom of God has become the world.

Why do both attempts (which despite their distinctiveness still mean basically the same thing) end in this way? Because both overlook the abysmal reality of *sin* in the world. Because both great systems of socio-ethical thought still believe in the *goodness* of man, even if they only believe there is a remnant of good in the unredeemed person. In both systems what the hymn states is impossible: "Even in the best of lives *our* deeds are useless!" [*Es ist doch unser Tun umsonst auch in dem besten Leben!*][27] The divine order of the world, the natural order just as much as

---

26   Sasse was aware of such attempts especially by the Ecumenical Movement as expressed, for example, in the first "Letter Missive" of the Council of the Federal Council of Churches of Christ in America in 1908, the World Mission Council of Edinburgh in 1910, and at the Stockholm 1925 Conference on Life and Work. RF

27   From *Aus tiefer Not*, Luther's metrical paraphrase of Psalm 130, stanza 2 (1523). RF

the legal order [*Rechtsordnung*], is the order which God gave to his fallen creation. Because of sin, law, state, government authority, and the sword are present. And only when sin is done away with, when [our] redemption has been completed in the new creation, will the order of this world cease. Only when God has completed the last judgment will there be no more law [*Recht*]. The Christian, however, stands in this world bound to its orders as true orders of God, and yet in faith in Christ he is already a member of the kingdom of God. What to the modern man appears as a contradictory morality, as an unallowable compromise between official and private morality—when for instance the Christian in his vocation [*Amt*] must use the sword, yet must not do so as a private man—this is only an expression of the eschatological tension in which all Christian lives exist according to the NT. We are in the world and yet not of the world, sinners and at the same time righteous; we are redeemed, but "what we shall be has not yet been revealed" [1 John 3:2]. He who would resolve this tension—perhaps by the famous "either-or" of so-called "radical Christianity"—ought ask himself whether or not a secret faith in man is hidden in his attempt. And he ought know that he has put an end [*auflöst*] to the message of the NT, since he places a rational morality in the place of the Gospel of the forgiveness of sins. The Reformers were concerned with the pure doctrine of the Gospel when they formulated the social doctrine of the [Augsburg] Confession, and as certainly as the Gospel applies to the world today, so certain is it that the Lutheran social doctrine also has something to say to the present.

To be sure, it will only have something to say to our time if it doesn't merely exist in old books which no one but theologians read. It must be preached to present-day humanity in modern language and in living discourse with the vital questions of our day. But for this to happen it is necessary that it be thought through anew and *reformulated in the spirit of our confession.* It is one of the most serious omissions of the past that our Evangelical Church has failed to do this until very recently. A host of problems are arising. The problem of [private] *property*, for instance, which has completely changed in the world of modern capitalism. What does the modern man who assembles securities of various forms, perhaps from diverse countries, have in common with the farmer or a craftsman at the time of Luther? To conclude we shall briefly enter into two other problems, because here lie particularly acute omissions in the doctrine of the Augustana.

The first is *the question of the state.* What is meant by "legal government authority" [*rechtmässigen Obrigkeit*]? We are separated from the time of the Reformation by a long history, in the course of which all the governing authorities of that time have tumbled by revolution and been replaced by new powers.[28] Can such powers be *legitima ordinatio* ["legal orders"]? If so, how? There can be no doubt that every revolt against the legal governing authority is a grievous sin

---

[28] For instance, the 1918 revolution in Germany, which effectively brought to an end the "Constantinian Era" of church and state relations. RF

according to Lutheran doctrine. It can happen that governing authorities are overthrown because of grievous guilt, that the revolution comes as the judgment of God upon them. But the insurgent never has legal right [*niemals . . . im Recht*]. He can be the instrument of divine wrath, but his rebellion remains guilt. As God does his "alien work" in the midst of war, so may he also allow the outbreak of human sin in revolution in order to fulfill his angry judgment. Anarchy follows revolution. From anarchy a new power arises, and the question is whether such new power can be a legally constituted governing authority [*rechtmässige Obrigkeit*].

We must answer this question in the affirmative. For as far back in history as we are able to see, every governing authority once arose from anarchy. *Legitima ordinatio* is not only that governing authority which can trace its legitimacy back through an ancient past by letters of investiture and deeds, rather every political power *may* [*kann*] become the "governing authority." How can this happen? Doubtless not by the acknowledgement of men through a national assembly or a vote of the people. The assertion "the power of the state arises from the people" is false according to Lutheran doctrine, if it would be more than a formal description of the proceedings in a modern state by which a government is formed. The power of the state proceeds from God. One last reminder of this lives on in the religious formulas and forms with which modern peoples still surround the state and civil life. Any political power which has arisen out of anarchy may become a God-given governing authority, if it fulfills the tasks of the office of governing authority. This task is the assurance of peace and the maintenance of law through external power, the symbol of which is the sword. The governing authority is a "servant of God, the avenger for those who do evil" [Rom 13:4]. Legal governing authority is distinguished from religious power in that it not only (as does the latter) possesses power [*Macht*], but it also uses its power in the service of law. Both belong to the essence of the state: power and law [*Macht und das Recht*].

A governing authority which bears the sword in vain, which no longer has the fortitude to decisively punish the law breaker, is in the process of burying itself [*gräbt sich selbst das Grab*]. A state which removes the concepts "right" and "wrong" from jurisprudence and replaces them with "useful" and "injurious," "healthy" and "ill," "socially valuable" and "socially inferior," [a state] which in the place of the principle of remuneration places the principle of inoculation [*Unschädlichmachung*], a state which in its civil law dissolves marriage and family— [such a state] ceases to be a constitutional state and thus the governing authority. A governing authority which knowingly or unknowingly makes the interests of social position or class the norm for the formation and definition of law, or which allows the norms of the law to be dictated by the so-called "legal consciousness" of the time, sinks to the level of raw power.

This danger exists now—and this is not addressed by the Augustana—for all governing authorities, and shall for all time. It exists especially in the modern democratic forms of government and in the dictatorship. For the result of the secularization process of the last century has been that the consciousness of eternal legal norms which are not determined by man has nearly perished. But where this consciousness ceases to exist, there God-given power is changed into demonic power, resulting in its ruin among peoples and states. But wherever on earth a governing authority—irrespective of which form—is conscious of a [civil] righteousness independent of its will, exercises the power of its office, upholds the law and guards the peace, there it is "God's good gift," there it is "by the grace of God."

The task of the church over against the governing authorities is an especially difficult responsibility. It must guard itself against any illusion of a "Christian state" and must limit itself.

We cannot enter here into other questions very closely tied to the problem of the state, such as the question of the *Volk* and *Volkstum*,[29] which scarcely existed at the time of the Augustana, and the question of international law. Regarding the latter we simply note that for the Lutheran Church the important problem of international agreement and so-called "world peace" exists only as a question of a new international law and can never be discussed under the title "Peace on Earth." For international law has nothing to do with the Gospel.

The second problem which finds no sufficient solution in the Augustana is the question how *the church* can maintain its independence without the influence of secular power. The lack of an answer to this question is the reason that the secular authority has been able, with the tolerance and indeed the praise of theologians, to do what the Augustana so energetically forbids, namely, the "the forcible entrance into an alien office," that is, that of the spiritual power. There is, in other words, no doctrine of church government or organization. To be sure, according to Lutheran doctrine, in contrast to Roman and Calvinist doctrine, [ecclesiastical] organization does not belong to the essence of the church. But because of this truth, the fact that the question of ecclesiastical *order* was entirely neglected later has had bitter consequences. For the Augustana, to be sure, the old church organization still subsists in the episcopal office—at least in theory—understood of course in the Evangelical sense as the spiritual office in general, or the office of the Word and the Sacraments. Thus it could treat this question lightly. But in the time which followed, the lack of a fully formed doctrine of the order of the church had great consequence for the Evangelical Church of Germany and for world Lutheranism. The Augustana was the first Christian confession which gave a dogmatic definition of the church. But how the church of Christ, constituted by the pure preaching of the Gospel and the pure sacramental presence of Christ, the church as the communion of saints, that is, [the communion] of justified sinners, who in this world live as sinful people and are subject to the created order of the

---

[29]   Given the wide range of meaning possible for *Volk*, it has been left in its original; usually it is translated as "nation" or "people." *Volkstum* is very rare and has the meaning of "nationality" or "national characteristics." RF

fallen world and who as the justified are members simultaneously of the kingdom of God and stand under its orders, how this church as an empirical reality of this world should step forth as a visible reality [*in Erscheinung*]—this question our confession does not answer. The fact that German Protestantism in the last two centuries has so often been found wanting in the area of social questions no doubt is due to this omission. For only when the church itself is a living and ordered fellowship [*Gemeinschaft*] may it give a living and real answer to the great questions of human communal life [*Gemeinschaftsleben*].

1930

THE CONFESSION
OF THE CHURCH[1]

This essay was written with reference to the Jubilee celebration of the four hundredth anniversary of the Augsburg Confession.

Huss number 056c
Hopf number 026

=◁◁/◇/◇▷=

The intellectual disposition of the modern world has developed through a long, difficult struggle against ecclesiastical dogma—be it that of Roman Catholicism or that of old Protestant Orthodoxy. This explains the deep aversion of modern man toward dogmatic Christianity, indeed toward everything which confession, doctrine, and dogma mean. This aversion exists even there where one is rooted, to the very depth of his being, in the great Christian tradition of the past. There is scarcely any conviction today so widely dispersed as that which maintains that if Christianity is to have any future at all, it must be a religion of the love of God and people, an *undogmatic Christianity* of sentiment and deed ["Gesinnung und der Tat," Goethe]. This conviction has deeply penetrated the church itself. It is not an overstatement to say that the great majority of Protestant churches are actually no longer confessional churches. They would sooner be united by anything but the agreement in pure doctrine of which the confessional writings of the Reformation speak. Modern theology has provided theoretical justification for this development. It has raised the question whether the emphasis on "pure doctrine" is actually constitutive for the Christian church in the sense which the confessions of the sixteenth century thought it so, and it has answered this question in the negative. Religion is not doctrine; consequently, doctrine cannot belong to the essence of Christianity; rather it must be a secondary expression of Christianity. Doctrine belongs to the church. As such it is a concretization of Christianity. As Christianity, analogous to other religions, forms its social expres-

---

[1] This article was originally published as "Das Bekenntnis der Kirche" in *Christentum und Wissenschaft* 6.9 (September 1930): 321–33. The present translation was originally published as "The Church's Confession" in *Logia* 1.1 (Reformation/October 1992): 3–8.

sion, called churches, so it forms its philosophical-intellectual expression in dogmas, doctrines, and confessions. And in the same way that churches are very imperfect attempts to bring "Christianity" to manifestation in the world, so also "Christianity" finds a very insufficient expression in confessions. Indeed, church and confession are properly always a defection from genuine, living religion. The striving of modern Christendom for a nondogmatic Christianity finds its theoretic justification in these conceptions.

Into this situation has come forth—apparently at the most untimely moment—a new dogmatic movement. Study of the Reformation has caused the question of the right and import of "pure doctrine" to be raised again. Thus the entire modern theory of religion and its application to Christianity has been placed in question. How is Christianity to be explained if biblical revelation is not a particular case of a general religious-historical phenomenon called "revelation"? What is the church if it is not merely a sociological creation, nor merely a "Christian religious society"?[2] Should there perhaps be a history of the church [Kirchengeschichte] which is not only a Christian history of religion [christliche Religionsgeschichte] but is rather a history of the church of Christ, which is actually what the term says. We cannot enter into these questions here.[3] But it is clear that the question concerning confession will now come into new importance. The moment in which the church comes to occupy the central place in theological thought concerning the Christian religion, confession will necessarily experience a new critique. Thus the question of the *theological concept of the confessions of the church* has become an important problem. That this problem is not only theoretical but also has to do with the extremely important practical problem of the church needs no further explication in this year of Jubilee for the Augustana [1930].

1. TOWARD THE CONCEPT OF CONFESSION

The religious language of the NT uses the words ὁμολογεῖν ["confess"] and ἐξομολογεῖσθαι ["confess"] in a threefold sense: for the confession of sin, for the confession of the faith, and for the praise of God. These three meanings belong together in closest conjunction, and in their totality they constitute the Christian concept of *confession in the widest and most general sense.* How closely tied together and dependent they are upon each other is shown not only by the NT, but also by study of the classical liturgies of Christianity and great individual "confessors"

---

[2]　This is a reference especially to Schleiermacher's theology of the church as an association of like-minded people. RF

[3]　Concerning the question of the concept of the church and its dissolution in the modern theory of church history, see my article "Kirche und Kirchen" in *Credo Ecclesiam* (Festschrift for W. Zoellner; Gütersloh: Druck und Verlag von C. Bertelsmann, 1930), 295–317. HS

It was reprinted in *ISC*, 1:155–67. An English translation is found in this volume ("Church and Churches: Concerning the Doctrine of the Unity of the Church"). MH

such as Augustine and Luther.[4] None of these forms of confession is present without the others. But the three must be theologically distinguished. They began to be delimited already in the NT and this development continued in the history of the church. From the ἐξομολογεῖσθαι τὰς ἁμαρτίας ["confession of sin"] developed the liturgical confession of sin and the sacramental confession, the ἐξομολόγησις of the Greek and the *confessio* (as part of the sacrament of penance) of the Latin church. From ὁμολογεῖν, the ὁμολογία of faith in the NT, comes the corresponding expressions *confiteri* ["confess"], *confessor* ["confessor"], *confessio* ["confession"]. These obtained particular concrete meaning as "martyr's tomb," "confessional writing," and, in modern languages, as a "denomination" represented by a particular confession. The third meaning—praise of God—withdrew in the course of time and remained limited to liturgical language. What the concept of "confession" in the widest sense has meant for Christianity shall not be entered into here. It is of note, however, that the effects of the Christian concepts of confession are to be noted far beyond the religious sphere, indeed in all of Western culture. From the Christian concept of *confessio* in the sense of confession of sins [*Beichte*] has come the capacity of the European person to give account for himself, and to give account to others for himself and to describe his innermost thoughts. "Confessions" have become a form of literature, a secularized form of confession [*Beichte*]. Compare, for instance, the *Confessions* of Augustine and Rousseau. Even poetry has been understood as confession where Goethe describes his work as the fragment of a great confession. And confession as confession of faith lives on in secularized form in the manner in which philosophical systems and worldviews step forth as "confessions." So great is the power of the Christian *confessio* concept that the Western person still remains a confessor even if he has long since given up the world of the Christian faith.

There is a wider and [more] general concept of Christian confession as a speaking forth of the person seized by the revelation of the living God—a speaking forth in which the confession of sin, confession of faith, and praise of God ring together. From this we distinguish *confession in the strict sense*, the confession of faith of the church. It is a particular case of Christian confession. Here it is not an individual Christian who speaks, but rather the church of Christ. If an individual should express it, then he does so as a member of the church or in the name of the church. As far as its content is concerned, this confession is qualified by the fact that it is only a confession of faith. It does not comprise the confession of sin nor the praise of God, rather it presupposes that these sides of confession find their own expression. Distinct from the confession of sin and the praise which are directed only toward God, confession of the faith of the church is directed also

---

4 The correspondence of the three aspects of confession is plainly noticeable in Augustine's *Confessions*. For Luther, compare E. Vogelsang, *Der* confessio-*Begriff des jungen Luther, Luther-Jahrbuch* XII (1930), 91 ff. HS

toward people. It is in this sense that the oldest formulas of the NT are confessions in which the early church expressed its faith before God and the world. So also are the so-called ecumenical creeds, plus the confessional writings of the churches of the Reformation, and also the particular documents in which an ecclesiastical communion sought to present its doctrine as the correct Christian faith. As great as the formal differences between these confessions may be, they essentially belong together.[5] And as churchly confession they stand over against the personal confessions of individual Christians as something distinct. In what follows we are concerned only with these churchly confessions.

2. CONFESSION AND REVELATION

Where is the origin of the confession of the church to be sought? Fendt[6] finds it in the call of Jesus to discipleship: "The disciples *professed* adherence to . . . Jesus, while they *physically became his followers.* . . . The *physical following* of Jesus was the actual confession of adherence to Jesus, the actual *Confessio Apostolica* ['apostolic confession']. Thus it is a *praxis* while the *talk* remained the subject of Jesus, that is, to the end." After the earthly days of Jesus, in the place of the physical following came Baptism, again, as a praxis. "*Baptism* is a new *confessio*, the new confession of adherence to the same Christ." "That now in Baptism one confessed adherence to Jesus *verbally* was understandable. . . . When Christ was yet visibly in the center of his followers, to be sure, verbal expression on the part of the confessor was unnecessary. But now the muteness of Baptism was taken away by 'words addressed to Jesus,' by praying words. . . . These words which now accompanied Baptism were called 'confession,' thus we have *confessio* . . . a confession of the *second* order." "Baptism itself is confession of the first order, the allowing oneself to be baptized, the becoming baptized. On the other hand, the words, the confession of the second order, are only a sign of the confession of the first order, an interpretation *of* the real confession, a witness *to* the confession." According to Fendt it is in this sense that all ecclesiastical confessions are to be understood, including the baptismal confession of the ancient church, the confessions of the councils, and also the Augustana.

Fendt is correct in maintaining that the verbal formulation of the confession must not be overestimated or indeed absolutized. The boundary for every ecclesiastical confession is already indicated in the Sermon on the Mount, where the

---

[5]   When E. Peterson, *Heis Theos* (1926), 171, denies to the early Christian formula "*Kyrios* Jesus" the character of a confession, because it is an acclamation, he overlooks the fact that according to Rom 10:9 the formula was used—apparently in the case of Baptism—as a confession. There is no formal criterion for that which is "confession"; it is rather a matter of content. Formally, the Augustana is also something completely different than the *Apostolicum* ["Apostles' Creed"]. HS

[6]   [Leonhard] Fendt [1881–1957], *Der Wille der Reformation im Augsburgischen Bekenntnis*, 7 ff. I engage this book intentionally because among the numerous books published for the Augustana Jubilee it is most well known and is certainly the book which has made the greatest attempt to awaken a new appreciation for the confession of the Reformation. HS

mere speaking of the *Kyrios* confession is contrasted with real discipleship, the true following of Christ, which is confirmed in the doing of the divine will. Nevertheless, the judgment must be rendered that the confession of the *church* cannot be understood as Fendt attempts to explain it. A confession, also a baptismal confession, must not be viewed as "praying words to Jesus." Indeed, Baptism stands in close connection to confession, but it is not confession, for then Baptism would be understood in the same sense in which Baptists understand it.

The following of Christ is also something other than confession, even though both belong together. The first disciples followed Jesus before their belief in him had become clear. They did not know who he was when they followed his calling. The following of Christ was not yet a confession in the strict sense. The origin of ecclesiastical confession is not the call "Follow me" [Matt 4:19], but the question "Who do you say that I am?" [Matt 16:15]. It is very significant that according to the NT Jesus himself demanded confession, indeed, verbal confession from his disciples. This must be placed in emphatic contradistinction to all modern attempts to degrade confession to something subordinate to "the practical Christianity of the following of Jesus," or possibly even [something] superfluous—attempts with which a theologian such as Fendt has nothing to do. It was not the metaphysical curiosity of people or the appetite of theologians for speculation which called forth the formation of the confession of the church, rather the question of Jesus to his disciples, "Who do you say that I am?" In response to this question followed the first confession of the church, uttered by the mouth of Simon Peter: "You are the Christ" (Matt 16:16). That we are dealing here with a ὁμολογία, a genuine confession, even if it is yet something formally entirely different than the later symbols, is shown by John 9:22: "The Jews were already in agreement that whoever confessed him as the Christ [αὐτὸν ὁμολογήσῃ Χριστόν] would be expelled from the synagogue." Jesus answered the confession of Peter, according to Matt 16:17, by praising him (the only time which such praise of a particular individual occurs in the mouth of Jesus): "Blessed are you Simon, son of Jonah, for flesh and blood has not revealed this to you, but my Father in heaven."

These words are extraordinarily important for the understanding of confession. The confession of Peter presupposes a precise knowledge. What kind of knowledge is this? That Jesus is the Christ is not a rational knowledge, not some consequence which Peter had to draw from that which he had experienced with this Jesus. Justice is not done to this knowledge and the answer of Jesus is falsely understood if it is placed in the category of the irrational and viewed as one sort with the "divination" by intuition of the metaphysician or with the display [Schau] of the mystic. It is a knowledge which according to its subjective side must be designated faith-knowledge, according to its trans-subjective side, revelation-knowledge. The living God acts in his revelation, and faith answers him, not in the sense of an intellectual allowing oneself to be convinced, not in the sense of a decision accordant with the will, not in the sense of a stimulation of pious feelings. It is rather a matter of faith in which the person, the entire person, abandons himself to God, or better, is accepted by God. For it is God himself indeed who works faith. And this faith expresses itself immediately in a confession. Confession belongs to the essence of the believer; he cannot be without it. He cannot be silent. According to the NT (Rom 10:9–10) the faith of the heart and the confession of the mouth belong inseparably together.

And how does faith express itself? Not in a hymn, not in the gush of feeling, but rather in a confession, a sober judgment of being, in which the facts of revelation are attested: "You are the Christ!" This sobriety, this objectivity is characteristic of all genuine confession. Truths speak, not feelings. Its theology is throughout a theology of reality.[7] There is nothing more sober, more matter of fact, than the great confessions of the church. But in this sobriety lies their greatness. On their monumental factuality and simplicity are dashed to pieces all religious theories which are able to see only "doctrine," rational, doctrinaire assertions, as the opposite of "true," "living" religion. If that theory of a romantic aestheticism is correct, if confession in its factuality is really a spoiling or falsification of the "true" religion, then it must be admitted that this falsification entered with the earliest beginnings of the Christian faith. To faith in Christ belongs the confession of Christ as a sober recognition of reality, and in this respect the first confession of the circle of disciples (now becoming the church), the confession of Peter at Caesarea Philippi, does not differ from the confessions of the later church.

Thus confession may be described as *the answer to revelation*, and this the revelation which occurred once in history. In her confessions the church gives her answer for all time, the answer of faith in the revelation in Christ. These answers may be different, corresponding to the understanding of the faith of their day. They may be formulated very differently, but they desire to be, according to their deepest intent, nothing other than an answer to the revelation of Christ. Therefore, all confessions are confessions of Christ, that is, confessions at whose center stand declarations concerning Jesus Christ. This applies to the ancient confessions as much as to those of the Reformation and to the more recent attempts at formation of confession (Lausanne, Jerusalem, and the Social Creeds added at Stockholm).[8] Because Christian revelation is historical revelation all confessions look to the past. They point back to the once and there of salvation history ("suffered under Pontius Pilate").

Thus it makes sense that their content is understood not to be new, but rather old, truth. "The truth has already long since been found" stands invisibly as a

---

[7] *Theologie der Tatsachen*, a reference to the work by A. F. C. Vilmar entitled *Die Theologie der Tatsachen wider die Theologie der Rhetorik: Bekenntnis und Abwehr*. Sasse wrote an introduction to a reprint of this work in 1938. RF

[8] This is a reference to meetings of the three main branches of the Ecumenical Movement: First World Conference on Faith and Order, Lausanne, 1927; Third International Missionary Council, Jerusalem, 1928; First Universal Christian Conference on Life and Work, Stockholm, 1925. RF

preface to all confessions. Thus the [old Roman] baptismal symbol is antedated by the apostles, the *Constantinopolitanum*[9] by Nicaea[10] and the *Quicunque*[11] by Athanasius. Thus the Augustana begins with the confirmation of the *decretum Nicaenae synodi* ["the decree of the Council of Nicaea," AC I 1]. This is one of the most difficult stumbling blocks for modern man. He can only conceive of a confession which looks entirely to the present and, if at all possible, ignores history and its "salvation facts," a confession which expresses the religious experiences of the present man, or perhaps "revelation of the present." In order to give biblical basis for this demand the prophecy of John 16:12 ff. is happily called to service. One may try to understand this passage in the sense of Catholicism, which thereby justifies the production of dogma of the church as an expansion of the scriptural revelation. Or one may try to understand it in the sense of the enthusiastic *Schwärmertum* of all times, from the Montanists on, which finds there a promise of a new revelation which places that of Scripture in the shadows. But for the most part the close correspondence for the Fourth Gospel between the witness of the Paraclete and the apostle is overlooked. The prophecy of John 16 is not dealing with a continuance of the revelation of Christ nor with an expansion or replacement of this revelation by another, but rather with its realization. The revelation in Christ maintains its unique place. The Spirit "will not speak of himself. . . . He will glorify me, for he will receive that which is from me" [John 16:13–14]. The Spirit remains bound to the Word of Scripture, faith to the Gospel, confession to the revelation which occurred once in history. It is the task of the confession of the church to give answer to these facts and express them in a meaningful way. Whether that happened in the old confessions of the early church ("Jesus is the Christ," "Jesus is Lord"), or in the developed Christological and Trinitarian confessions of later times, or in detailed confessional writings in which Christianity or a portion of the same presented the fullness of the faith, the object of the confession is always the revelation of God in Christ. New sayings, forms, or symbols may be chosen, new categories of thought may be used, the meaning of revelation for every domain of life may come to be understood or expressed in entirely new ways, still, confession always remains the answer to the great question of Jesus, "Who do you say that I am?"

---

[9]   The creed known in the church today as the "Nicene Creed" is actually the "Niceno-Constantinopolitan Creed" of ca. A.D. 381. RF

[10]   A.D. 325. RF

[11]   That is, the Athanasian Creed, ca. A.D. 600. RF

3. CONFESSION AND CHURCH

Confession is the response to revelation. To this first characteristic we must add a second: it is always the *response of a fellowship* [*Gemeinschaft*] *of people*, the expression of a consensus. Thus ecclesiastical confession [*Bekenntnis*] is distinguished from Christian confession [*confessio*] in the widest and most general sense. And here is the point at which modern man most deeply misunderstands the confession of the church. He who knows the faith only as a private concern can present the confession only as the act of an individual who expresses his personal faith, his religious experience, with the entire force of "Here I stand, I can do no other."[12] His opinion gives rise to a congregation, when people, who have had the same experience and possess the same faith, unite and formulate their common possession in a confession. This confession of the congregation is always something secondary. Over against the living, definite, concrete confession of the individual, it necessarily appears to be pallid, abstract, and distanced from real life. Since religious experience is finally entirely individually defined, the confession of the congregation must reckon with individual differences. It must express the common or general and be subordinate to a broad interpretation. While the great confession-forming times in the history of the church created definite, concrete, unambiguous confessions, modern Christianity has sought to create confessions (the formulation of which was inevitable) which are as general and indefinite as possible.

Thus Jesus Christ is spoken of not as the Son of God, Lord and Savior, but rather as the divine Lord and Savior.[13] The confession "Jesus is Lord" is preferred, but it is forgotten that the early church chose this expression because it unambiguously designated the divinity of Jesus Christ, while modern Christianity loves it because the word "lord" in modern languages is wan and ambiguous. This tendency toward generalization in the formulation of confessions is explained by the fact that the confession of the church is understood from the individual outward, no longer the [confession of the] individual from [that of] the church. Congregation, church, and confession are understood from the starting point of the individual Christian: the congregation as the sum of the individual Christians, as an association—the great form of social life in all ages—in which the genuine [churchly] fellowship is destroyed. The church is understood as a general union of the congregations ("the church is built from the congregation up"), the confession as the condensation of the declarations which are common to all individ-

---

12 As spoke Luther at Worms, 1521. RF

13 Preamble to the constitution of the Federal Council of the Churches of Christ in America [1908]. HS

ual confessions. This is the false doctrine of the Social Contract in the church![14]

This is the reason that the confession of the church in its deepest sense is scarcely yet understood. And indeed this applies also to many of the so-called "confessional" school. For also here confession is understood from the basis of the individual. It is, as it were, the inviolable statute of union of the union "church." Those who do not acknowledge this statute as binding may leave the church! In the confessional controversies of the last century the warring parties occupied, as far as the concept of confession is concerned, the same ground. The only controversy was whether the statute of union was to be interpreted strictly or liberally, whether it ought to be left in its old form or formulated anew. And because there was basic agreement on the concept of the confession, the present, generally accepted compromise-solution could be arrived at in the German churches, namely, that the old forms retain their honor, but they are used very liberally. The controversy for us has been enclosed in the spirit of this compromise. But here there can be no doubt that the deepest and most difficult discussion of confession will break out the very moment in which the [present] conception of church union is acknowledged to be untenable. In theology this hour is already upon us.[15]

But how is the confession of the church to be understood if it is not the condensation of individual confession? Must not every confession first of all be formulated by an individual? Did not an individual disciple first confess the original confession of the church? That is in fact the case. But the import of the confession of Peter is that it was immediately taken up by the other disciples. Jesus had directed the question to all the disciples present: "Who do *you* [plural in German, as in Greek] say that I am?" [Matt 16:15]. And Peter answered in the name of all of them. The Gospel of John rightly understood this matter when it gave the answer in the first person: "*We* have believed and are convinced that you are the Christ" [cf. John 6:69]. This confession immediately became the confession of all the disciples, and it is no accident that after the profession of the first confession, for the first time the church is mentioned: "You are Peter, and upon this rock I will build my *ecclesia* ['church']" [Matt 16:18]. Confession and church belong together.

This applies also to the baptismal confession from the first primitive formulas of the NT to the final form of the *Apostolicum* ["Apostles' Creed"]. They appear understandably in the first person singular form of *credo* ["I believe"], since

---

[14] The "Social Contract" is described as "a supposed agreement entered into by men dwelling together in one place or country to organize a state or political constitution, establish a government, submit to its authority, and obey its laws" (*Dictionary of Philosophy and Psychology* [ed. James Baldwin; New York: Peter Smith, 1940], 2:534). Schleiermacher's definition of the church as a "voluntary association of men" comes directly to mind here. MH

[15] See Emil Brunner, *Gott und Mensch* (1930), 50 ff. HS

they are indeed spoken by every individual Christian. But while the individual speaks this *credo*, which is the confession of the church, he places himself within the consensus of the church. As soon as the confession is employed not only in the case of Baptism, but also in the worship of the congregation, it has the tendency to take on the first person plural form. The *Nicaenum* ["Nicene Creed"] of the Eastern church has been kept with this form until today, and it is noteworthy that Luther's composition of the *Credo* in song likewise makes use of the first person plural: "We all believe in one true God." The Augustana may be considered from this viewpoint. What sort of age must that have been in which a professor of theology could create a confessional writing which began with these words: *ecclesiae magno consensu apud nos docent*[16] ["Our Churches, with common consent, do teach," AC I 1],[17] and which was so truly born of the consensus of the faith that it was immediately accepted by the churches of the Lutheran Reformation as their confession!

What theologian would dare venture today to formulate what "our churches" teach, and should he venture it, what response would he get? This consensus, this being one in the great common possession of the faith, is the mark of all great epochs in the history of the church, and these are the ages which could create the confessions. They are the times in which the "church" is not only an old word or a sociological concept, but rather a reality which one experiences and in which one lives. They are in no way times in which "the concept of individuality was not yet developed." What a multiplicity of characters we meet in the early history of the church, in the epoch of the formation of dogma, and in Reformation history! What a multiplicity of antitheses and differences! The present possesses, in spite of all its individualism (or perhaps for that reason), much more spiritual unity than those times past. But to us is lost that which was the characteristic feature of the great ages of the history of the church: the inner harmony of person and fellowship in the reality of the church.[18]

If we could ask the men of the NT whereupon the deep consensus rests from which the confession of the church is born, they would be able to respond to us nothing other than that which we read today in our NT: "So in Christ we who are many form one body, and each member belongs to all the others" (Rom 12:5 [NIV]). Or the passage from Ephesians (4:4–6), which the Augustana quotes where it speaks of the unity of the church [AC VII 4]: "One body and one Spirit . . . one Lord, one faith, one Baptism, one God and Father . . ." They would say

---

[16] For the concept of the consensus, see the preface of the Formula of Concord. The *ecclesiae* are not the "congregations" (Fendt, Thieme), rather the territorial and state churches (Althaus in *Theologische Literaturzeitung* [1930], 357). HS

[17] The English translation is that of the *Triglotta*, 43. MH

[18] On this point see W. Elert, *Lehre des Luthertum* (2ed.; 1926), 105 ff., and W. Zoellner, *Die Kirche nach dem Epheserbrief* in F. Siegmund-Schultze, *Die Kirche im N.T.* (1930). For an account of the decay of the fellowship in the Catholic Church, see R. Guardini, *Vom Sinn der Kirche* (1922), 4–5. HS

to us that the unity of the confession does not rest upon our faith or our experiences, nor upon a similarity of human individualities, but rather upon the one Holy Spirit who works faith and confession in us. Already in the discourse of the sending out of the disciples in the Synoptic Gospels the confession of the martyr before the judge was designated as a work of the Holy Spirit (Matt 10:19–20). And Paul said that no one could speak the (liturgical) *Kyrios* confession "except by the Holy Spirit" (1 Cor 12:3). The church has never forgotten the correspondence between confession and possession of the Spirit.

We are reminded of this by three things: the representation of the confessors as bearers of the Spirit; the (ecumenical) synod as [believed to be] led by the Holy Spirit (a notion which, among other things, is tied to Acts 15:28); and by the charismatic teaching office of the bishop (culminating in the doctrine of Vatican I of the *charisma numquam deficientis veritatis* ["charisma of the truth which never fails"] of the pope). It is urgently necessary that the Evangelical Church not only refute the false doctrines of Eastern and Western Catholicism concerning the manner in which the Holy Spirit works in the church, but also that it is itself clear concerning what the NT and the Reformation teach concerning the Holy Spirit and how it has viewed the workings of the Holy Spirit in the church. Perhaps this reflection would lead to the realization that we, who have the correct doctrine of the Holy Spirit, have also misconstrued and forgotten his reality, and that would explain the terrible fact that the greater portion of Protestantism no longer knows what the confession of the church is.

4. CONFESSION AND PURE DOCTRINE

Confession is directed to God as the answer of the church to revelation. Therefore it has its place in the worship of the congregation; it belongs to the liturgy. All great, primitive confessions can be prayed, and they have been spoken with praying hearts, but they are as little prayers as the Our Father is a confession. Consider the confessions of a later time, such as the great confessional writings of the Reformation, in which were laid down the results of difficult dogmatic controversies. Perhaps they bear this liturgical character only in certain parts (passages from Luther's catechisms) or no longer at all. But in fairness it must be remembered that these confessions presuppose the classical confessions of the ancient church and their utilization in worship. But this question will not be further discussed here because it belongs to liturgics and not to dogmatics.

The very confession which is directed to God and thus is closely related to the prayer of the church is directed now toward the world. The moment the church gives its answer to revelation it delimits itself from everything which stands outside of the church. The great task of the confession is the separation of truth and error, of church and that which is not of the church. "Jesus is the Christ"—this confession separated the primitive Palestinian church from the orthodox synagogue (John 9:22; 12:42). The question was whether or not it yet had any place within Judaism. That the crucified Jesus should be the coming Messiah could in no way be united with orthodox teaching about the Messiah, but perhaps it could somehow find some slight toleration. Thus the oldest church lived in the form of a Jewish sect in the shadow of the synagogue.

It would be different in the case of the second great confession which the early church put forward: "Jesus is Lord." It belongs, as the *maranatha* shows, already to the Aramaic epoch of the church, but not until it was preached in the Greek language would the cleft between church and synagogue become entirely evident. *Kyrios* was the holy name of God of the Septuagint. To give to a man "the name above all names," to bow the knee in worship before a man, was for the Jew blasphemy, an infringement on the first commandment. The *Kyrios* confession set the boundaries for the church over against the pagan religions, the mystery religions with their "many lords" (1 Cor 8:5), and the Caesar cult, in which Caesar was honored as lord and god. Indeed, these strange religions had no opposition to the designation of Jesus as the *Kyrios*. They were very tolerant. All paganism is tolerant. But for the Christians there was only one who was the Lord! It was because of this Christian intolerance that the great persecutions of the church broke out.

Thus the church delimited itself from all other religions by means of its confession. Had it not done this, it would have been drawn into the rush of ancient syncretism and ceased to exist, just as all Christianity ceases to exist in the struggle of the great world religions, which is played out upon the earth, if it fails to delimit itself over against all [other] religions by means of its solid, unambiguous confession. Today the NT is avidly read (selectively, as in Europe) by non-Christian Indians and Chinese, and scarcely any pagan or Jew has any objection to praying the Our Father at inter-religious prayer meetings. Many American Jews pray it fervently. But the confession of Jesus Christ, as expressed in the great churchly confessional formulas, is the boundary between church and that which is not church.

Just as the confession distinguishes the church from strange religions, so also it distinguishes—this its task—truth from error, pure doctrine from heresy, the church from sect within Christianity. Thus rings the definition of confession in the introduction of the Formula of Concord: "Et quia statim post apostolorum tempora, imo etiam cum adhuc superstites essent, falsi doctores et haeretici exorti sunt, contra quos in primitiva ecclesia symbola sunt composita, id est, breves et categoricae confessiones, quae unanimem catholicae christiani fidei consensum et confessionem orthodoxorum et verae ecclesiae complectebantur." ("And because directly after the times of the apostles, and even while they were still living, false teachers and heretics arose, and symbols, i.e., brief, succinct confessions, were composed against them in the early Church, which were regarded as the unanimous, universal Christian faith and confession of the orthodox and true

Church.")[19] This setting of the limit of truth and error belongs to the essence of confession. If the *improbant* ["they (our churches) reject"] and the *damnant* ["they condemn"] (by which is designated the impossibility of church fellowship), which sound so harsh to modern ears are silenced, the Augustana ceases to be confession.[20]

If this drawing of boundaries is called "loveless" and "unchristian," then the same reproach is also directed toward the *Apostolicum*, every sentence of which was formulated against some heresy, and, above all, this reproach is directed toward the Bible itself. Just as the false prophets stand over against the prophets of God (Jer 23:21 ff.; 29:8–9; Ezekiel 13), [and just as] the false apostles stand over against the apostles of Christ (2 Cor 11:13), so the sect and heresy stand over against the church. And just as the struggle between truth and error rings through all of Holy Scripture, so also it runs through the history of the church, and the church would cease to be the church of Christ, messenger of the redeeming truth of the revelation of God to people, if it would cease to fight this battle. Here lies the greatest and most difficult task of the formation of confession. Here is shown whether or not Christianity still knows what the confession of the church means. The manner in which an age approaches this task shows what of courage and strength of faith, and what of humility and love are alive in Christianity. Here is shown whether the church knows of the reality of the Holy Spirit.

If the people of the Christian West, deep into the rank and file of the church, have forgotten this last sense of the confession of the church, then the reason for the downfall must not be overlooked. It happened because this struggle for the truth of the Gospel—the most difficult struggle which the church in the world has had to carry out—was not always fought with pure hearts and unsullied hands. Nowhere has the church failed so seriously as there where it should have struggled for the pure teaching of the Gospel. In the fight against apostasy from the church, the church has itself only too often forsaken Christ. Thus the confessing church has ever and again become the denying church. The history of Simon Peter, who was the first to express the confession of the church and the first to deny the Lord, has been repeated in the history of the church. But something else is also repeated therein: the tears of repentance and the reinstatement into the office, and this is the office of confession, of bearing witness, of martyrdom.

---

[19] The English translation is that of the *Triglotta*, 777. MH

[20] On this point, compare the article by Theodor Hoppe, "*Die* Augustana *als Bekenntnis unserer Zeit*" in the June [1930] issue of *Christentum und Wissenschaft* [vol. 6, no. 6]. HS

THE CHURCH AS *CORPUS CHRISTI*[1]

This essay was delivered at the Conference of German and English Theologians, the same series of conferences for which Sasse had presented his essay *"Kyrios"* in 1928.[2] This conference, held in March 1931 at the Bishop's Palace, Chichester, England, was "to get at the positive doctrine of the Church and the Sacraments."[3] The table of contents in the issue of *Theology* in which this essay was first published gives a fuller title to the essay: "The Church as *Corpus Christi:* The Nature of the Institutional Expression of the Idea." Following the conference, Sasse spent some days as a guest of Sir Edwyn Hoskyns at his home in Cambridge. In a letter of thanks to the Bishop of Chichester, George Bell, for his hospitality, Sasse explains that it was his first visit to England and adds: "I have learnt very much about Anglican theology, more than I could have learnt by reading many books, and I think this is true of all of us who had the privilege of taking part in the discussions at Chichester."[4]

Huss number 080-II
Hopf number 419

When the church is designated as the body of Christ in St. Paul's epistles, that is a thought for which every parallel is wanting in the history of religion. The church of the NT can be compared with the congregation (people) of Islam or with the congregation of Buddha; parallels can be drawn between the Hellenistic congregations of the Pauline period and the associations of the Hellenistic mystery religions. In that way remarkable sociological affinities result. But neither the relation of a band of disciples to their master nor the relation of a believing com-

---

[1] This essay was published simultaneously in German and English in *Theologische Blätter* 10.6 (June 1931): 156–58 ("Die Kirche als Corpus Christi"), and *Theology* 22.132 (June 1931): 318–23. The translation given here is a reprint of that published in the journal *Theology*. The translation of all the German papers in this series was by the Rev. L. Patterson, D.D. RF

[2] *"Kyrios"* is also printed in this collection. RF

[3] From the editorial introduction to the collection (*Theology* 22.132 [June 1931]: 301). RF

[4] April 2, 1931; Lambeth Palace Library, Bell Papers, vol. 63, p. 180. RF

munity to its founder nor the relation of a mystery guild to its cult-god was capable of being designated by an expression which would even only approximately correspond to the σῶμα Χριστοῦ ["body of Christ"] of the NT. The singularity, in the history of religion and sociology, of the ἐκκλησία ["church"] of the NT finds in its designation as the body of Christ its classical expression. But while the NT utters this peculiar thought, it avails itself naturally of an already existing world of ideas and terminology. It is above all worth while to know these presuppositions of thought and language, if we wish to understand the idea of the *corpus Christi*. We can only here indicate what is most important.

The first presupposition is the thought that a community of people can be understood as σῶμα ["body"] in the sense of an organism. "We many are one body" (1 Cor 10:17). "As the body is one and has many members, but all the members of the body, though they are many, are only one body" (1 Cor 12:12). "As we have many members in one body, but not all members have the same work, even so we, the many, are one body . . . and every one members in their reciprocal relation" (Rom 12:4–5). A plurality of members of different kinds and with different functions exists in the unity, the wholeness of the body, whereby the whole is more than the sum of the parts. Only in the relation to the whole of the body and to one another the members have their existence. They are not there for themselves. Even their functions are related to one another and are functions of the body (1 Cor 12:14 ff.). Between the members, which can only exist with and for one another, there exists the relation of συμπάθεια ["sympathy"] (συμπάσχει ["suffer together with"], 1 Cor 12:26). These thoughts are intelligible without any commentary. As they have been set forth here—namely, with the omission of Christ's name—they contain nothing specifically Christian. We find in them the Hellenistic thought of the organism, as it was developed in the classical philosophy of the Greeks and was disseminated by the later popular philosophy (cf. the Platonic doctrine of the state as a collective person, the Aristotelian doctrine of the superiority of the society to the individual, the Stoic thought of the organism of the world or [in Cicero and Seneca] of the society bound together into unity through the συμπάθεια τῶν ὅλων ["sympathy/shared feeling of the whole"]). St. Paul has borrowed the widespread image of the body, with the help of which the essence of human communities was made clear, from the storehouse of the thought of his time and applied it to the church.

The second presupposition is the thought of the spirit constituting the community, an Oriental, not a Greek thought. It is emphasized again and again that it is the πνεῦμα ["Spirit"] which creates the unity of the σῶμα ["body"]. "One body and one Spirit" (Eph 4:4). "We are all baptized through one Spirit into one body, whether we be Jews or Greeks, slaves or free men, and are all made to drink of one Spirit" (1 Cor 12:13). Even this thought is not specifically Christian, but it belongs to the prophetic religions of the East. The Pneuma, the Spirit of God coming upon people from above and dwelling in them, binds the individuals together into a unity, a "we," a collective person of the true people or the congregation. The community so understood is something else than that which is meant by the Greek doctrine of the organism. It is, if the words may be used, a "supernatural," not a "natural" community. In this sense the great religious communities of the East, founded on revelation, have been understood. The historically most significant example of this outside Judaism and the church is the "people," the congregation, of Islam. On Christian ground the Oriental idea of the church as the collective person constituted through the Pneuma has maintained itself most clearly in the churches of the East. (Compare the "we," the πιστεύομεν ["we believe"], in the Eastern confessions in contrast with the Western *credo* ["I believe"]; further, [compare] the doctrine of the infallibility of the collective person of the whole church represented in the Ecumenical Council in contrast with the Roman doctrine of infallibility; to the Eastern theory of Catholic truth belongs the corresponding doctrine of Muhammad: "My people will never consent to an error!")

The thoughts of the community as a σῶμα ["body"], an organism, and of the pneuma constituting the community, form the presupposition for the NT conception of the church as the *corpus Christi*, and indeed the thought of the pneuma stands in the first place. St. Paul gives these thoughts a fully new content when he asserts the following: (1) The Pneuma constituting the church as a community is the Holy Ghost. (2) The σῶμα ["body"] constituted through the Holy Ghost is the σῶμα Χριστοῦ ["body of Christ"].

The first of these sentences means that not every pneuma is identical with the Holy Spirit of God. The NT would frankly recognize that there are also other spiritual communities, collective persons (1 Cor 10:20–21), in so far as other communities could broadly appropriate the utterances of St. Paul about the pneuma constituting the community. The only question is, What kind of a pneuma it is which constitutes these other communities? Here we come upon the distinction characteristic for biblical religion between the pneuma in itself and the Holy Spirit of God and between the spirit of falsehood and the spirit of truth. On this fundamental distinction rests the self-limitation of the biblical faith in God against all religions which come forward with the claim to possess prophecy and revelation. This distinction, already existing in the OT in the distinction of true and false prophecy, is so completed in the NT that the criterion for the testing of spirits, "whether they are of God," is found in this: whether they bear witness to Jesus Christ come in the flesh (1 John 4:1 ff.) and as the Lord (1 Cor 12:3). The witness of the Holy Spirit is always witness of Christ, whether it be of him that comes as in OT and NT prophecy (John 16:13), or of him who is come in the flesh (John 15:26). Christ and the Holy Spirit belong together. They are not identified but are thought of as coexistent: *Ubi Spiritus Sanctus, ibi Christus; ubi Christus, ibi Spiritus Sanctus* ["Where the Holy Spirit is, there is Christ; where Christ is, there is the Holy Spirit"]. The presence of the Holy Spirit in the ἐκκλησία ["church"] is therefore not to be thought of without the real presence of the Crucified and Exalted One. In the light of this presence of the Lord and the

Spirit, the church is to be understood: *Ubi Christus, ibi ecclesia* ["Where Christ is, there is the church"] (Ignatius[5]); *ubi Spiritus Sanctus, ibi ecclesia* ["Where the Holy Spirit is, there is the church"] (Irenaeus). If one asks about the church, one may not first put the question "Where are the people who belong to the church?" but one must ask, "Where is Christ, where is the Holy Ghost?" And the answer to this can only be this: Christ is really present in the word of the Gospel and in the Sacrament; the Holy Spirit is really given (*ubi et quando Deo est visum* ["where and when God sees fit"]) through the Word and the Sacrament. Where the Gospel and the Sacraments are, there people are called into the church, there comes into being the congregation of the saints, that is, of the justified sinners—a community not to be understood by means of sociology. Within this congregation there exists what the *Apostolicum* ("Apostles' Creed") calls the *communio sanctorum* ("communion of saints") and what is called in the NT κοινωνία, community in the sense of shareholding. The members of the congregation share in the same Christ and the same Spirit (1 John 1:3; 2 Cor 13:13 [ET 13:14]; Phil 2:1) and stand therefore in the relation of κοινωνία to one another. Christ dwells "through faith" in their hearts (Eph 3:17; cf. Gal 2:20, where the "in faith" is likewise to be noticed). So the many become a unity, "one single new man" (Eph 2:15), the collective person of the church. Through the "I in them," they are "perfect in unity" (John 17:23).

Now St. Paul designates the community of the church created through the Holy Spirit as σῶμα ["body"] and applies to it in the parable of the body and the members the thought of the community as an organism. It could be asked whether the thought of the organism, taken from natural life, is generally applicable to the spiritual community of the church. It is applicable within the same limits as (let us say) the idea of the people. The designation of the church as a body is exactly so far metaphor as its designation as "people," and in the same way more than a metaphor—namely, an indication of a real relation, as it is not only a metaphor, but a reference to a reality, when we call the church "people," "people of God." The application of the image of "body" to the church would present no problem if St. Paul only said of the collective person of the church constituted through the presence of the Lord and the Spirit what we read in Rom 12:5: "So we, the many, are one body in Christ." How, then, is the transition from the expression "body in Christ" to the other "body of Christ," which we find in the exposition of 1 Corinthians 12, agreeing in thought with Romans 12, to be explained? If one cannot comfort oneself with the too-convenient explanation that St. Paul was not a keen thinker, and that his mystical language dispenses with strict logic, then there remains no other explanation but the assumption that St. Paul, in what he says about the σῶμα Χριστοῦ ["body of Christ"], quite consciously combines two originally different thoughts: the thought of the ἐκκλη-

---

[5]   Ignatius, *Epistle to the Smyrnaeans* 8:2. MH

σία ["church"] as the ἓν σῶμα ἐν Χριστῷ ["one body in Christ," Rom 12:5] and that of the σῶμα Χριστοῦ, the body of the exalted Lord. Dr. Rawlinson[6] has rightly drawn attention to the puzzle of the expression *corpus Christi* and to the Sacrament, especially the Lord's Supper, as the probable starting point of the thought of St. Paul about the body of Christ. Both ideas of the body of Christ, which is present in the Lord's Supper, and of the one body, which the church represents, so coincide in 1 Cor 10:16–17 that one can speak of an identification of both. The church is the body of Christ, is identical with the body of Christ, which is really present in the Lord's Supper. The participation in the body and blood of Christ present in the Lord's Supper is synonymous with membership in his body. How seriously St. Paul takes this relation between the church and the glorified body of Christ may be concluded from the fact that he designates the bodies of the faithful, which indeed must be changed into the same form as the glorified body of the Lord (Phil 3:21), as members of Christ (1 Cor 6:15). But if this interpretation of St. Paul's thought is right, must not one then speak of an identification of the church with Christ? The question is on this account to be denied because, in spite of the occasional abbreviation "Christ" instead of "body of Christ" (e.g., 1 Cor 12:12), a distinction is always made between Christ and his body. That is clear in the epistles to the Colossians and Ephesians: Christ remains the "head" (e.g., Col. 1:18), the Savior (Eph 5:23) of his body, and the relation between him and the church is understood as the prototype of marriage (Eph 5:22–23). The collective person of the church constituted through the Holy Ghost is not Christ. Not "Christ existing as a congregation," as has been said, but Christ in his congregation and his congregation in him; that is the sense of the Pauline doctrine of the church as the *corpus Christi*. Its significance for dogmatics lies in this—that, like no other utterance about the church which we find in the NT, it expresses the fact that the essence of the church can only be understood in the light of Christology, and that means only in the light of faith in Christ.

---

[6] *Mysterium Christi*, 225–26. HS

1933

THE LUTHERAN CONFESSIONS
AND THE *VOLK*[1]

The notion of the *Volk* as nation and German people became dominate in the ideology of the Third Reich. Thus, Sasse was, in this essay, treading on very sensitive ground.

Against any notion that the German *Volk* might be unaffected by original sin or be a chosen people, Sasse described the church as a people, "a community of sinners, that is, a community of the godless, that is, a community of those human beings who are lost."[2] In response to a concept of the "religio-moral values" of the German *Volk*, Sasse declared that this people of God "is indeed not to be recognized in the particular religious or moral qualities of these historical communities, but rather in the presence of the pure doctrine of the Gospel and in the administration of the Sacraments according to their institution."[3] And later: "Its only notes are the purity of the doctrine of the Gospel and the proper administration of the Sacraments, not the religious or moral standing of its members."[4]

The so-called *völkisch* movement provided the historical roots and constituted the organizational as well as the ideological starting point of National Socialism. In *Mein Kampf* Hitler wrote: "The basic ideas of the National Socialist movement are *völkisch* and the *völkisch* ideas are National Socialist." In the summer of 1933, only six months after Hitler became chancellor of Germany, the Nazis formed a "German National Church," the *Deutsche Evangelische Kirche* (DEK, "German Evangelical Church") to which Sasse makes reference in this essay.

---

[1] Entitled "Das Volk nach der Lehre der evangelischen Kirche," this essay was originally published in *Auslanddeutschtum und evangelische Kirche Jahrbuch 1933* (ed. Ernst Schubert; Munich: Chr. Kaiser, 1933), 20–39. It was reprinted in Bekennende Kirche 20 (ed. Christian Stoll; Munich: Chr. Kaiser, 1934). MH/RF

[2] From the "August Confession" of the "Bethel Confession" by Sasse and Dietrich Bonhoeffer, VI, 3a, § 48, "Of the Church," in Guy C. Carter, "Confession at Bethel, August 1933" (Ph.D. diss.; Marquette University, 1987; Ann Arbor: University Microfilms International, 1987), 323a. RF

[3] As confessed by AC VII 1; the quote is from the Bonhoeffer-Sasse Draft of the "Bethel Confession," § 38, in Carter, "Confession at Bethel," 324. RF

[4] "August Confession," VI, 3a, § 51, in Carter, "Confession at Bethel," 324a. RF

Here, then, is perhaps Sasse's most thorough and pointed treatment of the idea of *Volk*.

Huss number 106
Hopf number 049

—◦∾◦—

PART 1

If we are to come to some understanding of the teaching of the Evangelical Church on the question of *Volk*,[5] then it is a given that we must begin with the *confessions* in which our church once gave testimony to its faith and doctrine. At first glance this appears to be a completely inappropriate, if not absurd, undertaking. How shall the confessional writings of the sixteenth century provide answers to the real questions of our day, questions which perhaps did not even exist then? And even if we were to find such answers in these documents, what authority would they possess for us? In the Evangelical Lutheran Church there is no dogma in the sense of Roman Catholic Church doctrine. There is no system of irrevocable doctrinal decisions with binding authority for all times, no *theologia perennis* ["perennial theology"]. Even the confessions themselves desire to be nothing other than a "witness and explanation of the faith, how at that time the Holy Scriptures were understood and explicated in controverted articles in the church of God, by those *living at that time*, and how the doctrine contrary to these Scriptures was rejected and condemned" [FC Ep, Preface, 8].

These confessions themselves demand critique when they establish the principle that all their assertions are to be examined on the basis of the *norma normans* ["ultimate norm"], the Holy Scriptures [see FC Ep, Preface, 7–8]. And the idea that somehow the era of the formulation of confessions was closed after the Formula of Concord would be absurd to its authors. No, we do not grab hold of the confessions in order to allow the theologians of the time of the Reformation to answer the questions of the twentieth century. We do so rather to encounter the church which still possessed the courage and the authority to produce confessions. This was the church in which there was not merely a chaos of individual opinions of lone pastors, professors, and ecclesiastical leaders, but rather the great consensus of the "we believe, teach and confess,"[6] the consensus of genuine churchly fellowship.

---

5   The translation of *Volk* is, of course, problematic. There simply is no precise English equivalent. "People" or "culture" at times comes close to sufficing but is still inadequate. We have, therefore, left the terms *Volk*, *Völker* (plural), and *Volkstum* (i.e., "*Volk*dom") untranslated in most instances. Sasse's article was a response to the elevation of the concept of *Volk* by the National Socialists under Hitler. MH

6   The Formula of Concord used this expression. The ancient ecclesiastical concept of a consensus brought about by the Holy Spirit (e.g., the theory of the synod from Acts 15 on) was taken up again by the Augustana (Articles I and VII). HS

This consensus has been destroyed in the Evangelical Church in the past two centuries. And thus the living process which allows for churchly development of doctrine and confession has come to a standstill. The modern Protestant who understood religion as a private matter ("God and the soul, the soul and its God"), and the church as the association of individual believers, viewed the church's confession primarily as the individual Christian's expression of religious conviction. For him the church's confession could only be the condensation of countless individual confessions of faith. Often a new form of confessional document has been sought, in the preambles of church constitutions, in the "*Biblika*" of the new Agendas, or in synodical pronouncements regarding questions of the day. There these new forms of confession must be as wan, general, and ambiguous as possible, in order to find acceptance. But nobody pays attention to them. Only a concrete, definite confession seizes hearts and unites individuals. Thus further development of doctrine was left to theological specialists. But these men have achieved no other consensus than that perhaps possible within various scholarly schools and points of view. Thus the Evangelical Church has become helpless over against the great political groups and worldviews which have become confessions in themselves.

The Evangelical Church of our day has only a few very general religious-moral convictions to counter the great teachings regarding *Volk*, state, and humanity, as they have been preached by Socialism and Communism, or by civil or revolutionary Nationalism. People gather to these movements as they once did around religious confessions. Whenever the church desired to give concrete answers, naturally it was directed to the widely divergent private opinions of individual theological viewpoints and schools. If present-day Protestantism is to overcome this weakness—and it is on its way to doing just that—then it can begin nowhere else but with a look at the Evangelical Church of the past. That church was still prepared, *magno consensu* ["by common consent"],[7] to answer the questions of its day and to carry out its work in the world by means of its doctrine. If our church is again to become a confessing church, then the struggle for a new confession must begin at the place where a torrent of living confessional creativity once flowed, which now has become torpid and stagnant. Thus it is self-evident that the spiritual productivity of the last century, whether positive or negative, is of the highest significance for the future.

This connection with the classical confessions of our church is also necessary for another reason. If we ignore it we will lose our connection with the Reformation. We cannot simply ignore the confessions and return directly to the Scriptures as though they [the confessions] did not exist. To be sure, Scripture remains the source and norm of all doctrine. We know of no tradition as source of revelation. But no one can read the Bible without his understanding of the

---

[7] These opening words of the Augsburg Confession, Article I, "Ecclesiae magno consensu," are cited often by Sasse. RF

same being determined by the experiences of the history of the church. No living person, be he Protestant or Catholic, theologian or non-theologian, can read the NT as though there never were an Athanasius, an Augustine, or a Luther, as though he never learned a catechism. Even the text or translation of the Bible we read is determined [*mitbestimmen*] by the history of the church. This history forms a commentary on the Holy Scriptures. And no one can entirely free himself from this context, not even the scholar who appears to study the Bible at his desk without presupposition in order to develop a system of Christian doctrine. Thus, for the one who seriously seeks the correct Evangelical teaching on crucial modern problems, there is no other way than the way which leads through the confessions of the church to Holy Scripture as the source of truth.

PART 2

He who approaches the confessional writings with our theme in view is immediately disappointed. The confessions do contain what we are accustomed to call "social ethics." They discuss marriage and family; the relationships of parents and children; property and domestic economy; authority and state; obedience over against civil law and its limitations; law, administration of justice; taking oaths; authority to punish; war and military service. They discuss, in passing, everything which belongs to the so-called questions of social ethics. But on the question of our theme we find nothing. The confessions of our church contain no teaching regarding the *Volk*. How can we explain this?

One can give the easy answer and say that the Reformers simply did not face the modern problems of *Volk* and nation. The modern concepts of *Volk* and nation, as they have developed in the wake of the Enlightenment, Idealistic Philosophy, and Romanticism (from various sources and in various contents), existed for them as little as did the modern national state. The state, with which the German Reformation had to do, was the Holy Roman Empire of the German Nation on the one hand, and the small territorial states on the other. This concept of state was based not upon a national principle, but on the idea of the universal empire [*Reich*] (which to be sure, has long since become fiction) and upon the dynastic principle. But even though it would be quite foolish to try to find in the Reformers a position over against the modern questions of *Volkstum* and the national state, still it is worth considering that the sixteenth century already encountered its questions regarding nation, even if in very different forms than those encountered by the modern world. And so it is quite astonishing that these questions are not taken up in the confessions.

The beginnings of the Reformation coincide with the rise of a great, new national consciousness in Germany. One need only be reminded of Luther's powerful document "To the Christian Nobility of the German Nation"[8] and the effect

---

[8]   1520, *LW* 44:115–217. RF

that it had. It is a document which is among the greatest monuments of our
national and political history. In this writing one speaks who with daring auda-
ciousness called himself "apostle and evangelist in German lands," even a
"prophet of the Germans." He spoke as Reformer of the church, but his words
were perceived as those of the spokesman of a people whose national consciousness was awakening. Those first years of the German Reformation are an entirely unique example of the coinciding of a renewal of the faith and a national upris-
ing. Germany never experienced anything like it again, not even at the time of the
war of independence.[9] One can well understand how our contemporaries ever and
again turn their attention to the high point of our history, where "faith and *Volk*,"
"Gospel and *Volkstum*" appeared to become one. Even when the great national
and political reform movement was shattered, when the great enthusiasm was
choked by the blood of the peasant revolt, when Luther had disavowed national
and social revolution in order to preserve the Gospel for his people, the Lutheran
Reformation never denied its national character.

What would Luther have been without the love for his people [*Volk*], which
he, with all his greatness, weaknesses, and mistakes, possessed like none of his
contemporaries! How this love is expressed, even when he, with the wrath of a
prophet, censured the sins of the German nation, the princes and the *Volk*. And
what has the Lutheran Reformation meant for the development of the German
Volk! It gave the German *Volk* the Bible, the Catechism, the hymn, and the Divine
Service in the vernacular. But the confessions only mention Germany and the
German *Volk* very infrequently. Luther, for instance, speaks in the foreword to the
Smalcald Articles of his fear "that [God] may cause a council of angels to descend
on Germany and destroy us utterly, like Sodom and Gomorrah."[10] In the Large
Catechism he speaks of how, but for the prayers of the pious which have guarded
against and hindered the might of the devil like an iron wall, "the devil would
have destroyed all Germany in its own blood."[11]

One could blame the humanist Melanchthon for the fact that the Augustana
and Apology do not refer to Germany and the German nation (except for the historical and political arguments in the preface). But in other writings, especially his
preface to the *Germania* of Tacitus, Melanchthon demonstrates that he in no way
lacked love for his German *Volk* or pride in its history.[12]

The preface to the Book of Concord says that God, in his mercy, "after the
darkness of papistical superstitions [granted] the light of His Gospel and Word,
through which alone we receive true salvation, [to] arise and shine clearly and

---

[9] Germany against Napoleon I, 1813–1815. MH

[10] SA, Preface, 11; the English translation is from Tappert, *BC*, 290. MH

[11] Large Catechism, Lord's Prayer, 31. MH

[12] Compare Werner Elert, *Morphologie des Luthertums* (1932), 2:133. Regarding what follows please note the
definitive presentation of the relationship between Lutheranism and *Volk* by Elert, 125–90. HS

purely in Germany, our most beloved fatherland."[13] This expresses both the ecumenical and national character of the Reformation and its teaching. But this
emphasis on things national is completely lacking where the teaching is explicated. Consider how differently the papacy is dealt with in the Thirty-nine Articles
of the Church of England and in the Smalcald Articles. In the former there is a
national protest against the papal claims to ruling authority: "The Bishop of
Rome hath no jurisdiction in this Realm of England."[14] In the latter we find the
churchly and theological polemic against the pope as the Antichrist. In the former the Reformation is the freeing of a national church from the "foreign jurisdiction" of Roman rule. In the latter the Reformation is the rediscovery of the
pure doctrine of the Gospel, which is valid for all of Christianity.

From this perspective one can understand that the national question barely
plays any role at all in the confessions. The confessions are about the Reformation
of the church. They do not intend to lay the foundation for a German national
church. They desire, rather, to proclaim the pure doctrine of the Gospel, which
ought be the same for Christianity among all peoples. What they teach regarding
Christology and justification; faith and works; marriage and secular authority;
church and state is only an explanation of the one Gospel which has validity for
Christians in all lands and among all peoples. Here is the reason for the great
effect which these confessions have had far beyond the borders of Germany. And
their influence has also spilled over the boundaries of the Lutheran confession.

The Reformers' view of the church explains how they could have spoken in
such a way. Lutheranism knows that the church appears in various external forms,
among individual peoples and language groups, countries and provinces. It is of
the opinion that the social form of the church, its governance and outer order as a
public institution, the forms of its worship, *ritus aut cerimoniae ab hominibus institu-
tae*[15] ["the rites or ceremonies instituted by people"], are to be adapted to the forms
of life of every individual people group [*Volk*] within which it exists. The medieval
Roman Church with its hierarchical constitution with the papacy above all, and its
uniformity were done away with and thereby freedom for new developments was
created. The adaptation of the external form of the church to the peoples
[*Volkstum*] among which it finds itself now makes it possible for the Gospel to be

---

[13]   The English translation is from the *Triglotta*, 7; cf. *BS*, 3; Tappert, *BC*, 3. See the words following shortly thereafter: "in our beloved fatherland, the German nation" (*BS*, 4; *Triglotta*, 6). RF

[14]   Article 37, "Of the Civil Magistrates." This article, which corresponds to Article XVI of the Augustana,
begins: "The King's Majesty hath the chief power in this Realm of England." While the Lutheran
Confessions made such generally applicable pronouncements regarding the doctrine of the state and sec-
ular authority, so that they could be appropriated by churches of other countries without alteration, the
English confession only speaks of England and its dominions. This has occasionally presented
Anglicanism with great difficulties, for example, in the case of the Declaration of Independence of the
United States. The Lutheran Confessions, often vilified as "doctrinaire," have proven to be not only a
protection for Evangelical doctrine, but also for church formation [in lands and times outside sixteenth-
century Germany]. HS

[15]   AC VII 3; see also Ap VII/VIII 30. RF

preached and to penetrate every people as much as possible so that the church of Christ can sink roots as deep as possible in and among various peoples.

Thus the language of the people must become the language of the Divine Service. The liturgy of a mystery religion can, if necessary, be celebrated in a foreign language, and it can still have its effect upon the "spiritually enlightened." The Word of God can only be preached in the language of the people, or it remains without effect. We cannot enter into specific detail here about what effect this principle has had for the national development of Germany and the countries in which the Lutheran Reformation took hold.[16] We will only mention Bible translation. It is always an epoch-making event in the linguistic and literary history of a *Volk*, in many cases the very beginning of this history, when the Holy Scriptures are translated into its language.

But this principle does not signify the dissolution of the unity and catholicity of the church. That is the great misunderstanding which the Reformation has ever and again encountered among Catholics and Protestants. In the fourteenth century, the Western church found itself in the irreversible process of disintegration. The logical conclusion of this disintegration was the separation of the universal church into a series of *national churches*. It is no accident that the concept of the nation first began to play a great political role at the reform councils. The English Reformation is an example of an event which could have happened in other lands (though probably in other forms) even without Luther. Even in Germany in the early years of the Reformation the possibility existed for a similar development. A series of national churches, whose doctrine would have been a compromise between medieval dogma and the spirit of the Renaissance, was certainly a possible outcome of the great crisis of the Western church. In certain ways it would have paralleled the disintegration of the ancient church of the empire.

This result was hindered by Luther and the other Reformers. Thanks to the Lutheran Reformation the idea of the *catholicity of the church* was saved. When the Lutheran Reformation took up the true concept of the national church and maintained that the church in every nation and among every people of every age may and should develop forms corresponding to these circumstances, it simultaneously rejected the false doctrine that connection to country or *Volk* is of the *essence* of the church:

> Therefore let no one think that the church is like any other external polity,[17] bound to this or that land, kingdom, or nation, as the Pope of Rome[18] says; but it certainly remains true, rather, that that house and men are the genuine

---

[16] See the detailed presentation of Elert, *Morphologie des Luthertums*, and the most recent Lutheran literature on missions, in which the fruitfulness of this principle for the present has been pointed out. HS

[17] That is, *politia*; we would perhaps say "social form." HS

[18] Here it is clearly recognized that the idea of the national church and the idea of the Roman Church, in spite of external contradictions, are deeply connected. The universalism of the Western Catholic Church was indeed defined (and actually finally destroyed) by the fact that it is the Church of Rome and thus

church which is scattered throughout the world, from the rising to the setting of the sun, who truly believe in Christ, have *one* Gospel, *one* Christ, [and
the] same Baptism and Sacrament, are governed by *one* Holy Spirit, even
though they may indeed have dissimilar ceremonies.[19]

Here the definition of the church found in the Augustana is explained (the
first confessional definition of the concept of church which was ever rendered in
the history of dogma). It is no accident that there is no reference here to the connection between church and *Volk*. The significance of this is clear when we compare it with the following confession in which a number of German Catholics of
our day, partial to National Socialism, express their hope for one national church:
"We believe in God the Creator, and in Jesus, the Redeemer, and in the Holy
Spirit, who gives life, and in the one true holy catholic church, and, within her, in
one holy Christian church of the German nation."[20]

The Reformers would never have agreed with such a confession, even if it
were formulated in a better way. And for precisely this reason: here something has
been drawn into the definition of the church which does not belong there. It does
not belong to the *essence* of the church that it exists in any particular sociological
connection. It can also exist, and has in fact existed, where it had no part in the
existence of *Volk* or nation (e.g., in the cultural milieu of the *Imperium Romanum*
["Roman Empire"], particularly its metropolitan cities). And we should never forget that the church of the NT existed in precisely this situation! And the church
has existed in those chaotic periods of the migration of nations
[*Völkerwanderungszeit*]. The expression of the Augustana (*quod una sancta ecclesia
perpetuo mansura sit* ["that one holy church shall perpetually remain," AC VII 1])
can never be read as though it meant a *Volks*-church. But this is just what must
happen if we desire to *believe* in a church of the German nation, as we believe in
one, holy church. Then we would have to believe in the eternity of a nation!

The *essence of the church* is defined in purely theological terms by our confessions, and never anthropologically or sociologically. The church proceeds *from
God and not from men*. Distinct from all other confessions, Lutheranism knows of
only two *notae ecclesiae* ["marks of the church"]: the Word of God and the
Sacrament. Where the Gospel is clearly and purely preached and the Sacraments
are administered according to the institution of Christ, there is the church, there
the church will be. The church is not constituted by any human qualities (not our
faith or the holiness of our lives) nor by any sociological state of affairs (a partic-

---

stands over against the national churches not as a universal church, but as the Imperial Church of the
Imperium Romanum ["(Holy) Roman Empire"]. HS

[19] Ap VII/VIII (11), *BS*, 236 (lines 14–22, German); see also page 238 where it is expressly emphasized: "We
are speaking not of an imaginary church, which is to be found nowhere; but we say and know certainly that
this church, wherein saints live, is and abides truly upon earth" [*BS*, 238, lines 40–44; *Triglotta*, 232]. RF

[20] Published by S. Ohlemüller, *Nationalsozialismus und Katholizismus*, 2 (Berlin 1933), 66. Compare this to
the symbol of German Catholics of 1845, Prot. R.E. IV, 585 ff., where the concept of the nation was not
yet forced into the definition of the church. HS

ular form of structuring the relationship of congregation and office of the ministry). The church is constituted only by the *real presence of Jesus Christ the Lord,* who in his Gospel and in the Sacraments is really and personally present. And through these he builds his congregation on earth. Everything else—our faith, our love, the external appearance of the congregation, its worship, its caring associations [*Bruderschaft*], its configuration as a legal organization—is a consequence of this church-constituting presence of Christ.

This strictly theological and Christological definition of the church, which was a result of the Reformation, has since then all but been lost by the Evangelical Church and her theology. We are accustomed to have an understanding of the church based upon man, proceeding from human piety, as though the church were merely the social form of "Christendom." We note the fact that this "Christendom," like all religions, is determined by natural arrangements and the historical vicissitudes of human life. We see that the various *peoples* [*Völker*] have developed not only various forms of church, but even various *forms of Christian piety.* There is in fact a German, English, Russian, or American Christendom. The Reformers would grant this also. But they would explain that the church can never be understood with this "Christendom" or these types of "Christendom" as the starting point. They would not argue that the manner in which the people of a *Volk* receive the Gospel and the expression it manifests are conditioned by the character of that people. But they would most decisively reject the idea that any particular characteristics of these peoples [*völkischen Besonderheiten*] make the *consentire de doctrina evangelii* ["agreement in the doctrine of the Gospel," AC VII 2] impossible. There is no German, Spanish, English, or French Gospel. There is only the one Gospel of Jesus Christ, and therefore only *one* Christian truth. There is finally no faith which is peculiar to any race or culture [*artgemässen*]. There is only true or false, strong or weak, Christian faith.

That the Western Goths, and then also a series of other predecessors to the Germanic peoples, became Arians is a historical accident. What did Arius have in common with the German soul? The Christology of those at Chalcedon was, for the Reformation, as little an expression of Greek piety as the doctrine of justification was for it an expression of German faith. What did the *articulus stantis et cadentis ecclesiae* ["the article of faith by which the church stands or falls," that is, justification], which the Reformation was about, finally have in common with things German? Lagarde[21] and other advocates of "German" faith view it as a Jewish remnant, as a doctrine with which Paul falsified the true Gospel of Jesus. The Jews, since the days of Paul, have perceived this doctrine as the destroyer of all morality, and thus the very opposite of genuine Judaism, just as its anti-Semitic opponents today perceive it as un-German.

---

[21]   Paul Anton de Lagarde (Bötticher; 1827–1891) was an orientalist and philosopher who desired a new national church "with a faith welling up out of the collective heart of the people" (*Lutheran Cyclopedia,* 456). RF

It is common to view German mysticism, from Meister Eckart through to German idealism, as the typical German expression of Christianity. But the Lutheran Church has excluded from the church of the Gospel this German mysticism, and all that is consequential to it (including far and away the greater part of modern theology), with the hard *damnant* ("they [our churches] condemn") of the Augustana. For this the German soul has found its revenge in that a well-known and authoritative book on "German piety" (much read in the youth movement) did not even mention Luther. Luther himself in the Smalcald Articles places the "German" religion of the "experiencing of God," in which we have all been raised, in the category of fanaticism, of one kind with Islam and the papacy [cf. SA III VIII 3–6, 9]. One could easily multiply such examples.

The existence of the various forms of piety, conditioned by the innate characteristics [*Seelentum*] of various peoples, is incontestable. But whatever meaning these may have, according to the confessions, they can never limit the possibility of the *consentire de doctrina evangelii* ["agreement in the doctrine of the Gospel," AC VII 2]. If the church really does stand and fall together with the article of justification, then it stands and falls with this article in Rome, in England, in China and Russia, just as much as in Germany and Sweden. But beyond all the different spiritual tendencies, which work themselves out in forms of worship and church formation, among those who hear the Gospel it must be possible to come to a *consensus de doctrina evangelii*. Unanimity of faith and confession is created by the Holy Spirit. For he is indeed the one who creates faith. It is impossible to come to some unified view of the various national religions and the definite types of piety found among varying peoples or races. Nor is it at all possible for theology to define the "essence of Christendom," in view of the countless contradictory manifestations of the Christian religion throughout history.

But if one proceeds from God and not from man, not from human religion, nor even from the Christian religion, but from the Gospel, as do the Reformation confessions, it is possible to understand the church. If one has understood what faith in the Evangelical sense is, worked by the Holy Spirit himself, and never "by my own reason or strength" [SC, Creed, 6]; that the Holy Spirit creates faith in the Word God; and that this is quite different from all human religions within the bounds of pure and practical reason, then it is possible to understand the church as the Reformation understood it. This church is not built by us. It is created by God himself. And this is so as surely as God is God, as surely as Jesus Christ is the Lord, as surely as God's Word is the Word of the Creator and Consummator, the Judge and Redeemer, the greatest power on earth.

The concept of the church of Luther and Lutheranism originates from faith in this Word. In this definition of the church, man, as individual or as *Volk*, can never have a founding or co-founding role. He is passive. One does not decide to join the church; he is rather called to the church. We do not build the church ("Arise! Let us build Zion!"); we are only the stones used to build it, or at most the tools used to build it. The church of the Word is the church of the *sola gratia* ["by grace alone"]. *It is the true catholic church, because it alone is the church of God,* not a Roman or German church, not Reich or national church, not *Volks*-church or free will church,[22] or whatever other adjectives we place beside it. These adjectives finally have no other intent (even though we hide them with the scientific mask of religious sociology, which is more often than not what is done) than to smuggle man back into the definition of the church. All these names serve finally only to deny the unity, holiness, and catholicity of the church.

Because the Reformers knew this church as a reality in the world—though it is indeed "hidden" from the eyes of men as the body of Christ and the *Volk* of God, but knowable in the preaching of the Gospel and in the Sacraments—they could allow such wonderful freedom regarding the church's external form. Thus they could leave free the forms of congregational formation, the office of the ministry, and the Divine Service. This holy catholic church can be present "where two or three are gathered in my name" [Matt 18:20] or where an entire *Volk* hears the Word of God. It is there where an individual bearer of the office of the ministry sets about to proclaim the Gospel to a pagan *Volk* for the first time.

The congregation which comes to exist as a result of the Word—be it a house congregation, a local congregation, or the congregation of an entire country and among an entire people [*Volk*]—borrows the external forms of its life from the world. And these forms remain of the world. A language, for instance, is not sanctified because the Bible has been translated into it. This church may and should enter into the world and be a Jew to the Jew, a Greek to the Greek, a Roman to the Roman, a German to the German, an American to the American, "in order to save some" [1 Cor 9:22]. This true catholic church does not need "catholic" forms, for its catholicity consists in Jesus Christ, who is Lord over all and who has sent his church to all peoples, and even to those who are not yet or no longer a *Volk* or a nation. This church does not need to legitimize itself as a national or *Volks*-church before any *Volk* and its demands. For it is the *Volk* of God.

Here lies the deepest reason why the Evangelical Confessions have no regard for the national question, or even the national question of the sixteenth century and the German *Volk* of that time. They speak of the church of God and its pure doctrine. But this was perhaps the greatest service which they could render to the German peoples [*Völker*]. Perhaps even today the Evangelical Lutheran Church of Germany can render no greater service to its people [*Völker*] than that it tell them what the church of Christ is. It could be that all our theological and untheological talk regarding *Volk* and *Volkstum* will remain unfruitful if we do not first know and say what the church is. For it may be that only one who knows what a *Volk* is is he who has understood the *church* as the *Volk* of God.

---

22   This is a reference to Schleiermacher's *Freiwilligkeitskirche*, "voluntary church." RF

PART 3

But the confessions speak not only of the church, they also speak of the world in which this church becomes a reality and of the men to whom this Gospel is preached. And indeed, neither this world nor these men are present apart from God, who has created them and still preserves them. Man remains God's creation also after the fall.[23] The condition of fallen humanity lies obscured by darkness. Everything which any pessimistic philosophy has ever taught on the nature of humanity pales in comparison to the depiction of human nature in the Augustana (AC II). For man is born laden with guilt and has merited death, already at the moment of birth. "This unspeakable injury cannot be known by reason, but only from the Word of God" (FC Ep I 9). God could well have destroyed this creation, but did not:

> And here pious Christian hearts justly ought to consider the unspeakable goodness of God, that God does not immediately cast from Himself into hell-fire this corrupt, perverted, sinful mass, but forms and makes from it the present human nature, which is lamentably corrupted by sin, in order that He may cleanse it from all sin, sanctify and save it by His dear Son. (FC SD I 39)[24]

Therefore in the Catechism the Christian thankfully praises the fatherly goodness and mercy of God, who "has made me and all creatures ... and still preserves them" (*adhuc conservet* [SC, Creed, 2]).

This concept of preservation (*conservare*) plays a great role in the Lutheran understanding of faith in God. God's governance of the world is revealed in this preservation (*conservare*) and in his *maintaining* fallen creation until judgment day. This boundary which is established by the last day ought never be forgotten. So also in Scripture the concepts of creation and the end belong inseparably together. This must be very clearly expressed because today the words "creation," "creation faith," and "order of creation" are regrettably misused. This misuse gives the impression that the article of faith regarding creation is a truth of reason, and that creation could be discussed without considering the end and the last judgment. *The end belongs to the [doctrine of] creation.* For the world is not eternal. Only he who is the Alpha and Omega, the Beginning and the End is eternal. Whoever speaks otherwise of creation is finally a pantheist. The time between creation and the end is the time of preservation, the time of *God's forbearance* (2 Peter 3).

God's preserving grace, God's forbearance, is revealed in the inviolable *orders* through which he governs the world. These divine orders (the confessions call them *divinae ordinationes* or *ordinationes Dei*) we find above all in the form of *orders of nature*. The *leges temporum* ["laws of seasons"], such as the exchange of summer

---

[23] "Nature also after the fall is still a creature of God and remains so" (FC Ep I [2]). HS

[24] The English translation is from the *Triglotta*, 871. MH

and winter, are called such *ordinationes* ["ordinances"] by the Apology (Ap XVI 6). No one can avoid their inviolable force. We are reminded here of the divine promise after the flood: "So long as the earth remains, seed time and harvest, cold and heat, summer and winter, day and night shall not cease" (Gen 8:22). This order serves to maintain the creation: "I will henceforth never again curse the earth because of men" (Gen 8:21). This order of nature is inviolably in effect until it shall be done away with in the new creation ("There will be no night," Rev 21:23 ff.). The promise of a new creation is seen in the miracles to which the Bible bears witness. *Marriage* too belongs to the legitimate order of nature. But unlike all other human orders, of which we shall speak later, marriage is rooted in nature itself.

> For likewise, by the word of Genesis 1, where God says, "Let the earth produce vegetation and plants and so on," the earth has been so created that it not only bore fruit in the beginning, but that it produces vegetation, plants, and other growing things, so long as nature continues. And so also man and wife were created to be fruitful, so long as this nature continues.

> And we speak here not of inordinate passion, which came in the wake of Adam's fall, but of the natural attraction between man and wife, which also would have remained in nature if it had remained pure. . . . Thus now the divine order and the created nature of things neither can nor shall be changed by anyone. Thus it follows that the estate of marriage may not be done away with by any human statute or vow. (Ap XXIII 7 [German])

As in the case of the other orders of nature, this one too will only be suspended in the new creation of the coming aeon: "In the resurrection they will neither marry nor be given in marriage" (Matt 22:30).

In the divine order of marriage the second area of the *divinae ordinationes* is alluded to. We call it the *legal order* [*Rechtsordmung*]. "We can accept no law regarding the unmarried state," says the Apology, "because it contradicts divine and natural law" ("quia cum iure divino et naturali pugnat," Ap XXIII 6). The explanations of the Apology on the divine order of marriage are the only passages in the confessions in which the concept of natural law is referred to: "Because this creation or divine order in man is a natural law, therefore the jurists have said wisely and correctly that the marriage of man and woman is a natural law" (Ap XXIII 9). This "natural law," it says further, is unalterable, and so this order which God implanted in nature must remain (Ap XXIII 9; cf. Ap XXVII [51]).

In the discussion of the other orders of human life, the concept of *natural law* has (apparently intentionally) been avoided [by the confessions]. This applies to the civil orders (*ordinationes civiles, ordo politicus* ["political order"] in the wide sense; compare the preface of Ap XVI [1 (53)]) and the *public and legal orders* of human life in society, which fall into the categories of the domestic and political orders (*oeconomia* and *politia*). *Marriage* and *family* on their civil-legal side belong to the domestic order (*ordo oeconomicus*), just as do *domestic matters* such as work, property, business, and so on. The various *civil-legal institutions* (governing authority, legislative power, and administration of justice, the authority to punish, make war, state leadership) belong to the political order (*ordo politicus* in the strict sense). There has never been a fully developed system of doctrine regarding these *ordinationes*. Even Luther's doctrine of the threefold order (*triplex ordo*), which has become so important for later Lutheran ethicists, is only an attempt at a system. It is present in the Large Catechism in basic outline (explanation to the Fourth Commandment) but is not presented as a system. Therefore only its basic concepts are viewed as confessional Lutheran doctrine, and not a hard and fast use of the threefold division of divine orders.[25]

The basic question regarding this second realm of divine orders, the orders in the sphere of law, is to what extent genuine divine orders are present and recognizable within existing *human orders*. The orders of God cannot simply be equated with human orders. Only the legitimate orders (*legitimae ordinationes*) are to be respected as divine orders, and thus the orders which obtain may in fact no longer be legitimate and divinely willed (AC XVI). If, for instance, the governing authority oversteps its bounds and tries to force us to sin against God, then we must obey God rather than men [Acts 5:29]. Or when we speak of war as a possibility within the limits of Evangelical Lutheran ethics, then this possibility is expressly limited to the "just war" (*iure legitimae*). That the *iure* is here defined as little as that *legitimae* changes nothing of the significance of this limitation.

As long as this world endures, these legal orders have as much inviolable validity as the natural orders. The *Gospel* suspends them as little as it suspends "natural law." It wills that we uphold the legal orders (*conservare tamquam ordinationes Dei*, "preserve as the orders of God" [AC XVI 5]) and exercise love as Christians within these orders, because behind them stands the divine legal order. The attempt of fanaticism to replace the order of law with the order of love in the kingdom of God already in the here and now was rejected and labeled sin against God.[26] We are to live as Christians within the legal orders. The existence of these orders is the presupposition behind the fact that the Gospel can be understood and that the kingdom of God can take root in hearts. This will be so until the day when God will destroy the legal order of human life as well as the natural order, in the last judgment. No one can remove himself from the legal order. Neither can the church do so, in so far as it is a human corporation, which exists as a public and legal institution.

When we pull together the expressions of the confessions regarding these orders, the following picture emerges:

Natural orders:
> "natural law"
> marriage (family)
> domestic realm (*oeconomia*)

---

[25] Compare the presentation and critique of this doctrine by W. Elert, *Morphologie des Luthertums* (1932), 2:49 ff. HS

[26] Compare AC XVI and the Apology on the same article. HS

Legal orders:
    marriage (family)
    domestic realm
    political realm (*politia*)

The orders of marriage and family belong to both groups, in so far as they are part of the domestic realm (*oeconomia*—work, household) and in so far as they have both a natural and a legal side. And thus there is an indissoluble connection between the two groupings. And the political realm (*politia*) too is dependent upon marriage and family and indirectly connected with the natural order. No one of these orders is present without the others. They form a whole, not in the sense of a system based on the means of human reason, but in the sense of the unity of the unfathomable divine, creating and preserving will.

These orders (natural and legal) have their basis in the gracious will of God. But can we define them more precisely? One is accustomed to ask whether and to what extent these are orders which were established with creation itself. And thus, were they applicable before the fall? Or were they or to what extent were they given to a fallen world? The Apology, as we saw, raises this question in respect to marriage. Before we can give an answer to this question, we need to understand that the *primeval history* [*Urgeschichte*] of which the first chapter of the Bible speaks is not history in the common sense of the term. The creation of the world lies before and over all of history. Even if we could stretch our historical comprehension over every age past, right to the beginning of the world, we would still know nothing of the creation of the world. It is inconceivable. We cannot comprehend it. We can only believe in creation. We cannot classify the beginning of time and space within our understanding of the world, limited to space and time.

Creation is a super-temporal event. It continues to happen today. For we believe in the God who is still the Creator. He is the Creator of every creature. He is my Creator. And as little as we can conceive of creation, so little can we conceive of the fall, because we are all fallen men. Neither can we pinpoint the date of the fall into sin on a timetable of history, because we cannot conceive of that "then" when we all (we, who were not even yet born) sinned "in Adam." That we are fallen, that we are sinners, this we do not know as natural men. And even the refusal of these "unreasonable" concepts is part and parcel of our existence as fallen beings, as those whose nature has been perverted. Our reason neither can nor will allow us to recognize the truth about ourselves. We know this truth only from God's Word. Because this is the case, we cannot sketch a picture of the "primeval history" [*Urgeschichte*], in which the original source of any individual [created] order is demonstrated. We can only demonstrate the inner connection of that order with creation and the fall into sin. And here Holy Scripture must lead the way. And so it is the case that any individual order is connected as much to the creation as to the fall, and thus any separation of *creation* and *preservation* is absolutely impossible.

The natural order appears at first to have nothing to do with the fall into sin. But passages such as Gen 3:17; 8:21–22; 9:13; Romans 8; and the messianic prophecies indicate that such a correspondence does in fact exist. And when one considers how man has intervened in nature and completely changed the face of the earth, this correspondence cannot simply be dismissed as mythological. The legal order, on the other hand, appears to us to be the earliest, if not the only elusively preservational, order for fallen man. It is certainly this, so far as it appears in the form of the state, the governing authority, and the legal right to punish. The *coercive* power of government and thereby the state, as we know it from history, certainly belongs to the sinful world (there was no "sword" in paradise). But the "Thou shalt" and "Thou shalt not" existed already before the fall into sin (Gen 2:16–17). And if the office of governing authority is derived from the office of father, as Luther maintains [in the explanation to the Fourth Commandment], then the legal order was present, at least in preliminary form, before the fall into sin.

Thus the confusing term "order of creation" [*Schöpfungsordnung*] should be avoided where possible.[27] The order of the state, for instance, does not have anything *directly* to do with creation. The expression "order of preservation" is problematic, because it is not specific enough (preservation of the world in general, or preservation of the fallen world). Theology would do well to return to the old term "divine order" [*göttliche Ordnung*] or "God's order" [*Gottesordnung*].

PART 4

If this, in broad strokes, is the teaching of the Evangelical Confessions regarding the divine orders, which are the foundation of all of life, then questions arise. Where in the structure of these orders does the *Volk* belong? Why are the confessions completely silent about it? Have they simply forgotten it? It is not so simple. We have seen indeed that the sixteenth century too, in its own way, had to face the question of *Volk* and nation. How would the Reformers answer us if we were to pose to them our questions regarding the nature of the *Volk*, the meaning of *Volkstum*, and the idea that the nation fulfills its historical calling in becoming a politically organized *Volk*? To put it very simply: Where does *Volk* have a place in the structure of these orders?

The Reformers would respond to us [in this way]: *Volk* has no place within *these* orders. It certainly stands in very close connection with them. But it does not belong within them. *Volk* is connected with marriage and family, with domestics, law and governing authority. It cannot be thought of apart from these. These orders are certainly present wherever there is *Volk*. No *Volk* can exist without

---

27   The confessions do not use the term. The closest they come to using the term is "creatio seu ordinatio divina" ["creation or divine ordinance"] (Ap XXIII 9). Only in the nineteenth century did Lutheran theologians begin to speak of an "order of creation" [*Schöpfungsordnung*] or (better yet) "order of the Creator" [*Schöpferordnung*], e.g., Harless. HS

them. They also achieve their full development when they become the orders of a *Volk*. But they are also present where there is no *Volk*, where it has not yet existed or no longer exists. These orders exist "so long as the earth endures" [Gen 8:22]. Human life is inconceivable without them. But there is human existence which does not exist in the form of the *Volk*. We Western men, we men of the present cannot conceive of an existence without *Volk*, because each one of us was born a member of a *Volk*. But there has certainly been human life on earth which was not yet bound together with what we call *Volk*. Marriage and family, law and governing authority, and what we call domestic matters existed already in forms of life which are completely foreign to us. It is one of the most dangerous heresies to be of the opinion that law and governing authority are somehow dependent upon the existence of a *Volk*.

If we did not know all this, then the Bible would teach it to us. And a skeptic himself, who saw only myths and sagas in the "primeval history" [*Urgeschichte*] of Genesis, would perceive it as a problem that such a view of history could have been conceived in which human existence was not yet thought of in terms of *Volk*. And there has been human life which has ceased to be determined in terms of *Volk*, as demonstrated by periods when various peoples [*Völker*] have ceased to exist. Talk of *Volk* as an order of creation, therefore, should finally cease. We fail to recognize the proper essence of *Volk*, the uniqueness which differentiates this order from the primeval orders of God [*Ur-Ordnungen Gottes*], and at the same time grant it inordinate value when we seek the origin of *Volk* at the wrong point.

Where does the *origin* of *Volk* lie? What is it that makes that which is not *Volk* become *Volk*? It is no accident that every sociological theory has foundered on the problem of *Volk*. This failure is explained not merely by the difficulty of placing definitions on life. Everything living finally defies definition. No, there has got to be some particular difficulty here. And this difficulty is not in understanding and bringing into some harmony all the factors which play a part in a *Volk* coming into existence (consanguinity and race, country and climate, language and culture, custom and religion, and whatever else may be mentioned). Someone may thoroughly understand all these factors, both individually and in their indissoluble unity, and still, he may finally never understand what a *Volk* is. Common blood and home, confraternity of language and thought, common custom and religion may all be present, and still the men bound together by them might not be a *Volk*. And on the other hand, men who do not share these commonalities may become a *Volk*. A mystery shrouds the origin of every *Volk*. Scholarship expresses it by the term "history" [*Geschichte*]. It is the mystery of historical time.

The order of the *Volk* and *Völker* is something other than the orders which we have discussed thus far. The *orders of nature* are always the same. The stars run their course, the seasons change, seed time and harvest follow each other, man and wife meet, children are born, farmers till the soil, and the earth produces its fruit today as it has for thousands of years. The *legal orders* too, as divine orders in the view of the Reformation, have always essentially remained the same through the course of the development of positive historical law. The norms established in the Decalogue for the relationship of men with each other possess inviolable validity for all men, and all peoples [*Völker*]. Where they are set aside, human life is destroyed. A society in which parental authority no longer exists, in which marriage has been destroyed, in which murder, theft, and lying are no longer viewed as illegal, in which violations of law are no longer punished has collapsed. *The Volk* stands over against both of these constant orders *as a completely different order*.

The order of *Volk* and *Völker*, the order of history, bears a completely different character. Here everything is in *motion*. Under the same sky, on the same soil, within the same race, one *Volk* after another appears in order to live out its history, a history that is never repeated. Men who had hitherto lived unhistorical lives, whose lives ran their course just as did the lives of their fathers, now awaken to a historical existence. Life takes on a new significance, it begins to move toward a goal, an end. It begins what we call historical development. The bearers of this life, this tempestuous, historical existence, in which every moment and every era earns its significance, are the *Völker*. An unsolvable riddle shrouds the origin of every *Volk*, the riddle of historical "contingency," of historical "time." Augustine said of it, "If you do not ask me what it is, then I well know it. But ask me, and I know it not." It appears suddenly in history like a star in the evening sky, a *"we,"* *which labels itself a* Volk *and experiences a common history as a* Volk.

Another definition of *Volk* cannot be given. For every *Volk* invests the concept of *Volk* with new content. The Athenians at the time of Pericles were a *Volk*, even though the twentieth century understands something else by the term *Volk*. What changes has the concept of the *"Populus Romanus"* gone through! How variant are the *Volk*-concepts of Western *Völker*? We must understand that the concept of the *Volk* and the nation, which began to sweep through Germany since the national revolution of 1933, has not been experienced by the other Western nations. Nor can this concept be read into the great documents of German history. Every nation and every age has a particular concept of *Volk*, which at the same time contains an ideal notion of *Volk*. There have been and are still today *Völker* in which the concept of race plays a decisive role. And there are others in which this is not the case. There have been *Völker* whose *Volkstum* rested completely upon the commonality of religion, as the history of the East shows. Indeed, the more seriously we modern Germans struggle to come to a new understanding of *Volk* and *Volkstum*, we shall be all the more convinced that there is no concept of *Volk* which is valid for all time.

From this perspective it is perfectly understandable that neither the Holy Scriptures nor the confessions of our church have canonized a particular concept of *Volk*, be it that of the first or the sixteenth century. But perhaps for precisely this reason they have something to say, which no one else can say, to the German man of the present, as he struggles for a new understanding of *Volk*.

What is the mystery of *historical time?* What does the Evangelical faith say about the riddle of the coming and going, the birth and death of *Völker?* It knows of the God who is the *Lord of history* and who has revealed himself in the here and now of human history. It knows of the Redeemer, who "suffered under Pontius Pilate" [Apostles' Creed], whose cross stood at a "then," outside the gates of Jerusalem. Here, in the Christian faith, history is taken seriously, more seriously than in any philosophy. Here history is understood, and with history is also understood the order of the *Volk* and *Völker*. For here is uncovered the deep connection which exists between God and the *Volk, God* and the *Völker*. Why has the concept of *Volk* been perceived as something sacred [*sanctum*], even by our secularized culture? Why does the name of God ring out in the modern national hymns, while "enlightened" Germans of the nineteenth and twentieth centuries had removed it? Why do the "enlightened" Americans celebrate their *Thanksgiving Day?* Why are the proclamations of the government of the German Reich again speaking of God? Because humanity has never entirely forgotten that a divine mystery stands behind the *Volk*.

Volk is a "vocation." Paul once described the congregation of God at Corinth with this word ["vocation"] (1 Cor 1:26). He meant by it a fellowship which is not held together by "natural" bonds, whose existence is not dependent upon nature, but rather upon the *call of God*, which occurs in the here and now of history. If the church is a "vocation" in this sense, founded by the call of God in the Gospel, then we may define *Volk* also, in a certain sense, as a "vocation." The *Volk* too does not owe its existence to any contingencies established naturally at creation, but to the call of God, which transpires in history. Were the *natural situation*, the existence of which we do not deny, the most decisive thing (as modern naturalistic nationalism believes), then the fellowship of blood and race would finally be that which makes a *Volk* a *Volk*. But then history in its entirety would be meaningless, because there would have been genuine *Völker* in prehistoric times, spoiled in the course of history, which could only have become *Völker* again by some sort of return to their natural origins or nature [which is, of course, impossible].

The naturalistic view has a relative legitimacy as a reaction against certain *Volk*-theories which, with a false idealism, overlook the natural side of *Volkstum*. But when such a forgotten truth is absolutized, it finally ends in absurdity. The Christian faith takes seriously the body and corporeality of man as the foundation of all human history, so seriously in fact, that to the horror of all modern Naturalists it speaks of a resurrection of the body. The Bible also knows of the curse and the blessing of heredity, and this more realistically than the modern race theorists, because the men who speak in the Bible have made their observations in the context of real life, and not at desks and in museums of anthropology. And from this knowledge of real life they understand the origins of *Völker*. The *Völker* are called into being by God. His call summons that which has lived hitherto without a history to history. He makes that which had not been a *Volk* a *Volk*. He calls the Philistine and the Aramean; the Assyrian and the Babylonian; the Egyptian and the Persian onto the stage of world history. He called the *Völker* of primeval time to the beginnings of human history. And he will call the *Völker* of the end time to the last, most fearful history which our earth will experience. He called Israel, his own *Volk*, to a particular history, for the salvation and admonition of all *Völker* of the earth. He calls every *Volk* to its particular task, which he alone knows. And just as his call to this task is the beginning of a *Volk's* history, so his *judgment of rejection* means the end of this history. If this judgment has been pronounced upon a *Volk* then neither the highly developed nature of its culture nor the purity of its race can delay its demise. This demise stands at the end of the history of every *Volk* like death at the end of human life.

This, according to the Christian faith, is the mystery of the *Völker*, their becoming and their passing. It is from this view that Evangelical teaching understands the remarkable "we" of *Volk*-confraternity [*Volksgemeinschaft*] as a collective person. This teaching is more profound than any theory of *Volk* as a mere natural organism or as a purely intellectual, linguistic, and cultural fellowship. This teaching understands the final, deepest unity of a *Volk*. We, the German people of all centuries, the Germans also of this time, so decisive for our *Volkstum*, whether we are Protestant or Catholic, Christian or decidedly non-Christian, are by virtue of a "vocation" to a historic task one in the sight of God. We share in the same blessing and the same curse. We bear the same common guilt, we are directed to the same mercy, and we will one day—precisely as a *Volk*—be judged by God.

The call of God makes that which is not a *Volk*, *Volk*. And this call has come to all Völker, the *"heathen"* who do not know from whence it comes, and the *"Christian"* who has long since forgotten. But because this call is no longer heard or no longer understood, because the *Völker* have met it with *disobedience*, the history of the world and the history of every *Volk* hastens toward judgment day. At one high point of apostolic proclamation, in the discourse of Paul at the Areopagus [Acts 17], the meaning of the history of *Völker* was once described this way: God allows every race of people to dwell on the face of the earth "from one blood." He establishes the spatial and temporal boundaries of their existence and places before them the task "that they should seek the Lord." But men have rejected him and served idols and images "made by human art and invention." "But now," the apostle continues, announcing the call of God which demands repentance of all men, and he places before them "one man," who is the Savior and Judge of all.

This "one man," this Jesus Christ, belongs to all *Völker*, and therefore to each individual *Volk*. Every *Volk* with its history stands connected to him in some way. And this is so even when we cannot understand this connection (e.g., as in the case of *Völker* which have gone out of existence not having heard his name). Just as the history of humanity can only be understood as a unity from the vantage of this one Christ, so the *history of every Volk* receives its meaning and its unity through its *connection to Christ*. It is always the greatest event in the history of a *Volk* when the Gospel is preached to it for the first time. For this means not only that a new religion has been brought to it which can provide it with one more bond of unity to sling about its members—the Gospel's call to repentance can and must also bring about separation, and as the history of many an emigration for the sake of the Gospel shows, in extreme cases the Gospel's call can even lead to a tearing of the unity of a *Volk*—but this preaching of the Gospel means, moreover, that the call of God is repeated. God reminds this *Volk* of its forgotten "vocation." He also calls the men of this *Volk* to become the true, eternal *Volk* of God, which he assembles from all the *Völker* of the earth. And this is truly a genuine *Volk* in a much higher sense than any historically bound *Volk*, because in it the intended character of the genuine *Volk* is fulfilled: "You shall be my *Volk*, and I will be your God" [cf., e.g., Lev 26:12; Jer 31:33; Ezek 36:28; Rev 21:3].

From this it is clear what the existence of the *church among a* Volk means. It does not mean that an institution is present which alongside other useful cultural institutions accepts the responsibility for spiritual life and the awakening of the deepest spiritual powers among this *Volkstum*. The church is not about the elevation and internalization of a particular culture [*Volkskultur*]. It is about the *existence of a* Volk *as* Volk. For if the existence of a *Volk* depends upon the call of God, then its existence or nonexistence, its life or death is dependent upon the renewed hearing of this call. The place where this happens is the church. And for every *Volk* which has at one time heard the Gospel, it is literally a question of life and death that in its midst, hidden from the eyes of the world and yet recognizable in the proclamation of the pure Gospel, the church of Christ be, the *Volk* of God.

1934

THE LUTHERAN CHURCH
AND THE CONSTITUTION
OF THE CHURCH[1]

This brief article is significant in that it continues that series of writings which warn of the threat of the control of the church by civil authorities, in this case, the National Socialists (Nazis). Even the journal in which it was published was controversial. Its editor from 1934 was Sasse's Erlangen colleague Friedrich Ulmer, who appears to have had a poor rating with the Reich officials. Ulmer "often picked an argument with the National Socialists. And his journal *Lutherische Kirche* was perpetually forbidden,"[2] or at least occasionally banned.[3] After Ulmer was no longer allowed to continue, Sasse became its editor until it was forced to cease publication.

Huss number 123
Hopf number 062

Lutheranism is the only great Christian confession which knows of no particular external order as being of the essence of the church. All other confessions know of a definite constitution as being of the church's essence because it has been commanded by God in the NT and must therefore be present where the true church of Christ is supposed to be. Thus for Roman Catholicism the Roman episcopal constitution, with the papacy at its summit, belongs to the essence of the church. Also the Orthodox churches of the East and the non-Roman Catholic churches of the West—to which, among others, we count the Anglican Church—know of a quite definite, divinely willed order of the church. To this belong the threefold office of bishops, presbyters, and deacons, together with the principle of apostolic

---

1   This essay, "Lutherische Kirche und Kirchenverfassung," was first published in *Lutherische Kirche* (Erlangen) 16.3 (May 1, 1934): 45–47. RF

2   Taped interview with Pastor Hans-Siegfried Huss, September 29, 1989. RF

3   One issue in 1938 published only its cover with this announcement: "By order of the Secret State's Police, State's Police Office, Berlin, the bimonthly journal *Lutherische Kirche* in Erlangen was forbidden for the period of three months," that is, February 15–May 15, 1938. RF

succession. Calvin knew of the order according to which the Lord willed his church to be governed. This order, the presbyterial and synodical constitution, which he felt obliged to read out of the NT, is, so far as the Reformed Church is concerned, instituted by God's command as *sacra et inviolable* ("holy and inviolable"). In this sense the French Reformed of Old Prussia declared in 1930: "For us Reformed, a discussion about the correctness and applicability of this church constitution is . . . just as much out of the question as say a discussion on the dogma of the Trinity or the doctrine of Holy Communion or the Sacraments is for other Christians. For us the question of the constitution is a confessional question." The other Protestant churches similarly have their firm principles in the matter of order, for example, the Congregationalists and the Baptists; but I do not want to go into details here.

Among all these confessions, the Lutheran Church stands alone. She recognizes no particular *constitution* as "a mark of the church." The marks of the church consist alone in the preaching of the Gospel and the administration of the Sacraments according to their institution [AC VII 1]. Where these two marks of the church are present, there Christ's church is present, in whatever outward form she may appear. The Lutheran Church has thus been able to assume the most diverse of forms.

She has been able to exist as a state and national church in Europe, as a free church in the United States and other countries, as an episcopally constituted church with apostolic succession in Sweden, without succession in other Nordic lands. She has been able to survive under constitutions presbyterial or consistorial; indeed, she assumed almost independent churchly forms, and on her mission fields quite new formations of the church appear to be developing.

Space does not permit establishing this viewpoint of Lutheranism here. Suffice it to say that Lutheran teaching on the constitution of the church is not explained by the underdeveloped appreciation of Germans for definite forms. Certainly, this deficiency in the German character has shown up not only in our political history but also in that of German Lutheranism. But with it that axiom of our confessional writings has nothing to do. Otherwise it would be quite inconceivable for the Lutheran churches of other countries to have accepted the axiom without ado and yet to have produced significant ecclesiastical formations.

The Lutheran view of church order results from the Lutheran understanding of the Gospel. The latter is no sacred law book, *but the glad tidings* of the sinner's justification. And it results from the view of the church *which is not founded by people and by human orders, but alone by Jesus Christ*. God has given his church his Word and his Sacraments that she remain true church.

But this side of Lutheran teaching on church order, on which there is complete agreement among the Lutheran churches, is only one side. One might, if this view were taken in isolation, arrive at the most incorrect conclusions. *This is happening in Germany today.* It is completely wrong to conclude, on the basis of the above, that we can shape the church as we will, or that we can even leave the regulation of church order and the outward governance of the church to the state or other worldly powers. *Though we acknowledge that there can be no church constitution which is the only one that is right, yet we must emphasize that there are constitutions that are false.* There is no constitution which *absolutely* guarantees preservation *of the pure doctrine* to the church, but there are constitutions *which in the long run must necessarily destroy the pure doctrine.* To this type belongs the old ecclesiastical regime under the temporal sovereign. This made some sense as long as it was conceived of in terms of the emergency measures of the Evangelical territorial lord seen as the *membrum praecipuum ecclesiae* ("first member of the church"). But this was to have been only a temporary emergency law, until an ordered church government was instituted. What developed out of it—and *in conflict with our confessions*, particularly AC XXVIII, which teaches the separation of spiritual and worldly power—was a right of the worldly authority to the governance of the church. And this right was even upheld *when the territorial lord converted to another church*, indeed even when the state became the guardian of equality for all religions. Even if the present state be described as a "Christian state" (a thoroughly inaccurate and theologically impossible expression), *yet thereby no right is granted it with regard to the formation of the Lutheran Church.*

The state has no right, for example, to coerce the Lutheran churches into a union with Reformed or Union churches and to impose upon them *a church regime which cannot be recognized as Lutheran Church government in terms of our confession.* Today we have to take this axiom seriously: *that church constitution alone is tolerable to the Lutheran Church which does not contradict* what our confession teaches about the church, about the unity of the church, about her spiritual office and her ecclesial government. From this perspective we must test both the constitution of the German Evangelical Church, as well as the many laws by which the regulations of this constitution have been already in part invalidated. And to the "Reich" and the church governments the following questions must be addressed: *Is the Church of the Augsburg Confession, publicly and legally recognized in Germany since the year 1555, to be accorded the right to exist in the motherland of the Reformation?* Is Lutheranism to become merely a theological direction within German Protestantism? *Is the Evangelical Lutheran Church to be no more tolerated as church in Germany?* We are not able to believe that the government of the German Reich and even a church government of the Reich would be ready to execute *the judgment pronounced against our church* four hundred years ago at Rome: *Non licet esse vos!* ("You are not allowed to exist!")

1934

The Church and the Word of God

Toward a Doctrine of the Word of God[1]

It is important to note the ecumenical setting of this essay. Sasse presented this paper at a meeting of the Continuation Committee of Faith and Order, at Hertenstein, Lake of Lucerne, Switzerland, on September 4, 1934. On that occasion both the German original and an English translation ("The Conception of the Word of God") were available in mimeograph form. At Hertenstein he was elected to be one of seven members of the Executive Committee and secretary of the Commission on the Church and the Word. The essay presents Sasse's agenda and vision for the Ecumenical Movement and particularly for the World Conference on Faith and Order.

Huss number 129b

〜〜〜

PART 1

Of all the questions before us, the theme "The Church and the Word" presents our conference with the most difficult, indeed the final question we have to answer. If we would have found a common answer to this question, and not merely a compromise formula, but rather the expression of consensus existing among us, then the World Conference on Faith and Order would have attained its goal. For if we were united on what the church and the Word of God are, and the relationship in which they stand to each other, then absolutely nothing would stand in the way of the union of our churches. All the other questions which we find so difficult, such as the question of mutual recognition of our offices and inter-Communion, would then be only technical questions of ecclesiastical organization. What separates us today, and indeed, so deeply separates us that human eyes

---

[1]   This essay, "Die Kirche und das Wort Gottes: Zur Lehre vom Worte Gottes," was presented at a meeting of the Continuation Committee of Faith and Order on September 4, 1934. It was published in *Lutherische Blätter* 34.123/124 (New Year 1981/1982): 3–15. The present translation was previously published in *Logia* 2.4 (Reformation/October 1993): 9–14. MH/RF

147

see no possibility of spanning the chasm, is the question posed by our theme, the question of the relationship between the church and the Word of God.

For we do not have to do here with one of the many controverted theological questions which have always existed and will always exist in the church. We are rather faced with the question which once shattered the unity of the Western church when the Reformation posed this question to Christianity. By it the Reformation distinguished itself from other events in the history of the church and made clear its meaning for the church universal. The Reformation has posed the question to all of Christendom concerning the deepest essence of the church, and this question absolutely demands a clear response. No denomination can avoid the necessity of answering this question with a clear yes or no. There are churches in India and China and in the mission fields among the primitive peoples of the world which otherwise know nothing of European church history. These must nevertheless give an answer to the question posed by the Reformation on the relationship of church and Word of God, just as they must decide for or against the Nicene Creed.

And though over four hundred years ago the unity of the Western church was shattered by this question, the resulting parting of ways must not simply be compared with other schisms and splinters in the history of the church. At that time not only did new ecclesiastical fellowships arise out of an old communion through excommunication and separation, but the form of existence of the entire church was also changed. Luther and his followers were expelled from the communion of the Papal Church. After this, in spite of the papal claim to the one holy catholic church, the Evangelical Lutheran Church rallied around her confession to the truth of the Holy Scriptures and stepped before the world, a self-aware confessing church.

Since then, in like manner, the other Western communions had to take on at least the form of confessional churches. They had to do this even if this form did not suit their peculiarities, as was the case for instance with the Church of England, for which the Thirty-nine Articles have always presented a certain dilemma. Indeed, the Roman Church had to make this change along with the others as well. The Council of Trent in effect meant for it the passage from its form of existence as universal church of the medieval West to one of the great confessional churches of the modern world. Thus the one holy catholic church, which previously existed "in, with, and under" the world church of the Middle Ages, now exists, since the Middle Ages, "in, with, and under" a number of confessional churches. By "confessional church" we mean an ecclesiastical communion which by an expressed consensus measured by confession is unified in its answer to the question posed by the Reformation.

If this form of existence of the church is to be replaced by another, in which the confessional antitheses are removed, it can only happen in the following way. The lack of agreement of the sixteenth century concerning the relationship of church and Word of God must be replaced by consensus. Any attempt to unify churches by circumventing the question posed by the Reformation would from the outset be doomed to failure. We can go back to the days before the Reformation. The call "Back to the Middle Ages!" is as unfeasible as the call "Back to the old undivided church!" This applies all the more to the call "Back to the Reformation!" There is no such return because neither the unrepeatable recurs, nor can that which has happened be made not to have happened. The *dissensus* ["disunion"] in which the age of the Reformation left Christianity cannot be removed from the world in a way that ignores the question of the Reformation. It can only be overcome if the question answered incompletely and incorrectly in the sixteenth century by the confessional churches is finally answered completely and correctly. Since our World Conference has called the church to do just that, it has called the Christianity and the theology of all confessions to a task of world-wide, historical greatness.

It is self-evident that everything we have to say today on the theme "Church and Word" can only be something preliminary. The humble work of entire generations of theologians in all churches will be required if the great dialogue between the confessional churches, which was carried on into the seventeenth century, shall again be taken up with real consequence. And it is also self-evident for our conference that this dialogue will only lead to a good end if, in the course of this interaction, churches encounter one another as churches. For we have not to do with the uniting of theological professors, but rather with the uniting of churches, which in any case, is after all the more difficult task. Therefore, in everything we have to say regarding our theme, we must have in view not so much our private opinions as our positions as teachers of the church.

PART 2

Canon Hodgson[2] in his remarks on our theme rightly called attention to the fact that the question of the relationship of church and Word of God can only be discussed on the basis of a clear conception of revelation: "What do we understand by revelation? What do we mean when we speak of Christianity as the religion of revelation?"

We must indeed proceed from this question, and not because Scripture and church doctrine [*Kirchenlehre*] point us in this direction. Neither the Bible nor the ecclesiastical confessions contain a theory of revelation. We must rather proceed because the struggle over the authority of the Bible and the church in modern times has become a struggle over the concept of revelation. The appreciation for that which church and Word of God properly are has been shaken and finally destroyed for the greater part of Christianity by the criticism which modern philosophy since the Enlightenment has often leveled at Christendom's concept of

---

[2] Leonard Hodgson was canon of Winchester Cathedral and general secretary of Faith and Order (1933–1948); from 1938 he was professor at Oxford University. RF

revelation and its claim of revelation. The essence of what revelation means for the Christian faith and what it is as the presupposition for the existence of the church and the Holy Scriptures can be clarified directly in light of modern criticism of revelation, and in light of what of the concept of revelation is granted validity by modern thought.

In one of the first writings on the philosophy of religion at the time of the Enlightenment, *De Veritate* ["On the Truth"] by Herbert of Cherbury[3] (1624), a theory of revelation is found which anticipated everything which was later leveled against the Christian concept of revelation. The chapter "De revelatione" discusses the conditions which must be met for the acknowledgement of supernatural revelation by philosophy. Among other things the following conditions are mentioned: "Ut tibi ipsi patefiat; quod enim tanquam revelatum ab aliis habenda est" ["That it is evident to you; that it is also believed to be revelation by others"]; furthermore: "Ut afflatum divini numinis sentias" ["That you feel the blowing of the divine will"]. Here we find already clearly expressed the three conditions which must be met before the modern man, so far as he is concerned about religious matters, is prepared to acknowledge revelation: (1) Revelation must not be sought only in Christianity; Christian revelation is rather only a particular case of a general revelation of which all religions have a part. (2) Revelation is for me only that which I experience as a self-manifestation of the divine, but not what another recounts to me as his experience. (3) Historical events in which those in the past experienced revelation cannot be of value as revelation today.

These three conditions have been tirelessly repeated since—indeed, as much by the alleged conquerors of the Enlightenment as the representatives of the Enlightenment themselves. Thus Fichte[4] repeated Lessing's[5] protest against the nature of revelation as "accidental historical truths": "Only the metaphysical saves, and by no means the historical; the latter only makes it intelligible," and: "One should not say, 'What harm does it do should one hold to these historical [phenomena]?' It is harmful when peripheral matters [*Nebensachen*] are placed on the same level as the chief thing, or even passed off as the chief thing, which is thereby suppressed, and the conscience is tormented about grasping and believing what it can no longer believe under such compulsion [*Anweisung*]." This same Fichte said positively: "Religion is not a matter of *believing* on the assurance of others that there is a God, rather that one have and possess an immediate vision of God in his own person and not via another, with his own spiritual eyes and not through the eyes of another."

Hear the young Schleiermacher express this theology in his *Speeches on Religion: "What is revelation? Every new and original perception of the universe is a rev-*

---

[3]   Lord Herbert of Cherbury, a Deist, wrote of a natural religion common to all and independent of revelation. RF

[4]   Johann Gottlieb Fichte (1762–1814) was a philosopher. RF

[5]   Gotthold Ephraim Lessing (1729–1781) was a philosopher and dramatist. RF

elation, and each individual best knows what is to him original and new, and if something in another which was original is still new to you, his revelation is also a revelation for you, and I will counsel you to consider it well."[6] And further:

> Every man, a few choice souls excepted, does, to be sure, require a guide to lead and stimulate, to wake his religious sense from its first slumber, and to give it its first direction. But this you accord to all powers and functions of the human soul, and why not to this one? For your satisfaction, be it said, that here, if anywhere, this tutelage is only a passing state. Hereafter, shall each man see with his own eyes, and shall produce some contribution to the treasures of religion. . . . You are right in despising the wretched echoes who derive their religion entirely from another, or depend on a dead writing, swearing by it and proving out of it. Every sacred writing is in itself only a mausoleum of religion, a memorial that a greater spirit was there, but is now no more. Were this spirit still alive and at work how could he place such great worth upon dead letters, which can only be a weak impress of himself? The one who has religion is not the one who believes in a holy writing, rather the one who needs none, and indeed, can produce one himself.[7]

There is no need for further proof that the Christian faith has not the least to do with what Schleiermacher here calls religion and revelation. Our faith understands by revelation an event which does not happen wherever there obtains a higher spiritual life and thus "religion." Revelation is not a general phenomenon of religious history, of which the Christian revelation is a particular case. Furthermore, the revelation which is the presupposition for the Christian faith is bound throughout to "accidental historical truths." Angelus Silesius[8] wrote: "Were Christ born a thousand times in Bethlehem, and not in you, you would be eternally lost." Thus speaks the mystic who knows only a timeless revelation. The Christian faith would assert the direct opposite: "Were Christ born a thousand times in your heart, and not in Bethlehem, you would be eternally lost." That is, the truth of our faith, the fact of our redemption depends upon "accidental historical truths," on the ἐφάπαξ ["once"] of salvation history. The truth of our faith depends upon the fact that Jesus Christ appeared *once*, was sacrificed *once* for us (Heb 7:27; 9:26, 28), that he suffered "under Pontius Pilate" [Apostles' Creed]. Should it be shown that the NT recounts not historical truth in its witness to Christ, rather only a myth, the apostles would be false witnesses (1 Cor 15:15). Then what Paul wrote would apply: "Your faith is futile; you are still in your sins! Then also those who have fallen asleep in Christ have perished" [1 Cor 15:17–18 NKJV]. And finally, Christian revelation, directly because of this historical char-

---

[6]   Friedrich Schleiermacher, *On Religion: Speeches to Its Cultured Despisers* (translated by John Oman with an introduction by Rudolf Otto; New York: Harper & Row, 1958), 89. MH

[7]   See Schleiermacher, *On Religion*, 91. Here Oman's translation has been altered to represent more literally Schleiermacher's original. MH

[8]   That is, Johannes Scheffler (1624–1677), the mystic. The son of a Lutheran Polish noble, he became a Roman Catholic (*ODCC*, 64). RF

acter, is bound to the witness of history and thus also the witnesses of history. It is bound to their word and to the written record of this word.

The contents of the Christian faith are not simply the objects of our experience. The incarnation, the death, the resurrection of Jesus Christ are not facts which we can know from our own experience. We know of them only through the testimony of the Scriptures. Thus that which is revelation for Herbert of Cherbury, Lessing, Fichte, the young Schleiermacher, and the entire modern world, insofar as these all have a religious interest in the matter, does not interest the Christian faith at all. And that which is revelation for the Christian faith, by which revelation it stands or falls, does not interest the modern world. For the modern world, the Christian idea of revelation is unbelievable, or indeed meaningless.

But this not only for the modern world! Biblical revelation is an "offense" for the religious and moral man of every age, just as it is "foolishness" to the philosophies of all ages [cf. 1 Cor 1:23]. It is a foreigner also in the world of religions. According to Acts 17:32, the most difficult obstacle which the Greek world found in the apostolic preaching lay in its insistence that the life of one historical man, which had been lived only shortly before, should be *the* revelation. The myths of dying and rising divinities were beautiful, but the message of Christ was hideous and senseless. The myth of the dying and rising of Osiris[9] contained a "necessary reasonable truth," namely the unchanging law of life and the world of "death and coming to be." The proclamation of the "accidental historical truth" of the death and resurrection of Jesus Christ met with rejection. It spoke of a onetime, unique happening, of a revelation which occurred once, not of a "revelation" which obtains always and everywhere. This message is no general religious-moral truth to draw upon.

The content of all other "revelations" in the history of religions can be expressed in the form of general theses, for the reception of revelation there always means the knowledge of some theoretic truth. The content of Bible revelation cannot be expressed in any theoretical thesis, neither in a thesis concerning the love of God and men, nor in the form of "the fatherhood of God and the brotherhood of men." The content of biblical revelation is much more the truth as a person; it is Jesus Christ. "To Him all the prophets witness that, through His name, whoever believes in Him will receive remission of sins" (Acts 10:43 [NKJV]). This is the content of the Gospel, the content of the Holy Scriptures. From the first page to the last every word points to him. "Behold the Lamb of God who takes away the sin of the world" (John 1:29).

---

[9] In Egyptian mythology, Osiris was the god of the dead. The Egyptian goddess Isis was his sister and wife. RF

PART 3

Insofar as this unique revelation, to which the Bible bears witness and which also presents a riddle for those who study the history of religions, finds no place in the categories of the history of religions [*Religionsgeschichte*], it can only be understood by one who understands its bearers and witnesses. They are the apostles and prophets. [Like the Christian concept of revelation,] for these offices as well there are no proper analogies in the history of religion. Indeed, the "disciples" of Jesus may be compared to the disciples of Socrates and Buddha. But as apostles, they are without parallel. For it belongs to the essence of an apostle, according to Acts 1:22, that he be a "witness of the resurrection" and that the Lord himself has called him. This office belonged to a single generation of history, thus it is unrepeatable in the church. Prophecy has its apparent parallels in other religions. Here we need only mention Zarathustra and Muhammad, whose forms of "prophecy" are most similar to biblical prophecy. These apparent parallel forms are the "prophets," that is, the ecstatic seers and speakers in whose mouths a message is placed, which they received in a state of inspiration. But in the Bible itself there is a clear distinction between one who in the Eastern religions is called a "prophet" and one who is a genuine prophet, who really is "no prophet nor the son of a prophet" (Amos 7:14), rather of whom the unprecedented applies, that the almighty God himself has spoken to him: "Behold, I place my word[s] in your mouth" (Jer 1:9), and who can say of himself: "The word of the Lord came to me" [see, e.g., Jer 1:4; Ezek 3:16; Zech 4:8].

In contrast to the office of apostle, the office of prophet is found throughout salvation history; indeed, it still exists in the church. Both offices, that of the prophets and that of the apostles, point to Christ: "Concerning this one all the prophets testify" [Acts 10:43]—even though they apparently speak of something completely different, [such as] the judgment of God on Israel and the nations, or whatever may be the exact content of the message they bear. They all point to Christ with an outstretched finger as did the last of the prophets before Christ, who was indeed more than a prophet: "Behold the Lamb of God" [John 1:29, 36]. And the apostles testify of him and only of him. They know nothing other than Jesus, the Crucified: "That which was from the beginning, which we have heard, which we have seen with our eyes, which we have looked upon, and our hands have handled, concerning the Word of life . . . that which we have seen and heard we declare to you. . . . And these things we write to you" (1 John 1:1, 3–4 [NKJV]).

Apostles and prophets—the NT names them in this order [Eph 2:20; 3:5; Rev 18:20]—are the bearers of the revelation. They are men to whom a word has come and this word is to be given to others. *God's revelation is God's Word*. Even where the prophet must say, "I have *seen* the King, the Lord of Sabaoth with my eyes" (Isa 6:5), the revelation remains God's *Word*. And also there where the content of all the promises, the incarnate Word, became *visible, where "Many prophets desired to see* what you see and did not see it" (Luke 10:24) came true, still, the One seen remains the *Word*. Thus the consummation of revelation, the incarnation of the only begotten Son of God is described in this sentence: "The *Word* became *flesh* and dwelt among us, and we *beheld* his glory" (John 1:14). The characteristic feature of biblical revelation is that it is *historical* revelation. This feature belongs together with a second, namely, it is a revelation of the *Word* [*Wort-Offenbarung*]. Because God came forth out of the hiddenness of the "light, where no man can approach" [cf. 1 Tim 6:16] only in his Word, the revelation of God is identical with his Word. Indeed, God "had not left himself without a witness" (Acts 14:17) even among the pagans. But he has remained for them the unknown God, for he speaks his name only there, he makes his essence known only there, where he *speaks:* "I am the Lord, your God" [e.g., Ex 20:2; Is 43:3], and thus he makes himself known only in his *Word*.

He does not tell us who he is in the works of creation, which at the same time both bear witness to him and yet veil him, rather he does so only in the revelation, of which the beginning of the Letter to the Hebrews says: "God, who at various times and in various ways spoke in time past to the fathers by the prophets, has in these last days spoken to us by His Son, whom He has appointed heir of all things, through whom also He made the worlds; who being the brightness of His glory and the express image of His person, and upholding all things by the word of His power . . ." [Heb 1:1–3 NKJV]. Only this revelation through the Word is real revelation. For in it God tells us *who* he is when he addresses us. Certainly for us humans words [*das Wort*] are the only means by which one person can communicate with another or really make himself known to another. Only when God has first spoken to us in Christ, that is, in his person, in his Word-revelation— which can also happen through the OT, for the OT is also revelation which already had its aim in Christ; the OT speaks of him even where his name is not yet mentioned, and can only be understood from him as the Alpha and the Omega and the center of the entire Bible—can we conceive that God also speaks the Word of his power and love in creation.

The Word of revelation is the Word which God has spoken "to the fathers by the prophets" and, finally, "in [his] Son" [Heb 1:1–2]. It is a Word which has been spoken in history (e.g., the dating of the calling of the prophets and the prophetic messages such as Isa 6:1; Amos 1:1; etc.; and the dating of the life and arrival of Jesus such as Luke 3:1; furthermore, the "under Pontius Pilate" in the Creed). Because it actually entered history, the Word of God had to take on the form of the human word, similar to the way the eternal Son of God, who entered history, actually became a man. Because the Word of God is spoken to people and heard by people, it partakes of the fate of that word which is comprehended by people: it fades away, it is forgotten, it remains without effect if it is not passed on and preserved by those two means for the propagation and preservation of words—oral proclamation and the written record. Thus the Word of God spoken in history becomes a human word, and yet it does not cease to be God's Word. The "revealed" Word becomes the "proclaimed" and "written" Word.

We agree with Karl Barth[10] when we distinguish between the three forms of the Word of God as the *revealed Word*, the *preached Word*, and the *written Word*. And we maintain with Barth that we actually have to do here with three distinct *forms* of the *one* Word of God. They belong inseparably together, yet must be distinguished. In their distinctiveness and in their unity Barth compares them with the three persons of the Trinity.

The three forms of the Word of God are already present in the prophets of the OT. "The Word of the Lord came to me"—this is the revealed Word. "Go and tell this people . . ." (Isa 6:9)—this is the proclaimed Word. "Take a scroll and write on it all the words" (Jer 36:2)—this is the written Word. That these three forms of the Word of God are already clearly perceivable in the salvation history of the old and new covenants must mean this: "And the three are one." The power which the *revealed* Word possesses indwells the *proclaimed* Word. Thus God can say to the prophets: "Behold, I have placed my words in your mouth. Behold, today I appoint you over nations and kingdoms to uproot and tear down, to destroy and overthrow, to build and to plant" (Jer 1:9–10). And [as proof that the power of the revealed Word also indwells the written Word] the Son of God himself availed himself of the *written* Word, for example, as a weapon in the fight against the devil (Matt 4:4, 7, 10; cf. Eph 6:12[–17]). The three forms of the Word of God are really one. That which can be said of the Word of God itself can be said of all three forms of the Word, namely, "Your Word is a lamp to my feet and light to my path" (Ps 119:105), that it is "living and powerful, and sharper than any two-edged sword . . . a discerner of the thoughts and intents of the heart" (Heb 4:12 [NJKV]). It applies to the Word of God in its unity as much as to each of its three forms that we humans live from it (Matt 4:4).

PART 4

What the Evangelical Lutheran Church teaches regarding the relationship of the Word of God and the church is to be understood from the vantage of this view of the Word of God, as it was discovered anew at the time of the Reformation. Here we can only briefly draw a cursory sketch of this doctrine, which after all agrees with the doctrine of the Reformed Church at essential points.

In the Apology to Article XIV of the Augsburg Confession, the Evangelicals declared that they were prepared to continue to acknowledge the old canonical form of church government and the authority of the Catholic bishops if the bishops would allow the pure preaching of the Gospel. The doctrine of the Gospel could under no circumstances be given up. Because the ecclesiastical authorities demanded this and thereby desired something which violated the commandment

---

[10]   *Die Kirchliche Dogmatik*, vol. 1: *Die Lehre vom Wort Gottes*, part 1 (Munich, 1932), 89 ff. HS

of God, thus they determined to "let the bishops go and be obedient to God and know *that the Christian church is there where the Word of God is correctly taught*" [Ap XIV 3–4 (26–27), German]. Here, with absolute clarity at the moment when the church of the West was disintegrating, the fundamental Evangelical truth proclaimed that the Word of God stands over the church, that the church is born of the Word of God, and that the Word of God is also the final and highest authority for the church.

In order to understand the position of the Evangelical Lutheran Church on this question, it is best to proceed from Article V of the Augsburg Confession, which treats the spiritual office (*de ministerio ecclesiastico*). Here we read: "Ut hanc fidem (namely, the justifying faith in the merits of Christ alone, of which Article IV spoke) consequamur, institutum est ministerium docendi evangelii et porrigendi sacramenta. Nam per verbum et sacramenta tamquam per instrumenta donatur Spiritus Sanctus, qui fidem efficit, ubi et quando visum est Deo, in his qui audiunt evangelium" ("That we may obtain this faith, the Ministry of Teaching the Gospel and administering the Sacraments was instituted. For through the Word and Sacraments, as through instruments, the Holy Ghost is given, who works faith, where and when it pleases God, in them that hear the Gospel").[11]

That this faith might be obtained God has given us humans something, and not, as one might expect, the Holy Scriptures. The old Evangelical Church still knew that the Scriptures are only one form of the Word of God. To be sure, they also knew Holy Scripture actually is one form of the Word of God. They knew that the Bible contains everything which is necessary for us to know for our salvation. But they also knew that Jesus Christ did not leave behind a holy book in the same way Muhammad left behind the Qur'an, rather that he left behind the ministry of teaching the Gospel [*ministerium docendi evangelii*], the charge to proclaim his Gospel to all peoples and all generations of world history.

For the church of the Reformation, both belong inseparably together: the written and the proclaimed Word, the Bible and the "preaching office or oral Word" [*Predigtamt oder mündlich Wort*], as Luther said in Schwabach Article VII, the forerunner of Augustana V. This homogeneity explains how the church sank roots among hitherto pagan peoples. If the Word of God were identical with the Bible, it would suffice to send the Bible in their own language to the people concerned. But because the Bible and the Word of God are not identical, there is sent to every people one or more preachers of the Word.

But neither would it suffice were these preachers to come without the Holy Scriptures, bearing the Word of God only in their heads and hearts. The Scriptures and the preaching office, the written and the proclaimed Word, belong together. The content of the Scriptures must be preached, and not *only* read in private. And the preaching office should expound the Scriptures, as the content of

---

[11] The English translation is from the *Triglotta*, 45. MH

its sermon is bound throughout to the Scriptures. But because every form of the Word of God is truly the Word of God, the church of necessity can never be deprived of one of these two forms.

We have in the history of the Evangelical Church (e.g., in the Hapsburg lands) many cases where the pastors were expelled, the ecclesiastical organization destroyed. But the church remained alive because the Bible remained in individual homes and because a new preaching office and a new congregation arose from the use of the Bible. On the other hand, we also know—for example, from the history of missions—of cases where Bible is not yet translated into the language of the people, thus it is essentially not yet available for the mission congregation. In these situations the content of the Bible is present in the proclaimed Word. The greatest example of this is the early church, which indeed from the beginning possessed the Holy Scriptures, namely the OT, but not yet the writings of the NT. It is completely inverted to say that in this case the church produced the Holy Scriptures. It merely delineated the canon in the very same way the synagogue once delineated the canon of the OT. But the church produced the Letter to the Romans or the Gospel of John as little as the Israelite or post-exilic synagogue produced the prophecies of the OT.

The Word of God, the written and proclaimed Word, creates and builds the church. There is no other means to build the church of Christ. For the Word of God alone creates faith. Certainly the Sacraments belong to the Word, and it is the experience of church history that wherever the significance of the Sacraments is misunderstood or neglected, the Word will also be despised or falsified. But the Sacraments ever exist only together with the Word, with the Word of the institution and the Word of promise. Thus the Augustana says that through the Word and the Sacraments the Holy Spirit is given, who works faith, "where and when it pleases God" [AC V 2]. This means we cannot prescribe the effectual power of Word and Sacrament. It is God's free grace, should he bring a person to faith through them. But we have the promise that the Word of God "shall not return void" (Isa 55:11). Thus the church will exist everywhere the Gospel is rightly preached, but only there. And it must be the continual prayer of the church that it be and remain the true church of Christ, as we pray in Luther's hymn in the worship service: "Lord, keep us steadfast in your Word." Herein as we pray we also admit that we cannot keep ourselves steadfast in this Word, nor can the church by itself do so.

The teaching of the Reformation on the Word of God and on the relationship between Word of God and church was directed against two opponents, against *Schwärmertum*, that is, against the fanatic [re]baptizers and spiritualists (e.g., Schwenkfeld[12]), who subordinated the revelation of Scripture to a direct rev-

---

[12] Kasper von Schwenkfeld (ca. 1489–1561) was a Protestant mystic. He was never ordained and after initial support for the Reformation, he came to reject justification, Scripture as the only source and norm of faith, the efficacy of the Sacraments, and infant Baptism (*Lutheran Cyclopedia*, 707). RF

elation in the present; and against the Roman Church, which subordinated the Bible to the teaching office of the church by declaring that only this teaching office could legitimately interpret the Scriptures and could also announce doctrines which go beyond what the Scriptures teach. Both these opponents charge that the Evangelical Church restricts the living revelation of God by a dependence upon the letter of the Bible.

Over against both opponents the churches of the Reformation have emphatically asserted that any alleged revelation which goes beyond the Scriptures goes beyond Christ, who is the truth in person, and thus is no revelation, rather illusion. Nor can John 16:12–13 be cited in this regard. All the great heresies of ancient (Montanus, Mani, Muhammad) and modern times have done this. Where the Word of Scripture has been forsaken by proceeding beyond it, there the unadulterated office of proclamation has also been lost. But then that which is preached does not long remain the revealed Word of God. For the revealed Word, the proclaimed Word, and the written Word of God are only forms of the one unique Word, in which God has revealed himself to humanity and upon which the church is founded.

1934

THE CENTURY OF THE PRUSSIAN CHURCH

IN COMMEMORATION OF CHRISTMAS 1834 IN HÖNIGERN[1]

It is with heavy irony and not a little wit (or with a great amount of satire) that Sasse parodies the events that took place in a small Silesian village one hundred years previous to the writing of this essay. It is through this remembrance that Sasse would recall for us a significant event in a not-so-significant village. What is more, as he was given to do elsewhere, he links the significance of a nineteenth-century event with events of the present time: he speaks of the struggle of church with state in nineteenth-century Hönigern in a way which his readers could not help comparing with the church struggles with the German Reich of the 1930s.

Here his strong critique of the Prussian Union Church is done in the context of his own experience, as he explains: "The author of this essay himself stood in the service of this church for some fifteen years."

Huss number 132
Hopf number 063

PART 1

On the 11th of September 1834 a commission, sent from the royal consistory of Breslau, appeared in the village parish of Hönigern in the district of Namslau. It consisted of the district magistrate; the royal superintendent; the official representative of the church patron, the Duke of Württemberg; and the district secretary, a retired captain. The police-escorted commission came in order to break the obstinate resistance which the young Pastor Kellner had mounted for years against the order of the authorities to introduce the new Prussian Agenda.

---

[1] This essay was first published as "Das Jahrhundert der preußischen Kirche: Zur Erinnerung an das Weihnachtsfest 1834 in Hönigern" in *Zeitwende* 11.3 (December 1934): 129–40. It was reprinted in *ISC*, 2:184–93. RF

Kellner was a student of the Breslau theologian Scheibel, who fought energetically against the Union. Connections among relatives also bound them together. Kellner was among those theologians who rejected the Union of the Lutheran and Reformed churches in Prussia (which the king initiated on Reformation Day 1817) as contravening the confessional writings of the Evangelical Lutheran Church. He unreservedly declined the use of the new Agenda (which had been composed by the king) as a document of this Union and a means of its introduction. The pastoral endeavors of the accountable superintendent, Ribbeck, in Bernstadt to dissuade Kellner from this theological concern remained fruitless. So did the administrative measures to which the ecclesiastical and secular arm of the royal Prussian state government resorted, both in alternation and in combination, against the obstinate pastor. Even a direct order to make use of the Agenda on a particular Sunday produced no further fruit than that the district executor was able to collect the threatened twenty-*Taler* penalty to the benefit of the state treasury.

It had become a matter of grave concern for the state authorities that the example of the recalcitrant pastor from Hönigern and his like-minded compatriots in the office of the ministry [*Predigtamt*] would revitalize anew resistance also in those places where one had come to accept that the king would enforce his will in any and all circumstances. But it must have appeared as especially dangerous to the state that not only the pastors but also more and more congregations themselves became bearers of opposition. Nothing tends to be more conducive for the unfolding of church life and the awakening of congregations from their church-sleep toward independent action as actual or supposed oppression through the state.

Consequently, the congregation at Hönigern experienced an unprecedented upswing in its church life during these months. The Divine Services [*Gottesdienste*] were full to overflowing. The neighboring villages participated in the "confessional struggle." Within eight weeks the parish which numbered some two thousand communicants counted three thousand people as having come to Communion. What appeared to the congregation as a true awakening appeared to the authorities to be the consequences of church-political agitation. As a result, the commission of the consistory which arrived in Hönigern on September 11 was able to see only a tumultuous throng in the two thousand people who gathered with the singing of chorales around their pastor.

In front of the assembled congregation, Kellner negated the question posed him by the superintendent as to whether or not he would be prepared to accept the Agenda. When the superintendent retorted with the announcement of his suspension from office, Kellner declared that he is unable to recognize the suspension, since the *Union* consistory does not have the right to suspend him, a *Lutheran* pastor. When the district council thus demanded the surrender of the keys to the church, it turned out that they were no longer in the possession of the pastor. He had for some time, in anticipation of his removal from office, appointed forty congregational deputies. With the approach of the commission, he had entrusted them with the keys, the congregational finances, and the official seals. Those deputized declared that they did indeed possess the keys, but that they were also not going to surrender them. Despite lengthy negotiations they persisted in their refusal and declared that they were unable to recognize either the suspension of their pastor or the appointment of the parish administrator [*Pfarrverweser*] which the commission had brought along. In the meantime, the congregation continued to sing chorales. They also kept the area in front of the church doors densely occupied, thereby preventing the forcible opening of the door. They were not willing to open their church to an alien, anti-confessional Divine Service.

Thus the commission had to leave Hönigern on September 11, having left matters unresolved. It could only be of small comfort to them that they achieved something of a victory in Kaulwitz, where the circumstances had been similar. Here they managed, by way of breaking a window, to enter the church forcibly and thereby to open the doors, the keyholes of which had been plugged from the inside. In this manner the parish administrator who had been appointed by the consistory was able to take possession of this Lutheran Church building.

On the next Sunday, the 14th of September, the congregational deputies of Hönigern asked their pastor to hold the Divine Service as usual. Since he had not recognized the suspension, he had no misgivings about fulfilling this request. The Divine Service culminated with a large celebration of the Lord's Supper with some five hundred communicants. Subsequently, the church was immediately locked again. It was the last time that Pastor Kellner officiated within this church; on Tuesday, after having again refused to recognize his suspension, he was taken into custody by the district magistrate.

He was brought to Breslau, where he was able to procure a private residence under the following conditions: he would not leave the city without permission from the royal government; he would abstain from all pastoral functions; he would utilize any inevitable and unavoidable contacts with his previous congregation only to warn against resistance to the authorities; and he would avoid any contact with the separated Lutherans in Breslau. When, after some time, he came to declare that he was no longer able to maintain these conditions willingly, he was immediately arrested and held in custody in the police prison. Yet because of illness he was temporarily released at Christmas.

In the meantime, the congregation in Hönigern continued with its resistance, even though several people had been thrown into prison in Namslau because of their disobedience to the regulations of the authorities. Several attempts by the local council to seize the church by means of a surprise ambush were thwarted by the watchfulness of the alert congregation. For three months the church was watched day and night. "When autumn weather set in," reported Wangemann,[2] "two wooden sheds were built at either end of the church. On Sundays everyone

---

[2] Wangemann, *Sieben Bücher Preußischer Kirchengeschichte* (1859), 2:82 ff. HS

gathered, on the east side the Poles, on the west the Germans, and edified each other through common singing and the reading of the pericopes for the Sunday, as well as with the praying of the general prayer for the church and the gathering of offerings for the families of those who were in prison."

Finally the king, in order to restore the authority of the state, came to what to him seemed a highly desirable resolution: he ordered military action against the rebellious congregation. On December 22 another commission, which included among others the chief of police, the district magistrate, and the chairman of the consistory, Hahn, failed in its attempt to come to a peaceful understanding. On December 23 the military, which had positioned itself ready for action in the vicinity of Hönigern, advanced upon the town with four hundred infantry, fifty dragoons, fifty hussars, and two cannons. In the early morning of December 24, the soldiers surrounded the church and the two hundred congregation members who were keeping watch. After repeated, albeit fruitless demands to clear the area, the command was given to load the rifles. But as the assault was ordered, blows with rifle butts and the flat sides of swords sufficed to put the crowd to flight. A few who were wounded remained lying upon the ground. The rifle of one soldier accidentally discharged, but without inflicting any injury. The church doors were broken down with the butt end of rifles.

The authority of the state was thus secured, and the Evangelical Lutheran Church at Hönigern was opened to the new Agenda and with it to the Prussian Union. In a manner of speaking it had now been, as one of the last congregations of this state to struggle so bravely for the confession of the fathers, "incorporated" into the organism of the new Prussian State Church as it began to emerge from the Napoleonic period. With this the century of the Prussian Church also began for this congregation.

This century was ushered in with the Christmas Day service of December 25. This service proved to be a church review launched with high-powered ammunition. At the altar stood three clergymen: the consistorial magistrate, who now had also qualified to become the general superintendent; the superintendent, who solemnly handed the new Agenda to the parish administrator, Pastor Bauch (the pastor of a neighboring congregation); and finally the pastor himself. Pastor Bauch, as the new pastor of Hönigern, proceeded to complain in his Christmas sermon "that the congregation shows him so little love, indeed, that it speaks ill of him even though he has only sought to follow the royal decree." The congregation did not sympathize with this lament and was in fact only poorly represented at this service. But attendance at church soon improved when it became known that the soldiers were not going to leave the town until "order in church attendance is reestablished." As a result, practically the whole congregation was at church on the Sunday after Christmas. When the occupation had ended, however, attendance again fell off alarmingly. But with the exception of a small group, which remained faithful to its Lutheran Confessions, the congregation acquiesced to the will of its earthly king. With a letter of "deep contrition" it submitted itself to him and thereby even attained the gracious remission of the high debt incurred by the military campaign for which they had been made accountable.

PART 2

The story of the conquest of the church in Hönigern is so "amusing" that it is worthwhile to wrest it from oblivion on the occasion of the one hundredth anniversary celebration of the event for this reason alone. It is well to remember that church history also possesses elements of humor, in the midst of a time which has come to experience the history of the church as so gravely serious. What remarkable comedy surrounds this church struggle of the early Victorian period! What grotesque incongruity is revealed here between the means and the end! An Agenda is introduced into an empty church with a show of military might. The armed forces of the state take up their positions with live ammunition in their gun chambers. All the while, the fatherly heart of the king and the churchly conscience of the crown prince—who spoke his mind to Baron Kottwitz, revealing to him how difficult this day was for him—quiver with the thought that it might come to bloodshed. To preclude this possibility, and in order that the effect of the use of weapons might remain a purely moral one, the consistorial magistrate—while not possessing military authority—was given ecclesiastical authority to execute the military campaign and the mission itself. Such were his own words.

Doubtless a happy solution! This representative of the *ecclesia militans* ["church militant"], proud as a victorious field commander, was ready to submit a report from Namslau to the minister von Altenstein on the afternoon of Christmas Day: "With a joyful heart I hurry to give to your excellency a most humble preliminary account of the fortunate success which our mission to Hönigern had. Not a drop of blood was shed, and it may now be said that the foundation for a new order of the ecclesiastical affairs in this not-insignificant parish has been laid." The names of the secular commissars are mentioned in glowing terms: the chief of police, Heinike, "who consistently acted with insight and energy, as well as with meekness and earnestness, so that I have learned to love and esteem him highly"; the district magistrate, von Ohlen, "who displays the most upright zeal everywhere and who operates very efficiently through his personal and local knowledge, as well as through timely pronouncements."

What noble harmony! The phrase of Theodore Storm, "The ecclesiastical, the secular, how well they understand each other," could have also have been applied here. And so

> we divided the work among ourselves: the gentlemen of the commission dealt with the mayors and judiciary primarily from a civil perspective, from which they had to be regarded as rebels; I regarded them from the religious-ecclesiastical standpoint, and so as primarily erring and misled. I therefore took pains to free them from their misunderstandings and to inspire them

with new trust for the intentions of His Royal Majesty and the ecclesiastical authorities.

Even the military fits harmoniously into the whole of this state-church or, perhaps better said, this church-state: "Major von Stoeßer and his officers behaved in a most admirable manner; to a man they first of all exhorted and warned repeatedly, even setting religious motives into motion. Only when everything else had failed to reach the intended goal did they employ force, yet again in such a manner that some individuals were jostled about and even had to be beaten but no one was injured." In these sentences the spirit of the Prussian state of the nineteenth century expresses itself with a candidly touching naivete. It is the spirit of that Prussia in which the most recently released and today still-binding Agenda for the state church bears the same publisher's insignia as that of the field-service regulations, the drill regulations, and the gunnery manual of the infantry.

PART 3

But unfortunately this episode in Hönigern does not have only a comical side. Rather, hidden behind the grotesque scenes of the conversion of a Lutheran Church to the Union by military means is the great tragedy of the end of the independent Lutheran Church in Prussia. Those courageous, obstinate congregational members in Hönigern and in a host of other places believed they were struggling *for* the legitimacy of the Lutheran Church and *against* the forcible introduction of the Union.

Yet the purity of their motives have been subject to suspicion, both then and now. One conjectured that these simple farmers and laborers did not have the ability to evaluate the complicated legal and theological issues at hand. They were, as the quick submission of so many was to prove, not completely clear as to the dogmatic questions at hand. Their struggle was therefore to be understood not as a struggle for the preservation of their confession but as an outbreak of separatist tendencies. And there is something of a truth in this. No such struggle is ever carried out without ulterior motives, and never could such simple congregational members as the laborers of Hönigern understand the dogmatic problems of the Union in all their depth.

One would find it understandable that they would attach themselves somewhat to an authority. It should not be dismissed out of hand that the pastor who has been responsible for their care appears more trustworthy to them than a smooth consistorial magistrate from the capital city. Yet one will have to concede this to these confessing pastors and the congregations which were entrusted to them: in distinction to the learned theologians and the lofty church officials of their time, they were able to recognize clearly the mendacity of the Union which was to be forced upon them, as well as the illegality of the state's measures and were therefore able to draw the consequences. They mistrusted with justification the promise given by the king, even though he sought to reassure them that their confessional position would not be touched and that the acceptance of the Agenda would not constitute assent to the Union. When a royal decree in 1834 declared that only the acceptance of the Agenda was obligatory but coalescence with the Union remained optional as before, it had to be maintained that up to a few years earlier repeated royal decrees had also assured congregations that the Agenda was also not to be forced upon any congregation.

How should anyone retain confidence in the words of this king when he himself appealed to the contradictory decrees and commentaries in the question of union? According to the order in cabinet of September 21, 1817, "the Reformed churches" should not cross over "to the Lutherans, nor vice versa, but both should become a newly vivified Evangelical Christian Church in the spirit of its holy founder." In this sense the intention of the new Agenda, according to the cabinet order of May 28, 1825, was "to give again the original pattern of doctrine to the Evangelical churches in the royal states," that is to say, to further the coalescence of the hitherto-separated churches into a dogmatically unified church.

However, subsequent to the Jubilee celebration of the Augustana in the year 1830, a decisive Lutheran confessional opposition had arisen in Breslau, and this after a celebration was to have advanced the "salutary work of the Union." When this opposition had gained widespread support in subsequent years, the king embarked on a decisive change of course with the order in cabinet of February 28, 1834. Under the pretense that it dealt only with corrections of misinterpretations and erroneous points of view which were being spread by the opponents of an ecclesiastical peace, an interpretation of the Union idea was now given which "stands in diametrical opposition to the concept and inclinations of the Union which people such as these have made acceptable."[3] "The Union," states the cabinet order,

> does not propose nor mean the relinquishing of the existing confessions of faith. Furthermore, the authority which the confessional writings of both the Evangelical confessions have had up to now is also not annulled by it. Joining the Union is nothing other than the expression of a spirit of tolerance and mildness, which simply no longer permits the differences of individual points of doctrine of the other confession to be valid as the basis for denying external church fellowship. Entry into the Union is a matter of free decision, and it is therefore an erring opinion which connects the introduction of the revised Agenda with a necessary joining in the Union or which regards it as contributing to it indirectly.

Which concept of the Union should now be regarded as valid? Either the Lutheran and Reformed churches were able to unite within a single church containing different directions, or they remained two separate churches between which the spirit of tolerance and mildness continues to rule. But they could not

---

[3]   Wangemann [cited above]. HS

become one church and at the same time remain two churches. This is impossible for reasons of logic alone.

The question of a union between the Lutherans and the Reformed has been one of the great problem of Protestantism since Philip of Hesse.[4] One could say either yes or no to the question whether this union is possible, depending upon the confessional and theological conviction which one represents. Zwingli and Calvin said yes, Luther said no. It was also answered differently in Germany during the nineteenth century. In Bavaria, in Hanover, and in the other state churches which remained Lutheran, one said no to the possibility of a Union. In the Palatinate, in Nassau, and in various other West German churches, one said yes to it.

If one says yes to it, then one has to annul at least some portions of the old confessions which are contrary to the Union and replace them with new formulations, as was indeed done in the Palatinate. But one cannot simply assert the perpetual validity of the Lutheran Confessions and tacitly or expressly exempt from this validity those articles which condemn Reformed church doctrine. Either these condemnations are true, or they are false. They cannot be both at the same time.

But if they are false, if it has been determined that the demarcations of the sixteenth century are no longer to be upheld, then the confessions must be revised. A Union, that is, a unification of Lutheran and Reformed churches into a single Evangelical Church, is only possible at this cost. All discussions about the Prussian Union tend to circumvent this decisive point. One can never substantiate *this* Union with the proof that a Union between both churches is quite possible and necessary. If it is possible, then only under the condition that the old confessions are annulled and replaced by a new confession which, under certain circumstances, could adopt a large portion of the old confessional writings again.

That is what the Prussian theologians, the Lutheran as well as the Reformed, should have told Frederick William III at that time. This they did not do, though there were a few exceptions. Either they were lacking in character, or they were floating in the higher dimension of some philosophical system. The unanimous protest which the church and theology should have raised was left to the few pastors and courageous congregations which later formed their own church fellowship in the form of the Old Lutherans [*Altlutheraner*].

There is insufficient space here to recount the story of the rise of this first independent [*staatsfreien*] Lutheran Church, which began its lonely trek back in the heated battles in Silesia, of which the episode in Hönigern is but a single scene. In a country where constitutional freedom of religion and conscience was guaranteed, these Lutherans were persecuted with the most gruesome police chicanery. The holding of a Divine Service held a fifty-*Taler* fine; attendance at the service one *Taler*. The children who did not attend confirmation in the Union church were not allowed to leave school early to attend their classes. Occasionally

---

[4]   Philip of Hesse (1507–1567) engaged in various efforts to unite Protestants. RF

they were dealt with as though school-aged minors until they were conscripted. Even the most elementary right, by which the religious laws of the sixteenth and seventeenth centuries permitted dissension from the conviction of faith of the territorial ruler—the right to emigration—was withheld from these Lutherans for a long time. Eventually they did attain this right.

Yet as the emigrants headed for the ships while passing by the castle at Potsdam[5] and the people of Potsdam came to learn who the emigrants were, the complete senselessness of this state-Christianity was revealed. Frederick William III was indeed a good man deep in his heart. He also desired to be a just king. Yet in his unholy church politics with respect to the Lutherans, he was himself a victim of his own state-church system.

But he was also a victim of his stubbornness which prevented him from making good again the mistakes which had been made. The contradictions which appear in the interpretation of the Union as they appear in the cabinet orders of 1817 and 1834 can be explained by the fact that the ideas of 1817 were already outdated by 1834. The Union was already an anachronism in the commemorative year of the Augustana in 1830. But the king was neither able to recognize his error nor able to admit it. When his son and successor attempted to make good again the injustice which had transpired, he was certainly able to correct specific mistakes and heal some wounds. But the breach of rights and the damage inflicted upon the confessions remained.

How horribly this has wreaked vengeance upon the "Evangelical Church of the Prussian Union," the largest Evangelical Church of Germany, and with it of all German Protestantism is clearly evident today. The church, by having made the confession of the fathers the object of mockery and by casting it away, has robbed itself of the weapon with which an Evangelical Church is alone able to mount resistance to the insurgency of purely secular forces in the modern world. And indeed how rich the Prussian State Church was in flowering congregations and upright, faithful pastors, in notable personalities! How many of the regions of the church in eastern and western Germany were blessed from the past with strong spiritual life!

And yet the Union had inflicted a paralysis upon this church. Consequently they were unable to resist the process of secularization. The pastoral office [*geistliche Amt*] had to disintegrate, for over the ordination vow hung the great untruthfulness of a nebulous Union. The congregation, indeed, the church governments no longer knew to which confession they belonged. The *itio in partes* ["traveling in parts"] in the high church consistory, that is, the separate meeting in caucus of Lutheran and Reformed members of the collegium for the making of separate resolutions concerning the inner affairs of their respective confessions, as it had indeed been established by law, was never carried out. Therefore at present only one Lutheran congregation exists in Berlin in the strict sense of church law:

---

[5]   Potsdam was the official residence of the kings of Prussia. RF

Bethlehem (Bohemian) Lutheran Church. But only descendants of the old Bohemian immigrants are allowed to be among its actual members. If a Lutheran were to move from Munich or Hanover to Berlin today, he could naturally attend the Divine Service of a confessionally Lutheran pastor, given that he as a stranger would be able to find such a pastor. But he could not remain in the state church if he should want to become a member of such a Lutheran congregation. He would have to join either the Old Lutherans [*Altlutheraner*] or another of the Lutheran Free Churches.

This state of affairs can be depicted no more clearly than was done a few years ago in the following official announcement in the official newsletter of the Berlin consistory which read: "The bearer [*Inhaber*] of the formerly Reformed parish [*Pfarrstelle*] in the . . . church of Berlin . . . has been installed as bearer of the previously Lutheran parish in the same church." Is it by chance that this is the same church in which a religiously ideological society which denied the basic truths of the Reformation and for many years has rejected the "Jewish" Old Testament enjoyed the rights of hospitality under the eyes of the High Consistory while celebrating worship services which were contrary to church articles and bylaws? Is it by chance that this High Consistory has for all intents and purposes now been abolished and that the church of the Old Prussian Union actually no longer exists as an independent church today? Or does all of this constitute the unfolding of church historical principles? After all, what should become of a church in which one is able to make of Lutheran and Reformed pastors, who were bound through their ordination vows to the confession of a particular church, interchangeable bearers of previously Lutheran and Reformed parishes at will?

Part 4

No one should construe that which we have just recounted about the Old Prussian State Church and its Union to be a pharisaic accusation. The author of this essay himself stood in the service of this church for some fifteen years. As such he had come to experience its dire plight in the congregational pastoral office [*Gemeindepfarramt*] and participated in the struggle of the Prussian Lutherans for the restoration of an Evangelical Lutheran Church in the old Prussian provinces. He does not speak as an outsider, but as one who knows of the great solidarity of fate and guilt which binds together all of the Evangelical churches of Germany.

To be informed about this solidarity is the presupposition for the success of the great rebuilding of the church with which we have been charged. We cannot approach this rebuilding as though church history has its beginning with us. We may not ignore the exhorting and warning voice of history. One also does no one a favor, least of all the congregations of the Old Prussian Church in which the struggle for the Gospel rages even today, if one keeps silent the accusations which the tragic history of this church levels against all of us. Nor does one do them a favor if one leaves those questions unanswered which this history poses to the whole of German Protestantism. If anywhere, then the deep plight of German Evangelical churchdom [*Kirchentum*] is revealed in this chapter of German church history, the plight which grows out of the false relationship between church and state, which is indeed a plight for both the church and the state and for the people who at the same time belong to the church as well as the state.

This is what the simple farmers and laborers of Hönigern, the Lutherans who opposed the Union, came to recognize with complete clarity: in the events which transpired they were able to perceive that secular authority had trespassed over the limits which God set before it and arrogated to itself rights in the church which it had never possessed. Even those who categorically approve of the Union would have to admit that secular authority has absolutely no right to further the Union or to introduce it by means of force.

If it lays claim to this right for itself, it also claims for itself the right of arriving at decisions in dogmatic questions. For the question whether or not Lutherans and Reformed can form one church without falling away from the church of their fathers is a dogmatic question. The absurdity of these claims of the state became even more evident when the territorial ruler claimed the use of the liturgy [*ius liturgicum*] for himself. The right to order the *cultus* and to prescribe the liturgy, which must necessarily correspond to the teaching of the church, can be claimed only by that church government upon whom the teaching office is also incumbent. The king of Prussia, by proclaiming this right for himself, exceeded all authority which the territorial rulers of earlier times had possessed. With this act he laid claim to a kind of papism for his church.

But the deterioration of the episcopacy of the old territorial rule into an unconditional lordship over the church in a time of the absolutist state had long been set in motion. With respect to the Union, Frederick William III could point with justification to the endeavor of his predecessors: "My enlightened ancestors who now rest in God, the elector John Sigismund,[6] the elector George William,[7] the great elector king Frederick I,[8] and King Frederick William I[9] already had, as the story of their rule and their lives prove, taken aim with pious zeal to unify both divided Protestant churches, the Reformed and Lutheran, into one Evangelical Christian Church in their land. I gladly join their ranks, in their memory and to the honor of their salutary work. I wish for an achievement which is pleasing to God. Yet this very work was met by insurmountable difficulties amidst the unhap-

---

[6] John Sigismund (1572–1619) was the prince elector of Brandenburg and the first Hohenzollern to convert to Calvinism, in 1613. RF

[7] George William (1595–1640), son of John Sigismund, reigned from 1619 until 1640 and in 1621 became duke of Prussia. RF

[8] Frederick William (1620–1688), called the "Great Elector" after Prussia defeated Sweden at the Battle of Fehrbellin in 1675. RF

[9] Frederick William I (1688–1740) obtained the title "King of Prussia"; he was the father of Frederick II, Frederick the Great. RF

py sectarian spirit back then, and I thus wish for the influence of a better spirit, which eliminates the adiaphora and holds on to the chief articles of Christendom, wherein both confessions are one—this I have come to accomplish in my state." The king presupposes that his predecessors also had laid claim to the right for such action. That this is indeed true, Prussian history has shown.

Beside the great elector, we will only take Frederick William I as an example here. He felt himself justified to prohibit chanting, candles upon the altars, making the sign of the cross, choir gowns, and liturgical vestments under threats of severe punishments because "such practices were erroneously retained after the Reformation." Thus the rule of the absolutist sovereign over his state church had in fact arisen out of the territorially ruled church government.

However, under Frederick William III an event of as yet obscure significance occurred. Yet it was an event which entailed presuppositions for the entire church politics of the king. Previously Brandenburg-Prussia had one church government for each of the Lutheran and Reformed churches. Through them the territorial ruler carried out his church government. In accordance with the Stein-Hardenberg[10] state reform, the existing church governments—the Lutheran High Consistory, the Provincial Consistory, and the Reformed Church Directorate—were dissolved as of December 16, 1808, and the function of the previous church governances was transferred to a department of the state government—the ministerial section for public worship and education.[11]

This was a revolutionary act. In fact it violated imperial law, for the Peace of Westphalia (1648) was still the law which was in force. It also violated an international treaty, the Peace of Stockholm, in which the Prussian king had promised "with his royal word" to obligate himself and his descendants to maintain a separate church governance for the Lutheran Church of his land. None of the statesmen who advised the king, least of all he himself, were conscious of the significance of this breach of the law. It was a legislative act in the spirit of the Enlightenment, a time which no longer knew of the church, but knew only religion, the maintenance of which was the task of the state, as was the maintenance of all other cultural areas.

The noble protest of the dismissed church officials faded away. Both of the churches which arose at the time of the Reformation on the territory of the Brandenburg-Prussian state as legally constituted churches disappeared. A clean slate [tabula rasa] had been made and one could now proceed to the building of a completely new church, the Prussian State Church, which was to become the soul

---

[10] Reichsfreiherr H. Karl von und zum Stein and Prince Karl August von Hardenberg were ministers in the government of Frederick William III. Under their plan of reform there was a separation of education from religion, and the limitation of clerical influence to the religious sector (H. W. Koch, *A History of Prussia* [New York: Dorset Press, 1978], 167). RF

[11] Compare the instructive work of Erich Foerster entitled *The Development of the Prussian State Church* (2 vols.; 1905–1907). HS

of the newly rising Prussian state after the ruin of the Napoleonic period. The new state wanted a new church, a church which would be ruled by it and which would determine the legal and dogmatic limits with respect to other churches. That this was an impossible dream, that such a church had nothing more to do with the church of the Augsburg Confession, the Christmas Day celebration at Hönigern had already revealed in 1834. This church is now one hundred years old. In the years 1933 and 1934 its governing agencies were eliminated just as their royal founder and supreme bishop had once eradicated the legitimate church government of the legally existing Evangelical churches of his land. He had thereby come to eradicate these churches themselves.

CHURCH GOVERNMENT AND SECULAR AUTHORITY ACCORDING TO LUTHERAN DOCTRINE[1]

This is doubtless one of the most thorough discussions of the relation of church and state, not only in Sasse's corpus, but also in any English language literature.

The title gives a hint of the context of this essay or book. Very soon after it had come to power in 1933, the National Socialist party (Nazis) made quick moves to coordinate the churches with the nationalist revolutionary state. To secure the confidence of the churches, Hitler had announced guarantees for the churches on March 23. Within a few weeks the churches had dropped their reservations about Hitler and began to give him increasing political support. At the meeting of the first Reich conference in Berlin at the beginning of April 1933, the so-called "German Christians," with support of the National Socialist party, called for a single Reich Church and unconditional political and social collaboration with the new Reich. Events moved swiftly: by the middle of July the constitution of the German Evangelical (Reich) Church had been confirmed by Reich law.

The issues involved became very open in the following year with the formation of the "Confessing Church" movement, for instance. It is to be noted that this essay itself is published as a volume in a series by that name. Sasse himself would later become one of the editors of the series.

Sasse wrote this book in late spring of 1935. It was, as he notes in his preface, "one of the most pressing questions in the church of our day." Once again it reveals his astute insight into the events around him. He himself described the setting succinctly some years later in a letter to Tom Hardt of Stockholm: "It was written in the church struggles at the time of Hitler."[2]

Sasse was writing to Hardt in circumstances which, while not as politically dramatic perhaps, were nevertheless compelling enough for him to make a com-

---

[1] This work originally appeared as *Kirchenregiment und weltliche Obrigkeit nach lutherischer Lehre* (Bekennende Kirche 30; ed. Christian Stoll; Munich: Chr. Kaiser, 1935). MH

[2] Letter of Sasse to Tom Hardt, October 30, 1958, Karin Hardt Collection, Stockholm. RF

parison: the parliament of Sweden was forcing the ordination of women to the ministry on the Church of Sweden. It seems that the day that this book may "be forgotten" (as Sasse suggests at the end of the preface) will be later rather than sooner.

Huss number 133
Hopf number 067

—⟨⟨⟨∕⟩⟩⟩—

PREFACE

This volume is an expanded lecture regarding one of the most pressing questions in the church of our day. The undersigned could not turn down the request to have it published, though he would have been quite pleased to be able to give the work a different configuration, perhaps more in line with the subject treated. Such as it is, may this little book simply cause the reader to note what stands in the confessions of our church. These confessions are so readily quoted, yet hardly understood, and taken with too little seriousness. When this service has been rendered, may this book be forgotten.

Erlangen
Holy Trinity 1935
H. Sasse

OUTLINE

1. The New Ordering of the Relationship between State and Church as a Task for the Present

2. What Is the "Lutheran Doctrine"?

3. The Basic Principle of the Separation of Powers

4. The Church Government of the Territorial Lord [*landesherrliche*] in the Light of the Lutheran Doctrine of the Church
   The Rise of the Church Government by Territorial Lord; Middle Ages; The Church of England; Theological Foundation; Luther's Position over against Medieval Thought; The Surrender of the Medieval Synthesis; The Residual Effect of the Medieval Relationship; The Appeal to the Territorial Lords; Christian Government; Contradictions in Luther; The Doctrine of the Confessions; Duties of the Secular Authority in General; Duties of Christian Government; No Church Government by the Secular Authority

5. The Lutheran Doctrine of Church Government and the Relationship of Church Governance and Secular Authority
   The Freedom of the Lutheran Church on the Question of Church Constitution; Misunderstanding of This Freedom; False Interpretation of the Separation of

Powers; Church and the Legal Order; Reformation and Canon Law; Positive Doctrine of the Constitution of the Church; Divine and Human Law in the Church; The Concept of Church Government; The Authority of Bishops; To Whom Does Church Governance Belong? Office and Congregation; Church Government and Secular Authority; Points of Contact between Church and State; Church Property and Laws of Marriage; The Rights of the Secular Authority

6. The Lutheran Church under Church Government by Territorial Lord
The Unavoidable Fact of Church Government by Territorial Lord; The Consequences; How Could the Church Tolerate It? The Insufficiency of the Safeguards; Territorialism

7. Can Church Government by Territorial Lord Be Renewed?
The Unrepeatable Nature of the *Summus Episcopatus;* A New State Church?

1. THE NEW ORDERING OF THE RELATIONSHIP BETWEEN STATE AND CHURCH AS A TASK FOR THE PRESENT

The correct ordering of the relationship between state and church is one of those great problems which throughout the history of the church must always be solved anew. A people [*Volk*] to whom the Gospel has been preached for the first time and among whom the church of Christ has begun to become a reality faces this task just like any other people among whom the church has existed for a thousand years and whose history has essentially been determined by the existence of the church. The members of the church may only amount to a vanishing minority within their culture [*Volk*]. Church membership and membership in a culture [*Volkszugehörigkeit*] may be essentially coterminous. The church may be poised to fulfill its mission task among a particular people. Or a people may be in a state of full, irreversible apostasy from the church of its fathers.

Still, no matter what circumstances may obtain, solving the problem of "state and church" is always one of the greatest tasks of an era. Genuine statesmen and pedantic bureaucrats, men of the church with real spiritual authority and narrow-minded church officials with clerical ambition, profound thinkers and hollow prattlers, brutal politicians of power and other-worldly enthusiasts [*Schwärmer*], utopian *literati* and men full of practical force and an understanding of reality, cool skeptics and glowing fanatics, believers and non-believers, convinced Christians and decided non-Christians have throughout all of history striven for a clear, decisive, conclusive solution to this problem. But every time someone believes he has found such a solution, joy over the discovery is quickly followed by profound disillusionment. Again and again men have been forced to acknowledge that there finally is no one answer, valid for all time, to the question of the correct relationship of state and church.

Why is there no such answer? There cannot be because it does not have to do with a task which amounts to correctly constructing a theory and then pragmatically defining two human institutions which we are free to form as we choose. That is the way the "Enlightened" modern world of the eighteenth and nineteenth centuries understood the problem. They could view the state and the church as nothing more than phenomena of human culture. The state was the political, the church the religious organization of a people or a group of men. If this were all state and church were, then it would be extremely simple to solve the problem. In fact, we would only have to ask how these two great social structures need be organized in order to correctly fulfill their functions.

The Enlightenment, and those solutions to this problem based upon its principles, tried to find a state constitution correct for all times and peoples, because it is based upon general laws of reason. Later theories tried to find that ordering of state life which fits a particular people [Volk] with its particular disposition and needs and which therefore is the natural or appropriate [artgemässe] ordering for a certain people. In both cases it was a question of human reason and authority—or even of human unreasonableness and powerlessness—whether man could erect such a state or not, and whether or not the remaining organizations of human culture could be arranged or coordinated in conformity with it.

But how can this be accomplished if the state is something else altogether? Indeed, it may be that what makes the state the state is the fact that it is a divine order (divina ordinatio), the governing authority established by God. Since the days of the apostles this is how the Christian faith has understood the essence of the state. And it could also be that the church is not at all what theologians and non-theologians since the eighteenth century have thought it to be, namely, a religious society [Religionsgesellschaft].[3]

What if that which makes the church the church is not our religion, not even our Christian religion? What if it is rather, as the church teaches of itself, the real and personal presence of Jesus Christ the Lord in the preaching of the Gospel and in the Sacrament? Then the question of the correct ordering of the relationship between state and church is not finally a question of our thought and organizing. Nor is it a question of legislation in matters of state and church, though this all must of course take place. It is primarily much more a question of the obedience

---

[3]   It is entirely misleading to say: "In the Weimar Republic the church was, on account of the state, made a 'religious society.' " This had already happened in the absolute state of the eighteenth century. It was not the Weimar Republic, but already the Prussian King Fredrick who had first completed "this dispossession of its essence and its dignity." Compare, for instance, the definition of the church in the general territorial law [Allg(emeine) Landrecht], Part 2, Tit. 11, paragraph 11: "Religious societies which have bound themselves to the public celebration of the Divine Service will be called church societies [Kirchengesellschaften]." There accordingly, "church" or "church society" is a particular case of "religious society," namely, a religious society which has united to the end of exercising public worship [Kultus], and maintains the right of the public exercise of its worship, quite irrespective of whether or not this worship is Lutheran, Roman, or generally Christian, or whether it be Jewish or another non-Christian religion. HS

of people over against the command of the Almighty Creator and Lord, whose divine order (*ordinatio*) stands behind the human ordering of the state. And at the same time it is a question of the faith of people in Jesus Christ.

But the demand of obedience to the commandment of God and the call to faith in the Redeemer are issued to all people, to every generation of history. And every generation must hear these for itself. No one else can believe for me. To be sure, there is a blessing of obedience and faith which stretches "to a thousand generations" [Deut 7:9; cf. Ex 20:6]. And this blessing works itself out in every generation of a people, just as the curse of the disobedience and unbelief of our fathers and forefathers has its effect in our lives. And so the condition of the state and of the church, and the relationship which exists between them, is connected to the obedience and disobedience, the faith and unbelief of our fathers. But the extent to which there exists today among our people a genuine state and a genuine church, and whether or not the correct relationship between them obtains, finally depends upon the extent to which there exists a living respect for the immutable commandments of God among our people, and to what extent there exists faith in the saving Gospel of the forgiveness of sins for the sake of Christ.

Here is why every generation of history faces the problem of "state and church" anew. This is why no generation can solve it for those which shall follow. This is why there can be no final solution to the problem. All the attempts at solutions which have arisen in the course of history and all the legal forms by which the terrible struggles over the relationship between church and state have at times been settled and been expressed via extant institutions are an eloquent testimony of how much or how little obedience to the command of God, how much or how little faith in Jesus Christ has been found among those living at the time. But to understand this we must learn to see the underlying course of church history behind the external events.

We have seen fit to place these propositions at the beginning of our discussion in order to prevent misunderstanding regarding our presentation of the Evangelical Lutheran doctrine of the relationship of state and church. It is not our view that the great problem of the correct ordering of the relationship between state and church would be solved simply by formulating correct theories about it and then giving these theories their corresponding form in civil-ecclesiastical law. It should be unnecessary to have to avert this misunderstanding, but unfortunately, we must do so.

An opposition to orthodoxy has enveloped Protestantism in the last two centuries. A general contradiction of all ecclesiastical law has forced its way into modern theology on the basis of senseless theories regarding the nature of religion. But these theories have no basis in Holy Scripture. This is why even in ecclesiastical circles and in theological scholarship, an appeal to a confession which has validity in the church and to valid ecclesiastical law is scarcely understood. Such an appeal is met with an anguished cry in the face of the specter of "dead" orthodoxy and "juridical-rational" thought. But we do not hear the voice of the church of God in this anguished cry. We hear only the voices of the Pietists, those of the Enlightenment, and the Romantics, all of the past. In what follows we will not let them confuse us as we seek to answer the following question: What does the Evangelical Lutheran Church teach regarding the correct relationship of state and church?

We know that how this relationship is ordered is finally not a doctrinal question, but a question of life, a practical question. We are not so foolish as to think that we would solve this question simply by gaining acceptance for certain theoretical norms. We are convinced that a fundamental settlement of the connection between the new state and the Evangelical Lutheran Church is the pressing task which today is so urgent for the sake of the future of the German people [*Volk*]. But this problem cannot really be solved if we are not clear on those basic and inviolable principles inherent in the doctrine of our church regarding the relationship of state and church. Among the possibilities which are publicly being suggested for a future settlement of this relationship are some with which the church can under no circumstances agree. By doing so it would be forced to confess basic principles which contradict its confession. If for some reason (say to avoid conflict) the church were not to reject such legal formulations, it would deny the very doctrine which it confesses before the world as the correct explication of the Word of God, and thereby destroy itself as church.

In what follows we shall briefly present those inviolable principles regarding the relationship of state and church. To surrender these principles would mean the surrender of the church itself as church. Here we must presuppose knowledge of what the Evangelical Lutheran Church teaches regarding the state or secular authority as a divine order, and also of what our church teaches regarding the nature of the church and the office of the ministry. Here and there in the course of our presentation we also will have something to say regarding them. But the question which is posed to us is the question of the *connection between state and church*, between secular authority [*weltlicher Obrigkeit*] and the spiritual office [*geistlichem Amt*], and especially the question of what rights and duties secular authority has over against the church.

2. WHAT IS THE "LUTHERAN DOCTRINE"?

The question of which rights and duties secular authority has over against the church according to Lutheran doctrine can never be answered by simply pointing out the legal state of affairs which existed earlier or which still exist today. The legal relationship between the Evangelical Lutheran Church and the state in the various countries in which Lutheran churches exist has at times been arranged quite variously (e.g., in Germany, France, Holland, the East European and Baltic States, the Scandinavian countries, the United States of America and Brazil, and the countries of the British Empire and in East Asia). And in each individual country this relationship has undergone various changes in the course of historical development. We can never assert on the basis of a *historical* judgment (e.g., by asserting that a definite form had already existed at the time of the Reformation) which legal forms which have resulted from such a process are legally correct and which not, according to the doctrine of the Lutheran Church. Much less can we do so by judging its practical usefulness (e.g., by asserting that one definite form has proven to be in the best interest of the church and state).

The criterion for every decision is much rather only the question of whether the legal forms being debated are in harmony with the *Evangelical Lutheran doctrines* of the church, of the office of the ministry, of civil order [*Staatsordnung*] and secular authority. If the ecclesiastical-legal forms are examined from this viewpoint, the circumstances will show that very old, and apparently also very sound, formations of the legal relationship between church and state are false.

The "Evangelical Lutheran doctrine," which must form the basis for that judgment is of course not the doctrine of this or that famous Lutheran theologian. Nor is it the doctrine of a particular theological school which confesses Lutheranism. It is rather that which is valid doctrine in the Evangelical Lutheran Church, that is, the doctrine of the *confessions* in which our church once expressed its understanding of the Word of God and which it confesses yet today.

To be sure, the other doctrinal documents of our Reformation, especially those of Luther himself, ever and again attract our interest as a necessary commentary. But we fundamentally maintain that that which is to be regarded as doctrine of the Lutheran Church is not simply what can be gleaned from the writings of Luther. Our doctrine must be taken first of all from the church's confessions. For the Evangelical Lutheran Church has certainly not adopted every individual thought of the Reformer as its doctrine and placed each under the "we believe, teach, and confess" of its confession. In expressing this, we are not establishing a new principle. We are only repeating what the confessions themselves teach regarding the authority of Luther in the church.[4]

3. THE BASIC PRINCIPLE OF THE SEPARATION OF POWERS

According to the doctrine of the Lutheran Church, the spiritual office and secular authority have entirely different tasks. Their realms of authority and functions dare not be mixed and interchanged.

"For the consolation of consciences" Augustana Article XXVIII [4] teaches "the difference between the spiritual and secular power, sword and government." And then it warns "that both governments and powers, for the sake of God's command, should be honored with all devotion and well maintained as two of the greatest gifts of God on earth" (AC XXVIII 4). Over against the ascetic and theocratic errors of the Papal Church and those of fanaticism [*Schwärmertum*], this "high necessary article" regarding secular authority shows "what a gloriously

---

4   See what the Formula of Concord (SD VII [34 ff.]) says about Luther as the "most important teacher of the churches which confess the Augsburg Confession" [SD VII 41] and regarding the authority of his writings. HS

great office" the office of secular authority is (Ap XVI 13 [65, German]). It admonishes the spiritual office to be mindful of its limitations and to acknowledge and honor the office of secular authority with its tasks and value.

> Therefore the spiritual power has its commission to preach the Gospel and to administer the Sacraments; and it is not to invade an office which is not its own, should not set up or depose kings, should not annul secular law or undermine obedience to authority, should not make or prescribe laws for secular authority regarding secular dealings (*non praescribat leges magistratibus de forma rei publicae constituendae*), as Christ himself said: "My kingdom is not of this world." (AC XXVIII 12–14 [quoting John 18:36])

These words from Article XXVIII explain the admonition: "Therefore the two governments, the spiritual and secular, should not be mingled or confused" (AC XXVIII 12).

Does this commingling of powers (*commiscere potestates*) occur only by the spiritual office overreaching its sphere? Or is there also an "intrusion into the office of another" (*irrumpere in alienum officium*), an illicit reaching into the realm of a foreign office, which occurs on the side of the secular authority? The latter is also a problem. In the preface to the "Instruction for Visitors" of 1528 [*LW* 40:262–320] Luther indeed calls upon the elector to take upon himself to remedy the ecclesiastical abuses and to call for the visitation. But Luther directly asserts in this passage, which otherwise places upon the elector a large measure of responsibility for the church, that "[he] is not obliged to teach and to rule in spiritual affairs."[5] He saw clearly at that time the danger that the secular authority could arrogate to itself functions of the spiritual office.

In his last years he spoke bitter words which display his great disillusionment over the intrusion of the secular authority into the sphere of the church:

> Therefore they should either become pastors, preach, baptize, visit the sick, give the Sacrament, and do all things ecclesiastical, or they should cease confusing vocations, see to their courts, and leave the churches to those who have been called to them, who must give account to God. . . . We desire ecclesiastical office and the court to be separate, or [we shall] abandon both. Satan goes on being Satan. Under the pope he mixed up the church in politics. In our time he desires to mix up the political realm in the church. But we will resist with God's help, and strive to keep the vocations separate.[6]

---

[5]　WA 26.200.29 [the English translation is from *LW* 40:273]; on this passage see below. HS

[6]　Letter to Daniel Greiser in Dresden, October 22, 1543 (Enders-Kawerau, 15, 256, 10). Compare also the letter to Amsdorf of July 21, 1544, where Luther complains: "The [royal] court is useless; its government is pure crayfish and snails. It won't continue to stand and will likely fall altogether. Christ looked after the church well by not entrusting the administration of churches to the court. The devil would have nothing to do if he did not have Christian souls to gobble up" (Enders-Kawerau, 16, 52, 13). Behind this complaint we see not only the disposition of the old Luther, but theological principles which the Reformer had constantly advocated. This is demonstrated by his answer to Melanchthon's question from

Here Luther asserted the validity of the warning of Augustana XXVIII [12], which was produced under different circumstances: "Therefore the ecclesiastical and civil powers are not to be commingled" (*non igitur commiscendae sunt potestates ecclesiastica et civilis*). Now it was directed against the claims of the state. Whatever may make both powers guilty of overstepping their legal bounds, in every case it remains the sin of "the intrusion into a foreign office." Therefore according to Luther and Lutheran Church doctrine, the rule "It is not to rush into an alien

---

the Augsburg Reichstag, whether or not ecclesiastical traditions (*traditiones*) could be imposed with binding authority by the government [*Obrigkeit*] and thus also by the bishops, if they were not in opposition to the Gospel, something like the way pious kings of Israel had ordered fasts (WA Br 5.476 f.). Luther's answer of July 21, 1530, said, among other things:

> First, since it is certain that these two administrations are distinct and diverse, namely, the ecclesiastical and the political, which Satan wonderfully has confounded and mixed through the papacy, we must be extremely diligent here not to confound them again ourselves, nor allow or consent to anyone else who does so. For this would make us thieves and robbers, because here the authority is divine, and it prescribes that these be kept diverse and unmixed, saying: "Not so with you." (WA Br 5.492.10; cf. Matt 20:26)

These words, as is the case with AC XXVIII, are directed in practice against the bishops, who were simultaneously holders of the spiritual office and secular authority, and demanded obedience to their orders in the name of God. The significance of this passage is that it shows how Luther appropriated AC XXVIII. Finally, we note Luther's explanation of John 2:13 ff. (WA 46.725 ff. [*LW* 22:225 ff.]) of 1537, where he deals with the doctrine of the separation of governments on the basis of the account of the purification of the temple:

> And from now to the end of the world these two realms [*zwei Regiment*; see further *LW* 13:147, note 4] are not to be confused, as was done in the Jewish nation during the period of the Old Testament. Henceforth they are to remain distinct and separate from each other, if the pure Gospel and the true faith are to be preserved. ([WA 46.]734.21 [*LW* 22:225; the English translation here and in the following quotes in this note is from *LW* 22])

> And the civil governments—the princes, kings, the nobility in the country, and also the judges in the villages—take it upon themselves to wield the oral sword and to tell the pastors what and how to preach and how to administer their congregations. But you say to them: "You fool and stupid dunce, attend to your calling. Don't try to preach, but leave that to your pastor!" On the other hand, the schismatic spirits will not content themselves with the oral sword and will reach rebelliously for the secular sword and will insist on reigning in the city hall. All this is due to the devil's maneuvers, who will not desist until he has brought about confusion with respect to these two swords. ([WA 46.]735.10 [*LW* 22:225–26])

> But I exhort you who are one day to instruct consciences in the Christian Church to take heed that you abide by the distinction between the two realms. For if these are confused, neither will prosper. ([WA 46.]736.4 [*LW* 22:226])

> You will discover that the devil will again confuse the two. ([WA 46.]736.13 [*LW* 22:226])

> It is not likely that the pope will harm us or rob us of the Gospel, for he is too badly beaten. But the young noblemen will—the members of the nobility, the princes, as well as the evil jurists. They go about nowadays with an air of authority and try to dictate to the pastors what they are to preach. They want to foist their will on the people with reference to the Sacraments, arguing that as the secular government they are entitled to obedience. And thus they merge the spiritual and the secular realms. The pope did this too. ([WA 46.]736.22 [*LW* 22:227])

> But if the princes continue to jumble the two, as they are now doing, then may God in his mercy shorten our lives that we may not witness the ensuing disaster. For in such circumstances everything in the Christian religion must go to wrack and ruin. This is what happened in the papacy when the bishops became secular princes. And if the secular lords now become popes and bishops and insist on sermons that defer to their wishes, then let the wretched devil preach to them; for he preaches too. But let us pray God that neither the spiritual nor the secular realm abuses its office that way! ([WA 46.]737.27 [*LW* 22:228]) HS

office" (*non irrumpat in alienem officium* [AC XXVIII 13]) also applies to the secular authority.

It is a terrible misfortune that Lutheran theology of the past did not always and on all sides clearly teach the resultant consequences of the propositions of Augustana Article XXVIII [regarding the state's intrusion into the church]. Thus it is only reasonable that the following warning applies to the state: "It shall not abrogate the laws of the church, nor take away legitimate obedience . . . nor prescribe laws to bishops concerning the forms of constituting the church"(*non abroget leges ecclesiae, non tollat legitimam oboedientiam . . . non praescribat leges episcopis de forma ecclesiae constituendae*).[7]

4. THE CHURCH GOVERNMENT OF THE TERRITORIAL LORD [*LANDESHERRLICHE*] IN THE LIGHT OF THE LUTHERAN DOCTRINE OF THE CHURCH

THE RISE OF CHURCH GOVERNMENT BY TERRITORIAL LORD

A mixing or confusing of ecclesiastical and civil functions would occur were the secular authority to lay claim to the government of the church or only a portion of the same. Therefore, the Confessions of the Evangelical Lutheran Church do not acknowledge a participation of the secular authority in the governing of the church.

This assertion will surprise many a reader who is not familiar with the Confessions of the Lutheran Church. The amalgamation of Evangelical Lutheran Churchdom of the sixteenth century with the state has been treated as something so self-evident that even today it is still inconceivable to many that this relationship could perhaps be in essential disagreement with the Reformation, and even stand in direct contradiction to the teaching of the Evangelical Lutheran Church. And yet it is in fact the case that the system of church government by territorial lord [*landesherrliche Kirchenregiment*], which at that time represented the amalgamation of state and church, resulted neither from the doctrine of Luther nor had its basis in whole or in part in the Confessions of the Lutheran Church. In order to prove this thesis, which is absolutely essential to our entire presentation, it will be necessary first to take a look at the origin and the beginnings of the system of church government by territorial lord and the amalgamation of state and church which obtained within it.

MIDDLE AGES

Church government by territorial lord and the ordering of the established connection between state and church which went along with it triumphed for the

---

[7] Sasse uses the words of AC XXVIII 13, but reverses the "powers." Thus the original: "It shall not abrogate the laws of civil rulers, nor take away legitimate obedience . . . nor prescribe laws to civil rulers concerning the form of the Commonwealth." MH/RF

first time with the Reformation. And it was carried out above all in the Protestant countries. But it certainly does not follow that this form of church constitution is a child of the Reformation. It was much rather an idea which had already existed before the Reformation, and it was in many instances simply a reality of political life. Not only in the emerging nation states of Western Europe, but in Spain, France, and England the king claimed an ever-increasing right over the church. But also in Germany increasingly the territorial lords who were becoming sovereign princes were guaranteed the principle which had already been ascribed to many of them in the fifteenth century: "he would be in his land pope, Caesar, and German master all in one."[8]

The idea that the secular prince could also govern the church is precisely a medieval idea. It presupposes a *medieval society* which is both state and church, in which all members are so bound by the unity of faith that the heretic cannot be guaranteed any civil or even physical existence. In this society, which as a "Christian body" (*corpus Christianum*) represented a great synthesis of church and world, of state and church, the two powers which stood at the head, the spiritual and the secular, wrestled for primacy.

Thus the history of the Middle Ages is defined by the claims of both powers and by the guilt of each as it intruded into the realm of the other, whether the spiritual power usurped rule over the state or the secular authority claimed rule over the church. The serious collapse of the papacy in the fourteenth century, above all its forfeiture of moral credit since the great schism, or for that matter the complete inner apostasy of the church in the centuries of the late Middle Ages, necessarily resulted in the ascendancy of the power of secular princes in all ecclesiastical affairs.

As always, the codification of church law follows church-political developments. If one part of the *corpus Christianum* broke down, should not the other intervene? Was not the office of the Caesar and of secular authority in general also from God? Had not the glimmer of a holy and divinely established institu-

---

[8]   Consider also the well-known saying: "The Duke of Cleve is pope in his land" (*Dux Cliviae est papa in terris suis*). On the origin of this expression and its many parallels, see Justus Hashagen, *Staat und Kirche vor der Reformation* (1931), 550 ff. In his comprehensive work, which continues and expands Werminghoff's studies on the rise of church government by territorial lord, Hashagen comes to the following conclusion:

> The rich development which church government by territorial lord experienced already previous to the Reformation sufficiently demonstrates that the determinative roots of this church-political manifestation of the Lutherans reach well back into the medieval past. Whoever is convinced of this will view as hopeless every attempt to explain the derivation of this form of church government of the Lutherans purely on the basis of a new and specifically Lutheran fundamental viewpoint. An inherently necessary connection between state and territorial church thought and traditions on the one hand, and the genuinely new forms of Lutheranism on the other hand, did not obtain.

Calling upon H. Boehmer, von Below, Haller, Kahl, and others, Hashagen asserts:

> Church government by territorial lord, at least in its theoretic and practical fundamental outlines, was throughout a medieval inheritance . . . . As such it had nothing to do with the innovations of the Reformation. With its unmistakable medieval idiosyncrasies, it much rather appeared to be a completely foreign phenomenon in this innovation. (pp. 558–59) HS

tion, without which Christianity was inconceivable, shone about the office of the Roman Caesar since ancient times? Was not the Caesar as bearer of the secular power the "protector" of the church, her mighty patron, and guardian of her legal right in the world? Did this not result in rights and duties of the secular authority over against the church, rights and duties which in the written and unwritten law of the empire and church were established, but which, because of an ever-changing historical situation, had to be defined anew?

Thus in the late Middle Ages there arose among princes and churchmen, lawyers and theologians, theories of canon law which contradicted the claims of the papacy of the high Middle Ages to unlimited world rule. Such theories defined anew the relationship of the two powers to each other. Among these theologians it was Occam, the "master" of theology,[9] in whose theology Luther was later trained. In the second quarter of the fourteenth century, barely two hundred years before the Reformation, Occam decidedly contested the papacy's claims to world rule, and he did so calling upon the Bible and natural law. He fought to limit the pope's legal right to the spiritual realm, and he asserted the proper legal right of secular authority.

At the same time the famous lawyer Marsilius of Padua[10] was also fighting for similar goals. His *Defender of the Peace (Defensor Pacis)* was an insightful anticipation of state and canon law theories of the modern world.[11] In his presentation of the relationship between the spiritual and secular powers, he goes even beyond Occam. He teaches not only that in secular affairs (e.g., taxation) the hierarchy is subject to secular authority and its judgment, but he even ascribes to secular authority a legal right which directly entails a right of supervision over the spiritual functions of the church. The bearer of the governing power should have the right to hold bishops and other clergy to the fulfillment of their ecclesiastical duty (e.g., the administration of the Sacraments). He should also possess the right to call a council. And at such a council, alongside the clergy, the laymen are also to take part. Of course, they should be laymen who are believers. The right to determine laws for the faithful (*legislator fidelis*) can only be granted to the Christian bearer of the governmental office.[12]

---

[9]   William of Occam (ca. 1280–ca. 1349) advocated the independence of civil rule. He was excommunicated in 1328 (*Lutheran Cyclopedia*, 586). MH/RF

[10]   Marsiglio dei Mainardini (ca. 1275–1342) was rector of the University of Paris in 1313. He wrote *Defensor Pacis* in 1324 which was condemned by the pope in 1327. He fled to Nuremberg and found protection in the court of the emperor, Ludwig of Bavaria, who himself had just been excommunicated. According to Marsilius,

> the State is the great unifying power of society to which the Church must be completely subordinated. . . . The Church . . . has no inherent jurisdiction whether spiritual or temporal. All her rights in this regard are given her by the State. . . . The principal authority in all ecclesiastical matters is the General Council, which should be composed of priests and laymen. These ideas, which ran counter to the whole medieval conception of society, have led to Marsiglio of Padua's being claimed as a forerunner of the Reformers, modern democracy, and even totalitarianism. (*ODCC*, 1043) RF

[11]   No need here to enter into the question of sources and collaborators of Marsilius of Padua. HS

[12]   [Marsilius of Padua, *Defensor Pacis*,] 2:20. HS

These concepts, which the pope proceeded to condemn as heretical, were of course not likely to prevail. They were at the time the insightful ideas of an individual thinker. But they spread gradually and exercised great influence. They formed the theoretic basis of the above-mentioned claim of greater and lesser princes each to be "his own pope" in his land. It is not surprising that from this claim and those ideas would arise new forms of church constitution when the attempt of the medieval papacy to reassert its power in the wake of political decline finally came to nothing or some other catastrophe befell the obtaining hierarchy. The new "popes" stood ready to claim the inheritance of the Roman papacy in the case of such a catastrophe. It was not to be expected that they would waive their claims when some future theologian raised objections and constructed other doctrines regarding the governance of the church, such as the *Defender of the Peace (Defensor Pacis)*. *The rule of the territorial lords over the church was a historical fate which was unavoidable when papal rule finally broke down*, quite irrespective of what finally caused such a breakdown.

THE CHURCH OF ENGLAND

The new form of church governance had little to do with the Reformation of Martin Luther and the doctrine of the Lutheran Church. It was much rather deeply rooted in medieval Catholicism, which was now ending. This is shown by the fact that the church in which church governance by territorial lord established itself as something completely self-evident, and in which it found its most complete fulfillment, was a church which Luther and his Reformation most emphatically rejected: *the Church of England*. The king who was such a decided opponent of the doctrine of Luther that he held the title "Defender of the Faith" (*Defensor fidei*), given to him by the pope, became the founder of the most powerful state-church system in Europe (here we need not take into account Russia).

Just when in Germany the emerging Evangelical Lutheran Church had confessed its doctrine before the world at Augsburg, the Convocations of Canterbury and York confessed their adherence to the new dogma of the Church of England, namely the thesis that His Majesty the King is the lord protector, the lord and supreme head of the Church of England, so far as the law of Christ allows. This thesis has been repeated ever and again in the history of the English Church. It is an integral component of its confession. This confession gave dogmatic foundation for the king's rule of the church when in Article 37 it asserts that in the English Empire His Majesty the King "has the highest power. And he has the supreme governance of all the estates of this kingdom in all cases, whether these are ecclesiastical or not" ("summam habet potestatem, ad quam omnium statuum huius Regni, sive illi ecclesiastici sunt sive non, in omnibus causis suprema gubernatio pertinet").[13]

---

[13] E. F. K. Müller, *Die Bekenntnisschriften der reformierten Kirche* (Leipzig, 1903), 519–20. HS
This is from Article 37 of the Thirty-nine Articles, "Of the Civil Magistrates." RF

The king is, accordingly, the "supreme governor of the church."[14] He is not entitled to exercise the functions of the spiritual office, the proclamation of the Word and the administration of the Sacraments, but he indeed possesses the highest jurisdiction over ecclesiastical business.[15] For instance, no one may consecrate a bishop, nor may anyone be legally elected or consecrated a bishop in the Church of England who has not been nominated by the king for the office concerned. The correlate of this royal supremacy was the end of papal jurisdiction in England, and thus the cited Article 37 contains the assertion that the bishop of Rome possesses no jurisdiction in the English Empire.

THEOLOGICAL FOUNDATION

The question of just how this position of the territorial lords over against the church was *theologically* grounded is extremely important. There can be no doubt that the late-medieval theories regarding the rights of secular rulers in the church were determined by ancient philosophy regarding the state. This is completely evident in the philosophy regarding the state of the Renaissance. But already Marsilius shows the influence of ancient thought regarding the state. His view that the church should be subordinate to the state in all matters, that it should be a matter of state governance to stipulate the number of clergy, to appoint pastors and bishops, to have control of church property, to set laws for the church and to exercise jurisdiction over the clergy, to call councils and supervise ecclesiastical life, has nothing to do with any sort of religious or theological convictions. It is the view of a man who had very definite philosophical convictions regarding the state as "the entity encompassing all the life functions of humanity in which a perfected society is not obtainable without human happiness."[16]

It is of the essence of this state that it be concerned not only for the temporal or mundane (*temporale sive mundanum*), but also for the eternal or heavenly (*aeternum sive caeleste*) in the lives of its citizens. The exercise of the public *cultus* is just as much a civil matter in this state as it was in the ancient state. Just as Constantine[17] once transferred the religious functions of the Roman Caesar as the *Pontifex Maximus* ["supreme pontiff" or "priest"] into the Christian and ecclesiastical realm, so the same mistake was repeated again here by importing the humanistic doctrine of the state into the realm of legal theory regarding state and church.

It is clear that there is no interest here in a theological foundation for the right of the ruler over the church. Marsilius of Padua did not need such a foundation. It was otherwise in the case of the Church of England however. To be

---

[14] This title in 1559 replaced the older "supreme head" (*supremum caput in terris, post Christum, Ecclesiae Anglicanae* ["supreme head of the Anglican Church on earth, after Christ"]), which was used by the first draft of the confessions, the Forty-two Articles of 1552. HS

[15] "Jurisdiction over the state ecclesiastical" (*status ecclesiasticus*) according to the Constitutions and Canons Ecclesiastical of 1603 (text and translation from C. Fabricius, *Corpus Confessionum*, 24:465 f.). HS

[16] A. Hauck, *Kirchengeschichte Deutschlands*, 5:503. HS

[17] Constantine I, "the Great" (ca. 280–337), was Roman emperor from 306 until 337. MH

sure, the political and civil law theories of Humanism played a great role in the founding of this church which was born completely of the spirit of the Renaissance. But royal supremacy had to be theologically justified over against the papacy and its religiously grounded claims.

How this happened is shown by the Second Canon of the Constitutions and Canons of the Church which threatens with excommunication anyone who "asserts that His Majesty the King does not have that same authority in ecclesiastical affairs which *the blessed kings had possessed among the Jews and the Christian Caesar in the ancient church.*" Consequently here it is claimed that the Christian or believing ruler possessed explicit legal authority over the church of his land, that the "pious magistrate" (*pius magistratus*) possessed rights over against the church which did not belong to the office of magistrate in and of itself, just as Marsilius in the *Defender of the Peace* had ascribed legal authority over the church to the "faithful legislator or his ruling authority" (*legislator fidelis aut eius auctoritate*).

Since there was no support for this in the NT, the example of the pious kings of Israel and the Christian Caesar of the ancient world were put forth. Thus *David* and *Constantine* were constantly held up in the Middle Ages as types for the Christian rulers and their relationship to the church. The particular rights of the secular ruler in ecclesiastical matters consequently depended upon their relationship to the church. According to this view, the pious King Hezekiah possessed rights in Israel which no longer belonged to his son Manasseh, the idol worshiper. Constantine possessed rights which in no way were possessed by his predecessors.

According to this theory, Constantine the Great obtained these rights over the church the moment he took the church under his protection. That assuming the duty of protection did not yet mean conversion to the church, that the brutal politicians of power among the Caesars of the fourth and fifth centuries, for whom the church was only an object and means of political maneuvering, cannot be called "Christian Caesars" without great qualification, are historical judgments which lay outside the purview of men of the passing Middle Ages and the time of the Reformation. But the concept of the pious, God-fearing or Christian government which possessed particular rights over the church is just as unclear as the concept of the ancient "Christian Caesar."

The bearers of secular power possess these rights not merely as persons who govern. Nor do they possess them as Christians or pious men. They possess them only because they are *simultaneously persons having secular authority and Christians.* Thus the concept of the "Christian" or "pious" government is a typically medieval concept. In it lurks the medieval ideal of the Christian government or the Christian Caesar, who not only possesses a secular but at the same time an ecclesiastical office. Thus this concept is a testimony to the medieval synthesis of church and state. And the same is true of the right of church governance which that "Christian" government possessed. Can there be a more obvious testimony to the medieval synthesis of church and state than the idea of a right which the Christian government possessed, not because it was government, nor because it was Christian, but insofar as it was both at the same time? But this and nothing else is the legal right of the so-called church government by territorial lord.

LUTHER'S POSITION OVER AGAINST MEDIEVAL THOUGHT

From what we have said, it is clear that it is completely impossible to deduce the arrangement of the connection between state and church which we have designated "church government by territorial lord" from the *Lutheran Reformation*. Luther is as little the founder of this form of church constitution as he is the founder of Anglicanism. Luther and the other Reformers much rather entered a situation in which the claims of the secular authority to church governance or an essential portion of the same already obtained. They lived in a world in which the ideas behind these claims were already an intellectual force.

The question they faced was only *one of how they would position themselves in respect to these ideas. Would they, or to what extent would they* compromise with the development of a state and church legal arrangement defined by these ideas? Would they oppose it, and if so, how would they bring to bear their opposition? If Luther's views in the early years of the Reformation are considered from this vantage, then in many respects they do not appear as new and revolutionary as has often been thought. There is much which is new and revolutionary in the powerful appeal "To the Christian Nobility of the German Nation" [WA 6.404–69; *LW* 44:115–217]. Note, for instance, the unrelenting consequence of thinking through to its end the concept of the general priesthood of believers,[18] or the inexorable seriousness with which the often-expressed vexations of the German nation were expressed here and given form as a convulsing complaint of an entire people against the papacy.

But the ideas of calling upon the secular authorities for assistance, of impressing upon them that it was their duty to lend their assistance or forsake the spiritual office, of ascribing to them the right to call a council were not new concepts. They are certainly not concepts which resulted from a new understanding of the Gospel. They are concepts which had been generally advanced in the now-fading

---

18   Compare the self-evident assurance with which Luther (WA 6.407.34) answers in the affirmative the question of whether or not a small group of Christians who have no ordained priest can choose one out of its midst and ordain him to the office of the ministry, with the vagueness of the *Utopia* of Thomas More of 1516 on this question. We read here ("On Utopian Religions"):

> Not a few joined our religion and were cleansed by the holy water of Baptism: But among us . . . there was, I am sorry to say, not a single priest; they were initiated in all other matters, but so far they lack those Sacraments which with us only priests administer. They understand, however, what they are, and desire them with the greatest eagerness. Moreover, they are even debating earnestly among themselves whether, without the dispatch of a Christian bishop, one chosen out of their own number might receive the sacerdotal character. It seemed that they would choose a candidate, but by the time of my departure they had not yet done so. [*St. Thomas More: Utopia* (edited with introduction and notes by Edward Surtz, S.J.; London: Yale University Press, 1964), 132]

Here we see very clearly Luther's advance over Humanism and at the same time the difference between the concept of church of Lutheranism and that of Anglicanism and humanistic Catholicism. HS

Middle Ages and which Luther in this document appropriated because they were as self-evident to him as to all of his contemporaries who earnestly labored to remedy ecclesiastical abuses. The breakdown of the spiritual estate was so appalling at the time how could the most pressing problems possibly be remedied unless the secular authority stepped in to help? Who else had the power to oppose the persistent legal aberrations of which the high ecclesiastical authorities had become guilty?

THE SURRENDER OF THE MEDIEVAL SYNTHESIS

If Luther in his appeal to the government still operated completely within the patterns of thought of his time, how then is his view of the relationship between spiritual and secular power different from that of any of his contemporaries? What new ideas did the Lutheran Reformation produce in this matter? This is not an easy question to answer. And indeed, the difficulty lies in the fact that Luther on the one hand *sharply and fundamentally distinguished spiritual and secular authority* and decisively opposed every attempt to mix them. But on the other hand, he was not prepared to free himself fully from the *effects of the medieval synthesis of church and state*, spiritual and secular, and to actually carry to its conclusion this correctly acknowledged principle.

We noted above that the concept of the *"Christian governing authority"* with its particular rights and duties over against the church, which were derived neither from its governmental nor its Christian character, is a typical example of the medieval synthesis of church and world. It had its sole basis in the fact that its bearers were both governing persons and Christians. Consequently, to be a Christian Caesar, for example, meant more than being a Caesar and a Christian. The rights and duties of the Christian Caesar could not simply be divided into those which had to do with the Christian and those which had to do with the Caesar. There were rights and duties which belonged neither to the Caesar as such nor to the Christian as such, which were possessed only by the Christian Caesar.

How did Luther and the Lutheran Reformation view such offices (be it that of the Caesar, a territorial lord, or a collegial municipal government) in which civil and ecclesiastical tasks were bound together in a manner characteristic of the medieval synthesis of church and world? Karl Holl[19] once said it was Luther's great deed that he "finally gave up that confused concept of a spiritual-secular Reich." That is correct. Luther of course knew that he lived among a people [*Volk*] who became members of the church and the society through Baptism. He knew the difference between a pious and a godless prince. He knew therefore that

---

[19] *Luther und das landesherrliche Kirchenregiment, Ges. Aufsätze*, I, Luther 6, p. 344. HS

Sasse had been a student of Karl Holl (1866–1926) at the University of Berlin (1913–1917). Holl's famous lecture on Reformation Day 1917 is said to have begun the rebirth of Luther studies in the twentieth century: "What Did Luther Understand by Religion?" (*Ges. Aufsätze*, I, 1 ff.). RF

church and state can never be so separated from each other as though they stood next to each other as two neighboring states.

But from the beginning of his work as Reformer, Luther maintained what the Augustana later stated the following way: "Therefore the two governments, the spiritual and secular, should not be mingled or confused" (AC XXVIII [12]).[20] When he spoke of the rights and duties of Christian government, as a rule he more or less clearly differentiated between that which the government as *secular government* and that which persons in government as *Christians* were responsible for or entitled to do.[21] Thus already in the address "To the Christian Nobility," a distinction is made between reforms which the secular government as government can direct to eliminate abuses in the church (such as the abolition of benefices paid to the pope, payment for the pallium,[22] etc.; furthermore, the elimination of the alleged rights which the pope claimed over the German bishops and thus over Germany) and other measures which would have to be directed by a council, for instance the purely ecclesiastical reforms in the realms of liturgy [*Kultus*] and church discipline.

In this document as elsewhere Luther ascribes to secular government in the then-current situation of the church the right and duty to call a council. It is interesting to note how this right or duty was at times justified. In "To the Christian Nobility" the third of the three walls of the Romanists against which Luther mounts an attack is the assertion that no one but the pope could convene a legitimate general council. He overturns this assertion on the basis of Scripture and shows that

> when necessity demands it and the pope is an offense to Christendom, the first man who is able should, as a true member of the whole body, do what he can to bring about a truly free council. No one can do this so well as the temporal authorities, especially since they are also fellow-Christians, fellow-priests, fellow-members of the spiritual estate, fellow-lords over all things. Whenever it is necessary or profitable they ought to exercise the office and work which they have received from God over everyone. (WA 6.413.27 [*LW* 44:137])[23]

---

20   See part 3 above. HS

21   Further details may be found in the above-cited essay by Karl Holl and in the chapter "Die Staatsauffassung Luthers" in Werner Elert, *Morphologie des Luthertums* (1932), 2:313 ff., especially pp. 329 f. HS

22   "The pallium is a woolen shoulder cape. It is the emblem of the archbishop's office and must be secured from Rome. The bestowal of the pallium is a very ancient custom and was so referred to by Gregory I (590–604). Canon law prescribes that the archbishop-elect must secure the pallium from Rome within three months of his election; otherwise he is forbidden to discharge the duties of his office. Luther's contention that it was originally a free gift of good will is correct, as is his contention that the pallium (i.e., an archbishopric) was bought in his day at a fantastic price" (*LW* 44:148, note 71). MH

23   The English translation of this and the following quotes from "To the Christian Nobility" is from *LW* 44. MH

If a fire were to break out in a city every citizen would be duty bound to lend assistance, even without the authority of the mayor: "How much more should this be done in the spiritual city of Christ if a fire of offense breaks out, whether in the papal government or anywhere else!" (WA 6.413.37 [LW 44:137]). The right—or, more properly, the duty—of secular government to call a council in the case of necessity is derived from the fact that the bearers of the governmental office are members of the church and as such may exercise the rights and duties which every believer has authority to exercise as a member of the general priesthood.

When Luther said, "The temporal power has become a member of the Christian body" (WA 6.410.3 [LW 44:131]), it is completely clear from the context that he intends to say nothing other than that persons in government are members of the church.[24] There is nothing said here of government as such necessarily having a office in the church. In addition to the apostolic council, which was not convened by Peter, but by all the apostles and the elders of the congregation, Luther uses the example of the Council of Nicaea and the other "general Christian councils" convened by the Caesars in order to make his point regarding the right to call a council. It is absolutely clear from the context that Luther is of the opinion that the Caesars had convened those councils insofar as they were Christians and in doing so exercised a right which was theirs as members of the church.[25]

In light of these facts we may maintain with Karl Holl that the "confused medieval concept of a spiritual-secular Reich" had been given up by Luther. The presupposition for all Luther's principles regarding the rights and duties of Christian governing authorities over against the church was that there are rights and duties which the secular government as such possesses, quite irrespective of the faith of the person governing. And there are rights and duties which believers possess, whether or not they have an office of government.

Here the views of the Reformer are completely clear. He no longer had the unclear and confused concept of offices in which spiritual and secular, churchly and civil functions were combined. From the very beginning he limited the spiritual office, particularly that of the bishops and in the early years of the Reformation also that of the pope, to its spiritual functions.

So also he limited the tasks of the secular government to those functions which secular government as such possesses according to God's ordering. He contested the idea that the Caesar as Caesar had an office in the church, as the Middle

---

[24] "Since those who exercise secular authority have been baptized with the same baptism, and have the same faith . . . . For whoever comes out of the water of baptism can boast that he is already a consecrated priest, bishop, and pope" (WA 6.408.8 [LW 44:129]). HS

[25] Luther expressly says this in "On the Councils and the Church" (1539). See the description of the Council of Nicaea which begins with the words: "The praiseworthy Emperor Constantine had become a Christian and had given the Christians peace" (WA 50.548.25 [LW 41:54; the English translation is from LW]). HS

Ages had taught when it treated the Caesar as *defensor* or *advocatus ecclesiae*, as the guardian and protector of the church, bound to vindicate the church with the power of the sword against her enemies and destroyers and claiming special rights in the church to do so.

Thus in the document "On the War against the Turk" of 1529 [WA 30^{II}.107–48; *LW* 46:155–205], Luther turns against the Roman view of the wars against the Islamic invaders as a struggle which "the Caesar as the protector of the church and defender of the faith" should mount against the "enemy of the Christian faith" (WA 30^{II}.132.30 [cf. *LW* 46:188]). "Consequently, the Caesar is not the head of Christianity nor the protector of the Gospel or the faith. The church and the faith must have a lord protector other than Caesars and kings. They are commonly the worst enemies of Christianity and the faith" (WA 30^{II}.130.27 [cf. *LW* 46:185]). The protector and advocate of the church is Christ alone, her Lord. When the Caesar makes war against the Turks he fights not for the church, but for Germany, and acts solely as secular governing authority: "Caesar's sword has nothing to do with the faith. It belongs in corporal, secular matters so that God may not get angry with us for overturning and mixing up his order of things" (WA 30^{II}.131.8 [cf. *LW* 46:186]).

The Augustana understands the war against the Turks, which is a task of Caesar's office, in the same sense when in the article on "The Cult of Saints" we are told to note the example of the good works of the saints "each of us in his own calling. So His Imperial Majesty may in salutary and godly fashion imitate the example of David in making war on the Turk, *for both are incumbents of a royal office which demands the defense and protection of their subjects*" (AC XXI 1).[26] When we remember what role the examples of David, "who is the example for all princes" (WA 11.275.13 [cf. *LW* 45:122]), and the other "godly kings" of the OT have played in attempts to understand the office of ruler as a simultaneously secular and ecclesiastical office, when we consider, for instance, that canon of the Church of England noted above, then it is clear that Luther's separation and delineation of the functions of the secular government and the spiritual office were something quite revolutionary.

It was really a turning point in the history of the church when Luther's remark "For this reason one must carefully distinguish between these two governments. Both must be permitted to remain"[27] was elevated to a doctrine of the Evangelical Lutheran Church by Augustana XXVIII when it stated, "Therefore, the two governments, the spiritual and the temporal, are not to be mingled or confused" (*Non igitur commiscendae sunt potestates ecclesiastica et civilis*, AC XXVIII 12).

---

[26] The English translation is from Tappert, *BC*, 46. MH

[27] "Temporal Authority: To What Extent It Should Be Obeyed" (1523), WA 11.252.12 [*LW* 45:92; the English translation is from *LW*]. HS

THE RESIDUAL EFFECT OF THE MEDIEVAL RELATIONSHIP

This completely clear and fundamental contradiction of the medieval synthesis of church and world, spiritual and secular, was what was new in Luther's teaching on the connections between state and church. But even so we ought not underestimate just how strong the effect of this synthesis was on the thought and dealings of the Reformer. And this is completely understandable. How could Luther and his contemporaries have conceived of a world which was not ruled by that synthesis! Educated within the intellectual world and the cultural forms of the late Middle Ages, this was the only world they knew. And they could not conceive of just what formations and state-church law would finally result from the principle "The two authorities, the spiritual and the temporal, are not to be mingled" (*Non commiscendae sunt potestates ecclesiastica et civilis*).

If Luther had attempted to formulate such a conception then he would have given play to his imagination and written a *Utopia* like those which philosophical civil theories have always produced. But he was no dreamer [*Phantast*] or utopian idealist. He was a Reformer. And Luther, like the Confession of the Lutheran Church, constantly guarded himself from the misunderstanding that the church, as he understood it on the basis of the Gospel, was a sort of "Platonic republic" (*civitas Platonica*) and that the Reformation was the attempt to realize some church ideal which was purely a mental construct (Ap VII/VIII 20).

For Luther and those who worked with him, what was at stake was much rather that Christianity of the sixteenth century, which before their very eyes was experiencing a time of the dissolution of the old and the institution of new forms of culture and society, hear anew the Gospel so that the true church of Christ would increase within these forms. *Thus for Luther society as it obtained at the time was a given. In this society church and state, Christendom and culture, spiritual and secular were tied together by countless connections.* This was the field upon which the seed of the Gospel would sprout and bear fruit. It was a society which, in spite of everything new which was astir within it, continued to bear the essential outline of the Middle Ages. It was a society in which the differentiation of citizenship from church membership was something purely theoretical and in which it was simply inconceivable that both could actually diverge. And thus it was a society in which the secular government was accustomed to meddle in ecclesiastical matters, and by no means only because it was eager for power (though this indeed happened). In many cases it did so out of a deep sense of duty to God.

THE APPEAL TO THE TERRITORIAL LORDS

It is not surprising that Luther presupposed the existence of this society. On the contrary, it would be quite astonishing if it were otherwise. But then the problem arises of whether or not in light of the factual ecclesiastical, social, and political connections of the sixteenth century Luther's differentiation and separation of the powers (*potestas*) had to remain something purely theoretical. The significance of this question becomes clear when we consider the church visitation in electoral Saxony, which in 1527 began the establishment of the Lutheran territorial church system.

The letter to Elector John of November 22, 1526, in which Luther proposed a church and school visitation, clearly shows why the Reformer believed he had to appeal to the secular government. It is the duty of government in a time of the disillusion of the old order, when young people are in danger of being completely neglected, to lead the youth back to discipline and order. The need of people compels a concern for "schools, preachers, and pastors." But then the administration of church property must also be ordered anew. This was the task of the secular authority after the administration by the bishops had ceased: "But now that popish and spiritual coercion in Your Electoral Grace's kingdom is out, and all cloisters and convents have fallen into your hands and you are in charge of them, you also have the duty and burden to organize such things."[28]

Consequently for Luther there are governmental and administrative measures which no one else but the prince of the country can carry out. In the preface to the "Instruction to Visitors" Luther distinguishes with the same clarity found in his address "To the German Nobility" between the tasks which the ruler is required to fulfill as secular authority and others which are incumbent upon him as a Christian. Luther bids the elector not to somehow assume a form of the episcopal office—the Reformer could not have conceived of allowing this possibility—rather to appoint visitors to temporarily exercise the episcopal office of visitation of the pastors and congregations within the elector's territory since the sitting bishops had forsaken this duty.

But when Luther does this, he turns to the elector as to "the prince of the country and our certain secular authority ordained of God." But he unmistakably expresses that what he bids the elector to do is a service of Christian love and not an act of secular governmental authority. His Electoral Grace should appoint visitors and organize the visitation "out of Christian love (for you are not obliged in these matters according to secular authority)" (WA 26.197.25 [cf. *LW* 40:271]). The service which is here requested of the Christian ruler is a service which he is to render as a *Christian*. But it is precisely requested of him because *as ruler* he has the power to render it.

If in the case of necessity, every Christian is called upon to render the service of love, and the authority of his participation in the general priesthood of believers renders him capable of exercising spiritual functions, there still obtains between Christians the greatest difference of respective power to help and of the ability to make use of their spiritual rights. Indeed, there have to be differences of

---

[28] WA Br 4.133.21. Luther here calls the elector literally "highest head" [*Oberstes Haupt*], not as "supreme head of the church" (*supremem caput ecclesiae;* see the section "The Church of England" above), but as the bearer of the highest governmental authority. HS

obligation. For the measure of ecclesiastical obligation naturally rises with the measure of ability to assist the church.

This is how the Reformers understand and justify their appeal to the bearers of governmental authority. They do not confer to them particular *rights*, they rather expect of them certain *duties*. The ruler has as a Christian no other rights than does any other member of the church. However, as "chief member of the church" (*praecipuum membrum ecclesiae*) because of his secular position of power which makes him a member of the church preeminent to other Christians, a maximum of duty is laid upon him.

It was quite foreseeable that out of this maximum of duty would be derived very quickly a corresponding claim to rights. For in the sphere of law, also state-church law, rights and duties always stand in a precise relationship to each other. But Luther did not realize the legal consequences which his appeal for help to the bearer of the governmental authority would finally have. When, in the dire situation the church faced, Luther appealed to the love of a Christian brother in the person of the ruler of the land, he did not realize that this very appeal itself, if correctly understood by pious princes, could only serve to strengthen the longstanding tendency to subordinate the church to the state.

CHRISTIAN GOVERNMENT

Now no matter how much the attempt was made to distinguish the functions which the ruler exercised as secular governing authority from those in which he acted as "chief member of the church" (*praecipuum membrum ecclesiae*), in practice *the office of Christian governing authority, as an office combining both civil and ecclesiastical functions, was restored in a different form.* Luther had corrected the confused and convoluted idea of an office which was as much ecclesiastical as civil by the clear principle of the separation of both governments. But under the mask of the general priesthood of believers, it sneaked back into the church in a new form. The power of the general sociological, political, and legal development of the time was so great that Luther was able to uphold his principles only in theory, and even this became increasingly difficult.

In the preface to the "Instruction to Visitors" Luther discusses the question of what was to happen if individual "undisciplined heads" should wantonly and maliciously oppose the legitimate orders of the visitors. Here Luther is at pains to distinguish between the powers (*potestates*) even as the visitations are carried out. Such people should be excommunicated. Further measures are left to the territorial Lord:

> While His Electoral Grace is not obliged to teach and to rule in spiritual affairs, he is obliged *as temporal sovereign* to so order things that strife, rioting, and rebellion do not arise among his subjects; even as the Emperor Constantine summoned the bishops to Nicaea since he did not want to tolerate the dissension which Arius had stirred up among the Christians in the

empire, and constrained them to preserve unity in teaching and faith. (WA
26.200.28 [*LW* 40:273])[29]

Here the distinction between spiritual and temporal government is completely clear. The task of the spiritual government is "teaching" and the governance of the church, as for instance through organizing visitation teams or by
calling a synod. If the elector should allow the visitations to occur, he does so, as
is clearly stated in the passage cited above, not as secular governing authority, but
as "chief member of the church" (*praecipuum membrum ecclesiae*). In Luther's view
this is precisely the respect, and not as Roman Caesar, in which Constantine
called the first ecumenical council [A.D. 325]. But the task of secular authority is
to safeguard the public peace from "strife, rioting, and rebellion."

As much as the functions of the two governments are here clearly and dogmatically separated, so much so are they inseparably bound together in the actual situation of life in the instance under consideration. We encounter here once
again the phenomenon of Christian governing authority, whose functions simply
do not allow themselves in practice to be parceled out as those belonging to secular *authority* as such and those belonging to *Christian* bearers of this office. We
encounter once again the Christian governing authority whose essence consists in
it being *simultaneously* both Christian and governing authority. Constantine could,
in Luther's view, convene the ecumenical council because he was both Christian
and Caesar alike. He could not have done this simply as a Christian nor as Caesar.
And it is the same in the case of the electoral Saxon church visitation. The elector could carry it out because he was both elector and a member of the church.

But in Luther's view the connection between governing authority and ecclesiastical tasks goes even further in both cases. If it is in general the task of secular
authority to prevent strife and rebellion, then it is also the task of Christian governing authority to put down the strife and rebellion caused by heresy within
Christendom of its territory. For were not the most fateful and, for the state, most
dangerous "sects" those which had religious roots and were the result of a heresy
(there were several instances of this in electoral Saxony and elsewhere at the
time)? Thus Luther understood the battle of Constantine against Arianism as
both a civil and ecclesiastical necessity. The same applied to the measures which
the elector took in order to maintain Christians in "unified doctrine and faith" in
his land.

CONTRADICTIONS IN LUTHER

We have now reached the point at which Luther was not prepared to carry
through his separation and differentiation of the functions of the spiritual and
secular powers. *Here the Reformer contradicts himself.* The one who emphatically

---

[29]   The English translation of this quote is from *LW* 40. MH

maintained that the territorial lord "is not obliged according to secular governing authority" to carry out the visitation demands of him that he "as secular authority" see to it that the visitation not come to nothing because of the obstinacy of individuals. He who reminded the elector that it is not commanded of him "to teach and rule in spiritual matters" held before him the example of a Caesar who maintained Christians in "unified doctrine and faith." The same Reformer whose "great deed" it was to "give up the confused medieval concept of a spiritual-secular Reich" finally at one point did not overcome the medieval synthesis of church and state. He ascribed to the *Christian territorial lord* the duty to demand the *pure doctrine* of the Gospel in his land, to defend it against *heresy*, and to work for the *unity of the church*.

Luther was never of the opinion that the secular authority as such could know what the Gospel is or that it could even teach it. But he was always of the opinion that the Christian in governing office could and ought to know what the pure doctrine of the Gospel is and that it be his duty to protect and advance this doctrine and to oppose heresy. It is in this sense that his pleas for the Christian governing authorities of his day to take it upon themselves to reform the church are to be understood.

Thus for instance on July 20, 1525, he bids Elector John to expect the heads of the cloister at Altenburg to reform the liturgy [*Gottesdienst*] in use up to the present or, as Luther proposes, dispense with "their hitherto traditional, un-Christian conduct," which has resulted in "divine non-service" [*Gottes Undienst*]. The elector is to point them "to the Word of God and to the example of other Christian communities" (WA Br 3.545, no. 904).

Consequently, Luther expected of his territorial lord that he instruct the Altenburg canons on correct Divine Service and that he forbid them certain forms of liturgy. If this instruction cannot finally be understood as something which every Christian brother is justified in doing and, in the case of necessity, even bound to do—namely, when those called to do such things are silent—this prohibition comes from the territorial lord as secular governing authority.

But then what meaning does Luther's delineation of spiritual and secular power (*potestas*) have when he states that the elector "is not commanded to teach and rule in spiritual matters"? There is a real contradiction in the thought of the Reformer at this point. It cannot be allayed by asserting that for Luther *the confessional unanimity of the civil realm* was the self-understood presupposition for the stability of the state and thus for Luther the restoration of this unanimity was a duty of the territorial lord as secular governing authority. This is correct insofar as Luther in fact could not conceive of a state which would be governable if it tolerated numerous, contradictory forms of the public exercise of the Christian religion.

Luther was committed to the view that dissenters should not be persecuted if they were not revolutionists and did not threaten the existence of the state. The private exercise of their religion was to be guaranteed, or they at least had to be granted the possibility of emigration. And here Luther's views on compulsion and freedom of faith are different from those of the Middle Ages. But Luther could conceive of one state which encompassed several equally legitimate confessions as little as could most of his contemporaries. And this is one of the clearest effects of the medieval synthesis of church and world, state and church, in Luther's thought regarding this question. Under the effect of this idea, he treated certain measures of the territorial lord, in which we perceive an intrusion into church governance, as purely civil, administrative measures.

But even if we acknowledge his conscious intention to remain true to his principles, there remains an objective contradiction between the delineation of the powers (*potestas*) in principle and their amalgamation in practice. This contradiction is nowhere more clearly expressed than in the fact that Luther not only compromises with the actual double position of the governing authority in the state and in the church and, in spite of often loud and plaintive protests, accepts the concurrent and constantly arising amalgamation of the powers (*potestas*): even he himself constantly falls back into medieval conceptions and terminology when he ascribes tasks to the princes and gives them a position in the church quite to the contrary of what he had otherwise thought and expressed on the matter.

Thus Luther writes to Duke Henry[30] of Saxony at the beginning of July 1539: "But because His Princely Grace nevertheless is the territorial prince and protector established by God, he is therefore responsible to God to put down such gruesome, terrible, blasphemous idolatry,[31] and in the same way Duke George[32] deliberately protected the devil and condemned Christ, Duke Henry should on the contrary protect poor Christians and condemn the devil."[33] The duke should forbid the masses in the cathedral churches at Meissen, Stolpen, and Wurzen for the following reason: "For the princes, wherever they can, should quickly undo Baal and all idolatry, the same way the kings of Judah and Israel did previously, and afterwards Constantius, Theodosius, and Gratianus.[34] For princes and lords are just as bound to serve God and the Lord Christ in the way they can as anyone else."[35]

---

[30] Henry "the Pious" (1473–1541) was Duke of Albertine Saxony from 1539 until 1541. He was the brother and successor of George the Bearded; he introduced the Reformation into Albertine Saxony in 1539. RF

[31] Namely, the Mass, which was still celebrated in the cloister at Meissen. HS

[32] The brother and predecessor of Henry, who decisively opposed the Reformation from the beginning. HS
      George the Bearded (1471–1539), duke of Albertine Saxony, persecuted Lutherans, sponsored the Leipzig Debate in 1519, and banned Luther's publications (*Lutheran Cyclopedia*, 329). MH

[33] Enders, 12, 188, 22. HS

[34] Luther is probably referring to Constantius II, who ruled from 337 until 361. Theodosius I ruled from 379 until 395, and Gratianus ruled from 375 until 383. RF

[35] Enders, 12, 189, 30. HS

When we remember with what clarity Luther, in the passage noted above, rejected the claim of the Caesar to be lord protector of the church because, among other things, "the church and the faith must have a different lord protector than those who are Caesars and kings," then the appeal to the Saxon prince to be cognizant of his office as lord protector and to "protect" poor Christians is as troubling as the comparison of George and Henry to the pious kings of Israel and the ancient Christian Caesars who fought against idolatry. Here we have exactly the concept of the office of the Christian ruler which we found in the canons of the Church of England.

Is it any wonder that the Evangelical Lutheran princes of Germany now demanded the same authority in the church which the rulers in other confessions justified by holding up the example of "the pious kings of the Jews and the Christian Caesars in the ancient church"? Is it any wonder that the very spirit of the times, which everywhere pressed for church governance by the state, proved more powerful than Luther's principle of the separation of the governments? After all, the Reformer himself under the influence of the time was finally not able to overcome ideas stemming from the medieval synthesis of church and state.[36]

Luther's position on the question of the connection between state and church is such that on the one hand the Reformer emphatically advocated the principle that the powers (*potestas*) were to be strictly separated and not to be confused. But on the other hand the authority of the state in this relationship is given ever-increasing influence in the ecclesiastical sphere, and the state cannot be denied this authority. Consequently the position of the confessions on this problem is particularly important. Remember what we said above regarding the relationship of the doctrine of Luther to the doctrine of the Evangelical Lutheran Church.[37] Our church did not appropriate every thought of the Reformer and elevate it to

---

[36] J. Hashagen, *Staat und Kirche vor der Reformation* (1931), 563, comments on the inherent contradiction in Luther's position on the emerging system of church governance by territorial lords:

> Along with Karl Müller we will certainly evaluate this ground-gaining retreat movement in Luther, which so fatefully influenced the entire future of German Lutheranism to the present, in light of the powerful "advance of the Evangelical movement." But we must remember that signs of the late Middle Ages accompanied this retreat and even facilitated it. Why did Luther so completely muzzle the voice of his conscience which was otherwise so dear to him? It must have warned him time and again against granting so much intrusion of the secular authority into the ecclesiastical-religious sphere. Indeed, he had often enough publicly and widely expressed the idea that secular authority in this area should be sharply reduced. So how could he have allowed secular authority so much room in this sphere? How could he tolerate the establishment and rise of the system of church governance by territorial lord?

> Hashagen explains this especially when he states that "for Luther the background of the late Middle Ages still always projected into his own time and environment but did not overthrow it." "It always necessarily continued to exercise a certain effect on Luther, even if he himself was perhaps no longer aware of it. The terrible inner struggle which the toleration of the governance of the church by the territorial lords certainly brought him could have been lessened for him [if he had realized] the fact that it was actually nothing new, rather tied to a long and firm tradition." HS

[37] See part 2 above. HS

church doctrine. Thus every time we come upon an important statement by Luther on any dogmatically significant question, we must ask how the doctrine contained therein relates to the doctrine of the church's confessions.

THE DOCTRINE OF THE CONFESSIONS

If we take this point of view in inquiring of the confessional writings of the Evangelical Lutheran Church what their doctrine on the connection between church and state is, the results may be expressed in the following four theses:

1. The Lutheran Confessions teach the strict separation of the divinely established orders of secular authority and the spiritual office and forbid any mixing of their respective functions.

2. The Lutheran Confessions place upon Christian bearers of governmental office, in addition to all duties incumbent upon such an office, the special duties involved in the protection of the church and the insistence on the pure doctrine of the Gospel.

3. The Lutheran Confessions place particular duties upon the spiritual office [geistliche Amt] and the members of the church over against the government, which may also be expressed in the form of rights of the government over against the church.

4. Still, these rights of the government, even the Christian government, according to the Lutheran Confessions, do not include the right to church government or a part of the same.

Of these four theses we have already dealt with the first because it has to be the point of departure for our presentation. It is the principle thesis of the Lutheran doctrine of the relationship between church and state. The third, which treats of the duties of the church over against the state, will have to be the object of a special section dealing solely with it. Thus the immediate task is to explain the second and fourth theses.

DUTIES OF THE SECULAR AUTHORITY IN GENERAL

There are *duties incumbent upon all secular government on earth*, no matter of which faith or confession it may be. These include the duties of the upholding of the law and thus to be guardian and protector of the subjects of such government. This of course includes the duty of maintaining legal tolerance for the church. This duty too is independent of the faith of the bearer of the office of secular authority (thus for instance, Christians in Turkey). If the governing officials are Christians, as secular authority they have absolutely no tasks beyond those of any other government.

But these tasks are for them infinitely more serious and consequential than for such as do not know the living God. How much more seriously will an earthly king take his office if he knows that he has received that office from the one who is the King of kings and the Lord of all lords! How much more will an earthly king be cognizant of his responsibility if he knows that he carries out his office in view of the one who "will come again to judge the living and the dead" [Apostles' Creed]! And yet the content of the office is not altered. The relationship of the ruler to the church is quite different still. In Luther's view, Emperor Charles V had different duties than Sultan Suleiman II [ruled 1520–1566], in whose kingdom a church also existed.

DUTIES OF CHRISTIAN GOVERNMENT

The Apology spoke of these *particular duties incumbent upon the ruler who is at the same time a member of the church* when it asserted that the command of God demands "of all kings and princes that they should as much as possible have a hand in, salvage, and protect divine matters, that is, the Gospel of Christ and the pure divine doctrine on earth, and in the place of God protect and guard proper Christian teachers and preachers against an incorrect use of power" (Ap XXI 44).[38]

The Treatise on the Power and Primacy of the Pope says the same thing of kings and princes, whom it describes as the "chief members of the church": "Especially does it behoove the chief members of the church, the kings and the princes, to have regard for the interests of the church and to see to it that errors are removed and consciences are healed. God expressly exhorts kings, 'Now therefore, O kings, be wise; be warned, O rulers of the earth' (Ps. 2:10). For the first care of kings should be to advance the glory of God."[39] ("Inprimis autem oportet praecipua membra ecclesiae, reges et principes, consulere ecclesiae et curare, ut errores tollantur et principes, consulere ecclesiae, sicut Deus nominatim reges hortatur: 'et nunc, reges, intelligite, erudimini, qui iudicatis terram.' Prima enim cura regum esse debet, ut ornent gloriam Dei," Treatise, 54.)

The view of the duties of the Christian governing authority which Melanchthon expressed in this passage is essentially the same as that which we found in Luther's call to the Christian territorial lords to organize the visitation and to carry out the Reformation.[40] The territorial lord is to be concerned that in his land no idolatry is advocated, no heresy spread, rather that the pure Gospel is

---

[38] The [German] text is the very free translation of J. Jonas. The original Latin states: "ut res divinas, hoc est, evangelium Christi, in terris conservari et propagari curent, et tamquam vicarii Dei vitam et salutem innocentum defendant" ["that they be concerned that divine matters, that is, the Gospel of Christ, be conserved and propagated on earth, and as vicars of God, defend the life and well-being of the innocent"]. HS

[39] The English translation is from Tappert, BC, 328. MH

[40] See our discussion of Luther above. Thus we find Luther's subscription next to those of Jonas, Bugenhagen, Amsdorf, and Melanchthon under "Three Concerns of the Theologians at Wittenberg regarding Self-Defense," which among other things says:

> In this case we conclude that every prince is in duty bound, consequently and especially, to protect and maintain Christian and correct Divine Service against all illegitimate power . . . . Yes, this protection is demanded of the princes in a much greater and higher manner, as the Scriptures often advise and command secular regents, that they should protect correct preachers and teachers. (EA 64.271) HS

preached. And this is what Luther demands in the preface to the Small Catechism when he advises that the prince expel from the land "such rude people" who will not learn the catechism.[41]

Thus the confessions place upon Christian governing authority a *maximum of duties* over against the church. These go above and beyond those which every governing authority as such is to fulfill. It is self-understood that these duties are incumbent only on the *Christian governing authority*. Melanchthon bases them as much on the divine command directed to the kings and princes of the OT as upon the reference to princes as the "chief members of the church" (*praecipua membra ecclesiae* [Treatise, 54]).

Properly speaking, these are two different bases. And indeed, the more the divine command to the kings or the duty to love arising out of the fact that the prince belongs to the church is applicable, the more those duties can be understood as duties of the Christian *governing authority*, or as duties of the Christian invested with an office of government. In the first case, the Christian character of the governing authority appears to be the norm. The governing authority as such then is to be what God demanded of it in the commands of the OT to the kings and princes: guardian of the law, and indeed, the whole law; "guardian of both tables of the Law" (*custos utriusque tabulae legis*), as Melanchthon put it. This is how the author of the Apology and the Treatise later provided a basis for the duties of the governing authority: "The magistrate is the guardian of both tables of the Law . . . but it is clear that idolatry and blasphemy are forbidden by the First and Second Commandments. Therefore, it is necessary that the magistrate remove and be concerned about external idolatry and blasphemy so that pious doctrine and pious *cultus* be advanced." ("Magistratus est custos primae et secundae tabulae legis . . . manifestum est autem in primo et secundo praecepto prohiberi idololatriam et blasphemias: ergo necesse est, magistratum externam idololatriam et blasphemias tollere et curare, ut pia doctrina et pii cultus proponantur.")[42]

The duties of the governing authority over against the church resulted from its character as governing authority because it was the norm that the governing authority was Christian. In the case that this were not true, it could only be "guardian of the Second Table" (*custos secundae tabulae*). This theory, which Melanchthon later ever more emphatically advocated, led to the idea of a Christian state. It laid the groundwork for the modern state-church system which

---

[41] *BS*, 503, line 43 [*Triglotta*, 534; Tappert, *BC*, 339, § 12]. HS

[42] *Corpus Reformatorum*, 16:87. Note similar statements on pp. 95 ff., and in III, 467. Compare John Fredrick II's [1529–1595] (Weimarer) *Ordnung und summarischer prozess des fürstlichen consistorii* of 1561: "When we then, as the territorial prince, because of the princely office placed upon us by the demand of God Almighty, and because of commanded concern and protection [*custodie*] which has to do with both tables of the Law, the first as much as the second, are willing and prepared . . . to protect . . . all those matters encountered in the divine Word" (E. Sehling, *Die evangelischen Kirchenordnungen des 16. Jahrhunderts*, I, 1 [1902], 230). HS

began in the age of absolutism insofar as it finally derived the ecclesiastical functions of the Christian governing authority out of the nature of governing authority.

But if we proceed from the idea of the prince as the "chief member of the church" (*membrum praecipuum ecclesiae*), that governing authority is the norm which is simply secular authority and therefore is only the guardian of the Second Table. As such, governing authority has the task of upholding civil righteousness (*iustia civilis*) and the public peace of the country. It is the governing authority of which Articles XVI and XXVIII of the Augustana speak, the governing authority which Luther had in view when he ever and again so very emphatically taught the necessity of the separation of the governments [*Regimente*].

Only if the bearer of this governmental office is at the same time a member of the church does he as "chief member" (*praecipuum membrum ecclesiae*) possess new tasks. Only then may he also be guardian of the First Table and be concerned to do away with idolatry and heresy and advance the pure preaching of the Gospel. In the first instance, the duties of the governing authority are demands which the church poses to the state. In the second instance, they are demands which the church makes of one of its members.

NO CHURCH GOVERNMENT BY THE SECULAR AUTHORITY

Both of these possible ways of understanding the nature and particular tasks of the Christian governing authority are found side by side, undeveloped in our confessions. These expressions can be understood more in the sense of Luther's call for help to the Christian territorial lords or more as a stop on the way to Melanchthon's later doctrine of the Christian state.[43] We can find in the confessions the idea that the spiritual and the secular powers are to be separated and the idea that both are divine orders and therefore overlap each other.

But however the statements of the confessions were *later* understood, whatever has been read out of them, there is still one thing no one has ever found in them. They contain neither directly nor indirectly, neither as express doctrine nor as a veiled suggestion, the view that the secular authority, even if it should be

---

[43] In order to avoid any possible misunderstanding, let it be firmly stated here that neither Luther nor the Lutheran Confessions know anything of a "Christian state." Such would be a state which as state confesses Christianity and sees in Christendom one of its fundamental elements, so that it necessarily is of the *essence* of its governing authority that it be Christian. In distinction from the theocratic view of Zwingli, who bound the authority of the governing authority to its Christian faith and consented to the overthrow of the governing authority in the event that it was no longer obedient to the commands of Christ,* the Lutheran Confessions expressly teach that the confession of faith does not change the character of governing authority as such: "The Gospel does not introduce any new laws about the civil estate, but commands us to obey the existing laws, whether they are formulated by heathen or by others" ("Nec fert evangelium novas leges de statu civili, sed praecipit, ut praesentibus legibus obtemperemus, sive ab ethnicis sive ab aliis conditae sint," Ap XVI 3 [55]; the English translation is from Tappert, *BC*, 222–23). *[In support of his statement about Zwingli, Sasse cited this:] "But if it is untrue or exceed the bounds of Christ, it may be overthrown with [the help of] God" (*Schlussreden*, 42, in Müller, *Bekenntnisschriften*, 5, 4). HS

Christian and take its duties ever so seriously, possesses a right to exercise governance in the church or even only a part of the same. Whatever rights the secular
government and, in particular, a governmental authority whose bearers are
Christian may have—we will have to address these rights shortly—it does not
have the right to govern the church. And this includes even the privilege to
administer the external affairs of the church. This assertion was our fourth in the
series of theses in which we summarized the doctrine of the confessions on the
relationship between church and secular authority. Since we have raised this point
at the conclusion of this section, we return to our starting point.

*It is generally to be granted that the Lutheran Confessions never directly speak of
church governance by the territorial lord or of Christian governing authority in general.*
But what does this silence mean? Was not the governance of the church by the
territorial lord so self-evident when Melanchthon wrote the Augustana, the
Apology, and the Treatise that there was no need to justify it more fully? Did it
not already obtain when the Evangelical estates of the empire—and thus secular
governing authorities—presented the Augustana to the emperor? Was it not the
necessary consequence of the duties which in the confessions were expected of the
territorial lord as the "chief member of the church" (*praecipuum membrum ecclesiae*)? And thus had not many a territorial lord already begun to fulfill this duty?

To be sure, the beginnings of the governance of the church by territorial lord
had existed since the recess of the Imperial Diet at Speyer of 1526 and since the
first visitation in the realm of the emerging Evangelical Lutheran Church. But the
full authority which the imperial law of 1526 gave to the imperial estates in
respect to the church was only considered something temporary, until the council should render final judgment. And Luther treated the involvement of the territorial lord as a temporary measure in an emergency and even later had always
designated the elector only "emergency bishop,"[44] whose office should expire
after the ecclesiastical emergency had passed.

Thus it lies completely outside the purview of our confessions that with the
Reformation a new form of church constitution had taken the place of that which
had hitherto obtained, the mark of which was the participation of the secular
authority in the governance of the church. Just as our fathers did not found a new
church but only desired to reform the existing one, neither did they devise a new
constitution for the church. They rather acknowledged as good human order the
constitution as it had historically existed, and this included the Catholic episcopal
system [*Bischofsverfassung*]. They only demanded that the degenerate and completely secularized spiritual government be transformed back into a genuine
church government, in accord with Evangelical doctrine. To this end—and this
the confessions do state—the Christian princes were to assist.

---

[44] For example: "Our only emergency bishop [*Notbischoff*], because no bishop will otherwise assist us"
(March 25, 1539, to the visitors of Saxony, EA 55.223) [St. Louis ed. XXI b, 2318, no. 2520]. HS

The confessions also state that certain secular functions of governance which up to that time had been exercised by the bishops, but which properly belong in the realm of the secular authorities (e.g., laws regarding marriage), should return to the territorial lords (Treatise, 77–78). But the confessions never in the slightest way indicate that the territorial lords become bishops or, as the followers of the bishops, should take in hand the governance of the church.

If this were the view of our symbolical books, it would have to be expressed somewhere in them. We would at least expect that the estates of the empire which presented the Augustana to the emperor would have somehow expressed their contingent claims to governance of the church. But this was not the case. They presented "a confession of our pastors' and preachers' teaching and of our own faith, setting forth how and in what manner, on the basis of the Holy Scriptures, these things are preached, taught, communicated, and embraced in our lands, principalities, dominions, cites, and territories."[45]

To be sure, these princes speak as spokesmen of their churches, but not as bishops. They do not say: "Thus we teach!" They say: "Our churches teach with great unanimity" (*ecclesiae magno consensu apud nos docent*, AC I 1). But even the confessions themselves could not silence it if according to Evangelical Lutheran doctrine the secular government as such, or because it is of the Christian faith, had a right to governance of the church or a part of the same. Anyone who has seriously considered the well-thought-out and well-balanced statements of Augustana XVI and XXVIII regarding the governing authority, together with the argumentation of the Apology, and considered the effects which this first confessional presentation of the doctrine of governing authority proceeded to have on all of sixteenth-century Christianity cannot be satisfied with the response that at that time it was not believed necessary to state something regarding the right of the governing authority in the area of church governance.

Why do the other confessions speak of this? The Anglican Confession established the right of the English king as the highest ruler of the church of his land.[46] In the same way, where the Reformed confessions treat the matter, they strongly assert the participation of the secular authority in the governance of the church.[47] It is a methodological error to believe that the authors of the Lutheran Confessions, either because of thoughtlessness or because it was something self-

---

[45]   Preface to the AC, 8 [the English translation is from Tappert, *BC*, 25]. HS

[46]   See the section "The Church of England" above. HS

[47]   For example, Thesis 36 of the Zwinglian *Epilogue* [*Schlussreden*] (1523): "Alles so der geistlich (genennt) stat, im zugehören rechtes und rechtes schirm halb fürgibt, gehört dem weltlichen zu, ob sye christen sein wöllend" (Müller, *Bekenntnisschriften*, 4, 36). Thus the church governance by the Zürich [City] Council is explained. HS

An English translation reads as follows: "Everything that the so-called spiritual estate claims by right or for the protection of its rights belongs properly to the secular authorities, if they have a mind to be Christians" ("The Sixty-Seven Articles of Ulrich Zwingli [1523]," *Confessions and Catechisms of the Reformation* [ed. Mark A. Noll; Grand Rapids: Baker, 1991], 43). RF

evident for them, did not say something about the right of the governing authority to govern the church. The only possible explanation for this is the admission
that they knew nothing of such a right. However great the concessions were
which Luther and the Confessions of the Evangelical Lutheran Church made to
the idea of the synthesis of state and church inherited from the Middle Ages, as
much as they may have on occasion endangered the principle of the separation of
the governments in the question of whether governance of the church can belong
to the secular authority, they remained inviolably true to the basic principle: "The
ecclesiastical and civil powers are not to be commingled" ("Non igitur commiscendae sunt potestates ecclesiastica et civilis," AC XXVIII 12).

5. The Lutheran Doctrine of Church Government and the Relationship of Church Governance and Secular Authority

If, according to the doctrine of the Lutheran Church, the governance of the
church is not granted to the secular authority, and if our confessions do not give
any indication of the theories advanced later by Melanchthon and others that at
least a participation in governance of the church is a right of the Christian governing authority, then the following questions arise: *To whom then does the governance of the church belong according to the doctrine of our church?* Which are the *rights
of the secular authority* over against the church, and what is the positive relationship between these two "governments" which are not to be mingled?

The Freedom of the Lutheran Church on the Question of Church Constitution

The answer which our confessions give to these questions, as we might have
expected, is not one that involves a developed theory of *church organization* or constitution [*Kirchenverfassung*]. Nor are there legally binding directions regarding
how the church shall be ordered in individual circumstances. Unlike the other
confessional churches of Christianity, Catholic as much as Protestant, the
Evangelical Lutheran Church knows nothing of a definite form of church constitution ordered by Jesus Christ himself. For the other confessions, a definite constitution is of the essence of the church, be it the episcopal constitution of the
ancient church or the constitution of the Roman Papal Church, the Presbyterian
or the Congregationalist-independent constitutions, or that of the Irvingites[48]

---

[48] Edward Irving (1792–1834), a Church of Scotland pastor, was charged with heresy in the doctrine of the
Trinity. He accepted Pentecostal phenomena, especially speaking in tongues. He was charged with heresy
regarding the sinlessness of Christ and was deposed from the ranks of the clergy in 1833 by the presbytery of Annan, Scotland. His followers, known as Irvingites, formed the Catholic Apostolic Church
(*Lutheran Cyclopedia*, 419–20). MH

with the renewal of the office of the apostle. Indeed, from a confessional stand-point it is maintained that this or that particular ordering of the church must be present if the church is to be the true church of Christ, if it is to be identical with the church of the NT. And they all maintain, consequently, that the church would be disobedient to the Word of God and necessarily apostatize or even cease completely to be church if it were not to preserve the constitution legally imposed upon it by divine mandate.

Lutheranism could never confess such a view. On the contrary, Lutheran theology clearly acknowledged that none of the forms of constituting the church, each allegedly sanctioned by divine institution—neither the ancient office of bishop with apostolic succession nor the honorable institutions of the presbytery and synod, neither the Congregationalist ideas of the church of God gathered about the Holy Scriptures, awaiting the working of the Spirit, nor any other visible form of the church—could accomplish what it was thought to insure, namely, that it be a bulwark against the church sliding into heresy. The witness of church history shows again and again that precisely those churches—and certainly not only the Catholic Church—have fallen into the most pernicious heresies which had specifically asserted that the church must have a particular form of constitution in order to be identical with the church of the NT and to preserve the doctrine of the apostles.

The Lutheran Church, furthermore, could never grant that the NT contains legal prescriptions for the form the church's constitution must take. Lutheranism viewed it as a false understanding of the NT when attempts were made to systematize the more or less explicit beginnings and fragments of primitive Christian church organization contained in it, and to treat this system according to the model of OT Law as a holy codex of canon law with divine commands for the *cultus* and ordering of the church as the New Israel.

There never was such a system. At the beginning of the history of the church there was no unified way of constituting the church, rather a multiplicity of forms of constitution. Thus sentences such as that which we find in Calvin's *Confessio Gallicana* would be inconceivable in the Lutheran Confessions: "Concerning the true church, we thus believe that it must be governed according to the legally mandated ordinance of our Lord Jesus Christ, that namely there be pastors, elders, and deacons, that the purity of doctrine be guarded, the wicked be suppressed and removed and the poor and troubled be assisted in their need, and the assemblies be held."[49] "We believe that all true pastors . . . have the same status and authority under one single head, one single Lord and only highest Bishop, Jesus Christ."[50] "We believe that none has the right to arbitrarily assume the gov-

---

[49] Article 29. German cited according to the official text of Ernst Mengin, *Das Recht der französisch-reformierten Kirche in Preussen, Urkundliche Denkschrift* (Berlin, 1929), 56. HS

[50] Article 30. HS

ernance of the church, rather that this must happen by election, so far as it is possible and God allows it."[51]

We have cited these theses which have at least partial validity[52] also in the Reformed Church of Germany and are in some quarters very highly regarded[53] because we see in this opposing view the uniqueness of the Lutheran doctrine of the constitution of the church. Our church maintains that it is a false understanding of the NT when there is found in the account of the appointment of the seven (Acts 6:1 f.) or in the other passages of the NT which speak of the office of deacon (e.g., 1 Tim 3:8 ff.) a "legally mandated ordinance of our Lord Jesus Christ," according to which there must be deacons in the church.

Neither may a law regarding the equality of rights of pastors nor regarding election as the normal procedure for the calling of a person into an office of the church be read out of the NT. Nor can such a law be proclaimed as an article of faith. Were it to confess such views, our church would have to surrender its entire understanding of the Holy Scriptures and their concept of the faith and what constitutes an article of faith.

For the Reformed Church the doctrine of the correct constitution of the church is an article of faith. And as E. Mengin said, a discussion regarding the correctness or applicability of this doctrine is as impossible "as a discussion regarding the dogma of the Trinity or the doctrine of the Lord's Supper or the Sacraments might be for any other Christian."[54] For Lutheranism, however, the question of the constitution of the church is always an open question. Because the Lutheran doctrine of the church knows nothing of a definite ordering of the church which Christ has mandated and therefore must be "holy and inviolable,"[55] because the constitution is not a mark of the church (*notae ecclesiae*), because the forms of constituting the church are much more of the *bene esse* ["(mere) well-being"] and not the *esse* ["very essence"] of the church and therefore must be considered fundamentally changeable, our church possesses a freedom over against the question of constitution which is foreign to the other confessions.

MISUNDERSTANDING OF THIS FREEDOM

This freedom of the Lutheran Church in the question of constitution has always been subject to the greatest misunderstanding. To explain this freedom as a deficiency (perhaps inherent in the character of the German people) of the German Reformer regarding organizational adroitness and a sense for institutions is to view it falsely. However the deficient capacity of the German people for the

---

[51] Article 31. HS

[52] See Mengin, *Das Recht der französisch-reformierten Kirche*, 4ff. HS

[53] See Bourdriot, *Ref. Kirchenzeitung* (1935), no. 21, p. 122. HS

[54] Mengin, *Das Recht der französisch-reformierten Kirche*, 33. HS

[55] [Calvin,] *Confessio Gallicana*, 25. HS

establishment of fixed forms of societal life may have worked itself out in the history of German Lutheranism, this freedom cannot be explained on this basis. And a glance at the Lutheran churches outside of Germany demonstrates this.

The principle that the constitution of the church is not of its essence is understood in a completely false manner also when it is asserted that our confession knows only an invisible church. The church of which it speaks, the church "in which the Gospel is purely taught and the Sacraments rightly administered" (*in qua evangelium pure docetur et recte administrantur sacramenta* [AC VII 1]) is a reality in this world. The proclamation of the Gospel in the sermon and in the absolution, its consummation in Baptism and the celebration of the Holy Supper are dealings which take place within the empirical congregation [*Gemeinde*].

The great error which underlies that false view and which is finally the most disastrous misunderstanding encountered by the Lutheran doctrine of church and which it continues to encounter time and again today is the opinion that Lutheranism has in general no interest in the question of the ordering of the church and leaves the formation of church constitution to the contingencies of historical development. Indeed, according to this misunderstanding, according to Lutheran doctrine the constitution of the church is in general a "secular thing," a question of law. And thus it is a matter of secular government as the guardian of the law, as are all legal questions.

In this sense, a political writer of our day can declare:

> *The ordering and law of the church* come under the domain of the state. The church must be able to gather its members in the name of Jesus Christ undisturbed, so that the Gospel is rightly preached and the Sacraments correctly presented to them. How this happens, in which ordering and under which law, is already an earthly concern. If the state allows the church to manage its own affairs, it does so for practical reasons. The church can demand nothing in these matters.[56]

This view is so popular in our day because it claims to be a correct interpretation of the statements of the Lutheran Church regarding its own essence.

FALSE INTERPRETATION OF THE SEPARATION OF POWERS

The great canon law teacher Rudolf Sohm once proposed the thesis *that church law is always in contradiction with the essence of the church.*[57] For it is incon-

---

[56] W. Stapel, *Die Kirche Christi und der Staat Hitlers* (1933), 65; emphases in original. HS

Wilhelm Stapel was a journalist of great influence in drawing the ties between God and *Volk*. " 'The German Volk,' he wrote in 1922 . . . 'is not an idea of humanity but an idea of God's.' This, in a sentence, was the new recognition and the content of the starting point of political theology" (Klaus Scholder, *The Churches and the Third Reich* [London: SCM Press, 1987], 1:104; cf. also 1:420). Stapel's book *Die Kirche Christi und der Staat Hitlers* went through four impressions with a total print number of twelve thousand copies. RF

[57] Rudolf Sohm, *Kirchenrecht* (1892), 1:1. HS

ceivable that the kingdom of God should bear human forms of constitution, that the body of Christ be subject to human (legal) rule.[58] Sohm maintained that one of Luther's greatest discoveries was that he renewed the "conviction of earliest Christianity" that "the church of Christ did not intend to be a church of law [*Kirchenrecht*]."[59] Thus Sohm understood the Lutheran separation of the "governments" in such a way that finally the *essential* functions of the spiritual office consist only of the preaching of the Gospel and the administration of the Sacraments. Everything in the sphere of the legal functions of the church, consequently everything which we commonly call governance and administration of the church as a legal corporation is secular business foreign to the essence of the church. As such, Sohm believed, these functions do not belong to the spiritual office.

The great and profoundly pious law professor was personally much too churchly a man to draw the consequences of his theory that the state should govern the church.[60] But a theology which dreams of a "Christian world" and which learned from an earlier generation that it is the task of the church to merge into the state does come to this conclusion. Thus we read in the writings of a theological student of Sohm the following interpretation of the Lutheran doctrine of the separation of the spiritual and the secular powers:

> The distinction lies in the means: the preaching office works though Word and Sacrament, the governing authority through compulsion and law. And they have separate spheres: one works on souls, the other on bodies. But all external dealings [*actiones externae*] of religion also fall into the corporal realm, indeed its entire manner of appearance, its societal life, its form. *This all is the subject of secular governing authority.*[61]

Rudolph Sohm (1841–1917), jurist and church historian, was professor of German and canon law at Leipzig from 1887. "He developed the view that, while the Church was wholly spiritual, law was wholly secular; hence the development of canon law . . . was an abandonment of the primitive ideal of the Church" (*ODCC*, 1514–15; see also *Lutheran Cyclopedia*, 726; *New Schaff-Herzog*, 10:496). MH

[58] Sohm, *Kirchenrecht*, 1:2. HS

[59] Sohm, *Kirchenrecht*, 1:460 ff. HS

[60] Sohm was of the opinion that the Evangelical Lutheran Church—like the early church, according to his theory—must have the power of faith to exist without legal form. But the "reformational men of the second rank" were not able to do this and thus repeated the fall into sin of the post-apostolic age:

> The church as such has only the Word. According to the Lutheran Confession, *all* coercive power and with it *all* legal power belongs *only* to the governing authority. *If* the church *intends* to be legal and compulsory, then it *must* be governed by the *secular governing authority*. . . . *If* in the church of Christ there is to be legal ordering and legal government, then according to Lutheran principles, the church governance of *the territorial lords must* be established. (Sohm, *Kirchenrecht*, 1:634)

For his view Sohm calls upon Otto Meier, who in his document *Die Grundlagen des lutherischen Kirchenregiments* (Rostock, 1864) likewise based church governance by the territorial lord on the idea that compulsion and law are according to Lutheran doctrine foreign to the essence of the church. HS

[61] Erich Foerster, *Die Entstehung der Preussischen Landeskirche* (1905) 1:11 (emphasis added). HS

CHURCH AND THE LEGAL ORDER

Here we cannot enter into a detailed critique of Sohm's theory of canon law. It has recently often been the subject of a penetrating examination.[62] Many of Sohm's dogmatic views—his idea of Christendom, church, and law, as much as the theories which encompass and intertwine these concepts—as well as his historical assertions regarding early Christianity and the Reformation have been shown to be either untenable or in need of correction. Here it will suffice to point out the following. If the thesis is valid that ecclesiastical law stands in contradiction to the essence of the church, then it must be granted that the church has always lived in contradiction with its own essence. *For the church has never existed without legal order* [*Rechtsordnung*].

Sohm has failed in his attempt to demonstrate that the church of primitive Christendom was a church in which there was not yet a legal order and [in which there was] only a communal life ruled by the free rein of the Spirit and brotherly love. His picture of the primitive church (viewed in the perspective of intellectual history) is just one in a long line of idealistic views of the church which have been read into the NT.

The church did not order itself legally as the result of a fall into sin. Nor did such a fall separate the NT age from early Catholicism. This legal ordering did not arise out of the "weak faith of a bygone Christian age." It is rather as old as the church itself. Insofar as the church, whatever it may otherwise be, is also a fellowship of people, it can certainly not exist without law valid within it and for it. *As a fellowship of people* living among the other human fellowships and tied together with these by countless connections, *it possesses a law* which is established with its existence, that is, with its very institution. This law is delimited by the law of other communal aspects of life, for instance, by the law of the state.

But it is not bestowed upon the church by the state. For it is indeed a great error to believe that all law proceeds from the state. During the great persecutions, the Roman Empire [*Imperium Romanum*] spoke its "You are not allowed to exist" (*Non licet esse vos*) to the church. And this was done by means of imperial law, formally and correctly issued. But by so doing, the state encroached on the law of the church. And this law it had not legislated and was not capable of eliminating.

It is also a great error to think that law must essentially be accompanied by compulsion and that there can only be law where there is also the power to carry out the claims of the law. When the church exists as a fellowship of people in legal connection to other human associations, it too is a legal fellowship. For in its midst is valid law so that its members, however else they may be bound together, are also bound together by legal connections with each other.

---

[62] See Günther Holstein, *Die Grundlagen des evangelischen Kirchenrechts* (1928), and the discussion which resulted from this book. HS

This cannot be otherwise insofar as the church is a fellowship of people—and, indeed, of sinful people—and not a fellowship of angels or saints. For all earthly fellowships, even for instance those of marriage and family, whatever else they may be, are also legal fellowships as long as we humans are sinners and stand under the Law of God. A fellowship which would be only a fellowship of love does not exist in this world.

Thus, since the days of the primitive congregations of Jerusalem, a legal order has existed in the church. The outpouring of the Holy Spirit on the day of Pentecost resulted in three thousand coming into the church. And this had legal consequences, just as every Baptism had, among other consequences those which were legal. *Therefore ecclesiastical law belongs*—we direct this assertion against the theories of Sohm and his students—*to the essence of the church of God as a fellowship of sinful people in this world.*

REFORMATION AND CANON LAW

We believe there is sufficient reason for making this assertion. Indeed, we must make it with particular emphasis in view of the great revolution which the *Lutheran Reformation* meant for the history of the church and canon law. Even if Sohm's understanding of the primitive church as a church in which there were indeed certain external ecclesiastical forms, but not yet legal forms, is not justified, if in fact the NT itself bears witness that already in the time of the apostles legal forms and legal claims existed, Sohm's interpretation of the Reformation could still be correct. In view of the nullifying judgment which Luther—especially in the early years of the Reformation, but later too—had rendered not only on existing canonical law, but also on spiritual law in general, it is quite understandable that Sohm believes that on December 10, 1520, Luther burned not only the currently applicable canonic law but also ecclesiastical law in general.

"Did Luther perhaps desire a different, improved spiritual law book, a different, better canon law? Absolutely not! He desired the complete nullification of applicable canon law from the first letter to the last. And he wanted nothing else put in its place. . . . Only when no 'Roman law' and consequently no canon law existed any longer would Christianity 'be well.' "[63] If we are to see in these thoughts expressed by Luther himself an essential component of his Reformation understanding of faith, then we cannot spare him the accusation that he himself, at a crucial point, surrendered the Reformation. And Luther is the guilty party if all is not "well" in Christianity according to his own measure.

We may be able to harmonize his readiness to maintain the existing canonical constitution—indeed, not as a binding legal order, but as a good human order freely to be accepted—with his fundamental rejection of the canonical law. We may find no contradiction in the fact that he burned the canonical law in 1520 and

---

[63] Sohm, *Kirchenrecht*, 1:462–63. HS

yet in 1542 borrowed directions from it for the installation of a bishop. Still, the fact remains *that Luther not only tolerated the establishment of a new ecclesiastical legal order, he himself instigated it with the visitation of 1527.*

As the result of a new understanding of the Gospel, the Lutheran Reformation issued a powerful, vehement, and conclusive protest against the false canon law of the Papal Church. But this in no way meant the abandonment of ecclesiastical law altogether. The dissolution of ecclesiastical law would have meant the dissolution of the church as an earthly fellowship of people! *The Lutheran Reformation no more set aside ecclesiastical law than it did dogma.*[64] It only redefined and returned it to its scriptural sense.

POSITIVE DOCTRINE OF THE CONSTITUTION OF THE CHURCH

What our *confessions* teach on the question of the *constitution of the church* can only be understood with the presupposition that the Lutheran Reformation did not do away with ecclesiastical law or the church as a legal institution. The freedom of outer form in the area of church constitution, of which we have spoken above, can certainly not be explained by a devaluation of order in the church. The Lutheran Church too knows what role questions of church order play in the NT. It knows that the oldest church orders, as we possess them in the letters of Paul, originated before the gospels obtained their final form.

Just how seriously our Reformers took what the NT said regarding the ordering of the church is demonstrated by the vast number of old Lutheran church orders. And these orders are the best defense against the assertion that Lutheranism in its zeal for dogmatic questions forgot the tasks of church formation. It is clear that in view of the false canon law of the Papal Church, which had nearly destroyed the church of Christ, the theologians of the emerging Lutheran Church had one intention. They had to keep from again crowning human thoughts, desires, and claims with the halo of divine Law. They had to clearly distinguish in the church between that which is the unchangeable expression of divine will and that which is established by men and therefore a changeable ordinance.

This fundamental distinction is carried out in our confessions with complete clarity. They acknowledge on the basis of Holy Scripture the "ministry of teaching the Gospel and administering the Sacraments" (*ministerium docendi evangelii et porrigendi sacramenta*) as *divine institutions*, completely independent of the will and establishment of men, and which are of the essence of the church [AC V]. This *ministerium* is not to be confused with the persons who occupy it. It is an office, a service (*diakonia*), which is to be carried out in the world because it is the will of God. This office exists "not from men nor through men" (Gal 1:1), but only "by

---

[64] Sohm's thesis is reminiscent of the thesis which von Harnack posed a few years earlier regarding the dissolution of dogma by the Reformation. Sohm's thesis is an intellectual-historical parallel to Harnack's theory of dogma. HS

the will of God" (1 Cor 1:1). Men could never have thought it up. It is a divine
order, a divine institution in the strict sense just as are the offices of the father and
secular governing authority.

But unlike these offices rooted in the will of God the Creator and Preserver,
it is rooted in the will of God the Redeemer. It entered earthly history through
the institution of Jesus Christ: "As the Father has sent me, so I send you" [John
20:21]. The sending of the Son, as it were, finds its continuation in the *ministerium ecclesiasticum* ["ecclesiastical ministry, spiritual office"]. For he himself, the
crucified and risen Lord, is really and personally present in the proclamation of
the Gospel which occurs through this office and in the Sacraments administered
by this office.

Thus this office is a gracious gift of God. It is a gift of one who in this office
wills that his Gospel be preached to the ends of the earth and until the end of
time. Article V of the Augustana which treats *De ministerio ecclesiastico* and immediately follows the article of justification is to be understood accordingly: "To
obtain such faith—that is, saving faith in Jesus Christ—God has established the
preaching office . . ."[65] Yet let it be noted that this did not mean the establishment
of an office separated from the congregation, a clergy standing over the laity.
Certainly "properly called" pastors are the bearers of this office. But it is equally
certain that this office—even as a duty to proclaim the Gospel—is also there
where the ordinary pastoral office, for whatever reason, is not yet or no longer
present.

Thus the presence of this office is of the essence of the church. For church
can only be present where the proclamation of the pure Gospel and the administration of the Sacraments in accordance with their institution is carried out [AC
VII 1]. Therefore it is God's will that the spiritual office be present. On the other
hand, the *forms* in which it is organized are not prescribed by divine command,
according to Lutheran church doctrine. It can be organized as the pastoral office
alone, or it can appear in a number of forms—perhaps as the office of parish pastor, as the office of bishop or archbishop.

And likewise, the congregation—be it the local congregation [*Gemeinde*] or
the congregation of an entire country—which as the "assembly of all believers"[66]
that has arisen from the proclamation of the Word and the administration of the
Sacraments and that consequently as a whole bears the ecclesiastical office may be
organized in entirely various ways. The church must have legal forms. But there
is no law regarding such forms in the Holy Scriptures. All legal forms of the
church are rather among the "human traditions" or the "rites and ceremonies
established by men" of which Article VII of the Augustana teaches. Thus agree-

---

[65]   The text of Schwabach Article VII says expressly "the preaching office or oral word" (*BS*, 59, line 4). HS

[66]   *Congregatio sanctorum*, the congregation of sinners justified by faith, as the expression of AC VII is to be
        understood. HS

ment therein is not *necessary* for the true unity of the church. And Article XV states that these forms should be maintained "if they can be maintained without sin and serve peace and good order in the church."

DIVINE AND HUMAN LAW IN THE CHURCH

Thus our confession strictly distinguishes between that in the church which is of divine law (*de iure divino*) and that which is of human law (*de iure humano*). But practically all external legal forms of the church, of the congregation and the office belong in the sphere of human law. Does not then this differentiation necessarily lead to the consequence that all external organization of the church is left to arbitrary human action? Must it be surrendered to anyone who usurps power in the church, and must not every existing form of church constitution be acknowledged or tolerated?

The great freedom which Lutheranism possesses in all questions of the external formation of the church has been misused. It has often meant that the question of correct human law has not been taken seriously enough. It has even been declared that it is quite immaterial how the church is constituted. But our confessions do not intend to make the external orders of the church indifferent. Friedrich Brunstäd[67] correctly takes exception to this point: "If legislation [*Rechtssatzung*] is no creedal truth, nor creedal truth a matter of legislation, it still does not mean that they should have nothing to do with each other."[68]

Whether or not candles burn on the altars of Lutheran churches is indifferent. But because of this, the command of the Reformed King Frederick William I to do away with altar candles is not yet binding ecclesiastical law. It is indifferent whether or not there are bishops in Pomerania or East Prussia. But because this is so, the court preachers decorated with the titles of bishop and archbishop by Frederick William III are not yet legal Christian bishops.

It is not true that the only concern is that the Gospel be preached and the Sacraments be dispensed but that it is indifferent how this happens. According to Article XIV of the Augustana, it matters greatly who exercises the preaching office, namely, whether the person in question is legitimately called (*rite vocatus*) according to correct ecclesiastical order. Luther also knew that the call (*vocatio*) causes the devil a great deal of woe.[69] Accordingly, he was convinced that bearers of the office who did not possess their office through an orderly call were quite pleasing to the devil. Therefore, the defenders of the view that the external legal orders of the church do not matter if only the Gospel is preached cannot call upon

---

[67] Friedrich Brunstäd (1883–1944) was a professor of philosophy at Erlangen and a systematic theologian at Rostock. He wrote *Theologie der lutherischen Bekenntnisschriften* (*Lutheran Cyclopedia*, 114). MH

[68] Friedrich Brunstäd, *Die Kirche und ihr Recht* (1935), 22. Regarding what follows we refer the reader to this recently published document. HS

[69] WA TR 1, no. 90. HS

the confessions for support. Our confessions, in order to oppose the wanton actions of the Papal Church and its false canon law, do sharply distinguish between divine and human law in the church.

But this does not mean that there need be no distinction made between legitimate human law and illicit human law. Nor does it mean that our church despises that *law which serves for peace and good order in the church*. The Lutheran Church once declared in its confessions its readiness to "help maintain old church ordering and the episcopal government, which is called canonical polity" (*canonicam politiam*) under the condition that the bishops would tolerate the pure doctrine of the Gospel [Ap XIV 1 (24), German]. This declaration presupposes that there are ways of constituting the church which the Lutheran Church can under no circumstances acknowledge, for example, the constitution of the Papal Church as it existed at the time of the Reformation. And there are other forms which it can acknowledge, for example, the episcopal constitution of the *old* canonical law.

Our confessions never expressed (at least in the period before the Religious Peace of Augsburg [1555]) which conditions a particular way of constituting the church must fulfill in order to be tolerable for the Lutheran Church. Nor did they indicate which ways of constituting the church in addition to that of the old canonical law can be discussed in our church. Nor could they have done so. The desire was not to found a new church, but only to reform the existing church. Thus the problem of constituting the church was not a question of which new way of doing so could be introduced. The question was rather about what had to happen to break the tyranny of the false hierarchy over souls and congregations which had obtained, in order that the corrupt ecclesiastical office with all its duties and all its members could again become a true spiritual office in the sense of the Gospel so that the entire church could be renewed.

But today when the church in a completely different situation is asked which conditions a church constitution must fulfill if it is to be acknowledged by the Lutheran Church as legitimate or possible, then the answer must be this: According to Lutheran doctrine the church is correctly ordered when its constitution provides a maximum of possibilities for the spiritual office to carry out its service of the proclamation of the pure Gospel and the correct administration of the Sacraments in the name and by the mandate of the Lord of the church and when it provides a maximum of possibilities for the congregation called by Jesus Christ himself through the Word and Sacraments, which in faith in him is a "congregation of saints,"[70] to lead its life in the world and to accomplish its service to people as is mandated the church of God.

This answer continues to assure evangelical freedom in matters of the external formation of the church. Lutheranism could give up this freedom only by giving up its understanding of the NT. A multiplicity of ecclesiastical forms of life

---

[70] In the sense of AC VII: *congregatio sanctorum*. HS

are possible as long as they do not preclude unity in the faith and thus the unity of the church. The external forms of the church may be adapted to the necessities of times and peoples. The constitution of a church may indeed undergo development. With this answer we avoid the *legalistic misunderstanding* that there is one definite and only correct ordering of the church prescribed in the NT. But we also avoid the *libertine misunderstanding* that according to Lutheran doctrine there is no such thing as a false way of organizing the church. We know that no external ordering of the church can assure purity of doctrine. But we also know just as well that *the doctrine of the church is never independent of the external ordering of the church* and that there are constitutions which make it impossible for the church to preserve its pure doctrine.

Those in the Church of the Reformation should never have forgotten this. And if what false canon law once meant was forgotten, then the experiences of the Lutheran Church in Germany, perhaps the experiences in Brandenburg-Prussia since the seventeenth century, certainly had to open the eyes of even the most blind to the connection which obtains and must obtain between church constitution and church doctrine because the church is a spiritual-corporal reality in the world.

THE CONCEPT OF CHURCH GOVERNMENT

Still more inconceivable than the view that according to Lutheran doctrine the external form of the church is completely indifferent is the *assertion that Lutheranism surrenders the external governance of the church*, which we today call *"Kirchenregiment,"* to the *secular governing authority*. The "church governance" of which Augustana XIV and XXVIII spoke is something completely different from what we understand when we think of the governance of the church. We mean by this the legal oversight of pastors and congregations, calling and dismissing bearers of ecclesiastical office, the decreeing of ecclesiastical laws, the administration of church property, and whatever else church leadership entails.

The Augustana however understands by church governance the proclamation of the Word, the administration of the Sacraments, the hearing of confession and the imparting of absolution, excommunication and absolution in the exercise of the Office of the Keys. The spiritual care which the superintendent or bishop exercises toward pastors and congregations may be counted among this church governance. But the means at the disposal of the spiritual office are Word and Sacrament alone.

Consequently, only those functions appertain to it which the pastor or bishop accomplishes by means of the Word and the Sacrament. All legal and administrative dealings may be withdrawn from the spiritual office for it does not have at its disposal the power of compulsion without which there can be no governing functions. Thus according to this view compliance to church law could not be left merely to free obedience and under certain circumstances must be by compulsion.

When a church government does this, it is a governing authority [*Obrigkeit*] and exercises governmental functions. But it could only derive this authority from the office which God has entrusted with maintenance of the legal order and to which he has entrusted the power of compulsion. But according to the clear doctrine of the Augustana that is secular governing authority. Consequently, [we are told] secular authority possesses the exercise of the legal functions of church governance.

We must begin our answer to this view by noting what we said above regarding the theory of Rudolf Sohm. For we have to do here merely with a repetition of Sohm's thought[71] and with the consequences which have been drawn from it. Above we answered Sohm's thesis that church law contradicts the essence of the church with our proposition that the church has never existed without ecclesiastical law and that it cannot exist without it because it is a fellowship of people. Thus we offer the following opposing thesis to this theory of church government: *The church has always existed with a church government which is not derived from the secular governing authority. This church government was exercised by the members of the church or by the ecclesiastical office,* and the church could not exist as an empirical church without such a church government.

If the Sohmian theory is valid in general for the church, as it ostensibly claims to be, then it must also be applicable to the ancient church, the church in Turkey in the sixteenth century, the church in modern China, on so forth. From whom did the martyred bishops of the ancient church receive the authority to govern their churches? What right did the provincial synods of the third century have to legislate ecclesiastical law? If the church as church can establish no law nor legislate any binding law for its members nor form any church governance, then all of this was of course illegitimate. Then valid law has only existed in the church since the time of Constantine, who procured legal recognition under valid law in the Roman Empire for a church which up to that time had been illegitimate.

We cannot say that the time when the church was persecuted represents a period when a sort of emergency law obtained. For the church can either always establish laws, or it cannot. We cannot further discuss here the necessary consequences this question would have had for church government of the churches under Suleiman II and for the governance of modern mission churches in China and Japan.

THE AUTHORITY OF BISHOPS

But were we to accept the idea that the Reformers so understood the separation of the powers (*potestas*) that the functions of the proclamation of the Word

---

[71] See the notes above regarding Sohm in the section "False Interpretation of the Separation of Powers." Already the old dogmaticians of our church had to confront the error that to the *ministerium ecclesiasticum* there could not and must not be ascribed any power (*potestas*) in the sense of a legal authority, for example, Johann Gerhard (Loci XIII, 13 f.). HS

and the administration of the Sacraments were not only the essential tasks of the spiritual office, but under all circumstances its only tasks, and that any activity of governance within the church by the spiritual office would be a usurpation of secular governmental functions, then one thing would be completely unthinkable. Then our church in its confessions would never have expressed its willingness in the situation which then obtained to acknowledge under certain conditions the *canonical constitution of the church*. For this constitution presupposed that the bishop not only exercised functions of spiritual care, but also governmental functions in the church in the narrower sense.

Nor can this be otherwise, as a glance already at the Pastoral Letters demonstrates, which from that very time have served as direction for carrying out offices of spiritual supervision. The admission of a woman to the ecclesiastical status of widow, of which 1 Tim 5:9 ff. speaks, is indeed not only a spiritual matter having to do with the care of souls, it is as an ecclesiastical-legal dealing with financial consequences for the church treasury.

Have the theoreticians who would limit the bishop and the pastor to the proclamation of the Word and the administration of the Sacraments ever considered that both cost money and that from the time the Lord first sent out his disciples (Matt 10:8–10; Luke 10:7) to the last "church order" of the NT (1 Tim 5:18; cf. 1 Cor 9:7 ff.) the question of the "pastor's salary" and the "church tax" has played a role?

And in which area of the dealings of church government does the following direction belong: "Do not receive an accusation against a presbyter except from two or three witnesses" (1 Tim 5:19)? The man who here—in the church of the NT!—has charge of disciplinary proceedings is the same one who ordains presbyters and deacons to preach the Gospel and oppose false teachers. And so it remained in the church. If the Reformation had come to the conclusion that this were a false understanding of the spiritual office, that the spiritual office must only deal with Word and Sacrament and that the administration of the externals of the church must be left to the experienced entities of the secular governing authority, how loudly they would have proclaimed this renewal! But they did not view it this way at all.

The demand our confession places upon the bishops is that they once again become real bishops. They should "not get involved in an office which is not theirs" [AC XVIII 13], they should not appropriate rule over areas which according to God's ordering belong to the secular authority. They are reminded that their incidental secular rule as imperial princes [*Reichsfürsten*] is granted them from the emperor and has nothing to do with the office of bishop:

> According to divine right, therefore, it is the office of the bishop to preach the Gospel, forgive sins, judge doctrine and condemn doctrine that is contrary to the Gospel, and exclude from the Christian community the ungodly whose wicked conduct is manifest. All this is to be done not by human power but by God's Word alone. On this account parish ministers and churches are

bound to be obedient to the bishops according to the saying of Christ in Luke 10:16, "He who hears you hears me." On the other hand, if they teach, introduce, or institute anything contrary to the Gospel, we have God's command not be obedient in such cases. (AC XXVIII 21–23)[72]

Here it is completely clear how the spiritual or episcopal office is understood. To preach, absolve, teach, condemn heresy, excommunicate the godless—the administration of the Sacraments could be added, as otherwise occurs—these are the functions which constitute the *essence* of this office. There are functions which the bishop has by divine right (*de iure divino*). But while this is so, it is not said that according to applicable human law in the church he must not and may not exercise other functions. Already in the passage cited "pastors and churches" are in duty bound to be obedient to the bishops so far as they do not "teach, establish, or institute something contrary to the Gospel" ("contra evangelium docent aut constituunt"). The rules they may make in view of circumstance—and they are never to introduce these as though they were the doctrine of the Word of the Lord, "He who hears you hears me" (Ap XXVIII 18–19 [quoting Luke 10:16])— are taught by Augustana XXVIII with unmistakable clarity.

Precisely against the background of the sharp protest against the anti-scriptural laws with which the Roman hierarchy had burdened the souls of Christianity and troubled their consciences, against the background of the struggle for Christian freedom which must be preserved in the church,[73] in a quiet matter-of-fact manner the right of the bishops to give instructions in the area of church governance for the sake of peace and order is maintained:

> What are we to say, then, about Sunday and other similar church ordinances and ceremonies? To this our teachers reply that bishops or pastors may make regulations so that everything in the churches is done in good order, but not as a means of obtaining God's grace or making satisfaction for sins, nor in order to bind men's consciences by considering these things necessary services of God and counting it sin to omit their observance even when this is done without offense. . . .

> It is proper for the Christian assembly to keep such ordinances for the sake of love and peace, to be obedient to the bishops and parish ministers in such matters, and to observe the regulations in such a way that one does not give offense to another and so that there may be no disorder or unbecoming conduct in the church. However, consciences should not be burdened. (AC XXVIII 53, 55)[74]

---

[72] The English translation is from Tappert, *BC*, 84. MH

[73] "It is necessary to preserve the teaching of Christian liberty in Christendom, namely, that bondage to the law is not necessary for justification, as St. Paul writes in Gal. 5:1, 'For freedom Christ has set us free; stand fast, therefore, and do not submit again to a yoke of slavery' " (AC XXVIII 51–52). [The English translation is from Tappert, *BC*, 89.] HS

[74] The English translation is from Tappert, *BC*, 89–90. MH

To be sure, here only instructions in the area of the Divine Service are dealt with expressly. But the authority which is prescribed to the bishops and pastors in this area fully suffices to show that our confessions understand the spiritual office in its essence, consequently in the sense of a divine institution, as a "ministry of teaching the Gospel and administering the Sacraments" (*ministerium docendi evangelii et porrigendi sacramenta* [AC V 1]). However, they grant to it authority which must be defined in terms of church-governmental functions in the modern sense of the term.

A statement of the Formula of Concord regarding the spiritual office shows that the Augustana has more in mind here than temporally conditioned concessions to the bishops who found themselves in office at that particular phase of the process of unification. The Augustana rather intends to make a fundamental assertion regarding the spiritual office, valid for all times (quite aside from the question of wherein consists the authority of the "spiritual fathers who rule and preside over us by God's Word," which Luther asserts in the Large Catechism, Fourth Commandment, 158). Article X of the Solid Declaration speaks of duties which "the servants of the Word have as leaders of the community of God."[75] The Latin text, which comprises the first commentary on the Formula of Concord, spoke of a "ministry of the Word of God (as those whom the Lord appointed to rule his church)," "ministri verbi Dei (tanquam ii, quos Dominus ecclesiae suae regendae praefecit)" [SD X 10]. It designates the "ruling of the church" (*regere ecclesiam*) expressly as a task given by the Lord and consequently reckons this "ruling" among the functions which are given to the spiritual office by divine right (*de iure divino*). The "ruling of the church" (*regere ecclesiam*) is then identical with that which Augustana XIV calls "church government" and which is exercised through the proclamation of the Word and the administration of the Sacraments.

But certainly no one will assert that according to the intent of the Formula of Concord the occupants of the spiritual office do not possess those—as we commonly call them—"church governmental" [*kirchenregimentlichen*] functions to exercise which the Augustana ascribes to bishops and pastors. Otherwise alongside the pastors as "leaders of the community of God" [SD X 10], there would have to be still other leaders who possess necessary church-governmental authority for the sake of order.

But our church does not know of any such leaders who would be more along the lines of the presbyter of the Reformed Church.[76] First of all they know nothing of a law that the secular governing authority should have the right to carry out the church-governmental dealings necessary for maintaining order in the church. That was already excluded when Article X of the Formula of Concord, "On

---

[75] SD X 10. Luther too declares that it is the task of the pastors that they "preach and lead the churches" (WA 46.735.12). See the discussion, note, and texts cited in part 3 above. HS

[76] Of course in accord with the doctrine of our church nothing is here said against the church for appropriate reasons creating a presbyterial office as good human order. HS

Church Usages," which we cited, ascribed to the church the right to introduce "ceremonies and church usages which in God's Word are neither commanded nor forbidden." And this was in full agreement with the other confessional documents.

TO WHOM DOES CHURCH GOVERNANCE BELONG?

Now we have come to the central question of our investigation: *According to Lutheran doctrine, to whom does church governance belong?* The completely unanimous answer of the confessions resounds, as Wilhelm Kahl[77] correctly formulated it: "The *ecclesia* itself, whose head is Christ." If we are questioned further about what is meant here by the word "church," we must answer this way: the one holy, catholic and apostolic church, which we confess in the Creed, the hidden church, which yet is not a Platonic republic (*civitas Platonica*), but rather a reality in the world, perceptible in its two marks—the pure preaching of the Gospel and the scriptural administration of the Sacraments; "the multitude of men . . . who here and there in the world, from the rising to the setting of the sun, truly believe in Christ, who then have one Gospel, one Christ, one and the same Baptism and Sacrament, are ruled by one Holy Spirit, even though they indeed have different ceremonies" (Ap VII/VIII 11 [German]); the church which is the body of the Lord, the people of God, the bride of Christ, the temple of the Holy Spirit; the church which wends its way through the peoples of the world and the centuries of history and to which the promise is given that the gates of hell shall not overpower it; the church in whose Word and Sacrament Jesus Christ is actually present, though our eyes do not see him.

This church, according to Evangelical Lutheran doctrine, is the possessor of ecclesiastical authority [*Kirchengewalt*]. The power of the keys (*potestas clavium*), which is the chief part of ecclesiastical authority, is not the possession of only one of the apostles. It does not belong to one individual ruling office in the church, nor was it first given to particular persons. It was given to the church, which is the body of the Lord:

> It is necessary to acknowledge that the keys do not belong to the person of one particular individual but to the whole church, as is shown by many clear and powerful arguments, for after speaking of the keys in Matt. 18:19, Christ said, "If two or three of you agree on earth," etc. Therefore, he bestows the keys especially and immediately on the church, and for the same reason the church especially possesses the right of vocation. (Treatise, 24)[78]

---

[77] *Der Rechtsinhalt des Konkordienbuches* (1910), 27 f. HS
[78] The English translation is from Tappert, *BC*, 324. MH

OFFICE AND CONGREGATION

Consequently, with the power of the keys (*potestas clavium*) the church is also given the right and the task to confer [*übertragen*] the "ministry of teaching the Gospel and the administration of the Sacraments" (*ministerium docendi evangelii et porrigendi sacramenta* [AC V 1]), that is, to call men to the preaching office to carry out the task given it by Christ to proclaim the Gospel. By church is always meant here the one inseparable church which is the body of Christ.

But this church never appears in our space-time world and in this sinful humanity in its totality, and never in full purity. We perceive its presence in faith in our historical, empirical churchdoms in the pure preaching of the Gospel and in the correct administration of the Sacraments. Wherever we may say in faith "Here is the church of Christ," there we may also assert, "Here is the ecclesiastical authority which Christ has given his church—the right and duty to install pastors, for preaching and absolution, for administration of the Sacraments, for the orderly establishment of the Divine Service, and so on."

The church of Christ can be and is present where "two or three are gathered" in his name (Matt 18:20). It can manifest itself as the local congregation or in a group of congregations or even in a territorial church. It is completely false always to immediately apply what our confessions say of the congregation [*Gemeinde*], the *congregatio sanctorum*, to the local congregation. Those "called saints" in Rome [Rom 1:7] at the time of Paul apparently only very rarely came together all in one place. And the introduction to the Letters to the Corinthians testify that already at that time "all the saints throughout Achaia" belonged to the "church of God in Corinth" [2 Cor 1:1].

But in whichever form the church appears, where it really is present, there is ecclesiastical authority. Here we cannot enter a discussion of the unique relationship which according to Lutheran doctrine obtains between the spiritual office (*ministerium ecclesiasticum*) and the congregation (*congregatio sanctorum*). But let this be stated. The indissoluble mutual connection which according to the doctrine of our church obtains between congregation and office of the ministry—neither is present without the other, neither produces the other, neither is lord over the other—makes it completely understandable that certain functions of church governance, such as the arrangement of "church usages" and "ceremonies," are ascribed sometimes to the office of the ministry (AC XXVIII 53 f.) and sometimes to the congregation [*Gemeinde*].[79]

In every case they are functions of the church, whether exercised immediately by the congregation or by the bearers of the spiritual office as the organs of the congregation called thereto. The church is the sole possessor of ecclesiastical

---

[79] FC Ep X 4: "We believe, teach, and confess that the community [*Gemein*] of God in every locality and every age has authority to change such ceremonies according to circumstances, as it may be most profitable and edifying to the community of God." [The English translation is from Tappert, *BC*, 493.] HS

authority, and indeed, not only ecclesiastical authority in the narrow sense of the power of the keys (*potestas clavium*), but also in the wider sense of the legal functions of church governance.

CHURCH GOVERNMENT AND SECULAR AUTHORITY

If this is the view of our confessions on church governance and its basis, then it is understandable that *according to Lutheran church doctrine the secular governing authority as such can have no part in church governance.* Of course the occupants of government office, so far as they are members of the church and participate in the rights of the Christian congregation, may exercise such church governmental functions to which the members of the congregations may be called commensurate with good order in the church. But such actions are the result of belonging to the church and not possessing governmental office.

This would also apply to the incidental participation of the territorial lords in church governance as "chief members of the church" (*praecipua membra ecclesiae* [Treatise, 54]). Thus Luther himself, as we have seen, understood it when he called the Christian princes of Germany to "the office of love" [cf. WA 26.197.25; LW 40:271]. We can also understand it completely that "the most important member of the church," to whom as a Christian a maximum of duty in service of the church was given, now possessed a maximum of rights. And consequently he was not only owed thanks and respect but also given the highest measure of participation in the governance of the church, which a member of the church who is not endowed with a spiritual office can in general hold.

If the basic principle had been preserved that the church alone can wield ecclesiastical authority, the result would have been that secular governing authority as such would have been granted no right to the governance or co-governance of the church. But this did not happen in the confessions, and it can hardly be seen as an accident. When we consider what Melanchthon in the Apology and in the Treatise entrusts to the princes in respect to the protection of the church and the demand for pure doctrine,[80] when we furthermore realize how much development the government of the church by territorial lord had already undergone by the time of the Treatise (1537), then it is quite surprising that he does not here already draw the consequence which he had drawn in later writings.

Even in the broadest statements on what the princes are in duty bound to do and thereby justified in doing, the territorial lord remains the lord protector of the church, but he never becomes the bishop.[81] The later theologians who sought to understand and justify the long-since established governance of the church by

---

[80] In addition to the passages already cited, compare Ap XXIII 71. HS

[81] For example, Treatise, 56: "It is especially incumbent on the kings to restrain the license of *the pontiffs and see to it that the church is not deprived of the power of making judgments and decisions according to the Word of God.*" [The English translation is from Tappert, *BC*, 329–30; emphasis by Sasse.] HS

territorial lord, such as Johann Gerhard,[82] were not able to do so by calling upon confessional doctrine. They formulated a completely new theological theory when they transformed the Lutheran *doctrine of the three estates* to which Christians belong (the domestic, political, and ecclesiastical orders—*ordo oeconomicus, ordo politicus,* and *ordo ecclesiasticus*) into a doctrine of the three estates which constitute and participate in the governance of the church. A glance at Luther's explanation of the Fourth Commandment in the Large Catechism proves that this theory is not identical with the old doctrine of the three estates.[83]

Thus the doctrine of the Lutheran Church on church governance, viewed in its totality, is a *confirmation of the basic principle* that both of the powers ordained of God—the secular governing authority and the spiritual office—should not be confused. But of course, our fathers knew just as well as we do that state and church don't exist on different planets. They knew just as well as we that they ate by the sweat of their brow and consequently also belonged to the domestic or economic order (*ordo oeconomicus*). This and nothing else expresses the profound doctrine of Luther and the old Lutheran Church regarding the three estates, to which we all belong.

Therefore our confessions know that there are areas of life in which the tasks of the state concern those of the church and where, as a consequence, there may also be conflict. And they furthermore knew of the rights which the state had over against the church, and the secular government had over against the spiritual office. And they knew thirdly of the grave responsibility which state and church, secular authority and spiritual office, had for each other and both together for the people in whose service they had been placed by God. Regarding this we have something very important yet to say in conclusion to this section.

POINTS OF CONTACT BETWEEN CHURCH AND STATE

The areas where state and church intersect are not the same in all periods of history. This is because the functions of the state are not always the same. How many and which functions the state reckons within its sphere of responsibility are conditioned by the current dominant concept of the state. In the case of the state—as with the church—a distinction must be made between essential and accidental tasks. The only essential tasks are the maintenance of the law and the preservation of peace. Lutheran Church doctrine very keenly recognized this on the basis of the Holy Scriptures. And we ought to guard ourselves against seeing in this limitation only the alleged narrow-mindedness of a Reformation which occurred in the context of a very small and undeveloped ideal of state.

---

[82] Johann Gerhard (1582–1637) was the "archtheologian of Lutheranism" (*Lutheran Cyclopedia*, 329). MH

[83] Large Catechism, Fourth Commandment, 141 ff.; 158 ff. On the doctrine of the three estates, compare the article by A. F. C. Vilmar under the same title, *Kirche und Welt* (1872), 1:207 ff., and also Werner Elert, *Morphologie des Luthertums* (1932), 2:41 ff. HS

The fathers of our church well knew what tremendous tasks were incumbent upon the state in maintaining the legal order and preserving the public peace. They knew and believed the old German legal proverb that God is the beginning of all law. And they did not yet mock the "night watchman state" as was done in the enlightened police state of later times. The Reformers well knew, as Luther's demands of the princes and councilmen demonstrate, that the secular authority can still take on other tasks. In case of emergency it is in duty bound to assume the duty of forming schools, to take up the concern for the preservation of the church which goes beyond the self-evident maintenance of the law, and yes, in certain cases even to attempt the solving of purely domestic problems.

But these functions are not of the essence of the state. The state remains the state, even if it should not perform these tasks, while it ceases to be the state if it neglects the tasks mentioned previously. Thus the ancient state maintained that the commissioning of public worship [Kultus] was its task. The duty of its formal details however was always left to private organizations. The modern state throughout the world thinks in directly inverted terms.

On the other hand, there are indeed essential functions which remain those of the church, namely, the proclamation of the Word and the administration of the Sacraments. But the church also exercises accidental functions. Among these are the fulfillment of organizational tasks in the area of the formation of laws and the domestic side of ecclesiastical life (diaconate and the maintenance of the ecclesiastical organization) of which we have spoken. The church would also remain church if it finally did not exercise these functions, although their continuing neglect would finally destroy the church because it is at once a spiritual-corporal organization. Thus the nullification of its outer organization would necessarily mean the destruction of the spiritual office and the Christian congregation [Gemeinde].

It is similar to the domestic functions of the secular authority, which are not essential to it and without which the proper tasks of the state cannot continue to be accomplished. Also with the church now we note a hesitation in respect to these accidental functions. The ancient church, for instance, had gradually to form its own legal system, or episcopal justice. When the Roman Empire went under and the secular authority was temporarily completely eliminated, it was a necessary service of love when the spiritual office, as the only authority remaining, offered assistance and took over the functions of the secular authority. This was the opposite counterpart to the service of love which Luther expected of the secular authority at the time of the dissolution of the medieval church. And the same misfortune occurred that those called to the "office of love" did not know when this office was to end.

There have been times when the church took care of the entire educational system and when the ecclesiastical diaconate helped preserve society. There were times when the church retreated from these spheres or when state and church encountered each other and therefore a legal regulation of the relationship was necessary. In the age of the Reformation, the medieval inheritance of the religious involvement of the princes [*geistlichen Fürstentums*] was a primary problem.

How differently indeed would the Reformation have run its course if the bishops had been only bishops and not also continued to be secular authorities in their realms. The solution which the Augustana has for this problem is completely clear. As secular princes of the empire, the bishops are subject to the emperor: "In cases where bishops possess temporal authority and the sword, they possess it not as bishops by divine right, but by human, imperial right, bestowed by Roman emperors and kings for the temporal administration of their lands. Such authority has nothing at all to do with the office of the Gospel" (AC XXVIII 19).[84] The emperor alone therefore has the right to confer (*collatio*) to the bishopric the status of imperial princely rule (Treatise, 35 f.). This question was generally no problem for the Reformation. Here they only had to point back to the claims of the medieval spiritual office to secular rule.

CHURCH PROPERTY AND LAWS OF MARRIAGE

More difficult was the question of how the rights of state and church to two spheres were to be delimited where for all time civil and ecclesiastical competencies and interests encountered each other: These were the spheres of *marriage law* and *church property*. Article XXVIII of the Augustana explains regarding this: "Whatever other power and jurisdiction bishops may have in various matters (for example, in matrimonial cases and in tithes), they have these by virtue of human right. However, when bishops are negligent in the performance of such duties, the princes are obliged, whether they like to or not, to administer justice to their subjects for the sake of peace and to prevent discord and great disorder in their lands" (AC XXVIII 29).[85]

Consequently it [AC XXVIII 29] deals with "power or jurisdiction" (*potestas vel iurisdictio*)[86] for "legally investigating certain cases" (*congnoscendis certis causis*) which the bishops possess by human right (*de iure humano*), and indeed not as princes of the empire, rather as bishops [*Ordinarien*]; that is a jurisdiction which according to valid law was incumbent upon the ecclesiastical courts, though this jurisdiction could as well have been exercised by the secular court.

---

[84] The English translation is from Tappert, *BC*, 83–84. MH

[85] The English translation is from Tappert, *BC*, 85. MH

[86] Both words are used here in a difference sense than in Ap XXVIII 13, where the old separation of powers of the bishop into the power of orders and the power of jurisdiction (*potestas ordinis* and *potestas iurisdictionis*) is taken up as a possibility (*placet nobis*) in the Evangelical Lutheran doctrine of the office: "Therefore a bishop has the power of the order, namely, the ministry of Word and sacraments. He also has the power of jurisdiction, namely, the authority to excommunicate those who are guilty of public offenses or to absolve them if they are converted and ask for absolution." [The English translation is from Tappert, *BC*, 283.] The power of jurisdiction (*potestas iurisdictionis*) is consequently identical with the power of the keys and has nothing to do with the right of ecclesiastical legislation, which according to Augustana XXVIII the bishop like all bearers of the spiritual office possesses by human right (*de iure humano*) [cf. AC XXVIII 19, 29 ff.]. HS

The Augustana is prepared to further acknowledge this human arrangement (*ius humanum*) just as much as the spiritual leadership of the princes as a part of the civil order which obtained at the time. But since in principle the spiritual office can exercise no jurisdiction in secular matters, in case the bishops should forsake that authority or jurisdiction (*potestas vel iurisdictio*) it passes to the secular authority as the appointed judge. Consequently, according to Lutheran doctrine, the secular authority—Luther expressed this already in his "Address to the Nobility"—has the *jurisdiction* and thus with it also a *legislative right* in questions of church property.

It is self-evident that in these questions there is also an *inherent legislative right which belongs to the church*. But this is not spoken of. It is indeed presupposed in other passages that there is church property which is at the disposal of the church and which is designated for ecclesiastical use. The secular authority only has the right and duty to be concerned and certainly if need be use compulsory means to see that the property of the church is correctly managed, revenue is used for ends in accord with the church's institution, and occasional illegalities are punished according to the principle of strict justice.[87]

Also *jurisdiction in the area of marital law* belongs fundamentally to the state. Therefore "temporal magistrates are compelled to make these decisions if the bishops are negligent" (Treatise, 77).[88] Other matters for the secular authority to nullify are the false ecclesiastical marriage law (e.g., "the prohibition of marriage between godparents," Treatise, 78 [German]) or the prohibition of the remarriage of innocent parties of a divorce or the prohibition against priests marrying,[89] and secretly contracted marriages ("without the knowledge or consent of the parents") are not to be acknowledged (Treatise, 78). However, the establishment of special courts to judge marital cases is proposed.

THE RIGHTS OF THE SECULAR AUTHORITY

With this we already face the question of *which rights the secular government has over against the spiritual office*, [the question of] *the state and the church*. These rights arise from the character of the secular authority as the divinely established protector of the law and the peace.[90] All people, and this includes the members of

---

[87] "They themselves should remember that riches have been given to bishops as alms for the administration and profit of the churches. . . . Wherefore they cannot possess these alms with a good conscience. Meanwhile they defraud the church, which needs these means for support of ministers, the promotion of education, the care of the poor, and the establishment of courts, especially courts for matrimonial cases" (Treatise, 80). [The English translation is from Tappert, *BC*, 333–34.] HS

[88] [The English translation is from Tappert, *BC*, 333.] This of course applies only for a secular authority which still knows the Sixth Commandment, consequently not for governments which have enacted the *Allgemeine Landrecht* ("general territorial law") or the Bolshevist marriage law. HS

[89] Compare AC XXIII and the Apology where the divine right (*ius divinum*) of marriage is equated with the natural law (*ius naturale*), for example, Ap XXIII 6: "Laws concerning celibacy . . . therefore we cannot approve, because they are against both divine and natural law." HS

[90] Compare on this point AC XVI and its explanation in the Apology. HS

the church and those who occupy its spiritual office, are subject to its [the secular authority's] statutory authority [*Befehlsgewalt*]. It has claim to the respect and obedience of members of the church and all bearers of the spiritual office if it remains within the boundaries of its call to govern people according to the principles of civil righteousness (*iustitia civilis*). And indeed, this obedience, which includes willingness to actively cooperate in all the tasks of state government, is to be performed as a willing service, as proof of Christian love. It is owed to the governing authority as a *legitima ordinatio*, as a legal order.

This legitimacy is certainly not to be understood as a state-legal-historical [*staats-rechtlich-historischen*] principle of legitimacy. Every ruling power which carries out its office in the sense of the Second Table of the *Decalogue* is a legal order (*legitima ordinatio*). Here the bearers of the governing office need not be Christians. The Apology expressly declares that the secular authority has claim to our obedience as God's order even if its office bearers do not belong to the church. Just as the father retains the office of father as a divine order even though he is not a believer, so also the secular authority remains such independent of its confession of faith or philosophy [*Weltanschauung*].

It would only cease to be secular authority, it would descend to the level of raw power if it were no longer the guardian of the law, if it were to suspend the commandments of the Second Table and were to compel us to sin against the commandments of God.[91] If this should be the case, Christians act according to Scripture, "We must be obedient to God rather than men" [Acts 5:29]. And then they must be prepared just as was the early church to bear the consequences of such a refusal to be obedient.

We could question whether or not this is all something quite self-evident and need not be specially mentioned as a particular right of secular authority. But since the eighteenth century in the West, there are scarcely any truths which are self-evident regarding these matters. A service has been rendered to the state, however great it may be and on whatever ideological principles it may rest, which no one else can do, when the truth is preached to its citizens, above all its youth: "For there is no authority except from God, and the authorities that exist are appointed by God" (Rom 13:1 [NKJV]).

No philosophy of the state can say this to them, for no philosophy understands this. This is a proposition which is not found in any human philosophy [*Weltanschauung*], however profound it may be and no matter how much influence it may have upon people. This is a proposition which only the church of Christ can speak. Ever since it was proclaimed to the peoples of the West, the fate of every European state stands and falls with this proposition. Should this truth finally no longer shed its light upon the German state and people, then the polit-

---

91 There is no need here to demonstrate that and why the Lutheran Church does not treat the use of weapons in service of the state, the taking of oaths, and so on, as sins. We simply refer the reader to AC XVI and the Apology. HS

ical history of Germany would be past. Peoples to whom the church has not yet come can live because they have an inkling of the truth of this proposition. But peoples who have rejected this truth can find nothing with which to replace it.

Therefore the state has a real right over against the church that the doctrine of secular authority as the servant of God be correctly proclaimed. In the same way, the secular authority has an inviolable right to be remembered in the prayers of the church. Modern people who no longer know what prayer really is treat this prayer as a sort of polite formality. For the church it has never been such. The prayer of the church in the name of Jesus is not polite talk. It is a power, and it does not remain without effect.

Perhaps the time is coming when among our people the destructive effects of the Enlightenment of the eighteenth and nineteenth centuries will finally be overcome. Then we will again understand the claims which the secular authority has over against the church in these matters. The other rights of secular authority will seem insignificant by comparison. These rights consist in the state being the protector of civil righteousness (*iusitia civilis*) among a people and being granted legal right to exercise that *oversight* over the external administration and legal life of the church (of which we have spoken in dealing with the question of church property and marriage law). And secular authority furthermore has the right and duty to see to it that the struggles and discussions which will always exist in the church are so carried out that the *public peace of the country* is not disturbed and they do not result in insurrection.

The state cannot prevent schisms. But it can and ought to demand and be concerned that a division in the church not lead to division of the nation and the dissolution of the state. These are all questions and tasks which every people and generation of history faces anew. We see in the attempts to solve these timeless problems what of genuine state and genuine church was living at the time. We see in them whether the men of the church and of the state understood themselves only as combatants who wrestled with each other for positions of power or as men who carry out a God-given office in the service of God and men.

6. THE LUTHERAN CHURCH UNDER CHURCH GOVERNMENT BY TERRITORIAL LORD

THE UNAVOIDABLE FACT OF CHURCH GOVERNMENT BY TERRITORIAL LORD

It cannot be seriously denied that there is a profound contradiction between the doctrine of the Evangelical Lutheran Church on the relationship of church and state, and the actual forms which this relationship took on in state-church law of sixteenth-century Germany. We found this contradiction already in nascent form in the thought and work of Luther. On the one hand, from the earliest days of his reforming work until the last years of his life, he emphatically advocated the principle of the separation of the governments. And he directed increasingly sharp criticism at the secular authority. But on the other hand, he was not fully able to free himself from the idea of an ecclesiastical office of the Christian governing authority.

As the Middle Ages were passing there arose from this idea the beginnings of the system of governance of the church by territorial lord, which now in the sixteenth century began to experience its heyday. The Reformation did not create it, least of all the Lutheran Reformation. But as the structure of the Roman hierarchy came apart in much of the West, governance of the church by the Christian secular authority became the normal form of church constitution.

That was a historical fate which none of the new churches could avoid. For how could a theological theory of the relationship of church and state, however correct it may have been, no matter how deeply it may have been based on the doctrine of the Bible, have prevented the development of the medieval European forms of the state into those of the modern world? The establishment of the governance of the church by territorial lord cannot merely be viewed from the standpoint of church history. We must always recognize its political significance as an important step in the development of the modern state and princely absolutism.

Over against this development the Reformation was powerless. What deep resignation was expressed by Luther as he complained about the way the territorial lords in the period of nascent absolutism had become guilty of overstepping their bounds! "Satan goes on being Satan!" (*Satan pergit esse Satan!*)[92] What did the governance of the church by the territorial lord as it now unfolded have to do with the confessions? What had the claim of the territorial lord that he as such had a right to govern the church of his land to do with the duty of the *cura ecclesiae*, the "care for the church" which Luther and the confessions had expected of the Christian princes?

As far as our confessions are concerned, as we have demonstrated, the former right can never be derived from the latter duty. *The doctrine of our confessions knows of no territorial lord as* summus episcopatus ["chief episcopate"]. *Indeed, they preclude it by their positive doctrine of church governance.* Luther was right in speaking of an office of "emergency bishop" assumed by the territorial lords.[93] But he viewed this only as a temporary service of assistance by the princes on the basis of the general priesthood, a service which was to end when an ordered church government had finally been reestablished.

Not once do the confessions speak of the office or title of "emergency bishop." They understand by the episcopal office precisely the office of a clergyman

---

[92] Letter to Daniel Greiser in Dresden, October 22, 1543 (Enders-Kawerau, 15, 256, 10), quoted above. RF

[93] See the end of part 4 above. HS

called for the proclamation of the Word and the administration of the Sacraments. And thus they exclude the possibility that the title of bishop can be applied to the territorial lords, even in only a conveyed sense.

Accordingly, if the governance of the church by the territorial lord, or—as it was later called—the *summus episcopatus*[94] of the territorial lord, is to be treated as an anti-confessional institution, and indeed not because it is not found in the confessions, but because it is in open contradiction to their doctrine, then the question arises of *how the Lutheran Church for centuries could tolerate this form of church government?* And how is it that it still bears this form of government in the Scandinavian countries?

THE CONSEQUENCES

First, as in the case of churches of other confessions, the Evangelical Lutheran Church bore the fate of the governance of the church by territorial lord not without suffering serious detriment to its spiritual and organizational life. The life of the congregation, the activity of the general priesthood of believers, the responsibility of individual Christians for the life and the work of the church necessarily suffers where the secular governing authority administers the affairs of the church and congregational members are left scarcely any activity other than attending the Divine Service.

How different was a Lutheran congregation in the time after the Thirty Years' War [1618–1648] from the picture of a Christian congregation which Luther had painted in his great Reformation writings! How quickly, in the age of ecclesiastical territorialism, did the ecumenical breadth which characterized the thought of the Reformation regarding the church narrow when the borders of countries became the borders of churches! Where in later times did the eye for the catholic, universal church remain, of which the Apology knows to speak so comfortingly and so forcefully, the eye for the church which is not bound to one country or one place but stretches from the rising to the setting of the sun!

And how the spiritual office had to suffer harm in respect to its very essence when pastors more and more became princely officials. Our church was rich with pastors full of character far into the seventeenth century. They were pastors who did not fear people and took up the cause of the poor and the oppressed even against the mighty of this world. How fearlessly a Valentin Ernst Löscher[95] at the

---

94 *Summus episcopatus* is merely another name for governance of the church by the territorial lord. It ought not be separated from this governance and be grounded on some alleged conferring of the episcopal jurisdiction to the Evangelical territorial lords by the Religious Peace of Augsburg [1555]. Such a conferral was not part of the Religious Peace, which only declared that the episcopal power rests with the Evangelical dominions. HS

95 Valentin Ernst Löscher (1673–1749) was the son of a Wittenberg professor of theology. He founded the first theological periodical (*Unschuldige Nachrichten*) and was the last great orthodox opponent of Pietism, syncretism, and unionism before all of these and Wolffian philosophy swamped what had been an orthodox Lutheran Church in Germany. His motto was *Veritas et Pietas* ("Truth and Piety"). Of the six doctoral dissertations written under Sasse at Erlangen, the first was by Paul Schreyer, *Valentin Ernst Löscher*

beginning of the Enlightenment spoke the Word of God even to the most powerful men on earth! But then princely absolutism and the doctrine of the Enlightenment on state and church made large numbers of Lutheran pastors servants of princes and state officials. And the governance of the church by the territorial lord was not without fault.

And is not the present condition of German Evangelical Christendom a crying lament against a past epoch of its history in which the capability of the congregations and the spiritual office to organize the body of the church was stunted and died? We need only cast a glance at the writings and lectures in which well-meaning professors of theology in the winter of 1918/1919 sought to get hold of the situation created by the collapse of church governance by territorial lord[96] in order to understand why sooner or later this collapse had to be followed by a catastrophe involving all of Evangelical Christendom in our fatherland.

What a conceptually rich and as yet inexhaustible body of literature was written for us by Lutherans and other theologians in the years between 1830 and 1870 regarding the basic questions of church law and constitution. They saw the end of the princely episcopate coming, and they had hoped that the Evangelical churches of Germany would finally assume the outward form which they had not been able to achieve previously, having been captive to the fetters of German territorialism and the absolute state. But this literature was forgotten.

To deal with the inferior questions of "cybernetics" [*Kybernetik*] is regarded as unworthy of theology. This is left to the men of proven ecclesiastical practice. And in the face of the partial approval and partial criticism which cries out to them in the *Quousque tandem* ["Which way then?"] of the professional theologians, these experienced "practical" men can accomplish nothing more than to erect that orgy of ecclesiastical parliamentarianism which is proudly called "the century of the church."

Who can be surprised that in the revolution of 1933[97] political territorialism in Germany came to a frightful end? What we experience today are the consequences of the government of the church by the territorial lord. We cannot say that this form of church government has existed in other countries and still exists there today and that the church is doing fine there. In reality government of the church by the territorial lord has only been maintained where the old monarchial form of the state has been at least superficially preserved. And even where this is the case, it finds itself in a latent crisis.

---

und die Unionsversuche seiner Zeit (Schwabach: Verlag J.G. Schreyer, 1938). Löscher also happened to be an ancestor of Sasse on his mother's side. MH

96 That was the consequence of the revolution in Germany following World War I. The constitution of the German Republic adopted by the National Assembly at Weimar in August 1919 declared church and state separate (*Lutheran Cyclopedia*, 331). RF

97 A reference to January 30 when Adolf Hitler became chancellor of Germany and/or July 11 when the constitution for the German Evangelical Church (DEK) was passed and then confirmed by Reich law on July 14. RF

In England, for instance, the classic country of the supremacy of the king, where because of the unique character of the people such old forms have been preserved with particular faithfulness, the necessary reform of the liturgy can no longer be accomplished through legal channels.[98] The parliament, whose members in large part do not belong to the Church of England but to the British free churches, as is well known rejected the reform agenda which intended to strengthen the Catholic elements. Only with difficulty was a solution to this situation found. But it only temporarily delivers church and state from a dilemma which in the long run cannot be solved except by "disestablishment," or the dissolution of the old bonds between state and church.

The governance of the church by territorial lord is in a state of crisis everywhere. That its effects on the church in Germany were much more devastating than in other countries is explained by the fact that the political chaos of Germany had of necessity to lead to an ecclesiastical chaos. He who would maintain that the territorial *summus episcopatus* was correct must grant that a change in boundaries such as the annexation of Hanover by Prussia meant that the Prussian king now became the legal highest bishop of the Church of Hanover. But this then means that the decision regarding who according to God's will should govern a particular church can be rendered on a battlefield along with other decisions.[99] There is no need to waste words over the fact that no church can live in perpetuity under a system of constitution which leads to such consequences without being severely hindered. If the Lutheran Church once had endured the government of the church by territorial lord without sufficiently protesting against it on the basis of Scripture and confession, then it must seriously repent of this historical guilt.

HOW COULD THE CHURCH TOLERATE IT?

But why did the Evangelical Church not once clearly protest against this governance of the church by territorial lord which is contrary to its confession? Why did the complaints of Luther over the self-interest and the overreaching of the princes not become a protest of basic principle? The answer is that no one entirely understood the significance of the development of state-church law which was

---

[98]   The attempt to reform the liturgy of the Book of Common Prayer (1662) in 1928 failed due to conflicts in parliament. RF

[99]   Sasse elsewhere explained:

> After 1866 things began to change. It has been said with a good deal of justification that the Lutheran Church of Germany suffered its decisive defeat on the battlefield of Koeniggraetz. The annexation of Hanover, Schleswig Holstein and electoral Hessia confirmed the dominant position of Prussia. This meant that the leadership of Protestant Germany was taken over by the church and state authorities in Berlin and sealed the predominance of the Prussian Union.

> This quote is from "Zur Lage des Luthertums nach dem Zweiten Weltkrieg" (Erlangen, July 1945, typewritten manuscript). The English translation used above is that of George Wolfgang Forell, "The Situation of the Lutheran Church" (unpublished), 4. The German original was reprinted in *ISC*, 1:287–302 (Huss number 251). RF

occurring at the time. Not even the individual territorial lords themselves were clear on what they were attempting to do, and did.

The history of the Reformation would be unthinkable without the nobility, those truly pious princes, or without the councilmen of the German cities who were profoundly gripped by the message of the Gospel. They rendered the service Luther expected of them out of the deepest commitment to their duty to care for the church (*cura ecclesiae*), in real responsibility before God, as real "chief members of the church" (*praecipua membra ecclesiae* [Treatise, 54]). And how could the history of Evangelical Germany be conceived of if, even in the later centuries, such men had not ever and again rendered their service as Christian governing authority, convinced that God would demand a reckoning from them regarding their office? The Evangelical Church will never forget this. Theology must never forget those men who in the most difficult times of our history were real protectors of the church and the Gospel, so far as men can be such. But the institutions are to be distinguished from the men. There is a history of the governance of the church by territorial lord which is not simply the history of its bearers.

Quite aside from the ruling territorial lords desiring it of their office as "chief members of the church" and no matter how the Reformers viewed it, the general political and social circumstances rooted in the thought of the time regarding the state and the actual exercise of the protection of the church gave rise to the institution of governance of the church by territorial lord. It was fully developed by the Religious Peace of Augsburg of 1555 and was anchored in imperial law. All at once it was there. Who could have gotten around it? With it the Evangelical Church at the time would stand or fall as a communion acknowledged by imperial law.

But for the Lutheran theologians there could only be one question: Can the church render her service of the pure proclamation of the Word and the right administration of the Sacraments under this form of church constitution as it had come to exist in the terrible struggles of the time of the Reformation? The answer then had to be this: It can do so as long as the incumbents of the governing authority know that they are bound to the pure doctrine of the church in the exercise of ecclesiastical power. Melanchthon, for instance, who for the most part had acceded to the theological grounding of the governance of the church by territorial lord and had even experienced its consummation after the Religious Peace of Augsburg, had always maintained that the government in its church-governmental dealings is only the "minister and executor of the church" (*minister et executor ecclesiae*).[100] Thus they [secular authorities] have to protect and advance the pure doctrine of the church in the world.

---

[100] "Although we have distinguished the powers, nevertheless it may be observed that civil power ought to be subject to the church for the sake of discipline. . . . For we ought all obey the ministry of the Word, thus the magistrate in the republic is minister and executor of the church." ("Quamquam distinximus

But the decision regarding what is pure doctrine belongs to the church as a whole, consequently also to the teaching estate and the congregation.[101] Here Melanchthon constantly and emphatically emphasized that the principle of the separation of the powers should not be infringed.[102] Thus where possible he also still maintained the fundamental delimitation of the governmental authorities which is expressed in Luther's remark to the elector that he "is not commanded to teach and govern in spiritual matters" [WA 26.200.28; cf. *LW* 40:273].

As long as this limitation was heeded, church governance by territorial lord could be tolerated for the sake of necessity. Church governance by the king in the Scandinavian countries today still is based upon the presupposition that the territorial lord in his ecclesiastical dealings is strictly bound to the confession of his church. Consequently, for example, he only nominates a man to the office of bishop who is qualified for the office according to Lutheran doctrine. But the moment this adherence of the territorial lord to the confession of the church and his joyous affirmation of this confession should cease, this form of church government, tolerable in the case of necessity, would no longer be tolerable. For the existence of the church as church would be illegally threatened.

THE INSUFFICIENCY OF THE SAFEGUARDS

This moment came when the presupposition of the prince as chief member of the church that was self-evident for Luther, the confessions, and the Religious Peace of Augsburg disappeared. It was self-evident to them that the territorial lord should belong to the church whose government he led. Hans Leube[103] once remarked how peculiar it is that Paul Gerhardt[104] in his valiant struggle for the right of the Lutheran Church in Brandenburg had never considered contesting that the *Reformed* elector could be *summus episcopatus* over the *Lutheran* Church.

---

potestas, tamen animadverti potest, quod potestas civilis servire debeat Ecclesiae propter disciplinam. . . . Omnes enim debemus obedire ministerio verbi, sic magistratus in republic minister et executor est Ecclesiae. Debet enim et ipse obedire ministerio verbi," *Corpus Reformatorum*, 16:124). HS

[101] "Because it is not always certain which opinions are blasphemy or impious; therefore precedence must be given to another jurisdiction, namely, knowledge of doctrine. But this pertains not only to the magistrate, but to the church, that is, not only to the clergy, but also to the laity" ("Quia non semper constat, quae opiniones sint blasphemae seu impiae; ideo debet praecedere aliud iudicium, videlicet cognitio de doctrina. Haec autem pertenet non solum ad magistratum, sed ad ecclesiam, h.e. non tantum ad presbyteros, sed etiam ad laicos," *Corpus Reformatorum*, 4:468). HS

[102] For example, *Corpus Reformatorum*, 16:96: "In order that the distinction between the ministry of the Gospel and the magistrate be maintained . . . we do not confuse the offices" ("Ut conservetur discrimen inter ministerium Evangelii et magistratum . . . non igitur miscemus officia"). HS

[103] *Kalvinismus und Luthertum im Zeitalter der Orthodoxie* (1928), 1:401. HS

Hans Leube (1896–1947) was a professor of church history at Leipzig, Breslau, and Rostock; he was a student of H. Böhmer (*Lutheran Cyclopedia*, 468). MH

[104] Paul Gerhardt (1607–1676) studied theology at Wittenberg (1628–1642) and became a pastor in Berlin in 1657. He was a noted hymnist. In 1666 he was dismissed from his position as pastor for refusing to sign syncretistic edicts of Frederick William I of Brandenburg. In 1667 he declined the opportunity to return to his position. In 1669 he became an archdeacon in Lübben, where he remained until his death (*Lutheran Cyclopedia*, 329). MH/RF

So firmly was the thought rooted already in the seventeenth century that the governing authority as such was to govern the church of its land, quite independent of its confession.

When the Saxon Electoral House for the sake of the Polish crown returned to the Catholic Church, it was viewed as intolerable that a Catholic ruler should himself exercise the governmental functions of the church. But no one contested that they belonged to him as territorial lord. It is well known that his rights and duties over against the church of his land were looked after by three ministers *in evangelicis* ["in things evangelical"]. And the general principle was adopted that the Catholic territorial lord indeed possessed the episcopal right (*ius episcopale*) over his Protestant subjects but allowed it to be exercised by Evangelical officials. With this the governance of the church by the territorial lord had come to the point of complete absurdity (*ad absurdum*). The princes continued to possess what they had once taken over as the "chief members of the church" (*praecipua membra ecclesiae*), even after they had ceased to be "members of the church" (*membra ecclesiae*)!

TERRITORIALISM

Consequently a man could now become the bishop of a church even though his doctrine was false! And one door after another was opened to appalling "territorialism," that theory of church law born of the absolute state and the Enlightenment, according to which the governance of the church is a civil matter. The exercise of religion is subject not only to the supervision of the state government, but also the leadership of the state. Thus the church had become purely an institution of the state.

This is the theory of church law of all men of the Enlightenment, from Marsilius of Padua to Thomasius[105] and the Prussian state philosophers. It is the church-law theory which has ruled Germany since the eighteenth century. Its dangerousness was not recognized because it was hidden away behind the pious mask of the old Evangelical doctrine of the duties of the princes as the "chief members of the church" (*praecipua membra ecclesiae*).

Finally the mask was allowed to drop. In Prussia on December 16, 1808, contrary to all public and valid law in Germany and in Prussia which had stood since the Reformation, a cabinet order of the Reformed *summus episcopatus* dissolved the existing church governments of both the Lutheran and the Reformed Church. The administration of the church was transferred to a division of the Ministry of the Interior which was also in charge of the royal theater.

---

[105] Christian Thomasius (1655–1728) was a lawyer and lecturer in Leipzig who was forbidden by the consistory to teach in 1690. He went to Berlin, gathered a large following, and laid the foundations for the University of Halle, where he later taught. "In a series of works on church law, he recognizes the State as purely secular and the Church as a society within its domain." He was a strong advocate of territorialism. A descendent, Gottfried Thomasius (1802–1875), taught theology at Erlangen (*New Schaff-Herzog*, 11:429–30). MH

But the responsible men of the state, stuck in a fog of pietistic feelings, of idealistic thoughts about the state and romantic episcopal dreams, finally never understood what they had done. They never realized the fact that by their actions the curse which lay upon an institution in which the orders of God had been violated had been carried out. Thus the government of the church by territorial lord necessarily led the Evangelical Christendom of Germany, and also the German princely houses, into an abyss.

7. CAN CHURCH GOVERNMENT BY TERRITORIAL LORD BE RENEWED?

It really ought to be unnecessary to have to note that *the government of the church by territorial lord is an unrepeatable relic of the past* and cannot be renewed. But recently it has been seriously proposed that the problem of the new ordering of the relationship between church and state be solved by a reinstitution of the old legal form of the *summus episcopatus*. And so something has to be said regarding this by way of conclusion.

THE UNREPEATABLE NATURE OF THE *SUMMUS EPISCOPATUS*

There are institutions which, after they have finally died, can never be resurrected. They are the temporally conditioned result of a particular historical situation which is unrepeatable. The governance of the church by territorial lord is such an institution. We can renew the relationship between state and church which it represents as little as we can reestablish the state and the church of the sixteenth century. Its presupposition is not only a unanimity of confession shared by ruler and people, but also the confessional unanimity of the people.

Thus finally both of the following legal principles are essential to this form of church constitution: "He who rules determines the religion of his dominions" (*Cuius regio, eius religio*)[106] and "Where there is one ruler, there ought be one religion" (*Ubi unus dominus, ibi sit una religio*). The governance of the church by territorial lord is at best conceivable where citizenship and church membership are coterminous and where the territorial lord is in agreement with his people regarding which is the pure doctrine that he is bound to advance and protect.

A portion of such unity of faith is today still present in the people who have been spared confessional division and in whom the Christian heritage of the past remains a force in determining the nature of their lives as a people. But even there only a portion of this unity is living, and the principle "He who rules determines the religion" (*cuius regio, eius religio*) is no longer possible even there.

Already soon after the Peace of Westphalia [1648] it was no longer sustainable in Germany. And the ideas of the eighteenth century and the political and

---

[106] The principle stated in the Peace of Augsburg (1555). RF

social changes of the nineteenth century have since made it completely illusionary. The government of a modern state which in principle tolerates individuals belonging to various churches and which must do so on ethical grounds can indeed no longer assume the duties which were inseparably bound together with the old *summus episcopatus*. It can no longer force citizens to send their children to Christian religious instruction if they refuse to do so for reasons of conscience. It cannot be intent on suppressing heresy.

No government of a modern state can decide the question which the territorial lords of the sixteenth century believed themselves authorized, indeed required, to decide—namely, whether the doctrine of the Roman or the Evangelical Church is correct. There can be a number of churches in one state, churches which the state acknowledges and protects and over whose external affairs it claims a right to oversight. But it cannot govern them. An Evangelical Church can be governed only by a person who maintains that its doctrine is correct and the doctrine of Rome false. Only someone who can render a judgment on the orthodoxy of pastors and bishops, and therefore on the doctrine of the church, can appoint them.

"For the doctrine of the church is not like a civil law code, which we can apply even if we are not convinced of its correctness. Its correct understanding and correct application rather presupposes inner faith and faithful inquiry," said Friedrich J. Stahl[107] in a time in which the incompatibility of the government of the church by territorial lord with the modern, nonsectarian state was generally acknowledged by all statesmen and theologians. It was the time when Frederick William IV,[108] as he was elevated to the throne, was considering the abandonment of the *summus episcopatus*. In the plans of the Reich and state constitutions of 1848, for the first time in German history, the separation of church and state was announced and everywhere in the Evangelical churches of Germany discussion began regarding possible new formations of the church. The government of the churches by territorial lord among our people was at its irretrievable end. It had lost the last remnant of its meaning. What remained of it was a spiritless state-church bureaucracy, which in November of 1918 met its inglorious demise.[109]

---

[107] *Die Kirchenverfassung nach Lehre und Recht der Protestanten* (1862), 2:360. HS
Friedrich Julius Stahl (1802–1861) was a jurist and statesman.

> He held that the three systems, episcopal, territorial, and collegial, represented different views of the nature of the church government, and were the outgrowths of the prevailing sentiment of three epochs of development; respectively, the orthodox, the Pietistic, and the rationalistic. Stahl advocated the Episcopal order. In his Die lutherische Kirche und die Union (1860) he opposed a formal union of the two Protestant churches. (New Schaff-Herzog, 11:61) MH

[108] Frederick William IV (1795–1861), King of Prussia (1840–1861), issued the "Generalkonzession" on July 23, 1845, which permitted Lutherans who remained separate from the Prussian Union to organize free churches (*Lutheran Cyclopedia*, 312). MH

[109] This is a reference to the "revolution" in Germany at the end of the war. The Kaiser fled the country and a republic was proclaimed. "As far as Protestantism was concerned, the revolution not only meant the

A NEW STATE CHURCH?

There is no possibility of reviving church government by territorial lord. But something else is theoretically conceivable. It is conceivable for the doctrine of territorialism in the relationship of state and religion to experience a revival. It is conceivable that there could be a revival of the doctrine that looking after religion ought be a task of the state. This was the view of the ancient world which was revived by the civil theories of the Renaissance. It has been the view of "enlightened" men of all times, from Marsilius of Padua to the Prussian state philosophers of the nineteenth century.

The Enlightenment indeed knew of a religious freedom, but it only granted individual people the freedom to believe or not to believe. The Enlightenment did not assert the freedom for the church to preach its message unhindered because it did not believe that any church had a message given by divine revelation. It viewed churches only as religious societies disseminating their private religious views. And thus precisely the most decided advocates of the Enlightenment were time and again able to harmonize their demand of individual freedom of faith with the concession that *public* doctrine and *public* exercise of religion are a civil matter.

Is it really entirely unthinkable that the result of the Enlightenment of the eighteenth and nineteenth centuries for the Western peoples of the future should limit itself to that personal freedom of the individual to believe or not to believe, but that the *public* doctrine of the faith and the *public* cultus again would be declared a monopoly of the state? Does a revival of the *Cuius regio, eius religio* in an entirely modern sense really lie outside the realm of possibility if we consider the terrible changes which the state has gone through recently, and certainly not only in Germany?

If so much which was previously a matter of the individual is declared to be a matter of the entire people [*Volk*][110] and subordinated to the rule of the state, why should religion be an exception? If there is no longer "freedom" in science, no "freedom" in art in the sense of Liberalism, why should a "freedom" in religion still exist? The proposition "religion is a private matter" has completely lost its meaning in a world which finally no longer views human beings as autonomous individual personalities, but first as members of a people [*Volk*]. There is absolutely no reason why religion should be viewed as a private matter after art, science, philosophical and political worldviews have ceased to be private matters of the individual citizen. Thus there in fact exists a *theoretical* possibility that the *Cuius regio, eius religio* of times past shall experience a resurrection in our century.

---

end of its traditional legal order; the revolution also robbed it of its political support, endangered its economic foundations and spiritually was nothing less than a catastrophe" (Klaus Scholder, *The Churches and the Third Reich*, 1:3). RF

[110] A central feature of National Socialist theory. RF

But it is still only a theoretical possibility. For anyone who has lived through the last two years of internal German history knows that this history has demonstrated two things. First, it is a fact that today it is no longer possible to declare one of the great Christian confessions the religion of the state, and second, it is a fact that these confessions still possess so much power over souls that every attempt to replace them with another state religion would throw Germany into the worst confessional struggle of its history.

Thus the German state of our day does not, as many a theoretician believes, face the task of assigning religion a new position within the bounds of public life. It faces rather the old question which has ruled the history of our people for a thousand years, the question of the correct ordering of the relationship of the state to the church of Jesus Christ. Whichever solutions are found to these problems of our century, however the civil-ecclesiastical law of the future in Germany may appear, this law will really serve the state and the church and thus be a blessing to the people who belong to both only if it preserves the basic principle which the Lutheran Reformation once learned from the Holy Scriptures and proclaimed to the world—that the divine orders of the state and the church are not to be mixed or confounded.

1935

NON-OBLIGATORY PROPOSAL TOWARD THE SPIRITUAL LEADERSHIP OF THE CHURCH[1]

The original document was dated January 12, 1935. It was presented to the Lutheran Council [*Lutherischer Rat*] by Sasse and his Erlangen colleague Friedrich Ulmer. These theses address a group of questions especially about the office of bishop in the Evangelical Lutheran Church.

They are in the context of the Nazi government's encroachment on the ordering of the churches (see, for example, reference to a Führer in thesis 11). They also comment on the relation of church and ministry. They are written in the context of the German *Landeskirche* ("territorial church") setting. Thus, when they speak of "church" they do not refer only to congregation (e.g., thesis 10). They conclude with a brief, clear statement of the doctrine of the two governments (thesis 12).

Huss number 134.1

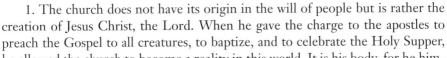

1. The church does not have its origin in the will of people but is rather the creation of Jesus Christ, the Lord. When he gave the charge to the apostles to preach the Gospel to all creatures, to baptize, and to celebrate the Holy Supper, he allowed the church to become a reality in this world. It is his body, for he himself is in it, concealed in Word and Sacrament, present until the world's end.

2. Wherever the pure Gospel is preached and the Sacraments are administered, there, according to the promise of God that his Word shall not return void [Is 55:10–11], springs into existence a congregation of believers, sanctified in the faith (*congregatio sanctorum*, AC VII).

---

[1]   This essay was originally published as "Unverbindlicher Vorschlag zur Geistlichen Leitung der Kirche" in *Lutherische Kirche* 17.3 (February 1, 1935): 39–41. It was published over the names of both Sasse and Friedrich Ulmer. MH/RF

3. The charge to proclaim the Word and administer the Sacraments is for all time accomplished by the office of the ministry [*kirchlichen Amt*] (*ministerium ecclesiasticum*, AC V).

4. This office of the ministry does not at its very essence come into existence out of the will of the congregation; it is rather the creation of Christ [*aus der Stiftung Christi*]. The relationship of office and congregation is to be understood in such a way that neither is present without the other and neither is master over the other.

5. Jesus Christ has prescribed to his church no specific order [*Verfassung*] to be drawn from the NT, but he has willed that his church have an ordered existence (1 Cor 14:40 and 14:33; 1 Corinthians 12; Ephesians 4; and Romans 12).

6. A church is then correctly ordered when its constitution [*Verfassung*] makes possible the right preaching of the Gospel and the right administration of the Sacraments. Any ordering of the church [*Kirchenverfassung*] which makes the fulfillment of this charge impossible or endangers it cannot be reconciled with the essence of the church.

7. In a correctly ordered church, the ecclesiastical office (which is not dependent upon people) and the congregation (whose Lord is Jesus Christ and not people) must find a form which makes possible the fulfillment of the particular tasks of each, which are to be accomplished cooperatively and independently. Still, these ordered tasks can never be so allotted that explicit functions of the church are simply the responsibility of the office of the ministry [*geistliche Amt*] alone or the congregation alone. Thus the congregation is responsible for the purity of the Word which is proclaimed and the administration of the Sacraments, and with this also the presence of a properly ordered office [of the ministry]. On the other hand, the office of the ministry [*geistliche Amt*] is to see that the congregation actually exercises the rights and responsibilities of the "spiritual priesthood" (1 Peter 2).

8. The spiritual character of the church excludes the separation of the proclamation of the Word from the administration of external matters [*externa*] so that the latter may be allowed to become entirely or partially extra-ecclesiastical entities. For finally, all external matters of the church serve the proclamation of the Word. Their administration can therefore never be without the influence of this proclamation.

9. The tasks entrusted to church government are as follows: the supervision of pastors and their preaching, and with this the purity of doctrine; the supervision of the life and the order of the congregation; and the administration of the external matters of the church. These appointed tasks are inseparably bound together.

10. This church government appertains to the entire church (FC SD X 9) and will be exercised at every level of the church's life (local congregation, provincial church, territorial church) in continuous cooperation with the office of the min-

istry [*geistliche Amt*] and the congregation. To this end the church has the power to create entities [*Organe*] which are necessary to accomplish its functions.

11. Such entities have been—since ancient times—the office of the bishop and the organization of synods. Insofar as the authority of the bishop surpasses that of the other holders of the *ministerium ecclesiasticum* ["office of the ministry"] and the authority of the synod exceeds that of the congregation, these orders [*Ordnungen*] are *iure humano* ["human law"], to be understood as "good order," if the church—which has the authority to do so—introduces them. Here the synod is not to be conceived of as an ecclesiastical parliament, nor the bishop an ecclesiastical parallel to the secular Führer. The dangers of sliding into a religious parliamentarianism or into an unevangelical clericalism will not be avoided by legal institutions. It will rather only be avoided by this: that the bearers of positions in church government are led by faith in the Gospel and that they therefore know that all external orders of the church only serve to build the church when God's Holy Spirit works among them.

12. The relationship of church to state in the Lutheran Church is clearly laid down in AC XXVIII. Both the secular and the spiritual government are "governments" given by God, and each has its proper value. Yet at the same time, their functions are differentiated from each other. The connections which exist between church and state in the sphere of public law must always be regulated anew. In this the church acts in accordance with the words of her Lord: Give to Caesar what is Caesar's [Matt 22:21]. That means the church will grant to the state those rights of oversight over ecclesiastical properties, including the related questions regarding property rights and external legislation, which rights the state needs in order to fulfill its God-given commission. The church will, in joyful obedience to God's Word, honor and acknowledge the right of the state and at the same time maintain that her own right [of existence] does not originate with the state, but from God, who has established the church alongside the state.

1935

CONFESSIONAL UNREPENTANCE?
REMARKS TOWARD UNDERSTANDING
LUTHERAN CONFESSIONALISM[1]

Sasse here gives one of his strongest critiques of the Union churches of Germany. He himself was raised in, educated in, and at first served in the largest such church, the Prussian Union. He once explained that he did not know Lutheranism until he visited the United States on study leave in 1925–1926. He also addresses, in very specific language, the challenge of Karl Barth to confessional Lutheranism.

In this essay we find a more confident, perhaps even belligerent theologian who speaks with a boldness not so much of self-confidence, but more from the seriousness of the situation facing the church. It is a time of "struggle" that threatens the very existence of the church, at least humanly speaking.

The essay however does not end in that polemical tone. At the end we find that confident hope for the church and for repentant churchmen that is centered in the Lord who still prays for his church.

Huss number 135
Hopf number 070

—◦◦◦—

PART 1

Since the time when princely despotism met its end in our fatherland, a number of Protestant princes and their court theologians were indeed successful—not at overcoming the ecclesiastical splintering of German Protestantism, but rather in increasing the number of Evangelical denominations in Germany from two to three. This happened through the introduction of the Union between Lutherans and Reformed. The difficult, but not all together hopeless task of the ecclesiastical unification of Evangelical Germany has become a problem something like the

---

[1] The German original of this article, "Konfessionelle Unbußfertigkeit? Ein Wort zum Verständnis des lutherischen Konfessionalismus," appeared in two parts in the *Allgemeine Evangelisch-Lutherische Kirchenzeitung* 68.11 and 12 (March 15 and 22, 1935): 245–49 and 266–74, respectively. MH

squaring of a circle. Until the Unions there certainly appeared, at first glance, to be a great tangle of territorial churches. But within them lived *both the Evangelical churches* which had existed since Reformation times, the "Evangelical Lutheran Church" and the "Church Reformed according to God's Word." Since the Religious Peace of Augsburg (1555) and of Westphalia (1648) they have been tolerated and acknowledged as denominations, but they have never been able to achieve the outer form necessitated by their confessional documents. For in the past, official German law had indeed guaranteed (in so far as it lay in the interest of the state) to the Roman Catholic Church, and later also to a series of small religious fellowships, the freedom of ecclesiastical formation. But for both the Evangelical churches which had their roots in sixteenth-century Germany, the corresponding right has always been denied.

Indeed, these Reformation churches also rejoiced over religious freedom in so far as they enjoyed legally guaranteed freedom of worship, ecclesiastical dogma, and the personal freedom of faith. But unlike other countries, particularly those speaking the English language, in our case *the free exercise of religion never included the unconditional freedom to organize the church* [*Kirchenbildung*]. Nor did this freedom in any way mean that the Lutheran and Reformed churches were granted the right to conform their outer order to the demands of their confessions.

Nothing is more significant for the lawful relationship of German Protestant churches than the fact that the Reformed Church in Germany has also been unable to have the church government which the teaching of the Calvinist Reformation demands [for its churches] to be the true church of Christ. The princes never granted this to the Reformed denominations. Only where the Reformed have lived in opposition to the temporal authority, as was the case with the "Congregation under the Cross" on the Lower Rhine, have they been able to establish their presbyterial and synodical forms of church government. But where this has happened, they have only been left an anxious respite in the territorial-church system. No one would maintain that the "Rhenish-Westphalian Church Order," which will soon celebrate its one-hundredth anniversary, is a genuine Reformed order, satisfying the requirements of the Reformed confessions. The Lutherans have faced an even worse situation.

In Prussia and other states, the Lutheran Church has been denied the right to a church government which accords with its confessions and which had been established by the Lutheran confession and acknowledged by the old Reich and state canon law. Some few thousand who, in view of the consequences which this move by state government would have for church and state, unswervingly maintained the demands of the confession were prepared to endure and sacrifice all for that confession. And they finally won the freedom to form a church according to the Lutheran confession. But they won this only for a Lutheran Free Church, not for the entire Lutheran Church of Germany. And the same thing happened in the case of the Reformed Church which was forced to exist with forms of church government determined by political and canon law territorialism. But these forms of existence were at essential odds with its essence. To borrow an example from natural science, they [these churches] were like minerals which, by unnatural manipulation, have been prevented from crystallizing into the form which corresponds to their essence.

It is therefore absolutely incorrect to cast blame upon German Protestantism for the fact that until 1933 it had achieved no greater unification than to have been an ecclesiastical federation of twenty-eight territorial churches. At the beginning of the Third Reich in Germany, there were exactly as many Evangelical churches as there were at the conclusion to the Peace of Westphalia, namely, two, the Lutheran and the Reformed, no more and no less. But both these churches throughout their existence have been able to establish ecclesiastical governments in accordance with their confessions only to the extent allowed them by public law. This is evident at every critical point in German history, whether in 1555 or 1648, 1806 or 1815, 1848 or 1871, 1918 or 1933.[2] Therefore all attempts to overcome the territorial church system [*Territorialkirchentum*] in earlier times were condemned to failure. Here we mean the efforts of German Lutheranism in the previous century to achieve an organic unity of the Lutheran territorial churches, just as much as the efforts in recent years for the formation of a Greater Hessian Church from church bodies which belonged in part to Prussia and in part to the Free State of Hesse. Only the complete setting aside of territorialism in the realms of political and state law (as we are now experiencing it), which had developed in Germany over the course of a long history, have made possible the freeing of the two Evangelical churches of Germany from the Babylonian captivity of territorial churchism.

PART 2

One can only hazard a guess at how simple the re-formation of German Evangelical churches in our day could have proceeded if that unhealthy inheritance of old territorialism, which has retarded every real attempt at a new ordering of ecclesiastical relationships, had not stood in the way: the false Unions of the nineteenth century. For these Unions were not born of ecumenical considerations or of an ecclesiastical consensus. They are rather the result of the worst provincialism. What was won for the church of Christ when the four (really! only four!) Reformed souls who lived in the Lutheran parish of Oranienburg[3] were

---

[2] 1555—Peace of Augsburg; 1648—Peace of Westphalia; 1806—the dissolution, with the empire, of the *Corpus Sociorum Augustanae Confessionis* (or simply *Corpus Evangelicorum*) of Protestant princes; 1815— events at end of Napoleonic era; 1848—the Great Revolution; 1871—formation of the modern German state under the leadership of Prussia (Bismarck); 1918—the revolution after WW I; 1933—the formation of the "German Evangelical Church" instigated by the Nazis. RF

[3] Sasse's first pastorate (as "fourth pastor") was in Oranienburg bei Berlin 1921–1928, a parish of ten thousand souls in two churches. RF

united with a thousand Lutherans to become one united congregation? Here the important aspects of both confessions relative to the Divine Service, the administration of the Sacraments, and catechetical instruction were treated as inconsequential for so long by one Lutheran and one Reformed pastor that finally no one in the congregation any longer knew (not even the pastors) to which confession they belonged. Or for that matter, they no longer even knew what an ecclesiastical confession was, indeed, what the church was in general. And this was supposedly justified then and still is today by this passage: "One body and one Spirit . . . one Lord, one faith, one Baptism" (Eph 4:4–5)!

The presupposition which lies behind the German Unions of the previous century was not a belief in the *una sancta ecclesia* ["one holy church"] as a divine reality in this world. It was not "this consoling article of the Creed" regarding the one true catholic church, which is not bound to this or that land but extends from the rising to the setting of the sun, an article of faith of which the Apology speaks so powerfully [Ap VII/VIII 9, German]. No, the presupposition of those Unions was the conviction that the ruler of the territory is also the bishop and lord of his church and that the boundaries of the visible church extent to the point where the rule of his Most Serene Highness [*Serenissimus*] ends. But when his Most Serene Highness is most graciously pleased to unite the churches in his land and thus finally to complete the Reformation, then the church is unified! No one asks about what has happened on the other side of the border. No one considers the consequences of that unification, that allegedly "divinely willed" work of establishing peace. The court preachers are in the best position to raise questions as they prepare the way for unification in their festival sermons. But they, of course, cannot conceive of the possibility that anything which his Most Serene Highness undertakes might not be greeted by the blessing of heaven. No one considers the possibility that all at once world history might possibly bring an end to these chapels which represent the good intentions of mediocre men who would be great [*Kapellen der Biedermeierzeit*].

A quick look at the centuries and the continents which have inherited the Reformers and the confessions of the sixteenth century shows that, though they speak of the catholic or universal church, no one any longer possesses, least of all the professors of systematic theology (who live partly in the study and partly in the arcane, ethereal regions of their systems), the theoretic foundation to justify what is happening in the church quite apart from their help. "Precisely the question," wrote Vilmar in 1856,[4]

> which has already begun to come to the fore in more recent discussions regarding the church is over its universality. And this is happening just as the terminology used by the unionists is losing its hold. To the unionists this is in fact entirely objectionable, or even completely inconceivable. Union churches are formed in Nassau and Hanau, in the Palatinate, in Baden and

---

[4] *Die Theologie der Tatsachen wider die Theologie der Rhetorik* (4th ed.; 1876), 51 ff. HS

Prussia, in Anhalt and Waldeck. But nothing more comes of it nor will come of it than insignificant little sectarian churches, short on confession and long on controversy, short on spiritual life and long on secular regulation, short on authority and long on rhetoric. That the Unions not only did not bring about a universal church but also did not clear the way for such a church has been shown by the fact that by excluding and repelling Lutheran and genuine Reformed Christians, while gaining one member, they have only increased the division of the church. But let it try to win another one for the Union! Perhaps only the Swiss, not to mention the Hollander, or to top it all off, the Scottish Independent. [And then see how much division results.]

How the history of the church of the previous generation has confirmed this judgment! If the Union possessed that inherent legitimacy which its disciples ascribed to it, if it really was able to bring about unification in churchly life, why has it never succeeded even in Prussia? Why, even after the political resistance of 1866 had long been defeated,[5] has the Prussian Church been unable to unite the churches of the new provinces with itself? Why were there still seven (with Waldeck, eight) distinct churches in Prussia in 1933? One could blame those "evil" Lutherans, but then why had the Evangelical Church of the Old Prussian Union (which arrogantly called itself the greatest Protestant church in the world) never even been able to generate enough gravitational pull to get the United Churches of Nassau and Frankfurt to join it? Lutheran confessionalism does not bear the least guilt in this matter. To what then were those once Lutheran and Reformed Christians united if after 1866 or 1918 the Prussian United Churches couldn't unite themselves? No, these Unions, allegedly serving to unify the church, have only created new divisions. Every false attempt to unify Christianity has had to bear the curse that, in spite of all the good intentions, disunity has only increased.

One need only be reminded of certain fellowships (from the beginnings of Pietism down to the modern day Disciples of Christ) which the scattered children of God desired to bring together from the various denominations on the basis of the simple biblical Gospel. In each instance a new denomination has thereby come into existence. The outcome was exactly the same with the Unions in Germany, Canada, China, and North and South India. The result was always the formation of a new denomination. This was not, of course, the intention. It was asserted that this was not the case. Hitherto every Union has begun with the assurance that no new denomination is being created, the intent being only the visible expression of the higher unity of the denominations which already exists. It is a celebrated highpoint of all Union synods when the participants later recount the unforgettable experiencing of this "higher unity" as a revelation. This

---

[5]   The battle of Königgrätz in 1866 confirmed the dominant position of Prussia with its annexation of Hanover, Schleswig-Holstein, and electoral Hessia. This meant that the leadership of Protestant Germany was taken over by the church and state authorities in Berlin, and that sealed the predominance of the Prussian Union. RF

"revelation" is perceived by them as the working of the Holy Spirit, but it is all too suspicious to theological critics. It was experienced in Toronto in 1925 and at the South Indian Union Synods of recent years, just as it was in 1846 in the Castle Chapel in Berlin when a confessing Union synod held forth the worthy reservation in the notorious *Nitzschenum*[6] "that a confession of the church shall in no way be erected here." But the nature of this so-called "higher unity" becomes evident whenever this tender plant, which bloomed in the warm greenhouse air of a synod, is uprooted by the rough storms of life. Indeed, every theologian needs to be absolutely clear about what the "higher unity" attained by the Prussian Union has meant. But many a German theologian, working in the realm of theory, often no longer knows anything of the realities of his church. One other example makes this clear.

What has actually come of the German emigrants who in the previous century emigrated from the lands of the Prussian Union to those portions of the world which still lie deep within the shadow of confessionalism? The Prussian emigrants in North America, in Australia, and in South Africa have returned to the churches of their fathers. They have again become Lutheran or Reformed so far as they have continued to belong to the church. Only in the United States did the idea of founding a church of the "higher unity" arise, a united church according to the German model, for German emigrants. This began in 1840 when two missionaries from the Rhenish and Basel Mission joined a pastor from Bremen and another pastor from Strasbourg. The "German Evangelical Synod,"[7] which was the result, had more than three hundred thousand members by the time just after the World War, and it represented nearly one-tenth of American Lutherans. Their confessions were the Augustana (the Variata[8] of course) and the Lutheran and Heidelberg Catechisms. On the basis of these confessions, the Synod

---

[6]   This was a document named for Karl Immanuel Nitzsch (1787–1868), a disciple of Schleiermacher. It was an attempt at a compromise in the ordination formula for the Prussian Union, according to which the candidate was to make profession of the great fundamental and saving truths instead of the church confession. But it did not include in such fundamental truths the doctrines of creation, original sin, the supernatural conception, the descent into hell and ascension of Christ, the resurrection of the body, the last judgment, nor everlasting life or punishment. Since by this formula the special confessions of Lutheran and Reformed were really set aside, the existence of a Lutheran as well as a Reformed church seemed to be abolished. Opponents made a play on words, substituting *Nitzschenum* for *Nicaenum*, the Latin title for the Nicene Creed; sometimes they would call this document the unfortunate *Nicaenum* of the nineteenth century (J. H. Kurtz, *Church History* [trans. John MacPherson; 2d ed.; 3 vols.; London: Hodder & Stoughton, 1893], 3:280–81). MH/RF

[7]   The Evangelical Synod of North America grew out of the Prussian Union. It was formed in 1840 at Gravois Settlement, near St. Louis, Mo., on the basis of a Lutheran–Reformed compromise. Eventually Reformed theology gained control and modernism followed. It eventually became a part of the Evangelical and Reformed Church (1934) and finally the United Church of Christ (1957; *Lutheran Cyclopedia*, 785). RF

[8]   The Variata refers to variant editions of the Augsburg Confession published by Melanchthon, especially that of 1540. Particularly controversial was the alteration of Article X on the Lord's Supper which made it more acceptable to the Calvinists. See "The Variata of 1540" in M. Reu, *The Augsburg Confession: A Collection of Sources with an Historical Introduction* (Chicago: Wartburg, 1930), part 2, pp. 398–411. RF

attempted to uphold the inner relationship within German Protestantism. It saw therein its obligation to guard and advocate to the other churches in the United States the "heritage of the Reformation" in the sense of the Old Prussian Church. But after the unavoidable move of the congregations to English as the ecclesiastical language had led them to strike the word "German" from the name of the church, the residue of Evangelical consciousness which had been preserved now immediately faded. While the strict Lutheran churches have managed to bring their confession over into the English language unabbreviated, the "Evangelical Synod" in recent years has surrendered its independence and been swallowed up by completely unevangelical sects. This is the fate of a church of the Augustana Variata, the fate of a church which sought to guard the "higher unity" which supposedly exists over and above the Lutheran and Reformed confessions, the "purely evangelical" church in the sense of the Old Prussian Union. It is the fate which sooner or later faces all German Evangelical diaspora in every corner of the world. And no Gustavus Adolphus Society,[9] no official church department in Germany will rescue it unless our emigrant congregations decisively renounce the false "higher unity" of the Union, which is finally nothing other than *confessionlessness*, and this before it is too late.

PART 3

The Union is confessionlessness. That is the lesson of nineteenth-century church history. The introduction of the Unions in Germany is the direct parallel in church history to the nullification of the Reformation confessions in the churches of Switzerland and in many other church fellowships formerly of the Reformed confession. The demand to dissolve the German Unions is nothing other than the cry for the reestablishment of the confessions. And this cry today rings throughout the church of Switzerland and other Calvinistic churches. That confessionlessness, which was naturally not intended by many of the advocates of Union, but knowingly strove for by others for generations, is also the deeper reason for *the impotence of the Union.* That the life of the church in the Rhineland is relatively strong provides no counter argument. This life was not produced by the Union— otherwise it would also be present in the Palatinate. It was rather the heritage of Pietism and a result of the [Confessional] Awakening, as was similarly the case in the Württemberg Church. It was a life which preceded the Union. But just how much the Union has weakened and destroyed that life may be clearly seen by anyone in the report which then president of the Rhine Provisional Synod, Walther Wolff, presented at the last German Evangelical *Kirchentag*[10] (1930) on "The

---

9   The Gustav–Adolf–Verein was formed in 1832 "to commemorate the bicentenary of the death of King Gustavus Adolphus of Sweden." It was founded to aid weaker sister churches (of all confessions) in the "diaspora" (*ODCC*, 723). RF

10   "Church Congress," which had begun in 1848 mainly for laity. RF

Right and Authority of the German Reformation for Church Formation." This report of the leader of the Rhineland Church contained precisely all the heresies which are so energetically fought against today in the Rhineland. The choice of this speaker, who has continued to be noteworthy, for a German *Kirchentag* in the anniversary year of the Augustana is the result of a quiet agreement between Reformed [Christians] of the Rhineland, friendly to the Union, and certain Berlin Protestants. Both of these groups had an interest in seeing that no one even once spoke seriously about the Augustana at the celebration at Augsburg. President Wolff also spoke so dubiously on the *notae* ["marks"] of the German Evangelical Church that no one could tell what kind of church the "German" Reformation actually had intended. He counted, among other things, the "German Catechism" as one of these "marks" of the church. Here one could supply whichever catechism necessary, Luther's Small Catechism or the Heidelberg Catechism.

This is the "higher unity" which the Prussian Union created. In other words, it is no unity at all, but rather a fraud, which comes to rule in every church in which the confession is destroyed. It was—at least in recent generations—no conscious fraud. For all these poor ecclesiastical councilors, general superintendents, and pastors had learned in their theological training the theology [*Weisheit*] behind this way of thinking. It is questionable, however, whether or not men in the first generation of the Union consciously cooperated in something they knew would nullify the church's confession. The notable interest which certain lodges with their Freemason "religion in which we all agree"[11] had in this happening would strongly confirm this, as well as the fact that later the Protestant Union became the energetic champion of the Union. It is also questionable whether or not at the General Synod of 1846, the only Synod in Prussia of any intellectual significance [*geistigem Format*], anybody actually realized what really happened in the Prussian Church. (The participants of this Synod were not elected but rather nominated by a king who had some sense for churchly matters.) But very soon untruthfulness came to pervade. It was believed that the "higher unity" had been found, but in reality unity was further away than at any time previously.

From the point of view of the Union, this is the most severe accusation which can be made against it. Even in its own midst it never achieved unity. The differences and antitheses between the Lutheran and the Reformed in Germany are certainly deep and serious. But they are nowhere near as threatening for the life of the church as the differences between the United [Churches]. There are individuals in these United Churches who, as far as they themselves are concerned, desire to be confessionally Lutheran or Reformed and, in fact, are such and only desire a common administration of external matters on the basis of church-organizational necessities. There are United individuals who desire to be neither

---

[11]　This quotation, used several times, is given in English in the original. RF

Lutheran nor Reformed but confess a particular type of evangelical Christianity. This "United" type of Christianity is at one time understood as a higher unity of Lutheran and Reformed [Christianity]. At another time, it is viewed as a common shrine, and one's confessional shoes must be removed before entering. Then it is seen as a higher scaffolding over the Lutheran and Reformed churches, erected by the arts of theological dialectic. The *pistics*[12] of the unsophisticated faith of the congregation are satisfied with the Lutheran or Reformed confession of the fathers and need to celebrate the Supper separately. The *Gnostics*, however, are producing the confession of the future in the higher spheres of a purely evangelical theology. This is how colleague *Herr* Bunsen[13] once depicted the structure of the church of the future.

In Prussia there are three or four types of congregations in the Union. The congregations have no idea to which type they belong, nor for that matter do the pastors know. Johannes Schneider[14] knew. Since his death no one any longer knows, not even the professors of practical theology. But outside the Prussian Union there are still the Nassau, Palatinate, and Baden types, and there are still others. There are United congregations which are absolutely committed to the great common Christian dogmas of the Holy Trinity and the divinity of Jesus Christ. There are other United congregations which have rejected such old "Greek" dogmas as outdated. Is it possible today that there are deniers of the divinity of Christ also in the Lutheran churches? Yes, this can be said. Unfortunately! But then such people are definite opponents of the Lutheran Confessions and disciples of the Union. There are United [Christians] who assert the authority of Holy Scripture over against all the pretensions of human reason. There are other United [Christians] who view the Bible only as a document of human religious history. It is said that these heresies have also arisen in the Reformed churches (as for instance in Switzerland, Holland, and Scotland). That is certain. But such Reformed churches have very definitely decided for the abolition of the old confessions and for union with all churches, and the Union has abolished dogma.

Is it not high time for the end of the disunity among the disciples of the Union? Is it not time for the disciples of the "religion in which we all agree" to tell us wherein this agreement really lies? For a century now we have heard daily

---

[12] Those trusting in faith alone rather than the "Gnostics" who trust in knowledge. RF

[13] Christian von Bunsen (1791–1860) was a German diplomatist and amateur theologian. He assisted in the preparation of the Prussian Union Agenda. While minister at the Prussian legation in London, he "was the chief instrument in the scheme for a joint Lutheran and Anglican bishopric in Jerusalem" (*ODCC*, 251). RF

[14] Johannes Schneider (1857–1930) was chiefly known as the founder and editor of the *Kirchliches Jahrbuch für die evangelischen Landeskirchen Deutschlands* (a yearbook sent to all Protestant pastors in Germany) from 1894 until his death. Sasse succeeded him as the editor (1931–1934), but its publication was stopped by the Nazis. In the 1932 edition, Sasse's essay on the ecclesiastical situation was critical of the Nazi party; it would soon cause much grief from party officials and acclaim from later critics. It was reprinted more than six times from 1932 until 1981. RF

how loveless, how unrepentant, how un-Christian it is that we do not agree with them. And whenever we ask wherein they properly agree and what it is to which we ought agree, this question is explained to us as a tactless meddling in the affairs of other churches, as audacious, inordinately ambitious confessionalism. And we are supposedly blind to the "higher unity" which is certainly already present. [After all] even a blind man himself would be able to *feel* it. And so it could only be evil intent which would cause us to deny this "higher unity."

How then do those of us who are confessionally minded proceed? There is hardly anything else we can do other than *leave the United to themselves for a time*, so that undisturbed by confessional interruption, they can come to some unity on what they actually teach and on whether or not they have one doctrine, one confession, and *whether the Union is a confession or not*. We will have to allow them their internal discussions. And in the meantime it would be good for those of us who uphold the confession of the fathers, whether Lutheran or Reformed, to join together in a federation [*Bund*]. We will fight shoulder to shoulder for the right of existence of the Evangelical churches born of the Reformation and against the truthlessness of the nineteenth century "religion in which we all agree." For we know that an "agreement" on religious sentiments and churchly organizations does not create the fellowship of the visible church [*die Gemeinschaft der sichtbaren Kirche schafft*], but only the *consensus de doctrina evangelii et de administratione sacramentorum* ["agreement in the doctrine of the Gospel and the administration of the Sacraments," AC VII 2].

We will not cease to pray and work so that the torn church of Christ may again become one. We are prepared to wrestle for the truth of the Gospel with all confessions [*Konfessionen*], whether Catholic or Protestant, so long as they confess the Nicene Creed. But a dialogue with the theologians of the Union will be impossible until they inform us on whether or not they advocate a confession and what their confession is. If in the course of time, such a confession is formed and the Old Prussian Synods one day are prepared to do what they are evidently unprepared to do today, namely, express a definite doctrine, then matters will be different. When they are ready to state their position on a matter such as the real presence of the body and blood of Christ in the Holy Supper and do so in a manner which makes clear why they are neither Lutheran nor Reformed, then we will be able to honorably strive with them for the truth. But if that is not the case, if these Unions refuse to be a confession and at the same time decline to return to the confessions of the age of the Reformation, and furthermore, if they assert that they represent a "higher unity," then we will see in them only a remnant of the mentality of the nineteenth century, which in no way can claim the legitimacy of a church and provides us no cause to enter into discussion. Either the Union will be a third confession along side of the Lutheran and Reformed confessions, if it has the courage and if it believes it absorbs both these old confessions, or it must be disbanded for the sake of the true unity of the church, which is only held up and hindered by the false attempt at union. These are the alternatives which face

German Protestantism today: *to make the Union a confession*, within which the other confessions may perhaps disband (that is if a real *consensus de doctrina evangelii et de administratione sacramentorum* would actually come about), or *the dissolution of the Unions* and the return of their congregations and believers home to the churches of the Reformation. *Tertium non datur* ["a third choice is not given"].

PART 4

Finally, a few personal remarks are in order. The arguments we have presented here do not win a person many friends. But it is necessary to say something about why a German Lutheran theologian has to speak in this way today. We say it in rejoinder to a series of articles which in recent months have advocated maintaining the Union, two of which we shall here discuss.

The first is the essay by the Bonn systematician Hans Emil Weber,[15] "Von Recht und Sendung der Union," which appeared first in the September 1934 edition of *Christentum und Wissenschaft*. Shortly thereafter it appeared in an expanded form and was given still wider circulation as a pamphlet in the Freizeiten-Verlag of the Essen pastor Fr. Graeber. We will not discuss its theological content here, for the ideas of E. Weber were all amply dealt with and refuted in the mid-nineteenth century. Here we simply note the theological opinion of the Erlangen, Leipzig, and Rostock faculties directed against the resolution of the Berlin *Kirchentag* of 1853 which declared the Augustana the common confession of the Evangelical churches of Germany. This was done in order to give the ecclesiastical unification of Germany a confessionally justifiable foundation. Weber makes precisely the same proposal—and he is hardly alone in this assertion. And indeed, he makes his proposal with the same reservation of the *German Evangelical Kirchentag*, that with their consent to the Augustana the individual churches can reconcile their particular confessions and particular doctrines, even the Reformed doctrine of the Supper rejected by the Augustana. That this is impossible is demonstrated by the theological opinion cited by Weber himself, *The Confession of the Lutheran Church Defended against the Confession of the Berlin Kirchentag by Certain Teachers of Theology and Canon Law*.[16]

There is only one thing to be said in response to Weber's article. We Lutherans are well prepared to heed the call to repentance, wherever it may come

---

[15] Hans Emil Weber (1882–1950), a student of K. Kähler, taught at Halle, Bonn, and Münster. RF

[16] [*Das Bekenntnis der lutherischen Kirche gegen das Bekenntnis des Berliner Kirchentags gewahrt von etlichen Lehrern der Theologie und des Kirchenrechts*] (Erlangen, 1853); reprinted in *Lutherische Kirche* (1935, no. 1). Whether this made any impression on Weber is quite doubtful. He apparently did not find it at all convincing. Here we have to do not with differing theological viewpoints within one church, but rather with churches which are finally in disunity. Only this can explain Weber's judgment on the perpetually most-troubling aspects of Brandenburg Union politics. One can see in Weber's thought why the formation of a Union confession has been in process for so long. For Weber will never understand that and why the question of the truth of the Lutheran doctrine of the Supper can only be decided with a "yes" or a "no" and never a "well yes, but also" [*sowohl als auch*]. HS

from. We are fully aware of the fact that unrepentance weighs heavy upon German Protestantism like a curse. We have not forgotten that the Reformation, like every previous epoch in the history of the church, began with the call to repentance. But we can only honestly repent for sins which we have acknowledged as such. If Weber, however, believes he can represent the viewpoint of confessional Lutheranism by the sentence "A confessionalism, however, which sets aside the basic principle that Holy Scripture stands above the confession should not expect to be taken seriously," then his call to repentance is illusionary. Where is *this* kind of confessionalism? If we, for good reasons, are of the viewpoint that the careful explication of the statements of the NT regarding the Holy Supper by the fathers of our church in the sixteenth century are still more correct than the opinions of modern exegetes,[17] is this really a subordination of the Scriptures to the confessions? Do Weber and the others who make this same accusation know how seriously we Lutherans take the *sola scriptura* ["by Scripture alone"]? Or are we again at a point where two churches stand at odds over against each other?

The second article to which we would like to respond is a series of theses published in the *Allgemeine Evangelisch-Lutherische Kirchenzeitung*, no. 9, entitled "Theological Reservations regarding the Struggle over the Union," wherein a position is taken for the Union and against its dissolution. It is an article which merits serious consideration. A succession of subscribers have given their thoughtful approbation to the document. Among them are, of course, men of the Positive Union. But have not the weapons with which this group desires to fight for the church proven to be too weak? The theologians of this group have led the Prussian Church to its present condition. They have never had the courage to oppose any heresy with the full authority of the ecclesiastical office. They have never been particularly concerned to uphold the confessional vow of the pastor and the confessional position of congregations. They do not want this. They indeed desire to defend the confession, but they are never able to say what is meant by the church's confession. We are not at all surprised to find the names of their theological champions appended to this article.

But there is one name which does in fact surprise us. That is the name of *Karl Barth*. Has the cessation of party strife, for which the first number of *Theologische Existenz*[18] (31 f.) so energetically reproached the young reformation movement [*Jungreformatorische*], been achieved? One is tempted to ask: "Just what is intended to be said about the nature of the church in a proclamation to which are appended, among others, the names Barth, Lütgert, von Soden, Wehrung, and Hertzberg?" To be sure, this proclamation does not speak *expressis verbis* ["explicitly"] of "the nature of the church," but it does speak of vital questions regarding the church in Germany, concerning which "Theological Reservations" are

---

[17] Weber wrote mainly in the area of the NT. RF

[18] *Theologische Existenz heute (Theological Existence Today)* was a periodical from Barth and his colleagues; the title reflects the existential emphasis of their so-called "crisis theology." RF

expressed. Is not one's judgment on the Union, and that means indeed the question of confession, more an indication of what kind of theology one has?

Just what does this manifesto, which claims to override and bind together theological antitheses, contain? It asks anew: "Has it been beneficial?" "Has it been beneficial to allow the recollection of 1817 and 1835[19] to be determinative as the ecclesiastical and theological questions of the Union are discussed?" The answer is of course no! This has not been beneficial. One must not only consider these two years. One must consider the three centuries from the defection of John Sigismund[20] from the Lutheran Church to the disciplinary proceedings which the last Reformed territorial bishop of Prussia in 1899 allowed to commence against Stöcker[21] when he urged the bishop to resign from his office. One must consider the persistent and brutal eradication of Lutheranism in Brandenburg-Prussia, and all the confessional battles which brought suspensions from office and political reprisals from 1614 to 1873! What kind of church must that be which has managed to live on through this history!

"Has it been beneficial to make the Union responsible for ecclesiastical difficulties and perils, which are also burning issues in confessional churches?" No, one is certainly justified in noting all the mistakes of the individual churches. In order to understand the effect of the German Unions, one must take note of the more recent history of all of Lutheranism and all of Protestantism in general. And when one considers that the majority of the German pastors were trained under faculties whose composition was determined in Berlin, it becomes absolutely clear how devastating the Prussian Union has already been for all of Germany!

"Has it been beneficial to hinder dealing with the theological-ecclesiastical problems of the Evangelical Union by considering only the most vexing extremes of either a purely confederative Union on the one hand or an absorptive Union on the other?" To this we have only to pose the counter question: "Has it been beneficial when immature young men, who have never seen a Lutheran or a Reformed church, who know neither the German nor the foreign church situation, who know nothing of the great questions regarding union on the mission fields and in emigrant lands and have no notion of the deadly seriousness of the question of confession, who perhaps have never even seen a confessing congrega-

---

[19] These were significant dates in the formation of the Prussian Union. RF

[20] John Sigismund (1572–1619) was elector of Brandenburg from 1608 until 1619. Raised as a strict Lutheran, he became a close friend of the Reformed Count Palatine Frederick IV while studying at Heidelberg. He became a decided opponent of the Formula of Concord. At first his change in sentiment was kept secret, but by 1614 he had in place a plan to subject his lands to the Reformed faith, and orthodox pastors were forced to flee. By 1618, however, opposition to his efforts was so strong that the attempt at changing the confession of Brandenburg was abandoned. Between 1613 and 1619 some 231 polemical treatises were published. The Lutherans were led especially by Leonard Hutter, Matthias Höe von Hoenegg, and Friedrich Balduin. See "Sigismund, Johann" in *New Schaff-Herzog*, 10:406–7. MH

[21] A prominent and controversial figure, Adolf Stöcker (1835–1908) founded the Christian Socialist Labor Party. He "remained an orthodox Lutheran, a conservative in politics, and loyal to the monarchy." In 1890 he was dismissed from his post as court preacher (K. S. Latourette, *The Nineteenth Century in Europe* [New York: Harpers, 1959], 123–25). RF

tion and confuse such an entity with a church-political club—has it been beneficial, I say, when such immature young men, who have learned nothing other than a bit of dialectic theology, contrive Unions and sketch them out on paper and now think Christianity must order itself accordingly?"

"Has it been beneficial to hamper dealing with the theological problem of confessionalism and also the theological productivity of the confessional inheritance by a juridical view of the confessional pledge?" The young theologians who are tormented by such problems would do well to spend a year as an assistant pastor in a Lutheran congregation in the forests of Canada or in the slums of Chicago. The juridical rationale for the confessional oath would have to be clear to anyone who perchance heard in Basel the lecture of a pastor from Münster in which it was asserted that there are two viewpoints in the church, the right and the left. And these

> represent the two essential sides of the one body and only in unison form the entirety of the church. . . . While the right views matters in a Trinitarian fashion in accord with ancient church dogma and believes in a triune God, the left views matters in a Unitarian fashion, since they do not make the Son equal to the Father. . . . The right, furthermore, sees in God a personal, higher ego, which stands over against the individual ego. The left venerates in God the super-personal, infinite Spirit, who is too great to be troubled over an insignificant human being. Today, the views of both sides are tending more toward the middle, so that a consensus concerning a conception of God does not appear impossible.[22]

No one in Basel can protest this mischief. Thurneysen,[23] who may be able to teach us Germans what "theological existence" is, has to tolerate this and apparently can tolerate it. For at his own pulpit is preached the very opposite of what he is convinced is the pure doctrine of the Gospel. If he were to contest the right of heretics, who for Luther and Calvin no longer belonged to the church (the deniers of the Holy Trinity and the divinity of Jesus Christ), to preach in the Evangelical pulpits of Basel, if he were to unleash an ecclesiastical fight over these matters, the church government would have to proceed against him. The very same men who perhaps are personally the most decided disciples of the doctrine of the old Reformed Church would be forced by legitimate canon law to protect the followers of Joris and Servetus[24] and to assure their right to occupy the pastoral office, in so far as they are only acting in accord with their understanding of Holy Scripture. That is the situation of a church which has given up its confession and nullified the old "juridical rationale" for the confessional oath.

---

[22] *Basler Nachr.*, 18, 2, 35, supplement to no. 48. HS

[23] Eduard Thurneysen (1888–1974), Swiss theologian, was pastor at the Münster at Basle and a close friend and colleague of Karl Barth. RF

[24] Jan Jorisz (1501–1556) was an Anabaptist, a spiritualist, and a self-styled "prophet." His followers were called "Davidists" or "Jorists" (*Lutheran Cyclopedia*, 431). Michael Servetus (1511–1553), an anti-Trinitarian, was arrested, condemned, and burned at Geneva (*Lutheran Cyclopedia*, 712). MH

A church can never exist in this world without church law. The question which it must always ask itself is whether its current applicable church law is correct or false. If the *legal* validity of the confession is done away with, then it is thereby declared that from henceforth both confessional and anti-confessional doctrine have an equal *right* to exist in the church concerned. To be sure, defection from the confession can occur in any church. Only a fool could think that the legal fixation of the confessional position and the "juridical view of the confessional pledge" can guard a church in the face of such defection. But in granting this, it is in no way granted that the legal acknowledgment of the confession is superfluous. The history of the Protestant churches of the last generation, and especially German church history of recent years, demonstrates most clearly that it is incomparably easier for a church to return from the errors of modernism and secularism to the Word of God when that church's doctrine (so far as it retains the Word of God as normative validity, even though it has been set aside) still enjoys legally binding validity. What would have been the result of these most difficult struggles within German Protestantism in recent years if our churches had no longer possessed the weapon of the confessions which were still documents of legally binding validity in the church!

If in the future there shall still exist a genuine Evangelical Church, if God in his longsuffering and mercy, quite apart from any merit or worthiness on our part, should maintain the church of the pure Gospel for our children and grandchildren, then future generations will extol it as a miracle of God's grace that the confessions of the sixteenth century had outlasted all the revolutions of intellectual life and the various legal situations in Germany and even modern theology. For if the tempestuous waves of false doctrine and defection from the Christian faith are ever to be calmed anywhere, it will happen on the smooth surface of the confession of the fathers, which today is still the confession of our church. It will not be brought about by we theologians of this generation, so weak in faith and thankless, nor by our vacillating [theological] systems.

Enough with the questions and counter questions about what has been "beneficial" in church politics today and what not! We refer to the important answers which Friedrich Ulmer[25] gave in *Lutherische Kirche*,[26] and which we are pleased to appropriate word for word. Let it finally be noted that the question "Has it been beneficial?" has, over the course of four centuries, brought the Evangelical churches of Germany to the place where they stand today, and it is time to turn our backs on all ecclesiastical pragmatism and finally, finally ask again, as our fathers asked at the time of the Reformation: "Has it been right?"

Finally, however, we direct a few remarks to *Karl Barth*, who now has "out Prussianed" us native Prussians and become the champion of the idea of the Union. There has scarcely been another theologian who has been listened to so

---

[25] Friedrich Ulmer was Sasse's Erlangen colleague and the editor of *Lutherische Kirche*. RF

[26] *Lutherische Kirche* (1935, no. 5): 78 f. HS

attentively by German Lutherans as Barth. In Germany his theology found greater response than in any other country, including Switzerland. For the Lutheran Church of Germany has never been so narrow-minded that it would not thankfully learn from the theologians of other churches, if only there were something which could be learned from them. We are not so ignorant of the world that we do not know that the history of the church and theology is played out also beyond the borders of our confession. Indeed, we have learned from Luther and from the confessions of our church that on the other side of the walls of the Evangelical Lutheran Church there also exists a true church of Christ and Christian theology. Thus German Lutheranism thankfully heard the powerful cry which Barthian theology signified for all churches which would ground themselves upon the Word of God, namely, the cry to come to the realization of just what this Word is. So even though he was very disappointed with the reception accorded his theological message in our theological circles, still Barth must grant that he always found much more attention among us than in the world of the Calvinistic churches. For when we look beyond individual, very decidedly, but very small circles of disciples which Barth has acquired in Holland, Switzerland, and in other regions of the Reformed Church, it must be maintained that the so-called "Group Movement"[27] within these Reformed churches has met with much more interest than has Barthian theology.

But the influence of Barth's theology on German Lutheranism must meet its natural end the moment it demands that the Evangelical Lutheran Church in Germany cease to exist as church and that it merge into a Union church, comprised of both Lutherans and Reformed. Barth made this demand in the theses which the "Free Reformed Synod" of Germany in January 1934[28] "took upon its conscience" and adopted as a resolution. But the Reformed theologians appear to have had reservations, and no further use has been made of this resolution. But Barth has continued unswervingly to make his demand. No hesitation by the Lutherans has had any influence upon him. He has been unwilling to recognize that the German Lutheran [Church] cannot declare its confession with its confessional delimitations null and void at the very moment that confession is needed as a weapon in the fight to maintain the external form of the church. He has been unwilling to recognize that such an invalidation of the old confessions with

---

[27] This is probably a reference to a movement more commonly known as the "Oxford Group" and later "Moral Re-Armament" under the leadership of Frank Buchman (*ODCC*, 247, 719, 1204–5). RF

[28] This was the Free Reformed Synod of Barmen-Gemarke at which Barth gave a speech entitled "Declaration on the Right Understanding of the Reformation Confessions in the German Evangelical Church of the Present." Elsewhere Sasse reports: "In an evening session of the Theological Committee of the Second Confessional Synod at Dahlem [in] 1934 the undersigned said to Karl Barth: 'You cannot demand of us the abrogation of the Augustana at this moment, when our bishops (Meiser and Wurm) have been robbed of their freedom' [i.e., placed under house arrest by the Nazis]. Barth's answer was: 'Why not?' " ("On the Problem of the Relation between the Reformed and Lutheran Church," *Quartalschrift* 46.4 [October 1949]: 238). The incident was similarly reported in "On the Problem of the Union of Lutheran Churches," *Quartalschrift* 47.4 (October 1950): 269. RF

their delimitations presupposes that we ourselves shall have been convinced that these delimitations are incorrect and unfeasible.

Barth has been unwilling to recognize that great [ecumenical] pronunciations between confessions, the struggle to overcome heresies within Christendom, and the struggle for the common knowledge of the truth must not remain limited to the Lutherans and the Reformed in Germany. For even if such a Union were to be accepted in Germany, what would this accomplish for the relationship between the Lutheran and Reformed churches of the world? We would then have only repeated the mistakes of the nineteenth-century Unions on a greater scale. All this Barth has been unwilling to recognize, and he has not been able to grasp the fact that neither his theology nor any of the ideas and experiences of churchly life in the most recent times have shown us a way to bridge the gap between the Lutheran and the Reformed doctrines of the Supper without inherent untruthfulness on either side. The demands which he placed before us were the demands of a man who believed himself called to reform our church, a church to which he does not even belong, in which he holds no office, which he finally does not understand, and which he has apparently not seriously been at pains to understand. No matter how attentively we have listened to Barth, we cannot acknowledge him as a reformer. We can in no way acknowledge that he has a divine task to reform *our* church. If he wants to reform something, if he believes he is called to reform a church, then let him address the churches of his homeland, then let him call the Reformed and Presbyterian churches of the world which have defected back to the confession of the fathers and to the Word of God. It is our intention as Lutherans, so far as it lies in our power, to do the same with the churches of our confession. The path of unconditional truthfulness alone is the path of responsible churchmanship. And the church of Christ must never let itself be swayed from this path.

For there still exists between the "Evangelical Lutheran Church" and the "Church Reformed according to God's Word" a deep divide regarding the doctrines of justification and predestination; regarding the Holy Scriptures and the relationship between Law and Gospel; regarding the Sacrament of the Altar, the office of the ministry, and the organization [*Verfassung*] of the church. We have not yet achieved that consensus without which, according to the teaching of Luther and the Lutheran Church, there cannot be full ecclesiastical fellowship. Still, we all acknowledge the apathy regarding dogmatic questions among the masses of our congregational members and the embarrassing ignorance regarding the doctrine of their church among so many of our pastors, schooled in a false theology. But these facts hide the depth of that divide; they cannot bridge it. And no theologian should be so foolish as to think that perhaps because the doctrine of the Supper plays no roll in our discussions in the present situation of our German churches that the question of the real presence of the body and blood of Christ in the Sacrament of the Altar is no longer a very great question which divides churches and confessions.[29] To be of this opinion one must be a German theologian whose theology is no broader than the confines of his study [Studierstubentheologe] and who knows nothing of the dire ecclesiastical circumstances and the confessional discussions going on today in the Christian world. But as long as that divide between the churches exists, we can do nothing else than go the way which insists upon absolute truthfulness, and go this way honorably and in love. Then the day may come in which God may graciously show us the path which leads into new realities which are a gift to his entire church. And this path may wend its way over the errors and imperfections of the existing confessions into a new future for the church. We hope for this day because we believe in the one who, as the merciful High Priest, intercedes with the heavenly Father for his church, that this church be one and that it be sanctified in the truth.

---

[29] So, for example, Karl Barth, Theologische Existenz heute 7 (January 26, 1934): 7:

> The dispute in the church today, and that concerning which we must "confess," does not have to do with matters of the Lord's Supper, but with matters of the First Commandment. In the face of this our need and task, that of the Fathers must recede, that is, there must still be serious opposition between the theological schools [i.e., between Lutherans and Reformed], but it must no longer be divisive and schismatic. RF

1936

UNION AND CONFESSION[1]

This essay addresses one of the most dramatic crises of the modern church, especially the Lutheran Church. Assailed from without by the encroachments of the powers of the Third Reich and from within by the rising domination of Barthian-Reformed churchmanship, the Lutheran Church of Germany was facing nothing less than its demise.

Sasse wrote "Union and Confession" under the duress of the times, dark times. From the formation of the *Deutsche Evangelische Kirche* (DEK—German Evangelical Church) in summer 1933, Sasse warned against the dangers threatening the church in Germany. The DEK was the product of Nazi interference, an effort to form one German church as a nationalist tool.

This was also the time of the culmination of efforts to bring the Lutherans into a "union" with the Reformed. Such efforts had been continuous ever since the formation of the Old Prussian Union of 1817/1834. Sasse had been raised, educated, and ordained in the Prussian Union Church and knew firsthand the difference between it and true Lutheran churches. The latter he "discovered" while on an exchange education program in the United States in 1925/1926 (see "American Christianity and the Church" in this volume).

The dangers thus were from within as well as from outside the church. The references to the Barmen Declaration and the "Confessing Church" (*Bekennende Kirche*) address the internal danger. Here Sasse gives one of his most explicit accounts of the famous synod at Barmen and his own role there. In a time when the compromising spirit of Barmen is greater than ever, Sasse's warning about the lie of unionism is important. "There is actually more unity of the church present where Christians of differing confession honorably determine that they do not have the same understanding of the Gospel than where the painful fact of confessional splintering is hidden behind a pious lie."

This lengthy essay was originally published in a noted series titled Bekennende Kirche (Confessing Church). In 1936 Sasse became an editor of the series, working together with colleagues Georg Merz and Christian Stoll. The title, the same as that given to a movement within the German church in opposi-

---

[1] This work originally appeared as *Union und Bekenntnis* (Bekennende Kirche 41/42; ed. Christian Stoll together with Georg Merz and Hermann Sasse; Munich: Chr. Kaiser, 1936). MH

tion to the Third Reich, may seem strange, for it is usually associated with Barthian churchmen of the period. However, as Sasse often wrote later, he and his confessional Lutheran colleagues were also founders of the "Confessing Movement."

Huss number 147a
Hopf number 079

PART 1

The lie is the death of man, his temporal and his eternal death. The lie kills nations. The most powerful nations of the world have been laid waste because of their lies. History knows of no more unsettling sight than the judgment rendered upon the people of an advanced culture who have rejected the truth and are swallowed up in a sea of lies. Where this happens, as in the case of declining pagan antiquity, religion and law, poetry and philosophy, life in marriage and family, in the state and society—in short, one sphere of life after another falls sacrifice to the power and curse of the lie. Where man can no longer bear the truth, he cannot live without the lie. Where man denies that he and others are dying, the terrible dissolution [of his culture] is held up as a glorious ascent, and decline is viewed as an advance, the likes of which has never been experienced. If, according to the irrefutable testimony of history, this is the judgment of God on the lie, should God then not also punish the lie in his church? Truly he who is the Judge of all the world will do this!

For the power of the lie extends right into the church. Since the days of the apostles this has been as true in the church as in the rest of the world. For men in the church are and remain poor sinners until their death. Lies have been told in the church because of cowardice and weakness, vanity and avarice. But beyond all these there is in the church one particularly sweet piece of fruit on the broad canopy of the tree of lies. There is the pious lie. It is the hypocrisy by which a man lies to others and the intellectual self-deception by which he lies to himself about what he actually believes. "In our time too the proclamation of the Word in received orthodoxy is unfortunately not infrequently the appearance of this lie." Thus the greatest ethicist of our church once spoke,[2] warning the theologians of his and our time about the most grievous sin, the lie to God.

The most fearful thing about the pious lie is that it will lie not only to people, but also to God in prayer, in confession, in the Holy Supper, in the sermon, and in theology. The pious lie has the direct propensity to become the "devotional" or edifying lie. It was once expelled from the church when it existed in the

---

[2]   A. F. C. Vilmar, *Theologische Moral* (1871), 1:313. HS

form of the legends of the saints and the fraud of relics. Then, in full view of pious eyes, it returned in a new form. Note the Luther legends, or in Pietistic times the almanacs and tracts containing the accounts of miraculous responses to prayer and equally miraculous conversions which either never happened or in which the kernel of historical truth was no longer discernable.

This "edifying" lie also forces its way into the sphere of the church, which teaches the truths of revelation. After sufficient preparation it can obtain the status of "doctrinal maturity."[3] Thus it becomes the *dogmatic* lie. We bid our Roman Catholic friends to believe that it is very difficult for us to use the word "lie" here, and we don't do so to offend them. We know that they affirm a dogma such as the immaculate conception of Mary out of deep conviction of faith, and they will accept the yet-awaited extension of dogma concerning Mary from the hand of the ecclesiastical teaching office with the same sincerity. But this changes nothing of the fact that in these dogmas false doctrines are established and that the Roman Church thus finds itself in a burdensome error.

But this is the biblical, the theological nature of the lie: though guilty of falsehood, deny the truth and proclaim that which is not truth, even if this guilt before God is hidden behind a human bona fides. Here the theological concept of the lie is distinguished from that of philosophical ethics. Theology knows that the most dangerous lies are those which are proclaimed with what the world calls a "good conscience." When we speak of the dogmatic lie we do not, however, have in mind only the celebrated dogmas pronounced by the Roman Catholic Church, which are elevated to the level of ecclesiastical dogma, have no basis in Holy Scripture, and are not true. We include here also precisely the dogmas with which modern Protestantism has been at pains to correct, to enlarge, or to replace the doctrine of the evangelical church, such as the false doctrine of Pietism concerning the church or of Rationalism concerning the person of Christ.

What a fearful thought it is indeed that things are taught in the church which are not true, under the guise of the eternal truth entrusted to her. No atheism, no Bolshevism can do as much damage and destruction as the pious lie, the lie in the church. In this lie the power of one is made evident whom Christ himself calls a liar and the father of lies (John 8:44). And indeed, this is no longer surprising. How can he who in his very essence is a liar passively look upon the fact that in this world of untruthfulness and error, upon the vacillating core of a world of relativity, there could be the "house of God, which is the church of the living God, a pillar and foundation of the truth" (1 Tim 3:15). But since he cannot storm this bulwark, which God himself has founded as the *columna et firmamentum veritatis*,[4] in open war, he slinks in under the mask of piety and occupies a position from which to make his conquest. And he attempts to topple the pillar of truth through the power of the pious lie. But does anyone think that Christ who is the truth per-

---

[3]   On this concept see Karl Adam, *Das Wesen des Katholizismus* (6th ed.), 168. HS

[4]   This phrase is simply the Latin version of 1 Tim 3:15. HS

sonified would allow the lie to come into his church uncontested? No, the judgment which he who is holy and true will render upon all the lies of the world begins, as with every judgment, with the house of God.

Among the lies which destroy the church there is one we have not yet mentioned. Alongside the pious and dogmatic lies, there stands an especially dangerous form of lie which can be called the *institutional* lie. By this we mean a lie which works itself out in the institutions of the church, in her government and her law [*Recht*]. It is so dangerous because it legalizes the other lies in the church and makes them impossible to remove. Such a lie exists, for instance, where the governance of the church grants to those who confess and those who deny the Trinity and the two natures in Christ [*Gottmenscheit Jesu*] the same legitimacy. It exists where the preaching of the Gospel according to the understanding of the Reformation enjoys the same right as the proclamation of a dogmaless Enlightenment religion, so long as the latter appeals only to the Bible. It exists where it is the rule that at a church with two pastoral positions one must be filled with a pastor of the "free" bent, so the "liberals" in the congregation do not have to go to another congregation with an "orthodox" pastor.

Such canon law (as it exists for instance in the Reformed Church in Basel, but in a similar form also in individual German territorial churches) makes it completely impossible to distinguish between truth and error, between true and false doctrine. A church so composed can no longer see that the Gospel is plainly and purely preached and heresy opposed. It must protect open heretics when the "orthodox" side denies that they possess an equal legitimacy in the church. The congregations of such a church, the youth who are educated in it, the people to whom it attempts to preach the truth of the Gospel must come to the conviction that it simply does not matter much what one believes or does not believe. Since what is to be believed or not believed in the sermon is left up to the individual, his inclinations and aversions, his worldview and soon also his faithlessness will become the norm for proclamation in the church. In place of the objective message of that which God has done in Christ, subjective religious feelings and convictions soon form the essential content of the sermon. Thus the church sinks to the level of an institution for the satisfaction of the manifold religious needs of people and ceases to be the church of Christ, the pillar and foundation of the truth.

It is self-evident that this falling away of the church from Gospel can also happen where its external organization [*Verfassung*] still appears to be in order. For no constitution, no statute [*Rechtssatzung*], no legal fixation of the confessional position can guard the church in the face of the defection from the true faith. Much less was this ever the teaching of the Lutheran Church, which in distinction from other confessions never knew of a form of organization [*Verfassung*] which God gave to his church to insure pure doctrine. We are unaware of Lutheran theologians ever teaching anything else. But the moment the falling away of the church from the Gospel finds its expression also in church law and thus is legitimized, the entire awfulness of what we have called the institutional lie applies. For this lie makes the return to the truth as good as impossible.

A church can fall into terrible dogmatic error, it can open door after door to heresy by tolerating it and doing nothing about it. With the help of the Holy Spirit, such a church can later repent, return to the pure Word of God, and take up the fight against false doctrine commanded by this Word. But if it has solemnly acknowledged the right of heresy in its midst, then heresy itself has become an organic component of the church concerned. It can then no longer fight against heresy, and a burning struggle against false doctrine in its midst would be an entirely illegal fight of one wing of this church against another.

Let me clarify this by an example: if in the *Frauenkirche* ["Church of Our Lady"] at Dresden or in the *Dom* ["cathedral"] at Magdeburg a pastor denies the propositions of the faith of the Nicene Creed, he is guilty of forsaking his ordination vow. The church government is, if it does not wish to bear heavy blame in the matter, required to proceed against him. If at the *Dom* at Bremen or in the *Münster* ["cathedral"] at Basel a pastor does the very same thing, he is completely untouchable [*unanfechtbar*], and his church government is required to protect his doctrinal freedom against eventual attack. It is clear that a church which is so composed can no longer remove false doctrine from its midst. One of the most important functions of the church, the elimination of error, which is the function essential to the very life of the church [*lebensnotwendige*], has in this case ceased.

How shall a church which suffers with this illness again become well? How can such a church body separate the true church from heresy? No one is so foolish as to think that heresy will ever of its own will give up the right granted it in the church. It is part of its essence that it cannot do this, for it lives on the basis of the claim to be the genuine church. It can only live in the shadow of the church and not as an independent religion or philosophy. And even when a particular heresy is forced aside in consequence of an altered philosophical situation and a change of the [ruling] theological system, it does not leave the visible center of church history without leaving its basic ideas, its power over minds, and its hard-earned right to exist, to other heresies.

There is nothing more foolish than the hope that the false teaching concerning the person and work of Christ, which has ruled a great part of Protestantism since the Enlightenment, would disappear with the philosophical view of the eighteenth and nineteenth centuries. No, it will return in entirely new and all the more dangerous forms—we have indeed experienced something of this already!— just as it had also been present in earlier centuries. The great heresies die as little as does the devil. They return in ever new forms—how many forms have Arianism and Pelagianism already taken!—and accompany the church through the centuries of her history as great temptations preparing her for the end times (1 Cor 11:19; 2 Pet 2:1).

The ancient church knew this, and we will have to learn it once again from her. Thus it is a foolish and simplistic hope that the false doctrine, which has been acknowledged in modern church government as equally legitimate with the pure doctrine, will finally disappear of itself. But where a church has made its pact with false doctrine and laid down the weapons with which it can and must fight heresy, there remains only the one last possibility for separating the church from heresy: the separation of the orthodox church from an image, which only bears the name "church," but in reality has nothing to do with the church of Christ.

This is the curse of the lie on the ecclesiastical institution. As far as human judgment is concerned, it makes the return to the truth impossible. This applies to the Protestant churches which have fallen sacrifice to the temptation of this lie, just as it applies to the Roman Church since Vatican I. For the papacy, as it has existed since the infallibility dogma of 1870, is indeed without a doubt the greatest example of the institutional lie in the church. Because the Roman Church in that dogma placed a clear *irreformabilis*, "not reformable," on the decisions of the faith rendered or yet to be rendered by its highest teaching office, it cut off its way back, even if a decision rendered then should later prove untenable. They have declared themselves a church which is no longer reformable.

But the Protestant churches, which in contradiction to the confessions of the time of the Reformation from which they came, and which now have granted false doctrine a basic right of existence within the church, have no right to be indignant over irreformable Catholicism. They have also cut off the return path to the truth of the Gospel. All these churches, whether they call themselves Catholic or Protestant, Reformed or Lutheran, are heading toward the judgment which the Holy and True One will render on every lie in the world, and which is above all a judgment of the lie in the church.

PART 2

Because we ourselves fear this judgment, because we do not desire that the Evangelical [Lutheran] Church of Germany fall into this judgment, because we cannot tolerate the thought that God could take from the people of the Reformation the church of the pure Gospel—for this reason, and this reason alone, we fight against the false Union. For the lie of the false Union is the curse which for more than a century has rested upon the Evangelical [Lutheran] Church of our country and poisoned her life.

Other churches have other enticements to deal with. The Roman Church in the modern world, in the face of the enormous seriousness of questions of Christian truth, is cursed with the false security of the Vatican decree. Anglicanism's temptation is canon law and the liturgy. Modern American Protestantism's temptation is so called "practical Christianity." A greater portion of the Reformed churches are enticed with a basic loss of confession or a churchless Biblicism. Our enticement in Germany has been the curse of the false Union. The great part of the German Evangelical [Lutheran] Church fell to this curse in the nineteenth century, and the remainder which at that time still avoided entering the Union is today making up for lost time.

Just as Satan loves to invade the church, posing as an "angel of light" according to St. Paul [2 Cor 11:14], so also the magnificent, church-destroying lie clothes itself ever and again in the deceptive mask of a renewal, an improvement, a reformation of the church. Therefore as a rule such lies, since time immemorial, have entered the church in an hour of deepest emotion and holiest enthusiasm, and where possible, with the singing of Veni, Creator Spiritus and the Te Deum. How rapturously was the Holy Spirit invoked before every session of Trent! How loudly the Te Deum Laudamus rang through the council hall in St. Peter after the announcement of the dogma of the infallibility! How often in evangelical churches people have sung "Heart and Heart in Unity"[5] or "Now Thank We All Our God" in a moment of intense emotion, only later to have to make the sober determination that the allegedly ostensible blowing of the Holy Spirit was in reality something quite different. September 20, 1853, is without a doubt one of the most celebrated moments in the history of German Protestantism. On that day the German Evangelical *Kirchentag* ["Church Congress"] at Berlin accepted the Augustana as a common confession of all of Evangelical Germany.

It was a powerfully gripping moment when the two thousand men from all districts of Germany joyously raised their hands to solemnly confess the Augsburg Confession as the oldest common document of publicly acknowledged Evangelical doctrine in Germany. Only eight hands were raised in opposition. It was a deeply moving moment when the great assembly joined in singing "Now Thank We All Our God."

Thus one participant recounted,[6] while another spoke of a "moment of historical world significance" before the ballot was taken. Now world history takes no notice of this moment. It only lives on in church history, but not for its greatness, rather for its ridiculousness; not, as was thought then, as the dawn of a new day in the history of German Protestantism, as the consummation of the confessional unification of the Evangelical churches of Germany, but rather as a classic example of the fact that the most celebrated hours in the history of the church can also be her most untruthful, and that the most untruthful hours are those in which a man lies not only to himself, but to others as well, and even to God the Lord, in claiming a unity which in reality does not exist.

---

[5] Why exactly this hymn has so often been used to express the deepest untruthfulness is understandable to anyone who has ever read the original wording of the hymn. HS

This reference is to the hymn by Nicholas von Zinzendorf which usually appears in translation under the title "Heart and Heart Together Bound." RF

[6] Kapff (*Prälat* ["prelate"] in Stuttgart), *Der religiöse Zustand des evangelischen Deutschlands* (1856), 53. HS

Everyone who takes part in ecclesiastical life knows the danger of such hours. Every serious theologian knows what a temptation to *Schwärmerei* ["fanaticism"] and insincerity interconfessional missions conferences, ecumenical events, yes also "Confessional Synods" and similar assemblies of adherents of various confessions (as we have experienced in the most difficult time of the German confessional struggle) can mean. To be sure, he will look back on such events and testify with thankfulness of the reality of the *sanctorum communio* ["the communion of saints"] which he has experienced and which transcends confessional lines. But he knows that what is true and untrue unity, what is real and what an alleged working of the Holy Spirit can only occasionally be determined by faith. For the presence of the exalted Lord, the working of the Holy Spirit can always only be believed, but never fixed, written down like the minutes of a meeting [*protokolliert*] and announced by the correspondents of the world.

The Holy Spirit, the Spirit of truth, is never present where lies are told. And there is actually more unity of the church present where Christians of differing confession honorably determine that they do not have the same understanding of the Gospel than where the painful fact of confessional splintering is hidden behind a pious lie. Or does the word "lie" appear too strong here? No, it was not only self-deception, it was not only ignorance, but rather it was a falsification of Reformation history when it was stated in the resolution of that *Kirchentag*:

> The members of the German Evangelical *Kirchentag* hereby announce that with heart and mouth they hold to and confess that confession delivered in the year 1530 at the Imperial Diet at Augsburg to Emperor Charles V by the Evangelical princes and representatives. And they hereby publicly testify to their agreement with it as the oldest, plainest, common document of publicly acknowledged Evangelical doctrine in Germany. And to this testimony they bind this declaration, that they maintain every particularity in the particular confessions of their churches, and [that] the United [churches] maintain their consensus, and that the various positions of the Lutherans, Reformed, and United on Article X and the unique relationships of those Reformed congregations which have never recognized it as a confessional document shall not be disparaged.

It was of course not unknown to the theologians participating in the *Kirchentag* that the Augustana was also directed against Zwingli and all deniers of the real presence of the true body and blood of Christ in the Holy Supper and that for this reason already in 1530 it could not be accepted by all German Protestants. And thus it is in no way the "common" confessional document of one "Evangelical" church made up of Lutherans, Reformed, and United churches. They knew that when Article X (and thus the entire doctrine of the sacrament, Christology, and everything else of ecclesiastical doctrine which goes with the Sacrament) was made irrelevant and nonbinding that this neither corresponded to Luther's view nor to the letter or spirit of the Augsburg Confession. Furthermore, they knew that the Augustana cannot be so separated from the other confessions, especially from the Apology and Luther's catechisms, that it can be said that the Augustana contains the common Evangelical doctrine, these other confessions contain the peculiar teachings of the Lutheran Church, and one finds oneself within the Church of the Augsburg Confession when one rejects these particular confessions and their doctrine and in their place accepts the Reformed confessions and doctrine.

Each individual theologian knew this. But as participants of the synod they made no use of this knowledge. It apparently sufficed for them that the *Kirchentag* "took full responsibility" for the declaration. Everyone knows that at especially ceremonious moments synods are prone to "take full responsibility" for things which individual participants can no longer be responsible for in any way. After the *Kirchentag* of 1853 the "teachers of theology and canon law" from Erlangen, Leipzig, and Rostock, who knew their ecclesiastical responsibility, rendered their opinion in an extremely valuable, pointed declaration[7] against the violation of historical truth and against the misuse of the Augustana and the entire untruthfulness of the decision rendered there. They were of course regarded as disturbers of the confessional peace and enemies of ecclesiastical unity.

This sinister power of the fanatical [*enthusiastischen*] mood, for which any calm consideration of reality is already a quenching of the Spirit and any critical question is blasphemy, laid heavy upon all the decisive hours in which the Union won its battles in the nineteenth century, and the Union has only this mood to thank for its success. The Union movement, which passed through Germany from 1817 on, belongs to the fanatical revolutionary movements which shake the church from time to time and which are not victorious because of truth, but because they satisfy emotional needs. This is demonstrated by many examples from the history of the Unions of the previous century. The most conspicuous example of this will suffice here: the appearance of the Prussian Union. Here we quote one of its theological founders, Chaplain and Bishop Eylert,[8] author of the cabinet order of September 27, 1817, which ordered the introduction of the Union. He describes very graphically from memory the remarkable events of the Reformation Jubilee in Prussia.[9] The celebration preceded a joint celebration of the Supper by the clergy:

> All the Evangelical clergy of both confessions, now united, took part in this Christian celebration with deep devotion and pious emotion, and received

---

[7] *Das Bekenntnis der lutherischen Kirche gegen das Bekenntnis des Berliner Kirchentags gewahrt von etlichen Lehrern der Theologie und des Kirchenrechts* (1853); it was reprinted in *Lutherische Kirche* (1935, no. 1). HS

[8] Rulemann Friedrich Eylert (1770–1852) was court preacher of Frederick William III at Potsdam (1806). He encouraged the king to initiate the inauguration of the Prussian Union (*Lutheran Cyclopedia*, 288). RF

[9] *Charakter-Züge und historische Fragmente aus dem Leben des Königs von Preussen Friedrich Wilhelm III*, part 3, section 2 (1846), 62 ff. HS

the Holy Sacrament as a meaningful symbol of internal and external union. The holy act was heart lifting. It lifted the souls of the prayerful heavenward to the Lord upon its wings. It was and remains to all who witnessed it and filled many eyes with tears. It is the historical beginning of a great, immortal work and *forms a new epoch in the history of the church*. It breathed of a life which is self-perpetuating and of which it is said that the old is past, behold, all things have become new.

Then the graphic account of October 31 in Potsdam:

The sun shone mild and glittering against the clear blue autumn sky. . . . The earth seemed to celebrate the festive day and the heavens to bless it. . . . The fully packed Court and Garrison Church resonated with drums and trumpets. The hymn "Lord God, We Praise You" rose to heaven and every heart sang "A Mighty Fortress Is Our God." The king was present with his entire family and all were dressed in state's uniform. Chaplain General Offelsmeyer preached a perfect sermon on this text: "Remember your teachers, who have spoken the Word of God to you; consider the outcome of their way of life, and follow the example of their faith" (Heb 13:7). He spoke golden words on the diversity and unity of the Protestant church. He ingeniously tied in *the Union accomplished with the help of God*, and he proved that the Union was in *the spirit of Luther* and traces a masterful characteristic from him. The conclusion to the sermon was that we could not honor Luther, Calvin, and all the Reformers more highly nor show more gratitude to God and the Redeemer than if in the entire country we formed one strong, united Evangelical Church out of hitherto Lutheran and Reformed churches and [we] were of Christian affection. The respectful stillness of deep devotion reigned over the great assemblage, and all were truly edified. Now the *Holy Supper* proved the preeminent point of the high celebration. After *long separation before the countenance of Jesus Christ* since the ancient days of Christianity, it would be *a meal of union*, unity, and harmony. The Words of Institution—"The Lord Jesus Christ, in the night in which he was betrayed"—were spoken and the choir began to sing "Lamb of God, you take away the sin of the world," and so on. Then the lord defender of the Evangelical Church of Germany, the king, approached and with him the crown prince and the rest of his children. The king appeared wan and was very serious. The peace of God rested upon his noble countenance and a tear shimmered in his pious eye. He appeared as one who had prayed and had found the Redeemer, as one who had done a good work, and then received the Holy Supper. He received the bread with the words of Christ "This is my body which is given for you; this do in remembrance of me" and the wine [with Christ's words] "This is the cup of the new testament in my blood which is poured out for you; this do in remembrance of me." With the sign of the cross *these deep words of the Supper* were directed to the king but spoken over the entire United Territorial Church. And the ancient but eternally new song of praise rang out: "Glory to God in the highest! Peace on earth! And good will toward men." It was as though one had felt the harmony of a better world. *Certainly the Lord was in this place; how holy the place from which flowed a stream of life over millions! Here was God's house, here the gates of heaven.* The king knelt and prayed; he prayed for himself and his subjects. The crown prince followed in the warmth of devotion, then his brother, the attendants, and a great multitude of men and women from all stations of life. No longer separated by varying confessions, now united, clergy of the church remained long, breaking bread. And all who took part in the Union celebration knew that the moment had lasted an eternity. The festival service lasted very long. After it was over the king traveled to Wittenberg in order to be present at the dedication ceremony for the memorial and statue of Luther in Luther's old city.[10]

This account should be read again and again. It should be translated from the style of the general chaplain into sober and dispassionate language. Even then it would remain fanatical enough and a witness for the *schwärmeristic* ["fanatical"] character of the church founded at that time. Those men obviously deceived themselves if they thought they would renew the church of the Reformation, an original, Evangelical church which existed before the separation of Lutherans and Reformed. "Remember your teachers, who have spoken the Word of God to you"—the Reformers obviously had in mind an entirely different "Word" than that of the Prussian chaplain general.

And what did this supper of brotherhood [*verbrüderungs-Abendmahl*], celebrated with pietistic feelings and rationalizing thoughts, still have to do with the Sacrament of the Altar as the Fifth Chief Part teaches it? The church which came into existence on the 31st of October in Potsdam was no longer the old Lutheran Church of Brandenburg-Prussia of the time of Paul Gerhardt. Nor was it any longer the Reformed Church of the great elector. In reality, it was a new church, the Prussian Territorial Church so long desired, the soul of the Prussian state which was rising in greatness and coming into global political significance. What this church had to do with the Reformation is documented by the trip which the king took immediately after the Union supper. He traveled from Potsdam to Wittenberg, which had shortly before come into Prussian hands and lost its university. Thus Eylert recounted further that in Wittenberg

> it could not be forgotten that the old university in large measure, with its generous public funding, had been transferred from there to Halle and only retained a seminary. Still Frederick William III won the hearts of the residents by his dignified seriousness, his virtuous benevolence, his natural, simple nature, *especially by the true reverence which he felt for Luther*, with which he honored the day. The great man and valiant Reformer—who there lived, dwelt, taught, and worked; who there is buried next to Melanchthon in the University Church; and who is constantly remembered now and will be into

---

[10] *Charakter-Züge und historische Fragmente*, 80 ff. The emphasis here and in the previous citation is my own. HS

the future—will always be called a *saint*. But since that time a monument was erected to him in the town square on the main thoroughfare so one can catch sight of him just as he was, standing, Bible in hand. Luther has been *deified* [*apotheosirt*]. Visitors stand in contemplation and residents pass by with quiet veneration.[11]

That was the coronation of this curious celebration of the three-hundredth anniversary of the Reformation. What did Claus Harms have to say in his seventy-fifth thesis regarding the impending Union? "Indeed! Do not consummate the act over Luther's bones! They will come to life and then woe to you!" Poor Claus Harms, you "foreigner," as Bishop Eylert called you, you don't understand Prussia![12] Luther no longer stands at the borderline of black and white. And such a disturbance of the public order would have hindered the military police in an emergency, as happened in Silesia, Pomerania, and Brandenburg—where they absolutely refused to allow the Lutheran monuments in their lands.

Frederick William III dedicated the first of these monuments himself. Indeed, he was an honorable venerator of Luther who drew from Luther's liturgical orders and prayers the best direction for his attempts at liturgical art [*liturgisches Kunstgewerbe*]. With this monument he would repeat his own sin and the sins of his fathers against Luther's city: the prohibition for the subjects of Brandenburg-Prussia to study at the *Cathedra Lutheri*, the stronghold of Lutheran doctrine in Germany, until the disbanding of the university and its transference to Prussia. While for the new Territorial Church new United faculties were formed from the outset (faculties such as those at Bonn and Berlin), in Wittenberg the lecture halls were desolated. Only with great difficulty was the appearance of a theological tradition maintained by the establishment of a United seminary whose theology had a fatal similarity to the familiar scent of an empty flask.

The doctrine of the Lutheran Church was nullified in Prussia. It has been rendered harmless, it no longer challenges anyone. And though the prophecy of Claus Harms was fulfilled throughout the rest of Germany around 1830, when the doctrine of the Lutheran Church experienced a resurrection, this doctrine no longer occupies any professor's chair in Prussia. For the Prussian Church indeed

---

11 *Charakter-Züge und historische Fragmente*, 84. HS

12 "In the honor of sound reason, which eagerly accepts what the voice of truth speaks; in honor of the humanity, which in agreement and accord with public opinion always has an effect upon the law (*vox populi est vox Dei*), I will gladly grant that the opponents of the Union were really convinced of the arguments which they used against it. . . . The first who arose as such was a foreigner, the Preacher Claus Harms in Keil. An old Lutheran in body and soul . . . he wrote theses. In these audacious, rigid, final, dogmatically formulated theses, he treated the Reformation as a task completed by Luther. He remained within the limitations of everything which was so excellently discussed with Calvin and Zwingli regarding the doctrines of the Supper and predestination, and then axiomatically codified particularly in the Augsburg Confession. But he took all this out of context. He treated the greater part of the discussion, carried on in allegoric diatribe, as though it were also in the sphere of the Confession, and he considered this as the norm, from which one must not deviate" (*Charakter-Züge und historische Fragmente*, 108 f.). What an unbelievable abyss of ignorance! HS

venerates Luther in the sense which the founder of the Union did so; it also calls
Luther philologists and Luther archaeologists to its lecture chairs. But of course,
no theologians who maintain that the Union of 1817 was irreconcilable with the
doctrine of the Lutheran Church are so called. If the Prussian state no longer tolerates such theologians in the pastoral office, rather removes them, imprisons
them, or compels them to emigrate, then such theologians certainly will not be
granted lectureships in the first place.

The young theologians on the Prussian faculties (and this immediately means
most German faculties) begin to develop an aversion to Lutheran confessionalism
from the moment they begin to suckle the theological milk bottle. The person
who studies in Berlin and Bonn, in Halle and Greifswald, in Breslau and
Königsberg, and then if possible finishes his study at the Wittenberg Seminary or
the Berlin *Domkandidatenstift* will, as a rule, be as immune to the theology of the
Formula of Concord—there are a few remarkable exceptions—as the absolvent of
the *Collegium Germanicum* in Rome is immune to Protestantism. For it is a law of
intellectual life, which applies also in the church, that only that doctrine can be
passed on and planted in hearts which the teacher concerned is absolutely convinced is true. A doctrine such as that of the Lutheran Church regarding the
Sacrament of the Altar has to be borne witness to. If it is no longer attested, but
only presented as an historical antiquity, even though it be presented with great
care and correctness, it dies. But this has necessarily now become the fate of the
entire Lutheran Church in Prussia.

But at the very moment this doctrine disappears as ecclesiastical dogma, the
veneration of Luther begins. Now Luther is actually "deified," as Eylert said so
candidly. The Luther scholars who now occupy the position of the guardian of
Lutheran doctrine now gather Luther's relics and display them in the Luther
Hall. The pilgrimage trains arranged by the Evangelical Federation view these
relics with the same veneration with which the pilgrims once viewed the relics
assembled in Wittenberg [*Allerheiligen-stift*]. The indulgence is indeed no more to
be had, but not because Luther had done away with it, rather much more because
of the reason Claus Harms had given in thesis 21.[13] And what about the appeal to
Luther? This also occurred on the anniversary of the Reformation in 1817, if not
at Wittenberg, certainly in the Garrison Church in Potsdam. On November 1,
the second day of the great celebration, which was celebrated as a holiday for the
youth throughout Prussia, our friend Eylert invoked Martin Luther in the middle of the sermon:

> Honorable, great, gentle, and kind man! How you deserve our admiration
> and thankfulness! We stand quietly in serious contemplation before your
> noble image, and our hearts pound in your presence [*unser Herz schlägt dir*

---

[13] "The forgiveness of sins at least cost money in the sixteenth century; in our day it is obtained for nothing, for everyone rewards himself with it." HS

entgegen]. We admire you in your valiant strength, which with powerful hands lifted the world from its hinges. And we love you in your gentleness, which allows you to kindly stoop down to children, in order to bless them with eternal benefits. Behold! Today, a host of millions of children is gathered together in a celebration dedicated to you, in the presence of God and Jesus, to whom you have led them. And with the hymns of praise of heaven and earth are joined our praises, and those of our children.[14]

How powerfully would Luther denounce the pathetic lies coming from the mouth of this offensive idol worshiper! The previous day the doctrine of the Lutheran Church was invalidated in Prussia, and now Luther is addressed in prayer. Both happened in the same church, at the same pulpit. How with mighty anger the Reformer would have unmasked this vexatious Luther worship, which the Evangelical Lutheran Church had never known, but which arises wherever the doctrine of the Lutheran Catechism is set aside. Such Luther worship is satanic fanaticism which seeks to eradicate the pure doctrine of the divine Word. For it whispers in the ears of man the lie of all lies, the original lie: "You shall be like God!" For the word "deify" [*apotheosieren*], which the babbling Garrison preacher used so thoughtlessly, means just this. And it is indeed finally not Luther who is placed upon the monument foundation in such festive "deification," but man himself.

To all the magnificent "heart lifting" celebrations in Potsdam and Wittenberg; to the supper celebrated as a feast of brotherhood [*Verbrüderungs-Abendmahl*] and the rapturous sermons; to the harmonious music of organ, tympani, and trumpet; to the emotional tears and all the energetic speeches; at the anniversaries, Reformation festivals, the placing of wreaths, church-day celebrations, national synods, rifle matches, and theological sessions which have made Wittenberg a museum upon the place where a genius once worked, Luther would have remarked very soberly with that which he once wrote in the Smalcald Articles concerning the serious sin of fanaticism, which darkens divine revelation and grieves the Holy Spirit:

> All this is the old devil and old serpent, who also converted Adam and Eve into fanatics. . . .

> In a word, fanaticism inheres in Adam and his children from the beginning to the end of the world, having been implanted and infused into them by the old dragon, and is the origin, power, and strength of all heresy, especially of that of the Papacy and Mahomet [Muhammad].[15]

---

[14] *Charakter-Züge und historische Fragmente*, 99. HS

[15] "Das is alles der alte Teufel und alte Schlange, der Adam und Eva auch zu Enthusiasten machte. . . . Summa, der Enthusiasmus steckt in Adam und seinen Kindern von Anfang bis zum Ende der Welt, von dem alten Drachen in sie gestiftert und gegiftet, und ist aller Ketzerei, auch des Papsttums und Mahomets, Ursprung, Kraft und Macht" (SA III VIII 5, 9). HS

The English translation is largely from the *Triglotta*, 495, 497. MH

It is the strength of all heresy, even the heresy of Potsdam and Prussian Wittenberg.

PART 3

We will not multiply examples demonstrating the fanatic character of the Union movement which began in Germany in the year 1817, though this would be easy to do. We would need only to proceed from Potsdam to Bernburg and Dessau or to the southwest German regions, become acquainted with the colleagues of Chaplain Eylert in these places, and attend their festival services to see the erstwhile Most Serene Highness and *Summus Episcopus*[16] in his full brilliance as "Guardian of the Evangelical Church," completing the Reformation in his lands. The grotesque comedy represented by the greater portion of these pathetic celebrations only veiled the deep seriousness of the ecclesiastical revolution which had taken place at the time.

And it is indeed not the case that merely the inadequacy of that generation laughably distorted a serious and great matter. The outbreaks of fanaticism were not only a phenomenon of the Union movement in Germany of the nineteenth century; they belong, rather, at their very essence, to this movement and therefore are present through the entire history of the movement down to our own time. The very same fanaticism which made it possible for the Union to be accomplished in a series of German territories in the decade after 1817 abruptly appeared again around 1846 (the year of the Berlin Church Conference, the Prussian General Synod, and the Evangelical Alliance) and led to the fanatical plans for a *Reichskirche* ["National Church"] which had its modest beginnings in the first German Evangelical *Kirchentag* beginning in 1848 (we have already mentioned the *Kirchentag* of 1853).

Times of fanatic hopes and plans for a "church of the future," in which the unification of the denominations [*Bekenntnisse*] is brought about, always coincide with times of great national and political excitement. This was the case after the founding of the Reich of 1871 and in the years from 1914 to 1919. This was especially true in the ecclesiastical revolution of 1933, which followed National Socialism's conquest of Germany. Perhaps to later generations it will one day appear as the classic example of the advent of fanaticism in the church, which cannot be explained by means of psychology. Here we have in mind not only the revolutionary movement of the "German Christians,"[17] which destroyed the structure of the ecclesiastical bureaucracy with a loud crash.

---

[16] *Summus episcopus* ("chief bishop") was a title assumed by territorial rulers serving, at first in an emergency role, the juridical functions of bishops. RF

[17] The *Deutsche Christen* was a pro-Nazi group which tried to bring a synthesis between National Socialism and Christianity. RF

Perhaps characteristic of the sinister nature of the power of this fanaticism is the effect which it has upon people who otherwise would essentially have nothing to do with it. It is not surprising that under the circumstances there would be people willing to become bishops. That ecclesiastical bureaucrats do not know what can happen in the case of such people is also not surprising. For that which most of German Protestantism called church government was overdue for the judgment which has now ensued, and as church history shows, revolutionary bishops can never long maintain their positions because they lack any inherent authority.

Remarkable and disquieting in the highest degree, however, was the remarkable defection of so many of our best theologians in the pastoral office, teaching office, and church government. Like the needle of a compass which for inexplicable reasons suddenly loses its bearing, these men lost the gift of discerning the spirits. Their theological judgment was lost. They made decisions which they never would have made earlier and would never make today. They said yes where, according to their entire being, their deepest convictions, they had to say no. Where they wanted to speak, where they had to speak, because it was the last irretrievable hour, they were silent. Thus the constitution of July 11, 1933, came to be, which was so unacceptable that it was as useless as a logarithm table established upon the presupposition that two times two equals five.[18] Thus the "German Evangelical Church" came into being, while its founders did not know for certain whether or not it would be a church. Thus the National Synod came into being in Luther's city, Wittenberg, through which German Protestantism experienced its deepest degradation.[19]

But who will blame individual men? Who feels safe from the authorities which seek to destroy the church in such times? "For our struggle is not with flesh and blood, but against principalities, against powers, against the rulers of the darkness of this age, against a spiritual host of wickedness in the heavenly places" [Eph 6:12]. Those "red cards" [roten Karten] of the "confessional front" [Bekenntnisfront] have no regard for these spirits. Yes, it may be that fanaticism dies in one part of the church only to come to life anew at an entirely different place, just as a fire dies down at one place in a burning house after it has done its destruction only to flame up at another place. Only with deep terror does one notice the blindness with which the leading men of the so-called Confessing Church[20] appear not to notice the strange fire of a wild fanaticism which has

---

[18] This reference is to the constitution of the German Evangelical Church (DEK), passed on July 11, 1933, and confirmed by Reich Law on July 14. RF

[19] This reference is to the First National Synod of the DEK in Wittenberg on September 27, 1933. RF

[20] The Bekennende Kirche was the group most opposed to the German Christians and to the Nazi control of the churches. In 1934 it became an opposition group which established alternate administrations (Bruderräte) at all levels where the official administration was German Christian. Sasse had been a participant in the movement, at least in its early days. Note also the title of the series in which this essay was published. RF

already begun to engulf their own house in flames. In a lecture recently delivered for pastors in St. Gall,[21] Karl Barth maintained that the errors of neo-Protestantism signify "a defection to the errors of Arius and Pelagius, already condemned in the ancient church," and that in the characteristic assertions of neo-Protestantism one hears not the voice of the Good Shepherd, but the voice of the stranger.

> Still, we are together under the roof of one church. But what will happen if our church is placed before these questions, as [is] today the case with the Evangelical Church in Germany? . . . I fear that the deep disunity in which we already find ourselves today, should it become entirely public, will make schism as unavoidable as it is in Germany.

To this we pose the following question: Under what circumstances and how long then can orthodox Christians in general remain together in one church with Arians[22] and Pelagians? According to the basic principles of our church we would answer that erring brothers should be borne in love in the hope that they will repent and return to the truth, but that *false doctrine* must not be tolerated. If false teachers have found their way into the church, they must be opposed. This struggle must also be waged against a church government which protects false teachers and thus makes itself a participant in their evil works.

If these basic principles are correct, then the following question arises which we hereby address publicly before the Christian world to Karl Barth: Why do these principles apply only in the case of Germany and not Switzerland? And if they apply in theory for the Swiss, why are they not put into practice there? What basic difference is there between the German Arian and the Swiss Arian? We can see no difference of great theological consequence. The state church is happy to have them both. It has always been the nature of Arianism that, because it does not know the real Lord of the church and because it does not believe that Jesus Christ really possesses all authority in heaven and on earth, it always seeks an earthly protector for the church. Whether the Arians of the fourth century, who lay in the dust before Caesar and pleaded with him that he help them obtain power; whether the English Arians of our time, who expect the House of Commons to protect them from the victory of Anglo-Catholic orthodoxy; whether the Prussian Arians, who during constituting assemblies of the church made their appeals to the Social Democrat and today make them to the National Socialist government so that orthodoxy not win the day; or whether someone in the Canton of Switzerland gives up the idea that the intellectual freedom [*Freisinn*] of Arianism needs to be forsaken—finally it is all the same. All Arian churches need a civil protector for their existence. Whether this protector is a

---

[21] *Theologische Existenz heute* 29 (1935): 33 f. HS

[22] Does Sasse mean us to hear also "Aryan" when he speaks at length in this section about the "Arians"? RF

Constantius who sends the orthodox into exile or a Theodoric who assures them of tolerance, finally there is no essential difference.

> We live in a divided church, and it is such that the situation will have to be tolerated. And since we have for the time being no order to separate us from each other, we can only be concerned with the question of how we, in spite of this most recent division, can manage to live with one another.

So far Barth. We have no desire to force ourselves into the ecclesiastical discussions of the Swiss. We do not begrudge the Swiss Church its inner freedom and can only wish for it that it may come to a renewal of its life and order without the crushing struggle which we in Germany have had to experience. But directly in view of what he wrote with such great influence in the first volume of *Theologische Existenz heute*, we must ask Karl Barth the following question: How does he know that God has commanded separation in Germany, but "for the time being" not in Switzerland? How has it happened that in Switzerland it is possible to know that the divine commandment is not in effect at present? There is also a voice of God in history, and the Swiss Christians must be very careful not to misunderstand this voice and perhaps to believe that because God has forbidden making compacts with Arianism in Lörrach it is also forbidden in Basel.

Finally, we must in all seriousness ask why God has granted the northern border of Switzerland a significance so theologically weighty and so important for the history of salvation [*heilsgeschichtlichen Bedeutung*]. Why must it be that in Basel, Zurich, and St. Gall, Arians and Pelagians still govern the church, while the territorial bishops of Würrtemberg and Hanover cease to be legitimate church government if they engage Arians and Pelagians in negotiations on their return to the church? If God makes this distinction, is there an explanation for his gentleness over against the Swiss and his strong hand with German church governments, or must we see therein a mystery of his hidden will?

It is necessary for us to direct these questions to Karl Barth for the following reason. His students, calling upon him and that which they have learned from him regarding the impossibility of compromise and individual peace agreements [*Burgfriedens*],[23] have announced their obedience to their hitherto legally acknowledged bishops, and with the approval of the liberal and Arian foreign press do not miss the opportunity to praise into heaven the "stalwart" confessors from Dahlem and Oeynhausen, along with their followers, at the expense of the "cautious" bishops, "prone to compromise."[24]

---

[23] For example, *Theologische Existenz heute* 1, p. 3. HS

[24] This reference is to the second and fourth synods of the Confessing Church. The first had been at Barmen at the end of May 1934; the second, at Dahlem, October 20, 1934; the third in Augsburg, May 22–26, 1935; and the fourth at Bad Oeynhausen, February 17–22, 1936. Why Sasse selects these two is not clear; Dahlem was the occasion on which the Confessing Church declared itself to be the only legal church in Germany. Oeynhausen was significant in that it manifested sharp divisions within the movement. RF

Now there is absolutely no doubt that the authority of a bishop has ended where he has forsaken the confession of his church, and where he demands his pastors act contrary to that confession. I must as a pastor refuse obedience to a church government which demands something of me which is contrary to my ordination vow. To be obedient in such a case would be sin. The Lutheran pastors in Prussia who after 1817 accepted the Union and Agenda without opposition bear a heavy burden of guilt. The pastors and congregations which rejected them and would sooner suffer all than be subject to the demands of a church government which contradicted their confession, and was therefore illegitimate, were correct. No matter how small the company which finally remained, this small number is absolutely correct in designating itself the "Evangelical Lutheran Church in Prussia," even if the state does not acknowledge the name. So also the Lutheran Free Churches, which came into being in similar struggles in the Hessian region and in Baden, are the legal Evangelical Lutheran churches in the applicable regions of Germany.

It is completely conceivable that also in our time the true confessors of the doctrine of the Gospel could be forced by an illegitimate—in the ecclesiastical sense—church government into what one Lutheran theologian once called "holy separation." But in such cases, everything depends on knowing exactly what the confession is from which one "cannot take anything away or give anything up, even if heaven and earth should fall and nothing remain." A man must know that and why it is the truth for which he must be prepared to lose body and life, and upon which he hopes finally to die consoled. Were this confession not the truth, then the man who confesses it, despite all his subjective honor, in spite of all of his "confessing attitude," is not a confessor of the truth, but rather a sectarian. Thus Scheibel in the great Prussian confessional struggle more than a century ago was a true confessor.[25] His contemporary, J. G. Oncken, founder of the German Baptists, was, in his confessional struggle against the Hamburg state and church government, a true sectarian.[26]

Does it not belong to the essence of a true confessor that he ever and again ask himself, as did Luther, "Are you alone wise? Have the others all erred and remained in error for such a long time? What if you are in error and lead so many people into error all to be eternally damned?" And does it not belong to the essence of the sectarian that he no longer even reckons with the possibility of error? If this is so, then it is among the most astonishing and troubling marks of our ecclesiastical situation that "confession" and "confessing" are spoken of with limitless self-assurance, even superficiality, without it being at all clear what the

---

[25] Johann Gottfried Scheibel (1783–1843) was a professor of theology at Breslau in Silesia who opposed the introduction of the Prussian Union. He was suspended in 1830 for championing Lutheranism. RF

[26] Johann Gerhard Oncken (1800–1884) joined the Continental Society whose purpose it was to oppose rationalism on the Continent. He established Baptist congregations in Germany, Holland, Scandinavia, and Eastern Europe (*Lutheran Cyclopedia*, 590). RF

proper content of confession is, or which propositions there are of which nothing can be given up, even if heaven and earth fall and nothing remain.

What is the confession which the "Confessing Church" in Bremen poses over against the German Christians? Is it so definite, so unambiguous that adherents of Bremen Liberalism are *eo ipso* ["by that very fact"] excluded from the confessional fellowship? Or is one as broadminded as the *Bruderrat*[27] of one large, east German city, which at the complaint that deniers of confessionally correct Christology also belong to the "Confessing Church" gave this naive answer: The question now is not about Christology, but about whether Jesus Christ alone is Lord of the church! What does this *Bruderrat* have in mind when it calls Christ "Lord" of the church! What confession does the Confessing Synod of the "Evangelical Church of the Old Prussian Union" advocate? If they wish to be a continuation of the Old Prussian Church from 1834 to 1933 (which is apparently their intent), then they must advocate two confessions. For the Old Prussian Church knew of only the Lutheran and the Reformed confessions.[28] There was no confession standing over both of these or contained in both. How does it come about that this church makes the following communication to its congregations?

> We thank Herr Professor Doctor Barth for the decisive service which he has rendered to the Evangelical Church. Through his theological work he has again ratified the Word of God among us as the only rule for doctrine and order in the church.

This cannot be said to the Lutheran congregations, which are indeed the great majority. For the Lutheran Church will ever thankfully acknowledge what Karl Barth did to rouse a sleeping Christianity. She will also learn from him that which she can, just as she has also happily learned what the great theologians of the Orthodox, the Medieval Roman, the Anglican, and the Reformed churches have taught of real Christian truth. But just as she has not taken over all of Tertullian nor all of Augustine, so must she also decidedly reject the error of Barth (for instance, his false doctrine of the relationship between Law and Gospel and his false concept of faith). The poor congregations in Prussia were misled by a demonstration of the kind in favor of Barth. They were, for instance, led to the view that Barth's explication of the *Credo*[29] repeats the church's doctrine, while it actually completely contradicts the explanation of the Creed in Luther's catechisms, as a passing glance at the definition of "faith" already shows, where there is no longer any talk of trust in the promise of the Gospel, nor of the proper heart of the evangelical concept of faith.

---

[27] The Brotherhood Councils, administrative councils or consistories within the Confessing Church, were alternatives to the official church governments. RF

[28] Here and later Sasse refers to the cabinet order which brought the Prussian Church into being. He wrote a separate essay in the anniversary year, "The Century of the Prussian Church: In Commemoration of Christmas 1834 in Hönigern," which is included in this volume. RF

[29] This is a reference to Barth's outline of dogmatics based on the Apostles' Creed, published in 1935. RF

Nor can the old Prussian *Bruderrat* be spared the accusation that it has not fulfilled its duty to guard the confession of the congregations to which it knows it is answerable as must happen. We happily grant to it that its members are deficiently instructed on the question of confession, but this of course does not exculpate it. Thus one could wander through all the territorial churches of Germany and ask each one, "What does the Confessing Church teach here?" In Baden do they confess what question 33 of the catechism used there says, after quoting several Bible passages, explaining the first article: "We learn to know God through his revelation in nature, in the history of man and within ourselves, but most especially in the Holy Scriptures"?

In the Palatinate do they make the article of the confession there their own according to which the Protestant Evangelical Christian Church accepts no emergency Baptism, so that parents should let their child die unbaptized if a pastor cannot be obtained? What is the confession upon which the Württemberg confessional pastor will judge the confessional faithfulness of his territorial bishops when they accuse him of acting contrary to the confession when he works to have German Lutherans placed under a spiritual leadership bound to the Lutheran confession? If these pastors oppose the demand of the Lutheran Convention at Hanover[30] that the Lutheran Church has a right to a Lutheran church government, how can they then sanction and even praise the church struggle of the Silesian Lutherans[31] of 1830 and the Hessian *Renitenz?*[32]

It is the deplorable consequence of the obvious ignorance of our pastors in individual churches of Germany regarding nineteenth-century church history that when the church struggle of 1933 broke out, the great church struggles of the past were not immediately before their eyes. It is all the more gratifying when these struggles are studied, as happened with representative thoroughness in the circles of the confessional pastors of Württemberg.

But what is to be said of the fact that they have not noted that those Lutherans of the nineteenth century struggled not only for the freedom of the church, but also and above all for the right of their church to a church government bound to their confession as the confession of pure doctrine. Oncken's Baptists also struggled for the freedom of the church, and we will grant to our Baptist fellow Christians without further ado that the goal of their struggle has been none other than this, that Christ alone, and not man, is the Lord of the church. The Silesian Lutherans struggled not against the territorial government,

---

[30] The Deutsche Lutherische Tag, Hanover, was held July 2–5, 1935. Sasse was one of 117 participants. RF

[31] This is a reference to a group which formed an independent synod in Prussia (and Saxony) after the decree of Frederick William III which mandated the Union Agenda for all Lutherans and Reformed. This group eventually came into fellowship with The Lutheran Church—Missouri Synod. RF

[32] This is a reference to a group in Hesse who refused to accept the royal Prussian order of 1873 which made the Church of Hesse an integral part of the Prussian State Church. *Renitenz* means "resisting": the group organized an autonomous Free Lutheran Church. The group likewise came into fellowship with the Missouri Synod. RF

but rather against a United church government, when they refused to acknowledge it. And the struggle of the rest of the Lutherans can only be understood with the presupposition that any church government which was not bound to the confession of the Evangelical Lutheran Church as the correct explication of Holy Scripture was for them intolerable.

All the brave fighters in the confessional struggles of the last century fought for the content of a definite confession. Where is the definite confession of the "Confessing Church" of the present? For the "confessing attitude" is not a confession. There is no real confession which cannot be confessed *in actu* ["in practice"]. The assertion of certain church governments that in their domain the confession is "inviolably" in force, though no use is made of it, is so laughable that no one takes it seriously. The territorial church of Mecklenburg is only Lutheran in so far as that in it the Word of God is actually preached according to the understanding of the Lutheran Confessions, and Luther's Catechism is taught. Insofar as in its government, practice, and teaching it is un-Lutheran, it has to that extent fallen from Lutheranism and is in need of repentance, a repentance that can be made easier because the legal confession is still Lutheran. Thus heresies are illegal and therefore can be more easily fought.

But it is meaningless to conclude from the fact that the definite content of the confession has been paralyzed that the correct confession amounts to only a "confessional attitude." Already the ancient church knew that the worst heresies produce their confessors and martyrs. The martyrs of the Marcionite church prove the truth of their doctrine as little as the martyrs and confessors of modern sects in Russia. And it is conceivable that wherever a "Confessing Church" among us stands engaged in the struggle against the German Christians and fights with heroic sacrifice for what it calls the lordship of Christ alone, that it is, however, in truth a sect or a group of sectarians. Whether it is acknowledged by us as a true church or not—we do not know God's judgment, nor do we make his judgment for him—can only be decided on whether its doctrine is pure or not. For no "Confessing Church" anywhere has seen it as its duty to clearly state what it confesses, to state which are the propositions of the faith from which nothing may be taken away or given up, even if heaven and earth fall and nothing remain.

But as soon as we direct this question to the German Confessional Movement of the present—we do so not from the outside, but as one who is committed to it with all his heart—the entire great predicament of this movement becomes evident. There is no sense in trying to hide this problem. The "Confessing Church" cannot say what it confesses. It can as little tell the world or Christianity what it believes and wherein its faith differs from the faith of other communions as can the "German Evangelical Church." Regarding the question of the confession of the "Confessing Church," we are answered by a chorus, no, a chaos of contradictory voices. First we hear those who with many variations assure us, "Our confessions are several and indeed, diverse."

Future historical accounts will perhaps see the real great act of the Confessional Movement of these years in that—in spite of all attempts which it has encountered to the contrary—it has firmly maintained the definition of the German Evangelical Church as a "federation of German confessional churches," as Barmen put it, or a "federation of confessionally defined churches," as it has been described since the Dahlem Synod. That is, it has acknowledged that the joining together of the territorial churches on July 1933 can only be understood in the sense of a federation, because the various Evangelical churches of Germany lack precisely that which makes unity and church fellowship possible in the church militant: the *consensus de doctrina evangelii et de administratione sacramentorum* ["agreement in the doctrine of the Gospel and the administration of the Sacraments," AC VII 2].

If this thought has not perished in Germany, if it has repeatedly been solemnly witnessed before world Christianity and the government of the German Reich, then this is the historical service of the churches united in confessional fellowship, but especially of the Lutheran Church. But alongside this view, from the beginning there were other voices. The theory of the federation of confessional churches is laden with the question which since 1817 ever and again deeply moved German Protestantism: Could, or to what extent could, a United Church [*Konfession*] also belong to [one of] the Evangelical churches [*Konfessionen*] (at the *Kirchentag* of 1848 it was already presented as a particular confession alongside of the two older confessions), and what was the nature of the United Church's confession? But then came the ever louder call for the full unity of the Confessing Church as the "German Evangelical Church," completely united in confession and organization. This goal would be advocated by all on the Reformed side, in accordance with the tradition of the Reformed Church. Already on the fourth of January 1934, the Free Reformed Synod at Barmen accepted a declaration composed by K. Barth in which it, in view of the heresies of the German Christians, calls upon

> the communions [*Gemeinden*] united in one German Evangelical Church, no matter whether they be of Lutheran, Reformed, or United origin and accountability, to acknowledge the sublimity of the one Lord of the one church and therefore the essential unity of their faith, their love and their hope, their proclamation through Word and Sacrament, their confession and their task. Thereby the notion is rejected that it must or needs be the authorized representation of Lutheran, Reformed, or United "interests" which supersede the demands of the common Evangelical confession and practice against error and for the truth.

Here it is bluntly said that there is no German Evangelical Church. It is the sum of individual communions. These communions are of various confessional origin and accountability, but they share an essential unity in the faith so that they can, in the present situation, confess as one. In the introduction to this declaration Barth expressed himself on the old differences which exist between Lutherans and Reformed. They are to be taken seriously but today must not prevent church fellowship:

> The dispute in the church today, and that concerning which we must "confess," does not have to do with matters of the Lord's Supper, but with matters of the First Commandment. In the face of this our need and task, that of the Fathers must recede, that is, there must still be serious opposition between the theological schools [i.e., between Lutherans and Reformed], but it must no longer be divisive and schismatic.[33]

How deeply this thought is rooted in the hearts of the Reformed is shown by the fact that Karl Immer programmatically repeats it in the conclusion to the *Report on the Confessional Synod at Augsburg*,[34] although in the meantime the Confessional Synods of Barmen and Dahlem, in agreement with all the Reformed, have declared that the "German Evangelical Church" can only be understood as a federation of confessionally defined churches (not as communions!) [*nicht etwa Gemeinden!*]. On the very same day on which the Lutheran Convention at Hanover solemnly declared as a demand of Lutheran churches bound to their confession, the basic proposition that a Lutheran Church can only be legally governed by a church government bound to the Lutheran confession— a proposition so self-evident that it needs no discussion at all among thinking people—Immer developed yet again the Reformed program as though no Synod of Barmen or Dahlem ever existed. He did not even shy away from demanding that the episcopal government [*Verfassung*] of the Lutheran Church be replaced by an allegedly divinely revealed *Bruderrat* government. He spoke of

> the enormous task that the German Evangelical Church, from congregation to congregation, from land to land, be reordered according to the nature of a church which is "under the Word." With this we will not avoid the question: How will the future church be defined? By the structure and history of intact churches, or by the brotherly, truly communal structure which the Confessing Church would represent in areas which have been destroyed?

Then follows a lament over the fact "that hitherto it has not led to altar fellowship without reservation." The fellowship of the "Confessing Church" finally must shatter on this inner contradiction between the view of the German Evangelical Church as a federation or the unionistic view of the same. The Lutheran bishops of Germany, insofar as they belong to a confessional fellowship, became guilty of serious untruthfulness over against their church when they transferred the spiritual leadership of the Lutherans in the German Evangelical

---

[33] *Theologische Existenz heute* 7 [January 26, 1934]: 7. With this last sentence he adopts, after all, the formulation of Schleiermacher which he otherwise might have avoided (e.g., *Sämtliche Werke* I, vol. 5, p. 341). HS

[34] *Report on the Confessional Synod at Augsburg*, 94. HS

Church to men who neither know the Lutheran confession nor desire to have a church of the Evangelical Lutheran confession.

It is absolutely impossible to explain the contradiction between both lines of thought within the "Confessing Church" and in its discussions which occurred in Oeynhausen and in the proceedings at the Confessional Synod convened there. To be sure, also in these events the positive and negative personality traits of the men who took part played a role, their wisdom or their foolishness, their action and inaction. But that the "Confessing Church" has not been able, nor yet today is able, to say what it properly confesses is not the fault of men. On the contrary, all the participants were of the opinion that they had to and could speak. For what is a Confessing Church if it does not confess? Have not its pastors, its congregations, its bishops, and its *Bruderräte* done this daily, even hourly? Have they not given valiant witness against the terrible heresies in the church, against lawlessness and violence? If a thousand, if a hundred thousand individuals confess, why should not they do it jointly? If Lutherans and Reformed bear witness individually, why should not they do it jointly?

Thus, corresponding to the admonition of Barth and the Reformed synods, the Barmen Confessional Synod sought to confess a common witness against the heresies of the times to the German Evangelical Church. The participants also believed that they achieved this, but that conclusion will not be so self-evident to later generations. Already today no one any longer ascribes to it the epoch-making significance which those who produced it, in particular its real author, Karl Barth, give it. In the meantime it has been proven that the only intent of the document which all sides agreed upon was the rejection of the doctrine of the German Christians. But everything else, especially all the positive theses, could and would be understood according to the Lutheran or the Reformed view.

In the third thesis of the Barmen Declaration, for instance, what is said regarding the presence of the Lord, if it is not to be empty talk, can be understood in the sense of the Lutheran or in the sense of the Reformed doctrine of the person and presence of the exalted Christ. That the following thesis on obedience and order of the church can likewise be understood in a Lutheran or Reformed manner has also been demonstrated. It is not so, as was thought at Barmen and as our Reformed brothers are pleased to assert, that one "community under the Word" in Nuremberg hears the same thing from this Word which is heard in Elberfeld, and that they have not remained "under the Word" if they have not heard from it Reformed church doctrine. For Lutherans hear from the NT entirely different propositions on the organization of the church than the Reformed. A theologian such as Barth had to have known and considered this.

Thus the Barmen Declaration is in no way only the afterword to a conquered ecclesiastical boundary between Lutheran and Reformed. Nor, according to the preamble, was its intent to eliminate this boundary.

It was also emphatically called a "theological declaration" and not a "confession," as in a similar manner the Prussian General Synod of 1846 accepted the

Nitzschenum[35] with the reservation that it did not thereby wish to establish a new confession. But in the text the word "confession" was indeed used, and finally, a binding declaration on what is pure and false doctrine is always a confession.[36] Thus the document has entered church history of our time as the "Barmen Confession." It has been boisterously greeted by the friends of a new Union as the dawn of the coming day of a unified Evangelical Church in which "Lutheran" and "Reformed" are only designations for varying theological schools, but no longer names of differing churches.

Soon the Barmen Declaration had won such dignity in wide circles of the "Confessing Church" that it was placed next to, yes even above, the confessions

---

[35] This was a document named for Karl Immanuel Nitzsch (1787–1868), a disciple of Schleiermacher. It was an attempt at a compromise in the ordination formula for the Prussian Union, according to which the candidate was to make profession of the great fundamental and saving truths instead of the church confession. But it did not include in such fundamental truths the doctrines of creation, original sin, the supernatural conception, the descent into hell and ascension of Christ, the resurrection of the body, the last judgment, nor everlasting life or punishment. Since by this formula the special confessions of Lutheran and Reformed were really set aside, the existence of a Lutheran as well as a Reformed Church seemed to be abolished. Opponents made a play on words, substituting *Nitzschenum* for *Nicaenum*, the Latin title for the Nicene Creed; sometimes they would call this document the unfortunate *Nicaenum* of the nineteenth century (J. H. Kurtz, *Church History* [trans. John MacPherson; 2d ed.; 3 vols.; London: Hodder & Stoughton, 1893], 3:280–81). MH/RF

[36] The attacks which have been directed against me because of my rejection of the Barmen Confession, since they contain aspersions and false reports and are still being spread today regarding the position I took at that time, necessitate a personal word. Hindered by real illness (not faked, as one church historian suggested to his readers), I could not participate in the preliminary discussions of a draft. I asserted in the debate that what Barth (who was closely connected with the declaration of the Reformed Synod of January 4, 1934) propounded was impossible. In the course of this discussion, Asmussen came to Erlangen at the behest of others higher up, and we produced another draft. This has yet to be discussed because Barth stood on his text as the basis for discussion, and unfortunately in the case of many the following applied: *Bona locuta, causa finita* ["Good has spoken; the case is closed"]. My main difficulty from the beginning was this, that a mixed synod cannot produce joint doctrinal declarations without making it clear that the Lutherans speak only for Lutherans and the Reformed for the Reformed. My positive proposal was that the synod (referring to the fact that the heresy of the German Christians would be condemned as much by the Lutherans as by the Reformed) should proclaim the right of the confessional churches bound to the confessions of the Reformation over against the illegitimacy of the German Christians. When I arrived in Barmen before the official beginning of the synod, it had already been decided in the preliminary discussions that there would be a common doctrinal declaration. As soon as I learned of this at the Lutheran Convention [the separate meeting of Lutherans at Barmen], I protested against it and declined a nomination to the committee which had the task of finalizing the formulation of the declaration. At the compelling entreaty of my territorial bishop, I cooperated with this committee in order to improve the declaration as much as I possibly could, but under the clear reservation that I did not believe the synod was authorized to produced a common doctrinal declaration for both confessions. I asked in vain to be able to present my reservations in the plenary or at least in the Lutheran Convention. It is inaccurate when J. Gaugen (*Die Chronik der Kirchenwirren*, 2:221) asserts that I was given plenty of opportunity to make my views known. I was able neither in the synod nor in the Lutheran Convention to give reason for my position, rather only in the secrecy of a small committee. When I noted that the schedule of the synod would not allow a dissenting view to be presented also to the plenary, I left the synod after having delivered a written explanation. I have not published this explanation so as not to give weapons to the opponents of the confessional fellowship and accordingly [risk] the possibility of destroying the fellowship of those who desire to fight for the confessions of the Reformation, and with them the substance of the church. For this reason, I have thus far been silent in the face of the hateful attacks. HS

Sasse's "written explanation," an essay entitled "Against Fanaticism," is also published in this collection. RF

of the Reformation. The participants of the Confessional Synods were allowed to depart from the Augustana. A dissention in matters of the Barmen Declaration was already more serious. Barth saw with a critical eye the worldly and human unity of the Unions of the nineteenth century, based upon untruthfulness, indifference, and subtle design. But no less than this Karl Barth strongly asserted that the Union consummated in Barmen could be "a heavenly unity, worked in the church by the Triune God." And in a paper widely disseminated, entitled "The Possibility of a Union of Confession," he made this so plausible that scarcely a reader could doubt that this was the case:

> Looking back at all the marks of the Barmen Union I would venture to state: This is genuine union! And it could be that here there occurred visibly a heavenly unity, worked by the Triune God. Precisely because it is such an unpretentious thing—a few completely preliminary theses—for precisely this reason I would say: There is every appearance, we venture to hope, that it has been spoken in obedience.

Full of astonishment, one asks: Is this still the old, sober Karl Barth who wrote *Quousque tandem?* Has he become a visionary? Has he seen heaven open? "Certainly the Lord was at this place; how holy was the *place from which flowed a stream of life over millions! Here was God's house, here the gates of heaven*," said Eylert on the founding of the Union in Potsdam. How is this any different from Barth's belief that not the Potsdam but rather the Barmen Union has been established by God? Has it become visible that God has worked in the unpretentiousness of the claims made by the Barmen document? What kind of doctrine of revelation is at work here? And are the claims really so unpretentious? "We believe that in a time of common difficulty and tribulation a common word has been placed in our mouths."

When one considers how the Bible speaks of the word which God places in the mouths of men, which is always the word of revelation received by prophetic inspiration (e.g., Num 22:38; 1 Kgs 17:24; Jer 1:9; cf. Is 6:7), this thesis of the Barmen Declaration will, at the very least, be viewed as very unfortunate. And it is regrettable that the many biblically literate participants in the synod let it pass. Asmussen's commentary on this thesis of the Theological Declaration of Barmen shows where it leads when words are no longer weighed temperately and calmly. He states: "Accordingly, it is before the eyes of the entire world that God has already long since placed a common word of faith in our mouths."[37] This assertion now crosses even the limits of the millennial kingdom, for there at its earliest it will be "before the eyes of the entire world."

But do we find ourselves at the beginning of the millennium, or perhaps rather in the end times? Is perhaps the unity of the church which is sought no longer at all the unity of the church militant, as it is described in the seventh arti-

---

[37] *Verhandlungsbericht*, 15. HS

cle of the Augustana, rather already that of the church triumphant, which is exempted from the struggle for pure doctrine? Then that remarkable "demand" about which we have questioned Karl Barth, which applies in Germany but not yet in Switzerland, is understandable. It would then be similar to the demand which led the holy church from the four winds to Pepuza and Tymion[38] for an encounter with her Lord, and which people since, throughout the history of the church, have so often believed they have heard. But it has never been the demand of God the Holy Spirit, but rather the demand of another spirit.

No one who understands this question will understand our critique falsely. Its purpose is not to cripple the Confessional Movement of our day, nor is it to place a stain upon the church history of Evangelical Germany since 1817. We are only and solely interested in an answer to a question which persists at the very heart of our being. Just how is it that every founding of a Union between the Evangelical churches of Germany has also simultaneously been an outbreak of Enthusiasm?

PART 4

There is only one possible explanation for this incontestable historical fact. There must be such a close correspondence between the boundary which separates the Lutheran and Reformed, on the one hand, and the boundary which separates the church bound to the *sola scriptura* ["by Scripture alone"] from Scriptureless Enthusiasm, or Enthusiasm which does violence to Scripture, on the other hand, that the opening of the one boundary is automatically followed by the opening of the other. Whether fanaticism opens the door to Union or Union to fanaticism may vary in individual cases. But both always hang inseparably together. At first this appears absolutely untrue. For both confessions, Lutheranism and Calvinism, see in fanaticism their common enemy. Both fight for the sole validity of the Scriptures against the

> enthusiasts—that is, the spiritualists who boast that they possess the Spirit without and before the Word and who therefore judge, interpret, and twist the Scriptures or spoken Word according to their pleasure. Münzer did this, and many still do it in our day who wish to distinguish sharply between the letter and the spirit.[39]

One would think that this struggle against the common enemy of both confessions could be much more effectively carried out if they were united in one church. But the paradoxical experience of church history of the last century is repeated also in this case. For those Protestant churches which have set aside their

---

[38] According to the early church heretic Montanus, Pepuza, a small town in Phrygia, was the new Jerusalem, the earthly center of the true church. Tymion was a neighboring village, united with it in this honor. All Christians were to gather here. RF

[39] SA III VIII 3. HS

The English translation is from Tappert, *BC*, 312. MH

particular doctrine in order to join federations or Union churches to fight a common opponent have been much less consequential, indeed, they have suffered terrible defeat much earlier than the confessional churches which fight hopelessly
according to human measure.[40] The churches which have opened themselves
widest to the Union are always the quickest to fall to fanaticism, as indeed also the
German Christian movement, after a prelude in the southwest German churches
(Nassau, Baden) organized itself in the Old Prussian Church as a church-political
power and already by 1932 achieved a great victory. From there it began to seize
the Lutheran Church. And to be sure, it took over those first in which the
church's confession had for the most part already disintegrated (Schleswig-
Holstein, Thuringia, Saxony).

At this point we must confront a misunderstanding which has time and again
distorted the debate on the Union question. The German territorial churches
cannot be divided into those which are united and those which are not, as though
they fall into two groups, namely, those who have accepted the Union, and others which have remained untouched by it. Nor is it the case that only a few of
these churches are responsible for the introduction of the Union, while others to
the contrary had no part in it. The Union arose out of the ecclesiastical relationships of the early nineteenth century, as the "ripe fruit of its unripe time" (thus
Wangemann,[41] and also Scheibel). The great political revolution of the
Napoleonic era had produced many states (which had up to that point possessed
unified territorial churches) into confessionally mixed regions. Problems which
resulted, which in individual regions of Germany had already been discussed for
generations, were now solved in accordance with the spirit of the times. Civil government from above was renounced. (Only in the Palatinate was a balloting by
house fathers actually brought about.) The Enlightenment had made the church
a society within the state. And idealism—which finally had no place for the church
at all, but only for an institution for the cultivation of religion as one benefit to
civilization, alongside other things beneficial to it—had further developed the
idea of the power of the state over the church.

Shrugging their shoulders, those in Berlin ignored the protest which arose
from churchmen against the horrible and illegal act of December 16, 1806. With
the stroke of a pen, and against all the prevailing laws, the century-old form of
church government was eliminated, and a section of the civil government, which
also supervised the royal theater, took over the government of the Lutheran and
Reformed churches. Who at such a time could have mounted an effective protest
against the governmental introduction of the Union? All the efforts for union in
the past finally failed because of the faithfulness with which the church held to her

---

[40] The struggle of the churches in the United States united in the Federal Council against the modern god-
    lessness has been, for instance, much less effective than that of the independent confessional churches.
    HS

[41] Hermann Theodor Wangemann (1818–1894) was the director of Berlin Missionary Society. RF

confession, but there was no greater power than the desire for a unified state [*Staatsraison*]. But Pietism and the Enlightenment had done their church-destroying work. At just this point of the greatest weakness and degradation of German ecclesiastical life, the state government could solve the confessional problem to its benefit in the spirit of the times, and that meant in the spirit of indifferentism.

What a lonely bird on the roof was Claus Harms with his powerful protest! The reason not all of Germany had accepted the Union at the time was that there were not enough Reformed congregations, for where there are no Reformed congregations the Union could not be introduced. At least that was the view at the time. Today it is quite something else. There were large German territories where there was not a single Reformed Church. They maintained the Lutheran name but didn't deserve it. A few of them actually became Lutheran again, and this by the grace of God alone which can also raise dead churches again to life. The Church of Saxony would also have joined the Union in the seminal years in which the Gustavus Adolphus Society[42] was founded (in Saxony the light of the Enlightenment radiated longer than elsewhere), but there were not enough Reformed churches. There were many Lutheran churches in Germany whose virginity was like the celibacy of a young woman who had not found a husband. And where would all the Reformed come from? In Silesia there were, according to Schleiermacher, four Reformed congregations over against some seven hundred Lutheran. It was a similar situation in all of the provinces east of the Elbe. The numbers were more favorable only where the exiled Huguenots had once found asylum, and especially in Berlin and in a few other places in Brandenburg. But the congregations in the east were all (except for Berlin) small, and their number and membership was on the decline. Only in the western provinces of Prussia were there Reformed Christians in great number and in sizable congregations. But all in all, at the beginning of the century in the Prussian Empire, there numbered only thirty-four French and one hundred twenty-five other Reformed congregations over against some seven thousand Lutheran congregations.

It has been said correctly that in most of the regions of the Prussian State, the Union meant that hitherto Lutheran congregations were declared united. For the most part the Reformed congregations continued to exist. The allowance of dispersed Reformed Christians as guests at the Lutheran Supper had already been introduced by church law in the eighteenth century. The only consequence of the Union was that the Lutheran Church was gradually robbed of its Lutheranism. Today *most of the congregations within the Old Prussian Union are de jure Lutheran*, but they do not know it; they have forgotten their confession. Thus the boundaries between United and not United churches [*Kirchentum*] are fluid, and there is without doubt in many areas of Prussia a more Lutheran consciousness among pastors and congregations than in many a Lutheran Church in which the Union

---

[42] This was a Protestant, unionistic society, organized for the purpose of subsidizing evangelical churches in Roman Catholic countries. RF

is only known by hearsay. There is at least one church in Germany which returned to Lutheranism from the Union. This is the Bavarian Territorial Church, which for a generation, from 1818 to 1848, was actually part of the Union, insofar as also the Reformed congregations in Bavaria west of the Rhine and the United churches of the Palatinate were under the jurisdiction of the Munich *Oberkonsistorium* ["High Consistory"]. Here a church government had succeeded in releasing entire regions of the church from its oversight in order to become a church government genuinely bound to its confession.

This brings us to the question of the common responsibility of all the territorial churches for the Union. The return to the confession was possible in Bavaria because the Roman Catholic *Summus Episcopus* allowed it. How often has the thought arisen in pious Prussian hearts that it might have been better if John Sigismund would have defected to the Roman Catholic instead of the Reformed faith in 1613.[43] The Jesuits could have already been gotten the best of in Berlin, just as the Lutheran Church outlived the Jesuits at the court of Dresden. It was indeed much more difficult to outlive the "Protectorate" [*Schutzherrschaft*] of the Berlin Hohenzollerns.[44] For the service of protection was rendered upon the condition of complete rule of the church, down to the right of the king to determine what the Evangelical Church should be. "Never had a pope had power over the Catholic Church like the Reformed King Frederick William had from 1808 over the Lutheran Church," said Wangemann, who was a royal loyalist.[45]

How great this power was is illustrated no more clearly than by a fact which must be designated an irony of history: the men who today fight for the freedom of the church are zealous advocates of the Unions, which stand among us today in the church as the living monuments to *territorialism* and *royal absolutism*. Insightful princes had understood the senselessness of this entire system of church government. It was bound to be assailed no later than 1866 by those who by their ordination vows were in duty bound to be concerned about the maintenance of pure doctrine. For the Prussian crown was overwhelmed with its oversight of the most diverse churches.

Here we see plainly the common guilt of all the German territorial churches. If the Unions were incompatible with the Lutheran confession, then they

---

[43] John Sigismund (1572–1619) was the elector of Brandenburg who became heir of the Duchy of Prussia in 1618. Though he was raised as a strict Lutheran, he embraced the Reformed confession in 1613 and became aggressively active on behalf of Calvinism and the union of Lutheran and Reformed churches. For an excellent English study, see Bodo Nischan, *Prince, People, and Confession: The Second Reformation in Brandenburg* (Philadelphia: University of Pennsylvania Press, 1994). RF

[44] There were also other Hohenzollerns, for instance, the brave confessor whose name stands at the end of the Augustana and whom Bezzel once held before the last king of Prussia as a model. HS

The Hohenzollerns were a German royal family. The "brave confessor" was George von Ansbach (1484–1543), margrave of Brandenburg, called "the pious" and "the confessor" (*Lutheran Cyclopedia*, 329). Hermann Bezzel (1861–1917) was one of the most important leaders of Lutheranism in Sasse's day. He became a successor to Löhe at Neuendettelsau and was opposed to all unionizing. RF

[45] *Sieben Bücher Preußischer Kirchengeschichte*, 1:17. HS

should never have been granted ecclesiastical recognition. Those churches which remained Lutheran had indeed accepted the fact of the Union, but at the same time they should have seen the definite consequences of this acceptance. The catechisms of Baden and the Palatinate contain such a weak echo of Evangelical [Lutheran] doctrine and are so beset with false doctrine and open the door to every heresy that the Lutheran Church must warn its members who move to Baden and the Palatinate not to join these churches and urge them to join the Free Church. A Lutheran Christian cannot receive the Sacrament at a territorial church altar in Heidelberg or Speyer because there the doctrine of his church on what makes the Supper the Supper is publicly denied.

This is not lovelessness, but a simple requirement of truthfulness. For as a Lutheran Christian I do not go to the Table of the Lord to experience some meaningful religious moment of celebration, nor to celebrate an undefined "most holy union" with my Redeemer. I go because I believe that in the Sacrament of the Altar the true body and the true blood of my Lord Jesus Christ, under the bread and wine, are given to me to eat and to drink. The pastor there may be an upright, pious Christian and a beloved man. But he will tell me during the celebration of the Supper, either directly or indirectly, in the address or in the liturgical formulas, that precisely that which I seek in the Supper is not found there, that my faith here is not the correct Christian faith, rooted in the NT, rather the controverted private view of a Lutheran theologian. Therefore I cannot receive the Supper in this church. (In this day and age when people move and travel widely [*Zeitalter des Verkehrs*], this is not necessarily implicit. Why must everything always be made as easy as possible?) And I cannot send my children there for confirmation instruction.

The Lutheran churches should instruct their own members on this matter and then in all Christian love, but absolutely unambiguously, discuss this matter with the United churches, especially the Old Prussian Church. Indeed, the Old Prussian Church never introduced a new confession, rather in far and away the majority of congregations it left all the Lutheran Confessions, except the Formula of Concord, "inviolably" in force. On this basis the Lutheran churches believed they could also maintain church fellowship with the Prussian Church, although the choice was given to anyone belonging to a Lutheran territorial church moving to Prussia, to join the so-called Old Lutherans by simply declaring his preference for the "Evangelical Lutheran Church of Old Prussia."

But if the Prussian Union Church should claim to be the continuation of the Old Lutheran Church which existed before 1817, how is it that her confession has been so ignored? How many people from all over Germany have moved to Berlin? But it is precisely in Berlin that congregations of the old confession have not been allowed to exist. For Lutherans who came to Berlin there was no possibility within the territorial church to join a congregation of the Lutheran confession. It is still the case today that any Reformed Christian who travels to Berlin can join a Reformed congregation in which his children can receive confirmation instruction according to his confession. But any Lutheran who moves to Berlin becomes a member of a definite parish in which the pastors—in contradiction to their ordination vow—are duty bound to preach according to both confessions which have validity in the congregation. Perhaps he has been able to find a pastor somewhere to give his children Lutheran confirmation instruction. But the religious instruction which his children receive in school will be imparted exclusively by teachers who have had no opportunity to learn that something like a Lutheran Church even still exists.

What severe guilt have the Lutheran Church governments incurred by letting this happen! It cannot be said that the church governments before 1918 could not possibly have spoken because they were for the most part civil governments [*Man sage nicht, den Kirchenregierungen sei es vor 1918 nicht möglich gewesen zu sprechen, weil sie halbe Staatsbehörden waren*]. They have been silent even when they could have done so without difficulty. What good does it do to maintain the confessional position, what good is it to carry out doctrinal discipline in a Lutheran territorial church (if the pastors are indeed bound to the confession) if the other entities which are teaching within the domain of the church concerned, and at times teaching very effectively, are bound to no doctrinal norm?

Lutheran churches such as the Bavarian and Hanoverian churches must say to the great independent associations and societies, to domestic and foreign mission societies, to the Gustavus Adolphus Society and to the Martin Luther Bund, to the Pastors' Alliance and to the Evangelical Federation, to the publishers, the women's groups, the youth organizations which have taken over a great part of the ecclesiastical work: We are happy that it is the purpose of your program to serve our congregations with your practical work. But if you desire to *teach*, if you desire to preach God's Word to the various age groups in the church and to the parishes as members and office holders, if you wish to tell them what faith, [what] church, what a Christian congregation is, then you are bound to the confession of the church and subject to its discipline as much as anyone else who teaches in the church.

What are your newspapers like? What have you brought into all the homes of Evangelical Germany with the great editions of your publications? The Lutheran churches have got to speak this way. They must finally, finally, say this. In the Unions of the nineteenth century a clear historical *fate* is revealed which has affected all of German Protestantism. It has affected one church more, another less, but no realm of German church life has gone unaffected. And if we must speak of *the guilt of unionism*, of the guilt [of] frivolous, untruthful Union-blundering [*Unionsmacherei*], which has lied to itself and others about a unity which is not present at all, then there is not a single territorial church in Germany which is free of this guilt. Thus the entire German Church must bear the consequences of the false Union. And the question of what will become of these Unions is one that gets at the very existence of all the territorial churches.

The moment the boundary between the Lutheran and the Reformed churches was removed by the German Unions of the previous century, the dike which should have protected the church of the *sola scriptura* against the raging flood of fanaticism broke. Why did this happen? How is this connection explained? The moment both Evangelical churches were no longer able to say what separated them, remarkably they also lost the ability to withstand fanaticism with a clearly confessed word.

The Union is, in many respects, more eloquent than any confession. It does not tire of drumming up recruits and extolling its merits. It speaks more of "confessing" than of the confessions. It rouses itself, like an intellectual poet of the Enlightenment, to wax poetic on the obligation of praising and thanking, but no longer praises and thanks. When it comes to serious confessing, the Union is struck dumb. There is no *Union confession*, or more correctly, there are so many varying confessions that none of them is taken seriously and viewed as a real confession. The "Evangelical Protestant Church in Baden" has a confession. "The United Protestant Evangelical Christian Church in the Palatinate" also has a confession. But neither agrees with the other.

Why has no friend of the Union come up with the idea of uniting the United churches of Germany? That would be a magnificent accomplishment. The obstinate Lutherans could simply be left aside and the attempt be made to unite all the United churches of Germany with one confession. It is possible. The Palatinate Union has this motto (it is in its catechism and at the head of the church newspaper of the Palatinate): "It is of the deepest and holiest essence of Protestantism henceforth to bravely forge on in the way of well-proven truth and genuine religious enlightenment with undefiled freedom in matters of faith."

What do the Halle Pietists who today are at pains to figure out whether they should be Lutheran or Reformed, both or neither, have to say about this Union? The attempt to have the Prussian Union declare what it actually confessed continued down to our own time. But no one has been able to get it to do this. What a struggle for the church's confession has raged throughout the history of the Old Prussian Church, from the cabinet orders of 1817 and 1834 to the General Synod of 1846, down to the organizational and ecclesiastical struggles of our own day. What different understandings the Lutherans and the Reformed have of the Union, both of whom are pledged to the unabated continued legitimacy of their confession. What different understandings have the adherents of the Positive Union, the Protestant Alliance, and the Middle Party! For all this it must be quite easy to determine what Lutheran and Reformed have to confess in common over against the Catholic churches, fanaticism, and neo-paganism! If one can say what the Lutheran and Reformed confessions have in common with the Roman Catholic and Eastern Orthodox confessions, namely, the truths of the Nicene Creed, then it must be quite a simple thing to determine the consensus between both Evangelical confessions. Dorner, Nitzsch, and Julius Müller did this. Their attempts may be read. Wilhelm Lütgert and Arthur Titius put this consensus down on paper in five minutes. Unfortunately, these two attempts do not agree with each other, and they have not found any adherents.

The result is always the same. Doctrinal formulations are abandoned and there is a hasty retreat to the Bible. But this pious retreat is what all heretics make, as everyone knows. Think only of the fight against the *homoousios* based on the fact that the word does not occur in Scripture.[46] This retreat can be made in a Pietistic manner, or more in accord with Enlightenment sensibilities when the appeal is made to the advance in the science of exegesis. The Biblicists of both parties can only be answered in the following way: If you have really come to a new understanding on the basis of the Scriptures, formulate it! Don't just talk about it, formulate it! For confessions are nothing other than *formulations of the understanding of Scripture*. If you really believe you have come to some new understanding of the Lord's Supper which supersedes the doctrines of the Lutheran and Reformed churches, then formulate it in clear language, as did the catechisms of the time of the Reformation. But hitherto, unfortunately, such theses have not been produced for discussion. Nor is the other way out of this problem possible, namely, Karl Barth's "Confessional Union" [*Bekenntnis-Union*]. He would reduce the church-dividing antithesis between Lutheran and Reformed to a difference of theological schools which can exist alongside each other in one and the same church. He thinks it is

> not comprehensible why modern Lutherans could not explain that the *improbant secus docentes* ["they reject those who teach otherwise"] of Augustana X was directed against Zwingli and the *Schwärmer* ["fanatic"] of the sixteenth century as an important delimitation of the Lutheran doctrine of the Supper against a particular heresy, without thereby asserting the ridiculous notion that the modern Reformed are also included in this *secus docentes*, and from whom there must also be ecclesiastical separation.

He believes this is possible because the controversy in the church today is not over the Supper but the First Commandment. It is remarkable that a theologian who is so intelligent and familiar with the Lutheran literature can make this judgment. Doesn't he notice that his proposal finally says the same thing as the definition of the Union given in the cabinet order of 1834:

> The Union proposes and intends no giving up of confessions of the faith hitherto in place; neither is the authority which the confessional writings of both confessions have had up to this point done away with. The introduction of the Union is only the expression of the spirit of moderation and charitableness which will no longer allow the differences in individual points of doctrine of the other confession as grounds for denying external ecclesiastical fellowship.

Over against this legally binding definition of the Prussian Union, Barth today would only add this support: Because the fight today is not regarding the

---

[46] *Homoousios* is the word used in the Nicene Creed to express that the Son is "of one substance" with the Father. RF

Supper, the doctrinal differences on this question can no longer be church-dividing; moreover, the condemnation of Augustana X does not apply to the Reformed today. But to this we simply say that what the Lutheran Church intended with its condemnations is clearly enough stated. It had in mind with its condemnations always definite false doctrines which are not confined only to one age. Just at it appropriated the ancient church's condemnations of the Valentinians, Arians, Eunomians, and so forth, so also the condemnation which was expressed in Augustana X has to do with a doctrine which can always reappear and is in fact alive to this day. Indeed, it has conquered a great portion of Lutheranism itself. And this is the doctrine that in the Sacrament of the Altar the true body of the Lord is not given to us in, with, and under the bread.

Our church also expressly broadened this condemnation to include the doctrine of Calvin. Even if others do not, Barth should know what this view of the Sacrament, what the Fifth Chief Part of the Catechism, means for all of Lutheran doctrine. And if he perhaps asks who still advocates this doctrine, we also beg to ask him who still advocates the doctrine of original sin and the great doctrines of the Reformed Church? It is of course very easy to ask with a certain amount of irony whether there is today still a Lutheran Church at all. The same question can be put about the Reformed Church, or even the church in general. The matter does not depend upon how many or how few people confess the doctrines of the Reformation, but rather whether these doctrines are still preached and believed. As long as this happens, the old churches of the Reformation era are still a reality. Lutherans and Reformed, whether few or many, still stand united with their fathers by the same confessions of the faith, even as both churches still stand over against the other. There is no actual Evangelical Church in Germany outside of both these confessions. The Union churches also live, whether they know it or not, from the remnant of ecclesiastical content which they have salvaged from the time when the confessional churches were separate, down to the present. This is demonstrated by a quick look at their catechisms.

PART 5

Evangelical Christianity in Germany stands before the greatest organizational task which it has ever faced in its four-hundred-year history. The old forms in which it has existed and into which it was forced have been forever broken in the revolution of our day, and it must create a new form of existence. But a new ecclesiastical structure has never come about without the tiresome labor of many years. It is self-evident for every serious theologian that this form cannot be a single unified church, since we have in Germany differing Evangelical confessions. A "German Evangelical Church" which claims to be more than a "federation of confessionally defined churches" would be the worst conceivable untruthfulness so long as German Protestantism is not united in confession. The last remnant of true Evangelical church life [*Kirchentums*], which has maintained itself in Germany until our day, would inevitably die in this lie.

In the interest of the German people, which is made up not only of theologians, and therefore which has the naive opinion that the church ought actually be what it is called, the following ought to be considered. Should not the misleading name "German Evangelical Church," a creation of Schleiermacher, the man of a thousand tricks,[47] who brought so much false terminology into circulation in theology and church, be gradually removed from circulation? This could of course occur only with a loyalist understanding and in full agreement with the Reich government, for whom the terminology employed by theologians has won the significance of state-church law. Here is a wonderful new opportunity for the Ecclesiastical Committee of the Reich [*Reichs-kirchenausschuss*], which knows of course just as well as we do that the "German Evangelical Church" is not properly a church. The members of this committee are theological advisors, extraordinarily well acquainted with the area of ecclesiastical language, and it would not be difficult for them to coin a new expression to replace the long-since antiquated expression of Schleiermacher. It could be popular and yet at the same time express the facts without any misunderstanding that the alliance of the Evangelical territorial churches signifies the closest conceivable *confederation* of those historic churches of the Reformation, yet that these churches have not ceased to be *confessional churches*.

Within such a confederation, constructed upon the strictest principles of truth, the relationship of the Evangelical confessions toward one another can and must then finally be arranged anew. As a presupposition to this, the question must first be settled as to whether and to what extent there is one united confession, alongside of the Lutheran and Reformed confessions. The friends and champions of the Union must give the Lutherans and the Reformed an answer to this question, which has been directed at them now for over a century. Whether they will be able to give a united answer is entirely doubtful, as we have indicated above. If the churches of Baden and the Palatinate have entirely different conceptions of the Union and of the applicability of Reformation confessions, how will they come to an agreement on this question with the churches of East Prussia and Silesia, which have never had a catechism other than the Lutheran catechism?

It is always conceivable that a portion of German Evangelical Christianity might gather itself around a new conception of Union, and the Lutherans and Reformed be united by definite, confessional theses of some kind. If such attempts should succeed, then that part of German Christianity could not be denied its own particular character as a type of confession. But under no circumstances is it the case that those who happen to live in "United" churches comprise a "United

---

47 See, for example, the letter to Cölln and Schulz, 1831 (*Sämtliche Werke* I, vol. 5, p. 701); *Vorrede zu den Augustanapredigten*, 1831 (*Sämtliche Werke* I, vol. 5, p. 704). HS

confession," because the word "United" in East Prussia has a meaning completely different from that in the Palatinate. East Prussia has practically no United
congregations, while the Palatinate has only United congregations. The
Evangelical Church of Silesia binds its pastors to an entirely different doctrine
than the churches of Baden and Nassau.

It is impossible and should be unworthy of German theologians to justify the
Union by asserting that the congregations, and even the theologians, today no
longer understand the difference between "Lutheran" and "Reformed." And if
this is so, then they must learn it again. For if ignorance is what dictates what the
church is and is not to teach, what will be left to teach? Should the Sacrament of
the Altar, celebrated as it has been in the churches of Nuremberg since the time
of the Reformation, be divested of its confessional character, so that it gives no
offense to "enlightened" people? Is it Christian love to demand this? Is it
Christian love to comply with such a demand?

But at the very least, the Union is justified by the practical necessities of life.
We certainly do not wish to make light of the problems which once occurred in
Anhalt where a Lutheran pastor got his beer from a "Reformed" brewery, and
where in another situation a Reformed glazier repaired the window of a Lutheran
Church, which had very serious consequences for the desired state of affairs. But
if in these and other circumstances, as they are presented today as sufficient
grounds for the necessity of a Union, the practical men of the church know of no
other way out than that two churches change their dogma, then they only prove
that they have made all too little use of the intellectual gifts which our dear God
has given to them.

From the difficulties which are brought about by more than one confession
existing side by side, and which today among most Christian peoples are a hundred times greater than in Germany because we only have very few confessions,
there is derived the necessity of a Christian, brotherly life together, of an ordered
mutual relationship. But these difficulties can never necessitate the Union. *The
Union can always only be justified dogmatically*. The friends and disciples of the
Union are obliged to present this justification to the advocates of the Lutheran
and Reformed confessional churches. But not as though they could be convinced
that their views are not correct. That would be as pointless as the corresponding
attempt to do this between the Lutherans and Reformed. But if this wrestling
over these issues in our day is able to accomplish what the nineteenth century
could not, namely a Union confession of more than purely personal or territorial significance, then it will be given the attention to which every ecclesiastical
confession has claim. We are ready and willing to limit our proposition, that the
Union has no confession, to the past. But we can only do that if the disciples of
the Union clearly tell us what they *magno consensu* ["with common consent"; cf.
AC I 1] believe, teach, and confess on the questions dealt with in the catechism.

Furthermore, the relationship of Lutherans and Reformed within a confederation of German confessional churches must then be based upon a new basic

situation. We must proceed from the knowledge which has arisen from the painful experiences of the history of the Union, and from the bitter experiences of the present ecclesiastical struggle. The reason both confessions speak past one another, which has made these struggles so difficult, has its deepest cause in the fact that the Lutheran and the Reformed churches do not have the same *concept of the Evangelical Church*.

For the Reformed, the Lutherans are part of the Evangelical Church in so far as they are on the way toward the completion of the Reformation. It is the task of the Reformed to help the Lutherans in this regard, for instance, to help the Lutherans free themselves from the realistic doctrine of the Supper, from the one-sided emphasis on faith over obedience, among other things.

For the *Lutherans*, the Reformed no longer belong to the church of the *pure* Gospel. They have moved in a direction which has departed from the Reformation. They have surrendered biblical truths, such as the realistic doctrine of the Supper, which cannot be given up. They have muddied and partially lost the fundamental knowledge of the proper distinction between Law and Gospel.

From his viewpoint, Calvin thought he was entitled to direct the affairs within the Church of the Augsburg Confession. He thought he was [a confessor] and desired the recognition of the Reformed as kindred confessors of the Augustana. The Lutherans, however, could in no way grant that Calvin's doctrine of the Supper, which denied the real presence of the body and blood of Christ in the Lutheran sense, was compatible with the Augsburg Confession. It of necessity abandoned everything which Luther had taught on the Fifth Chief Part of the Catechism. V. E. Löscher bid the Reformed in his "Peaceable Address to the Reformed Congregations in Germany" to think through the situation of the Lutheran Church around 1570 and to place themselves into this situation:

> Suppose at that time the entire theological faculty at Geneva were secretly Lutheran, the faculties at Zurich and Basel were for the most part headed in the same direction, and the faculties at Heidelberg and Marburg would not or could not do anything to oppose this; men who were secretly Lutheran were shoved into offices everywhere, and we demanded this secretly, but denied it publicly. What then would have the remaining Reformed, for instance in Holland, done to maintain their religion? Certainly nothing less than our theologians did through the Formula of Concord and otherwise, to conserve their confession.

The consciousness of Calvinism over against Lutheranism, its conviction that the Reformed Church must lead the Lutheran Church to a completion of the Reformation, is completely understandable from a human point of view. But the naivete with which this view has been played out, from the days of Laski's[48] exiled congregation—because of its Calvinistic faith it had been expelled from London

---

[48] Jan Laski (1499–1560) was a Polish humanist who became a reformer. He emigrated to England where his Calvinistic theology was quite influential under Edward VI. Edward had given him the task of orga-

and requested not only asylum in Copenhagen, then Rostock, Wismar, and Lübeck, but also the acknowledgment that its doctrine of the Supper was alone scriptural—to the politics of the Union in Brandenburg, Prussia, and the church politics of today's Reformed Confederation, has deeply confused the relationship between both confessions.

This explains why the Lutheran resistance has been so intense. For down to the present day, the natural demand of the Lutheran Church for a church government bound solely to its confession has been viewed as a disturbing of the confessional peace. Paul Gerhardt, who simply would not sit by silently as the Lutheran Church in Brandenburg was forcibly calvinized, is viewed as a destroyer of the peace. The Great Elector,[49] who out of deep conviction sought to calvinize the Lutheran Church, is viewed as the paragon of an Evangelical prince.

Will this state of affairs change? Will both Evangelical churches, which stand over against one another in German speaking lands, ever come into a relationship in which each finally has respect for the faith of the other? Then they will be able to speak to each other. Before this happens they cannot but speak past one another. We are completely prepared to hear the grievances which the Reformed have to bring against Lutheranism and its church politics. For only when the *church political* misunderstandings and mistakes have been settled can both confessions truly speak to each other in a churchly and theological way. But if this happens, it will truly be a churchly and theological dialogue.

For it is not the case, as one who had a superficial knowledge of our age of orthodoxy stated, that a Lutheran is bound to see in the Reformed Church a form of the "devil's church." That would be entirely un-Lutheran, nor did orthodoxy have this view.[50] In all its unambiguous rejection of those things which were viewed as false doctrine, and in all its struggles against the church-political meth-

---

nizing a congregation of foreign Protestants. But when Mary came to power in 1553, Laski and his congregation were exiled and wandered from place to place, finally obtaining asylum in Frankfurt. MH

[49]　Frederick William (1620–1688). RF

[50]　The meaning of the condemnation formulas of our confessions is authentically interpreted in the foreword to the Book of Concord (*BS*, 11.41 [the following translation is from the *Triglotta*, 19]):

> As to the condemnations, censures, and rejections of godless doctrines, and especially of that which has arisen concerning the Lord's Supper. . . . It is in no way our design and purpose to condemn those men who err from a certain simplicity of mind, but are not blasphemers against the truth of the heavenly doctrine, much less, indeed, entire churches, which are either under the Roman Empire of the German nation or elsewhere; nay, rather has it been our intention and disposition in this manner openly to censure and condemn only the fanatical opinions and their obstinate and blasphemous teachers, (which, we judge, should in no way be tolerated in our dominions, churches, and schools,) because these errors conflict with the express Word of God, and that, too, in such a way that they cannot be reconciled with it.

> Our church has never taught "that the other church does not have nor pray to Christ, but an idol" (Asmussen, *Theologische Existenz heute* 24, p. 30). The Lutheran Church never even asserted this about the Papal Church. What of the true Gospel the Reformed also have has always been acknowledged. Thus from 1653 to 1806 [Lutherans and Reformed] could stand together over against the empire and Catholicism. HS

ods to calvinize all of the German lands, it never denied that the church of Christ is also in Scotland or Switzerland. But that false doctrine must be fought, and that there could be no church fellowship where there is no unity on the basic understanding of the Gospel—that was indeed an understanding which had been learned from Luther, and which neither the Old Lutheran Church nor the Evangelical Lutheran Church of later times could have given up. Whoever does give it up—as the Enlightenment and Pietism did—abandons the Reformation. And not only that: he abandons the church altogether.

For since the Reformation raised the great question of the pure doctrine of the Gospel for all of Christianity, the church exists only in, with, and under the form of confessional churches. No one can belong to the church, no one can desire the church, unless he affirms a confession—be it old or new. That these confessions contradict each other, that we from our understanding of Scripture, out of deep conviction of faith, must view another view of Scripture as mistaken, that is the cross which the church must bear as *ecclesia militans* ["church militant"]. But if one is tempted to doubt the correctness of the proposition that full church fellowship presupposes the full fellowship of faith, doctrine, and confession, let him study the unspeakable and deplorable plight of the churches of the Reformation, seen in their deepest humiliation, in the history of the modern Union. This history can teach us what the church's confession is and what the struggle for God's truth in the *ecclesia militans* means for a world which faces the threat of being swallowed up by the lie.

1936

AGAINST FANATICISM[1]

When Sasse left the Confessing Synod at Barmen on the early morning of June 1, 1934, he had been instructed by his bishop to utter no public critique of the proceedings. Now, some two years later, Sasse is able to break his silence. The group which remained at Barmen came to call itself the "Confessing Church" [*Bekennende Kirche*]. They were chiefly followers of Karl Barth and his view of confessions. Sasse here explains that "We understand something different when we speak of the Confessing Church."

It will be helpful to know a little of the history of the Confessing Movement. The First Confessing Synod was at Barmen in late spring 1934; the second was at Dahlem, a suburb of Berlin, at the church of Pastor Martin Niemöller in the following autumn. In some parts of Germany, the Confessing Church formed an alternate church government.

Huss number 154
Hopf number 084

—◦◦◦—

The "Provisional Leadership of the German Evangelical Church" [DEK] in Berlin, whose church-government-like claims of the confessionally loyal Lutherans have ceased to be acknowledged for some time, now sends out a "Word concerning the Confessional Question of the DEK" that is suitable to mislead the pastors and congregations of Evangelical Germany. It will properly be rejected by the responsible organs of the Lutheran churches. For the sake of the urgency of the matter, however, the undersigned, by request of the editor of this journal, now makes a personal statement about some points of that declaration.

1. As a Lutheran theologian, as a member of the confessional fellowship of my territorial church, and as a participant of the Barmen Synod, I object to this assertion: "He who today, as Lutheran or Reformed, actually desires to confess the confession of his church can no longer ignore the doctrinal decision of Barmen. When the Theological Declaration of Barmen is not recognized, the

---

[1] The original German, "Wider die Schwarmgeisterei," was published in *Lutherische Kirche* 18.15 (August 1, 1936): 237–40. MH

confessions of the Reformation are in truth surrendered." I declare, to the contrary: He who recognizes the Theological Declaration of Barmen as a *doctrinal* decision has thereby surrendered the Augsburg Confession and with it the confession of the orthodox Evangelical Church. What is pure and false doctrine, what is and is not to be preached in the Lutheran Church can only be decided by a synod which is united in the confession of Lutheran doctrine, and not an assembly at which Lutherans, Reformed, Consensus United, Pietists, and Liberals were all equal participants, as was the case in Barmen.

Among the participants of the Barmen Synod were many for whose strength of faith and earnest desire to serve the Lord of the church we all have respect. But many of these same participants are guilty of doctrinal errors—some quite serious—which our confessions reject. Our preparedness to fight shoulder to shoulder against common enemies can never lead to our allowing those with whom we have confessional disagreement to render doctrinal decisions which are binding on our church. The representatives of the Lutheran churches, against the warnings of the undersigned, finally found themselves prepared, in brotherly accommodation, to present a theological declaration in common with the adherents of another confession. But in so doing they have not established a new confession which should in any way take a position next to the confessions of the Reformation or be an authentic and binding explication of the same. That was expressly declared. How, for instance, could the delegates of the churches of Bavaria, Württemberg, and Hanover[2] have returned home with a new confession which should henceforth be binding for the pastors and congregations of their churches? By doing so they would have violated not only the constitution, but also the confession of their churches.

Only if the Barmen Declaration is expressly acknowledged by the authorized authority of a Lutheran Church as *confession* (with doctrinal decisions and the decree of confessions) would it win the character of a binding doctrinal decision. Then the question would arise whether such an equality didn't alter the character of the church in question. But so long as the Barmen Declaration was not solemnly received in this manner by the Lutheran churches of Germany, it has no higher authority than a document like the pronouncement [*Kundgebung*] of the *Kirchentag* ["Church Congress"] of 1930, directed to the church question, which was also a "theological" declaration. It was a denial of brotherly love and a breach of trust over against the Lutheran bishops when, soon after the Barmen Synod, Barth and Asmussen trumpeted this declaration as a new "confession"[3] and the basis of a new Union, though they know what Bonhoeffer[4] says today in plain language, namely, that with this view of the synod and its declaration "the Augustana

---

[2]   Three of the Lutheran *Landeskirche* ("territorial churches"). RF

[3]   See also "The Barmen Declaration—An Ecumenical Confession?" in this collection. RF

[4]   *Evangelische Theologie* (1938, no. 6), 227. HS

has already been decisively abandoned." Here Bonhoeffer was as imprudent as Asmussen. He, shall we say, let the cat out of the bag a little early. And he did this also by openly declaring that the Barmen Confession is God's Word: "If we take this message of the synod with absolute earnestness, we must then confess that God the Lord himself is responsible for this message."

Then he asks: "What has God said regarding his church and the direction it is to go if he has spoken through Barmen and Dahlem?" This is pure *Schwärmertum* ["fanaticism"], which ends in blasphemy. This is the result if the *Barmen Confession* is declared a binding doctrinal decision. We can only declare to the "Provisional Leadership" that what they understand by "Confessing Church," namely, a church comprising Lutheran, Reformed, and United [Christians], based upon the *Barmen Confession*, which appeared in Barmen as the result of a divine miracle, is a sect, and indeed, one of the worst we have experienced in Germany. We understand something different when we speak of the Confessing Church.

2. A word on the question of the Union. It is absolutely clear that the "Provisional Leadership" has accepted that the German Evangelical Church [DEK] is a "federation of confessionally distinct churches." But nevertheless, this they view according to Barth's conception of Union, namely, as an emerging church which today already has *a* confession (namely, the *Barmen Confession*). And it is governed by *an* ecclesiastical leadership. If they had taken seriously the concept of federation, then in the time since the Dahlem Synod they would have had time enough to structure all entities relative to church leadership according to confession (as decided at Dahlem). They did not do this, though it would have been possible. It would have been possible even in Prussia to so structure at least the pastoral leadership (ordination and visitation) so that Lutheran and Reformed would each be under leadership of their own confession.

What does it mean to appeal to the confession over against the world when this confession is not taken seriously in the church? The Old Prussian Church, as church, indeed knew of no other confessions than the Lutheran and the Reformed. Thus the authority of the "Confessing Church" in Prussia has been nullified by the great inner untruthfulness which has arisen. The *Bruderrat*[5] in Pomerania, for example, which assumed emergency ecclesiastical authority for church government over 550 Lutheran and three Reformed congregations was not established in order to "take up anew and advance the dialogue between Lutheran and Reformed [churches] which had not advanced since the days of the Reformation," but rather to govern a church, threatened by death, in accordance with the confession of the fathers. Now it has demonstrated that it cannot do this, and this *Bruderrat* is not the only one in this situation. So there is no need to wonder why the ecclesiastical right of necessity is proclaimed yet again.

---

5   The Brotherhood Councils of the Pastors' Emergency League were part of the Confessing Church organization which, in effect, formed an alternative church government. They in effect were a presbyterial form, replacing the superintendents or bishops of some territorial churches. RF

The hour of the Lutheran Church has come. May all those who still know what the confession of the Lutheran Reformation is hear the cry. Otherwise our ecclesiastical life will be drowned in pure *Schwarmgeisterei* ["fanaticism"].

1936

THE THEOLOGIAN
OF THE SECOND REICH

THOUGHTS ON THE BIOGRAPHY
OF ADOLF VON HARNACK[1]

Adolf von Harnack (1851–1930) was a towering figure in the academic world of Germany at the turn of the twentieth century. He "was prob[ably] the most outstanding patristic scholar of his generation."[2] But his critical attitude to traditional Christian dogma evoked strong opposition from conservative theologians. He was professor at Berlin (1888–1921) when Sasse was a student there (1913–1916): "My main teachers in Church history were Harnack and Holl."[3] He was the son of Theodosius Harnack (1817–1889), described here by Sasse as "a real theologian."

In this essay Sasse gives a critique of historicism and describes the relationship between history and dogma: "All history is based upon dogmatics."

Huss number 156
Hopf number 088

In his memorial lecture for Adolf von Harnack in the Prussian Academy of Science in the year 1931, Hans Lietzmann spoke of the famous lectures held a generation ago on *Das Wesen des Christentums (The Essence of Christendom)*.[4] He

---

[1] Most people are familiar with the phrase "the Third Reich [Empire, Kingdom]," describing Hitler's Nazi regime, which was to endure for a thousand years. The First Reich refers to the Holy Roman Empire (800–1806). The Second Reich was the German Empire (1871–1919), which had been united by Bismarck. This essay deals with Adolf von Harnack, whose worldview and theology were shaped by the idealism typical of the Second Reich. MH

This essay was first published as "Der Theologe des Zweiten Reiches: Gedanken über Lebensbeschreibung Adolf von Harnacks" in *Zeitwende* 12.12 (September 1936): 346–54. It was a review essay of Agnes von Zahn-Harnack's book, *Adolf von Harnack* (Berlin-Tempelhof: Hans-Bott, 1936). It was reprinted in *ISC*, 2:194–200. RF

[2] *ODCC*, 736. RF

[3] "Reminiscences of an Elderly Student," *Tangara* (Luther Seminary, Adelaide) 9 (1976): 4–5. RF

[4] This famous course of lectures by Adolf von Harnack stressed the moral side of Christianity to the exclusion of the doctrinal. The English translation is officially entitled *What Is Christianity?* (1901). RF

asserted how inadequate the view of the Christian faith developed therein appears to the present generation. And he added this remark: "But let he who is of this view willingly survey this image a while. The rays reflect the evening radiance of the beautiful sunny day which God in the nineteenth century allowed to ascend and descend over the German nation."

Not only is that book strikingly characterized with these words, but at the same time Harnack's entire life's work. When the famous theologian of the era of William [II] died on the tenth of June 1930, the last absolutely great proponent of the nineteenth century left us. The splendor which shone about his life and work was the splendor of the nineteenth century, the happiest era of German history. Born in the middle of the century, he was one of the heirs of the great intellectual world of German idealism from the first third of the century. He carried this heritage over into the time of German realism, which we might describe as the era of Bismarck and William II, so fortuitous in external matters, and so inwardly impoverished.

To understand Harnack one must view him against the backdrop of this heritage of idealism. In the universality of his scholarly interests and in the manner of his dealing with the world, but also in his impetus to translate knowledge to deed, he is the successor of Leibniz and Goethe. That he became a historian was a necessity. For only in the areas of historical scholarship was idealism still able to live on in the second half of the century. That he became a theologian was really a mistake, even if a productive one. For what theology is in its deepest essence, Harnack never understood, though he could have learned it from his father, Theodosius Harnack, who was a real theologian. The tragedy of his [Adolf Harnack's] life is in the fact that he who studied so many theologians of all eras, of whom he possessed an intimate and personal knowledge, never was able to grasp what makes a theologian a theologian and distinguishes him from a scholar of religion.

Perhaps one needs to have been his student and have experienced for years the charm of his personality, the brilliance of his thought, and his gift for teaching in order to understand the depth of this tragedy. Thus he will not live on as a theologian—what remains of his work are important historical discoveries, but all his theological ideas are today already antiquated.[5] He will live on much more so as his students guard his countenance in their memory. He will live on as the Goethian man—none of our contemporaries was as similar to Goethe as he—for whom the history of Christendom became the object of scholarly investigation, and thereby also the stuff for the construction of his intellectual world.

Thus the scholarly work of his life belongs not so much to the history of theology as to the chapter of the German intellectual history which bears the inscrip-

---

[5] In a letter to Tom Hardt (November 7, 1962) Sasse remarked: "In your studies on *Dogmengeschichte* ("history of dogma"), consult [Friedrich] Loofs, a very good textbook, though somewhat out of date like Harnack and Seeberg." RF

tion "the end of German idealism." Yes, one may say that Harnack's work played no small role in this. For the collapse of the great intellectual world of German idealism was completed in three stages. The first was the catastrophe of the collapse of German philosophy in the generation after the death of Hegel. At that time philosophy lost not only its position as the intellectual leader of culture [*Volk*], which it had enjoyed at the beginning of the century, but also the leading position in science. The second was the collapse of modern Protestant theology, which began in the years of the [First] World War. Idealism, which had long since been routed in all other areas of life, had in *modern theology* fled to the church. Here Lessing and Kant, Fichte and Schleiermacher, Goethe and Hegel were still taken seriously. They had taken their asylum in the halls of theology until, in the years after the World War, a new generation replaced them.

The third stage of that collapse is the dissolution of the German *university* of the nineteenth century. In it German idealism had once created its means for influencing a nation. There had been scholarly presuppositions upon which this great institution rested, such as the idea of presuppositionless scholarly investigation and the idea of the unity of all disciplines of scholarly study (the *universitas litterarum*). Since these ideas had already long since fallen into decline, the university itself began its irretrievable fall in the years after the World War. One must view the scholarly life's work of Adolf von Harnack in this connection in order to understand how "it reflects the evening radiance of the beautiful sunny day which God in the nineteenth century allowed to ascend and descend over the German nation."

Something of this "brilliance" shines about the biography of Adolf von Harnack, which we owe to the pen of his daughter, Agnes von Zahn-Harnack.[6] It is certainly a risky undertaking when a daughter attempts to present the life of her father, especially when, as is the case with Harnack, the father was such a publicly controversial personality with such a rich and altogether significant life. But the risk paid off. This biography of Harnack is not only a historical execution based upon careful use of all the available sources, it is—much like English biography—also a humanly significant and literary work of high standing, one of the most beautiful German biographies of recent times.

Memoirs, letters, and biographies have become very popular again in our time in Germany. Thus this book will also find many thankful readers, who trace the unspeakably full and happy life of Harnack, from his days as a child in Dorpat and Erlangen, to his years of study in Dorpat and Leipzig, until the great scholarly life's work in Giessen (since 1879), Marburg (1886), and Berlin (1888), and see him climb to the highest levels of life and scholarship. To be sure, one should not seek in this book anything other than a portrait of the *man* Harnack. The *theologian* Harnack can only be presented by a theologian, and this the author is not.

---

[6]   [The biography, *Adolf von Harnack*, was published by] Hans-Bott-Verlag, Berlin-Tempelhof, 1936, 579 pages. HS

For instance, the relationship to his student, friend, and later Berlin colleague Karl Holl, so rich and informative for [understanding] the theological position of Harnack, is keenly depicted in its human dimension. But the book does not deal with points where difference of character and worldview produced opposition [between the men]. As keenly as the atmosphere of Dorpat, Erlangen, and Leipzig is depicted over against Giessen, Marburg, and Berlin, the book has nothing to say regarding the ecclesial and theological views which finally separated these two worlds.[7]

It must be acknowledged that the author makes a serious attempt to avoid simply taking the view of the *Berlin Daily* and the *Christian World* in her presentation of the great church-political struggles in which Harnack was a central figure. These include the controversy regarding the Apostles' Creed of 1892 and others in which he took part, such as the case of Jatho and that of Traub.[8] Those papers portrayed these as cases where the evil orthodox were persecuting the pious liberals and wanting to burn them at the stake. But because there is finally no attempt to get at the basic motives of the opponents of Harnack, the ecclesial and intellectual reasons for these struggles remain hidden.

The incentive to clarify his motives could have been given by the generational problem, important for every attempt at biography. This problem became evident in the conflict with his father, the faithful guardian of the Lutheran tradition at Erlangen and Dorpat, and with his student Karl Barth. Notably, in the book the father is the only "orthodox" individual who, in his opposition to Harnack's theology, is credited with pure motives: "Theodosius Harnack always struggled with his son against subjectivism and for the church, which he himself had served his whole life, with all his might."

After the appearance of the first volume of *The History of Dogma*, the elder Harnack wrote to his son in Marburg: "Our difference is not theological, but rather one which is profoundly and directly Christian. Thus if I would ignore it, I would deny Christ . . . since he who . . . views the resurrection as you do . . . is in my view *no longer a Christian theologian.*" This too was the view of the Evangelical High Consistory, when, in accordance with its duty, it protested against Harnack's call to Berlin. At best this attempt at church governance by the highest church authorities of Old Prussia, undertaken with insufficient means, can be described with the words which King Ludwig II applied to his Munich archbishop: "The flesh was willing, but the spirit was weak."

But finally the High Consistory was right. And he who is willing to grant only a qualified correctness to the judgment of Theodosius Harnack regarding the the-

---

7   Sasse here draws the contrast between the father, Theodosius, and his son. RF

8   Carl Jatho (1851–1913), a pastor in Bucharest, Boppard, and Cologne, was defrocked in 1911 for pantheistic preaching. Gottfried Traub (1869–1956) was dismissed from the ministry in the Westphalian Church for defending Jatho. Jatho and Traub all took part in the *Apostolicum* Controversy, which sought to abolish the obligatory status of the Apostles' Creed. Adolf Harnack was also involved in these attacks on the Creed. RF

ology of his son cannot hold that the protest of the Old Prussian Church leadership was unjustified. The biography, which is here before us, does not give nor can give answers to any of the questions here raised. Here it needs supplementation. But since a presentation of the theology of Harnack will presumably never be written, simply because he was never a real theologian in the strict sense, it will be the task of a history of the nineteenth century to produce this supplementation. It will have to give the great ecclesial, intellectual, and historical background to the human portrait which Agnes von Zahn-Harnack's book paints.

No German theologian since Schleiermacher has had such a profound impression upon intellectuals as has Adolf von Harnack. When one recalls how deep the cleft between *church* and *education* was in the years between 1870 and 1900—never has Germany had such an unintellectual pastorate and never such an unchurchly intelligentsia as then—then one can grasp the affect which resulted from Harnack. "A man such as *Mommsen*,"[9] recounts Agnes von Zahn-Harnack, "experienced in Harnack theology as science—a connection which he had never encountered in such a radical way. He experienced in him religious character, and through it was profoundly influenced in his view of Christendom as a historical phenomenon."

Gustav *Schmoller*,[10] the national economist, confessed of himself that he was swept up in the intellectual breeze of David Friedrich Strauss[11] and that he ever recoiled at "what the common pastors presented." He wrote to Harnack regarding *The Essence of Christendom*. The lectures in this book meant for him "an edification, a confirmation of things hoped and inklings had, a dispelling of doubt— indeed, I might say, a revelation—the revelation of the historical Christ, in the only way in which he is a possibility today for the intellectual and scholar."

There are men yet living among us who after the turn of the century were torn away from the superficial materialism of that day by Harnack's famous lectures and led again to a higher view of the world. For the first time they encountered again Jesus Christ, to be sure, a Jesus "only . . . possible today for the intellectual and scholar," that is, as he was comprehensible at that time to the cultured citizen. The discovery of a Jesus freed from the veil of dogmatic conceptions and from all the superhuman and miraculous elements was perceived as a new reformation.

Otto Harnack, the literary historian, during the controversy over the Apostles' Creed, called his brother to the reformatory act, to the full renunciation of the Creed. Harnack, however, felt himself neither then nor later called to be a

---

[9]   Theodor Mommsen (1817–1903) was one of the most influential German historians of the nineteenth century; he was a specialist in Roman history. From 1858 he was professor of ancient history at the University of Berlin. RF

[10]   Gustav von Schmoller was the leader of the Historical School of Economics. Schmoller wished to free German economics from the doctrines of the classical school. The Historical School of Economics opposed the idea that unchanging natural laws ruled economic life. RF

[11]   David Friedrich Strauss (1808–1874) taught a mythical theory of the Gospels, especially in his very controversial book *The Life of Jesus* (1835). RF

reformer, and in many questions he took a mediating position, which to radical Liberalism always appeared as a denial of the acknowledged truth. Finally, it was indeed his Erasmus[-like] nature which shunned tumult, which only hoped for a gradual cure, brought about by wise pedagogical methods, which kept him from drawing the consequences from his views.

For these views, if they are really thought through to the end, necessarily lead to the destruction of *dogma* and the destruction of the *church*. That was the flip side of his missiological effectiveness among the intellectuals. The fate of so many apologists was repeated in him: He won men, but he gave up that for which he desired to win them. He won the intellectuals at the cost of dogma and the church. And this price was too high.

Therein is also the profound *tragedy* of his life. The famous scholar of the history of dogma came to the conclusion that dogma does not belong to the essence of Christendom—in the early church there was as yet no dogma, and since the Reformation it really no longer exists—rather that it was a sort of transitory, necessary evil. The famous church historian ended with the conviction that there is no "church," rather only "churches," which are not comparable to each other, and that the "misleading colloquial use of the term 'church' " should really be done away with. The author of *The Essence of Christendom* would, through a return to original Christendom, establish what the Christian religion properly is. In so doing, he sought the historical Jesus and his Gospel. But he found a Jesus who is no longer the coming Messiah and a Gospel which in its primary form should no longer contain the message regarding the Son of God—a view which today no serious historian would any longer dare to advocate.

Everything which falls in the sphere of Harnack's thought, be it the greatest reality, was changed into a mere concept and dispelled like a puff of smoke. That is a sure sign that his thought is an ill, a false thought. This became particularly clear as soon as it dealt with practical questions. On July 1, 1911, Harnack wrote to Gustav Krueger in a discussion of the *Spruchkollegium* among other things: "The time will certainly finally come when also the positive [conservative Christians], such as in Switzerland, will come to see that they do not betray the most holy cause if they remain in an external church fellowship which desires to embrace everything which is religion among us, so far as it is not Catholic or Jewish. But at the present time we are not so far advanced." One can only read such a sentence with profound alarm. The sergeant major of our company[12] had this view of the Evangelical Church when he had the Catholics step out to the right, and the Jews to the left, and let all who remained, including the Baptists and dissidents, march off to the Evangelical Divine Service. One does not need to have studied theology for forty years or to have written the most famous history of dogma in four editions in order to have this view of the church!

---

[12]   This is a reference to Sasse's experience in the army during the First World War. RF

And is then such a church really such a high ideal so worthy of effort that one must regrettably maintain that the state of affairs is not yet achieved "that the territorial church is no longer a confessional church"? For Harnack it was self-evident that this state of affairs would finally come about: "The Prussian Territorial Church stood with Hengstenberg[13] in 1866, with Kögel[14] in 1890, and with Goltz in 1900, and now it stands with Dryander, Kahl, and Kaftan.[15] That is a powerful advance, and the wheels of history cannot be driven faster." No, it really does not move so quickly. For "God's millstones grind slowly, but exceedingly fine; what in patience he leaves, he mills again through harshness." In 1930 the Prussian Church stood with the students of Adolf von Harnack. In 1933 it stood with Ludwig Müller[16] and Joachim Hossenfelder.[17] It is scarcely conceivable that the "powerful advance" will proceed much farther in this direction.

Two generations ago Friedrich Nietzsche wrote his untimely treatment *Of the Advantage and Disadvantage of History for Life*, in which he perceptively depicted the dangers of "historical sickness." Is any one really surprised that the disciples of a theology can learn to believe nothing more from the history of the church when their master has learned so little from it? What sort of illness has become evident in this failure of historical theology at the end of the nineteenth and beginning of the twentieth centuries? It has to do not only with the theology of Harnack, but also with the entirety of that theology whose greatest advocate he was, next to Ernst *Troeltsch*.[18] After Troeltsch's death, the historian Friedrich Meinecke wrote the words which apply to all the great historians of the last generation, including Harnack. They are perhaps the best description of the illness of "historicism":

> His friends, who . . . in him have lost one of the strongest sources of light of their life, must often admit when sharing impressions about him amongst themselves that his positive and furtive thoughts and goals stood in a certain disjointed relationship to the phenomenal richness of his sublime historical views. His great ability to express matters verbally, strangely enough, often failed when it was needed finally to develop his own will and thoughts without doubt.[19]

---

[13] Ernst Hengstenberg (1802–69), a Lutheran professor at Berlin, opposed rationalism and unionism. RF

[14] Theodor Kögel (1829–1896) was court preacher in Berlin. He championed Prussian Union and orthodoxy in opposition to liberalism. RF

[15] Julius Wilhelm Martin Kaftan (1848–1926) was a professor at Berlin. RF

[16] Ludwig Müller (1883–1945), leader of the *Deutsche Christen* ("German Christians"), was elected bishop of the Reich in September 1933. He attempted to unite the German Protestant churches in harmony with Nazi party principles. RF

[17] Joachim Hossenfelder (1899–?) was a pastor who joined the Nazi party in 1929. RF

[18] Ernst Troeltsch (1865–1923) was professor of the history of philosophy and civilization at Berlin from 1915. He was a leader of the History of Religions School, seeking truth in the comparative study of all religions. Both Harnack and Troeltsch were students of Albrecht Ritschl and gave emphasis to the history of Christian thought. "His originality as a theologian lay in his application of sociological theory to theology," notably in *The Social Teaching of the Christian Churches* (1912; ET 1931) (*ODCC*, 1643). RF

[19] Cited in *Deutsche Nation* (March 1923), by Friedrich von Huegel, in the introduction to *Ernst Troeltsch, Historicism and Its Demise* (1924). HS

But how is this failure, this illness, to be explained? It cannot be explained on the basis of the mistakes and weaknesses of one particular man; it must rather be rooted deep in the essence of modern history, and along with it, in modern historical theology. That became completely clear in the entirety of Harnack's work. *For him history is what dogmatics was for theologians of previous generations.* Harnack demanded from theologians above all knowledge of ancient church history, "otherwise the theologian gets lost in his evaluation of later history, as soon as he must explain it theologically, that is, from a position of original Christendom." Theological judgments are for him—in the same way they once were for Erasmus—thus historical judgments, because that is theologically correct which is consistent with original Christianity. The impossible undertaking to set forth *The Essence of Christendom* by means of historical treatment is understood on this basis.

This valuing or overvaluing of history corresponds to the despising of metaphysics which Harnack shared with his teacher of dogmatics, Albert Ritschl.[20] But it also corresponds with the devaluation of all genuine dogmatics. "We relegate the dogmaticians to the sphere of beautiful literature," he [Harnack] said to the students who helped him unpack his library in Giessen. Today the dogmaticians exact their revenge from him when they relegate *The Essence of Christendom* to the realm of the devotional literature of Liberalism. Yes, one might often think that Harnack deliberately intended precisely to reverse that (for him unbearable) claim of Cardinal Manning[21] that one must overcome history through dogma.

Here now the most profound reason for the mistakes of the theology of Harnack becomes clear. All history is based upon dogmatics. For all historical perceptions and judgments presuppose norms which determine the selection and point the way for the investigation. Otherwise the vastness of historical investigation is simply beyond our grasp. The historian is like a seafarer who travels across a seemingly endless and trackless sea. All about him it is night. For history is, in and of itself, dark. Therefore he needs the stars which shine above the surging sea, unmoved by the storms of this world. The historian who forsakes dogmatic norms and, in the place of these, establishes his own norms by which he will direct himself, drawing only from history itself, is like the seafarer who fastens a lantern on the bow of his ship and now navigates by it. He does not know where he will end up. He does not know whether or not he travels in a circle. He never reaches his destination. Here lies the most profound reason for the mistake of Harnack's the-

---

[20] Albrecht Ritschl (1822–1889) was a German Protestant theologian who had an immense influence through the turn of the twentieth century. He was the founder of the so-called "Ritschlian School." His system, with its emphasis on ethics, has been called the "Theology of Moral Value." It had two foci, reconciliation and especially the kingdom of God, neither of which resembled the confessional statements of Lutheranism. Harnack's father, Theodosius, was one of Ritschl's most noted critics. RF

[21] Henry Manning (1808–1892) was ordained in the Church of England and a member of the Oxford Movement. He left the Church of England for Rome in 1851 and became cardinal archbishop of Westminster in 1865. RF

ology and that of those of like mind. We have something to learn from their fate. But it would not suffice for us to think that the historian or church historian must have *a* dogmatics. He must have the *correct* dogmatics. It would not suffice to fix one's gaze at a favorite star. For even the stars travel their course, move, and disappear over the horizon. We need him who in the Holy Scriptures is called "the Bright Morning Star" [Rev 22:16].

Friedrich von Huegel, the Catholic philosopher of religion in England, recounted how his friend Ernst Troeltsch in 1901 informed him that in his life and thought as a German philosopher of religion there was a *salto mortale* ["leap of death"]. That is, based upon the presuppositions of his thought, he was not able to come to certain conclusions in a normal and logical manner. But certain truths of the faith were so evident that he dared make the leap, which could be so deadly for a philosopher.

The great and venerable thinker here points to a uniqueness of all genuine theological thought. The most basic theological knowledge is not gained on the paths of normal scholarship, neither that of history, nor philosophy or philosophical dogmatics. To understand a theologian means that one must understand his "leap of death" [*salto mortale*]. It means to grasp where and why he, contrary to all demands of reason and all philosophical presuppositions, dares to make the leap into the bottomless, indeed, to fall into the arms of God. Where is this point with Adolf von Harnack? It is there where he, to the greatest vexation of his theological friends, and against his own theoretical convictions, during a sermon [which he preached],[22] cited the following verse:

> The ground on which I'm grounded
> Is Christ and his blood.
> This makes it that I find
> The true, eternal Good.
> For my life and me, there is nothing on this earth.
> What Christ to me has given,
> That is love's worth.[23]

It is a verse from his favorite hymn, as he then finally lived from the hymns of Paul Gerhardt. He had lost the confession—so far as it was deposited in the symbolical books—of the church in which he was baptized, the church in which he was confirmed, the Evangelical Lutheran Church of his fathers and his own father above all, who is one of the great, unforgettable theologians of Lutheranism (his great works on the doctrine of Luther and his writing on church governance have been republished in our times). But the confession of this church

---

22 Sasse once remarked: "Just as with Harnack, sometimes suddenly the Lutheran heritage could come out when he stood in the pulpit" (letter to Tom Hardt, August 29, 1959). RF

23 From "If God Himself Be for Me" by Paul Gerhardt (cf. *Lutheran Worship* 407, stanza 2; *The Lutheran Hymnal* 528, stanza 3). RF

as it lives in the hymns of the confessor Paul Gerhardt had not died in him. He lived from this.

And yet something else was there. In his *Marcion* (1921) he put forth this untenable thesis: "The rejection of the OT in the second century was a mistake. . . . Its maintenance in the sixteenth century was a fate. . . . But to continue to preserve it in the nineteenth century as a canonic document in Protestantism is the result of a religious and ecclesiastical paralysis." But in stating this he did not at all draw the consequences of this thesis for himself. On his last birthday [celebration], May 7, 1930, as the countenance of death was about him, as the heaviest struggles over his last great achievements were occurring regarding the Kaiser Wilhelm Society for the Promotion of Sciences, he conducted the evening devotion in his home on the great text from Is 40:27–29. This text speaks of the Creator and Lord of the world, who gives strength to the weary and power to those grown faint. "But how deeply his soul was stirred," recounts his daughter of this final, struggle-filled birthday, "we came to know only after his death. For in the Bible, which he used for this devotion, he had written at this passage: 'I know not, for great sorrow, where to turn.' "

God is greater than our heart! And the Word of our God remains forever (Is 40:8)! All theology ends with this realization.

1937

Luther and the Teaching of the Reformation[1]

In a letter to Theodore Tappert in May 1938, Sasse offered the following brief description of this essay: "It does not contain anything new, yet is a sign of interest in Luther among modern Anglicans."

Among those modern Anglicans was Edward Gordon Selwyn, dean of Winchester Cathedral, the editor of the collection of essays in which the English version of this essay first appeared. He and Sasse had probably met for the first time at the second British-German theological conference in Eisenach in August 1928 (see *"Kyrios"* in this collection) and then again at the third conference in Chichester in March 1931 (see "The Church as *Corpus Christi*" in this collection).

Huss number 163
Hopf number 096

———◈◈◈———

PART 1

The Reformer came not from the ranks of noble, scholarly, and devout bishops who, like Nicholas of Cusa, strove for a thorough revival of the decayed church. Nor did he come from the circle of learned humanists, who, like Erasmus, sought to revive the church by a return to the pure original sources of Christianity. Still less did he come from the extreme critics of the church, the heretics and the revolutionary enthusiasts. Like the great reformers of the church in the centuries of the Middle Ages, he came from a monastery. He was a Catholic monk whose views on the church were impeccably orthodox. In 1505, in accordance with a

---

[1] While the text of this essay was originally in German, the German text was not published until 1950: "Luther und die Lehre der Reformation," *Lutherische Blätter* 2.13 (special supplement; Festival of the Reformation, October 31, 1950): 1–11; it was reprinted in *ISC*, 1:38–49. The English edition was first published in *History of Christian Thought* (ed. Edward Gordon Selwyn; London: originally John Heritage, the Unicorn Press; later the Centenary Press, 1937), 106–24. The translator was C. H. Jeffery. There was a second English edition of the volume, with different pagination (and the word "short" in the title as had originally been intended by Selwyn): *A Short History of Christian Thought* (London: Geoffrey Bles, 1949), 80–92. The translation given here is a slightly revised version of that translation. RF

vow taken under duress from the fear of death, the twenty-two year old Master of Arts, after just beginning his legal studies at Erfurt, entered the Augustinian monastery there. His father, who, working as a miner, had risen from humble peasant origin to an assured middle-class existence, was very angry at this frustration of all the material ambitions he had cherished for his highly gifted elder son. His friends explained that a vow made in such extenuating circumstances was invalid. But Martin Luther remained faithful to his decision. At the command of his superiors, he began his study of theology immediately. He was ordained priest in 1507, and in 1508 began his career as a lecturer, first in the faculty of arts in the newly founded university at Wittenberg, then for a while at Erfurt, and later at Wittenberg again as lecturer on the *Sentences* of Peter Lombard. Against his own will, he was obliged, by the orders of his superiors, to take his degree of Doctor of Divinity in 1512 and to undertake the professorship of biblical studies. It was during the next few years, between 1513 and 1518, that he gave his lectures on the Psalms and the Epistles to the Romans, Galatians, and Hebrews, which are so important for the beginnings of the Reformation. This professorship was the public position which Luther retained until his death in 1546. His lectures consisted of an exegesis of the books of the Bible, until at last, from 1535–1545, he gave his exposition of Genesis. During his years as a monk he also filled various offices in his order. As one of the disciplinarians known as the Observants, he was in Rome during the years 1510–1511. Occasionally, too, he helped in the ministerial office. It was while acting for the pastor of the town church of Wittenberg that he had his experiences in the confessional box. This led him to draw up his theses on indulgences. This church was also the scene of his great sermons during his professorship. But these offices are much more than the mere outward circumstances which form a background to Luther's life and work. It is only through them that Luther can be understood as a Reformer. There is no worse misunderstanding of Luther than to see in him, as the ages of Enlightenment and Liberalism did, the originator of modern culture who freed the individual from the fetters of the church and of medieval society and exalted reason to the position of arbiter over the doctrine of the church. Luther was never a modern in this sense of the word. In many respects, indeed, he strikes us as anything but modern in comparison not only with Erasmus but also with the great minds of medieval Catholicism. When we remember Luther's appeal to the Word of Holy Writ against the doubts raised by reason and his insistence on the fact that at the Last Supper Jesus had given his body and blood to the disciples to eat and to drink, it is impossible to describe him as the founder and forerunner of the age of Enlightenment.

This might perhaps be said of Zwingli. But did not Luther oppose all the authorities of the world at Worms with his brave words "Here I take my stand; I cannot do otherwise"? And was he not thus the forerunner of "private judgment"? Certainly, at that time, Luther stood alone—incidentally, these words are legendary—and he could truly say, as he looked back later on this hour of his life:

Tunc eram ecclesia ["At that time I was the church"]. But these very words show how he himself understood his aloneness. He did not oppose society as an individual, or the corporate body of the church as a singly isolated Christian. He was conscious of his duty as defender of the true teaching of the real catholic church of all ages against those errors, which, despite their widespread nature, are none the less untrue. For Catholicism in the sense of universality is no criterion of truth. Nothing in the world achieves such quick and complete universality as the great errors of humanity. In this connection Luther himself was often troubled throughout his life by the thought that the error might lie on his side. "Can I believe that all previous teachers were ignorant? Must all our fathers have been fools? Can I, then, have remained the nest egg of the Holy Ghost until this generation? Would God have allowed his people to remain in error for so many years?"

These doubts show us that it is impossible to see in Luther the modern individualist who heedlessly opposes his own personality to the needs of the community and proclaims the right of personal conviction. Still less can he be regarded as the great revolutionary, the destroyer of the established authorities. This is proved by the conclusion of his famous speech at Worms:

> Let me, then, be refuted and convinced by the testimony of the Scriptures or by clear arguments, for I put no trust in the mere authority of the pope or the councils, since it is obvious that they have often been mistaken and have contradicted each other. Otherwise I am forced by the words of Holy Scripture, which I have quoted, and I am a captive in my conscience to the Word of God. Therefore I cannot and will not recant anything, for it is neither safe nor expedient to act against conscience. So help me God. Amen.

It is just as wrong to see in Luther the great enemy of the Catholic Church and to try to understand the Reformation on the grounds of this hostility. The young Luther was a most faithful son of the Roman Church. Even later, when he was involved in his fierce struggle with the papacy and regarded the pope as antichrist, he drew a sharp distinction between the Catholic Church itself and the alien elements which had crept into it. In the papacy itself, as it had developed in the last few centuries, he could see only the "abomination of desolation" [cf. Dan 9:27; 11:31; 12:11; Matt 24:15], but he know that this "abomination" had grown up in the very Holy of Holies of the true church of Christ.

This point indicates a characteristic difference between Luther and Calvin. Calvin considered those churches under the papal obedience to be "more synagogues of the devil than Christian churches," and could find in the Catholic Church of the Middle Ages only a slight resemblance to the true church, for example, in its Baptism. Luther combined with his severe criticism of the papacy surprisingly conservative views of the Catholic Church. He burned collections of papal canon law with the bull of excommunication. It was a protest against the misuse of the law in the name of God, and against a law which owed its origin to a forgery. Even so, he was always ready to acknowledge the *Ius antiquum* ["rule of old"], for example, in connection with the episcopal office, as a godly piece of church discipline. Although in his book on the Babylonian captivity of the church and in the Smalcald Articles, he unmasked and condemned the idolatry which had crept into the Mass, he admitted that the Roman Mass was still a valid Eucharist. And so he did not, like Zwingli and Calvin, introduce a new liturgy. The Lutheran liturgy was merely a Mass without the invocation of the saints and [without] the Roman conception of sacrifice. To Luther it was unthinkable that the unity of the Western church might be forever destroyed. He wanted to recall this church to what he was convinced was the pure teaching of the Gospel and, at the same time, the ancient teaching of the church.

Only from this point of view can Luther's actions be understood. He wanted neither to split the church nor to found a new church. Nor was it his ambition to become the reviver, the Reformer of the church. His conscience told him that he was merely carrying out the duties of his office in the church: the pure teaching of the Gospel. According to his own conception, his work consisted only in this: "to have reintroduced the Holy Gospel into the world."

PART 2

But what did Luther understand by "Gospel," and what distinguished his interpretation of the Gospel from that of the church of his day? We shall best answer these questions by showing how Luther arrived at his conclusions. Luther belongs to those men of genius whose greatness consists in their ability to wrestle strenuously with a problem to the bitter end, and not to rest until they have found a real solution. The problem which concerned Luther was the old problem of Western theology: the redemption of humanity. In the monastery Luther asked himself in desperation, "When shall I find a God of mercy?" Here he was only expressing once more the great question of Western civilization. It had been the dominating problem from the time of the Shepherd of Hermas, concerning the discipline of penance, up to the quarrel over indulgences in 1517. [This is the question:] *Quid sum miser tunc dicturus, quem patronum rogaturus?* ["(As a) wretched person, what can I then (on judgment day) plead? Whom can I ask to intercede (for me)?"] What shall I say, and who will be my advocate in that great day of which it is said, *Dies irae, dies illa solvet saeclum in favilla* ["Day of wrath, day when the world is reduced to ashes"]?[2] What distinguished Luther from others was his refusal to be satisfied with the answer given by the church of his day. The most faithful fulfillment of all his monastic duties, the mortification and the rigorous asceticism, his participation in the liturgical life of the monastery, the frequent confession and Communion—all these could give him no assurance that he was justified and that God's wrath had turned away from him. This experience of terror and temptation finds expression even in his later hymns:

---

[2]   These Latin phrases are from a Roman Catholic Mass for the dead. RF

Die Angst mich zu verzweifeln trieb,
da nichts denn Sterben bei mir blieb,
   zur Hölle musst' ich senken.

[My fears increased till sheer despair
Left only death to be my share;
   The pangs of hell I suffered.][3]

We come now to the secret of his personality, to what is known in secular language, not in that of theology, as religious genius. For the church knows that the measure of faith given to a man is not derived from any natural endowment. Luther had the gift of a particularly tender conscience, and connected with it, an unusually vivid consciousness of the reality of God. "Our God is a consuming fire" [Heb 12:29]. That was the preaching of the church of the apostles. People are inclined to rob this consuming fire of its terrors. This is only too often the effect of those systems of theology in which, by fine distinctions and great learning, the terrifying reality of God is changed into a harmless consciousness of God's existence. The medieval conception of God, based on Neoplatonism and Aristotelianism, had become but a faint reflection of the "consuming fire" of the NT. The conception of God in modern Protestantism since the age of the Enlightenment has completely lost every trace of terror. The God of Kant,[4] Schleiermacher,[5] and Ritschl[6] is no longer a consuming fire. If the modern man believes in God at all, he believes in him as the guarantor of his happiness. And so the thought of the existence of God has become, since the eighteenth century, a comforting thought. For Luther it was a most disturbing one. In bitter moments of grave temptation he often wished that God did not exist. For if God exists, and if he really is God, then man is lost. Created to do God's will, and incapable of its fulfillment, he is guilty of the judgment [of God]. And how can man hope to stand before the God of heaven and his unerring judgment?

At this point one side of Luther's teaching becomes quite clear. The Reformer himself and the Lutheran Church which followed him represent a teaching on the nature of man, which humanly speaking, seems to be the extreme of pessimism in its judgment of humanity. That man is a sinner, that he is fallen from God's grace, and that he is therefore in need of salvation—on this all Christians agree. But the extent of the change man has suffered by this fall and what capabilities of good

---

3   From stanza 3 of "Dear Christians, One and All, Rejoice." The English translation is from *Lutheran Worship* 353; cf. *The Lutheran Hymnal* 387. RF

4   Immanuel Kant (1724–1804) denied the metaphysical and considered morality to be the chief content of Christianity. RF

5   Friedrich Daniel Ernst Schleiermacher (1768–1834) is widely regarded as the founder of modern theology. He is also considered the "theologian" of the Prussian Union. RF

6   Albrecht Ritschl (1822–1889) was a German Protestant theologian who had an immense influence through the turn of the twentieth century. He was the founder of the so-called "Ritschlian School." His system, with its emphasis on ethics, has been called the "Theology of Moral Value." It had two foci, reconciliation and especially the kingdom of God, neither of which resembled the confessional statements of Lutheranism. RF

and thus of cooperation in his salvation he has retained are problems upon which
the various confessions disagree [with Luther]. The Lutheran Church agrees with
Luther in the answer it gives in the Formula of Concord of 1577:

> [We believe, teach, and confess] that original sin is not a slight, but so deep
> a corruption of human nature that nothing healthy or incorrupt in man's
> body or soul, in his inner or outward powers, remains, but as the church
> sings: "Through Adam's fall is corrupted all nature and human essence. This
> unspeakable injury cannot be discerned by the reason, but only from God's
> Word." [FC Ep I 8][7]

Even after the fall, man still remains man, a being of reason and will. He is
still a creature of God, and sin has not, as Manichaeism maintains, become his
very substance and nature. But God's image in man is lost. He can no longer fear
and love God. It is impossible for him to cooperate in his salvation. Sin has not
merely weakened his communion with God but quite destroyed it. So far developed is the corruption of his being that human reason is not longer able to realize the truth about humanity. God himself must reveal this truth to us, and this
he does in his Word. But when it is thus revealed, our reason revolts against it.
Human reason can never consider the teaching of Adam's fall as anything more
than a myth. It cannot regard the view that our sin is connected with the sin of
Adam as anything but an incomprehensible assertion which it is impossible to
prove. Finally, in the assertion that inherited sin is guilt and that a newborn child
is from its very birth condemned to eternal damnation, it can see only an offense
against God. That is the tragic situation of man since the fall. Man must deceive
himself about his own nature, and all the systems of anthropological philosophy
are, in the last resort, merely attempts of the human mind to deceive itself about
its relations to God and its wretchedness.

It is from this aspect that Luther's passionate protest against the heathen philosophy of Aristotle must be understood. To admit that one had much to learn
from the great philosophers of the ancient world in spheres of knowledge comprehensible to human reason was quite natural for Luther. He had been brought
up in the school of Occam; in 1531 he referred to Occam as his dear master, and
he definitely acknowledged the importance of Scholasticism in certain branches
of learning. But that one should adopt and introduce into theological systems the
doctrines of heathen thinkers about man and even about God seemed to Luther
an utter falsification of Christian teaching.

Thus the young Luther's conception of God represents the reversion from
the medieval theology based on a synthesis of biblical and philosophical thought
to the living God of the Bible. This thesis remains correct even when we remember that Scholasticism is not a unity and that Luther was not familiar with the
whole of medieval theology. Even if he had been better acquainted with Aquinas'

---

[7]   The hymn cited is "All Mankind Fell in Adam's Fall" (cf. *Lutheran Worship* 363; *The Lutheran Hymnal*
369). RF

teaching, in which greater value is attached to reason but all human accomplishments are traced back to the grace of God, his judgment of Scholasticism would not have been essentially different. In the Scriptures Luther found the living God, the God of jealousy and wrath, who imposes upon man tasks which he cannot fulfill and condemns him to judgment and death if he does not fulfill them. In the Scriptures the nature of man was revealed. "The essence of this epistle," begins Luther's lecture on Romans (1515–1516), "is the complete destruction and eradication of all wisdom and righteousness of the flesh, however great these may seem in the eyes of man and to ourselves, and however sincere and upright they may be, and the planting and firm establishment of sin whatever the degree of its absence or apparent absence." The Word discloses man as a sinner. It tears every mask from his face, even the mask of piety. It shows us that in our religion, in our moral striving, we seek not God but ourselves. It shows us that there is no righteousness which can be attained by man's own efforts: "There is none righteous, no, not one" (Rom 3:10 KJV). But moreover, Luther found in the Scriptures what he henceforth understood as the real meaning of the Gospel.

The decisive turning point in Luther's development, the experience of which he speaks in his great confession of 1545, in the preface to the collected edition of his Latin works [LW 34:323–38], was not a mystical experience like that of Jacob Boehme,[8] nor a conversion to obedience as in Calvin nor an emotional conversion to the certainty of redemption as in Wesley, but, as it were, a discovery in the sphere of exegesis. It was the new understanding of the righteousness of God which came to him in 1513, during his exposition of the Thirty-First Psalm, from Rom 1:16 ff. He realized that the righteousness of God revealed in the Gospel cannot be an exacting and punitive righteousness. For in that case, the Gospel would not be "the power of God unto *salvation* to every one that believeth" [Rom 1:16 KJV; emphasis added]. It can only mean the righteousness which God gives us and by which he makes us sinners righteous. This, of course, is a righteousness which must be revealed to us, for it contradicts our own moral criteria. According to our standards, it should not be the publican but the Pharisee who is meant in these words of the parable: "He went down to his house justified" (Luke 18:14). With God the judgment is reversed. We men declare him righteous who is righteous. God calls the sinner righteous, and only the sinner. That the prodigal son in the parable is nearer his father than the elder brother, that there is more joy in heaven over one sinner who repents than over ninety-nine just people, that the laborers in the vineyard who have wrought but one hour receive full pay, that the thief on the cross is saved, that the first are last and the last first, that Jesus calls sinners and eats with sinners—this miracle of divine mercy, so offensive to our rational system of morality, is revealed in the Gospel, and only there. Only the Gospel proclaims the fact so incomprehensible to our logic that the same man

---

8   Jacob Boehme (1575–1624) claimed that he was the recipient of mystical experiences and that he wrote only what he had learned personally from divine illumination (*ODCC*, 218). RF

who is a sinner and remains a sinner to his death can in God's judgment be a saint because Christ's righteousness has become his righteousness.[9] It is only from the testimony of the Scriptures, the promise of a Messiah in the OT and Christ's incarnation, crucifixion, and resurrection in the NT, that we men know of the divine mercy, to which we all must turn, St. Francis not less than the thief on the cross. But for Christ, God would remain the God of judgment and wrath who judges and condemns us all. In Christ alone, the Savior of sinners, who has borne the sins of the world, does God open his heart to us. "Dost thou ask his name? He is Jesus Christ, the Lord of Sabaoth, and there is no other God."[10]

That, then, was the Gospel for Luther: the Good News that God will give forgiveness of sins to all who have learnt to despair of themselves and to hope in Christ, and will for Christ's sake consider them righteous. Moreover, Luther did not understand this message of the justification of the sinner *sola gratia, sola fide* ["by grace alone, by faith alone"] as a theological theory. The Gospel was for him not a doctrine about the possibilities of the forgiveness of sins but the message of God to the sinner to desire forgiveness of his sins, and the promise of this forgiveness. When Luther and the Lutheran Church repeatedly speak of "the pure teaching of the Gospel" as the mark of the true church [e.g., AC VII], they do not mean a correct theory of doctrine, but the true proclamation of this message to sinners. For in this lies the real office of the church. Certainly the church should also proclaim the Law of God—how could it otherwise preach the Gospel? But the Law of God is taught in the synagogue too. That we should love God and our neighbor is to be found even in the OT, and the Golden Rule of the Sermon on the Mount [Matt 7:12] is known to the heathen too. The idea of man facing a last judgment was familiar to Zarathustra and Muhammad. Asceticism and monasticism exist in the religions of Asia, sanctification of life and hope of immortality in the mystery religions. But forgiveness of sins is found only in Jesus Christ. Just as it is his proper office to be the Savior of the world, so it is the true and most special duty of the church to call man to faith in him, and thus to forgiveness of sins. Neither can it be said that this is not enough, because forgiveness of sins is something negative, and that we men needed not merely the partial grace of forgiveness but the full grace of salvation from our sins. Whoever speaks thus has failed to realize the profound miracle of justification which Luther expressed in these words: "Where there is forgiveness of sins, there are also life and happiness" [SC VI 6]. There is not justification without sanctification, no forgiveness without renewal of life, no real faith from which the fruits of new obedience do not grow.

---

[9]   It has been correctly pointed out that this teaching of justification, which is performed by the act of God on the transcendental ego, which is not an object of our consciousness, brings to a conclusion medieval anthropology and prepares the way for later critical philosophy. In the same way, Luther's thesis from his teaching on the Eucharist, *Dextera Dei ubique est* ["the right hand of God is everywhere"], marks the end of the medieval conception of heaven. HS

[10] From stanza 2 of "A Mighty Fortress Is Our God" (cf. *Lutheran Worship* 297/298; *The Lutheran Hymnal* 262). RF

The Christian lives only from the daily forgiveness of sins for Christ's sake, but it is a real life which he thus enjoys, *peccator simul et iustus*, sinner and justified at once. That is the answer of the Lutheran Reformation to the thousand-year-old question in Western Christianity of the justification of the sinner.

PART 3

When in 1537 the long-awaited council[11] seemed about to meet, Luther was asked by his elector to name those articles of faith which he would not only defend as irrefragable before a council but which he would also be prepared to uphold in the last moment of his life before the judgment seat of Almighty God. In the Smalcald Articles, which were the result of this request, the Reformer says this of the teaching of justification by faith alone: "Of this article nothing can be yielded or surrendered, even though heaven and earth and all things should sink to ruin. . . . And upon this article all things depend which, against the pope, the devil, and the whole world, we teach and practice" [SA II I 5]. The importance of the teaching of justification is repeatedly emphasized in the Lutheran Confessions. Thus we find this in the Formula of Concord:

> This article concerning justification by faith . . . is the chief in the entire Christian doctrine, without which no poor conscience has any firm consolation or can know aright the riches of the grace of Christ, as Dr. Luther also has written: "If only this article remains in view pure, the Christian church also remains pure and is harmonious and without all sects; but if it does not remain pure, it is not possible to resist any error or fanatical spirit." [FC SD III 6][12]

If this article does not remain pure, if justification through faith alone is no longer taught, there arises in place of the righteousness bestowed upon us another righteousness attained by man himself, a human merit by the side of or even in the place of the merit of Christ. It is very significant that the Lutheran teaching of justification is opposed much more to modern Protestantism than to medieval, or even Tridentine, Catholicism. For this does at least recognize the merit of Christ, even if it admits too the coexistence of a human merit. But for modern Protestantism, as it has been defined by the age of Enlightenment, the Lamb of God who bears the sins of the world no longer exists at all. For them [the adherents of modern Protestantism] Christ has become merely a new lawgiver, a second Moses, who left behind him a moral and religious teaching. And then the salvation or damnation of man depends solely upon the obedience or disobedience to these laws. Luther actually recognized this opposition to his teaching in the "groupists," or "enthusiasts" of his day. And the growing Lutheran Church, in its confessions from the Augsburg Confession of 1530 till the Formula of Concord

---

[11]   The Council of Trent would not be convened until 1545; it met in three sessions and ended in 1563. RF

[12]   The Formula is quoting from Luther's comments on Psalm 117 (cf. *LW* 14:37). RF

of 1577 expressed most decisively its disagreement with them. Luther saw too the inner connection existing between the apparently heterogeneous enemies of the church of *sola fide* ["by faith alone"], between Roman Catholicism and the Enthusiast movement. The papacy and the Enthusiasm of Karlstadt, Münzer, and the Anabaptists both recognize another source of revelation beside the Holy Scriptures: the tradition which is put up beside the Scriptures, or the direct inspiration of the soul by the Holy Ghost, working independently of the Scriptures.[13] But wherever this second source of revelation is admitted, there appears the teaching of the cooperation of man in his redemption. And so for Luther there exists a permanent connection between *sola fide* ["by faith alone"] and *sola scriptura* ["by Scripture alone"]. Only upon the Scriptures can *sola fide* be founded, and only the article of justification can be "the key which opens the door to the whole of the Scriptures." Whenever one claims to find the Word of God elsewhere than in the Scriptures, and in the teaching of scriptural truths by the church, Christ is thus deprived of his honor as he in whose name alone salvation is to be found [see Acts 4:12]. But where that happens, the church ceases to be the church of Christ.

Since the teaching of justification by faith is the *articulus stantis aut cadentis ecclesiae* ["article by which the church stands or falls"], its decay is the decay of the church, its revival the reformation of the church. Only from this aspect is the Lutheran Reformation to be understood. Its sole object was to lead the church back to this biblical truth. By this standard all institutions and all doctrines were measured. Everything in the church which was reconcilable with the teaching of justification was retained, but everything which was contrary to it, and therefore to the Gospel, was rejected. The Lutherans were prepared to retain the canonical constitution of the church (Melanchthon [was prepared to retain] the papacy as well) so long as this was only a human institution. But they could no longer regard the hierarchy as an office instituted by Christ and necessary for man's redemption, with dominion over souls, and when they had to choose between obedience to the pope and obedience to the Word of the Scriptures, they had no difficulty in making their decision. They retained the Mass but excluded from it everything which was suggestive of a sacrifice offered by man, and of merit attained by man. They celebrated the most important saints' days, but they no longer recognized any merit in the saints themselves, since that would have impaired the unique merit of Jesus Christ. Only when compelled by circumstances did they build up their church, in cases where the bishops opposed the preaching of justification through grace alone, by faith alone. And this church testifies even today before the whole of Christendom the teaching of the Reformation: *verbo solo, sola fide* ["by Word alone, by faith alone"].

---

[13] To the Roman objection that tradition is older than the NT Scriptures, Lutheranism has always replied that the church only formed the *canon* of the NT; the Word of God exists as Scripture *and* as the living preaching of the church. HS

1937

THESES ON THE QUESTION
OF CHURCH AND ALTAR FELLOWSHIP[1]

This essay was occasioned by a significant event among the German churches. At a meeting of the Confessing Church of the Prussian Union held in Halle, May 10–13, 1937, the Lutheran, Reformed, and Union churches adopted a *Consensus de doctrina evangelii* ["Agreement in the Doctrine of the Gospel"] which declared altar fellowship among the churches. In the matter of altar fellowship, the Halle meeting denied the right of Lutheran or Reformed churches to exclude one another from Communion. It was also evident by this time that the Barmen "Declaration" had been elevated to the status of a "confession."[2]

This event was considered so momentous that a response was considered "necessary." Thus Sasse and others undertook such a response in the form of a collection of essays edited by Sasse, *Vom Sakrament des Altars* (1941). Sasse's own contributions to the volume, three out of ten essays, indicate the beginning of a lifelong concern to confess this doctrine.[3]

In addition, Sasse wrote these theses. Here he asserts most positively that the renewal of the church is dependent on the proper confession and practice of the Sacrament of the Altar.

The following theses were written in the fall of 1937 for a theological dialogue in view of the serious situation within the "Confessing Church" which arose in May of that year at the Prussian Confessional Synod at Halle. The synod had, in contradiction to the constitution of the church, declared general altar fellowship between Lutheran, Reformed, and United [Churches] on the basis of a compromise formula, against which decisive opposition arose within German Lutheranism. The Lutherans appealed to the authen-

---

[1] The original essay, "Zur Frage nach der Kirchen- und Abendmahlsgemeinschaft," was in mimeograph form. It was first published in *Lutherische Blätter* 2.6 (February 1950): 1–5, and then in *ISC,* 1:115–20. A separate English translation by Robert Kolb was published in *Concordia Journal* 26.2 (April 2000): 109–14. RF

[2] See the letters of Sasse to John W. Behnken, president of The Lutheran Church—Missouri Synod, dated October 23, 1958, and November 15, 1958 (Concordia Historical Institute, St. Louis, Mo., Behnken Collection). RF

[3] One is found in volume 2 of this collection, "The Formula of Concord's Decision about the Lord's Supper." Another, "The Lord's Supper in the New Testament," is available in *We Confess the Sacraments* (trans. Norman Nagel; St. Louis: Concordia, 1985), 49–97. RF

tic declaration of the preface to the Book of Concord.[4] They held that the condemnation of false doctrine regarding the Supper and the resulting refusal of altar fellowship does not mean the condemnation of persons who err in simplicity, much less of entire churches within and outside of the German Reich. Rather the condemnation is directed against false doctrine and against those recalcitrant "teachers and blasphemers, who we in no way intend to tolerate in our lands, churches, and schools." Radical theologians of the "Confessing Church" asserted, however, that a church is either a church of Christ or a devil's church. These theses were posed in opposition to this untenable assertion and do not claim to deal exhaustively with every aspect of the theme.[5]

Huss number 165
Hopf number 103

—◦◦◦—

1. As there is only *one* Christ, there is only *one* church, which is his body; only *one* Baptism, in which we through *one* Spirit are all baptized into *one* body; only *one* Table of the Lord, at which we all partake of *one* bread and thereby have the fellowship of the body of Christ. From this it follows that church fellowship is altar fellowship [*Kirchengemeinschaft Abendmahlsgemeinschaft ist*], as then "the communion [*Gemeinschaft*] of the body of Christ" (1 Cor 10:16) entails both participation in the *corpus Christi* ["body of Christ"] in the Eucharist and membership in the church as the *corpus Christi*.

2. The unity of the church, and with it the indissolubly connected unity of the Supper, will not be seen by the world. For since the days of the NT, where people believe in Christ and desire to belong to his church, they have been rent asunder by schism and heresies into various fellowships [*Gemeinschaften*], and there have been division and separation at the Supper. Already the first report of the administration of the Supper was occasioned by divisions of the community [*Gemeinde*] (1 Cor 11:18). It was not since the days of the rise of the confessional churches of the century of the Reformation when altar first stood against altar, but already since the days of Ignatius of Antioch, and since Rome hurled the anathema against Constantinople in the Middle Ages,[6] that the world could accuse Christians that the meal of love had become the object of contention.

3. The judgment of the world is that the church and the bond of love in the church did not exist because those who confess themselves disciples of Jesus were not able to commune at one altar. This cannot be taken seriously enough. The worst difficulty which the splintering of Christianity has brought can never be

---

[4]   *BS*, 755–56; Tappert, *BC*, 11. RF

[5]   *ISC*, 1:115. MH

[6]   This is a reference to the Great Schism of 1054. RF

overcome by simply declaring that the barriers between the altars are no longer present, and by pronouncing a general altar fellowship. Altar fellowship is only possible where a real church fellowship already exists. Should altar fellowship be pronounced, as was the case in the Unions[7] of the previous century, as the means and beginning of a prevailing church fellowship, not only is this fellowship not established, but the church is also destroyed. Such measures make the church a human religious society, and the Supper is made a mere religious celebration of such a society. This thesis has been confirmed by the experiences of all unions, which treat altar fellowship not as goal, but as point of departure for ecclesiastical unification.

4. An understanding of the question of church fellowship and altar fellowship is only possible when one has understood the causes of divisions of the church and separation in the Supper. The one church, which is the body of Christ, may be divided by no one. The Table of the Lord, at which the true body and blood of Christ is received, remains ever one and inseparable. As there is only one church, so there is only one Supper. The divisions of Christianity and the separation at the celebration of the Supper have a double cause. They are explained by the sins of lovelessness, which lead to schism and division of the congregation, or by the intrusion of heresy into the congregation, which leads to the formation of sects and necessitates the separation of pure doctrine from false, the church from the sect.

5. Schism and heresy are two allurements which constantly threaten the church. In view of the propensity to schism, admonitions in the NT, such as 1 Cor 1:1 ff.; 11:18; Eph 4:1 ff., are spoken to Christians and Christian congregations. He who destroys the unity of the Christian congregation sins against Christ. He who causes divisions of the congregation about the Supper celebrates the Supper unworthily and eats and drinks the body and blood of the Lord to judgment. In view of the propensity to heresy (e.g., 1 Tim 4:1; 2 Tim 3:1 ff.), the admonitions apply to be on guard for false doctrine and heretics (i.e., Gal 1:7 ff.; Titus 3:10; 1 John 4:1 ff.; 2 John 10 ff.). For if heresy comes to rule in Christianity, then the church may become the synagogue of Satan (Rev 2:9), and the Lord's Supper can become a sacrifice to idols (Rev 2:20). Thus Christianity has the duty to strictly avoid every church and altar fellowship with heresy, to examine individual believers, to instruct the erring in love, and to most strenuously advance church and altar fellowship within orthodox Christianity.

6. The fulfillment of this duty presupposes the clear knowledge of what pure and false doctrine, what church and heresy are. In their judgment regarding this, however, the denominations and confessions of Christianity differ widely. This is not merely since the Reformation, as, for instance, the example of the old African church demonstrates. There communions of the Montanists, Novatians, and

---

7   To various degrees, Lutheran and Reformed churches were forced into so-called United or Union (*Uniert*) churches, for example, Prussia and Nassau, 1817; Hanau and Rhenish Bavaria, 1818; Anhalt, 1820; Baden, 1821; Rhenish Hessia, 1822; and Württemberg, 1823. RF

Donatists raised the claim over against the Catholic Church that they were the true church. In the difficult debates of the ancient church over this question, a decision was rendered which has achieved authoritative significance for all Christianity until the present. Accordingly, all the churches which resulted from the Reformation confirmed it. The Catholic church father Cyprian argued that there is no salvation, that is, no forgiveness of sins outside the church, and therefore among the heretics there is neither Baptism or Supper (letter 70).[8] The church at that time decided that the Baptism imparted according to its institution is also valid when it is imparted by heretics, that is, in a heretical communion. Thereby, every fellowship of churches [Kirchengemeinschaft] which has acknowledged this principle grants that the church of God, or, to use Calvin's expression, "some vestige of the true church"[9] may also be found among the heretics because her existence is bound not to the faith of people, but to the means of grace. The judgment that another church is a heretical church, with which one may have not church fellowship, in no way entails the assertion that this church must then be treated only as a synagogue of Satan, or a "devil's church."

7. Thus he who asserts that another church must either be viewed as an equally legitimate true church or as a non-church and devil's church returns to the viewpoint of Cyprian and has the view of the entirety of Christianity of 1,700 years against himself. One may see therein an unbearable contradiction: that, to be sure, heresy comes from the devil, but that also among heretics the church of Christ may yet exist. Yet he must grant that this contradiction stretches through all of church history, from the controversy over Baptism by heretics to the struggle over the Baptism of rationalists. Also Luther and the Lutheran Church, though they have described the satanic origin of heresy with strong words, never denied that also in a heretical communion the church of Christ might still be believed [present]. They have also extended this judgment to the Reformed churches.

8. If the church of Christ may be believed also on the other side of the walls of our confessional church, then it is to be accepted that also there as with the Sacrament of Baptism thus also the Sacrament of the Altar—even if in disfigured form—is still present. In this sense our fathers constantly believed that their forefathers in the Papal Church still celebrated the Sacrament of the Altar and received in Communion the true body and the true blood of Christ in spite of the reservation of the cup, in spite of the abomination of the sacrifice of the Mass, and in spite of the doctrine of transubstantiation in the Mass. But they never drew the conclusion from this that one may thus commune at Roman altars. For he who

---

[8]   See Saint Cyprian, Letters (1–81) (vol. 51 of The Fathers of the Church: A New Translation; trans. Sister Rose Bernard Donna, C.S.J.; Washington, D.C.: Catholic University of America Press, 1964), 260–62. RF

[9]   Institutes, 4.2.11; cf. Institutes of the Christian Religion (The Library of Christian Classics 21; London: SCM, 1960), 1051. RF

would do that would deny the recognition which did not yet obtain in the Middle Ages, but which in the Reformation was born of the Holy Scriptures, that the sacrifice of the Mass is an abomination. On the other hand, we will not fundamentally deny that the Supper celebrated in the Reformed Church could be Christ's Supper, even though the celebrant [*Geistliche*] is convinced that he does not give under the form of the bread and wine the true body and the true blood of Christ to all who partake in the Supper to eat and to drink.[10] Still, there is for the Lutheran Christian no possibility, not even in the peril of death [*periculo mortis*], of taking part in the Reformed Supper. For through that participation he would confess that it does not matter whether one teaches the Lutheran or the Calvinistic doctrine of the Supper, so that thus the Calvinistic doctrine is perhaps a perverted, but still bearable theological theory, but no church-destroying heresy. Altar fellowship with the Reformed churches would only be possible if they were to deny Calvin's doctrine and teach the bodily presence of Christ under the forms of the bread and wine.

9. The Lutheran and Reformed churches currently consist of a plenitude of church bodies, but we may treat them as realities of church history, just like the Anglican, the Orthodox, the Methodist, and the Baptist communions. The raising of the question of altar fellowship between the Lutheran and Reformed churches is so unpleasant because, according to Reformed doctrine, the Lutheran denial of altar fellowship is the sin of schism, the loveless destruction of ecclesiastical unity. But according to Lutheran doctrine, the Reformed doctrine of the Supper is a heresy which denies the teaching of Scripture, destroys the Sacrament of Christ, and leads either to the dissolution of the church (Quakerism) or to the return to Roman Catholicism (Anglo-Catholicism). This tragic situation is not alleviated by the attempt to limit the charge of heresy to Zwingli's doctrine and to understand Calvin's doctrine as a possible or bearable explication of the passages regarding the Supper in the Holy Scriptures. For first of all, the Reformed Church has never condemned Zwingli;[11] second, the doctrine of Calvin in its substance was already rejected by the Augustana; and third, it cannot be justified on the basis of Scripture. The situation is this: that either the Lutheran Church can surrender to the Reformed doctrine, or the Reformed Church to the Lutheran doctrine of the Supper, but there is no higher unity transcending both. If it were somehow conceivable as a theoretic construction, it would nevertheless have no authority or lasting significance because it would be deficient in the area of scrip-

---

[10] "It does not rest on man's faith or unbelief but on the Word and ordinance of God—unless they first change God's Word and ordinance and misinterpret them, as the enemies of the sacrament do at the present time. They, indeed, have only bread and wine, for they do not also have the Word and instituted ordinance of God but have perverted and changed it according to their own imagination" (Luther, quoted in FC SD VII 32). This translation is from Tappert, *BC*, 574–75 (cf. *LW* 37:367). MH

[11] Calvin and Bullinger, Zwingli's successor in Zurich, reached agreement on the doctrine of the Lord's Supper in the *Consensus Tigurinus* of 1549. RF

tural basis. In the question of the "in, with, and under," of the *manducatio oralis*[12] and the *manducatio impiorum*,[13] there is only an either/or.

10. Thus the Evangelical Lutheran Church must reject church and altar fellowship with the Reformed until the Reformed churches have renounced their errors. This means, first of all, that it [the Evangelical Lutheran Church] fundamentally rejects church and altar fellowship with churches and fellowships which confess the Reformed doctrine of the Supper. It means, second, that the individual Reformed Christian, if he desires to receive the Supper in a Lutheran Church, may only be allowed if he confesses the doctrine of the Lutheran Catechism. For worthy reception of the Supper requires also correct faith, and this includes not only genuine trust in God's mercy in Christ, but also believing trust in the promise of Christ that he desires to give to us his body and his blood to eat and to drink. Therefore the participation of a Reformed [Christian] in a Lutheran Supper means his joining the Lutheran Church. The only exception in the matter of admission which can be made is in the admission of a repentant Christian, no matter of what confession, in the danger of death.

11. The weightiest objection which will be made against the preceding theses is that they can "no longer" be carried out in the practice of churchly life. To this we must immediately answer: If strict churchly and confessional principles can "no longer" be carried out in our time, then there is today no point in maintaining an Evangelical Lutheran Church. But then we would do well to ask ourselves whether the truths of the Reformation still apply today. Luther did not ask how the truths of the Reformation would play out. What is really true and right is just as difficult or easy to carry out in the twentieth century as it was in the sixteenth. Furthermore, it is to be noted that the church in other countries is in a still more difficult situation. The ecclesiastical situation of England, or certainly of the United States, presents completely different tasks than the new ordering of the relationship between Lutheran, Reformed, and United churches and congregations. How difficult, how hopeless are the dealings regarding the South Indian Union[14] and regarding the relationship between the Church of England and the English Free Churches. We will even have to learn to improve the diminishing abilities to think through ecclesiastical questions and to come to the correct con-

---

[12] Literally, "oral eating": the Lutheran teaching that Christ's body and blood are received into the mouth. RF

[13] Literally, "eating by unbelievers": that in the Sacrament even unbelievers eat the very body and blood of Christ. RF

[14] For Sasse, the example of the Church Union in South India was one of the most significant. This is indicated by his writings: *Church Union in South India: Some Considerations for Lutheran Theologians* (1963); also "Die Union von Südindien als Frage an die Lutherische Kirche" (Briefe an lutherische Pastoren 56), *Lutherische Blätter* 15.77 (June 1963): 43–60, parts of which were translated into English by Henry P. Hamann, "The Union of South India and the Lutheran Church," *Australian Theological Review* 37.4 (October–December 1966): 133–43. RF

clusions. Certainly any new arrangement will not be brought about quickly. What has been neglected for centuries cannot be made good in a few years. We must think in terms of decades. One thing, however, is sure. Today we at least understand the situation better than we did ten or thirty years ago. We know today what a perverted doctrine of the Supper and its corresponding practice has produced in our churches. It has nearly robbed us of the Sacrament and thus nearly destroyed the church. The renewal of the doctrine of the Sacrament, which we are experiencing today with astonishment, will be followed by the renewal of the correct celebration of the Holy Supper. And if this renewal is carried out first in a few places, and in smaller circles, if it is really the rightly understood and rightly celebrated Sacrament of the Altar, then the church will necessarily be renewed through it. For the church, which is the body of Christ, is built on earth when Christ feeds his community [*Gemeinde*] which truly believes in him with his true body and blood.

1937

CONFESSION AND CONFESSING

LESSONS FROM FIVE YEARS
OF THE CHURCH STRUGGLE[1]

The so-called "church struggle" [*Kirchenkampf*] was chiefly that struggle between the Christian church and the Nazi party of the Third Reich. But Sasse saw in it something more: it was also a struggle for the confessions of the church and their proper role. That meant a struggle not only between church and party but also between confessions. This is preeminently the case in the Prussian Union, the largest of the German *Landeskirchen* ("territorial churches"). But it was also very evident to Sasse in the position of Karl Barth who basically held (in Sasse's words) that the act of " 'confessing' or 'the confessional stance' is taken as the *decisive* criterion for membership in the 'Confessing Church' " and was thus more important than the content of the confession.

Beginning with the issue of the journal *Lutherische Kirche* in which this article first appeared, Sasse is designated as co-editor with his Erlangen colleague Friedrich Ulmer.

Huss number 168
Hopf number 105

On June 6, 1932, the recently founded "Faith Movement of German Christians"[2] adopted its "Guidelines," the work-and-battle program with which it entered the struggle for the Protestant territorial churches. The bitter election battle in the Evangelical Church of the Old Prussian Union, which ended with the German Christians taking a third of all seats in the church committees of Prussia, constituted the first phase of the church struggle.[3] Then in 1933 the acquisition of

---

[1]   This article was first published as "Bekenntnis und Bekennen: Lehren aus fünf Jahren Kirchenkampf" in *Lutherische Kirche* 19.5 (May 15, 1937): 50–55. RF

[2]   The *Glaubensbewegung Deutsche Christen* ("German Christian Faith Movement") was launched in Berlin in May 1932. On May 23 Pastor Joachim Hossenfelder was placed in charge of carrying out the electoral campaign for the Prussian Church elections. Three days later he issued ten guidelines for the new movement. By June 6, 1932, the movement had an organizational structure similar to that of the National Socialist party. RF

[3]   These elections were in November 1932. RF

power in most of the other territorial churches and in the developing Reich Church followed.

One needs to recall those events because in our myth-happy time a myth of the church struggle is already beginning to form. It is not the case that in 1933 suddenly a new (even if long-prepared) heresy had broken out in the church, a false doctrine which had suddenly discovered another revelation alongside Holy Scripture. One will find no new thought in the programs of the German Christians apart from the—also not very original—idea of transferring the "Führer"-principle to the church. They were not concerned with doctrines but with imposing a political will upon the church.

Certainly there was a considerable difference between the preaching of the new bishops and provosts from the ranks of the German Christians in Prussia and the preaching of the general superintendents and synodical bishops whom they had brought down. But, leaving aside the personal dimension and looking only at the ideas, the difference was that of the National Socialist and the bourgeois-national worldview. It was not a difference of church doctrine. That is why the old church government lacked the authority and courage to confront the undoubted errors of the German Christians. One could not honestly condemn in them what one tolerated—and indeed listened to with enthusiasm—in the pulpit of Berlin's cathedral, at the infield services of the Steel Helmets,[4] and in the gatherings of the Evangelical Federation [*Evangelischer Bund*[5]]. According to the constitution it was the highest duty of the Prussian Church authorities to watch over the purity of doctrine in the church, and this doctrine was to be none other than that of the Lutheran and/or the Reformed Confession.

The unwritten law of the "equal rights of religious directions" turned concern for doctrine into concern that the church's security might not be disturbed by questions of doctrine. How powerful this unwritten law was is demonstrated by the fact that the German Church [*Deutschkirche*] in Berlin was allowed to hold its services, which contradicted all confessional bases and all the orders of the church, as public congregational services of worship over many years before the eyes of four general superintendents and the whole central administrative authority of the church.

Is it really so astonishing that these superintendents then one day read in the newspaper that they were fired? How indeed is a church to oppose false doctrine if she is unable to confront it with anything other than the offer of a share of the synodical seats and bishops' chairs proportional to the number of adherents! Five

---

[4]　The *Stahlhelm* was a nationalist ex-servicemen's organization. It played a prominent role in politics in the 1920s and early 1930s (Louis L. Snyder, *Encyclopedia of the Third Reich* [New York: Paragon House, 1989], 331). RF

[5]　The *Deutscher Evangelischer Kirchenbund* was founded on May 25, 1922. It was the federal organization of the Protestant *Landeskirchen*. RF

years ago the Old Prussian Church was not able otherwise to confront the German Christians, her legitimate children. If the state today demands equality of rights for the religious directions within the German Evangelical Church and leaves the decision about doctrine and order in the church to the will of the church-tax payers, it is merely appropriating the principles by which, in contradiction to the Lutheran and Reformed confessions to which it was bound, the Prussian Church Senate ruled the largest German territorial church.

Therein lies the profound tragedy of the great labor of church construction achieved in German Protestantism under the standard-setting leadership of the Old Prussian Church in the post-war period. What an immense work was done by all those men—so capable in their way, honorable people, and certainly moved by the best of goodwill! However, this work has not served to build but to destroy the church—because it silently removed the presupposition on which alone the church of the Gospel can abide.

This presupposition is unanimity in the confession of the saving teaching of the Gospel. This does not mean uniformity of theological opinions. But it does imply that one can, in the unity of the faith, tell the world what the Gospel is. Neither the Church Congress [*Kirchentag*] nor even only the Prussian General Synod could do that. It could sing "heart to heart united," but it was unthinkable to recite the Apostolic Creed together (and would have been dishonest), let alone the confession of even one of the great doctrinal articles of the Augsburg Confession.

But wherever this unity of the church has been lost, something else must be available to hold churchly organization together. In Prussia this was, to a degree unknown elsewhere in German Protestantism, the political charge which the state gave the church. For the "Evangelical" Church, which arose in the Napoleonic era to replace the Lutheran and the Reformed churches as the soul of a renewed Prussia, is a state creation. Since 1817 the king decided what may and what may not be taught. Thus it was not the church but the state which determined the limits of church fellowship. If the will of the state is to abolish the border between two confessional churches, it is abolished. Frederick William III,[6] it has been said, exercised power over the Protestant churches of his territory such as no pope ever possessed in the Roman Church.

The whole "Confessing Church" of Old Prussia admires the heroic struggle of the confessors who defended the Lutheran confession a hundred years ago in Silesia.[7] That however does not prevent her—but for a few exceptions, whose

---

[6] Frederick William III was king of Prussia at the time of the Prussian Union. He ruled from 1797 until 1840. RF

[7] Silesia was the southeastern part of Prussia, where some pastors and people refused to conform to the enforced Union. In 1830 they formed the Evangelical Lutheran (Old Lutheran) Church (*Lutheran Cyclopedia*, 332). RF

confessional loyalty is then also called into doubt—from zealously defending the faith which Frederick William III at that time introduced into the town church of Hönigern[8] by force of arms. As to the doctrinal question whether a Union church government could be acknowledged by the Lutherans as their rightful church authority or not (which was the one point at issue in that struggle), the Prussian Councils of Brethren today stand almost completely on the side of the king. And that is the case only because for a hundred years his view was privileged to be taught in Prussian lecture halls.

So the Prussian Church has become a political church at her core. Indeed, she continued to play her political part even after the royal house which had charged her with it had long been brought down. "By force we are spatially separated," Wilhelm Kahl[9] called out to the East Prussians at the Königsberg Church Congress of 1927. "But *one* church, *one* fatherland, indissoluble spiritual communion in faith, love, hope, daily bonded in prayer: 'O Lord, make us free.' "

This mixture of church and world, Christianity and patriotism was more than rhetorical enthusiasm by a non-theologian. A speech given on the same occasion by President Wolff shows that. In it this celebrated leader of the Reformed Church called East Prussia "a holy land" because of its destiny as a border region and declared: "Under the sacred sign of the German Evangelical community of destiny, from East and West we give each other the hand of true loyalty. One kingdom, one people, one faith!" One could imagine that under the impress of such words, the Königsberg district military chaplain, Ludwig Müller,[10] would have matured toward the high twin office of provincial bishop of Prussia and national bishop [*Reichsbischof*].

The significance of the German Christian Movement is thus to be seen in its bringing a hundred-year development within the largest and most important of German territorial churches to completion and so plainly showing where this development had to lead. There is a direct line leading from Schleiermacher's *Speeches on Religion* to the views of the German Faith Movement, from Frederick William III and his court bishop Eylert[11] to Ludwig Müller, from the Prussian patriotic court, field, and festival preachers to the Thuringian national church people.

The end of this development however has to be the church's complete absorption into the state, as it is indeed today being demanded by the

---

[8]   On the significance of this place, see Sasse's essay "The Century of the Prussian Church: In Commemoration of Christmas 1834 in Hönigern" in this collection. RF

[9]   Wilhelm Kahl was a canon lawyer. RF

[10]   Ludwig Müller (1883–1945) was an army chaplain in Königsberg, where he met Hitler in 1926, "who in 1933 made him his confidential adviser in Church matters." In the same year Müller was elected bishop of Prussia and *Reichsbischof* (*ODCC*, 1124). RF

[11]   Ruhlemann Friedrich Eylert (1770–1852) was court preacher of Fredrick William III at Potsdam (1806); he encouraged the king to initiate the inauguration of the Prussian Union (*Lutheran Cyclopedia*, 288). RF

Thuringians.[12] And this in notable agreement, be it said, with the earlier religious socialists, who were of the view that society in the future would no longer distinguish between state and church. The merging of the church into the state is of course partly a nineteenth-century demand (Richard Rothe), partly a warning prophecy (August Vilmar). In wide circles of German Protestantism, it has now suddenly become clear that we face the fulfillment of this prophecy, if there is to be no turning in the last moment. This means that we face nothing less than the end of the Protestant [*evangelische*] church as church.

This has triggered the large confessional movement in present-day Germany. It is a great illusion to imagine that this movement can be explained on the basis of political motives. It is no anti-state movement. On the contrary, this is the great movement running counter to the process of self-dissolution which has been proceeding apace in the Protestant churches for several generations. In some regions of Germany, especially in those which experienced the "Awakening" a century ago, the confessional movement is already giving the impression of being a genuine revival, similar to the great awakenings of church history in being accompanied by the manifestations of sectarian Enthusiasm. In essence, however, it is nothing but an inner-church reform movement, in which the Protestant churches of Germany are returning to what causes the church to exist as church.

The church struggle of our days is therefore a genuine confessional struggle. In the face of the errors destroying the church, it began with reflection on the doctrine of the church confessions and, in their name, with the rejection of those errors. Because a large percentage of congregations, indeed even of the clergy, were completely estranged from the church's confession, many only intuitively sensing its meaning for the church rather than actually understanding it, that struggle necessarily had to become a battle for the understanding of that confession. This is the significance of the debates within the confessional movement. In it three different notions of the essence of the church's confession struggle with each other: the Neo-Protestant, the Reformed, and the Lutheran.

Though Neo-Protestantism in fact no longer possesses noteworthy theological representation in Germany, as the heir of the nineteenth century it is still a major force not only with the German Christians but also in the "Confessing Church." It understands the church's confession from the viewpoint of the individual's confession. There is genuine confession wherever a convinced "Here I stand, I can do no other" sounds forth. The church's confession comes about as the sum of individual confessions; the confessional church—or, as one prefers to

---

[12] The bishop of Thuringia, Martin Sasse (no relation) had reported to Hitler that "all the pastors of Thuringian Church, obeying an inward command, have with joyful hearts taken an oath of loyalty to Führer and Reich. . . . One God—one obedience in the faith. Hail, my Führer!" (Eberhard Bethge, *Dietrich Bonhoeffer* [New York: Harper & Row, 1970], 504). (Note: The index of the original edition of the English translation did not distinguish Hermann Sasse from Martin. See the index entry on page 863: "Sasse, Hermann, Bishop of Thuringia," a conflation, corrected in later editions.) RF

say in these circles, "the confessors" or the "Confessing Church"—comes about by the assembling of the individual confessors.

This point of view or its consequences is today encountered wherever "confessing" or "the confessional stance" is taken as the *decisive* criterion for membership in the "Confessing Church" and where, correspondingly, even people who publicly deny the fundamental truths of the Apostles' Creed or the Augsburg Confession and who strive to keep the church "confession free" are recognized as church members with equal rights. Countless examples could be adduced of how strong this Neo-Protestant concept of confession remains in the "Confessing Church" today and how well it supports the old idea of "equality of directions" (in religion) and so the phenomenon of indifference to true doctrine, examples that force every sober judge to face this question: How does the "new" (or "young") church actually differ from the "old"?

The Neo-Protestant view of confession is opposed by the Reformed and the Lutheran view. These share the presupposition that the confession of the church is indeed never present without the "confessing posture" of the individual (the plain term for that is "without confessors"), but that it can never be understood on that basis. Were it really in the first instance to depend on the confessing posture and only then on the content of the confession, the real "Confessing Church" in Germany would perhaps be the sect of the International Bible Students' Association.[13] The confession of an individual or of a community only becomes the confession of the church when the faith of Christ's church is witnessed to. Luther was thus able to say of his confessing at Worms: "At that moment *I* was the church," that is, as one individual he stood over against the whole church of his time and confessed the true faith of the genuine church of all times, not merely his personal conviction.

Though *Lutherans* and *Reformed* stand together in opposition to the Neo-Protestant concept of confession with its denial of the church and its neglect of church doctrine, at other points their understandings of the confession of the church diverge. "The Reformed confession of faith," Karl Barth maintains, "comes to formulation spontaneously and openly in a *locally circumscribed* Christian community, which in this way defines its character *for the time being* to those outside, and gives direction *for the time being* to its inner teaching and life. It is a statement of the insight given *provisionally* also to the universal Christian church concerning the revelation of God in Jesus Christ, which is witnessed alone in Holy Scripture."[14]

While the Reformed confession always wants to represent only a section of the church (thus the Confessio Helvetica, Gallicana, Belgica, Scotica, etc), the Lutheran confession is to be valid throughout the *whole* church. The Reformed

---

[13]   This was an organization of the Jehovah's Witnesses outside the United States (*ODCC*, 841). RF

[14]   *Die Theologie und die Kirche* (1928), 76 ff. HS

See the English translation of this important essay by Barth in *Theology and Church: Shorter Writings 1920–1928* (London: SCM, 1962), chapter 3: "The Desirability and Possibility of a Universal Reformed Creed (1925)." RF

Confessions are inscribed "until further notice" or "for the time being." They expect to be replaced by something better.

The fathers of the Formula of Concord however make their confession "in the presence of God and of all Christendom among both our contemporaries and our posterity . . . in which by God's grace we shall appear with intrepid hearts before the judgment seat of Jesus Christ" (FC SD XII 40).[15] In the same way Luther did in his great confession of 1528: "Hence if any one shall say after my death, 'If Luther were living now, he would teach and hold this or that article differently,' " he replies that he has well considered all the articles: "I know what I am saying, and I well realize what this will mean for me before the Last Judgment at the coming of the Lord Jesus Christ."[16]

The Lutheran Church can speak in this way because she can confess with her Reformer: "This is my faith, for so all true Christians believe and so the Holy Scriptures teach us."[17] Another occasion may allow us to speak of all that is embraced by this Lutheran concept of the church's confession and of why it is not evidence of the overweening human certainty of a confessional church but only of faith in the certainty and infallibility of the divine Word.[18] Here we are merely noting the difference in the concept of confession used by the churches, and we ask: Why is this difference being blurred today? Why today foist the Reformed concept of confession upon the German Lutherans by treating the Barmen Declaration as an allegedly new confession?[19]

For if that declaration is a confession, then it is a typically Reformed confession, a confession which indeed contains single correct statements—as in fact all Reformed confessions also contain truths to which we gladly assent—but that as a whole is not acceptable because it serves to mask the differences and to bypass the issue of truth, thereby opening the door to the enthusiasts. We will hopefully all agree on this (and this conviction has provided the confessional movement of these recent years with its strength): We are not permitted to treat the question of the truth of the church's confession with less seriousness that it was in 1577, 1530, and 1529.[20] If we fail to take it just as seriously as the fathers did in the sixteenth century, then the great confessional struggle is lost. But that would be the end of the Protestant church in Germany.[21]

---

[15]   The English translation is from Tappert, *BC*, 636. MS

[16]   *Confession concerning Christ's Supper* (1528), *LW* 37:360–61. The English translation of this and the following quote is taken from *LW* 37. RF

[17]   *Confession concerning Christ's Supper* (1528), *LW* 37:372. RF

[18]   For more on Sasse's discussion of the role of the confessions and especially the comparison between the Lutheran and the Reformed views, see Ronald R. Feuerhahn, "Hermann Sasse: Confessionalist and Confessor," in *And Every Tongue Confess: Essays in Honor of Norman Nagel on the Occasion of His Sixty-fifth Birthday* (ed. Gerald S. Krispin and Jon D. Vieker; Dearborn, MI: Nagel Festschrift Committee, 1990), 14–37. RF

[19]   See the essay "The Barmen Declaration—An Ecumenical Confession?" in this collection. RF

[20]   1577—Formula of Concord; 1530—Augsburg Confession; 1529—Marburg Colloquy. RF

[21]   In 1948 Sasse in effect declared this prediction fulfilled, at least for the Lutheran Church. See "Das Ende der lutherischen Landeskirchen Deutschlands," *ISC*, 1:303–8. RF

1937

THE BARMEN DECLARATION—AN ECUMENICAL CONFESSION?[1]

The Barmen Declaration, devised at the First Confessing Synod at Barmen in 1934, was one of the most significant documents of this period. What at the time of its inception had been promoted as a "declaration," not a "confession," soon came to claim confessional status. That is the case even beyond Germany.[2] This is one in a series of items by Sasse published on the subject; see, for instance, "Against Fanaticism" in this collection.

Huss number 170
Hopf number 106

———❦———

The misuse of the "Theological Declaration" of Barmen which is being propelled by Karl Barth and his disciples is getting worse all the time. This declaration was first accepted because it was to be a guide in the struggle to maintain the confessional churches, not because it was a new confession. "It will not supplant that which can only be declared binding for the Lutheran by a Lutheran Synod and for the Reformed by a Reformed Synod." Thus Territorial Bishop Dr. Meiser[3] declared at Barmen in a communication to his pastors, and so the Barmen resolutions, which bear a churchly responsibility, were at that time, in good faith, understood by all the delegates.

Irresponsible fanatics [*Schwarmgeister*], however, have since proclaimed this declaration a confession, binding the Lutheran and Reformed churches—yes as a

---

[1] The original German was published as "Die Barmer Erklärung—ein ökumenisches Bekenntnis?" in *Lutherische Kirche* 19.6 (June 1, 1937): 74–76. RF

[2] Thus see *The Constitution of the Presbyterian Church (U.S.A.)*, part 1, *Book of Confessions* (Louisville: Office of the General Assembly, 1991), part 9, "The Theological Declaration of Barmen," and part 10, "The Confession of 1967," especially § 9.04, which states: "The United Presbyterian Church in the United States of America acknowledges itself aided in understanding the gospel by the testimony of the church from earlier ages and from many lands. More especially it is guided by the Nicene and Apostles' Creeds from the time of the early church . . . and the Theological Declaration of Barmen from the twentieth century." See also Jan Rohls, *Reformed Confessions: Theology from Zurich to Barmen* (Columbia Series in Reformed Theology; trans. John Hoffmeyer; Louisville: Westminster John Knox, 1998). RF

[3] Sasse's bishop, Hans Meiser (1881–1956), was bishop of the Bavarian *Landeskirche* ("territorial church"). RF

word given by the Holy Spirit, which must be respected as God's word.[4] This mischief is even today taught in the theological periodical of the German Barthians, *Evangelische Theologie*. Karl Barth himself has not found it necessary to remove such assertions. He has, to the contrary, in a plan circulated en masse to every journal proclaimed a genuine "confessional union" to the people of the "German Evangelical Church." It is now public what evil he has caused, particularly with respect to congregational members who not of their own fault no longer know anything of church and churchly confession.

Now the Barmen "Confession" is even to be raised to the level of dignity of an ecumenical confession, binding all of Christianity, or in any case, all Evangelical Christianity. In the *British Weekly* of April 22, 1937, Barth demands that the English churches declare that the First Thesis of the Barmen Declaration "in its positive and negative content is the correct and necessary expression of the Christian faith at present and is therefore also our confession." A "voice from Scotland" which the *Reformierte Kirchenzeitung* of May 16 published without comment, and with evident agreement, shows how this alarm which Barth has publicly directed to all Reformed churches has affected the foreign world. It begins with these words: "The meaning and force of the Barmen Confession of Faith crosses the boundaries of the German Evangelical Church. When Luther had accomplished his act of confession, the Ninety-five Theses, the effect exceeded the sphere of his little congregation. Likewise, the Barmen Confession means not only a distinguishing of spirits in the German Evangelical Church, rather *it appeals for a distinguishing of spirits in all of Christianity!*" Then the writer, Rev. Arthur G. Cochrane of Edinburgh, explicitly establishes the demand that the *Reformed World Federation* appropriate the Barmen Confession.

We fully expect to see it again in the proceedings of the Reformed World Federation and its session in Montreal, or also in the proceedings of the Reformed Church of Scotland or in Germany. If they accept the Barmen Declaration as their own, then we will treat it as a Reformed confession. Against *one* assertion, however, we must strenuously protest, and we regret that the *Reformierte Kirchenzeitung* did not do this for us. The Barmen Declaration is neither a confession of faith, nor the confession or, even merely, a confession of the German Evangelical Church. Indeed, a German Evangelical Church as church— yes, exactly according to the Barmen Declaration—does not exist. Lutheran theologians true to their confession had, already before the Barmen Synod, expressed weighty concerns against the planned declaration. The confession was only accepted because most of the delegates did not understand it as an ecclesiastical confession. It was accepted without contradiction only because the order of business and the proceedings made it impossible for dissent to be expressed before the

---

[4]   See "Against Fanaticism" in this collection. RF

plenary. What would the Christians in England, Scotland, in the United States and Canada say to the Barmen Declaration if they knew that this declaration was accepted without free discussion and without really voting, and this in the face of manifest contradiction?

But let there be no misunderstanding about this: No German Lutheran is refusing to give an answer to the questions raised by the Barmen Declaration. But only a Lutheran Synod can decide to what extent the Barmen Declaration, which intentionally avoids the doctrinal differences between the Evangelical churches, agrees with Lutheran doctrine. Why have the disciples of the Barmen "Confession" never thought of submitting this "confession" to one Lutheran and one Reformed Synod for examination? Apparently for the same reason the father of the Barmen Confession demanded that the Reformed World Federation make his confession its own, but not the Church of Basel.

1937

THE CONFESSIONS
AND THE UNITY OF THE CHURCH[1]

It has been noted that Sasse frequently viewed the history of the church as being filled with crises if not tragedies. The time of the church under the Third Reich was, not only for Sasse to be sure, such a time of crisis and the threat of tragedy. Here the title again clearly states the theme: the role of the confessions and the unity of the church.

By the time of this essay, Sasse had been active in the Ecumenical Movement for ten years. His earnest appeal here for truth as well as, even before, unity represents the dedication found among the leaders of the first ecumenical meeting Sasse attended, the World Conference on Faith and Order, Lausanne, 1927.

Huss number 173
Hopf number 098

———⟨•/•/•⟩———

PART 1
SECTION 1

The Bavarian Territorial Church and its pastors, as well as a large number of people in the other Lutheran churches of Germany, are currently remembering with sadness and thankfulness the great churchman Hermann Bezzel.[2] The twentieth

---

[1] Sasse read this paper at a pastoral conference in 1937 in Nuremberg. It was originally published as "Die Konfessionen und die Einheit der Kirche" in *Korrespondenzblatt für die evangelisch-lutherischen Geistlichen in Bayern* 62.26 and 27 (June 29 and July 6, 1937): 229–31 and 237–40, respectively.

   The article is preceded by the following citation from Bezzel:

     Perhaps someone among us might think: What if the witness suddenly stopped at the end of the twentieth century because it had no more power? If a new faith came, where would we remain, [we] who are heralds and adherents of the old faith? Have no care, the divine witness does not become speechless, and the anointing from above does not fail, and the help of the truth will neither end nor fail! LG

[2] Hermann Bezzel (1861–1917) among other things served as rector of the Deaconess Institute at Neuendettelsau from 1891 until 1909 and as president of the Protestant Upper Consistory in Munich,

351

anniversary of his death occurs on June 8. Bezzel's untimely death was a terrible loss, and not only for our territorial church, in which we are still experiencing the blessing God bestowed on his life's work. His death was also a deep misfortune for all of Evangelical Lutheran Germany. When Bezzel was taken away from us we lost one of the few churchmen who clearly saw the great "either-or" which faced German Evangelical Christendom: National Church or Confessional Church? In losing Bezzel we lost the only church leader who would have possessed the spiritual authority to prevent the formation of the Church Federation, which began five years after he died and came to its inevitable end on July 11, 1933.[3] In 1916, over against the Reich Church plan of Weinel,[4] Bezzel formulated his view this way: "We do not want a national church as a convenient federation; we want an international church as a confessional fellowship." He based this assertion upon the doctrine of the church and its unity in the Augsburg Confession and appealed to the famous lecture of 1868 in which Kliefoth[5] had affirmed

> that Article VII does not maintain that we are to be satisfied if we are dissolved into individual congregations where there is Lutheran preaching and administration of the Sacraments within a German Evangelical National Church. We are rather obligated on the basis of this article to be and to remain a Lutheran Church with an organization and church administration which is determined by our confession.[6]

1909–1917, the position later called territorial bishop. An incisive theological thinker and a powerful preacher in the footsteps of Wilhelm Löhe, Bezzel left the Bavarian Territorial Church with a firm confessional Lutheran imprint. A leading concept in his theology was the condescendence of God in coming to save humanity, a concept which was an important corrective to the *kenosis* teaching of other Erlangen theologians (Heinz Brunotte and Otto Weber, eds., *Evangelisches Kirchenlexikon: Kirchlich-theologisches Handwörterbuch* [2d ed.; 4 vols.; Göttingen: Vandenhoeck & Ruprecht, 1962], 1:424–25). *Kenosis* is Greek for "an emptying," based on Phil 2:7: "[Christ] emptied himself." Some theologians interpreted this in the sense that Christ gave up his divine personality while on earth; Orthodox Lutherans on the other hand held that Christ, in his state of humiliation, did not always and fully use the divine properties but did not give them up. LG/RF

3 · The *Deutscher Evangelischer Kirchenbund* ("German Evangelical Federation") was founded on May 25, 1922; it was a federation of all Protestant churches in Germany. The constitution of the *Deutsche Evangelische Kirche* (DEK, "German Evangelical Church") was signed by representatives of all *Landeskirchen* ("territorial churches") on July 11, 1933. That the bishops signed was due to both political pressure and ignorance: "They did not understand at that time why this constitution should not be accepted" (Sasse, letter to Herman Preus, January 13, 1946, Archives of the American Lutheran Church, Luther Seminary, St. Paul, Minn.). RF

4 Sasse is referring to Heinrich Weinel (1874–1936) who led the syncretistic *Bund für Gegenwartschristentum* or "Federation for Contemporary Christianity," a group which included Martin Rade, Adolf von Harnack, Friedrich Loofs, and other famous liberals. LG

5 Theodor Kliefoth (1810–1895) was a major figure in the restoration of confessional Lutheranism in Germany. He was important both as an incisive theological scholar (systematics, history of dogma, liturgics) and as a preacher, practical administrator, and liturgical reformer. After 1844 he served as cathedral preacher and superintendent at Schwerin and after 1886 as higher church president (bishop) of the Lutheran Territorial Church of Mecklenburg. LG

6 *Neue Kirchliche Zeitschrift* (1918): 11. HS

Expressing his consternation "that such high-ranking Lutheran clergy false-ly expound the confessions of their own church," Weinel, in his rebuttal of Bezzel, instructed the Lutherans on how they should understand the Augsburg Confession:

> According to the Augustana, the confession is not the power which gathers the folk into the church, but the faith, outwardly recognizable in the preaching of the Gospel and the distribution of the Sacraments. . . . There is not a single word regarding a church as a confessional fellowship the way these Lutherans understand it, nor can there be, because the proof is presented in the Augustana that the Evangelicals are part of a true Christian, catholic church.[7]

This astonishing theological assertion shows that Weinel is absolutely ignorant of the doctrine of the church or even the concept of pure doctrine. But on this basis, sorely confused, he repudiates the position of Bezzel: "Just as the possibility of a German Catholic Church was once placed within the reach of Döllinger,[8] and that through him the new German Empire might have taken a different route and soared to inner greatness, so once again in Bavaria the decisive man has been found wanting at [a time of] growing churchly unification of our folk."[9] It is beyond Weinel how one could still hold the position "that in a church fellowship only the (Lutheran) Confession should be valid, even if the unity of the folk and the work for the folk suffers." Bezzel's sober assertion regarding the plans for a stronger union of the practical organizations of German Protestantism seems a loveless condemnation: "Fellowship of working together, without fellowship of faith, is self-deception." For Weinel it is nothing more than a haughty pronouncement of heresy when someone declares that he is not in the fellowship of faith, and thus not in church fellowship with Harnack and Baumgarten.[10]

Weinel is convinced that he and not Bezzel has the Augustana on his side when he describes the emerging Reich Church as follows:

> We need a great and living fellowship for our people, full of courage and power in all inward and holy things. It must extend over our entire folk. Those with the strongest faith and the greatest power must be their leaders

---

[7] Dr. H. Weinel, *Die deutsche Reichskirche* (Munich, 1917), 11. HS

[8] Johann Joseph Ignaz von Döllinger (1799–1890) was a Bavarian Roman Catholic historian who developed the notion of a German church free from state control and Rome but in communion with Rome. He was excommunicated in 1871 for refusing to submit to the decisions of Vatican I. He became a leader of the Old Catholics (*ODCC*, 496). RF

[9] Weinel, *Die deutsche Reichskirche*, 10. HS

[10] Sasse is referring here to the great liberal theologian and historian of dogma, Adolf von Harnack (1851–1930), and to Otto Baumgarten (1858–1934), a professor of practical theology at Jena and later at Kiel who was a prominent political and social activist. Baumgarten had served as a member of the German peace delegation in 1919. LG

[*Führer*]. Love must be the bond of unity, which binds together even the most diverse people, and it must become a lively certainty in word and deed for our folk. It must gather up the last, strong, holy vitality of our folk and help shape it into reality. He who has in his heart such faith and such a desire for his folk, is building toward the forthcoming church of our folk.

Bezzel would have judged the passionate summons which appeared in June 1917 under the title "The German Reich Church" no differently than he did Weinel's summons of 1915. He could have explained that this Reich Church lacks the very thing that makes the church the church. He could also have earnestly warned against the self-deception inherent in an ecclesiastical fellowship which rests on any other foundation than the genuine consensus of "We believe, teach, and confess" [e.g., FC Ep I 1 and passim]. He might have cited again the remark where Luther, in one of his last writings, warned against the misunderstanding that church fellowship might be established upon the unity of love, where the unity of faith was lacking: "Do not speak to me of any love and friendship where one would demolish faith or the Word. For not love but the Word brings ever-lasting life, God's grace, and all heavenly treasures."[11] But Bezzel was no longer able to say these things. He lay dying when Weinel instructed him concerning what the church might be according to the Augsburg Confession.

We have mentioned these exchanges—the last theological battle which Bezzel fought before God brought upon him the severe struggles of his own death—not only because the memory of June 8, 1917, is on our minds, [but also because] these debates have significance far beyond matters of biography or contemporary history. They are an important part of the great *struggle over the church's confession*, which is the real theme of recent German church history. No more important question has arisen since the rediscovery of the church in the nineteenth-century awakening of German Protestantism; none has moved intellects more deeply than the question of what significance the confession holds for the church and for the unity of the church.

The question about the church, which has agitated Christendom the world over and all confessions since the end of the Enlightenment, has ever and again in Germany been expressed as a question concerning the church's confession. For the Roman Catholic and the Anglican, the Reformed and the Methodist, the Congregationalist and the Baptist churches of the world, a church struggle is a struggle over liturgy and pastoral office, over form and order of the church, over freedom from the state and over influence upon public life. Among us, every church conflict that was kindled by questions regarding the Agenda or the office of bishop or the relation between the state and the church or between the church and the world has been a struggle regarding our confession. This is true of all of our church struggles, from the struggle for the confessions and against the Union

---

[11] Luther in a sermon on Ephesians 6 in 1531, WA 34^{II}.38 ff., cited by Bezzel in "Zum Jahresbeginn," *Neue Kirchliche Zeitschrift* (1917): 12. HS

by the Silesian Lutherans after 1830, to the heated battles regarding the church assembly and the National Church since 1846. It is true from Harnack's dispute over the Apostles' Creed and the incidences involving Schrempf, Jatho, and Traub,[12] down to the great church dispute of our days. The decisive question in these struggles has always had to do with the extent to which the church's confession also determines the boundaries of the church. It is the question posed by Article VII of the Augsburg Confession of whether the unity of the church is the *unity of doctrine*, or whether there is also a unity of the church where there is *doctrinal diversity*.

The contemporary significance of the controversy between Weinel and Bezzel is that during the war, and more precisely in the decisive year 1917, the question at issue was formulated with total clarity. Such clarity became necessary in the reconstruction of the churches after the collapse in 1918. The question was this: *National Church* or *Confessional Church?* This is the great question which will be permanently decided in our time, perhaps even this year. We must be clear that today, under the temporary (at least theoretically valid) constitution of July 1933, we live in a time of transition. For the "German Evangelical Church" is neither a Confessional Church nor an Evangelical Reich Church. It is still a temporary federation of territorial churches, stalled on the way to becoming a Reich Church. But if the remnants of the territorial churches are shattered this year—perhaps as the result of the church elections being undertaken for that purpose—then we stand at a parting of the ways.

It is clear that for the state the result of the elections is far less important than the fact that they are held. If the attempt succeeds to change the "German Evangelical Church" from a federation of territorial churches into a religious body of Protestant individuals in Germany who pay church taxes, then Weinel's conception of the church has won. Then the General Synod will be that which Weinel in 1917 called his "fundamental demand": "The representation of the entire German church folk within a Reich Church assembly based on a general, fair, immediate, and secret election." And he expressly added that in the Reich Church assembly every theological leaning, if it is serious, must be allowed to speak.

If now, twenty years later, this plan, an old dream of German Liberalism and an old demand of the "Protestant Society,"[13] is to be implemented, then the Reich

---

[12] Christoph Schrempf (1860–1944) was a religious freethinker who was dismissed from the ministry in Württemberg in 1892 for his liberalism and his outspoken opposition to the confession of the church. Carl Jatho (1851–1913), a pastor in Bucharest, Boppard, and Cologne, was defrocked in 1911 for pantheistic preaching. Gottfried Traub (1869–1956), who like Jatho was involved in the *Protestantenverein* (see following note), was dismissed from the ministry in the Westphalian church for defending Jatho. Schrempf, Jatho, and Traub all took part in the *Apostolicum* Controversy which sought to abolish the obligatory status of the Apostles' Creed. Adolf von Harnack was also involved in these attacks on the Creed. LG

[13] The *Deutscher Protestantenverein* ("German Protestant Society") was a society that began in 1863 in the wake of the "Agenda Storm" in Baden, a revolt against a reform liturgy with Lutheran tendencies introduced in 1855. The society opposed divisions created by theological differences and urged churches to

Church thus constituted will necessarily and immediately fall to pieces. For as little as it was possible for Bezzel and Weinel to be in the same church twenty years
ago, so little is it possible for their supporters and successors on either side to have
church fellowship today. We neither can nor shall ever recognize as church a
church whose unity does not consist in the unified teaching of the pure Gospel,
a church in which various conflicting confessions are recognized as equally valid, a
church in which pure doctrine and false teaching have the same right to exist.

The significance of the hour in church history in which we live is that it
places us before a question which must be answered. What was only a theological debate twenty years ago has today become a question of the very existence of
the church. And that question is this: National Church *or* Confessional Church?
One *or* the other. Either the boundaries of the nation are also the boundaries of
the church, or else the boundary of the confession is the boundary of the church.
The possibilities of reinterpreting the "either-or" into a "both-and" have been
exhausted. One cannot join even the most moderate German Christian in saying:
"National Church or German Church? Yes, indeed! But we are not willing to
infringe upon the confession." Nor can one say with the friends and pupils of
Harnack, Weinel, Rade,[14] and Baumgarten, who in the meantime have fled from
the threatening consequences of their own teaching into the Confessing Church:
"Confessional Church or Confessing Church?[15] Yes, indeed! But we must tolerate within the Confessing Church not only various theological tendencies—this
is of course self-evident in a really living church—we must also tolerate divergent
confessions, for example, both the Lutheran and the Reformed, and therefore we
cannot exclude anyone from the Confessing Church just because he perhaps
denies the articles of faith of the Apostles' or the Nicene Creed."

All these attempts at compromise led to complete absurdity in the history of
the German church after the winter of 1918–1919. For the time period from 1918
to 1933 was marked by the desire to build an Evangelical churchdom in Germany

---

proclaim divine love. Prominent in the Protestant Society were men who emphasized liberal theology
and the freedom or autonomy of the local congregation. A theological group which was supported by the
Protestant Society was the Evangelical Federation of 1922 (*Deutscher Evangelischer Kirchenbund;* see the
note on this above), which worked for the unification of the German Evangelical churches. The federation was interested in fostering the Union and in combating the influence of Roman Catholics. It was
involved in various forms of activism. Theologically it was committed to the development of the "Luther
Renaissance" and of "dialectical theology." LG

[14] Martin Rade (1857–1940), a follower of Albrecht Ritschl and Adolf von Harnack, was theologically a liberal and, as founder and editor of *Die Christliche Welt*, was deeply involved in the relations between religion and politics. A spokesman for complete freedom in theology and church matters, he energetically
supported Harnack, Schrempf, and Jatho. During the Third Reich, Rade boldly defended the persecuted Jews. LG

[15] Sasse distinguishes here between the *Bekenntniskirche*, "Confessional Church," meaning the church
which accepted the Lutheran Book of Concord, and the *Bekennende Kirche*, "Confessing Church," which
consisted of groups or conventicles which rejected the Nazi takeover of their territorial churches. The
Bekennende Kirche, consisting largely of individuals from the Union churches, regarded "confession" not
as an act of subscribing to the Lutheran Confessions but as an act of professing Christ across confessional
lines. LG

that would maintain the old confession but overlook the norms which the confession gave for the building of the church. Today we stand at the turning point which Bezzel foresaw for our church and expressed in these alternatives: National Church or Confessional Church? Put theologically, we face the question whether the great "it is sufficient" (*satis est*) of Article VII of the Augsburg Confession is true or false: "For the true unity of the church it is sufficient to agree concerning the doctrine of the Gospel and concerning the administration of the Sacraments" ("ad veram unitatem ecclesiae satis est consentire de doctrina evangelii et de administratione sacramentorum"). The answer which we must give to this great question regarding the true unity of the church, and which we all shall perhaps have to give this very year, cannot remain merely theoretical. It must be the answer which was once given at the time of the Interim[16] in a situation which, humanly speaking, was completely hopeless. That answer given by our fathers and the pastors and congregations of the Lutheran Church, by the grace of God, delivered the church in an hour when it seemed at the point of total ruin.

SECTION 2

Thus the question concerning the church and its unity has become a question regarding the confession of the church in German Protestantism in a way that it has not, or at least not yet, been experienced in *other countries*. Perhaps this is the great contribution which the Evangelical churches in Germany have to make to the enormous struggle regarding the church which has been experienced by all Christians for a hundred years. It is not as though we could vicariously carry on the battle of other churches for their confession. No one can believe for another, and so no church can vicariously confess for the other. However, our own confessional struggle can and should open the eyes of the other churches to the significance of churchly confession. The other Protestant church fellowships look with surprise, and even at times with dismay, upon the return to the confessions of the Reformation that is taking place in Germany.

We must be clear that in the nineteenth century a majority of these church fellowships completed their own break with the confessions of the Reformation period. The Anglican churches, if we may mention them at this point, have virtually robbed the Thirty-nine Articles of all their validity, even though they are still legally in force. The Methodists, who are the numerically largest Protestant church fellowship next to Lutheranism, possess no confession as we understand it. It is axiomatic for Baptists and Congregationalists that it is left up to the local congregation to accept the confessions or not. Even the majority of the Reformed churches have solemnly invalidated the confessions of the sixteenth century, although they are still in force in certain localities. For all these churches, their confessional writings from the sixteenth and seventeenth centuries today possess only a historical and in no wise normative significance. Consequently, humanly

---

[16]   The Augsburg and Leipzig Interims of 1548. RF

speaking, it is out of the question that these writings should ever again become anything more than venerable documents from a past long since relinquished.

People in these churches simply cannot understand how in Germany appeals are still made to the Augustana or the Smalcald Articles, or, in our Reformed congregations, to the Heidelberg Catechism and the Gallic Confession. And who can blame them for this lack of understanding when there are theologians in German Lutheran churches who openly say that to combat false teachings of recent times with the Augustana would be much like fighting the military battles of the twentieth century with the weapons of the sixteenth. One wonders which particular museum they intend to use to hide away the *Nicaenum* ("Nicene Creed") and the *Apostolicum* ("Apostles' Creed"). It is inconceivable to an American Congregationalist or Baptist that a confession, in which the church has testified to a biblical truth which cannot be surrendered and by which serious struggles over pure doctrine have been settled, could be valid not only for the generation which has pronounced it, but insofar as it testifies to the truth of Scripture, it may make the claim to be recognized always, everywhere, and by all (*semper, ubique et ab omnibus*).[17] For he knows the church only as the local congregation, here and now, which today confesses what is the conviction of its members at this very moment.

The Lutheran, however, should understand this. Included in his symbolical books are confessions which span some fifteen hundred years. And one symbol accepts and confirms the others. Our church knows not only the consensus of those now living but also the consensus which binds together the generations of the orthodox church of all times. Therefore, the return to the confession of the sixteenth century is for us anything but a repristination of the past. Truly, anyone who has experienced how theologians young and old—including those who for a whole lifetime had nothing to do with the church's confession—now have discovered the Augustana, or anyone who has seen how the Catechism has come to life again in the congregation, such a person knows that this has not been a romantic flight from reality.

The return to the Augustana in our time was the return home to the church. And this was the case with our fathers a hundred years ago. Regardless of how this homecoming to one's church may take place for people of other confessions—

---

[17] George Calixtus, a seventeenth-century Lutheran theologian with syncretistic tendencies, had defined the consensus of the church in the first five centuries as the sufficient basis for unity talks among the Lutheran, Reformed, and Roman churches. Thereby he borrowed a concept of Vincent of Lérins (flourished ca. 425), who described the catholic faith as that which had been believed "at all places, at all times, and by all Christians." Piepkorn commented of Calixtus and his followers: "Their tendency to reduce the necessary minimum of *credenda* ['believing'] to the baptismal creed and a sometimes overly great reliance on the consensus of the first five centuries . . . must be deplored as a case where a preoccupation with polemic and irenic concerns interfered with an adequate evaluation of the facts of the history" (Arthur Carl Piepkorn, "George Calixtus," *The Encyclopedia of the Lutheran Church* [ed. Julius Bodensieck; Minneapolis: Augsburg, 1965], 1:350). Piepkorn notes that the term *consensus quinquesaecularis* ("consensus of the first five centuries") was not used by Calixtus but introduced by Johann Georg Dorsch (1597–1654). The *consensus quinquesaecularis* became a leading concept in the unification attempts of the modern Ecumenical Movement. However, this kind of primitivism overlooks the controversies of the first five centuries and assumes a golden age with a consensus that never existed. LG

whether it be the return to a liturgy, to obedience over against an office, to an old constitution of the church, or to activity in the life of the congregation, or whatever else one might mention—for the Lutheran, going home to the church, whatever else it might mean, means returning to the confession of our fathers.

This reflection upon the church's confession in the Evangelical churches of Germany, which is often inconceivable or even offensive to Christians of other confessions, coincides in our time with the greatest movement toward unification ever experienced in the history of the church. "The call for unity" was the first topic of discussion at the World Conference on Faith and Order at Lausanne in 1927. And it reverberates mightily today through all Christendom, particularly through churches in the English-speaking countries. While Lutheranism, especially German Lutheranism, asks about one's confession, the rest of Protestantism asks about unity. The great question regarding the church among us is the question about one's confession. In the English-speaking churches the question about the church assumes the form of a longing for unification. In view of the soul-corrupting errors in the lies bewitching the church, we in Germany have come to understand that the eternal High Priest prays for his church: "Sanctify them in your truth; your Word is truth" (John 17:17). Anglican and Reformed Christendom in the world today concentrates upon the other petition of the high priestly prayer: "That they all may be one" (John 17:21). Today the theologians of our church lament to the very depths of their souls the apostasy from pure doctrine for which we all take responsibility. The theologians of those churches lament what they call the sin of division. For us true repentance in the church means becoming serious again about the confession of our church. For those churches this is proof of unrepentance, of stubbornness, of a new, evil defection from the true church of Christ. After all, he prayed, "That they all may be one," and therefore does not want the division but the unity of his disciples.

PART 2[18]

Only a few theologians in Germany have any real conception of the extent and influence of the *movement of unification* which today has enveloped Christendom outside of Europe. It is a result of the expansion of Christendom over the whole earth by the migrations of the Caucasian race and by world missions of the nineteenth and twentieth centuries. In the age of Napoleon, Christianity was still a

---

[18] Part 2, the continuation of this essay published in the July 6, 1937, issue of *Korrespondenzblatt für die Geistlichen in Bayern* (vol. 62, no. 27) is prefaced by the following citation from Bezzel:

> Believe you me, when testimony can no longer be given to the Gospel, then a burning, terrible thirst will pass among the people, and no one will be able to quench it. Great deserts will cover wide areas and no spring will refresh them. Heaven will become brazen and earth will harden, and the elements of life will turn themselves into as many powers of death. . . . A folk does not die from repentance but from its idols. A congregation does not die from the seriousness which it is offered but from the worship of people to which it succumbs. LG

European religion. The European countries were the stage upon which church history was enacted. Across the world's oceans there were daughter congregations and daughter churches of the European territorial churches. There were remnants of the Roman Catholic mission churches from the great period of Spanish and Portuguese colonization. And there were the beginnings of Protestant mission churches. The churches in the young United States of America were the most important manifestation of church life across the oceans. But they were small and confined to the Eastern seaboard of America.

Then in the nineteenth century the Caucasian race experienced rapid expansion over vast unpopulated areas of the earth, and this resulted in the expansion of the churches in these same places. If someone were to ask me what I thought was the most significant accomplishment in the history of the church in the nineteenth century, I should be inclined to answer thus: the building of the church in America. I would assign to second place the completion of the building of the Roman Catholic Church into a worldwide entity, and in third place the building of the Anglican Communion.

But this means that the most important events of church history, and especially those that are particularly significant for the future, have taken place outside of European Christianity. One can observe in the history of the individual confessions just how the influence of their non-European churches is growing. One hundred years ago, Lutheranism in America was simply a European mission in diaspora. Today, though along with the decline of the German language it has lost the German Bible of Luther, it has become the strongest column of Lutheran churchdom. The world-encompassing church of the Methodists started as a church in America. Since 1867, when the worldwide Lambeth Conference of Anglican bishops was established, the Anglicans of the United States and Canada have provided the most important stimuli to the conservative and stodgy state Church of England. Only a specialist could tell us how extensively the church politics of the Vatican today are influenced by considerations from other parts of the world. But it is obvious to anyone interested that an excellent foundation has been laid for winning Asians to Roman Catholicism.

This fact of the expansion of the various denominations over the whole earth has had very important consequences for their relationships to each other. Germany, on a smaller scale, experienced a great dispersion during the Napoleonic age when territorial boundaries were altered and thus began the formation of confessionally mixed regions. Meanwhile, the total population increased by almost forty million people, and great migrations within our country further interspersed the confessions. Christianity throughout the world has experienced a similar phenomenon on greater scale. The confessional distribution of Christianity followed geographical lines in an age which held to the principle of "he who has the rule determines the religion" (*cujus regio, ejus religio*)[19]—a say-

---

[19] Although this Latin phrase was not expressly included in the Religious Peace of Augsburg, 1555, that

ing which, as is well known, applied also in America until well into the eighteenth century. This has all increasingly subsided in the past generation. It has completely ended in the lands of immigration where the confessions are no longer contained within certain territories. For us Europeans, a church belongs to a province and a confession is part and parcel of the history of the country. But when Presbyterians from Scotland, Reformed from Zurich and Duisburg, Lutherans out of Lübeck and Stockholm, Roman Catholics from Würzburg and Milano all live together in a suburb of Chicago, when their children go to the same schools and become citizens of a new nation, then the confessional differences take on a different meaning than they have in Europe.

About ten years ago, the *Forum*, a respected American monthly, presented a series of religious confessions under such titles as "Why I Am a Catholic," "Why I Am a Lutheran," and so forth. If I had to give an answer to the question of why I am a Lutheran, then in all honesty I would have to reply in this way: Because in 1624 my ancestors lived in a territory in which the feudal lord had decided in favor of Lutheran teaching. This is why I am a Lutheran today, and indeed, a very deeply convinced Lutheran. This power of history, which is revealed in our confessional affiliation, is unknown in those other countries. The events of the sixteenth century, the men of the Reformation age and their writings are still an active force among us. In Nuremberg or in Augsburg, the stones themselves bear witness to the history which Christ's church experienced in those cities where decisions of faith were rendered which are still operative after hundreds of years. These events are as remote for the Christian in America as the events of Nicaea and Constantinople, Ephesus and Chalcedon are for the average Christian in Germany today. Therefore the confessions necessarily have a different meaning when they are removed from their native soil and placed amid the motley abundance and the chaotic confusion found in the new lands of the immigrants. A person cannot permanently remain a Lutheran in America just because he came from Hanover. He will remain a Lutheran only because he confesses the teachings of the Lutheran Church.

This explains why the Roman Catholics, the Anglicans, the Lutherans, and the strict Presbyterians—a minority within Reformed Christianity—have a sharply stamped confessional consciousness. The Lutherans in America are much stronger "confessionalists" than their fellow believers in Europe. And that third of the Presbyterian Church in Canada which did not participate in the union with the Methodists and the Congregationalists in 1925[20] has become a growing con-

---

treaty established the principle that the religion of a citizen should be determined by the religious preference of his ruler. This peace was a victory for the Lutheran Church because it officially recognized the Augsburg Confession and gave tolerance to rulers who held to it. LG

[20] Sasse is referring to the creation of the United Church of Canada in 1925, which was made up of Congregationalists, Methodists, and Presbyterians. After a controversy, the latter denomination split, with two-thirds joining the United Church of Canada and one-third remaining as a separate Presbyterian Church in Canada. LG

science for the Presbyterian churches of other English-speaking areas, for example, for the Church of Scotland. Consequently, the churches which are in a position to gather people around a certain doctrine—among the Anglicans this is no
longer the teaching of the Thirty-nine Articles but instead a reform Catholicism
based on the dogmas of the ancient church—are more and more defining themselves as confessional churches.

On the other hand, among the churches which no longer possess the unify-
ing bond of doctrine—and this includes the majority of Protestant communions—confessional consciousness is increasingly disappearing. They are the field
upon which the unionism and syncretism of modern Protestantism flourishes.
The official religious statistics of the United States list more than two hundred
denominations. Nearly one hundred different denominations carry on mission
work in China. It would be a mistake to describe these denominations as confessions. Many of them have no particular or distinctive doctrines of their own at all.
They have their origins in the confessions of the sixteenth and seventeenth centuries: from the Anglicans, from the Puritans, from the Baptists, and later from
the Methodists. We cannot describe in detail here this complicated ecclesiastical
world. But this is the world from which that mighty longing for unification proceeds. This is the world which is compelled to bring about unification.

We must be clear about two things in judging these at-times illusionary unification ideas and unification plans. First, we must note that the frightful fragmentation of Christianity outside Europe is the fault of European Christianity.
For these divisions are basically those of European Christianity which have been
transferred to other parts of the world. But they develop differently there because
the churches and denominations there are no longer divided by geographical
boundaries. Second, it is quite clear that no theological objection against frivolous
unions as they are consummated in the world today—whether raised by
Lutherans on a worldwide basis or the Lutheran and Reformed theologians on
the European continent—can change anything of the reality of these unions or
halt the great melting process.

For example, in a small town in South Dakota for many years the Methodist,
Baptist, and Presbyterian congregations have joined together in a federation and
now have only one pastor. Each year they alternate between a Methodist, Baptist,
and Presbyterian pastor. Elsewhere Quakers, who are not baptized, are pastors in
a Methodist congregation today and tomorrow officiate in a Baptist church. Lay
people, like the pastors, fluctuate from one church to another. In light of all of
this we must ask them this question: "What becomes of the church's doctrine?"
To this we would receive the simple answer: "Yes, but what else should we do?
Already for purely economic reasons it is impossible for every one of these
denominations to maintain its ecclesiastical apparatus." In the Great Depression
of recent years, thousands of congregations in America collapsed financially. In
order to salvage at least something, one local union after another was formed. "At
least the churches still stand and preaching still goes on," they say. But one can

well imagine what is preached in such churches. Thus the vicissitudes that every church which abandons its doctrinal substance faces are inexorably taking place in these Protestant churches. At first, it appears to be a liberation from the dead letter of dogmatics. One comforts oneself with the thought that one still has that living Christianity which is present in all confessions. Sermons are not dogmatic, but practical. But practical preaching means preaching ethics. Moral preaching, however, becomes preaching of the Law, and the Gospel disappears.

To find out where this leads, we hardly need look as far as syncretistic aberrations such as pulpit exchanges between churches and synagogues. It can be seen already at the highest levels of modern American Christianity, for example, in the great missionaries that Methodism has produced. At the great interconfessional missions conference which was sponsored by the Federal Council of the Churches of Christ this winter in America, one of the most famous missionaries, the renowned E. Stanley Jones[21]—some of his books about India have been translated into German—delivered a moving appeal to American Christianity to acknowledge Christ as its Lord and to obey his commandments. He said that America must decide between Fascism, Bolshevism, and the kingdom of God upon earth, that is, the establishment of a people's order of righteousness and love—which should then be God's kingdom on earth. And what if this order should not come to pass? What if the power of sin has not yet been broken? What if the coming of God's kingdom does not depend upon our will? Then, only the two other possibilities remain: Fascism or Bolshevism. What has become of the Gospel here! When we recall the periods in the history of our own church when the dogmatic substance of Christendom had been hollowed out to this degree, then we can only hope that this type of Christianity may quickly be granted an awakening. Nothing less will be needed for it to clearly understand why the one petition in the high priestly prayer, "That they all may be one," is inseparably connected with the other, "Sanctify them in your truth!" There must be an awakening which arouses a hunger and thirst for pure doctrine.

SECTION 3

Eighty years ago August Vilmar asserted in his *Theology of Reality* [*Theologie der Tatsachen*] that no article of Christian doctrine or life has been discussed more diligently in recent times than the article concerning the church. And he added the following prophecy:

> Suffice it to say, we must now experience and learn something which up to this point has not been experienced and learned. It is the unmistakable mark of these times, in so far as fellowship in Christianity is concerned, especially in the Evangelical [Lutheran] Church. By the power of eternal mercy it wres-

---

[21] Eli Stanley Jones (1894–1973), whose *Christ of the Indian Road* (1925) was translated into twenty languages. RF

tles for a new birth out of the maternal bosom of Christianity. And because it cannot happen any other way, it wrestles with violent pain to free itself for those things in which eternal mercy has taken its form. In the same way, the reality of the true divinity of the Son and of the true divinity of the Holy Ghost and the appropriation of salvation given by him have been experienced with great distress in contemporary Christianity, and in the same way the crucifixion and resurrection of the Lord have come out as the facts from which all others flow as out of a common source, together with most violent pains experienced by the holy apostles in the reality of this world.[22]

Nowhere else is the deepest meaning of the epoch of church history in which we live so deeply recognized and so wonderfully expressed as here. For since the late 1820s, when the theology of all confessions again began to ask, "What is the church?" (*quid sit ecclesia*), the doctrine of the church has been the chief topic of theology. We have seen how the quest for the one true church of God rings throughout Christianity today. It sounds forth as the most profound question of existence itself in the churches of the Old and the New World, as the quest for truth and for the unity of the church. We hear this question expressed on the mission fields in the scorn of people who see our fragmentation and ask us where the church is in all this. But we also see it expressed in the profound longing of lost humanity for salvation which is found in the church of God. We hear this question expressed in the perplexity of the statesmen of all nations who, in a time of world revolutions, stand before the riddle of the church. We hear the question regarding the church of God arising as a worldwide concern born of the attacks of the old evil foe against the church, which is the "pillar and foundation of the truth." We hear the question regarding the one, true church of God as the people of our folk, the members of our congregations, turn to us as pastors and seek answers. We hear how theologians of other confessions address this question to us Lutheran theologians. What do we have to say to these questions directly addressed to us?

We have, above all, one thing to say. Only the person who takes seriously the question of the *one* church and the question of the *true* church can understand the church of God. Modern Protestantism failed, during the eighteenth and nineteenth centuries, to take these questions with complete seriousness. It was not troubled by the fact that there were many churches. If the church was essentially only a human religious fellowship, as it reasoned, must there not be many churches, in view of the different natures, needs, and ways people think? Nor was it dis-

---

[22]   Vilmar, *Die Theologie der Tatsachen wider die Theologie der Rhetorik* (1856), 48. HS

August Friedrich Christian Vilmar (1800–1868) led a very checkered career as a noted scholar and writer in literature and history, as an active politician participating in the government of Hesse, as a superintendent in the State Church of Hesse, and, in his later years, as professor of theology at the University of Marburg. Vilmar, who moved from the rationalism of his youth to becoming a strict Lutheran, had a high view of the pastoral office through which, by Word and Sacrament, God granted salvation. The task of the pastors was "to lead their flocks to eternal blessedness" (Vilmar, *Dogmatik: Akademische Vorlesungen* [ed. K. W. Piderit; Gütersloh: C. Bertelsmann, 1874], 3). LG

turbed that the churches taught differently. If what churches teach simply amounts to people expressing their opinions about God and his revelation, then these teachings will necessarily be very diverse. How different it was at the time of the Reformation and during that often-scolded period of Orthodoxy! The sixteenth and seventeenth centuries knew something about the church because they took seriously the question of the one church. They knew that there can only be *one* church because the church is the body of Christ. They took just as seriously the question concerning the true church. Because the church's doctrine was for them testimony to the one revelation, because it was the correct exposition of the Bible, they could not therefore come to terms with the notion that there should be many and entirely diverse doctrines in the church. Every page of our confessions bears witness to how seriously they took the question of unity and the question of truth. For our fathers at the time of the Reformation the *one* church was not, like it was for the idealistic theologians of the nineteenth century, a "Platonic republic" (*civitas Platonica*):

> We do not speak of an imaginary church which is nowhere to be found, but we speak and know it to be true that this church, in which the saints live, truly is and remains upon the earth, namely, that some children of God are found here and there in all the world, in all kingdoms, islands, countries, and cities, from the rising of the sun to the going down thereof, who have rightly acknowledged Christ and the Gospel. And we say that this same church has these outward signs: the preaching office or Gospel and the Sacraments. And this same church is actually, as Paul says, a pillar of the truth [1 Tim 3:15], for it retains the pure Gospel, which is the true foundation. (Apology VII/VIII 20, German)

Only a total ignorance which knows neither Luther nor the confessions could have falsely ascribed to Lutheranism the view that it confines the true church to its own confessional boundaries.[23] Perhaps no other confession has gone so far as Lutheranism in recognizing the true church in other confessions. It knows that the pope is the antichrist—today we would only add this: not only the pope in

---

[23] Neither the Eastern churches claim that for themselves, nor even, strictly speaking, does the Church of Rome. Cyprian's statement that "outside the church there is no salvation" (*extra ecclesiam nulla salus*) stood in epistle 73 in a context where the validity of heretical baptism was questioned [see Saint Cyprian, *Letters (1–81)* (vol. 51 of *The Fathers of the Church: A New Translation*; trans. Sister Rose Bernard Donna, C.S.J.; Washington, D.C.: Catholic University of America Press, 1964), 282]. And, as Cyprian understood it, the statement was rejected by the Roman Church. With the recognition of the validity of baptism by heretics, it was basically decided that the church existed also outside the organization of the Roman Church. The famous controversial question of whether or not heretics belonged to the church was usually answered by Roman theology in the sense that they belonged to the "soul" but not the "body" of the church. The Roman Church is very generous, yes, much more generous than the Lutheran Church, in answering the question of the connection of the heathen with the church. The faith which is needed for salvation is not "catholic faith," and, as a Dominican explained it to the Section on Sacraments at the World Conference on Faith and Order, baptism does not need to be a baptism "in reality" (*in re*) but can be replaced by a baptism "of intention" (*in voto*). However, this concept could be stretched so far that every inclination of a heathen toward God, as he is revealed to him through the natural light of reason, could be understood in this sense. HS

Rome but other "popes" as well—but it knows that the abomination of desolation stands in the holy place of God, in the true church. It knows that the true body of the Lord is present in the Eucharist also in St. Peter's in Rome and that sins are also forgiven there and that in Holy Baptism souls are born again unto eternal life. "And the holy church is present among the fanatics" (*et sancta ecclesia est apud Schwermeros*) Luther could say, "except for those who deny Baptism, the external Word" (*exceptis qui negant baptismum, verbum externum*).[24] This is the reason why our church basically has never sent missionaries to Madrid or England. Even where, for the sake of eternal truth, it must unflinchingly judge falsehood, it has never claimed that Christians, among whom these errors are found, no longer belong to the Lord Christ or that they are even the devil's churches.

If anyone does not want to believe the celebrated words of the preface to the Formula of Concord, let him read the review by the Wittenberg faculty of over a thousand pages in 1664—"That the Calvinistic errors affect the foundation of the faith and are damaging to salvation"—or that which Abraham Calov[25] wrote about the meaning of the condemnations in the ancient church and in the confessions. To be sure, these old theologians took very seriously the question of truth and error in the understanding of the Gospel. They made no concessions to error, not even for the sake of the greatest earthly reward. Therefore they never yielded to the temptation which the Lutheran Church has faced ever and again in the course of its history. From 1529 until 1929 this temptation was connected with the name "Marburg," with the intent of achieving a common front of all "Evangelicals" or "Protestants" against Rome and so-called "Catholicism."[26] But we Lutherans would have to join such a "common front" with the so-called "Evangelicals" with both eyes closed. We Lutherans along with Luther certainly judge Rome more sharply than we do modern Protestantism. We know what the word "antichrist" means. But we fail to see why fanaticism [*Schwärmertum*] should be less dangerous today than four hundred years ago!

The position of our church over against the other confessions rests upon an unshakable faith in the *una sancta* ["one holy (church)"] as a reality in history and upon an uncompromising advocacy for the pure teaching of the Gospel. Therefore we see it as a prerequisite for all unification that the great confessions once more gather around the teachings of their own confessional documents. The majority of the denominations which separated from one another over small differences will disappear, but the large confessions will have to reunite and struggle

---

[24]   Cf. WA 40¹.71.6–7; *LW* 26:25.

[25]   Abraham Calov (1612–1686) was a chief proponent of confessional Lutheran orthodoxy against the syncretists of his day. RF

[26]   Sasse is, of course, referring to the Marburg Colloquy of 1529, in which Luther debated with Zwingli over the doctrine of the Lord's Supper. The debate showed the irreconcilability of Luther's doctrine, "This is my body," with Zwingli's doctrine, "This is not my body." A fine presentation of Marburg is given by Hermann Sasse in *This Is My Body: Luther's Contention for the Real Presence in the Sacrament of the Altar* (Minneapolis: Augsburg, 1959), especially 187–94. See also Lowell C. Green, "What Was the True Issue at Marburg in 1529?" *The Springfielder* 40 (September 1976):102–6. LG

over a new relationship to each other. The difficult experiences which the churches of all confessions have had in the battle against the enemies of the Christian faith cannot detract from the importance of doctrinal differences.

However, these experiences have changed the relationships of the churches to one another. This is proven by the call to establish a fellowship of the churches (κοινωνία τῶν ἐκκλησιῶν) which the ecumenical patriarch of Constantinople sent to all of Christendom in 1920. The ecumenical work of recent times has its foundation in these experiences. The meeting of the churches in the Ecumenical Movement has shown that there is a common possession of faith among all those who confess the great dogmas of the ancient church. Modern experts in the history of dogma and symbolics have not gotten it right (e.g., as Harnack presented it in his paper on the *Consensus quinquesaecularis*[27] ["Consensus of the First Five Centuries"], delivered before the Stockholm World Council).[28] They have maintained that these seemingly commonly held confessions are explained completely differently in the various churches, and therefore there is no longer any bond of unity. Although we in no way want to deny the differences, we confess the sentence in the Smalcald Articles that there is no quarrel or controversy over the lofty article of divine majesty among those who accept the symbols of the ancient church [SA, part 1]. Whoever denies this must then go a step farther with Harnack to the denial of the church altogether and prove that there is no church but only churches and that it would be better not to use the confusing word at all any more.

The significance of the consensus between the churches of various confessions which exists in the heritage of faith from the ancient church has been experienced anew by modern Christianity at the ecumenical conferences. Of course, this consensus is not sufficient for a reunion, as the Anglicans have learned. But it does open the possibility of an association of the churches in the form of church federations, and it creates the prerequisite for continuing the great debates among the confessions over questions which have remained controversial since the sixteenth and seventeenth centuries. We do not know how these discussions will end, what fruit they may produce, or what possible forms cooperation among the churches might take. But all depends upon our taking the question of unity and the question of truth just as seriously as our fathers in the sixteenth century. This means that we understand why the two petitions in the high priestly prayer belong together: "Sanctify them in your truth; your Word is truth" and "That they all may be one." We do not know how and when the unity of the church in the world will become visible. We only know that the merciful High Priest brings these petitions before his heavenly Father and that God will fulfill them—in his way and in his time.

---

[27] See the note on George Calixtus above. RF

[28] The First Universal Christian Conference on Life and Work, 1925. RF

1938

Church and Lord's Supper

AN ESSAY ON THE UNDERSTANDING
OF THE SACRAMENT OF THE ALTAR[1]

When Sasse finished this essay in the spring of 1938, it was as if he were writing for the events taking place more than half a century in the future. How timely his words are today. He related the story of the essay in a letter to his friend Herman Preus in 1956:

> In Germany during the church struggle, when the Confessing Church[2] under Reformed leadership had decided that there was no longer any hindrance to inter-Communion between Lutherans and Calvinists, I had to fight the battle with a small band of friends. I brought out *Kirche und Herrenmahl.*[3]

---

[1] This work originally appeared as *Kirche und Herrenmahl: Ein Beitrag zum Verständnis des Altarsakraments* (Bekennende Kirche 59/60; ed. Christian Stoll together with Georg Merz and Hermann Sasse; Munich: Chr. Kaiser, 1938). RF

[2] The Confessing Church was the group of Evangelical Christians "most actively opposed to the German Christian Church Movement," the Nazi-sponsored and -promoted church, between 1933 and 1945. It grew out of the "Pastors' Emergency League" founded in November 1933 by Martin Niemöller.

> In 1934, the Church opposition began to set up its own canonical authorities (esp[ecially] the Councils of the Brethren, the *Bruderräte*) at all levels in those regions where the official administration was "German Christian"; the Synod of Barmen in May 1934 issued the Barmen Declaration which laid the foundation for subsequent resistance to all attempts to make the Evangelical Churches an instrument of Nazi policy. Persecution of clergy and laity failed to prevent the opposition of the Confessing Church until the outbreak of War in 1939 brought open resistance to an end. Many of the younger confessional pastors were conscripted and fell in battle.

> At the end of the War, in 1945, leaders of the Confessing Churches met a delegation of the Provisional World Council of Churches under G. K. A. Bell in Stuttgart and made to them a "Declaration of Guilt." This action opened the way to a restoration of fellowship between the German Churches and the World Council of Churches, which gave considerable assistance to the Confessing Church. (ODCC, 394)

Sasse attempted to work with the Confessing Church in its earliest formation, but he was unable to sign the Barmen Declaration because it represented a significant compromise of the Lutheran doctrine of the real presence. For the sake of conscience in this matter, Sasse protested. His protest met with considerable scorn, and so he faced the disdain of both the Nazi party as well as the leaders of the Confessing Church. JS

[3] Sasse to Herman Preus (March 22, 1956); archives of the American Lutheran Church, St. Paul, Minn. RF

Other events in 1938 were to overshadow the debate at hand between confessional Lutheranism and the Reformed. The book appeared in dramatic circumstances, political as well as ecclesiological. To another correspondent, Sasse wrote this in 1956:

> We had the same situation in Germany when in 1937 one of the Confessing Synods decided that henceforth there could not be any reason for refusing altar fellowship with the Reformed. At that time, I began to write on the subject, since I was one of the founders of what then was called "the Confessing Church." In 1938, I brought out *Kirche und Herrenmahl*. I wrote it while the troops were marching past my house to "liberate" Austria or Czechoslovakia. I do not quite remember which. At any rate, it was a time when we had to hurry.[4] The book was quickly sold. Another edition was demanded, but Karl Barth, whose books appeared with the same publisher at Munich (Kaiser) did not like to see a definitely Lutheran publication appearing again in this house.[5]

The manuscript was at the printer by May. Sasse later considered this work to have been superseded in various ways by his book *This Is My Body*, published in 1959. That too was published in an urgent awareness that the distinction between Lutheran and Reformed sacramental theology was being eroded or ignored in North America. He believed that all the material contained in *Kirche und Herrenmahl* was incorporated in the 1959 book. Some, however, profess a preference for Sasse's earlier writings on the Sacrament, including his essays in *Vom Sakrament des Altars*, 1941, a collection of essays which he also edited.

But this essay is not only about the Sacrament of the Altar. It is also about the church—that "basic question facing all theology in all confessions." That is one of the reasons why this essay is still timely today. He speaks of the church under the cross, in all of its dependence on and relationship to the Sacraments. The church cannot be understood without an understanding of the Sacraments. For that matter, neither can the Word of God be understood. Here, then, he talks about all the things essential to a description of the church: Gospel, preaching, absolution, Sacraments. Here we find his exposition of that marvelous statement of Luther on preaching, *Haec dixit Dominus*, "God himself has said this." On the other hand, there can be bad preaching; thus it is comforting to hear that while "Christ can be forgotten in preaching, he cannot be forgotten in the Supper."

This essay, as implied in the title, is an exposition of how the church and the Sacrament of the Altar are interconnected and why altar fellowship is church fellowship and vice versa. Indeed, so many things are interrelated: "The firm handing on of doctrine within Christendom is simply inconceivable apart from the liturgical handing on of the Sacrament."

---

[4] The so-called Austrian *Anschluss* ("consolidation, joining together") took place in March 1938; the invasion of Czechoslovakia twelve months later. RF

[5] Sasse to R. E. Haugan (general manager of Augsburg Publishing House, Minneapolis; December 30, 1956); archives of the American Lutheran Church, St. Paul, Minn. RF

Could it be today, as Sasse observes in 1938, that "pastors simply no longer have any clear dogmatic convictions about the Sacrament of the Altar [but] content themselves with wavering subjective opinions that they choose according to personal taste and practical needs from that well-stocked warehouse of fashionable theological goods . . . since the time of . . . Friedrich Schleiermacher." Given the practices relating to the Lord's Supper reported today, it seems so. For those pastors—and laity—who wish to correct that weakness, this essay can be of great benefit. For all readers, Sasse states the confessional Lutheran view of the church and Lord's Supper in a clear, right, and beneficial manner.

Above all, Sasse here urges the importance of Luther's contention for the Sacrament and why "for Luther the struggle to preserve the Sacrament of the Altar as Christ instituted it and the struggle for the pure doctrine of the Gospel are one and the same struggle."

Huss number 189
Hopf number 121

—⟨∞⟩—

PART 1: THE QUESTION OF THE CHURCH

Suffice it to say that the unmistakable sign of the times for the communion of holy Christendom, and in the first instance for the Lutheran Church, is that we are now about to *live* and *learn* things that have hitherto not yet been lived and learned. By the power of eternal mercy, a new birth is struggling loose from Christendom's maternal womb, and those in whom eternal mercy has taken shape cannot undergo this struggle without violent pain. The facts of the true Godhead—of the Father, of the Son, and of the Holy Spirit—of the Son's true manhood, and of the appropriation of the salvation bestowed by him were likewise ascertained amidst the most violent pains of temporal Christendom. Just so the crucifixion and resurrection of the Lord, as the facts whence all these others flow, as from their common source, stepped forth into this world's reality and experience to the accompaniment of the most holy apostles' violent pains (John 16:21–22).[6]

---

[6] August Vilmar, *Die Theologie der Tatsachen wider die Theologie der Rhetorik* (4th ed.; 1876), 49–50. HS

August F. C. Vilmar (1800–1868), professor at the University of Marburg in Hesse, had a considerable influence on Sasse. He converted from Rationalism and from the Reformed Church to Lutheranism and became a leader of the confessional renewal movement in Germany. "In apocalyptic interpretation of history he predicted the downfall of his nation as a result of its apostasy from the living God and its unconcealed rejection of his law. . . . Clinging firmly to the Lutheran Confessions," he rejected "every false kind of unionism" (Friedrich Wilhelm Hopf, "Vilmar, August Friedrich Christian," *The Encyclopedia of the Lutheran Church* [ed. Julius Bodensieck; Minneapolis: Augsburg, 1965], 2442). JS

Sasse wrote an introduction to a reprint of the third edition of Vilmar's *Die Theologie der Tatsachen*. It was reprinted as the second volume in the series Stimmen der Väter ["Voices of the Fathers"] (Erlangen: Martin Luther-Verlag, 1938); Sasse's introduction was on pages 4–8. During this period (ca. 1937–1944),

With these prophetic words, in 1856, August Vilmar foretold an age of Christendom similar to the fourth and sixteenth centuries when questions about Christ's divinity and about justification stirred the church at the deepest levels of her life. The pivotal issues of this coming age would do more than top the agenda of theological scholarship. Along with the indissolubly related questions of the pastoral office and church government, and of the Sacraments and their relationship to the preaching of the Word, the question of the church would most profoundly affect the Christian congregation. Whatever we may make of Vilmar's notion of the epochs of church history, his prophecy has come true in our time.

The luminously splendid sunset of the 1800s occurred a generation ago in those outwardly happy years between the turn of the century and the outbreak of World War I. At that time, an educated German shuddered at the mere mention of the word "church," even if he still professed Christianity. For we learned from Harnack[7] that Protestantism could manage perfectly well without the church! Indeed, the whole meaning of church history since the Reformation seemed to be the liberation of Christianity from its imprisonment in the church. The trouble with Protestantism was thought to be the sixteenth century's historically understandable failure to effect this liberation. For a variety of psychological, national, and pedagogical reasons, it could be realized in the early twentieth century only to the extent that the mature adult Protestant could make the personal decision to forego churchgoing. For "the soul's solitude with her God is religion in the sense of Protestantism" (Heinrich Scholz).[8] In complete harmony with the *Weltanschauung* ["philosophy of life"], significant thinkers such as Harnack and Troeltsch[9] wanted the "misleading" expression "church" completely banned from

---

in addition to contributing introductions to works by Vilmar, Sasse also gave lectures on Vilmar (1943) and his doctrine of the holy office (1944). RF

[7] Karl Gustav Adolf von Harnack (1851–1930) was one of the great classical liberal theologians at the turn of the twentieth century, whose approach to Christianity was reduced to the maxim "The fatherhood of God and the brotherhood of man." He regarded the rise of Christian dogma as an aberration in the church's history and attributed it to the Greek influence in the church and thus considered it a distortion of genuine Christianity.

Harnack was one Sasse's professors at Berlin. When Harnack died, Sasse observed that he was the last great proponent of the theological liberalism that perished during World War I. Sasse compared the work of the nineteenth-century and early twentieth-century classical liberal theologians like Harnack to children who are playing outside and do not realize the sun is setting. In Sasse's later years, when lecturing on Adolf von Harnack and Karl Holl, he was reduced to tears, recalling how much he admired these men, yet lamenting how much damage they had done to the church with their theological theories. JS

[8] Heinrich Scholz (1884–1956) was a student of Harnack. He was influenced by the higher critic Rudolf Otto, who attempted to reconstruct the life and work of Jesus according to the precepts of higher criticism. Later in his career he was influenced heavily by Karl Barth and A. N. Whitehead (*Lutheran Cyclopedia*, 704). JS

[9] Ernst Peter Wilhelm Troeltsch (1865–1923) was a leading figure in the *Religionsgeschichtliche Schule* (the History of Religion School of thought), a term that was invented in 1904 to describe a nineteenth- and early twentieth-century school of thought that placed great emphasis on the historical and geographical environment of Christianity, oftentimes at the expense of scriptural truth. Troeltsch eventually became professor of systematic theology and concluded his career as a professor at Berlin. He was one of Sasse's professors. JS

theological discourse. For the men of this time, including the clergy themselves, the *pastoral office* was a source of embarrassment. There was a complete lack of understanding that this office might exist in the world for purposes other than giving its occupant the opportunity to communicate the ideas a superior education had given him about God and the world. By thus publicizing his views "to the city and the world" [*urbi et orbi*],[10] rather than keeping them to himself, he would bring about the religious enlightenment of the people and, as he thought, educate them. This church, which had turned into world, this "Christian world,"[11] as it called itself without noticing the irony of this catch phrase, tolerated the *Sacraments* in much the same way, and with no greater seriousness than it did the ceremonies of its Masonic lodges—that is, as antique symbols and piously guarded remnants of a past age. Belief that something happens in *Baptism* and that God gives something in the *Holy Supper* was regarded by this generation as an old-fashioned superstition.[12] People were firmly convinced that nothing else takes place in *confession* and *absolution* than when I recite Goethe's "Thou who art from heaven"[13] and thereupon grant absolution to myself, recalling this poet's observation that a man cannot live without having daily acquittal conferred on himself and others. This Christianity, bereft of church, ministry, and Sacraments, had completely lost the meaning of the Third Article, along with all that it says of the Holy Spirit, the communion of saints, the daily forgiveness of sins, and the resurrection of the body.

Today, this churchless "Christianity" has perished. Apart from a few stalwart children so immersed in their play that they did not notice the sunset, its adherents either have returned to the church or drifted away to new religions. Issues regarded as redundant a generation ago have hereby been placed with unprecedented solemnity on Christendom's agenda. No exaggeration lurks in the statement that the basic question facing all theology in all confessions is the essence of the church. If the "century of the church" had not in our time become just as ridicu-

---

[10] These words are part of the familiar blessing given by the pope, for example, from the balcony of St. Peter's, which is intended for both the people of Rome and for all the faithful of the world (*The HarperCollins Encyclopedia of Catholicism* [ed. Richard P. McBrien; San Francisco: HarperCollins, 1995], 1290]. RF

[11] Sasse is alluding to the periodical *Christliche Welt*, whose editorial policy was similar to that of *The Christian Century* in contemporary North America. JS

[12] "The ethical truth of our religion should move us to resist the lure of compulsion to be baptized in the three names (by which is meant the names of the Father, the Son, and the Holy Spirit)." So we read in the dogmatic article on Baptism in *RGG*[1] 5:1107. HS

[13] Johann Wolfgang von Goethe (1749–1832), the great German poet, abandoned the biblical instruction he had been given by his mother and instead embraced a form of pantheism. He had a high regard for classical antiquity and was caught up in Idealism and Romanticism. He did not believe in sin and hence had no use for the Gospel of salvation through the sacrifice of Christ. His rationalistic syncretism was expressed throughout his literary works, which were highly regarded by many German theologians, who themselves were moving further and further away from orthodox Christianity throughout the nineteenth century. JS

The reference here is to Goethe's poem *Wandrers Nachtlied*, in *Goethes Werke* (ed. Eduard Scheidemantel; Berlin: Deutsches Verlagshaus Bong and Co), 1:48. RF

lous a catchword as its predecessors concerning the "monistic" and other centuries, then we might realistically speak of an age of the church. The use of such terminology would not, of course, imply that the church's cause is prospering in the world. In 1926, a writer falsely prophesied when he maintained that

> in this hour, Lutheran[14] Germany is being given a Lutheran Church in the full meaning of the word. . . . Lutheran Germany is being pulled into a worldwide movement. Forces at work in the whole of Western culture are *bearing the renovated church upward*. . . . There is something glorious in flinging oneself in the face of the storm and lifting high the flag while the assault is mounting from all sides and the little band of the faithful is continually diminishing. It is here required that discipleship of Jesus hold its own in its full original sense and that the cross be carried after the Master. But it is not, therefore, any less a grace, and an unspeakably great grace at that, to be permitted *to sacrifice oneself for a cause to which the living God is pledging himself in visible forward strides*, a cause born by the *labor pains of a new age*.[15]

Those of us who have lived through the most recent installments of church history find it incomprehensible that, just a decade ago, someone could have appraised the church's situation so perversely. Lutheran Germany has, in fact, been pulled into entirely different movements.[16] The forces at work in Western culture have done other things than bear the church upward! We cannot describe any church in the world during this period of time as having made "visible forward strides." Apart from the fact that the date of these words' public appearance marked the completion of ten years of the greatest, bloodiest, and most radical persecution known to history—a persecution that ended in the complete uprooting of ecclesiastical organization from a great segment of the earth—where can we speak of any visible progress of the church on the part of Christendom that was spared this tribulation? An increasing number of typewriters clattering away in the ecclesiastical office buildings of the world and automobile-equipped general superintendents holding ever more conferences cannot justify intoning a *Vexilla regis prodeunt* ["the royal banners forward go"]. For such increased pro-

---

[14] The word here translated "Lutheran" is *evangelisch*. It is a translator's nightmare. Carrying few of the North American connotations of "evangelical," this adjective can mean "generically Protestant" or "specifically Lutheran," depending on the user's intention. Generally, I have chosen to translate it "Lutheran." JS

[15] Sasse does not give the source of this quotation. RF

[16] For example, the "German Christians" were Protestants who attempted to bring about a synthesis between Nazism and Christianity. Their more extreme adherents wished to eliminate the OT, Paul, and the doctrines of St. Augustine and to remove from the Gospels everything that was Jewish or "servile." They believed that the "Holy Land" was not found in Palestine but in Germany and that the Law of God was embodied in Adolf Hitler. They claimed to be completing Luther's Reformation. Because they hid their more radical tendencies and were heavily promoted by the Nazis, they were able to obtain a majority of elected positions in the church in July 1933. Ludwig Müller was the most influential person in the movement and became *Reichsbischof* ["Bishop of the Reich"]. He worked to incorporate the Evangelical Youth into the Hitler Youth organization. The "Confessing Church" arose as a response to the German Christian movement, which, during World War II, controlled more than half of the territorial churches in Germany (*ODCC*, 668). RF

ductivity has not yet done anything to alter the fact that the Western peoples, in "Catholic" and "Protestant" lands alike, are drifting away more and more from the sphere of the Christian message's influence, and that church attendance and participation in Holy Communion are almost everywhere on the decline. For the process of secularization, this avalanche—which threatens to bury alive all remaining elements of ancient, inherited churchly life—is accelerating as rapidly among professedly Christian people as it is in the rest of society.

If the actual percentage of those still confessing the basic dogmas of Christianity could be ascertained by polling the "Christian" population of the West, what religious nihilism would be shown to underlie the thin veneer of Christian culture! Then there would no longer be anything mysterious about the volcanic eruptions of atheism and hatred of Christ that have for the past two centuries continually threatened the existence of the church. Then we would understand that these phenomena reveal not just the will of individual people, but rather a mighty inner fate of Western culture, which stood for many centuries under the sign of the Crucified.

How can we expect the living God to stand by his church any differently in this age than he has in all others? The fact is that he will cause judgment to come down on her, as has been his practice since the days of the NT: "For the time has come for judgment to begin with the household of God" (1 Pet 4:17 [RSV]). He will act by bringing the dear holy cross upon her. For, according to Luther's profound saying, "the holy Christian people are externally recognized by the holy possession of the sacred cross. They must endure every misfortune and persecution, all kinds of trials and evil from the devil, the world and the flesh (as the Lord's Prayer indicates) by inward sadness, timidity, fear, outward poverty, contempt, illness and weakness, in order to become like their head, Christ."[17]

If God wills to arouse his church from sleep and to call a dying pastorate and a dying church to new life, then according to all the church's experiences in the many centuries of her history, he never does so by causing her to be borne aloft to outward grandeur on the wild billows of the age. Instead, he employs his miraculous, divine manner of acting, which was understood by Luther, the theologian of the cross: *occidendo vivicat* ["by killing he makes alive"]. Looked at from the outside, Christ's victory over the world was a defeat that took the form of his dying on the cross. Seen with the eyes of the world, the ancient church's triumphal march was a string of seemingly senseless martyrdoms. The church's renewal in the Reformation occurred outwardly in the smashing of its wondrous structure and the destruction of its unity. From this perspective, the events of contemporary church history force this question: What great things must God intend for his church on earth when he so chastises and judges her, as is manifest for all to see?

---

[17] From Luther's *On the Councils and the Church* (WA 50.641.35 ff.; the English translation is taken from *LW* 41:164). JS

The very fact of this *chastisement*, this *judgment*, this outward *dying* of the church poses to us the question of her *essence* in a completely fresh way. As with every new era in the church's history, the one God in his mercy may have reserved for us is also dawning "amidst the most violent pains of temporal Christendom." Experiencing this distress is, however, the precondition for understanding the church. By taking from the church so much that we believed to be necessary for her to exist, God is teaching us to turn our gaze from nonessentials to the essentials, from minors to majors, from the many to the one thing necessary. This is a painful yet needful instruction. The churches of the West had become rich in external possessions bestowed on them by the pious of past centuries. They had a powerful position guaranteed by public law in Christian nations and states. They had great influence on humanity. The life of an ancient culture, with all of its intellectual riches and systems of education, was available to the church. Perhaps all of this is now coming to an end. Even those churches still enjoying these goods will learn in the next centuries the truth of Matthias Claudius'[18] verse:

> That we here a land inhabit
> Where rust does iron gobble,
> And brittle is the state
> Of every throne and hovel.

The most bitter, yet most necessary aspect of these experiences will be the discovery that even Christians will have their full share in the fearful *impotence* and *nothingness* of man. This may come as a severe blow to many Christians and many churches. The church's bankruptcy, which is being realized before the eyes of the astonished and mocking world, is the *bankruptcy of the pious man*, whether this man be a cardinal or a poor soldier of the Salvation Army, a confessing pastor or an orthodox bishop, a pietist who has made good progress on the path of sanctification or a devout Benedictine, a confessionalist or a unionist. Not until we have acquired this knowledge through the bitter experiences of our own hearts will we be able to understand the sole factor that causes the church to be the church: *the presence of Christ alone.* He is present in the word of his *Gospel* and in the Sacraments of *Baptism* and *Holy Communion* and calls sinners to repentance, forgives them their sins, and makes them members of his body. We can imagine the church bereft of all external and internal goods, things, and persons that she possesses. In an emergency, the church can be without pastors and bishops, without congregations, and even without us Christians, for God can at all times raise up children for Abraham out of stones [Matt 3:9]: Christ alone is indispensable to her. *Ubi Christus, ibi ecclesia* ["Where Christ is, there is the church"].[19] Because this is so, the means of grace—Word and Sacraments—are the sole marks by which we may know for sure that "here is church!" We shall not yet truly understand the

---

[18] Matthias Claudius (1740–1815) was a Lutheran layman and defender of biblical faith in the age of Rationalism (*Lutheran Cyclopedia*, 182). He was also a hymn writer. RF

[19] Ignatius, *Epistle to the Smyrnaeans* 8:2. See the essay by Sasse with this title, also in this collection. RF

church so long as we ascribe to the pious man with his thinking and doing, his believing, loving, and hoping any other role in the formation of the church than that played by a stone in the construction of a house.

Because World War I taught us "that man is nothing and he should therefore learn to despair of himself and to hope in Christ," we learned to understand something of the essence of the church, which is born of Word and Sacrament. Among other consequences of our generation's experience has been the emergence of a theology that has again inquired into the objective *Word of God*, after trials once more taught people to pay heed to the Word. This earnest effort for a new and deeper understanding of the Word must go hand-in-hand with inquiry into the *Sacrament*. This is a lesson we should learn, not only by study of the Reformation, which regarded the Word as inseparable from the Sacrament , but also by the exigencies of our deeply troubled present-day church life. It is, therefore, a gratifying sign of our time that theology has again begun to devote itself to something it neglected for generations, namely, the question of the Sacraments.

The Word of God cannot be rightly understood when the Sacraments are not understood. One who does not know that the Sacraments are more than signs—and who does not believe that God does something in Baptism and that something *happens* in the Holy Supper—will never understand that the Word of Holy Scripture and scriptural preaching are, in every instance, God's Word. When I as a pastor have baptized a child, then I know that God has said to this child with unmitigated solemnity, "I have called you by name, you are mine" [Isa 43:1 RSV].

When I as a preacher stand in the pulpit, then I must know what God's Word is.

For a preacher must not pray the Our Father nor seek forgiveness when he has preached (if he is a proper preacher), but must say and boast with Jeremiah, "Lord, you know that what has gone out of my mouth is right and pleasing to you" [Jer 17:16]. Indeed, he must defiantly say with St. Paul and all apostles and prophets, *Haec dixit Dominus* ["God himself has said this"]. *Et iterum* ["and again"], "I have been an apostle and prophet of Jesus Christ in this sermon."[20]

Speaking in this way is not tantamount to having God's Word and Spirit at one's beck and call, but it does involve believing in God's promises with unshakable certainty and not letting the least doubt peck away at the pledges he has attached to the verbal and sacramental means of grace.

The benefit of the doctrine of the Sacraments for the understanding of the Word of God is that they are the way we learn the *unconditional validity of God's*

---

[20] WA 51.517.5 ff. [cf. *LW* 41:216]. Compare these words from Luther's confession in his "Reply to the King of England's Libel" (1527):

> For the sake of my person and life I will humble myself before anyone and beg grace and favor even from a child insofar as these people are not hostile to the Gospel. For I know that if it is strictly judged, my life earns me nothing but the abyss of hell. But for the sake of my office and doctrine, and even of my life to the extent that it conforms to these, let no one—particularly not tyrants and persecutors of the Gospel—expect any patience or humility from me. For in this respect they are to regard me as a living saint. (WA 23.33.33 ff.) HS

promises and the objective nature of divine grace and the means of grace—independent of all human activity. If there should be any misunderstanding in the case of the Word of God—whether man through his hearing, obeying, willing, or doing can and must cooperate with God—where the Sacraments are concerned there can be no shred of doubt that God is the sole willing agent and that man is the sole recipient. The *blessing* of the Sacrament is indeed dependent on faith, but its *efficacy* is not. Nor is there any doubt that this efficacy goes deep into the realm of the unconscious and even of the body itself. From the Sacraments of Baptism and the Supper we learn what it means that Christ is present, that Christ is active, that Christ is at work in our life even before we know of him at the cognitive level. *Ubi Christus, ibi ecclesia*—"where Christ is, there is the church."

The following pages intend to offer a modest reflection on the Sacraments that is so needed in our day. We aim to discharge this task by pondering a specific question that is equally significant for theological scholarship and for the life of every Christian congregation: the question of the *relationship between the Lord's Supper and the church*. We shall begin with the scriptural evidence for the links that exist between the Sacrament of the Altar and the church, hoping thereby to recall to our own and others' memory some of the great truths that our fathers in the ancient church and in the Reformation knew concerning the essence of the church of God.

PART 2: LORD'S SUPPER, CHURCH, AND WORLD

The Lord's Supper occupies a special place among the means of grace, which are at the same time the marks of the church. Without setting a limit to God's mercy, the church teaches that Baptism is necessary for the salvation of each individual. This is not said of the Supper. The Word of God is necessary for salvation, for "How shall they believe in him of whom they have not heard?" (Rom 10:14). It is necessary for salvation that a person be reborn in Baptism by water and the Spirit (John 3:5; Titus 3:5). People can be saved, though, even when they have had to do without the Supper. This does not mean that the Sacrament of the Altar possesses a lesser dignity than the other means of grace, but simply that it has a different place in the life of the church. The Supper is necessary for the life of the church, for in the celebration of this Sacrament the church keeps on becoming what, according to God's will, she is meant to be. Here she becomes visible as church in a totally unique way.

Because the *Word* of God is given to the whole world, it resounds throughout the world, which is why the Christian service of the Word has been a public event open also to non-Christians, as a matter of principle, since time immemorial. *Baptism* stands at the borderline of church and world, acting either by itself or in combination with the closely associated rite of confirmation to disclose to people the inner space of the church, which is forever hidden from the gaze and understanding of the world. For, according to the teaching of the NT, the church does not belong to the cosmos. She lives in the world but is not at home in it. As has been rightly said on the basis of Phil 3:20 and Heb 13:14, the church on earth is indeed a "colony of citizens of heaven," which here languishes on alien terrain. Her foreignness becomes clear at every celebration of the Lord's Supper. As the Sacrament proper to the church, the Supper is, therefore, as a matter of principle, not a public event. Thus, the most ancient church celebrated it behind closed doors (Rev 3:20). For centuries thereafter, the arcane discipline[21] kept the liturgy and doctrine of the Supper strictly secret from Jews and pagans, which is why those writings of the NT intended for the general public, like the Gospel of John, make no mention of the Words of Institution for the Supper or, like the older text of Luke, present only an allusive report of them.[22] Hence the horror stories told in the pagan world concerning the Christians' secret worship—the eating of the flesh of the Son of Man and the drinking of his blood (John 6:53)—as ritual murder and cannibalism. The "holy kiss" (1 Cor 16:20), a part of the eucharistic liturgy, was said to be an example of unchaste behavior.

These incidents taught Christendom very soon that even at the Supper it could not entirely leave the world.[23] So while the dismissal of the unbaptized with

---

[21] Sasse is referring to the *disciplina arcana*. In the very early years of the church, when persecution was most severe, the celebration of the Lord's Supper was witnessed only by the baptized. There was justifiable fear of those who might be spies of Christian proceedings, intent on doing damage to the church and causing harm to participants in the Lord's Supper. Thus, when it came time for the celebration of the Sacrament, the catechumens and other non-baptized persons, including those who had not yet enrolled as catechumens, were dismissed from the church and the doors were closed. Then the service of the Lord's Supper was held. The Christian mysteries were reserved for those who had been baptized and had made a proven commitment to the Christian faith. JS

[22] Compare Joachim Jeremias, *Die Abendmahlsworte Jesu* (1935), 44. The early church only rarely, and only then with good cause, broke its silence concerning the Sacrament, as, for example, in chapter 66 of Justin Martyr's *First Apology*. HS

Jeremias' *Die Abendmahlsworte Jesu* is available in English translation. See Joachim Jeremias, *The Eucharistic Words of Jesus* (trans. Norman Perrin from the 3d German ed.; London: SCM Press, 1966).

In his *First Apology*, Justin Martyr wrote:

> And this food is called among us Eucharist, of which no one is allowed to partake except one who believes that the things we teach are true, and has received the washing that is for the remission of sins and for rebirth, and who so lives as Christ handed down. For we do not receive these things as common bread nor common drink; but in like manner as Jesus Christ our Savior, having been incarnate by God's Logos took both flesh and blood for our salvation, so also we have been taught that the food eucharistized through the word of prayer that is from him, from which our blood and flesh are nourished by transformation, is the flesh and blood of that Jesus who became incarnate. For the Apostles in the memoirs composed by them, which are called Gospels, thus handed down what was commanded them: that Jesus took break and having given thanks said: "Do this for my memorial, this is my body," and likewise he took the chalice and having given thanks said: "This is my blood," and gave it to them alone. Which also the wicked demons have imitated in the mysteries of Mithra and handed down to be done; for that bread and cup of water are placed with certain words said over them in the secret rites of initiation, you either know or can learn. (Justin Martyr, *The First and Second Apologies* [translated with introduction and notes by Leslie Barnard; *Ancient Christian Writers* 56; New York: Paulist Press, 1997], 70–71) JS

[23] Perhaps one of the most dramatic examples of pagan suspicions of what actually went on during Christian worship gatherings is found recorded in the writings of a third-century Latin Christian apologist who recounted what was said by a certain Cornelius Fronto, a tutor of the great Roman Stoic emperor Marcus Aurelius. The following was a claim made by pagans:

the *Ite missa est* ["Go, the Mass is ended"] long formed an interruption between the Mass of the Catechumens and the Mass of the Faithful, in the long run this and other barriers amounted to little more than a symbolical pointer to the fact that the Supper is the celebration proper to the church, in which only a genuine member of the church may participate. It occasionally transpires in modern churches that a Jew or a heathen or some other kind of unbaptized person, say a Quaker, participates in the Supper. Such a state of affairs would have struck the Christendom of the ancient and Reformation epochs as an unimaginable profanation of the Sacrament of the Altar. This is the meaning of the ancient liturgical exclamation "the holy things for the holy ones," which *Didache* 10:6 enables us to trace right back to the primitive church: "Let him who is holy step forward, let him who is not holy repent" (i.e., let him become a Christian).[24]

Here lies the reason why our church still today requires announcement for the Holy Supper. For, even if the world has a precise knowledge of the external form of this celebration, and even if it is acquainted with every word spoken in

---

A young baby is covered over with flour, the object being to deceive the unwary. It is then served to the person to be admitted into the rites. The recruit is urged to inflict blows onto it—they appear to be harmless because of the covering of flour. Thus the baby is killed with wounds that remain unseen and concealed. It is the blood of this infant—I shudder to mention it—it is this blood that they lick with thirsty lips; these are the limbs they distribute eagerly; this is the victim by which they seal their covenant. . . . On a special day they gather in a feast with all their children, sisters, mothers—all sexes and ages. There, flushed with the banquet after such feasting and drinking, they begin to burn with incestuous passions. They provoke a dog tied to the lamp stand to leap and bound toward a scrap of food which they have tossed outside the reach of his chain. By this means the light is overturned and extinguished, and with it common knowledge of their actions; in the shameless dark with unspeakable lust they copulate in random unions, all equally being guilty of incest, some by deed, but everyone by complicity. (Robert L. Wilken, *The Christians As the Romans Saw Them* [New Haven: Yale University Press, 1984], 19–20)

Apparently, the grain of truth in such stories derived from libertine Gnostic sects who may have engaged in bizarre sexual rituals and perverted the Christian Lord's Supper and misused the agape meal that accompanied it. Sasse's point here is most profound and deserves careful reflection. The very fact that Christians were accused by pagans of cannibalism and child sacrifice, because they confessed that they ate and drank the body and blood of the Son of God, is powerful testimony to the early church's determined adherence to a realistic view of the presence of Christ in the Lord's Supper. How much trouble could have been prevented if only the Christians had been able, with Zwingli and Calvin, to confess merely a representative presence of Christ, explaining that the bread is simply bread only! They chose instead to suffer the misunderstanding and mistreatment of unbelievers rather than give up the doctrine of the real presence. JS

24 Matt 7:6 was quoted from the earliest times as a biblical support for this principle. Tertullian cites this passage in chapter 5 of the second of his two books [entitled] *To His Wife*, and he does so in a context that vividly illustrates the incompatibility of the arcane discipline with a mixed marriage. HS

Tertullian wrote, "Will not your husband know what it is which you secretly taste before taking any food? And if he knows it to be bread, does he not believe it to be that which it is said to be?" (Tertullian, *To His Wife* [trans. S. Thelwall; *Ante-Nicene Fathers*; ed. Alexander Roberts and James Donaldson; repr., Grand Rapids: Eerdmans, 1982], 4:46–47).

For a more detailed discussion of the liturgical expression "the holy things for the holy ones," see especially Werner Elert, *Eucharist and Church Fellowship in the First Four Centuries* (trans. Norman Nagel; St. Louis: Concordia, 1966, repr., 1998), 219–22. JS

the liturgy and with every idea the church links with the Supper, nevertheless, by virtue of inner necessity, the Sacrament remains incomprehensible to it. This must be so, for the world can only understand those things that belong to it and obey its laws. Although it is celebrated in a particular place at a particular time with earthly elements, the Supper does not belong to this world but always remains an intrusive alien element within it. Even for this reason, the church needs the Supper. So far as we humans can judge, a church bereft of this Sacrament would be swallowed up by the world and cease to be church, just as it has in fact transpired. Whenever the Lord's Supper has been permitted to decay, the boundary lines between church and world have universally disappeared and the church has been absorbed into the world. The Supper is thus the Sacrament in which the church's "foreignness from the world," and hence her essence as church of God, finds visible expression.

PART 3: IN REMEMBRANCE OF ME

However much the various confessions' conceptions of the Supper may otherwise differ, they have all faithfully held on to one thing: Whatever else it may be, the Supper of the Lord is a *memorial meal*. On this point Zwingli's doctrine of the Supper is in agreement with the Tridentine conception of the sacrifice of the Mass as the *memoria* of Christ's sacrifice.

In the Lord's Supper, a historical event is commemorated, and how! There is no event of world history, no date of birth or death, no fact of political or intellectual history that is constantly recalled to the memory of later generations as is the crucifixion of Christ. This remembrance is preserved neither in thoughts alone, nor only through the words of the scriptural tradition and the oral proclamation, but also through the *monumentum aere perennius* ["one perennial memorial"] of the continually repeated Sacrament of the Altar. Memories fade and words lose their force, but the Sacrament of the Altar indelibly preserves in the church the remembrance of Christ's death with undiminished vividness. The Christian faith's characteristic ability to remember a salvation history that took place many centuries ago, which then brought forth Western Christian culture's distinctive knack for historical thinking, is unthinkable apart from the Supper. The firm handing on of doctrine within Christendom is simply inconceivable apart from the liturgical handing on of the Sacrament. No one can understand the essence of Christian dogma and liturgy who does not know how closely connected the apostolic admonition "Remember Jesus Christ" (2 Tim 2:8) is with the Lord's command "This do in remembrance of me" [Luke 22:19].

The fact is that the Supper commemorates a historical event and immediately renders crystal clear the way it differs from the holy meals, the communion and sacrificial celebrations of other religions. The external kinship that undoubtedly exists here, already sensed by Paul (1 Cor 10:19 ff.) and going on to become a serious apologetic problem for Justin, can never blunt our realization that the "table of the Lord" is something completely different from the "table of Lord Sarapis"[25] or any other "table of demons" (1 Cor 10:21). This point must be conceded even by the unbeliever who does not know that Jesus alone is the "Lord," the *Kyrios* of whom we sing "And there's none other God!"[26] For the sacred rites and meals of the pagan *mysteries* lack the very ingredient that makes the Sacrament of the Altar the Sacrament of Jesus Christ, namely, the remembrance of what *once* occurred in a particular place and at a particular time for the redemption of humanity (e.g., the solemn emphasis of Heb 7:27; 9:18, 28). When did the death and resurrection of Osiris[27] take place, which the Egyptian mysteries can so movingly recount? This question is utterly bereft of meaning, for, like all *myths*, the Osiris myth proclaims abstract truths, propositions of perpetual and universal validity: through death to life, through night to light, through pain to joy, through dying to new birth. This is what is proclaimed in the myths; this is what is celebrated in the mystery cults in an inner personal experience shared with the cult deity, which experiences in itself the process of dying and becoming.

The church of Christ knows nothing of all this. It is said that Christian preachers proclaim such things at Easter, Pentecost, and Christmas. These are false preachers, who should have become newspaper reporters or poets or priests of Isis. The Gospel does not speak of an eternal process of dying and becoming. It speaks of the One who as the Lamb of God died "under Pontius Pilate" [Apostles' and Nicene Creeds] before the gates of Jerusalem and rose from the dead on the third day. Simply put, everything depends on this actually having occurred in this way. "If Christ has not been raised, your faith is futile and you are still in your sins" (1 Cor 15:17 [RSV]). Absolutely everything depends on this not being a myth.

We publicly accuse all theologians who use the word "myth" to describe facts of salvation history (such as the incarnation of the eternal Son of God, his atoning death, his resurrection, and his exaltation) of distorting the Christian message. By virtue of the fact that Holy Scripture applies the expressions and images of

---

[25] "There is one Zeus, Sarapis" was the enthusiastic cry adherents of the Sarapis cult would shout out. The Sarapis cult was a combination of Greek and Egyptian gods, begun under the Hellenistic rulers of Egypt, starting with Ptolemy I. It was popular among the cultural elite of ancient Rome, who viewed it as an outgrowth of Greek culture. Feasting and special festivals were associated with the cult of Sarapis. The god Sarapis was pictured with the face of Zeus. He was believed to be a healer of the sick, a worker of miracles, and a god who was superior to fate. It was believed that he spoke to his followers in dreams. Apparently, at some of his temples, there were persons known as *katochoi* ["kept down, held fast"], who believed they could not leave the temple grounds until Sarapis set them free. JS

[26] "And there's none other God" is from stanza 2 of Luther's hymn "A Mighty Fortress Is Our God" (*Lutheran Worship* 298; *The Lutheran Hymnal* 262). RF

[27] Osiris was an Egyptian god. The Egyptians believed that people (as well as sacred animals) were identified with Osiris, hence "Osirified," in the next life. During Hellenistic times, Osiris was associated with the worship of Sarapis. In Egypt, Osiris remained the god of the underworld. As the worship of Isis spread throughout the Roman Empire, Osiris was a central figure in the liturgical and ritual drama of the Isis cult. JS

ancient mythologies to Jesus Christ, they cease to be mythology.[28] The myth of the primal man, for example, is no longer a myth when it is applied to Jesus. It has absolutely no bearing on the validity of the message of salvation taught and celebrated in a Sarapic or Mithraic cult[29] if it tells of things that really happened. In company with the truth of a poem, the "truth" of such a message holds good independently of the question of its historical authenticity. *But the saving message proclaimed in the church stands or falls with the historicity of its content.* If it is true that Jesus Christ is the eternal Son of God delivered up for our sins and raised for our justification, then and only then are we saved. In this case, though, we are really redeemed and do not need to comfort ourselves with a mere hoped-for or dreamed-up redemption.

Only from this vantage point can we thoroughly appreciate the fact that the Lord's Supper calls the "in remembrance of me" more intensely into the world than any sermon. How often has Christian preaching been unfaithful to its mandate to bear testimony to the incarnate, crucified, and risen one! Christ can be forgotten in preaching, but he cannot be forgotten in the Supper. The ego of the pious man here recedes completely, and he [Christ] alone may speak: "Our Lord Jesus Christ, on the night when he was betrayed . . ." This *designation of time* has belonged to the eucharistic liturgy since time immemorial [see 1 Cor 11:23], just as the OT prophecies often give precise indications of date (Amos 1:1; Isa. 6:1). "Under Pontius Pilate" belongs to the Creed. This historical indication of time precludes classifying the *institution narrative* simply according to its form under the History of Religion's categories of "etiological cultic account" or "cult legend."[30]

We are not dealing with a myth here, but with a report of an actual historical event. Their textual variants demonstrate that the reports of the institution have certainly not been spared the usual inconsistencies to which oral and written traditions are subjected. Looked at as a whole, though, they furnish us with as good a tradition as we possess elsewhere in the ancient history of religion. Anyone who has sharpened his eye for history through the study of the primal history of such great extrabiblical religions of the East as Parseeism, Buddhism, and Islam knows

---

[28]   No doubt Sasse has here in mind theologians such as Rudolph Bultmann whose work at "demythologizing" Christianity was intended to remove the so-called "mythical" elements of the sacred Scriptures (the miracles of Christ, etc.) in order to apply the deeper "truths" in such myths to contemporary man. Sasse was in no uncertain terms opposed to such tampering with sacred truth. His criticism here is mild compared to what he has to say, for example, in his essay entitled "Flight from Dogma: Remarks on Bultmann's 'Demythologization' of the New Testament," which he wrote in 1942. An English translation of that essay is included in this collection. JS

[29]   The worship of Mithras was a Persian mystery religion which was incorporated into various forms of Gnosticism. Mithraism and these Gnostic groups posed a significant threat to early Christianity and attracted many followers because of their elaborate rituals. See Sasse's early review of R. Reitzenstein, *Das iranische Erlösungsmyterium: Religionsgeschichtliche Untersuchungen* (1921) in *Neugreichische Jahrbücher* 3.3/4 (1922), 421–26. JS/RF

[30]   As is done in the article "Abendmahl" in *RGG*² 1:9. HS

what excellent source material is contained in the NT, its fragmentary character notwithstanding.[31]

Whatever may account for the different tradition in John and the Synoptics concerning the date of Jesus' death, no one should ever doubt that Jesus' last meal was a *Passover meal*. The highly lifelike and detailed depiction of the preparation in Mark 14:12 ff. bears the stamp of historical authenticity. Recent scholarship has demonstrated with all the certainty achievable in questions of this kind how Jesus' actions and words at that meal fit smoothly into the context of a Passover meal.[32] That Jesus distributed the bread to his disciples with the words "This is my body" (probably *den hu gufi* in his mother tongue)[33] is just as sure as the fact that the content of the cup was designated, with its slight variants, as his covenant blood shed for many (cf. Ex 24:8) [Matt 26:26–28; Mark 14:22–24; Luke 22:19–20; 1 Cor 11:24–25]. Apart from the issue of the interpretation of these words, it remains an open historical question whether the command to repeat the Supper, which is transmitted in Paul and has thence made its way into the Lucan report, while remaining absent from Matthew and Mark, goes back to Jesus himself. Should this question receive a negative reply, this command nevertheless captures his meaning, that the Lord himself really intended this action to be repeated by his disciples.[34]

Now Paul's Supper narrative is far older than the present text of the Gospels. The absence from the latter of the command to repeat the Supper may not therefore be urged as proof positive of its spuriousness. This caution is underlined by the fact that Paul expressly includes this command in the tradition he received and that he traces back to Jesus himself (1 Cor 11:23).[35] Should one nevertheless be prompted by the textual evidence of the Gospels to believe that the command to

---

[31]   Here, as elsewhere in his writings, Sasse reveals that he was well informed about Eastern religions. RF

[32]   Substantial progress has recently been made on the question of the relationship between the Supper and the Passover by Joachim Jeremias in his penetrating study *Die Abendmahlsworte Jesu* (1935), to which we hereby refer in connection with the following pages. The bases for the contemporary discussion of the problem were laid in Gustaf Dalman's work *Jesus-Jeschua* (1922). A clear overview of the current state of scholarship is offered in August Arnold's excellent (Catholic) Tübingen prize-winning essay *Der Ursprung des Christlichen Abendmahls im Lichte der neuesten liturgiegeschichtlichen Forschung* (Freiburger Theologische Studien 45; 1937). HS

      Dalman's *Jesus-Jeschua* is available in English translation. See Gustaf Hermann Dalman, *Jesus-Jeshua: Studies in the Gospels* (trans. Paul P. Levertoff; New York: Macmillan, 1929). JS

[33]   Aramaic was a Semitic language known to have existed since at least the ninth century B.C. It was used widely throughout Palestine and other Middle Eastern countries as the language of commerce and government. The Babylonian Empire used Aramaic and, thus, after the Babylonian captivity, Aramaic became the daily language of the Jews. Jesus' original Aramaic words are used in the Greek NT when some of his final words from the cross were recorded (Matt 27:46). JS

[34]   Sasse is not so much questioning the historical accuracy of the biblical text as he is engaging his contemporaries, who, by and large, had been influenced negatively by classical higher criticism to believe that the recorded words of Jesus were not necessarily historically accurate, particularly if they were not duplicated in each of the Gospels. JS

[35]   The understanding of this passage intimated above sides with Jeremias, *Die Abendmahlsworte Jesu*, 72 ff., and G. Kittel against H. Lietzmann and others who understand "I received from the Lord" in the sense of a direct revelation. The supposition that Paul was instructed on the Supper during the experience he reports in 2 Cor 12:2 ff.—hence in "the third heaven"—is found, by the way, in old Lutheran theology, but naturally not in the sense that this revelation would have stood in contradiction to the tradition. See,

repeat the Supper may not be traced back to Jesus, it still remains an open question whether Jesus understood his Supper as a once-only event, and thus merely as an anticipation of the messianic table fellowship in the kingdom of God, or as a Sacrament to be repeated by his disciples on earth.

Anyone who opts for the first answer must draw a breathtaking conclusion: Notwithstanding the fact that we are dealing with the most ancient report preserved for us in NT Scripture, the Lord's Supper as it stands before us in 1 Corinthians is, strictly speaking, not something instituted by Jesus, but a sacramental action instituted by the most ancient church on the basis of a misunderstood, although historical act of the Lord. The only justification for resorting to this sort of hypothesis would be internal reasons making it, if not absolutely proven, at any rate highly probable that Jesus could not have entertained the idea that the Supper would be repeated. The difficulties presented by the Sacrament are swept away by the simple device of getting rid of the Sacrament itself! Yet the question remains whether this solution is possible.

The conscientious historian will regard the Lord's will to institute it as the point of origin of the Christian Supper as long as two obstacles stand in the way of the radical hypothesis. First, even though it is possible that the Supper is the result of an ancient error whose venerability does nothing to shore up its claim to truth, there is the testimony of the whole church of all times. Second, we have to consider the unanimous testimony of all those people whose knowledge—whether drawn from memory or from most ancient tradition—goes back to the earliest Christian celebrations of the Supper and indeed as far back as Jesus' Supper on the night of his betrayal.[36] Never has a last will found a more comprehensive and faithful fulfillment than has Jesus' command to his disciples "This do in remembrance of me." Never has the memory of a historical event been more faithfully preserved than has the memory of "the night in which he was betrayed" in the Supper of the church.

PART 4: FOR THE FORGIVENESS OF SINS

All confessions are agreed that the Supper is a memorial of the death of Christ. This memorial of his *death* is, at the same time, also its interpretation. The death

---

for example, *Kurtz Bekentnis und Artickel vom hl. Abendmahl* . . . , produced by the Saxon theologians in Wittenberg in 1574 (p. E1). HS

[36] To reinforce the fact that there are others who share this judgment we venture to quote the beautiful and correct sentences Simon *Schöffel* writes in his article "Offenbarung Gottes im hl. Abendmahl" (*Luthertum* [1937]: 367):

Can we really imagine that primitive Christianity had so little piety toward the Most Holy that it did not hold firmly even to what happened on that last night? Can we really imagine that soon after the death of the Lord the primitive community shaped a Sacrament, and can we think how it came about that the first witnesses passed on this theology (!) in place of fact? No, anyone who has preserved but an ounce of feeling for the holy alarm with which the first age hung to the words of the Lord can only be amazed at those who, instead of viewing her faith and her hope with reverence, credit the community involved in eucharistic celebration with inventing what never happened and with theologizing about something Jesus never dreamed of. HS

of Jesus Christ is not commemorated the way the world marks the death of a hero—namely, the end of his heroic course and his deification. Nor is the death of Christ understood as a martyrdom or as a great teacher's melancholy leave-taking from his mournful disciples—as in the case of Socrates' farewell or the Buddha's attainment of perfection.

In contrast to these views, the death of Christ is understood to be a *sacrificial death* in the strict sense of the word. We do not simply compare it with a sacrifice, as when we figuratively describe a mother's death for her children or a soldier's for his fatherland. The death of Christ is not like a sacrifice, it is the sacrifice.

If the words of the Bible and the church's proclamation allow for a shred of doubt whether the death of Christ is really the one, unique, fully valid sacrifice for the sin of the whole world, then the Supper ends this doubt. Christ's death on the cross is the grand sacrifice, a bloody sacrifice in the OT manner, the final, once-for-all-valid sacrifice "once" offered to God "outside the gate" (Heb 13:12) by the eternal and merciful High Priest, who is at the same time the Lamb of God who takes away the sin of the world. The first to understand Christ's death on the cross along these lines was neither the nascent church nor Paul with his "Christ, our Passover lamb, has been sacrificed for us" (1 Cor 5:7) nor an anonymous "community theology." On the contrary, *Jesus himself gave this interpretation of his death* by teaching in his Supper that he himself is to be understood as the Passover lamb and his blood as the blood of the new testament, which is shed for many.

The Supper's position in the Christian *Divine Service* is to be understood from this perspective. If the actual content of the Gospel is the joyful message of the forgiveness of sins for Christ's sake, and if this message is spoken to us in the Supper by Christ himself, with a forcefulness and urgency no sermon can achieve, then the fact that the Supper has from time immemorial been the centerpiece of the Christian Divine Service must be described as a thoroughly logical phenomenon. Then one understands the enormous importance of the Sacrament of the Altar for the preservation of the Gospel. However much this Sacrament may be distorted in the Catholic churches, genuine Gospel and genuine faith has been retained in their midst through Christ's Supper. When Roman Catholic Christians write "My Jesus, mercy!" on their graves and when they set over their high altar the inscription *Rex tremendae majestatis, qui salvandos salva gratis, salva nos* ("King of tremendous majesty, who gives us free salvation, save us"),[37] then the faith that speaks from these words has been kindled from the light of the Gospel in the Supper.

Was not the flame of the Reformation itself once ignited by this light that shone even in the very heart of the Roman Church? And did not the Lutheran churches in the age of the dreadful distortion of preaching in the eighteenth and nineteenth centuries likewise experience what the Sacrament means for guarding doctrine? There have been and there still are Protestant churches in which the

---

[37] This is from a hymn written by Thomas Aquinas' friend and biographer, Thomas de Celano, in ca. 1250. Compare the translation in *The Lutheran Hymnal* 607, stanza 8. JS

last surviving remnant of the Gospel, beyond the Bible readings, is supplied by the Words of Institution of Baptism and the Supper that are imbedded in some ancient liturgical formulas. This fact automatically answers the old theological question of how the Sacrament of the Altar relates to the *articulus stantis et cadentis ecclesiae* ["the article by which the church stands or falls"], the doctrine of the *justification* of the sinner through faith alone. This article cannot be purely preserved in the church apart from the celebration of the Supper, at which Jesus Christ himself preaches to us with his "for you" [Luke 22:19–20; 1 Cor 11:24]. The converse also holds true, namely, that the Supper cannot be kept from distortion without this article. Anyone who does not yet know it from another source can learn from Luther's Small Catechism both the meaning of "given and shed for you for the remission of sins" and also the kind of hearts that are required by this promise. Luther's great struggle for the Supper, of which we still have to speak in another context, can only be understood by someone who knows that for him the destruction of the Holy Supper as founded by Jesus must have as its consequence the destruction of the faith willed by Jesus. Justifying faith is indeed the faith with which we are to go to his Table. For Luther the struggle to preserve the Sacrament of the Altar as Christ instituted it and the struggle for the pure doctrine of the Gospel are one and the same struggle.

Luther learned from the *Roman Mass* how the Sacrament of the Altar suffers *degeneration* when the article of justification is not purely preserved. He never disputed—and in this the Evangelical Lutheran Church has followed his example—that even in this Mass the genuine Supper of the Lord still exists, albeit hidden underneath the additions and errors of people.[38] At what then does the Lutheran Reformation direct its opposition? This is not directed primarily against such

---

[38] In order to demonstrate the difference between his doctrine and that of the sacramentarians, in his 1534 "Letter concerning his Book on the Private Mass," Luther confessed

> before God and all the world that I believe and do not doubt, and shall also with the help and grace of my dear Lord Jesus Christ adhere to this confession until the last day, that where mass is celebrated according to Christ's ordinance, be it among us Lutherans or under the papacy or in Greece or in India, even if it is also only under one kind—which is nonetheless wrong and an abuse—as is the case under the papacy at Easter and otherwise during the year when they provide the sacrament for the people, nevertheless, under the form of bread, the true body of Christ, given for us on the cross, under the form of wine, the true blood of Christ, shed for us, are present; furthermore, it is not a spiritual or imagined body and blood but the genuine natural body and blood derived from the holy, virginal, true, human body of Mary, conceived without a human body by the Holy Spirit alone. This body and blood of Christ are even now sitting at the right hand of God in majesty, in the divine person called Jesus Christ, who is genuine, true, eternal God with the Father of whom he was born from eternity, etc. This body and this blood of the Son of God, Jesus Christ, not only the holy and worthy but also sinners and the unworthy truly administer and receive bodily, although invisibly, with their hands, their mouths, the chalice, paten, corporal, and what they use for this purpose when it is administered and received in the mass.
>
> This is my faith; this I know, and no one shall wrest it from me. (WA 38.264.26 ff. [the English translation is from *LW* 38:224])

This is precisely what the Evangelical Lutheran Church teaches. Discussion of the problem was occasioned in the age of the Reformation when the question kept arising whether our forebears in the medieval centuries, particularly since the dogmatization of transubstantiation in 1215 and the withdrawal of the chalice from the laity, had actually received the Sacrament of the Altar. If the Mass was only an

doctrines as those of the Fourth Lateran Council on transubstantiation and of the Council of Constance on concomitance, that is, the teaching that both the body and blood of Christ are present under each of the two kinds. Observe Luther's distinctly low-key opposition to transubstantiation in the Smalcald Articles, which he bases on 1 Cor 10:16 and 11:28, and how the Reformer there reckons with the possibility that the theological theory of concomitance might be correct (SA III VI 2–5). By way of contrast, in a judgment that goes far beyond other instances of the *damnamus*,[39] he turns with unprecedented vehemence against the *sacrifice of the Mass* and against those provisions of canon law that support it. For he regarded this issue as involving not only false doctrine, but pure insurrection against God. They "thus set themselves against and over Christ, our Lord and God."[40] The vigorous protest against Rome in part II of the Smalcald Articles shows to what extent this is the case. Concerning the doctrine of justification we read that

> nothing in this article can be given up or compromised, even if heaven and earth and things temporal should be destroyed. For as St. Peter says, "There is no other name under heaven given among men by which we must be saved" (Acts 4:12). "And with his stripes we are healed" (Isa. 53:5).

---

instance of execrable idolatry, then the Supper of Christ existed in the Middle Ages at most in small isolated communities, just as the Baptists have always maintained concerning Baptism. The Lutheran Church has never doubted that the genuine Sacrament existed hidden under the horrors of the sacrilege of the Mass in just the same way as she has never doubted the validity of medieval absolution. This conviction is the key to understanding the inner freedom with which she took over from the Roman Mass everything that she deemed worthy of preservation. An example of this process is seen in the Lutheran Church's adoption of eucharistic hymns of the Middle Ages such as Thomas Aquinas' *Lauda Sion salvatorem* and *Adoro te devote*. With some slight alteration of the verses teaching transubstantiation, the first of these, the famous sequence of the festival of *Corpus Christi*, was used in congregational worship (e.g., in the *Psalmodia* of Lukas Lossius in Lüneburg), and such theologians as Selnecker gladly cite it as the voice of the church. *John Gerhard* still quotes the second [hymn] at the end of his teaching *De Coena Domini* in the *Loci*, placing it alongside such authorities as the eucharistic prayers of the Eastern Church with their doctrine of the Lord's Supper as the *mysterium tremendum* ["tremendous mystery"] and Thomas' Communion prayers. Old Lutheranism was sufficiently ecumenical in its breadth of vision to find an expression of the evangelical truth of Christ's presence under the elements of the Supper in the verse Thomas composed on the basis of a passage in Albert the Great:

> Godhead here in hiding, whom I do adore
> Masked by these bare shadows, shape and nothing more,
> See, Lord, at thy service low lies here a heart
> Lost, all lost in wonder at the God thou art.Seeing, touching, tasting are in thee deceived;
> How says trusty hearing? that shall be believed;
> What God's Son has told me, take for truth I do;
> Truth himself speaks truly or there's nothing true.

[The English translation is that of Gerard Manley Hopkins from *Catechism of the Catholic Church* (Liguori, Mo.: Liguori Publications, 1994), § 1381.] HS

[39] *Damnamus*, "we condemn/damn," is a creedal or confessional condemnation of false teaching. It originates in St. Paul's words in Gal 1:8. See the antitheses in the Augsburg Confession and the Formula of Concord. For a study of the concept of the *damnamus*, see Hans-Werner Gensichen, *We Condemn: How Luther and 16th-Century Lutheranism Condemned False Doctrine* (trans. Herbert J. A. Bouman; St. Louis: Concordia, 1967). RF

[40] SA III VI 4; the English translation is from Tappert, *BC*, 311. JS

On this article rests all that we teach and practice against the pope, the devil, and the world. Therefore we must be quite certain and have no doubts about it. Otherwise all is lost, and the pope, the devil, and all our adversaries will gain the victory.[41]

Immediately upon this follows

Article II. The Mass in the papacy must be regarded as the greatest and most horrible abomination because it runs into direct and violent conflict with this fundamental article. . . . For it is held that this sacrifice or work of the Mass . . . delivers men from their sins, both here in this life and yonder in purgatory, although in reality this can and must be done by the Lamb of God alone, as has been stated above.[42]

Luther here finds the decisive point that forever separates him and the orthodox church from Rome.

Even if it were possible for the papists to make concessions to us in all other articles, it would not be possible for them to yield on this article. It is as Campegio said in Augsburg: he would suffer himself to be torn to pieces before he would give up the Mass. So by God's help I would suffer myself to be burned to ashes before I would allow a celebrant of the Mass and what he does to be considered equal or superior to my Savior, Jesus Christ. Accordingly we are and remain eternally divided and opposed the one to the other.[43]

This is, in fact, the actual point of conflict between Rome and ourselves in the question of the Supper. The whole contrast between our respective understandings of the Gospel is here laid wide open: Is there still another sacrifice in addition to the one sacrifice on Golgotha? Is the Lord's Supper a sacrifice that we men—whether it be the priest or the church—present to God? The Catholic Church here speaks a determined "yes." "Yes," for Paul already set the Lord's Supper in parallel to the sacrifices of Jews and pagans. "Yes," for it is written in Heb 13:10 that "we have an altar from which those who serve the tent (i.e., the Jews) have no right to eat." "Yes," because immediately after the days of the NT, the ancient church understood and designated the Eucharist as a sacrifice (e.g., the *Didache* and Irenaeus) and referred to it with such Bible passages as Mal 1:11. The Reformation's "no" is just as decisive as this "yes" of the Catholics. In his great work on the Council of Trent,[44] such a man as Martin Chemnitz declares it entirely possible to apply also to the Supper or "Eucharist" the concept of sacrifice that Scripture employs so comprehensively and sometimes even figuratively:

---

[41] SA II I 5; the English translation is from Tappert, *BC*, 292. JS

[42] SA II II 1; the English translation is from Tappert, *BC*, 293. JS

[43] SA II II 10; the English translation is from Tappert, *BC*, 294. JS

[44] See Martin Chemnitz, *Examination of the Council of Trent* (trans. Fred Kramer; St. Louis: Concordia, 1978), part 2, sixth topic, "Concerning the Mass," article 2, "In What Sense the Action of the Liturgy May, According to Scripture, Rightly Be Called a Sacrifice," pp. 443–45. JS/RF

Because the distribution of and participation in Communion, or the Eucharist, is done in commemoration of the unique sacrifice of Christ, and because the sacrificial victim, who was once offered on the cross for our sins, is distributed and received there, it could for this reason, and with this explanation added, be called a sacrifice, even though Scripture does not so call it.[45]

Chemnitz establishes that what is at stake for the Catholics is not a mere name, but the Tridentine teaching[46] that a true and actual sacrifice is offered to God in the Mass. The same Christ is said to be offered in an unbloody manner who once offered himself in bloody sacrifice on the cross. This is not the place to enter into the details of the Catholic doctrine of the sacrifice of the Mass, which in the face of Protestant opposition has, since Trent, taken such pains to exclude the idea of a repetition of the sacrifice of Golgotha and thus to understand the sacrifice of the Mass as but a memorial, setting forth (*repraesentatio*) ["representation"], and appropriation of the sacrifice of the cross.[47] Suffice it here to say that among Catholic theologians themselves no unanimity has hitherto been reached on the relationship between the sacrifice of the Mass and the sacrifice of the cross. There is not even any clarity over the extent to which in the sacrifice of the Mass, the priest, the church, and Christ are subject and object of the offering.

The very prayers of the Mass themselves demonstrate that clarity exists only on the point that, since man presents the sacrifice of the Mass and God graciously accepts it, man cooperates in his own redemption. Our church, however, regards this as doing injury to the honor of Christ. For his glory consists in the fact that he procures our redemption acting entirely alone and without receiving any assistance from anyone else. In this sense, the Supper is for us the memorial of the sacrifice, concerning which it is written: "For by a single offering he has perfected for all time those who are sanctified" (Heb 10:14 [RSV]). Since it is much more than a memorial and since in it the eternal High Priest gives us his true body and his true blood to eat and to drink, the Sacrament of the Altar makes fully present for us the sacrifice Christ—and he entirely alone—offered on the cross in infinite love for sinners.

---

[45] Martin Chemnitz, *Examen Concilii Tridentini* (Preuss ed.; Berlin: Gustaf Schlawitz, 1861), 384; cf. the Kramer translation cited in the previous note, part 2, p. 445. JS

[46] [This teaching was formulated at] session 22. HS

[47] And yet the Roman catechism of 1565 again spoke of the sacrifice of the Mass as "renewing" (*instaurare*) the sacrifice of Calvary. HS

The official catechism of the Roman Church continues to affirm the teaching of the Council of Trent and quotes it directly to explain the doctrine of the Mass as sacrifice:

The sacrifice of Christ and the sacrifice of the Eucharist are *one single sacrifice*: "The victim is one and the same: the same now offers through the ministry of priests, who then offered himself on the cross; only the manner of offering is different." "In this divine sacrifice which is celebrated in the Mass, the same Christ who offered himself once in a bloody manner on the altar of the cross is contained and is offered in an unbloody manner." (*Catechism of the Catholic Church*, § 1367) JS

PART 5: MARANATHA

In the Lord's Supper, the church looks back into the past to the historical hour of the first Supper in that room in Jerusalem "on the night when he was betrayed." At the same time, her gaze is directed to the future, to the great supper in the kingdom of God. Just as each Lord's Supper is a repetition of the first, even so it is at the same time a prolepsis of the heavenly meal Jesus himself had spoken of at the institution: "Truly, I say to you, I shall not drink again of the fruit of the vine until that day when I drink it new in the kingdom of God" (Mark 14:25 [RSV]; cf. Luke 22:18 and the parallel statements concerning the Passover lamb, Luke 22:16). Just as Jesus himself at the Supper looks into the future "until the kingdom of God comes" [Luke 22:18], "until it is fulfilled in the kingdom of God" [Luke 22:16], even so Paul says of the Lord's Supper in 1 Cor 11:26, "For as often as you eat this bread and drink the cup, you proclaim the Lord's death until he comes" [RSV].

The proclamation of Christ's sacrificial death is indissolubly connected with the prayer to the Exalted One that he would manifest his heavenly glory and enter into his lordship over the world. For only if Jesus was actually the Messiah could his death be the atoning sacrifice in the sense of Isaiah 53 and thus more than a hero's or martyr's death, or a moving farewell. The account of the disciples at Emmaus affords a most telling demonstration of the indissoluble connection in the faith of the nascent church between the statements that Jesus is the Messiah prophesied in the entire OT, that he must die, and that he rose again. These statements express a single conviction. The Emmaus account makes it clear how this faith is bound up with the Supper. At the breaking of the bread, "their eyes were opened and they recognized him" (Luke 24:31). The nascent church knew from Jesus himself that he was the suffering Messiah in the sense of Isaiah 53. This she understood in the Supper. From this perspective, proclamation of Christ's death and invocation of him as the returning Messiah belong indissolubly together in the primitive church's celebration of the Lord's Supper.

The origins of this invocation shine through the Emmaus story. Just as "Abide with us" [Luke 24:29] is still intended as a personal request but is nevertheless in truth already a prayer to the Exalted One, so likewise in the primitive church's invocation of Christ, the petition of the circle of disciples to their Master is in the process of becoming the church's prayer to her Lord now exalted at the right hand of the Father. A happy coincidence has preserved for us this most ancient prayer to Christ in the maranatha that still retains its original Aramaic form in the eucharistic liturgies[48] of the Pauline communities and of the *Didache* [10:6], while it already appears in the Greek language in Rev 22:20 ("Come, Lord

---

[48] One of the surest and most important results of recent research on the history of liturgy is the fact that the Supper of primitive Christendom fashioned fixed liturgical forms already at a very early date. These forms—and not the chaotic formlessness characteristic of occasional outbreaks of Enthusiasm—are the actual outcome of the workings of the Holy Spirit that Paul portrays in 1 Corinthians 12 and 14. The

Jesus!"). Here we cannot discuss the significance of this ancient liturgical expression for the history of Christological dogma. The statement must suffice that the maranatha, which next to the Words of Institution is the most ancient portion of the eucharistic liturgy, belongs on account of its content to every celebration of the Lord's Supper. The church has been praying it for nineteen centuries. For nineteen centuries, she has been hearing the world's sneering question, which is also posed by the mockers who arise in her own midst: "Where is the promise of his coming? For ever since the fathers fell asleep, all things have continued as they were from the beginning of creation" (2 Pet 3:4 [RSV]).

Humanly speaking, the delay of the ardently expected end of the world and return of Christ is possibly the severest disappointment ever experienced on earth. It remains one of the most plausible arguments for unbelief when people say that the NT was mistaken with the prophecy of the imminent return of Christ and draw the corollary that it has erred also with its statements that Jesus is the Christ and that his death is the death of the Lamb of God. What does the church say in response? She can give no answer other than that already delivered by the NT in response to this question, albeit to believers rather than to mockers: "But, beloved, do not forget this one thing, that with the Lord one day is as a thousand years, and a thousand years as one day. The Lord is not slack concerning His promise, as some count slackness, but is longsuffering toward us, not willing that any should perish but that all should come to repentance. But the day of the Lord will come as a thief in the night" (2 Pet 3:8–10 [NKJV]). The church can give no other reply. How is it possible for her to be content with this answer? How is it possible for her to avoid plunging into despair over the delay of the parousia, for her not to lose her faith on account of this? How is it possible for her to wait with unspeakable patience, as if the measurements and laws of earthly time did not exist for her, and yet with every moment to grow in joyful assurance of her cause?

> Zion hears the watchmen singing,
> And in her heart new joy is springing.
> She wakes, she rises from her gloom.[49]

---

ancient church's liturgical language grew out of the language of prophecy, of which *Didache* 10:7 still gives an indication. The image, still dominant today, of a formless primitive church with a formless Divine Service was thrust into the NT by enthusiastic pietism and needs to be revised in accordance with these facts. Already in the first century, the Divine Service had more similarity with the Mass of one of the Eastern churches than with the assembly of a Methodist community. In his shining work, *Messe und Herrenmahl* (1926), Lietzmann traced the origins of the Preface right back to the Pauline congregations. This—along with the Salutation, "The Lord be with you," and the Sanctus (Isa. 6:3), attested to in *1 Clement* [34:6]—is thus to be regarded as a very ancient component of the liturgy. The entire sentence found in 1 Cor 16:22–23, "Maranatha! The grace of the Lord Jesus be with you," which reoccurs in Rev 22:20–21, perhaps belongs to the ancient liturgy of the Supper. The formula "If anyone has no love for the Lord, let him be anathema" is also to be understood in this context as intending to warn unbelievers and the unworthy against participation in the Eucharist. The reason we know so little of the shape of the most primitive Divine Service is that Paul did not need to deal in his letters with matters of common knowledge. HS

49   From stanza 2 of the hymn "Wake, Awake, for Night Is Flying" (*Lutheran Worship* 177). JS

How is it possible for the church to feel the flow of time with such sentiments as these? What kind of hope is it that only becomes firmer and firmer with the delay of its fulfillment? How can one pray "Come, Lord Jesus!" Sunday by Sunday and day by day for nineteen hundred years and more?

All these questions find their answer in the Holy Supper. Because the church possesses this Sacrament, she can wait for centuries and millennia on end. The Supper bridges the space of time between Jesus' days on earth and his return. By us "upon whom the end of the ages has come" (1 Cor 10:11 [RSV]), it is celebrated between the ages of the world, that is, between the old aeon, which extends from the creation of the world to the last judgment, and the new aeon which has already begun with the resurrection of Christ as the firstfruits from the dead and goes on into blessed eternity. The Supper exists only "between the ages,"[50] where it is present for the church, which no longer belongs to the world and yet is still in the world. In the Supper, time touches eternity and the here and now meets the beyond. It is the meal of pilgrims, *cibus viatorum* ["food of travelers"], as our medieval fathers used to call it. It is eaten on the migration from the world to the kingdom of God, from time to eternity, from the here and now to the beyond.

The Supper is now received in much the same way as Israel ate the Passover—"your loins girded, your sandals on your feet, and your staff in your hand; and you shall eat it in haste. It is the LORD's Passover" (Exod 12:11 [RSV])—and was given manna and water from the rock on its journey through the wilderness (1 Cor 10:1 ff.). A type of the Supper can also be discerned in Elijah's finding bread and water under the broom tree: "And he arose, and ate and drank, and went in the strength of that food forty days and forty nights to Horeb the mount of God" (1 Kgs 19:8 [RSV]). Since the days of Paul, the church has continually invoked these OT types in explanation of the Sacrament, and, by so doing, she has constantly expressed the idea that the Supper is the *viaticum*,[51] fodder for the journey between the worlds, between time and eternity. Already in this life, it gives us a share in the goods of eternal life: "And I assign to you, as my Father assigned to me, a kingdom, that you may eat and drink at my table in my kingdom, and sit on thrones judging the twelve tribes of Israel" (Luke 22:29–30 [RSV]; cf. Matt 19:28, which lacks any reference to the Supper). This promise holds good not only for the apostles but for all who, as members of the church, partake at the Lord's Table. "Do you not know that the saints will judge the world? . . . Do you not know that we are to judge angels?" (1 Cor 6:2–3 [RSV]). While the world hastens toward the last judgment, "those who are invited to the marriage supper of the Lamb" (Rev 19:9 [RSV]) are removed from the divine

---

[50] Sasse here likely alludes to the magazine *Zwischen den Zeiten*, which was the mouthpiece of the "dialectical theology" movement associated with Karl Barth in the 1920s. JS/RF

[51] *Viaticum* is the Latin word for "food for the journey." When administered to a dying person, the Lord's Supper is said to be that person's food for his journey to heaven. RF

judgment of wrath (cf. also 1 Cor 11:31–32). The blessed world of the resurrection and eternal life awaits them, for to them applies the promise "he who eats my flesh and drinks my blood has eternal life, and I will raise him up at the last day" (John 6:54 [RSV]).

If the NT gives us to understand the Lord's Supper along these lines, it follows that the sacramental celebration is, in a certain way, exempt from the conditions of earthly time and space. The Supper involves both the beginning and the end of the way. It involves both the first Supper, founded by Christ's promise, and the final supper fulfilled in the kingdom of God. Yet nothing is altered in the Supper itself by the particular stage of wilderness wandering one happens to have reached; it does not matter whether the Supper is celebrated in the year 50 or 500 or 1500 or 2000. Each eucharistic celebration of the church is a repetition of the first Supper and a prolepsis of the final supper. Both these factors are expressed in the liturgy, the first by the faithful use of the Words of Institution, the second by our joining in the ancient Prefaces' expression of the praise and adoration which, according to Holy Scripture, are offered to God by the angels and archangels, the powers and dominions, and all the hosts of heaven. This twofold reference explains both the timelessness of the eucharistic liturgy and also the fact that in the Supper we join with believers of all ages in the prayer of unshakable Christian hope, "Amen. Come Lord Jesus!" whereby we proclaim the Lord's death until he comes.

PART 6: *SANCTORUM COMMUNIO*

The Supper directs the believer's gaze at once into the past and into the future, to the church's historical beginning in this world's time and to her eternal goal in the coming aeon of the kingdom of God. By doing so, the Supper acts as does nothing else to make believers aware of the church's deepest essence. We cannot learn what the church is from theological books. Nor can we learn this only from sermons, even though it should continually be said to us in sermons and we should hear it there. Rather, faith in the church—that is, believing knowledge of what the church is according to her deepest essence—arises from our experiences at the celebration of the Supper. This was the place where the disciples understood the reality of the church for the first time. The nascent church awoke to self-awareness in the celebration of the "breaking of bread," the "Eucharist."

Just as the early Christian congregations gathered around the Supper in the countryside of Asia Minor and North Africa, and in cities from Antioch and Ephesus to Rome, so likewise the church's altar has in all ages been the point of crystallization around which living congregations have assembled. In every respect, the Lord's Supper has been the center of the church. It even determined the beginnings of canon law and of ecclesiastical organization: A presbyter is one who, at the Eucharist, has a right to one of the front seats by the altar; a bishop is one who leads the celebration; and a deacon is one who "serves at table." The church's whole *diakonia* ["service, ministry"] proceeds from the altar, just as the fellowship of Christian *brotherly love* grows out of the Sacrament, which is justly called "Holy Communion." All attempts to build Christian congregations without placing at their center the congregation-forming Sacrament of the Altar are just as much condemned to failure as are efforts to renew the Divine Service without renewing the Lord's Supper. The sad experiences of the nineteenth and twentieth centuries in this area only confirm the lessons of the past. The enormous effort made in the area of church planting during recent generations must be regarded as a failure. It has produced a wealth of societies and card files, but not a single congregation.

Something similar must be said about the liturgical endeavors within Protestantism in recent times. They have produced liturgies galore for every conceivable taste, but they have hitherto proved unable to move people to go to church again in order to celebrate these liturgies. Where the custom of church-going has lapsed with the consequence that the Christian congregation is dead or dying, there is but one single means for getting people back to church. Hunger and thirst for the Lord's Supper must be aroused in them. Whenever this hunger and this thirst awake—and it obviously does not lie within our power to awaken them—people go to church again. In an emergency, hunger and thirst for God's Word can be satisfied in one's chamber, at least according to the pietistic theory with which the Protestantism of the last two centuries has preached its own churches empty. Except in case of grave illness, however, the Sacrament of the Altar can only be received in the house of God. The renewal of the Christian congregation and her Divine Service therefore begins, in a way that most theologians today still find incomprehensible, when we once again seriously learn and teach what the NT and the catechism say on Baptism and the Supper. That our church is today experiencing the beginnings of such a movement belongs to the promising signs of our time.

How is this community-forming character of the Lord's Supper to be explained? *Sociology* distinguishes two groups of human communities. The first comprises those structures of social life which have their origin not in the will of men but in the givens of human life. Not a voluntary decision but an accident of fate is responsible for one's belonging to a family, a clan, a race, a tribe, or a people. These communities, which have a basis in nature, exist before the individual, who is born into them. Alongside these there are other communities that come into being through voluntary association. One joins a circle of friends, a society, or a political party through a voluntary decision. The individual here exists before the social structure in question. In this case, community is created by the will of particular "self-associating individuals." The two groups of community structures are also to be found in the life of religious communities. The sociology of religion knows of religious communities that preexist the individual, who is simply born into the cultic associations that we meet in the paganism of all ages and which usually overlap with the family, the tribe, or the *polis* ["city"]. Alongside them this discipline knows of other associations that are formed by the will of individuals, such as the cultural societies of the Hellenistic mysteries or the faith community of classical Buddhism, which people freely join by pronouncing the so-called "formula of flight." Both of these forms of community life are manifested even within Christendom. It is a pure accident of fate that a child of Catholic parents is baptized and raised Catholic. If at a later date the child in question joins a religious order of his church or converts to another church, then his free decision is at work. Whatever nomenclature the sociology of religion may use for these two types of social formation on the soil of Christendom, their existence must be recognized as a fact. The great philosopher of religion Ernst Troeltsch[52] was at all events guilty of using misleading language when he claimed for them two words that lost for him their ancient meaning, namely, "church" and "sects."

The fact that the church does not really fit into either of these groups is prime evidence that her essence eludes sociological understanding. The forms of Christian community life sometimes belong more to the first and sometimes more to the second type. Deep down, though, they simply do not fit into this framework. People are neither born into the church, nor do they achieve membership by joining her *voluntarily;* rather, they are *baptized* into the church.

The sociology of religion points to the existence of two forms of Baptism, namely *infant* and *adult* Baptism. Troeltsch regards the former as symbolic of what he calls "church," that is, the Christian ecclesial community to which people belong by an accident of fate. He understands the latter as symbolic of what he labels "sect," that is, the ecclesial community people join voluntarily and that is thus founded on individual decision. No matter how important the distinction between these two kinds of Baptism may be for sociology, and no matter how much stress the Baptist communities may lay upon it because of their conviction that infant Baptism is no Baptism, while the church may certainly find this distinction to be useful on the practical level, she regards it as devoid of theological importance. Baptism's essence is in no way affected by its being administered to infants or adults. Because faith and Baptism belong inseparably together and rebirth cannot take place without faith, Luther was incontestably right when he championed this principle all the way to the corollary of infant faith in his catechisms and *Taufbüchlein* ["Baptism booklet"]. *Baptism is not a symbol* for something that man does or for something that is done to him. It is the very *act of God himself* by which he adopts an individual as his child and a fellow heir of Christ, forgives him his sins, and makes him a member of the church.

The essence of the community vouchsafed to us in the church consists in its being rooted in the Sacrament, that is, in God's act of love which takes place in the Sacrament. That is what distinguishes the church from all other worldly communities and even from the religious communities of the world. A late addition to the Western baptismal creed pinpoints the characteristic quality of this "community" that exists within the church as *sanctorum communio*. This expression may

---

[52] See note 9 above. RF

not be understood with Luther as a paraphrase of the concept "church." The very style of the Western creed, in which a fresh fact is introduced with each new word, precludes this assumption. On the contrary, this term describes the unique reality within the church which the NT has in mind when it speaks of the *koinonia* ["fellowship"] that binds the members of the church with their Head and with each other. As is well known, there are two ways of understanding the Latin expression *sanctorum communio*, namely, either as "communion of the holy things," that is, the Sacraments,[53] or else as "communion of the holy persons." For our immediate purposes, this ambiguity is of no consequence, since in each case the *koinonia* described is established and preserved among the members of the church through the Sacraments of Baptism and the Supper. Our whole understanding of the church depends on whether we understand this *koinonia* aright. It does not exist among those who belong to the communities of other faiths, religions, or ideologies. Muslims also know themselves to be a "people" enlivened by a single spirit which exists, so to say, as a gigantic collective person. "My people can never agree in an error," says Muhammad. The community of Buddha likewise knows of a mighty fellowship that unites all those who go the holy way. The attractiveness of the mystery religions in the large cities of antiquity was based, in large part, on the human community they offered to the homeless, uprooted individuals in their congregations. From an external perspective, community within the church is something very similar. Undoubtedly, there are historical, psychological, and sociological affinities between ecclesial and extra-ecclesial expressions of religious community life.

Yet what constitutes the essence of ecclesial community is not what it has in common with other communities, but what distinguishes it from them. This is the special *koinonia*, the "communion of holy things or persons" that is established by Baptism and the Supper. Would this *koinonia* also exist if the church had only the Word and not also the Sacraments? Obviously no answer can ultimately be given to this question since it happens to have pleased God to give his church both Word and Sacrament. Therefore, we cannot imagine a church without Sacraments. We only throw out the question in order that it might help us to reflect on the essence of the *koinonia* established by the Sacraments.

---

[53] Compare the exclamation "the holy things for the holy ones," *sancta sanctis*, mentioned in part 2 above. For further reference see, first, Dietrich Bonhoeffer's *Sanctorum Communio: Eine dogmatische Untersuchung zur Soziologie der Kirche* (1930), which has received far too little attention, and, second, Paul Althaus' *Communio Sanctorum: Die Gemeinde im lutherischen Kirchengedanken*, vol. 1: *Luther* (1929), which is especially informative on Luther. HS

An English translation of Bonhoeffer's *Sanctorum Communio* is available as *The Communion of Saints* (trans. Ronald Gregor Smith et al.; New York: Harper and Row, 1963) or *Sanctorum Communio* (London: Collins, 1963).

Note also, however, that Sasse was critical of Bonhoeffer's ecclesiology in *Sanctorum Communio;* see "Die Frage nach dem Wesen der Kirche" (Zum Oekumenischen Konzil III), *Lutherische Blätter* 14.74 (July 1962): 111. RF

We may say that there can never be a Sacrament apart from the Word—"For without God's Word the water is plain water and no Baptism. But with the Word of God it is a Baptism" [SC IV 10]—and hence that the Sacrament effects nothing that is not in the final analysis effected by God's Word. Yet it did in point of fact please God for our salvation to bind certain effects of his Word to the Sacraments. Therefore, we must say that we only share in these effects by way of the Sacraments. It is the sin of the Quakers that they want to have these effects apart from the Sacraments, that they want to have a Sacramentless church in opposition to the Lord, who gave the Sacraments to his church. The upshot of this rejection of the Sacrament is the loss of the other means of grace, the Word (among the Quakers the internal word is apprehended in holy silence through steps alongside and above the external Word of Scripture and preaching). This is precisely what happens to all those who say that the Sacrament does no more than seal the Word, which thus emerges as the means of grace that already gives us all we need. According to this view, the Word of God already creates the *koinonia* of the church, for where two or three are gathered together in Jesus' name for the hearing of the Word and common prayer, there he is according to his promise in the midst of them. The communal Supper adds nothing new to this fellowship but only expresses it and confirms it.

A warning is in order for anyone who undervalues and disdains the special blessing of the Sacrament of the Altar: Let him beware lest he lose the Sacrament altogether and along with the Sacrament the Word also! How often have people imagined themselves to be gathered in Jesus' name, when in fact they were only gathered in their own! How often have they believed themselves able to subject the presence of Christ to sense perception—we can only accept this claim on trust!—when in fact they have merely imagined this presence! How often have people believed themselves to have experienced the communion of saints when what they experienced was not the communion of the Holy Spirit but just a communion of the pious flesh! Hymns such as Zinzendorf's *Herz und Herz vereint zusammen* ("Heart and heart made one together")[54] have never been sung with greater ardor than in the worst sects known to church history.

Just as the Holy Spirit is not an object of our psychological experience but is only knowable by faith, and just as the church is not an "article of sight" [*Sehartikel*],[55] but rather an article of faith [*Glaubensartikel*], so likewise the communion of saints can only be believed. It is a state of affairs within the church that

---

[54] This work was written in 1725 and said to have been occasioned by strife in the Moravian Brethren's Unity, which was healed by common love for the Savior. The work contains a poetic rendering of our Lord's farewell discourse as recorded in John 14–17 (John Julian, ed., *A Dictionary of Hymnology* [2d ed.; London: John Murray, 1925], 517). RF

[55] Sasse uses the terms *Sehartikel* and *Glaubensartikel* also in his essay "Ministry and Congregation," *We Confess the Church* (trans. Norman Nagel; St. Louis: Concordia, 1986), 73. RF

is inaccessible to all psychological experience and to all sociological perception. We would not know anything of it if God's Word did not tell us that it exists. But now Scripture tells us that Baptism and the Lord's Supper give us a share in the communion which binds the members of the church with each other and with Christ: "For by one Spirit we were all baptized into one body" (1 Cor 12:13 [RSV]) and "Because there is *one* bread, we who are many are one body" (1 Cor 10:17 [RSV; emphasis added]). But when Scripture tells us that Baptism and the Supper establish the "communion of the Holy Spirit" (2 Cor 13:14) that exists in the church, we must accept this even when we are unable to comprehend how the Sacraments can "do such great things" [SC IV 9].

We do not know why we must be born anew and from above "by water and Spirit" (John 3:5). We do not know why "there are three witnesses, the Spirit, the water, and the blood; and these three agree" (1 John 5:8 [RSV]). Scripture's saying this must be sufficient for us. Nor can we dodge its clear statements by claiming that the idea that the Holy Spirit is given through the Sacraments is magic and therefore incompatible with the lofty spiritual and ethical heights of biblical religion. This reproach does not fall on us who ascertain the contents of the NT, but on the apostles who had obviously not reached the lofty spiritual and ethical heights of enlightened idealist philosophy. Idealist philosophy and the theology that it has spawned down the ages since Origen has always been deeply offended that the Holy Spirit is not given directly but through means, as the church's confession says,[56] and that not only the Word serves as means in this process but also the elements of water and of bread and wine that accompany Christ's Word in the Sacraments. This offense has led to an unremitting series of attempts to evade the NT's clear teaching concerning the means of grace by either reinterpreting it or else declaring it nonbinding. But this is to do violence to Holy Scripture. God's Holy Spirit surely has other ways of working than the human spirit. The antithesis of matter and spirit as we know it manifestly does not exist for the Holy Spirit. The incomprehensibility of the Holy Spirit's mode of operation is the reason why the NT's teaching concerning the communion of the church established by Baptism and the Lord's Supper eludes our understanding. The claim that the greatest, most profound, and most all-encompassing community of human history has been established by these unimpressive-looking Sacraments is just as offensive to our thinking as is the assertion that God's Holy Spirit is given along this path. And yet this is the case. For this reason the church herself remains an insoluble riddle for human reason, a pure article of faith like the article concerning the *sanctorum communio*.

In addition to the Bible passages already quoted there remains a further indirect proof that the Sacrament is truly the agent which brings this community into

---

[56] *Nam per verbum et sacramenta tamqaum per instrumenta donatur Spiritus Sanctus* ["For through the Word and Sacraments, as through instruments, the Holy Spirit is given," AC V]. HS

being. This is the description of the church as the *body of Christ* as we first find it in Paul. There is nothing intrinsically surprising in the church's being described as a body, a *corpus*. The comparison of a human community with a body is very ancient. That the church is a body because she is animated by the Holy Spirit is an idea that makes complete sense. "There is *one* body and *one* Spirit . . . *one* Lord, *one* faith, *one* Baptism, *one* God and Father of us all" (Eph 4:4–6)—this and similar statements contain nothing that the reader of the NT would not grasp immediately. The description of the church as a "body in Christ" which occurs in Rom 12:5 is also understandable without further ado: "so we, though many, are one body in Christ, and individually members one of another" [RSV]. On the other hand, the description of the church as the body of Christ remains a riddle. This formulation brings a totally fresh idea into the picture of the body, which indeed ceases to be a picture. Calling the church a body is to use a figure of speech that can also be applied to other communities. But calling her the body of Christ involves first of all the assertion that just as there is only one Christ so likewise the church is something completely unique. And second, this terminology establishes the most intimate union between the church and that other manifestation of the body of Christ, namely, the glorified body of the risen and exalted Lord in heaven to which our earthly "lowly body" will one day be conformed (Phil 3:21). This body is a reality in heaven. Furthermore, as we shall see in the next section, this body is the gift of the Lord's Supper, which is given to us with the bread and is thus a reality on earth in each celebration of the Eucharist. Alongside the body of Christ in heaven and the body of Christ in the Eucharist, there now steps the body of Christ as church. It is perfectly plain that in this expression the word "body" ceases to be a mere picture and participates in the same high level of reality as do the other expressions. There is the body of Christ in *heaven*. There is the body of Christ in the *Eucharist*. There is the body of Christ in the *church*. The body of Christ in heaven is made present on earth in the Lord's Supper. By virtue of believers being fed, the church becomes the body of Christ. One can say that this is speculation. Anyone who says this, however, must at the very least concede that this is a biblical speculation. For these statements about the body of Christ contain no thought that is not deduced from the NT, no thought that could be omitted by anyone who seriously intends to expound the NT. It is not theological speculation but unquestionably the teaching of the NT that when believers celebrate the Lord's Supper they become a body. This ecclesial body becomes the body of Christ. Belonging to the church means being a member of Christ's body, being incorporated into Christ. This incorporation occurs in the Sacraments of Baptism and the Lord's Supper in a way that we are completely unable to picture or imagine. The older theology was then in error when it thought that the church is only figuratively described as the body of Christ. The church is the body of Christ in precisely the same degree as it is the people of God and as it is the temple of the Holy Spirit. The body of Christ is as much really present in the church as it is both in the Eucharist and in heaven at the right hand of the Father. This is the clear teaching of the NT, which cannot be wrenched out of the Bible by asking whether and how the body of Christ can be at the same time in heaven and on earth, at the right hand of the Father and in the Eucharist, in the bread of the Supper and in the church that celebrates the Supper.

In response to the question concerning the historical roots of this conception of the church as the body of Christ, we begin by ascertaining that it is first expressed in *Paul*. To the further question of how Paul arrived at this conception, historical scholarship can answer only with conjectures. Even though it is certain that the *corpus* idea of ancient sociology and the multiple meanings acquired by the word *soma* ["body"] in the Hellenistic history of religion were not without influence on the apostle's thought and manner of expression,[57] these environmental influences are nevertheless unable to explain the connection forged by Paul between the body of Christ in heaven, the body of Christ in the Eucharist, and the body of Christ in the church. *Rawlinson* is right in saying that "it is permissible to support a connection between the use of the phrase 'body of Christ' as a description of the church and the use of the same phrase as a description of the sacramental 'body' of the Eucharist, for ecclesial rite surely precedes ecclesiastical doctrine."[58] It would then be appropriate to suppose that the church's first great theologian's understanding of the church as the body of Christ grew out of the Lord's Supper.[59] But behind Paul's thoughts and words looms as the final point of origin of all ideas concerning the connection between church and Lord's Supper the word Jesus himself spoke at the institution of the Supper, which is repeated at each eucharistic celebration: *"This is my body!"*

PART 7: THIS IS MY BODY

We thus stand before the saying that is surely to be reckoned among the most enigmatic utterances of human history. What differences have broken out within Christendom around "This is my body"! Ratramnus and Radbertus, Berenger and

---

[57] For further details, see Ernst Käsemann, *Leib und Leib Christi: Eine Untersuchung zur paulinischen Begrifflichkeit* (1933). HS

[58] A. E. J. Rawlinson, "Corpus Christi," in *Mysterium Christi: Christological Studies by British and German Theologians* (ed. G. K. A. Bell and D. Adolf Deissmann; London: Longmans, Green and Co., 1930), 225–244; [the quote is on page] 227. HS
This volume also included an essay by Sasse, "Jesus Christ, the Lord," on pages 93–120. RF

[59] In his essay "The Lord's Supper in the New Testament" (*Abendmahlsgemeinschaft?* p. 79), E. Käsemann assumes to the contrary that the apostle "already had this body of Christ as the church in mind when he spoke of the body of Christ of which we acquire a share in the eucharistic element." He is obliged to judge thus, since he is of the opinion that Paul was the first to give the realistic meaning to "this is my body." HS
Sasse critiques this essay by Käsemann in more depth in the essay "Why Must We Hold Fast to the Lutheran Doctrine of the Lord's Supper?" which is also included in this volume. Käsemann's essay is in the volume entitled *Abendmahlsgemeinschaft?* by Hans Asmussen et al. (2d ed.; Evangelischen Theologie, Supplement 3; Munich: Chr. Kaiser, 1938), 60–93. RF

Lanfranc,[60] Zwingli and Luther, Calvin and Westphal[61]—these names denote only those struggles concerning the Supper that have achieved historical fame. What stands behind them are not only intellectual conflicts between theologians and their schools, but also human bitterness, misunderstanding, and lovelessness, and grievous personal destinies! If we then ponder the effects of these eucharistic struggles on Christian congregations and entire churches, if we think only of the consequences of the difference in eucharistic doctrine for the relationship of the Lutheran and Reformed churches and then for their relationship to the various Union churches and for the formation of various types of Union churches,[62] and

---

[60]   Here Sasse mentions the chief antagonists in the great medieval controversies over the Eucharist. The speculation that the bread and wine of the Eucharist are actually changed into the body and blood of Christ (later called the doctrine of transubstantiation), along with the teaching that the Mass is the unbloody sacrifice, was championed by Paschasius Radbertus, (ca. 785/786–860/865), a Benedictine theologian. His treatise *Concerning the Body and Blood of the Lord* gave full expression to both of these medieval theories. Radbertus based much of his argument on interpretations of earlier church fathers, but he also relied heavily on miracles supposedly associated with the Eucharist. Ratramnus (died after 868), a Benedictine monk at Corbie, was instructed by the Holy Roman emperor, Charles II of France, to prepare a response. Ratramnus roundly rejected Radbertus' treatise and prepared a treatise of his own, with the same title. Ratramnus emphasized the symbolic and figurative nature of the Sacrament, emphasizing the Sacrament's great mystery. Eventually, it was the theory of Radbertus that won out in the medieval church. Later, Berenger (ca. 998–1088) built on Radbertus' position and declared that unworthy communicants cannot receive the body and blood of Christ. This position was rejected by Lanfranc (ca. 1008–1089), another Benedictine theologian. Berenger was eventually imprisoned for his theory, then signed a vacillating statement, but later again asserted his position. He again backed away when forced to do so, but upon returning to his native country, once again asserted his position. Finally, he once more recanted and died a lonely death. The theory of transubstantiation was adopted by the Fourth Lateran Council in 1215, affirmed again at the Council of Lyons in 1274 and the Council of Florence in 1439, and then finally confirmed as binding church dogma at the Council of Trent in 1551 (session 13, chapter 4). Alternative views were declared anathema. JS

Sasse describes this history in chapter 1 of his book *This Is My Body: Luther's Contention for the Real Presence in the Sacrament of the Altar* (Minneapolis: Augsburg, 1959; repr., Adelaide, Australia: Lutheran Publishing House, 1977); see especially pages 36–60 (1959 ed.). RF

[61]   Joachim Westphal (1510–1574) was a Lutheran pastor who was later a superintendent in Hamburg. He was a pupil of Luther and Melanchthon, known for his vigorous defense of Luther's doctrine of the Lord's Supper against John Calvin, the great Reformed theologian of Geneva. In no small measure, it was Westphal's controversy with Calvin that led to the Formula of Concord's clarification of the Lutheran doctrine of the Lord's Supper, which of course was adopted with the Book of Concord in 1580. JS

[62]   The phrase "Union churches" refers to a variety of declarations of church fellowship between historically Lutheran and Reformed churches in Germany. The first great Union between Lutheran and Reformed churches was the Prussian Union of 1817. The legacy of that Union led to the formation of the *Vereinigte Evangelisch-Lutherische Kirche Deutschland* (VELKD) ["United Evangelical Lutheran Church of Germany"], which was organized July 6–8, 1948, and also the *Evangelische Kirche in Deutschland* (EKD) ["Evangelical Church in Germany"], formed July 9–15, 1948. The VELKD claims to be a Union of various Lutheran territorial churches, but it is also a member of the EKD, which is a federation of Lutheran, Reformed, and other Union churches. Sasse worked very hard to prevent the formation of a false Union, as it is found in the forms of the VELKD and the EKD. He had prepared draft constitutions for both organizations for his bishop; neither was used in the proceedings of the formation. Thus, profoundly disappointed, Sasse was unable to stem the tide of the Union movement. Sasse's drafts were delivered to Bishop Meiser in preparation for the Church Conference in Treysa, August 27–September 1, 1945: "Entwurf einer Verfassung für die Vereinigte Evangelish-Lutherische Kirche in Deutschland" ["Draft of a Constitution for the United Evangelical Lutheran Church in Germany"] and "Entwurf einer Satzung für den Rat der Evangelischen Kirche in Deutschland" ["Draft of a Statute for the Council of the Evangelical Church in Germany"]. JS/RF

if we further consider how these struggles have been played out before the eyes of an increasingly hostile world, then we might well agree with the ancient complaint that the meal of love has turned into the hub of all quarreling and cover our heads at the mention of this biblical saying: "The name of God is blasphemed among the Gentiles because of you" (Rom 2:24 [RSV]).

If it is theoretically possible to pose such a question, must we lay the blame on *Jesus* himself? He could have avoided the entire struggle over the Supper, which was to rage through his church with more or less severity in all centuries from the very outset, simply by expressing himself more clearly and with less possibility for misunderstanding at the institution of the Supper. We must reply that it would indeed have been possible for him to prevent the Supper strife. He need only have said, "What I am doing is a parable. When I say, 'This is my body,' I actually *mean* only that the bread signifies my body. When I say, 'This is my testamental blood,' I don't mean that this is really what it is, but rather I am employing a figurative way of speaking." If Jesus had said this, if he had accompanied his action with the explicit explanation needed if it was in fact a symbolic action,[63] then everything would have been clear. Theologians would then indeed have believed themselves obliged to improve on this explanation just as they have considered that many an explanation he gave according to the Gospels stands in need of improvement or is to be reckoned as secondary material.[64] But the church would not have needed to take any notice of this and she would have been spared a conflict concerning the Supper. So, if Jesus did understand the Supper as a parabolic action, then he cannot be spared from blame for not speaking in a clearer way, less open to misunderstanding, and for obscuring the parabolic action with enigmatic words rather than explaining it with plain words. By enigmatic words we understand those words whose meaning is not expressed with the words, but which the hearer is rather to seek behind the words. Here lies an important reason why the fathers of our church held fast with such great tenacity to the simple verbal meaning of the Words of Institution: They could not think that Jesus was capable of leaving his true meaning wrapped in ambiguity in this decisive hour for the whole future of the church.[65] They neither would nor could make him respon-

---

[63] Just think of how Agabus' symbolic action is explained in Acts 21:11 or of Jer 19:10–11. HS

[64] For example, the parable explanations given in Luke 10:36–37 and Mark 4:11–20. HS

[65] Let us simply recall Luther's words from the *Confession Concerning Christ's Supper* of 1528:

Even supposing that our text and interpretation were uncertain or obscure—which it is not— as well as their [namely, Karlstadt's, Zwingli's, and Oecolampadius'] text and interpretation, you still have this glorious, reassuring advantage that you can rely upon our text with a good conscience and say, "If I must have an uncertain, obscure text and interpretation, I would rather have the one uttered by the lips of God himself. . . . And if I must be deceived, I would rather be deceived by God (if that were possible) than by men." . . .

Consequently, you can boldly address Christ both in the hour of death and at the Last Judgment: "My dear Lord Jesus Christ, a controversy has arisen over thy words in the Supper. Some want them to be understood differently from their natural sense. But since they teach me nothing certain, but only lead me into confusion and uncertainty . . . I have remained with

sible for the eucharistic conflicts that must necessarily arise if the Supper was in fact a symbolic action for which the Words of Institution offer only an obscure explanation, rather than a perfectly clear explanation. Jesus' lack of an explanation to ward off all misunderstanding, similar to his explanations of the parables, is a sure sign that Jesus neither regarded this action as a parable nor intended the Words of Institution as symbolic discourse. If these words were not intended as a parable, but as an explanation of his action, to be understood in the realistic sense of his words, then Jesus could not in fact have expressed himself with greater simplicity and clarity.

The only thing that might be construed as missing from the Words of Institution would be an explanation of *how it is possible* for the bread he held in his hands to be his body and for the wine in the cup to be his blood. Yet Jesus did not offer such an explanation on the occasion of any of his miracles, whether they were those he himself performed or those, such as the resurrection, that he predicted. An incomprehensible miracle must be involved in the Supper if it is not to be explained away as a parabolic action. Thus, the church has always connected the Supper with the miracle of the transfiguration, where Jesus' sinless body already experienced something of future glory, and with the miraculous feedings. The most that might be expected of Jesus in this situation is that he would have more plainly characterized the miracle as a miracle. But when we recall how tight-lipped he was in his miraculous deeds and made do with saying only what was strictly necessary, then we shall not be justifiably surprised that he did not say more in this case either. Nor would it have made any difference to the outcome if he had done so. He could have used thirty or three thousand rather than three or four words to say "This is my body."

Apart from the fact that many words would not have been any more impressive and that they may well have not have been preserved, the strife around the Supper would still have broken out over the many words, just as the words in John 6 are hotly disputed. For *the cause of strife over the Supper does not lie in the Lord's words but in the doubt of people who do not want to believe him in these words.* If the basis

---

thy text as the words read. If there is anything obscure in them, it is because thou didst wish to leave it obscure, for thou hast given no other explanation of them, nor hast thou commanded any to be given. . . .

"Now if there should be anything obscure about these words, thou wilt bear with me if I do not completely understand them, just as thou didst forbear with thine apostles when they did not understand thee in many things—for instance, when thou didst announce thy passion and resurrection. And yet they kept thy words just as they were spoken and did not alter them. Thy beloved mother also did not understand when thou saidst to her, Luke 2[:49], 'I must be about my Father's business,' yet with simplicity she kept these words in her heart and did not alter them. So have I also kept to these thy words, 'This is my body.' " (WA 26.446.18 ff. [the English translation is from *LW* 37:305–6])

These words reveal in its entirety the distinctive flavor of the Lutheran doctrine of the Supper, and above all—notwithstanding the assistance rendered by the theory of ubiquity—its completely unphilosophical character. Neither Zwingli nor Calvin could have spoken in this way. Nor could these words be pictured in the mouth of such a modern Reformed theologian as Karl Barth. HS

of the dispute lay in the words of Jesus, then either on the night of the Supper, or immediately after Easter, and at all events prior to the church's first controversy of church monies in Jerusalem (Acts 6:1), the first eucharistic controversy would have broken out around this question: What did Jesus mean with his words?

Yet neither the original apostles, who together experienced the first Supper, nor Paul and the church of the first generation felt that the question of what is received in the Eucharist was a problem. The first evidence we have for the view that Jesus could have meant something different from what he said in the eucharistic words and that they are to be understood symbolically occurs in the *Gnostics*,[66] and then in the churchly *gnosis* of late second-century *Alexandrian theology*. Ever since *Origen*[67] classically formulated this view and established the opinion that in the Supper believers are given to eat and drink not of Christ's flesh and blood, but of the Logos, a symbolic, spiritualistic understanding of the Supper has been read into the NT, and then read back out of it as a result of theological scholarship. To the extent that it was determined by *Neoplatonism*,[68] the whole of subsequent theology took over this understanding from Origen. In their doctrines of the Supper even *Athanasius*, the great theologian of the incarnation, and *Augustine*, the great theologian of the *sola gratia* ["by grace alone"], paid their tribute to the Neoplatonic philosophical disdain for earthly matter.

Therefore, no obscurity in the words Jesus spoke at the institution of the Supper is therefore responsible for the deeply regrettable eucharistic controversies, but only the assumption that he could not have meant what is expressed in the Words of Institution because these words as they stand assert something *impossible*. According to Calvin, for example, it is impossible for the bread that

---

[66] The Gnostics were adherents of the complex religious movement known as Gnosticism. Gnosticism took many different forms and was commonly associated with names of particular teachers, such as Valentinus, Basilides, and Marcion. There were certain common features of the movement as a whole. The most important feature of Gnosticism was its emphasis on obtaining the secret knowledge (*gnosis*) of God and of the origin and destiny of humanity, by means of which a person's spiritual nature would receive salvation. Christian Gnostics believed that the apostles imparted hidden truths in addition to the written accounts of Christ. There were great varieties of Gnostic sects and cults, some teaching that since the human flesh was of no value, a person could indulge the flesh in carnal pleasure. These were the libertine Gnostics. The ascetic Gnostics believed that the only way to liberate the spirit was through strict control of the flesh. Most Gnostic teachers believed that some people received a seed or spark of divine spiritual substance. Through Gnostic rituals and secret knowledge it was believed that the divine within a person could be liberated and rescued from the evil material body in which it was trapped. JS

[67] Origen (ca. 185–ca. 254) was a Greek theologian, originally in Alexandria. "His philosophical speculations often issued in audacious theories." He was anathematized in 553 at the fifth ecumenical council at Constantinople for, among other things, his mysticism and spiritualism (*ODCC*, 1193–95). RF

[68] Neoplatonism, a philosophical school of thought derived from Plato, considered physical matter to be inherently evil. Man's purpose is to strive to shed the fleshly and earthly aspects of his being and strive toward the spiritual. Neoplatonism, supposedly rejected by Christian theologians, laid the basis for the view that what is finite is incapable of the infinite, thus, in regard to the Supper, it is understandable how the earthly elements of bread and wine were viewed by Calvin and other Reformers as being incapable of hosting the Lord's actual body and blood. Augustine, though rejecting major tenets of Neoplatonism, retained enough of it to lay the foundation for what would finally result in the work of John Calvin, who in many respects was the most thoroughgoing student of Augustine at the time of the Reformation. JS

Jesus held in his hand at the institution to have been his body, which at that hour he still bore.[69] Nor could he possibly have meant that the wine in the cup was really the testamental blood that would be shed for many, for—quite apart from all other possible objections—his blood was not yet shed but still flowed in his veins.

The objection has continually been raised against the realistic doctrine of the Supper that it is unthinkable for the body of Christ to be at the same time in heaven and on earth, so this cannot be the meaning of the Words of Institution. One argument raised by *Zwingli* at the Marburg Colloquy against *Luther's* literal understanding of the Words of Institution was *Deus nobis non proponit incomprehensibilia* ["that God does not present us with any incomprehensible propositions"].[70] Luther's response was that God does indeed present us with much that is incomprehensible,[71] for example, that Christ is God and man. No one—and least of all Luther himself—disputes the uniquely and enormously *paradoxical* quality of the eucharistic dogma's claim that Christ's body is simultaneously in heaven and at each earthly Supper, and that already at the first Supper, in anticipation of his death and glorification, Christ gave to his disciples his body and blood to be eaten and drunk in, with, and under the bread and wine. We absolutely do not understand why this paradox should be thought any greater than those involved in the doctrine of the two natures of Christ or the doctrine of the Trinity.

It would never occur to anyone to deem the eucharistic dogma true if it were only a product of theological speculation. The facts of the matter precisely mirror those that obtain in the case of the dogma of the two natures in Christ or of the Trinitarian doctrine. We are dealing with nothing other than the issue of the faithful rendering of scriptural statements. Scripture alone bears responsibility for the indisputably paradoxical nature of the assertions made in the eucharistic dogma. But these scriptural statements are actually present in the text. Nor can they be explained away. In ancient and modern times the attempt has been made to give a different sense to the words that have been handed down. We cannot list all these attempts. They range from Karlstadt's[72] claim that at the words "This is my body," Jesus pointed to his body, to the very popular claim of modern theologians that the original meaning of the Aramaic *gufi* here is not "body" but "per-

---

[69] *Institutes*, 4.17.17 and 23. HS

An English translation of Calvin's *Institutes* is available as John Calvin, *Institutes of the Christian Religion* (trans. Ford Battles; ed. John T. McNeill; Library of Christian Classics 20–21; Philadelphia: Westminster Press, 1960). JS

[70] WA 30^III.120.29 [cf. *LW* 38:21]. HS

[71] *Quod multa proponat nobis deus incomprehensibilia* (WA 30^III.120.17–18 [cf. *LW* 38:22]). HS

[72] Andreas Rudolf Bodenstein von Karlstadt (ca. 1480–1541) was an early supporter of Luther, a member of the Wittenberg University faculty. Karlstadt's attempts to destroy all traces of Roman Catholicism in Wittenberg in 1521 precipitated one of the first internal conflicts of the Lutheran Reformation and forced Luther to return from hiding at the Wartburg Castle in order to quell the unrest and turmoil caused by Karlstadt's iconoclastic activities in Wittenberg. Karlstadt eventually ended up rejecting both the Sacrament of Holy Baptism and the Sacrament of Holy Communion as true means of God's grace. He was expelled from Saxony in 1524 and became associated with Zwingli and Bullinger, Zwingli's successor in Zurich. JS

son." The purely linguistic impossibility of this last claim is demonstrated by the fact that, in order to uphold it, one must with Otto[73] and Käsemann[74] declare the cup-saying spurious and as a later addition of the church. Moreover, all attempts to spiritualize "body" in the Words of Institution come to grief against the Fourth Gospel's replacement of "body and blood" with "flesh and blood." John thus translates the Aramaic word underlying "body" with "flesh," probably in conscious opposition to Gnosticism's attempts to spiritualize the Lord's Supper, which began already in the NT age.

If the NT reports of the institution of the Supper thus contain nothing that necessitates a symbolic explanation, if on the contrary, such an explanation leads to the conclusion that Jesus obscured the actual sense of the Supper and thereby gave rise to the later controversies, and if furthermore, it stands fast that the only real reason for all symbolic, spiritualizing interpretations are the intellectual difficulties involved in a literal understanding of "This is my body," then theology is compelled to stick to the literal understanding on the basis of the reports of the institution. A valid reason to depart from the literal understanding could never be found in a philosophical argument against the possibility of the real presence, nor could it ever be provided by a psychological consideration of what Jesus might and must have thought and said in that hour. No man can think himself into the soul of the God-man in that hour when he sanctified himself (John 17:19) as the Passover lamb of the NT and as the Lamb of God who takes away the sin of the world. The one and only justification for abandoning the literal sense would be the existence of a word of Scripture that teaches a different understanding of the Lord's Supper. Now in two passages of the NT we possess something that one may rightly think is missing from the Synoptic Gospels' reports of the institution: the tenth and eleventh chapters of 1 Corinthians and the sixth chapter of John's Gospel contain detailed *commentaries on the Words of Institution*. What do these passages teach concerning the Lord's body and blood in the Supper?

In view of the meager quantity of the extant source material, the historian regards it as a happy accident that the most ancient datable report of the institution of the Lord's Supper has been preserved for us by *Paul*, in connection with a commentary. Because the church cannot understand the emergence of the canon apart from the activity of the Holy Spirit, she discerns here a pointer to this activity. The Pauline report was fashioned before the first Gospel grew out of the oral and written traditions in which the memory of the historical Jesus lived on, which happened about twenty-five years after the first Supper. Conflicts within the Corinthian congregation, which led to divisions at the Supper and impaired its

---

[73] Rudolf Otto (1869–1937) was a classic German liberal theologian famous for his book *The Life and Ministry of Jesus according to the Historical and Critical Method*, which questioned much of the historical narrative of the NT concerning Christ's life and work. JS

[74] Ernst Käsemann was a German NT theologian. Influenced by Rudolph Bultmann, he has emphasized the necessity of "demythologizing" the Gospels, while at the same time strangely upholding the importance of the historical basis of Christianity. RF

celebration, obliged Paul back at that early juncture to remind the congregation of what it had once learned from him concerning the Lord's Supper. The fact that Paul had always taught along these lines considerably shortens the temporal distance between this report and the institution itself. Moreover, Paul's heavy emphasis that his report of the institution simply reproduces a tradition that goes back to Jesus himself[75] gives his record the quality of a first-class historical source. The authenticity of Paul's report is all the more strong because it agrees in all essential statements with what has been preserved for us in Mark's completely independent tradition of the institution. The fact that it was dispute and division at the celebration of the Eucharist that produced both the first written report and the first commentary on the Supper is not without deeper significance.

This sad state of affairs is proof positive that eucharistic controversies can have a highly productive effect insofar as they oblige the church to reflect on the essence of the Lord's Supper. Nor is it any accident that the famous *oportet et haereses esse*[76]—"for there must be factions among you in order that those who are genuine among you may be recognized" (1 Cor 11:19 [RSV])—originated in precisely this context. If the situation in Corinth had not obliged Paul at that time to address a question that he otherwise never touches in his letters, then, according to the tested methods of modern NT scholarship, the most learned books would have been written on the question of why Paul shows no awareness of the Lord's Supper. In all probability, the illuminating answer would have been given that, in Paul's time, the Supper did not yet exist. After all, contemporary scholars use the same logic to prove that the primitive Palestinian church's breaking of bread and the Eucharist of the *Didache*[77] had no connection at all with the death of Christ!

Here we cannot enter into a detailed exegesis of the Pauline statements on the Lord's Supper. We must be content to reply to the important question of *what, in Paul's opinion, is given to participants in the Lord's Supper*. The apostle himself places this Sacrament in a grand framework of the history of religion and at the same time sets it in the context of salvation history. The Lord's Supper has *analogies in the history of religions* in the shape of the sacrificial cultus of the Jews and the sacrificial and communion celebrations of the pagans: "Consider Israel according to the flesh: Are not those who eat the sacrifices partners (*koinonoi*) in the altar?" (1 Cor 10:18). Those who "sacrifice to demons" are correspondingly also "partners with demons" (1 Cor 10:20). "You cannot drink the cup of the Lord and the cup of demons. You cannot partake of the table of the Lord and the table of demons" (1 Cor 10:21 [RSV]). Just as participation in non-Christian sacrificial

---

[75] See part 3 above. HS

[76] *Oportet et haereses esse* is the way the Vulgate renders 1 Cor 11:19. A literal translation would be "it is necessary that there be heresies." The Latin *haeresis* is a transliteration of the Greek αἵρεσις, which in 1 Cor 11:19 means "faction." RF

[77] The *Didache* seems to have originated around the year 130, though portions could be significantly older. It was intended to be used as the source for instruction of those to be baptized. The description of the Eucharist in the *Didache* is realistic and parallels the teaching of the NT. Some speculate that the source for the *Didache* was a very early manual of instruction for Jewish converts to Christianity. JS

rites brings about a *koinonia* with the divinity honored therein, so likewise participation in the Lord's Supper establishes a *person's* koinonia *with Christ.*

Paul nowhere says that the Lord's Supper is a sacrifice. He means only that it occupies the same place in Christian worship as sacrifices occupy—albeit according to different understandings in each case—in Jewish and pagan worship. Moreover, this parallel is correct not only from the vantage point of the history of religions, but also in theological perspective, insofar as Christ's sacrifice on the cross (his great "for you") is celebrated in the Lord's Supper. The *koinonia* with Christ that is established by the Lord's Supper is incompatible with the *koinonia* of the demons. This is described more precisely by Paul as *a* koinonia *with the body and blood of Christ:* "The cup of blessing which we bless, is it not a participation (*koinonia*) in the blood of Christ? The bread which we break, is it not a participation (*koinonia*) in the body of Christ?" (1 Cor 10:16). In what respect is a *koinonia* with the body and blood of the Lord effected through the cup and bread? This "is demonstrated by 1 Cor 11:27–30, which expresses most clearly that the blood is drunk with the wine and that the Lord's body is eaten in the bread."[78] As Luther rightly perceived,[79] 1 Cor 10:16 and 11:28 are sure indicators that, according to Paul, the bread remains bread as the Supper is eaten and that the substance of bread does not cease to exist, as the Roman Church believes.

From this fact we may not, however, conclude with Calvin that the believer eats only bread and that the *koinonia* of the body and blood is a spiritual event that takes place simultaneously with the bodily eating as the believer's soul is spiritually fed with the Lord's body and blood in heaven while his mouth eats and drinks bread and wine. Calvin developed this notion in his endeavor to reconcile the statements of the NT with his philosophical worldview, which denied the possibility of a physical presence of the human nature of Christ. Nothing of the kind exists in Paul's thought. He nowhere indicates that our faith establishes communion with the Lord's body and blood, but rather says explicitly that the cup is the communion of the blood and the bread is the communion of the body.

With the same certainty that the bread is the body of Christ, as the Words of Institution are understood by Paul, so also participation in the bread and wine is participation in the body and blood of Christ, although the elements do not cease to be bread and wine. It is wrong when Paul's view is understood otherwise than in the sense of what later theological schools described as sacramental union— body and blood are united with bread and wine—and as *manducatio oralis* ["eating by the mouth"]—the Lord's body and blood are received with the mouth, albeit not in the manner of common earthly food. Accordingly, Paul teaches the so-called *manducatio indignorum* ["eating by the unworthy"],[80] the belief that the

---

[78] H. Lietzmann, *Handbuch zum neuen Testament* on 1 Cor 10:16. HS

[79] SA III VI; see part 4 above. HS

[80] There was a distinction, made at the Wittenberg Concord in 1536, between the *manducatio indignorum* ("eating by the unworthy," e.g., nominal Christians, those in doubt) and the *manducatio impiorum* ("eating by the ungodly," e.g., the heathen). While allowing the distinction, the Lutheran Confessions actu-

unworthy, that is, those who do not examine themselves and who do not distinguish the body of the Lord from other foods, receive Christ's body and blood for judgment, not blessing (1 Cor 11:27 ff.).

H. Lietzmann[81] makes the pertinent comment on 1 Cor 11:27 that from the words "This is my body," it follows "as Luther rightly explained in the sense of Paul that the bread is really the Lord's body: Whoever eats it unworthily sins against the Lord's body, and he will soon notice the consequences in his own body, [1 Cor 11:] 30." It is no accident that this verse names sickness and death as divine punishment. Poverty or distress may not be substituted for these penalties.

According to the common opinion of Christendom, just as the blessing of the Lord's Supper affects our body, to which resurrection and eternal life are guaranteed by this Sacrament, likewise God also attaches a bodily punishment to unworthy eating by giving man up to the fate of death. This is the clear teaching of Paul. If we could ask him if he would deem correct the description of the Eucharist as "medicine of immortality, antidote against death"[82] which Ignatius of Antioch[83] quotes from the Antiochene liturgy at the beginning of the second century, the apostle would presumably answer with a comfortable "yes." It goes without saying that Ignatius also knew that the Supper is not a miraculous medicine that works in a magical and mechanical manner apart from faith on man's part. Moreover, as the whole context of 1 Corinthians 10 and 11 shows, the meaning of Paul's warning against unworthy eating is precisely to safeguard against a brand of Christianity that rests on the sure possession of infallibly operating Sacraments.

Paul's clear and internally consistent view of the gift of the Lord's Supper becomes clearer yet when we consider the salvation-history context in which he places the Lord's Supper. Paul is not only acquainted with *analogies* to the Lord's Supper in the *history of religions*, in the shape of the sacrificial cultus of Jews and pagans, but also with *salvation-history prototypes*. In his translation of the Bible, Luther translates the Greek word *typos* with the German word *Vorbild*, that is, "type." This term denotes a "shadow of what is to come" (Col 2:17 [RSV]). Adam, through whom sin and death came into the world, is, according to Rom 5:14, the *typos* of the future Adam who brought grace and life. Thus Baptism and the Lord's Supper also have their prototypes in the OT, for "all our fathers were under the cloud, all passed through the sea, all were baptized into Moses in the cloud and in the sea, all ate the same spiritual food, and all drank the same spiritual drink. For they drank of that spiritual Rock that followed them, and that Rock was Christ" (1 Cor 10:1–4 [NKJV]). While the purpose for which the "spiritual food" and the "spiritual drink" were given is not explicitly stated, it can be established with cer-

---

ally see the two as the same. See Sasse, *This Is My Body*, especially pages 309–10 (1959 ed.); 250–51 (1977 ed.). RF

[81] Hans Lietzmann (1875–1942) was a professor at Berlin, specializing in NT, early church history, and liturgical theology. JS

[82] See note 103 below. RF

[83] Ignatius, *Epistle to the Ephesians* 20:2. HS

tainty from Paul's whole train of thought: for the miraculous preservation of the people of God on the wilderness wandering. To be sure, the *pneuma* ["Spirit"] food of manna and the *pneuma* drink of water from the rock did not assist everyone in the preservation of his life. In many, God had no pleasure because they fell into grave sin, namely, into sacrificing to demons, unchastity, putting God to the test, and murmuring against him. Therefore, they had to die. "Now these things happened to them as a warning [Greek: *typikos;* Luther Bible: *vorbildlich*], but they were written down for our instruction, upon whom the end of the ages has come" (1 Cor 10:11 [RSV]).

Even though it strikes the contemporary exegete with his modern scholarly methods as strange, and while it could never be achieved by our human means, this unquestionably correct interpretation of the OT by an apostle of Christ is a genuine aid to our understanding of the Lord's Supper—if we pay attention to what the Supper has in common with the OT "type," and to what distinguishes the two. God's grace, which preserves and protects from death, is the common factor.

Another common feature is that, on the one hand, this grace is effective for the chosen people of God—that is, for Israel according to the flesh on its journey through the wilderness into the promised land of earthly Canaan—and, on the other hand, for Israel according to the spirit on its journey through the comfortless wilderness of this world to the heavenly Canaan of God's kingdom. In both cases, God rescues his people from certain death by means of a miraculous feeding. He bestows supernatural, spiritual food and supernatural, spiritual drink. Whoever tastes this food and this drink is miraculously preserved. All who belong to the people have a share in it; they all eat the same food and drink the same drink. But the food and drink do not avail for the rescue of all. Many fall into idolatry and many into unchastity—the two mortal sins so frequently encountered in the ancient church—and many fall into putting God to the test and murmuring against him. God's judgment falls on them, even though they have tasted the *pneuma* food and the *pneuma* drink. The Lord's Supper and its type agree thus far.

To our surprise, in another important point, Paul establishes a further identity by teaching that Christ was already present in the OT prototype: "For they drank of that spiritual Rock that followed them, and that Rock was Christ." Christ is present with his church. In the Lord's Supper, he miraculously provides food and drink for the church on her journey through the wilderness. Paul teaches that Christ invisibly accompanied Israel on her wilderness trek and gave her spiritual food and spiritual drink.

One thing, though, he could not yet give the children of Israel—and here the new and unique quality of the Lord's Supper becomes plain. There was not yet any koinonia *of the body and blood of Christ in the OT*. The Christ who is already present in the OT is the eternal Son, the Logos. He is not yet the *Christus incarnatus*—the Logos made flesh. There were already *prototypes of the Sacraments* in the *old covenant*, for the beginning of 1 Corinthians 10 also speaks of Baptism. *But Sacraments have only been around since the incarnation.* Therefore, the practice of seeking Sacraments already in the OT involves either a misuse of language or a lack of appreciation for the indissoluble connection between the incarnation of the Logos and the institution of the Sacraments. The spiritual food and the spiritual drink that Christ gives us when we come as guests to his Table could not yet exist in the OT; Israel could not at that time receive them: they are the Lord's body and blood. Thus when the blessed bread and cup are said to be the *koinonia* of the body and blood of Christ, nothing else is meant than that we receive *the body of the Lord with the bread and the blood of the Lord with the cup* as spiritual, supernatural food and spiritual, supernatural drink. To get across this point, Paul could also say that we *eat the body* and *drink the blood* of the Lord.

But why does the apostle avoid these expressions? If he does this intentionally, then he certainly does not do so because they are wrong, but because they are likely to be misunderstood. The *Gospel of John* uses them without misgivings. Yet one can well understand how, when they made their way from the arcane discipline of the Christian Divine Service to within earshot of evil-minded pagans, sayings such as John 6:53 ("Unless you eat the flesh of the Son of Man and drink his blood, you have no life in you") led to the rumors of ritual murder, rumors which accompanied the ancient church for centuries. It also proves, by the way, that the primitive church understood the Supper neither in the sense of a commemorative meal, nor in the sense of a purely spiritual feeding. How else can one explain the fact that, in a world full of cultic meals and communion celebrations, people took such grave offense precisely at the Christian Supper and kept on calling out the police against it? Yet, even within the church itself, the "hard saying" (John 6:60) about *eating the body* and *drinking the blood of Christ* could provoke offense.

Can the body of Christ be eaten like ordinary food? Manifestly not, for all the churches of Christendom that adhere to the *manducatio oralis* have always emphasized that this is a different eating from eating for ordinary nourishment, which serves to build up and preserve physical life. We can understand how such considerations may have prompted Paul to avoid those expressions, resulting in his speaking of the "body" of Christ rather than of his "flesh." Yet at the moment when the protest against a false materialization would lead to a false spiritualization of the Lord's Supper, and when the "eating" of the body of Christ would be given up for fear that it might be misinterpreted along materialistic lines and thus would be replaced by a purely spiritual process that could only figuratively be described as eating, then Paul would have defended the eating of the body of Christ just as strongly as John does.

This is the meaning of the hotly controverted sixth chapter of John's Gospel, behind whose powerful words we are able to discern one of the first great debates on the Supper. It is universally acknowledged today that this chapter deals with the Supper. In earlier times, when the distinctive literary character of this Gospel had not yet been understood, John 6 was seen as containing at most a prophecy of the Supper. Even a theologian of Luther's caliber disputed the connection of this chapter with the Sacrament of the Altar. It is also universally acknowledged today that the passage breaks down into two clearly distinct sections, the *discourse on the bread of life* (John 6:32–51a), and the *discourse on eating and drinking the body and blood of Christ* (John 6:51b–63).

In the first discourse, Christ is the Logos, the true bread that comes down from heaven. Eating this bread means to believe in him. In John 6:51, the place of Christ as the object of eating is taken by his flesh. The absolute necessity of the sacramental eating and drinking is now taught with strong words. Realism is, so to say, pushed to the limit. It is not in any way retracted by the statement "It is the spirit that gives life, the flesh is of no avail" (John 6:63 [RSV]). These words are patently directed against the error of cross materialism—that is, against that "Capernaitism" which understands the eating of Christ's flesh in purely physical terms.

At the same time, these words do not intend to deny the fact and benefit of the incarnation. Even so, they do not intend to deny the eating of Christ's flesh and the benefit of this eating, which is the supernatural taking up of Christ's body into our corporeality and its effect on the whole person. The emphasis on the "flesh" in the Supper also must be understood in terms of John 1:14—"the Word became *flesh*" —which is the theme of the Fourth Gospel.

The reason why John is not content with the word *soma* (body), which sufficed for Paul, is that that the concept of *soma* came to be understood along thoroughly spiritualistic lines. The *Gnostics*, who emerged on the scene in the period of time separating John from Paul, did not dispute that Jesus had a *soma*, a body, but they did resolutely dispute that this body was an earthly body of flesh like ours.

The advocates of this tendency must have regarded themselves as the champions of the genuine Gospel, advocates who intended to preserve Christianity as a spiritual religion and to protect it from sinking into magical, materialistic notions. They were countered with the sentence *"The Word became flesh."* In the struggle against them, 1 John 4:2–3 established the standard by which the congregations were to distinguish between pure and false doctrine, between church and non-church: "Every spirit which confesses that Jesus Christ has come *in the flesh* is of God" [RSV]. The statements in John 6 on the eating and drinking of the Lord's flesh and blood belong in this context. The real, historically incarnate Christ *gives to his people his flesh to eat and his blood to drink in the Eucharist* and thus incorporates them into himself: "He who eats my flesh and drinks my blood abides in me, and I in him" (John 6:56 [RSV]). At the same time, he thereby gives them a share in eternal life: "He who eats my flesh and drinks my blood has eternal life, and I will raise him up at the last day" (John 6:54 [RSV]).[84]

---

[84] The creedal expression "resurrection of the flesh" is connected with this struggle against spiritualism. It goes without saying that the church knows with Paul that "flesh and blood cannot inherit the kingdom of God, nor does the perishable inherit the imperishable" (1 Cor 15:50). Yet she also knows with Paul that the "spiritual" or "heavenly" body is genuinely corporeal and that it is connected with the present earthly body, just as the plant is with the seed (1 Cor 15:42 ff.). HS

In light of all this, scarcely a shred of doubt remains that *the two great commentaries* that the NT provides on the eucharistic words teach the *real presence* of the body and blood of Christ under bread and wine. Only a violent exegesis can deny this. Nor can we concede the possibility of explaining 1 Corinthians 10–11 and John 6 in a variety of ways because of a supposed unclarity or ambiguity in their wording, which would make it possible for both the spiritualistic and the realistic doctrine of the Supper to appeal to them. We must hold fast to this refusal directed against *Calvin*, whose explanation of the Supper texts is determined by the preconception that Christ's body cannot enter into us.[85] For Calvin, the body of Christ as a truly human body exists in finite form and must, therefore, after the exaltation be as far removed from us as heaven is from earth.[86] The Lord's body thus cannot simultaneously be present in heaven and on earth, and in multiple locations on earth.[87] Calvin is not in a position to substantiate these assertions from the Bible, for he did not derive them from the Bible. These are metaphysical statements and ideological presuppositions that he uses to explain the Supper texts. Calvin does not realize how his procedure involves him from the very outset in rejecting precisely what we saw above[88] to be a presupposition in Paul's doctrine of the Supper, namely, the apostle's understanding that the body of Christ can be simultaneously present in heaven and on earth, and in many places in the Lord's Supper.

The upshot of this is that Calvin must necessarily have a wrong understanding of Paul's thought. A great volume of applause directed these days toward the great systematician of the Reformed Church[89] by all who wish to avoid the scandal of Christ's bodily presence is equaled by the contradiction of Calvin the exegete. Recent research has irrefutably demonstrated that 1 Cor 11:27–30 can be understood in no other sense than that of Christ's bodily presence in the Sacrament when considered from a purely linguistic and logical point of view.[90] The understanding of the Synoptic narratives of the institution of the Lord's Supper cannot remain unaffected by this finding. Even someone who is inclined to say with Zwingli that *Deus non nobis proponit incomprehensibilia* ("God does not present us with any incomprehensible propositions") and who thinks that

---

[85] *Quamvis in nos non ingrediatur ipsa Christi caro* (*Institutes*, 4.17.32). HS

[86] *Necesse est a nobis tanto locorum intervallo distare, quantum coelum abest a terra* (*Consensus Tigurinus*, 25). HS
On the *Consensus Tigurinus* see further in part 8 below. RF

[87] *Institutes*, 4.17.17. HS

[88] In part 6 above. HS

[89] Sasse is referring to his contemporary Karl Barth (1886–1968). Barth features prominently in many of Sasse's writings, because it was Barth around whom many German theologians rallied, including many Lutherans. Sasse never fails to point out the deficiencies of Barth's theology and wishes always to remind Lutherans that Barth was a Reformed theologian whose views on key issues are incompatible with the biblical truth confessed by Lutheranism. Barth was a student of Harnack, as was Sasse. JS

[90] Sasse doubtless is making specific reference to 1 Cor 11:29, "For anyone who eats and drinks without discerning the body," which was being interpreted as a reference to the "body" as the church rather than to the sacramental body of Christ. RF

Lutheran eucharistic doctrine requires people to acknowledge too great a miracle nevertheless must concede that the literal understanding of the *verba testamenti* ("Words of Institution") was already advocated by Paul. Let it be supposed, for the sake of argument, that the words of Jesus were unclear and that we could not with good conscience decide for the literal understanding on the basis of the Synoptic reports.

Even if this were the case, would not the commentaries of Paul and John still compel us to opt for the literal understanding? Do they not, after all, belong together with the institution narratives in an indissoluble unity? Do they not form with the latter a single great biblical testimony to the Lord's Supper? Must we not constantly keep this *total witness of the NT* before our eyes in order to be able to teach the Supper correctly? The fact that the most ancient report of the institution is immediately joined to a commentary is surely no accident but rather has a deeper meaning. If there is any authority on earth competent to give instruction on the Lord's Supper beyond what Jesus himself said, is it not the authority of the apostolic office?

One reason alone could justify the modern church's refusal to be taught by the biblical commentaries found in Paul and John, namely, the certain conviction that the testimony of these apostolic authorities is irreconcilable with what Jesus himself thought and taught on the Supper. The achievements of researchers in the History of Religion School, such as Heitmüller and Weinel,[91] in bringing about a new understanding of the Sacraments and worship in primitive Christianity have been universally acknowledged today by the theologians of all churches—Roman Catholicism included. The following sentences from Heitmüller characterize the way these scholars have sketched the development of the primitive Christian Supper:

> When Jesus in that solemn hour distributed his body and blood to his disciples as the basis of their union, he meant himself, his personality, what his personality determined and guaranteed by way of religious substance and experience: he meant a purely personal, spiritual, and ethical communion with himself. This elevated and pure tone was not maintained, and perhaps we must say that, to begin with, it could not be maintained. Naturalistic, mystical elements usurped this communion with Jesus, the idea of spiritual and bodily union with the exalted one forced its way in, and, in connection with this, there crept in, from the undercurrent of popular religion, a belief in the mediation of spiritual goods by external actions and "material" means.

---

[91]   H. Weinel has set forth his viewpoint most comprehensively and with the greatest clarity in the paragraphs dealing with the Sacraments in his *Biblische Theologie des Neuen Testaments* (2d ed.; 1913), especially paragraphs 66 ff. HS

Wilhelm Heitmüller (1869–1926) was a leader of the History of Religion School of thought. He was particularly interested in applying the *Religionsgeschichtliche Schule* theories to Baptism and the Lord's Supper, writing a number of books on the subject. Heinrich Weinel (1874–1936) applied the History of Religion School's theories to winning over the intellectuals of his day. In the attempt, he was willing to surrender much of orthodox Christianity. JS

The holy meal became supernatural food, bread and cup mediated Christ's body and blood: sacramental belief made its entrance. The first beginnings of this fateful development manifest themselves already in Paul, even though, in his case, communion with Christ in the spiritual and ethical sense stands in the foreground and the sacramental elements lie completely on the periphery. For the Mass of ancient Christian congregations this development was almost unavoidable: it needed mystery's external visible surety and allure. The kernel could only be preserved in this form that fitted the age.[92]

Any glance at recent theological literature on the Supper shows what a deep impact on theology has been made by this picture of history, which goes back ultimately to Harnack's understanding of dogma's ancient history. A generation after Heitmüller wrote his account, his influence is still found today among the very theologians who think themselves to have far outgrown the History of Religion School, albeit decked out with a few alterations to suit the times. There is no longer any talk of how, in his last meal, Jesus bequeathed to his disciples his personality and his religious experience, but something is expressed along the lines of how, in the Supper, Jesus gives himself to them as the one who dies for them. There is full agreement with Heitmüller that Jesus did not yet think and indeed, in view of his mental presuppositions determined by the OT and Judaism, could not have thought of distributing his flesh and blood as a supernatural substance to participants in the Supper. On the contrary, this understanding of the Words of Institution must be explained in terms of the influence of Hellenism on the nascent church. Even *Althaus*, who acknowledges the sacramental "realism" of 1 Cor 10:16, immediately poses "seriously the question whether Paul has not here taken over ideas prevalent in the syncretism of his pagan environment."[93]

Moreover, in the NT essay for the symposium volume *Abendmahls-gemeinschaft?* Ernst *Käsemann* explains how Paul succumbed to a "temptation" that "could scarcely be avoided in the Hellenistic age"[94] insofar as he pictures the elements of the Supper as partaking of the heavenly nature of the risen Lord. In the statements of 1 Cor 10:16 that teach that the bread and wine are no longer symbols of something else but rather the bearers of the heavenly gift of the Supper, Käsemann sees the effect of that fateful influence of the history of religions which kept nascent Christianity permanently entangled in Hellenism. Even if this were the case and we did in fact find a different understanding of the Supper in Paul and Jesus respectively, we would at least have to begin by asking

---

[92]　*RGG*[1] 1:51–52. Note how what is here labeled "folk religion," that is, "belief in the mediation of spiritual goods through external actions and means," is precisely identical with what is said in the statement from AC V quoted above (in part 6) and with what Luther continually reiterated, as, for example, in SA III VIII 10: "Accordingly, we should and must constantly maintain that God will not deal with us except through his external Word and sacrament. Whatever is attributed to the Spirit apart from such Word and sacrament is of the devil." [The English translation is from Tappert, *BC*, 313.] HS

[93]　P. Althaus, *Die lutherische Abendmahlslehre in der Gegenwart* (1931), 42. HS

[94]　Supplement 3 to [the series] Evangelischen Theologie, p. 90. HS

whether we are really dealing here with an unbridgeable antithesis, or perhaps rather with a necessary supplement. Might it not have pleased God to give us through the apostle's mouth not only a commentary on the eucharistic words, but also in this commentary tell us things about, for example, the connection between the body of Christ in the Supper and in the church which we do not learn from Jesus' brief words? At the very least, it ought to be conceded that Paul himself did not understand his explanation to be a reinterpretation but rather the correct interpretation of the historical words of the Lord. Should it then be completely unthinkable that "Hellenism" played a thoroughly legitimate role in this interpretation, just as did "Parseeism" in the exposition and further formation of the messianic prophecies in the later sections of the OT? Let not the enormous importance of Hellenism for the rise of the church be forgotten.

The Greek-speaking church grew out of the Hellenistic synagogue. As is well known, the Septuagint is not just a translation of the OT in a purely linguistic sense. It is also a transposition of the OT revelation into the mental world of Hellenism. As such, it was the oldest Bible of the Greek church, fully recognized by the NT as the inspired Word of God, alongside the Hebrew Bible. If it pleased the Holy Spirit to take a roundabout way via the Hellenistic synagogue and its Septuagint to enable the NT message to be expressed through the introduction into biblical language of the Hellenistic concepts of *cosmos, aion* ["time, age"], and *Kyrios* ["Lord"], who will forbid him to do the same for understanding the Supper through the adoption of the Hellenistic concept of *soma?* We do not wish to say more with this than that the substance Jesus was concerned with found its appropriate terminology in the Greek language's much greater possibilities of expression. The times are long and truly past—even for the Roman Catholic Church, by the way—when an anxious apologetic attempted to deny any influence on the language and thought-world of Holy Scripture by the surrounding religions.

If we bear all this in mind, then we shall have to be much more cautious about trying to find a contradiction between Jesus and Paul in the understanding of the Supper than is generally the case today. Above all, the whole development of recent theology will not permit our generation to get around the necessity of answering a question that a generation ago simply did not exist for the History of Religion School: the question of the *doctrinal authority of the Pauline epistles* for the church. We can get a clear grasp of the significance of this question from the following judgment rendered by Heitmüller on the meaning of Jesus' Words of Institution. He takes as his starting point the churchly interpretation that "the bread *is* really his body, indeed his *glorified* body. In and with the bread and wine the true body and blood are distributed and received." Heitmüller establishes that Luther stubbornly defended this interpretation, commenting:

> It is certain that this understanding is very ancient, that it was already present in ancient Christendom at least in a similar form in Paul, and that the writers and first readers of the Gospels understood the words in a similar

way. We sincerely admire the deep mysticism and believing ardor that have in all ages found contentment and experienced their culmination in this eucharistic faith. But none of this justifies the view that Jesus himself intended these words in this way. No less than everything speaks against this assumption.[95]

And then follows an account of the presumed thoughts Jesus is said to have joined to the Words of Institution. This is no more and no less than a claim that, while the realistic Supper doctrine of Luther and the church is taught in the NT, the passages in question may not actually be considered normative for the church, since they contradict the teaching of Jesus. This is basically the same line of argument that we find in all those who, while acknowledging "sacramental realism" in Paul, nevertheless immediately pronounce this facet of the apostle's thought non-binding because Jesus did not teach it and because Paul was influenced by Hellenism. This presupposes that there is no unified NT as such, only historical records of varying value concerning ancient Christianity. Historical proof is put in the place of scriptural proof. By taking from under Luther's feet the ground on which he waged his struggle against the Roman Mass and against Sacramentless Enthusiasm, which is to say by abolishing the firm basis of the biblical testimony to the Lord's Supper, they rob the Lutheran Church of the victorious weapon of the divine Word and thereby destroy the basis for her existence.

A theology that makes use of arguments of this sort bequeaths scriptural proof to the Roman Church, and Rome will not fail to make plentiful use of this surrendered weapon. Over against modern Protestantism, which rejects Paul's "sacramental realism" and contents itself with what remains of the Sacrament when the presence of the Lord's true body and blood under bread and wine has been removed, the Roman doctrine is purely and simply in the right because, despite all its errors, it stands closer to the real Gospel. Today there are perhaps entire countries in which, notwithstanding the sacrifice of the Mass, the Roman Sacrament of the Altar has preserved more remnants of the biblical Lord's Supper than has what the Protestants there celebrate—or no longer celebrate—as the Supper. Alongside his appreciation of the doctrine of justification, the greatest and deepest theological perception vouchsafed to Luther was surely his comprehension of what depends on whether the words "This is my body" are still understood or no longer understood. Not only the preservation of the Supper and the Sacraments in general depends on this, but also, as is confirmed by the melancholy experiences of four centuries of Protestant church history, the authority of the divine Word and the understanding of the Gospel as the message of the incarnation of the eternal Word. Therefore, when the Evangelical Lutheran Church, with the Reformer, fights for the proposition that served as the title of one of his great eucharistic writings—*That These Words "This Is My Body" Still Stand Firm*

---

[95] *RGG*[1] 1:33. HS

against the Enthusiasts[96]—it is not a superfluous quarrel among theologians, but a necessary battle for the church's preservation.

PART 8: THE PRESERVATION OF THE LORD'S SUPPER

We took as our point of departure the statement that the Lord's Supper stands as a foreign concept in the world. In the first centuries of church history it was the stuff of calumny and hatred, while, for the enlightened people of the modern world, it has been the target of mockery and scorn. Whether the ancient world waxed indignant over alleged cannibalism on the part of Christians or the modern world turns up its nose with Frederick the Great,[97] [saying] "that they eat their God," for both the wise and the fools of this world, the Supper remains in equal measure incomprehensible and insupportable—at the very least an insult to human reason. So it always has been and so it will always remain.

Explaining the Supper to people who do not believe in Christ as the Son of God crucified for their sins and raised for their justification is therefore an enterprise doomed to failure. What absolutely ought not to happen is the eclipse of understanding the Supper even within the church. While this should be unthinkable, it does, in fact, happen that even in a church the Supper is turning into a foreign concept. No sign testifies with such infallible certainty the death throes of a congregation, or a whole church, as the decline and decay of the celebration of the Eucharist. This is, however, the deadly serious situation in which a very large segment of these Protestant churches of the world finds itself.

At the time of the Reformation, the whole Christian world still realized that the Lord's Supper is the climax of all Christian worship. Even Zwingli and Calvin did not intend to rob the Supper of this place. Whether the Lord's Supper's removal to the back burner was not a necessary consequence of their eucharistic teachings is another question, but they certainly did not intend to dislodge it from the center of the church's life.

Having been purified from sacrificial ideas and rituals, in the Lutheran churches the "Mass" maintained its place without contradiction until Pietism and the Enlightenment broke up the ancient order of the Divine Service. With this development, the "Supper crisis," since the eighteenth century, has closed in on the churches of Lutheran confession also. This crisis is expressed in a way that everyone can understand in the statistical facts and figures of participation in the Supper.[98] For the theologian, this crisis is most shockingly revealed in the fact that

---

[96] This can be found in *LW* 37:3–150. JS

[97] This is a reference to Frederick II (1712–1786). He is not to be confused with Frederick William of Brandenburg (1620–1688), who was known as "the Great Elector." Frederick the Great was a religious skeptic whose religion was "duty." RF

[98] While there are 1,396 Communions (1,174 in the year 1931) for every hundred members in the Catholic Church (which means that, on average, every Catholic goes to Communion 14 times in a year), the com-

those pastors and theologians in Lutheran Germany who today still advocate the eucharistic doctrine of the Lutheran Reformation form a shrinking minority.

Neither the Reformed nor any other doctrine has taken the place of the Lutheran teaching in this process. Pastors simply no longer have any clear dogmatic convictions about the Sacrament of the Altar. They content themselves with wavering subjective opinions that they choose according to personal taste and practical needs from that well-stocked warehouse of fashionable theological goods which has been called "German evangelical theology" since the time of this firm's founder, Friedrich Schleiermacher. The events of recent years have already given us some inkling of the long-term consequences of this development. Today's normative theology is resolved, on principle, to learn nothing from history about issues of Christian doctrine. It even goes so far as to justify this refusal with these words of Karl Barth: "From the point of view of Christian language about God, answers from church history's so-called answers provide no answers to questions that need be put independently."[99]

This decision causes us to realize that even the worst neglect of one of the most important parts of church doctrine will not lead anyone to perceive in what direction a church is headed when it no longer understands the Sacrament of the Altar. The time could come one day when the question must be posed with full seriousness whether Luther would find a church with the sacrifice of the Mass more tolerable than a church that, for all practical purposes, has lost the Supper.

In light of everything we have said about the Lord's Supper on the basis of the NT, the fate of a church that has lost the Sacrament of the Altar is clear. A church that does not continually gather around the Supper must undergo *secularization*. It must irreversibly turn into a piece of the world, because the Supper establishes the boundary between church and world. This conclusion is confirmed by the experience of church history and especially of the history of worship in the last few centuries. The destruction of the Supper is followed by the disappearance of the living *remembrance* of Jesus from the hearts of Christians, especially of his suffering and death.

Thus, in the century of the Enlightenment, the fading away of the person of Jesus as the biblical Redeemer into an indeterminate universal teacher, who might just as well be called Moses or Socrates, was bound up with the decline of the Supper

---

municant figures for Protestant Germany in the year 1931 amount to 25 percent of the membership. Among the territorial churches, Schaumburg-Lippe (59 percent) and Bavaria (58 percent) stood in first place, while Hamburg (5.5 percent) and Bremen (5.6 percent) offer even lower figures than Berlin (8.4 percent). The overall picture in the last decades has been of a steady drop in percentage without regard to confessional allegiance within Protestantism. In the *Church Yearbook* of 1933 [ed. Sasse], P. Troschke draws on Dehmel to give the following informative numbers from the old days in Silesia, where the highpoint of eucharistic participation was reached around 1,700 (p. 63): in Görlitz, during the decade 1701–1710, the yearly average number of communicants was 196,526, while it dropped to 95,743 in the decade 1791–1800. At St. Mary Magdalene's in Breslau the number sank from 35,959 in the year 1701 to 9,505 in the year 1800. HS

[99] Karl Barth, *Church Dogmatics* (trans. G. T. Thomson; New York: Scribner's, 1936), 1.1.3. JS

as the celebration of his inextinguishable remembrance. We have already spoken at length about the connection between the Sacrament of the Altar and *belief in justification*. Where Jesus Christ no longer himself speaks to us in the Holy Supper the Gospel "given and shed for you for the forgiveness of sins," the message of the Lamb of God who takes away the sin of the world necessarily fades away.

Christ certainly speaks this, his Gospel, to us not only in the Supper, but also in each of his words. He certainly does not need the Sacrament in order to impress this message on us, but he is pleased to make use of it. Not only did he offer himself as the sacrifice for the sin of the world, nor does he merely keep on having this fact proclaimed, rather, he who is High Priest and sacrificial lamb in one gives us a share in his sacrifice here and now. The unique occurrence on the cross, which is at once a truly historical and truly supra-historical happening, is rendered present when Jesus Christ, the crucified and risen one, gives us his body sacrificed for us to eat and his blood shed for us to drink. Where this no longer happens because Christians have stopped celebrating the Supper, Christ's sacrifice turns from a reality into an idea, and the vicarious satisfaction for sins turns from a fact into a theory. In the place vacated by faith in the Son of God, "who loved me and gave himself for me" [Gal 2:20], steps the intellectual conviction of the correctness of the doctrine of reconciliation. This doctrine will then very soon turn into a topic for general philosophical discussion, bandied about in apologetics, and it will eventually undermine faith altogether as it fuels doubt. Thus, the Gospel itself dies with the Supper.

The same fate affects the church's blessed hope of the coming reign of God and the manifestation of Christ's glory. Where the church no longer proclaims the Lord's death at the altar "until he comes," the maranatha falls silent. Where people do not already have a foretaste of heaven and the beginning of the coming aeon in the Supper, in the long run they cannot endure the disappointment involved in the delay of the parousia. In that event, the eschatological promises of the Gospel are not taken seriously. For this reason a symbolic, spiritualistic doctrine of the Supper has, as a rule, resulted in a symbolic, spiritualistic doctrine of the last things.

This becomes especially clear in the matter of *belief in the resurrection*, which, since the days of the NT, has always been indissolubly connected with faith in the presence of the true body and blood of Christ in the Supper. Because Holy Scripture says nothing to us on this subject, we shall in this life never experience the precise connections that exist between the eating and drinking of the Lord's body and blood in the Supper, on the one hand, and our resurrection to eternal life, on the other. But on the basis of texts such as John 6:54, the church has always testified that a connection exists between the Supper and the resurrection.

In support of this position, the Reformer and the old Lutheran Church delighted to adduce the testimony of the church fathers, above all in the shape of statements by Irenaeus, Cyril of Alexandria, and Hilary. They did this because they found the correct exposition of John 6:54 in these voices of the fathers, for example, in the words of Irenaeus[100] that old Lutheran theology loved to quote: "As the bread taken from the earth" in the celebration of the Holy Supper "is no longer ordinary bread, but the Eucharist, which consists of two elements, earthly and heavenly, so also our bodies when they receive the Eucharist no longer belong to the perishable order, but have the hope of resurrection." When the orthodox church of all ages has ventured to make such statements, she has not allowed herself to be guided by speculations and hypotheses concerning the beyond that arose in the sphere of natural philosophy, but by the clear words of the NT, which is the only source and norm of all statements of this kind. The fact that in this area of doctrine, as in others, some individual theologians have occasionally overstepped the biblically imposed limits may never be used to disprove the scripturally attested fact that a connection exists between the Supper and resurrection. By continually reminding us of the promises of the NT and assuring us of the blessed hope of the resurrection, the Supper keeps the church from becoming a church without hope. If the Supper should be discarded, the church will turn into a this-worldly church or a spiritualistic community and cease to be the church of the risen Christ.

We do not, then, say too much in advancing the thesis *No Supper—No Church*. This becomes especially clear when we recall that, according to the teaching of the NT, the Sacraments of Baptism and Supper are the very forces responsible for the creation of *koinonia*, or the community of the church. We now understand why this is the case. The church is not something to which human history has been inclined to attach the label "intellectual community," in which case it would be a community of the like-minded who band together in an external formation and present themselves before the world as a *corpus* because they share common convictions of faith and a common will. On the contrary, from the beginning and according to her deepest essence, the church is a spiritual and bodily structure: "Because there is *one* bread, we who are many are one *body*" (1 Cor 10:17 [RSV; emphasis added]). The body even takes precedence in Eph 4:4: "*one* body and *one* Spirit." For by *one* Spirit we were all baptized into one body" (1 Cor 12:13 [RSV; emphasis added]). Man never belongs to the church only according to the spirit, but also according to the body. "Do you not know that your bodies are members of Christ?" (1 Cor 6:15). "Do you not know that your body is a temple of the Holy Spirit within you, which you have from God? You are not your own; you were bought with a price. So glorify God in your body" (1 Cor 6:19–20 [RSV]).

How can man's physical body—in its transitoriness, weakness, hatefulness, and lowliness—be a member of Christ? Of the coming Christ, we read in Phil 3:21, "who will change our lowly body to be like his glorious body" [RSV]. He will do this because this body already belongs to him, and that not just in the sense

---

[100] *Against Heresies*, 4.18.5 (cf. 5.2.3). This passage was very often quoted, for example, in the Wittenberg Concord [1536] and in the Mansfeld Preachers' Opinion of 1562 (German 1571). Compare also FC SD VII 14. We must here forgo proof that Irenaeus' mind was correctly understood by the Lutheran fathers. HS

that he is the Lord of this body, but in virtue of the fact that this body has become a member of his body. Our body has become this through Holy *Baptism*. *Luther* was thoroughly in tune with Paul, when, in the Large Catechism, he says the following concerning Baptism's effects on man's body and soul:

> This is the reason why these two things are done in Baptism: the body has water poured over it, though it cannot receive anything but the water, and meanwhile the Word is spoken so that the soul may grasp it.

> Since the water and the Word together constitute one Baptism, body and soul shall be saved and live forever: the soul through the Word in which it believes, the body because it is united with the soul and apprehends Baptism in the only way it can. (LC IV 45–46)[101]

Luther also understands the juxtaposition of *faith* and *eating*, of the spiritual and physical eating of Christ in the Supper. Both are necessary, since man is a spiritual and physical being: "The heart cannot eat it physically nor can the mouth eat it spiritually" (WA 23.191.19–20).[102] The soul cannot eat and the body cannot believe. Yet both, soul and body together, are meant to be united with Christ: "If we eat him spiritually through the Word, he abides in us spiritually in our soul; if one eats him physically, he abides in us physically and we in him" (WA 23.255.24 ff.).[103] What happens then in Baptism and the Lord's Supper—and Luther here superbly reproduces Paul's point of view—is that we are incorporated into Christ and that this *koinonia* is strengthened and preserved as a *koinonia* that is at once spiritual and bodily because we become Christ's members in both soul and body.[104] We now understand why the community of the church must at all times

---

[101] The English translation is from Tappert, *BC*, 442. JS

[102] The English translation is from *LW* 37:93. JS

[103] The English translation is from *LW* 37:132. JS

[104] The conception of the bodily effect of the Sacrament and of the spiritual and bodily nature of the church was first developed in the Eastern Church. It was formally received as church doctrine by the Evangelical Lutheran Church in Ap X [3] with the following words of *Cyril* of Alexandria [*On the Gospel according to John*, 10:2]:

> "We do not deny that we are joined to Christ spiritually by true faith and sincere love. But we do deny that we have no kind of connection with him according to the flesh, and we say that this would be completely foreign to the sacred Scriptures. Who has ever doubted that Christ is a vine in this way and that we are truly branches, deriving life from him for ourselves? Listen to Paul say, 'We are all one body in Christ' (Rom. 12:5); 'We who are many are one body, for we all partake of the same loaf' (I Cor. 10:17). Does he think perhaps that we do not know the power of the mystical benediction? Since this is in us, does it not also cause Christ to dwell in us bodily through the communication of the flesh of Christ?" A little later he says, "Therefore, we must consider that Christ is in us, not only according to the habit we understand as love, but also by a natural participation," etc. [The English translation is taken from Tappert, BC, 179.]

The Formula of Concord explicitly recalls the decision of the Apology and adopts the doctrine "that Christ dwells bodily in the Supper through the communication of his flesh in us" (SD VII 11). May one hope that the foolish chatter will now at last fall silent, according to which the doctrine of the bodily effect of the Sacrament in our church is allegedly a theologoumenon of "Neo-Lutheranism"? HS

See Norman E. Nagel, "Medicine of Immortality and Antidote against Death," *Logia* 4.4 (October 1995): 31–36. RF

remain incomprehensible for the world and why, even for ourselves, it is a matter of faith and not of empirical demonstration. We do not know from our own experience of a bodily community of the kind that is presupposed here. A particular set of circumstances prompted Paul to point in 1 Cor 6:15 to the remote analogy of the community established through sexual relations in order to make clear the essence of the church. Here, as in Eph 5:30 ff., Paul discerns in the relationship between Christ and the church the prototype—mark well the *prototype*, not the reflection!—of marriage. In this life we shall never fathom the whole depth of these biblical statements. However they are to be understood, the community of the church involves a spiritual and bodily community, the Sacraments of Baptism and the Lord's Supper involve a spiritual and bodily happening, and, therefore, the gift of the Supper involves a spiritual and a bodily gift. It here becomes plain that the Sacrament's mode of working is different from that of the Word. At the same time, it remains certain that the Sacrament may never be separated from the Word or elevated above the Word on account of its different mode of working. In the community of the church, as it is realized in the Supper, we are dealing with a spiritual and physical state of affairs between Christ and believers that affects the whole man according to soul and body, and the whole Christ according to his divine and human natures.

This community is only realized if it is actually the case that the whole Christ is really present according to both his divine and human natures, that there is a genuine oral eating of the true body and blood of the Lord, that his corporeality miraculously enters into ours, and that the Sacrament has an effect on both body and soul. If all this should not exist, neither would the church exist as the spiritual and bodily community we have described. The Supper would then not be a realization of this community, but only a confirmation of the community constituted by the Word even apart from the Sacrament. The celebration of the Supper would then only be a particularly festive form of the union of believers that is described in the saying "Where two or three are gathered together in my name, there am I in the midst of them" [Matt 18:20]. The church would then not be the *body of Christ* in the strict sense but would only be called this in a figurative sense. Christ would only be present in this world in the same way as he was prior to the incarnation, that is, only according to his divine nature. The church could then actually exist perfectly well without the Supper, if it would not involve her in disobedience to an express command of Jesus. She would have every spiritual possession, even apart from this Sacrament. "As a matter of fact we have everything that the Supper gives us every day in preaching, Scripture reading, and prayer. What other communion with the Lord should be possible than the one that is created by Word and Spirit!" With these words *W. Niesel*[105] superbly summarizes the Reformed position on this question.

---

[105] Wilhelm Niesel, *Calvins Lehre vom Abendmahl* (2d ed.; 1935), 97. HS

At the same time that the publisher, Chr. Kaiser, had produced Sasse's *Was heißt lutherisch?* ("What Is Lutheran?" available under the English title *Here We Stand*), it also published Niesel's *Was heißt reformiert?* ("What Is Reformed?"). RF

In the midst of the temptations of this world, the significance of the Sacrament consists in its presenting us weak people with "external signs . . . which confirm for us the word of promise"[106] and in its being a pledge of what God will do to us. With this understanding, the Lord's Supper does not belong to the deepest essence of the church. But where the Sacrament of the Altar is no longer understood as something that belongs to the essence of the church because it makes the church to be the church, there is, in the long run, nothing to prevent the decay of this Sacrament.

We wish to refrain from judging the development of the sacramental question and the emergence of the "Supper crisis" in other churches. Of our own church we can say the following on the basis of the experiences of the last two centuries: Everywhere that the Supper's needfulness with respect to the essence of the church was no longer understood, wherever people were allowed to think of the church as existing apart from the Supper, wherever the Supper was retained merely out of obedience or piety, but not out of a deep longing for the unique gift of this Sacrament—in all these places the Supper itself died with the hunger and thirst for the Sacrament, and the church died with the Supper.

Ever since that hour when, in the celebration of the first Supper on the night when he was betrayed, Jesus Christ, the incarnate Word of the Father, as at once the High Priest and the Lamb of God who takes away the sin of the world, distributed his true body and his true blood to his circle of disciples under bread and wine, thereby making them members of his body and bestowing on them forgiveness of sins along with life and salvation, *the heart of the church has been beating in the Lord's Supper*. Even when we do not know it, the heart of the church is still beating today in the Lord's Supper. If the celebration of the Supper should cease, then the preaching of the Word would be struck dumb, with the result that faith would be quenched, love would grow cold, and hope would die. Where the heart dies, the body dies also. *The church dies with the Supper.*

Our *fathers* in the century of the Reformation knew this. For this reason, and for this reason alone, they struggled with deep passion and with resolute earnestness *for the preservation of the Sacrament of the Altar* and of the pure biblical *doctrine of the Supper*. The world has no understanding of these disputes. It is just as unable to understand them as it is in a position to grasp what was being fought over. Luther's dispute with Karlstadt, Zwingli, and Oecolampadius; the conflict between Westphal and Calvin; and all the other controversies that preceded the decision of FC VII—all this "Supper strife" sticks in the memory of the world (and, therefore, when the chips are down, of all historical research also) as a case of theological logomachy, of opinionated wrangling over scholastic concepts and mere words. What other judgment will we expect from the world when Christian congregations and even theologians no longer have a shred of understanding

---

[106] Niesel, *Calvins Lehre vom Abendmahl*, 98. HS

about the titanic struggle waged by the churches of the Reformation around the Supper? Modern theologians untiringly assure us these days that the Lutherans acted on the basis of a giant misunderstanding when they were unable to unite with *Calvin*. They wrongly allowed the *improbant secus docentes* ["they (our churches) reject those who teach otherwise"] of AC X, which was originally directed against Zwingli, to be carried over into the condemnation of Calvin's teaching found in FC VII. It is broadly conceded today that Luther was in the right over against Zwingli at Marburg.

But does not Calvin teach something completely different? Did he not himself continually emphasize how he stood closer to Luther than to the Reformer of Zurich? Does Calvin not teach the "real presence" of Christ? Does he not teach that the Holy Spirit bridges the enormous spatial distance between heaven and earth? Doesn't the Holy Spirit bridge the gap between the glorified body of the Lord at the right hand of the Father, and the Supper on earth, in such a way that he feeds our soul with the true body and blood of the Lord while the bodies of communicants partake of bread and wine? In this process, there is certainly no sacramental union between the body and blood of Christ and the eucharistic elements. There is neither an oral eating nor an eating of the body by the unworthy. Do not the Lutherans also teach that we have to do here with a supernatural eating and not with a "Capernaitic," or a merely natural, eating? Does not the whole controversy then basically revolve around a mere difference of opinion *de modo praesentiae* ["concerning the mode of presence"], that is, concerning the manner and *how*, but not the *fact*, of the Lord's presence? And could we not arrive at a union on this matter along the lines proposed by the Reformed these past four hundred years: We are one in the faith *that* Christ's body and blood are present in the Supper, yet we are not one in our understanding of *how* they are present, but we leave this as an open question and will not deny eucharistic and church fellowship to each other on its account.

Why did our fathers in the sixteenth century not accept this peace offer? Why did they refuse the hand of brotherhood, not only to radical *Zwinglianism*, but also to much more moderate *Calvinism*, by which decision they invited odium for unbrotherly and unchristian dogmatism and the reproach of "impenitent" confessionalism, which still to this day sullies their name and that of our church?[107] On closer inspection, though, we notice how extraordinarily broad-

---

[107] On the issue of eucharistic fellowship, let only the following brief fundamental points be made. Eucharistic fellowship is church fellowship. For this reason, insofar as they take their confession seriously, the various confessional churches refuse each other admission to the Supper on principle. The sole exception to this rule is formed by the Reformed Church, which denies admission to Catholics but not to Lutherans and for her part demands admission to the Lutheran Supper because she acknowledges no ecclesial boundary in this case. For her part, the Lutheran Church has been obliged to refuse this demand, because she deems the Reformed doctrine of the Supper to be heretical. This does not mean, however, that she considers the Reformed Church to be a "devil's church." She has always recognized the existence of the church of Christ among the Reformed. Precisely the same state of affairs obtains here as

minded these men could be even on questions of eucharistic doctrine. They could allow for the validity of very many theological points of view *de modo praesentiae*. They demanded of no one that he profess a particular theory, whether it be Luther's doctrine of consubstantiation[108] or one of the other theological conceptions that were advocated at that time to help people grasp the miracle of Christ's bodily presence.[109] How broadminded they were toward Melanchthon, whose own opinions oftentimes lurched perilously close to Calvinism. They required but one thing, namely, acknowledgment of the bodily presence of Christ under the species of bread and wine. And this was precisely what Calvinism could not grant. The *Consensus Tigurinus*[110] of 1549 describes as a *perversa et impia superstitio* ["a perverse and impious superstition"] the belief that Christ is present "under the elements of this world."[111] Here lay the boundary line that Calvin could never

---

between the Roman and the Orthodox churches, which also have no eucharistic fellowship, although they recognize each other as church. The apparent contradiction is explicable in terms of the fact that, since the dispute over heretical Baptism, the whole of Christendom has recognized against Cyprian that the church's existence among heretics must be believed so long as they possess the means of grace. Yet we cannot realize church fellowship so long as they have not renounced their heresies. Thus Lutherans do not deny the Reformed the name of "brother," but they admit them to the Supper only when they have renounced their false doctrines. This is at all events the right churchly practice. HS

[108] The claim that Luther believed in "consubstantiation" has been widespread, for example, in *ODCC*, 408. This is so even among Lutherans, for example, Gustaf Aulen, *Eucharist and Sacrifice* (Philadelphia: Muhlenberg, 1948), 67, and Bengt Hägglund, *History of Theology* (St. Louis: Concordia, 1968), 242. Here Sasse is evidently describing the Reformed view of Luther's position. Elsewhere, he addresses the erroneous claim that Luther advocated the theory of consubstantiation; see *This Is My Body*, 101–2 (1959 ed.); 81–82 (1977 ed.). RF

[109] This is how, for example, Nicholas *Selnecker* writes on page E2 of his last eucharistic writing of 1591, *Concerning the Supper of the Lord*:

When our churches also use the ancient little words "the body of Christ is taken in the bread, with the bread, or under the bread," they do not postulate thereby any inclusio or consubstantiatio or delidescentia (i.e., "inclusion," "putting together," or "hiding underneath"), but nothing more or less than this alone, that Christ is truthful and that when he gives us the bread in the Supper, he at the same time gives us his body to eat, as he himself expresses it. So if we retain only the Lord's body in the Supper, it makes no difference to us whether people say "in the bread" or "with the bread" or "under the bread" or even omit these little words entirely. We will not let the body of Christ be taken from us even at the price of our body and life, honor, property, and blood. And we appeal herewith to the countenance, throne, and judgment of Christ, and we cite and invite thither all who counter his express testament and institution by dreaming up an absent body in the Supper or propounding a figurative interpretation. HS

[110] The continuing debates with Lutherans concerning the Lord's Supper motivated John Calvin to seek a definitive statement of the Reformed view of the Sacrament. This was accomplished with the *Consensus of Zurich*, also known as the *Consensus Tigurinus*. John Calvin prepared twenty-four propositions for the first draft in 1548. Calvin's document was annotated by Bullinger (Zwingli's successor in Zurich) and eventually took the form of twenty-six articles when it was adopted in 1549. It was adopted by various Swiss Reformed theologians and cities, thus creating unity among the Reformed, permitting them to be more organized in their opposition to the Lutherans. JS

[111] The following citation from the *Consensus Tigurinus* indicates the clear distinction between the Reformed and Lutheran teachings concerning the bodily presence of Christ in the bread and wine:

Though philosophically speaking, there is no "place" above the heavens, nevertheless, because the body of Christ, as the nature and mode of a human body calls for, is finite and is

cross. It was precisely for the sake of this boundary line that he reached this consensus with the Zurich reformation. He stood closer to Zwingli here after all than he did to the Lutheran doctrine. Let it be noted how the repugnance of many Reformed theologians for Zwingli—of which a contemporary example is seen in the school of Karl Barth—is neither shared by the whole of Reformed theology, nor has it ever moved the Reformed Church to issue a judgment against Zwingli, a judgment similar to those pronounced by the Lutheran Church against its great theologians Flacius[112] and Osiander,[113] and against certain teachings espoused by Melanchthon. This refusal on Calvin's part to concede the presence of the body and blood of Christ under the bread and wine made clear to the Lutherans that the point at issue was not a mere question *de modo praesentiae*, involving just "the *how*" of the presence. Against this understanding of the dispute, they always objected that this method would permit any theological controversy to be dismissed as a tempest in a teapot. Even Arius and Athanasius were agreed that "God was in Christ" and that "in him the whole fullness of Godhead dwells bodily" [Col 2:9]. They only disagreed *de modo praesentiae*, that is, on the question of how the whole fullness of Godhead might be in Christ. To the Reformed assertion that Christ's body could not be present *sub elementis huius mundi*] ["under earthly elements"], they [the Lutherans] objected that Scripture teaches this notwithstanding. For 1 Corinthians 10 and 11 cannot be understood otherwise. Against the objection that it was impossible for Jesus on the night of his betrayal to have distributed his body and blood to his disciples, they emphasized that he himself said so! To the objection that a body cannot be present at the same time in many places, they retorted that Scripture says so! If we do not take what Scripture says concerning the presence of Christ with complete seriousness, then we have a wrong understanding of Christ.

---

contained in heaven, as in a place, it is necessary that it be distant from us by so great an interval of space as heaven is removed from the earth. . . . For since the signs are here on earth, are observed with the eyes, softly touched by the hands, Christ, as far as He is man, is to be sought nowhere else than in heaven and not otherwise than with the mind and the intelligence of faith. (*Consensus Tigurinus*, 25, cited from Francis Pieper, *Christian Dogmatics* [St. Louis: Concordia, 1953], 3:339, n. 70) RF

[112] Matthias Flacius Illyricus (1520–1575) was the leader of the Gnesio-Lutheran (or "Genuine") movement that resisted the "Philippists," who looked to Philip Melanchthon for leadership after Luther's death. The Gnesio-Lutherans were intent on preserving intact Luther's teachings and not permitting the compromising spirit of Melanchthon to ruin the gains made by Luther in the mid-fifteenth century. Flacius led an aggressive campaign of polemical writing against all forms of error, both within and without Lutheranism. Unfortunately, his pugnacious nature and his inability to discern error in his own opinions alienated him even among his supporters, who found they had to criticize Flacius for overstatements. Only after his death was it possible finally to achieve a large measure of harmony among Lutheran theologians, politicians, and territories through the adoption and promulgation of the Book of Concord in 1580. JS

[113] Andreas Osiander (1498–1552) was a lifelong supporter of Luther, siding with Luther against Zwingli at Marburg and with Luther against Melanchthon when, after Luther's death, Melanchthon's timid nature led him to unfortunate compromises with both Roman Catholic and Reformed theologians. Osiander fell into error in regard to the doctrine of justification by grace through faith alone when he continued to defend the proposition that it is the indwelling of Christ within a Christian that makes the Christian righteous in God's sight. FC III settled the controversy and rejected Osiander's speculations. JS

Then we also have a wrong understanding of his church. Then we have a mental construct of Christ in place of the real Christ, and in place of the real church, in which Jesus Christ is really present according to both his divinity *and* his humanity, we have a dream church, a mere community of spirits in which Christ is only spiritually present just as he was prior to his incarnation. Then the church ceases to be what it has been in the world ever since the incarnation of Christ, his death and his resurrection, and the institution of the Supper, to wit, the place of God's love among people, a spiritual and bodily community in which we are in Christ and Christ is in us.

The reason why our fathers contended for the pure doctrine of the Sacrament of the Altar is that they knew all of this. They recognized the consequences that an inadequate and false understanding of the Lord's Supper must have for the whole doctrine and life of the church. We are not ashamed of their ardent struggle. For when she has followed the Reformer in taking with utmost seriousness the inextricably related questions of the faithful administration and the right understanding of this Sacrament, the Evangelical Lutheran Church has never been set on the enthronement of preferred opinions and confessional peculiarities. What is at stake for her is the supreme value for which the church can and must wage her warfare, namely, the absolute validity of the divine Word.

In times past and present, her struggle does not aim at securing a "Lutheran" Supper, but a biblical Lord's Supper, and therefore the *biblical* church and the *Christ of the Bible*. In this process, she has always acted on the assumption that Scripture's teaching on the Supper is not something yet to be discovered by future synods and theological conferences, but that it has already long since been found and can be seen by everyone who reads the NT in faith in Christ, without ideological preconceptions.

Perhaps the church of coming ages will be the first to understand what service the church of the Lutheran Reformation has performed for the whole of Christendom by this untiring testimony in doctrine and life: The Sacrament can be rightly administered only where the Gospel is purely taught, and the proclamation of the Gospel can remain pure only where Christ's Sacrament is rightly celebrated. Just as continued celebration of the Sacrament keeps the church's proclamation from ending up as mere doctrinaire theology, so likewise constant care for pure doctrine must protect the celebration of the Sacrament from sinking into cultic mysticism and magic. Word and Sacrament, Gospel and Lord's Supper belong indissolubly together, because Christ the Lord is present in them and through them builds his church on earth in divine omnipotence and love. This he does neither through the Word alone, nor through the Sacrament alone, but through both together.

The Church at the Turn of the Year[1]

The *loneliness* expressed in the title of this collection of essays is described in part in this essay. "Many of us are lonely and forsaken: pastors who at lonely posts in areas of the church where today the very things which had been the church's salvation through the times of the worst apostasy, the Word of the Holy Scriptures and the Sacraments of the Lord, are perishing." It is loneliness especially of pastors who desire to remain faithful to the confessions. Here is Sasse offering a comforting word to his *Amstbrüder* ("brothers in the office").

Huss number 194
Hopf number 129

—∿∿—

The church has a relationship to time quite different from that of the world. The world hastens toward its end. It has some inkling of this but yet will not admit it. The world sees death ahead as an inescapable fate and seeks to overcome it, though it well knows that it is the world that shall be overcome. The anguish of death and longing for "deeper, deeper eternity" speak alike from the great works of man, from the creations of his spirit, his will. In these he attempts to "immortalize" himself, to conquer eternity. But finally eternity is not his. Eternity belongs to the triune God, to the Father, the Son, and the Holy Spirit. It belongs to the one who is "the one blessed and only powerful, the King of all kings and Lord of all lords, who alone has immortality, who dwells there in light where no one can come, which no man has seen nor can see" [1 Tim 6:15–16].

The *world* does not recognize him. But the *church* believes in him. She sings her Gloria to him, "to the triune God, as he was in the beginning, is now, and

---

[1] This article originally appeared as "Die Kirche an der Jahreswende" in *Lutherische Kirche* 20.1 (January 1, 1938) 2–6. It was reprinted as "Deutschland: Wie treue Lutheraner ins neue Jahr eintraten" in M. Reu's *Kirchliche Zeitschrift* 62.2 (February 1938) 123–27. Theodore Engelder of Concordia Seminary, St. Louis, had read it there and reproduced it in part in the "Theological Observer" of *CTM* 9.10 (October 1938): 783–84. Another shortened reprint appeared in *Lutherische Blätter* 22.99 (January/February 1970): 1–5. MH/RF

shall be now and evermore." As in the days of the apostles she prays to the one who is the Alpha and the Omega, the Beginning and the End, who was and is and is to come, the Almighty: "Maranatha!" "Amen, yes, come, Lord Jesus!" [Rev 22:20]. The world trembles before the great day of the Lord. It lets its philosophers prove that there could be no last day, no judgment. But the church waits expectantly for the blessed last day. "Zion hears the watchman singing, And in her heart new joy is springing. She wakes, she rises from her gloom."[2] She hears the jeering question of the world: "Where is his promised advent? For after the fathers fell asleep, everything has remained as it has been from the beginning of creation" [2 Pet 3:4]. The world cannot wait. It is in a hurry because its time is nearing its end. It must always immediately have it all, otherwise it is too late. The church can wait. She has learned to do so in the course of nineteen centuries. She has a different relationship to time. For she belongs to one for whom a day is like a thousand years and a thousand years like a day [2 Pet 3:8]. She is not anxious in the face of unstoppable, inescapable, unrepeatable time. She knows she is the possession of him who is the Lord of time, because he is the Lord of eternity. Therefore when the church crosses the threshold of a new year, she can never do so with the feeling of worldly anxiety which we all know as natural men, the anxiety in the face of an unknown future. She rather enters the new year in firm faith: "My time is in thy hands." In this faith the church of God on earth heads into the new year, the *year of the Lord* 1938.

All of us who are participants in the ecclesiastical discussions of the present and whose hearts are often so heavy with fearful concern for the future of the church among our people need to allow ourselves to be summoned to this faith which produces joy and cheerfulness. Many of us are lonely and forsaken: pastors who at lonely posts in areas of the church where today the very things which had been the church's salvation through the times of the worst apostasy, the Word of the Holy Scriptures and the Sacraments of the Lord, are perishing. Young theologians face impossible tasks and are thrown into terrible conflicts of conscience. Instantly, at the very start of their life in the office, they learn to know the depth of the forsakenness into which God has always led his servants and which is the only way an entirely firm faith and a completely mature character is produced— faithful Christians who have proved true in life and in the service of the congregation and who must today experience how the judgment which passes over entire churches and their work also affects their own work. But how much lonely concern for the church is present even where the ecclesiastical circumstances still appear to be in order! Today he who praises Paul Gerhardt[3] for his heroic fight

[2]   From stanza 2 of "Wake, Awake, for Night Is Flying." The English translation is from *Lutheran Worship* 177; cf. *The Lutheran Hymnal* 609. RF

[3]   Paul Gerhardt (1607–1676) studied theology at Wittenberg (1628–1642) and became a pastor in Berlin

for the confession, for the pure doctrine of the church, may be certain of a joyful reverberation in the broadest ecclesiastical circles. But he must be prepared to meet with an icy silence who expresses the view that the doctrine for which Paul Gerhardt and his contemporaries fought was actually the pure doctrine of the church. This doctrine is as true today as it was in the seventeenth century, and if it no longer rings true today, it could not have been correct then. He stands alone who today in Germany advocates the Lutheran confession, as it has been understood from Luther to Bezzel,[4] in its completely serious regard for truth and with its strict rejection of error. Our readers know this, especially those who have learned to bear the burden and distress of this isolation in the Free Churches. In this situation we must all constantly allow ourselves to be reminded that he has reserved the worry for his church and her future entirely for himself. If there was ever a time to take this comforting statement seriously, it is now: "Cast all your anxiety upon him, for he cares for you" [1 Pet 5:7]. This is the test of faith which the present crisis of the church means for us all: Do we or do we not believe that Jesus Christ is Savior of his body? Do we still know what it means that he as the eternal, merciful High Priest is interceding with his heavenly Father for his church? Do we or do we not believe that he, to whom all authority in heaven and on earth has been given, is with us always, even to the end of the age [Matt 28:18, 20], in his Gospel and in his Sacraments, really present and therefore as near to our time as any other time in history? Do we believe in the power of his Word? Do we believe the hidden acts of the Savior which he also performs in our time through his Sacraments? If we have this firm, joyous faith, then we may proceed confidently into the new year, even in the midst of all the difficulties of the ecclesiastical situation. And we know that the church in Germany and in the world has a great future. For the future of the church is indeed not our future, but the future of Christ.

In this faith in the church of Christ as a great, divine reality in the present world, we ask about our *tasks*, the tasks of the Evangelical Lutheran Church. We know with Luther and with all our fathers that "holy church" is also found outside the boundaries of our confession. For where Christ is—and he is present in the Word of his Gospel and in his Sacraments—there is the church.[5] We also

---

in 1657. In 1666 he was dismissed from his position as pastor for refusing to sign syncretistic edicts of Frederick William I of Brandenburg. He wrote great hymns of comfort in the midst of the most trying circumstances (*Lutheran Cyclopedia*, 329). MH

[4]   Hermann Bezzel (1861–1917) among other things served as rector of the Deaconess Institute at Neuendettelsau, 1891–1909, and as president of the Protestant Upper Consistory in Munich, 1909–1917, the position later called territorial bishop. An incisive theological thinker and a powerful preacher in the footsteps of Wilhelm Löhe, Bezzel left the Bavarian Territorial Church with a firm confessional Lutheran imprint (Heinz Brunotte and Otto Weber, eds., *Evangelisches Kirchenlexikon: Kirchlich-theologisches Handwörterbuch* [2d ed.; 4 vols.; Göttingen: Vandenhoeck & Ruprecht, 1962], 1:424–25). On Bezzel, see especially "The Confessions and the Unity of the Church" in this collection. LG/RF

[5]   "Where Christ is, there is the church" was written by Ignatius in his *Epistle to the Smyrnaeans* 8:2. MH

know all the poverty and weakness of our church, and indeed not only the external poverty and weakness, which for four hundred years have been the marks of Lutheranism. No, we also know—we would no longer be the church of justification, the church of "through faith alone," if we did not know this—of our weakness of faith and our lack of love. We know that our church is a church of sinners and that the sins found in other churches are all found among us. But we know that God has entrusted to us a precious heritage not only for ourselves, but for all of Christianity on earth, and that he will one day ask us in the last judgment whether we have invested our pound or whether we have tucked it away. Neither our church nor any other is served if we allow the doctrine of our confessions to sink into the great sea of religious confusion which today threatens to engulf entire confessions. Nor is it love, much less Christian love or NT love, when merely not to cause another any more woe we no longer pose the question of truth and error. We should ask ourselves once more what service is rendered for the true unity and the true peace of the church by the indifference which no longer asks about pure doctrine or about the serious, conscious distinguishing of truth and error! "Suppose" says C. F. W. Walther, the church father of the Missouri Synod, in his Reformation sermon of 1876,

> when in the fourth century the doctrine of Christ's divinity was attacked by Arius, that neither Athanasius or any other person would have fought this falsification; suppose, when in the fifth century the doctrine of man's conversion only through grace was assailed by Pelagius, that neither Augustine nor any other person would have fought against it; suppose, when in the sixteenth century the entire doctrine of Christ had been falsified by the papacy, that neither Luther nor any other person would have fought against it; suppose, when at the end of the past century rationalism forced its way into the Christian Church, that no one would have fought against it, true there would have been infinitely less strife and dissension in the world, but where would the pure Word of God be now?[6]

And if for this reason we with our entire church since Luther and the Formula of Concord must also continue to bear the disgrace of people, we will gladly do it. Perhaps the time is not far off when a great many Christian people, who do not understand us today, will come to understand that this inflexibility of the Lutheran Church, this apparent dogmatic narrow-mindedness, has been a blessing for all of Christianity.

For we see enacted before our eyes today an intellectual-historical transaction of immeasurable importance. Protestant modernism has died along with the intellectual world of the eighteenth and nineteenth centuries, which formed the soul of that which a generation ago was called "modern culture." Those who

---

[6] *Amerikanisch-Lutherische Epistel Postille* (St. Louis: Concordia), 468. The English translation is from *Standard Epistles* by C. F. W. Walther (trans. Donald E. Heck; Fort Wayne: Concordia Theological Seminary Press, 1986), 486–87. MH

understand ecclesiastical life, wise observers of the religious developments in the various portions of the earth assure us that the most impressive thing about the ecumenical conferences of 1937[7] is the complete retreat of ecclesiastical and theological Liberalism. Already in Stockholm, 1925,[8] and in Lausanne, 1927,[9] it became evident how little this Liberalism still had to say. Since then this development has become even clearer and quicker. And indeed it is happening even in churches—for example, in American churches of Reformed and Methodist stamp—in which just five years ago no one could have dreamed of such a development. Its velocity in the peoples of the West has been increased by the collapse of the League of Nations[10] and pacifistic dreams. Today on the battlefields of China the "Social Gospel"[11] is dying in the terrors of the modern aerial war.[12] It had been discovered barely a generation ago in America and its doctrine amounts to this, that Jesus Christ came in order to transform this earth into the kingdom of God through an elevated ethics, through the instruction of unlearned people. Today Christians in the Far East are learning what it means to live in a forsaken world and that Jesus Christ came in order that all who believe in him not be forsaken, but have eternal life [John 3:16].

Thus modern Protestantism is like an army, advancing hastily from victory to victory, which has lost contact with its base of operations, with its point of origin. And now, quickly recognizing the untenability of its situation, it is in quick retreat to its original position. Will this Protestantism take up its position where the Reformation once won its victory with the truth of the Gospel? Or will this position also be surrendered? Will modern Protestant Christianity, as many observers believe, return to Catholicism and go the way to Rome because it no longer is able to find the way to Wittenberg? This is the opinion of many of our contemporaries. It is based on the fact that the entirely unexpected and completely inexplicable return to a dogmatic Christianity is connected with a return to the Sacrament, or more precisely, with a strong longing for Sacrament which has been lost in modern Protestantism. It is certainly no accident that in the most diverse churches questions regarding the Sacraments, especially the Lord's Supper, are beginning to occupy the central point in ecclesiastical and theological discussions. But should not exactly this development indicate that the Lutheran Reformation still has a mission to all Christianity? It is perhaps one of the very greatest tasks of our church—one among *many* tasks—that in this situa-

---

[7]   This is a reference to the Second World Conference on Life and Work, Oxford, and the Second World Conference on Faith and Order, Edinburgh. RF

[8]   The First Universal Christian Conference on Life and Work. RF

[9]   The First World Conference on Faith and Order. RF

[10]   While the league did not officially disband until April 1946, it had collapsed at the time of Sasse's writing or shortly thereafter, that is, by 1939. RF

[11]   Sasse addresses the "Social Gospel" especially in his essay "American Christianity and the Church" in this collection. RF

[12]   This is a reference to the Sino-Japanese War. RF

tion it proclaim to churches of other confessions Luther's deep understanding of the Sacrament in its indissoluble connection with the Word of the Gospel. For we are of the conviction that Luther at just this point understood the NT more profoundly than any other theologian. To be sure, this can only happen if the Lutheran Church first has herself appropriated anew the often forgotten doctrines of her Reformation, and if we all have learned anew to implore the Lord of the church with the profound earnestness of our fathers: "That we keep pure till life is spent Your holy Word and Sacrament."[13]

13 From stanza 2 of "Lord Jesus Christ, Will You Not Stay?" The English translation is from *Lutheran Worship* 344 (cf. *The Lutheran Hymnal* 292). Sasse quotes this hymn by Nikolaus Selnecker perhaps more than any other. RF

1938

WHY MUST WE HOLD FAST TO THE LUTHERAN DOCTRINE OF THE LORD'S SUPPER?[1]

In 1933 Sasse had come out of the Prussian Union Church of Mark Brandenburg to the Lutheran Territorial Church of Bavaria. He had "learned" of Lutheranism during his study visit to the United States in 1925–1926. In the late 1930s, the tension between the Lutheran and the Reformed confessions became a very great concern for him and that was evident in no greater way than in the Lord's Supper.

This then is one of several writings in this period, and later, which would highlight the doctrine of the Sacrament of the Altar. Here Sasse takes issue with a Lutheran theologian, the NT scholar Ernst Käsemann, a representative of Protestant modernism. Note how often Sasse refers to "modern scholarship" or "modern exegete" in this essay.

This essay is not, however, mere polemic. There is also a pastoral concern:

All these results of "modern scholarship" and many others, which we do not care to count here, are certainly not the object for honest grappling by the church nor a theology that is responsible toward the church. They should be the object, instead, of pastoral consultation, church discipline, and rejection as false teaching which destroys the church.

Huss number 198
Hopf number 124

---

[1] The original of this essay, "Warum müssen wir an der lutherischen Abendmahlslehre festhalten?" was published in three parts in *Allgemeine Evangelisch-Lutherische Kirchenzeitung* 71.3, 4, and 5 (January 21, January 28, and February 4, 1938): 53–55, 79–82, and 90–97, respectively. RB/RF

PART 1

In his contribution to the collection entitled *Abendmahlsgemeinschaft?*[2] H. Gollwitzer[3] states on pages 112–13 that

> all modern exegetes are in agreement that Luther's doctrine of the Lord's Supper, at least in the lack of ambiguity that it regards as so necessary, is called into question as a *non liquet* ["not clear"] and actually is denied by most of them. This fact has a very direct practical consequence for the Prussian Union Church. For every Lutheran who appeals to members of the Union Church to return to a confessional division can only make his appeal binding if he does not base it upon reasons of tradition or some confessional formalism, but upon exegetical reasons taking into account Käsemann's essay[4] demonstrating the current status of exegesis. He who belongs to the Union Church has by the Union been transplanted back to the situation before the churches divided. He cannot simply inherit the division from his fathers but would have to take such a step on the basis of his own conscious decision. Just as it was with his fathers four hundred years ago, he must be compelled by Scripture and nothing else. It cannot be denied that a genuine hearing of the Scripture is not a mere repetition of the exegesis of the Formula of Concord without honestly grappling with modern scholarship, devoid of preconceived notions. As long as current appeals to divide the churches are not undertaken this way, one would have to refuse any churchly legitimacy to appeals made to the Union churches in any other fashion.

We gladly respond to the challenge made here to show the biblical basis and thus the churchly legitimacy of the Lutheran doctrine of the Lord's Supper. We cannot do it, however, without correcting this completely false way of posing the question. Otherwise our response would at the same time acknowledge the requirement Gollwitzer places into his question. To be specific, he claims that there are churches in Germany whose pastors and members, through the Union, have been transplanted back to the situation before the division of the Lutheran and the Reformed Church. Now they would be asking us why they should decide for one confession or the other and which is the scriptural one. We cannot countenance this spectator role of the two churches and their four-hundred-year struggle in relation to each other, nor expect it of any Protestant Christian in Germany, not even in those Union churches which in contrast to the Old Prussian Church attempted to erase confessional differences. These churches and their members are not back to where they were *before* the split between the

---

[2] Supplement 3 in the [series] Evangelischen Theologie (Munich: Chr. Kaiser, 1937). HS

[3] Helmut Gollwitzer (1908–) was a theologian and at this time (1938–1940) pastor of the church in Berlin-Dahlem. He has been described as Karl Barth's "most controversial living disciple" (J. D. Douglas, ed., *New 20th-Century Encyclopedia of Religious Knowledge* [Grand Rapids: Baker, 1991], 362). RF

[4] This is a reference to "Das Abendmahl im Neuen Testament" ("The Lord's Supper in the New Testament"), Käsemann's essay in *Abendmahlsgemeinschaft?* 60–93. RF

churches, but rather they are in a world of enlightenment or pietistic indifferentism, which no longer has the power nor the courage to make dogmatic decisions and merely attempts to hide this weakness behind the mask of some pietistic Biblicism. It is dead wrong to confirm Prussian pastors in this spectator role which they learned from the theology of the nineteenth century. A clergyman in Silesia, Pomerania, or East Prussia who teaches the Calvinistic view of Baptism or the Lord's Supper because that view appeals to him more than the Lutheran one is breaking his ordination vow just as much as the Bavarian pastor who does so. If I admonish the Silesian pastor as well as the Bavarian to remain with Lutheran sacramental teaching, I am not appealing to him to break up the church. I am merely admonishing him to take an existing division seriously by keeping pure the teaching to which he once committed himself before the altar. It's quite understandable when modern theologians who personally doubt the truth of the Lutheran doctrine of the Lord's Supper now state that confessional obligations need not be honored. But then they should declare that openly. It is also understandable when modern theologians keep the confessional vow but soften it in the Reformed direction. The Reformed, after all, simply do not know the kind of confessing which runs from Luther's confession of 1528[5] to the Smalcald Articles right through to the Formula of Concord, the confession of faith made "before God and all Christendom, both those alive and those who will come after us" [FC SD XII 40]. This comes when the confessor has recognized the true faith from Holy Scripture with which "we also by God's grace with hearts unshaken wish to appear before the judgment seat of Jesus Christ and give account, and against which we wish neither to speak nor to write anything secretly nor in public" [FC SD XII 40]. They do not know the vow of a pastor to preach this doctrine and this one only, because it—*quia*, not *quatenus* ["because," not "insofar as"]—agrees with God's Word and to prefer to resign one's office if one can no longer do this. It is, as mentioned before, completely understandable when people come to the conviction that the Reformed type of confession, seeing faith statements as provisional and more or less correct, is right and preferable.

But whoever has this conviction is obligated to stand up for it *publicly*. This is one of the most serious accusations we make against the crusaders of Barmen and Halle,[6] that they *secretly* put the Reformed understanding of church, fellowship, confession, and confessional subscription in the place of what had held sway in the Lutheran Church of Germany for centuries. The Old Evangelical Church, like

---

[5] This is a reference to Luther's *Confession concerning Christ's Supper*, 1528 (*LW* 37:151–372). RF

[6] This is a reference to the meetings of the Confessing Church at Barmen (1934) and of the Confessing Church of the Prussian Union held in Halle (1937). Regarding the latter, see the earlier essay in this collection "Theses on the Question of Church and Altar Fellowship." At that conference, the Lutheran, Reformed, and Union churches adopted a *Consensus de doctrina evangelii* ("Agreement in the Doctrine of the Gospel") which declared altar fellowship among the churches. In the matter of altar fellowship, the Halle meeting denied the right of Lutheran or Reformed churches to exclude one another from communion. RF

every truly Lutheran Church today, obligated its pastors to the doctrine of the Confessions because it is the true exposition of the Holy Scriptures. After the decisions at Halle, the pastors are now merely obligated to it with the open question, insofar as the Confessions agree with Scripture. This question should now be decided, we are told, by a new "genuine hearing of the Scripture." One wonders whether it would not be wiser to follow the example of many Reformed churches and to restrict the vow simply to Holy Scripture as the *norma normans* ["the standardizing norm"]. In any case, we feel ourselves justified in taking the confessional subscription of pastors in the Old Prussian Church just as seriously as our fathers did and just as every confessionally bound Lutheran Church must take it. We are not doing this for "reasons of tradition and confessional formalism"—only a complete fool could expect to build churches with a motive like that. We do it completely and only because we are convinced in our heart of hearts on the basis of the most serious study of Holy Scripture and the history of the church that the doctrine of the Augsburg Confession is "taken from God's Word and is solidly and well grounded in it."

PART 2

Whoever dares in our day to make such a confession has to expect that Protestant Germany from Heidelberg to Königsberg, from Bonn to Breslau, will see him as an orthodox hypocrite or as a poor fool. Doesn't he know anything about Käsemann?[7] "*Only* by making the need for a division of the churches clear on the basis of exegetical reasons in light of *Käsemann's* essay demonstrating the status of exegesis" can one make his appeal for a Lutheran Church "binding." Luther or Käsemann—who is right? Luther, who found a clear teaching in the NT of the real presence of the body and blood of Christ in the Sacrament, or Käsemann, who cannot find it? That is the fateful question which Gollwitzer poses to the Lutheran churches of the world. It cannot be answered from the Formula of Concord, but only by a "genuine hearing of Scripture" and certainly not without a "grappling with modern scholarship, devoid of presuppositions."

We begin, then, "grappling with modern scholarship," although we admit at the start, rather than have you read it between the lines, that we cannot come up with the lack of presupposition (we're not talking here of human presuppositions, since we know neither Gollwitzer nor Käsemann) against "modern scholarship." "Modern scholarship" regarding the Lord's Supper can only become the object of the serious interest of the church and its theology with great reservation and then

---

7   Ernst Käsemann (1906–1998) was a professor of NT, last at Tübingen. He was influenced by Rudolf Bultmann; he emphasized the necessity of "demythologizing" the Gospels; he called for a "new quest for the historical Jesus" which would end the separation of the Jesus of history from the Jesus of faith (*The Blackwell Encyclopedia of Modern Christian Thought*, ed. Alister E. McGrath [Oxford: Blackwell, 1993]). Käsemann is the one with whom Sasse takes chief issue in this essay. RF

only in part. To point out the problems with "modern scholarship" we mention some of the scholarly results from the faculty of which Käsemann was a student. In a popular book about Jesus intended for a wide readership (1926), Käsemann's teacher Bultmann instructs Protestant Christians about how Jesus never spoke of his death, nor of his resurrection and its significance for salvation: "Of course, in the Gospels words about these subjects were placed into his mouth, but they originated in the faith of the church, and not even from the original congregation, but from Hellenistic Christianity. That's the case with the two most important words of this type, the words about ransom and the words concerning the Lord's Supper." These are called "liturgical sayings from the Hellenistic celebration of the Lord's Supper, which overshadowed the earlier source, now only shining through in 'traces' in St. Luke."[8] Here, just as in other findings of this cheerless Jesus book, we hear not the serious criticism of strictly historical research, but a skepticism which hacks away even at the established historical facts. How much more of a matter-of-fact outlook comes from the studies of another teacher and authority for Käsemann, the great religious psychologist Rudolf Otto,[9] recently deceased, who examined the Lord's Supper along with Bultmann and interpreted it on the basis of his deep knowledge of the spirit of Eastern religions! Can an interpretation of the Lord's Supper expect to be taken seriously as theology when its author does not even know what the church is? How can I take the church's sacraments seriously when at the same time I organize a "religious men's society" where Catholics, Protestants, Jews, Buddhists, and representatives of other Asiatic religions meet in order to "get to know each other and in contact with one another wait quietly and hope that this contact will be deepening and fruitful for all involved and will perhaps make room for new and unexpected things to break through"[10]? It is certainly not just coincidence, but a clear sign of the self-destructiveness of modern Protestant theology, that a third regular professor [*Ordinarius*] of the same faculty was moved by his studies on the Lord's Supper to arrange secretly for consecration as a bishop by a Catholic sect, so that he as a supposed successor of St. Peter could consecrate the elements properly and then secretly give the same power to other Protestant clergy.[11] All these results of "modern scholarship" and many others, which we do not care to count here, are certainly

---

[8] Rudolf Bultmann, *Jesus* (1926), 196. HS

 Compare the English translation, *Jesus and the Word* (New York: Scribner's, 1958), 213–14. See Sasse's critique of Bultmann (1884–1976) in the second volume of this collection, "Flight from Dogma: Remarks on Bultmann's 'Demythologization' of the New Testament," first published in 1942. RF

[9] Rudolf Otto (1869–1937) was a Protestant theologian and a professor of systematic theology at Göttingen (1898–1914), Breslau (1914–1917), and Marburg (1917–1929). One of his books was *Life and Work of Jesus according to the Historical and Critical Method*. RF

[10] Rudolf Otto, in the article "Menschheitsbund" in *RGG*[2] 3:2123, where the conclusion notes that "currently, the head of the Religious Humanity League is Professor Hauer of Tübingen." HS

[11] Sasse refers to Friedrich Heiler (1892–1967), professor of comparative history of religions at Marburg in the philosophy department. Heiler wrote a letter to Sasse in response to this article. He took issue espe-

not the object for honest grappling by the church nor a theology that is responsible toward the church. They should be the object, instead, of pastoral consultation, church discipline, and rejection as false teaching which destroys the church.

It sounds harsh when we say these things so openly, but they must be said for the sake of the truth. We theologians all have reason not to deny our part in this sin which has brought our churches to the edge of the abyss. We are not telling some secret but are simply stating what every student and many careful listeners to sermons already know: *present-day Protestant theology, despite the considerable efforts of the past two decades, has simply not found its way back to a real theological understanding of the Bible.* We have excellent biblical theologians, but we have no biblical theology. How many valuable exegetical bits of insight have been given us in recent years. We are not even mentioning the individual works of the younger generation of NT scholars who combine genuine historical scholarship and deep theological insight, and we remember the rich harvest of just one theologian's life, Adolf Schlatter,[12] and what he was able to do in his final years alone! Yet every newer commentary series or even Kittel's dictionary[13] shows how far away we are from the goal: that the individual insights should become stones to construct a whole biblical theology. If you ask today's scholars what the NT teaches on a given question, they respond with careful analyses of what has been discovered in the Synoptics and in John, in Paul and in the "deutero-Pauls," in Hebrews and in the other writings of the canon. To what extent these individual findings constitute a common witness and what that common witness might be, that they cannot say. No matter how many advantages modern exegesis has over against the Reformation, especially in the area of linguistic understanding, no modern exegete will dispute that those in the sixteenth century had a unified NT, which was much more than just the sum total of successive literary layers. Isn't that the reason why modern exegesis is unable to prove from Scripture the statements of faith contained in the Evangelical Confessions, which for the Reformers were completely evident truths of Scripture? We're told that no modern exegete can find Luther's doctrine of the Lord's Supper in the NT any more. May we ask in response, What article of the Augsburg Confession is modern exegesis willing to find grounded in Scripture? The statements concerning the Holy Trinity or of the

---

cially with the statement by Sasse that the ordination had been in secret, a claim, he acknowledges, made many times before by others. The ordination took place in August 1930 in the Gallican Church in Rüschlikon near Zurich. Finally he asserts to Sasse: "Anyhow there is a world of difference between my conception and the one of Bultmann" (letter of February 7, 1938, Bavarian Territorial Church Archive, manuscript 1833, correspondence of Dr. Hermann Sasse). RF

[12] Adolf Schlatter (1852–1938) was a Reformed theologian at Tübingen (1898–1922). "He held that the only sound foundation of Systematic Theology lay in biblical exegesis. . . . He vigorously opposed all idealistic interpretations of the Christian faith" (*ODCC*, 1463). He was held in high regard by Lutheran theologians, including Sasse and Martin Franzmann, as well as by Reformed theologians. RF

[13] Sasse himself had contributed to Kittel's *Theological Dictionary of the New Testament* until he moved to Australia in 1949. He then had to give up his work on it due to the lack of adequate resources. RF

natures of Christ? What do modern-day exegetes think about the person of the Holy Spirit, or of the virgin birth? The statements in St. Matthew 1:18–25 and St. Luke 1:35, which are the foundations of the doctrine of Christ's virgin birth, are, according to a big-name theologian of our time, "parts of the NT which even the most conservative Biblicist among scholarly theologians would hardly dare today to call 'Bible proof.' "[14] Theologians who count themselves among the defenders of the Evangelical faith against the liberalism of times past have given up on the doctrine of Christ's death as a punishment for sin or [on the doctrine] of the propitiatory sacrifice of the Redeemer. They deny that the doctrine of original sin can be found in the Bible. They make Jesus into a Pelagian who expects people to reach at least a relatively high level of perfection and who thinks little children are sinless. They protest the one-sidedness of making St. Paul's doctrine of justification into the center of the whole Scripture. To say it bluntly, there is scarcely a single point of the church's confession which contemporary exegetical theology (and we speak here only of those who wish to be consciously churchly) is able to ground in Scripture and defend against the faith stances of other groups. If someone triumphantly tells us that no modern exegete holds to the Lutheran doctrine of the Lord's Supper, we respond that of course we note that with some regret but could hardly have expected otherwise. And yet that in itself does not prove anything against the sacramental teaching of our church. It could simply mean that "modern scholarship" (and its views on the Lord's Supper) has proven its own poverty. In any event, the church has done right by not taking us theologians and the results of our research quite as seriously as we take ourselves. Sunday after Sunday the Christian church confesses "born of the Virgin Mary" without the least worry that the "scholars' findings," as Paul Althaus correctly observes, are "mostly negative or even skeptical." The church goes on singing the Agnus Dei and will sing it until the end of time without worrying about the views of each new wave of "modern scholarship" concerning the death of Jesus and its salvific meaning. Thus our church, without concern for the opinions, hypotheses, and discussions of modern scholars, just keeps on celebrating the Sacrament of the Altar, the Sacrament of the true body and blood of the Lord, in the same sense taught by the Confessions. The church doesn't do it with a guilty conscience arising from some false conservatism, but because her respect for the Word of God is still greater than any respect she has for the hypotheses of contemporary scholarship.

PART 3

What, then, is the NT picture of the Lord's Supper which Käsemann draws on the basis of recent scholarship? First, he speaks against the view recently

---

[14]   Emil Brunner, *Der Mittler* (1927), 289 [ET, *The Mediator*, 1934]. HS

expressed again by Joachim Jeremias[15] and Behm[16] that Christ's Last Supper is to be understood with the Synoptic Gospels as a Passover meal, despite the different version in John 18:28. Against the arguments of Billerbeck and Dalman, Käsemann believes the execution of Jesus on the first day of the Passover to be so improbable that he then rejects the clear indication of the Synoptics that Jesus celebrated the Passover meal with the disciples on the night before his death. He says the early church brought the Passover into the account of the Last Supper.[17] "With this position we have made a decision which influences further investigation very strongly, because it weakens our confidence in the historical accuracy of the Synoptic accounts and warns us to be wary of the data offered in the Synoptic text."[18] To be sure, one could hardly be critical enough of the gospel accounts if the entire report of Jesus' Passover meal is just a legend. Then Mark's version of the Words of Institution and Matthew's, which follow him, are sacrificed to these doubts. The text of the Words of Institution is taken from Luke 22, where verses 19b and 20 are missing in the oldest manuscripts: "Luke gives us in verses 15–19a and 29–30 the last historically verifiable bit of data in the whole of the Synoptic accounts on the Lord's Supper."[19] Then the institution reads:

> "I have eagerly desired to eat this Passover with you before I suffer. For I tell you, I will not eat of it again until it finds fulfillment in the kingdom of God." After taking the cup, he gave thanks and said, "Take this and divide it among you. For I tell you I will not drink again of the fruit of the vine until the kingdom of God comes." And he took bread, gave thanks and broke it, and gave it to them, saying, "This is my body. [. . .] And I confer on you a kingdom, just as my Father conferred one on me, so that you may eat and drink at my table in my kingdom and sit on thrones, judging the twelve tribes of Israel." [Luke 22:15–19a, 29–30 NIV]

If those are the Words of Institution, then "the explanatory word regarding the bread takes on a key position."

> "This is my body"—on this basis the *diatheke* ["testament"] gets its meaning, that Jesus' disciples very soon will share his heavenly meal at his table. Because they now become partakers of him, they shall also be partakers with him in the eschatological table fellowship. They now become partakers of him, since σῶμα ["body"] (like the Hebrew *gufi* ["my body"] underlying it) can mean "I myself." Jesus gives himself, his person, under the sign of the bread, gives himself as the dying one that he is in this hour of farewell. While he gives himself as the dying one and his death brings the dawn of God's

15 *Die Abendmahlsworte Jesu* (1935) [ET, *The Eucharistic Words of Jesus*, 1966]. HS

16 G. Kittel, *Theologisches Wörterbuch zum Neuen Testament*, 3:231 ff. HS

17 Käsemann, "Das Abendmahl im Neuen Testament," 70. HS

18 Käsemann, "Das Abendmahl im Neuen Testament," 62 f. HS

19 Käsemann, "Das Abendmahl im Neuen Testament," 67. HS

reign, he wishes in the sharing of bread broken, which represents his broken body, to institute a *diatheke* in view of his coming *basileia* ["kingdom"]. Whoever has received a part in him, the dying one, shall also receive a portion of the eschatological future, namely, the table fellowship, by his death.[20]

This institution "cannot intend a testament for later years in this world."[21] Only later did people understand the Supper that way in the "changed situation" after Good Friday and Easter, when the church realized that "the end of all things was not yet come with the death of Christ." Only then "was the last earthly meal, which anticipated the future heavenly one, replaced by another meal, constantly repeated in the church's worship, which apprehended the reality of God's new order in Jesus' cross under symbolical signs."[22] The Lord's Supper understood this new way and reported in the Words of Institution in Mark and Matthew thus becomes just an embellishment of the early church. It was not Jesus, but the infant church which made the Lord's Supper into a sacrament to be repeated. It was not Jesus, but the early church which placed the cup, originally just an "inaugural cup," after the "giving of bread" and then understood them as analogous. Thus the church gave the word "body" a new meaning, since it now paralleled the "blood." It was not Jesus, but the church which set this covenant blood into a parallel with the sacrificial blood of Exod 24:8.

"They will call it a construct," Käsemann says against his summary of this ancient development and admits that he, in fact, is offering a construct, but one which is "made incumbent upon us by the difficulty of the textual material."[23] Such a construct would certainly be fitting for a historian, but only after he had exhausted every other possible way of explaining the contradiction between Luke and the other Synoptics. It is utterly incomprehensible why Käsemann, who was commissioned to report the status of research, would so quickly and easily glide over the contributions that serious scholars such as Zahn and Schlatter, Leipoldt and Joachim Jeremias have made to the understanding of St. Luke. The suggestion instead that Luke would have left out the real Words of Institution, which he knew from Mark, since he was compiling a history intended for the public (just as the Fourth Gospel reports nothing of the Supper for the same reason) is such a simple answer which corresponds fully with the facts and does justice to the spirit of the early church. Any historian would surely prefer that to Käsemann's construct. Käsemann objects that Luke in that case wouldn't have been able to even allude to this secret. Then the words "This is my body" (Luke 22:19a) wouldn't have been allowed.[24]

---

[20] Käsemann, "Das Abendmahl im Neuen Testament," 66 f. HS
[21] Käsemann, "Das Abendmahl im Neuen Testament," 69. HS
[22] Käsemann, "Das Abendmahl im Neuen Testament," 73. HS
[23] Käsemann, "Das Abendmahl im Neuen Testament," 68. HS
[24] Käsemann, "Das Abendmahl im Neuen Testament," 64, 68. HS

Yet the history of rules of faith, whose wording was to be kept secret from non-Christians, shows that arcane discipline was entirely consistent with allusions to the secret. Käsemann's proofs here just don't cut it. One notes immediately that he is not serving as a man just reporting the status of research, but he is an apologist for his own construct. It is hard to imagine that this bloodless construct, so foreign to the real life of the early church, could find much acceptance with the book's readers. On the contrary, it will hopefully confirm the view which Käsemann attacks. It demonstrates with wonderful clarity where things lead when the Lord's Supper is separated from the Passover. Did not Jesus consecrate himself as the propitiatory sacrifice of the new covenant when he instituted the Supper in light of Jer 31:31–34 and Exodus 12? Did not he himself add the word over the cup about his blood of the covenant to the word regarding his body (cf. Exod 24:8, "This is the blood of the covenant that the LORD has made" [NIV])?[25] If he at that celebration envisioned a one-time thing which would only be repeated later in the kingdom of God, then the Lord's Supper as we find it in Mark, Matthew, Paul, and in today's text of Luke, in other words, the Lord's Supper of the NT, is merely a creation of the church which grew from a misunderstood and misinterpreted act of Jesus. Then the claim of Christians in every century and in every church that the Eucharist is rooted in the will of Jesus at the time of its institution is nothing but fiction. Anyone who thinks he can understand the history of the church and the Sacrament which stands at the center of its worship with that presupposition, let him try it. We admit freely that our historical conscience protests against a historical construct of this kind.

In addition, one ought not forget that our oldest report on the Lord's Supper comes from St. Paul. Long before the composition of our gospels, about twenty-five years after the Last Supper, Paul felt compelled by the church struggles and divisions which arose in the celebration of the Eucharist to discuss the Lord's Supper in detail, something he did not do otherwise in his epistles. We have this to thank for the oldest preserved report on the institution of the Lord's Supper, and at the same time the first commentary on it. The correct understanding of the biblical doctrine of the Supper depends upon properly understanding Paul's statements and their relationship to the Synoptics. If we ask how Käsemann understands the Lord's Supper in Paul's writings, we can be glad that he, to begin with, recognizes the realism of Paul's sacramental teaching and its central significance for an understanding of the church. He acknowledges that, for the apostle, the body of Christ distributed in the Sacrament and the body of Christ in the church are not different things: "Through the sacramental element called σῶμα Χριστοῦ ['body of Christ'] we are incorporated into the σῶμα Χριστοῦ as church."[26] In 1 Corinthians 10 and 11 the sacramental elements are understood as "bearers of

---

[25] On these questions, see the detailed explanations of Joachim Jeremias, *Die Abendmahlsworte Jesu* (1935), 77 f. HS

[26] Käsemann, "Das Abendmahl im Neuen Testament," 79–80. HS

heavenly power-substance." "Only because they are bearers of heavenly power-substance and impart a portion of the resurrected corporeality of Christ are they able to incorporate us into the body of the risen Christ, namely, the church."[27] With Paul bread and wine are "no longer symbolic representations of the *diatheke* ['testament'] on the cross" (as Käsemann claims they are with Mark and Matthew), "but they are bearers of heavenly spirit-substance, which according to the view expressed in 1 Cor 11:27 ff. in some cases even has power to curse people and cause illness and death."[28]

The correct and significant insights contained in these statements become confused again, however, through two deficiencies in Käsemann's interpretation. The first deficiency is a completely insufficient and basically contradictory notion of *pneuma* ["spirit"] as the gift of the Lord's Supper. "According to Paul, the Sacrament feeds us with *pneuma* in such a way that this *pneuma* proceeds from Christ and then, secondly, unites with Christ."[29] Where do you find that in the NT? Nowhere! Käsemann wrongly thinks he finds it in the "spiritual food" and "spiritual drink" of 1 Cor 10:3 f. In the same connection, however, he says of this *pneuma* that "according to 2 Cor 3:17 the *Kyrios* ["the Lord"] is the *Pneuma*, and he alone," and again, "for Paul and his contemporaries *pneuma* is thought of as a very real, supernatural, miracle-working power-substance and as such is also the basic building block of resurrection corporeality."[30] It's clear that here different things which must be kept separate are not being distinguished clearly enough, namely the "Lord" and the "Spirit." With Paul, they always belong together— where the Lord is, there is the Spirit; where the Spirit is, there is the Lord—but they are never identical. In addition, there is the distinction between the Holy Spirit known only by the church and the *pneuma* known also by the world, and finally [there is the distinction between] the gift of the Holy Sacrament and the Holy Spirit. According to Paul, the gift in the Sacrament is the body and blood of the Lord, and even though this body is certainly "pneumatic" body, it's just as certainly not to be simply identified with the *Pneuma*.

Käsemann's second deficiency is that he has to assume a deep contradiction between Paul's understanding of the Lord's Supper and that of the Synoptics. He speaks of a "significant shift" and stresses strongly what Paul and the Synoptics have in common: "The death of Christ is and remains constitutive for the establishment of a new divine order and also for the saving gift in the Lord's Supper, which participates in this divine order."[31] This is the difference between the Synoptics and Paul's view: "The saving power of Jesus' body of death, first grasped symbolically and then effectively conveyed by the authority of the Christ-

---

[27]   Käsemann, "Das Abendmahl im Neuen Testament," 80 f. HS

[28]   Käsemann, "Das Abendmahl im Neuen Testament," 76. HS

[29]   Käsemann, "Das Abendmahl im Neuen Testament," 75. HS

[30]   Käsemann, "Das Abendmahl im Neuen Testament," 75. HS

[31]   Käsemann, "Das Abendmahl im Neuen Testament," 88. HS

diatheke, is being replaced here with a substantial connection to the *Pneuma*-Christ resurrected from the dead."[32] "The character of the elements is no longer to represent something, but to actually convey Christ-power and Christ-substance. Here it is apparent that religious-historical influences have strongly invaded the sacramental teaching of the apostle."[33] Paul has fallen into a "temptation" which "one could scarcely escape in the Hellenistic era," namely, "to imagine the elements already as participating in the heavenly nature of the risen one." Thus the door was opened to a development which allowed Christianity "to get ever more deeply enmeshed in Hellenism."[34] This is seen not only from Ignatius,[35] but in John's Gospel. From John 6 it becomes clear that the phrases "eat my body, drink my blood" are already part of the church's sacramental terminology. Together with R. Otto, Käsemann understands this chapter to be the Fourth Gospel's attempt to pull the church back from its way leading to Hellenism by resorting to a "revolutionary simplification of the entire sacramental teaching."[36] Being fed by the *Logos* ["Word"] and appropriating the *Logos* by faith become the meaning of the Sacrament. Paul's misguided path has thus been left behind. But later Catholicism returned to it again by thinking in Paul's terms of "the elements as participating in the heavenly nature of the risen one"[37] and by assuming that reception of the Sacrament effects "a substantial connection to the *Pneuma*-Christ resurrected from the dead."[38] "It was only the Reformation which reignited this liberating solution" (that is, the Fourth Gospel's solution, according to Käsemann's view) "and did so in the sense of the Fourth Gospel with Luther's word, 'Believe, and you have it; believe not, and you don't have it!' "[39] Käsemann concludes his essay with this surprising finding. Then the question remains open whether Zwingli or Calvin was the real Reformer. Despite this quote of his which doesn't belong here, Luther has nothing to do with this "Reformation." One ought to know that, even in Marburg—or especially in Marburg.[40]

PART 4

For surface reasons, we cannot delve further into the sacramental question in John, which Käsemann himself only touched on briefly. As far as how we might respond otherwise to Käsemann's understanding of Paul's sacramental teaching,

---

[32] Käsemann, "Das Abendmahl im Neuen Testament," 76. HS

[33] Käsemann, "Das Abendmahl im Neuen Testament," 90. HS

[34] Käsemann, "Das Abendmahl im Neuen Testament," 90, 93. HS

[35] Käsemann, "Das Abendmahl im Neuen Testament," 90, cites Ignatius, *Epistle to the Ephesians* 20:2. RF

[36] Käsemann, "Das Abendmahl im Neuen Testament," 92. RF

[37] Käsemann, "Das Abendmahl im Neuen Testament," 90, also quoted above. RF

[38] Käsemann, "Das Abendmahl im Neuen Testament," 76, also quoted above. RF

[39] Käsemann, "Das Abendmahl im Neuen Testament," 93. HS

[40] This is a reference to the Marburg Colloquy (1529) between Luther and Zwingli. RF

we combine that with the positive answer to the question Käsemann asked us about the biblical grounds of our church's teaching on the Sacrament. That doctrine is built on the cumulative witness of the NT on the Lord's Supper. Since Luther understood the Words of Institution against the backdrop of this cumulative witness and could not understand them otherwise, he was in no doubt about what the "is" must mean. The words "this is my body" and "this is my blood of the covenant [*Bundes*]" only become problematic and unclear, like all other words of Scripture, when one tears them out of the context in which they wish to be understood. The witness of 1 Corinthians is part of this context. It is no coincidence in this oldest record of the Supper that the historical account, which is expressly followed back to a tradition reaching to Jesus, is joined to an apostolic commentary.

The exegetes wishing to understand the history of the institution, as they say, simply and on its own terms as if they did not know anything else regarding the Sacrament, and who then refuse to take the Words of Institution as they read, end up with these difficulties. They feel they must understand Jesus' act as analogical to other acts, whether those of cultic origin or prophetic parabolic deeds. In addition, they have to understand the psychology of Jesus' words. Both of these approaches are impossible. Despite surface comparisons with cultic ceremonies and sacred meals of the Jews and pagan [meals] already known to the early church, the Lord's Supper is something entirely unique. There is no parallel to it, just as the incarnation, the death on Golgotha, and the resurrection are without parallel. What exegete will seriously attempt to get into Jesus' soul at the Last Supper in order to explain his words psychologically? Why don't people just stop the learned, devotional sort of sentimentality that thinks it can tell us what Jesus could and must have thought or said at the time? We won't learn anything more from such an enterprise than what the Lord's Supper would be if it had been instituted by the professor doing the interpreting. We cannot find out anything more about what was going on within the soul of the God-man in his hour of departure, while he was sanctifying himself as the Lamb of God, than what has been recorded in his final disclosures. We don't find what Jesus meant by looking between the lines of the Gospels or peeking *behind* the Lord's words or talking about our hypotheses of what led up to the Gospels, and certainly not by searching ancient or modern Jewish or pagan parallels and analogies, but in the simple statements of Scripture.

And if people ask us, like Zwingli and Calvin[41] what "This is my body" could really have meant since Jesus was still in his earthly body when he said it, aside from the fact that Paul and the early church were aware of all that, we reply: And why not? If each celebration of the Sacrament done according to the Lord's institution is an incomprehensible miracle because of the supernatural presence of Christ, then why shouldn't the first Lord's Supper have been a miracle? Doesn't

---

[41]   *Institutes of the Christian Religion*, 4.17.17. HS

taking the Lord's Supper as a great miracle in which the Lord reveals his glory to his people shed much more light on this testament of Christ to his church than all those doubtful analogies arising out of the foggy history of religions? In point of fact, the institution of the Holy Supper has been understood by the church since ancient times as a miracle comparable to the transfiguration or the miraculous feedings. The presupposition of such an understanding, both of the first Lord's Supper and of the Sacrament in general, is faith in him who as true God and true man has received all authority in heaven and on earth. It is certainly not irrelevant to remind people that it follows that such a discussion on the Lord's Supper between adherents of different confessions is only possible on the basis of a common Christological understanding, just as the great disagreement between the Western confessional churches on the Sacrament assumes a common Nicene and Chalcedonian[42] Christology.

If one does not proceed with an interpretation of the biblical Lord's Supper based on the cumulative witness of the NT, but [if one] is restricted only to the Synoptics, then it is possible with the brevity of those accounts and using the Zwinglian-Calvinistic argument already mentioned to come to a different, a symbolical understanding of the Words of Institution—but only at a high price. One must abandon the sacramental teaching of Paul (we would include John also, but we will not go into that here) either by a massive reinterpretation of his original meaning, or one must reject it as false and nonbinding. The first solution is that of the Reformed Church; the second is the way of Protestant modernism.

Of course, within the *Reformed* Church there is the widest variety of ideas on the Lord's Supper, from the Zwinglianism which denies the real presence (he has been condemned by individual Reformed theologians, but never by the Reformed churches) down to classic Calvinism which claims to affirm the real presence. Yet all these parties agree in their denial of three affirmations: first, that the body and blood of the Lord are present "under the form of bread and wine" (AC X, German); second, that they are received with the mouth, though in a supernatural manner (*manducatio oralis*) ["eating by the mouth"]; and third, that even unworthy communicants receive the body and blood of the Lord (*manducatio impiorum*) ["eating by unbelievers" or "ungodly"]. Here is the boundary which the Reformed feel they cannot cross without falling back into Catholicism. Although Calvin was prepared to admit the real presence [*wirkliche Gegenwart*] of Christ in the Sacrament as well as the actual reception of the Lord's body and blood through the intervention of the Holy Spirit, he could not affirm it in the way those three sentences teach it [i.e., *die Realpräsenz*]. Yet that is the way in which Paul understands the Sacrament and what it gives. Paul sees the elements as the bearers and conveyers of what is given in the Sacrament. 1 Corinthians 10 and 11 only make sense against this backdrop, which Käsemann has very correctly recognized. But

---

[42] This is a reference to the Council of Chalcedon (451) which sought to give a clear definition of the church's Christology, that is, that Christ is one person in two natures (divine and human), which natures are united "unconfusedly, unchangeably, indivisibly, and inseparably." RF

then the Lord's body and blood are being received in, with, and under the elements, that is, orally [*mundlich*], not just spiritually at the same time the elements are being consumed, even though Paul avoids the "hard" expressions of eating the body and drinking the blood. He doesn't avoid them because they are false, but perhaps for the same reason that assurances against "Capernaitic"[43] or "sarcophagic" [from Greek; literally, "flesh eating"] misunderstandings are inserted at John, chapter 6. This accusation has constantly been leveled in the church, and the Reformed who accuse the Lutherans just as the Nestorians once did the Orthodox ought to ask themselves whether the accusation of "Thyestean banquet"[44] is not one of the surest historical proofs that the ancient church taught in a much more realistic way about the Supper than Calvin cared to admit. The *manducatio indignorum* ["eating by the unworthy"]—including the thought so repugnant to the Reformed, that the Sacrament can have physical effects, which Luther knew also[45]—is taught unambiguously in 1 Cor 11:27–30.[46] Only a violent exegesis could deny this, but unfortunately that is the exegesis of the great strong-willed systematician Calvin on many points. The consequence of such a misunderstanding of the "sacramental" in Paul is expressed by Käsemann in his book published in 1933, *Leib und Leib Christi*, with these words: "It is a fact that Catholic exegesis has had to defend this elementary state of affairs over against Protestant idealism and can legitimately accuse it of not taking Paul's notion of the 'sacramental' seriously, emptying it without proper cause through the introduction of some 'magical' idea."[47] For us there is no question that it is not just modern idealism, but already the sacramental teaching of the Reformed Church which has led to Rome seeing itself as the keeper of a biblical truth largely forgotten in the Protestant world in an important matter of church doctrine. There may even be entire countries nowadays in which the Roman Mass contains better remnants of the NT Eucharist than what the Protestants have in their Communion services.

---

[43]   Some charged the Lutherans "that as the people in Capernaum interpreted Christ's words in John 6:26, 52 as referring to physical eating, so the Lutheran doctrine could only mean that the communicants 'rend the flesh of Christ with their teeth and digest it as other food' " (Tappert, *BC*, 483 n. 9; see FC Ep VII 15; VIII 17). RF

[44]   Thyestes unknowingly ate the flesh of his own sons served him by his brother and rival (see Cicero, *Tusculan Disputations*, 3.12.26). RF

[45]   That the Sacrament has physical effects is not just the romantic hobbyhorse of the nineteenth-century "neo-Lutherans," since most of them spoke against it, but it is a teaching of the church seldom discussed in the Reformation because it was assumed and not a matter for debate. For more, see E. Sommerlath, *Der Sinn des Abendmahls* (1930), 81 ff. With regard to Baptism, why do people today diligently hide the great difference between the Lutheran and Reformed baptismal teaching, for example, on the question of regeneration? Recall Luther's words in the Large Catechism, Fourth Chief Part, on the power of Word and water over our souls and bodies. [On the physical effects of the Lord's Supper, see LC V 68–69; FC SD VIII 76.] HS

[46]   One should just try to think of other punishments in 1 Cor 11:30 instead of illness and death, and one will immediately see how Paul felt there was a strong link between the physical gift and the physical effects of the Sacrament. HS

[47]   Käsemann, *Leib und Leib Christi*, 128. HS

The other way of escaping Paul's teaching on the Lord's Supper is the way of Protestant modernism. People just determine this doctrine to be nonbinding on the church, a theological view of an apostle who fell into the dangers of Hellenism. With all desirable clarity, Käsemann's work demonstrates where this path is leading. It ends with *the disintegration of the NT and the denial of the Word of God.* Nobody disputes that there is a history of the Lord's Supper in the NT. But when the reconstruction of this history leads us to posit a pre-synoptic, a synoptic, a Pauline, and a Johannine Lord's Supper, each with a meaning different from the others, then the NT Lord's Supper has been destroyed. Nobody disputes the need to distinguish in the NT between passages with a greater or lesser doctrinal weight. But whoever tears at the cumulative witness of Scripture regarding the Supper, which is given us in the accounts of its institution and in the commentaries of Paul and John, and then tells us that Paul's commentary is a questionable interpretation which needs improving by the better version of John destroys both the unity and the authority of Holy Scripture. Nobody denies that the language and thought world of the NT writers were influenced by the religious history of the ancient world, just as nobody denies that there are parallels between the Christian sacraments and other religions. "Every dogma is as old as the world!" But whoever wants to tell us that Paul's teaching on the body and blood of the Lord is to be understood as Hellenistic influence and that he understands "This is my body" in a way completely different from the Synoptics or Jesus himself is tearing the wall down between the church and the heathen world and is abandoning the canon of Holy Scripture. Of course, Käsemann doesn't want that. He does not draw any of these consequences, but they are put in place by his premises, and it is amazing that the authors of this book did not notice that. Or maybe they did not want to notice it! Don't they see that the "Confessing Church"[48] makes its whole line about "Scripture and Confession" and its appeal to confess the Scripture unbelievable and even ruins itself as a truly Evangelical Church when it allows room for such argumentation? If one can hear the fact that Paul teaches not a symbolic, but a very real understanding of the "is" and can respond that this is correct, but that Paul's words do not matter, only Jesus' words—and even those are not as one finds them in our Synoptic Gospels, but somehow in what lies behind those Synoptics—then scriptural proof means nothing. Then it is totally impossible to prove or refute any article of faith from Scripture. Then we are surrendering the Scripture and the possibility of scriptural proofs to the Roman Church. Then we are neglecting the one powerful weapon used by our fathers in the struggle against Rome and the greatest heresy of all history. In place of the last Scripture proof there is only historical proof. With the help of that sort of proof we can excommunicate Paul from the church, just as old Liberalism did with the motto "From Paul to Jesus!" But he who rejects Paul rejects Jesus Christ also. *If Paul's Lord's Supper falls, then so does that of Jesus Christ.*

---

[48]   As is noted in the foreword of the collection of essays, many of them were presented to conferences of the Evangelical Confessing Synods (*Abendmahlsgemeinschaft?* 3). RF

Holy Communion has been the heartbeat of the church since that hour when the Lord gave his disciples his body and his blood in the wonder of the first Lord's Supper and left behind this meal as his testament for all subsequent time until the great banquet in the kingdom of God. That is why the NT church had no Sunday without the Eucharist. That is why there never is and never has been real "church" without the Sacrament. The church came to understand itself as the body of Christ by means of these words, "This is my body." That is why the Sacrament is one of the *notae ecclesiae* ["marks of the church"] together with the Word of God and Baptism. This also explains why the Lord's Supper has been the subject of discussion and debate. All questions of the life and teaching of the church ultimately led to the question of the Lord's Supper. That is why it is not a bad sign that not only in Germany, but in all Christendom, the question of the Sacrament of the Altar has become a life-and-death question for the church and is seen as such. If the question of the Word of God is taken so seriously as has been the case here in Germany since the World War, then the question of the Sacrament must also come alive. For Word and Sacrament belong together, and for the church there can be no greater concern than this: "That we your Word *and Sacrament* may pure retain until our end."[49]

---

[49]   Sasse ends this essay as he often does with a reference to the hymn *Ach Bleib Bei Uns*, "Lord Jesus Christ, Will You Not Stay" (cf. *Lutheran Worship* 344, stanza 2; *The Lutheran Hymnal* 292, stanza 2). RF

1938

QUATENUS OR *QUIA*[1]

The distinction here noted, which indicates the nature of one's stance toward the confessional documents of one's church, has been much debated, particularly since the nineteenth century. Does one subscribe to them *quia* ("because") they agree with Scripture, or merely *quatenus* ("in so far as") they agree. The latter is the confessional stance among Reformed churchmen, who from time to time revise and update their statements of faith.

In this essay, Pastor Höppl from Oppertshofen über Donauwörth responds to an earlier article by Sasse, "Why Must We Hold Fast to the Lutheran Doctrine of the Lord's Supper?" (1938), also found in this collection. In the earlier essay, Sasse commented on the role of confessions among modern theologians and how it reflects the Reformed attitude:

> It is also understandable when modern theologians keep the confessional vow but soften it in the Reformed direction. The Reformed, after all, simply do not know the kind of confessing which runs from Luther's confession of 1528 to the Smalcald Articles right through to the Formula of Concord, the confession of faith made "before God and all Christendom, both those alive and those who will come after us" [FC SD XII 40]. … They do not know the vow of a pastor to preach this doctrine and this one only, because it—*quia*, not *quatenus*—agrees with God's Word and to prefer to resign one's office if one can no longer do this. It is, as mentioned before, completely understandable when people come to the conviction that the Reformed type of confession, seeing faith statements as provisional and more or less correct, is right and preferable.

That is the setting for the following exchange between Pastor Höppl (who wrote the first section) and Hermann Sasse on the nature of confessional subscription.

Huss number 201
Hopf number 125

—◦◦◦—

---

[1] This interchange between Sasse and Pastor Höppl appeared in *Allgemeine Evangelisch-Lutherische Kirchenzeitung* 71.7 (February 18, 1938): 151–54. The editor of that publication added this note to explain the Latin terms in the title: " 'In so far as' or 'because.' The Reformed hold to the confession 'in so far as' it agrees with Scripture; the Lutheran holds to the confession 'because' it agrees with Scripture." MH

QUATENUS

What I have to say here is prompted by the basic assertion of the article by Herr Professor Doctor Sasse "Why Must We Hold Fast to the Lutheran Doctrine of the Lord's Supper?" What follows is not a contribution to the dialogue regarding the Lord's Supper. Neither is it meant to assert a position on the problem of the Union. I see a basic line of thought drawn by the author of the aforementioned article, which he has already often put before us and which raises many questions for him. The simple pastor [*Land-pfarrer*] could only inadequately dispute with the professor over many of these questions. But since we Lutheran pastors are addressed regarding our ordination and its meaning in Professor Sasse's article, I will hazard a few remarks. I do not know for how many I speak, but for me this is not essential. I will only publicly declare on my own behalf that I can in no way agree with the basic position of the article, but that I, too, have up to now been a Lutheran pastor.

In the article, the author's basic position is most clearly shown where he renders his judgment on the *quia* or *quatenus*. Every reader will certainly remember the appertaining passage. There Sasse labels it a Reformed view to accept a confessional document as a doctrinal norm under the condition of the *quatenus*, or "insofar as" it agrees with Holy Scripture. The Lutheran view, on the other hand, is the *quia*, or that the confessions are doctrinal norms "because" their agreement with Holy Scripture is once and for all time certain. By virtue of his ordination, the ordained pastor of a Lutheran Church has subscribed to the confessions in this sense. And thus he is to restrain himself in instances where modern exegesis would lead to an attack on particular formulas of a confessional document.

It is completely clear that the way of the *quia* and of the *quatenus* can diverge greatly. The problem is put to us Lutheran pastors as a decisive question: *quia* or *quatenus?* It might be good to ask for a moment whether the confessions themselves compel this decisive question, and whether they also have something to say regarding their own validity, quite to the opposite [of what Sasse asserts]. We leave that counter question to the celebrated experts on the confessions. Until now it has appeared to me that the important assertion of the confessions regarding themselves—*non obtinent auctoritatem iudicis* ["they do not claim the authority of a judge," FC Ep, Preface, 8] and everything which they assert regarding subordination to the *norma normans* ["norming norm," i.e., Holy Scripture as the final authority of the confessions; see FC Ep, Preface, 7]—at the very least would caution us from making the decisive question *quia* or *quatenus*.

But if this should be the decisive question, I hereby calmly and publicly declare that I accept the *quatenus*. It was because of this *quatenus* that I could become a pastor, and in holding this *quatenus* I can remain a pastor. If the Lutheran Church is found only on the side of the *quia*, then I am no longer a servant of the Lutheran Church. This is all simple and clear—if the author of the article is correct.

I am not concerned to answer this last question, nor am I the least compelled to do so. First let me declare with the openness which is to be expected of us pastors that I cannot go along with Herr Professor Sasse. I take the side of the *quatenus* because I cannot see how I can honorably remain a theologian and pastor in any other way. I am speaking here strictly for my own person, and I do not pronounce judgment on the conscience of others. I only know what I can do and what I cannot do.

Now to be sure, there would be much to say on this matter. As for myself, a completely free *quatenus* has always been the best way for me to be able to accept the assertions of the confessions with a clear, honorable *quia*. There may well be profound reasons for this. Whether one speaks of Subjectivism, Liberalism, or a confessionally Reformed view, I am not troubled by labels.

But can I as an ordained pastor answer the decisive question with *quatenus?* I have in fact done this, and indeed in full agreement with what, I assert, is the meaning of my ordination. I have allowed myself to understand my ordination as an ordination based upon Christ, the truth. It is not a matter of expressing this meaning of ordination more clearly in the formulas already in use. If I had not been led by way of my ordination to the firm conviction that my church would and could oblige me to nothing other, greater, beyond, or truer than the Christ, to seek and maintain as a student and teacher, then I would not have been ordained.

If there is to be a decision between the *quia* and the *quatenus*, an ordination so understood simply leaves no other choice but the *quatenus*. This remains my approach to the confessions, and even to the Bible itself. For if the approach leads to Christ as the final goal, then a *quatenus* is valid also over against the Bible. My basic position allows me freedom not only to acknowledge a declaration of the confessions as capable of being corrected and in need of correction on the basis of biblical exegesis, but also in biblical exegesis the *quatenus* which aims for Christ gives to me that free possibility of seeking Christ *through* the Bible. And no sacrifice of the intellect (*sacrificium intellectus*) is compatible with this. In the face of that free investigation, I cannot simply hide behind a "respect for the Word of God," which for me—to cite a specific example—would allow something like the *natus ex virgine* ["born of the Virgin"] to appear assured, in spite of the exegetical evidence. If my *quatenus* applied only in the case of the confessions, the *natus ex virgine* for instance would always continue to be assured for me by the [simple] wording of the Bible. But now the *quatenus* applies for me also over against the Bible. And something has happened in this one case which is quite different than what had been feared by those who see in such a view only evil subjectivism. When the *natus ex virgine* was no longer tenable for me, the wonder of Christ did not become less for me, but greater.

My way back to Christ remains that of the *quatenus*. Lose the *quatenus* and the light falls from Christ back onto the Bible and the confessions. This is my position relative to the confessions and the Bible. Now, am I a Lutheran pastor or not? I would be quite happy only to be a disciple of Jesus.

Pastor Höppl
Oppertshofen über Donauwörth, Bavaria

QUIA

We are thankful to Herr Pastor Höppl for pointing out the great inner distress which the theologian's obligation to the confession can mean, indeed, must mean, if he takes his ordination seriously. And if this distress consists in nothing other than a theologian, who joyously speaks the yes to the doctrine of his church, seeing how the pastor of another church, with the very same joyfulness, allows himself to be pledged to a doctrine which, according to his deepest convictions, is not the pure doctrine of the Gospel, [but] rather contains grievous errors—that would already be sufficient cause to seriously ask himself whether the *quia* of the Lutheran doctrinal pledge is necessary and whether it is theologically and ecclesiastically justifiable. How is this question to be answered?

1. There is not only a distress in this matter for the theologian, who pledges himself to the doctrinal confession of the church, but there is also a distress, and indeed an infinitely much greater distress or need for the congregation, which today, for the most part, no longer hears the Gospel preached because its pastor desires to preach something else. We know that this urgent state of affairs is long-standing and has its roots, at least in part, clear back into the eighteenth century. Such congregations have endured in their pulpits, one after another, Rationalists, Freemasons, Liberals, religious socialists, nationalist pastors,[2] and German Christians[3] of various bent. But who assists them with the proclamation of the Gospel? Who assists that congregation when it no longer pleases its pastor to administer the Sacraments according to their institution, so that it is the Baptism of Jesus Christ and the Lord's Supper? Perhaps one of the church governments, which today proudly declare that they do not wish to interfere in the preaching of the Gospel?

Anyone who has only a weak understanding of the enormous difficulty which has befallen not only our German ecclesiastical life, but also, and frequently in

---

[2]   *Stahlhelmpfarrer*, literally, "Steel Helmet pastors." The *Stahlhelm* was a nationalist ex-servicemen's organization formed in 1918. It played a prominent role in politics in the 1920s and early 1930s. In December 1933, Hitler decreed that its members be incorporated into the SA (Storm Troopers) or, in the case of the older members, into the SA Reserve (Louis L. Snyder, *Encyclopedia of the Third Reich* [New York: Paragon House, 1989], 331). Sasse refers to this organization in the essay "Confession and Confessing" in this collection. RF

[3]   On the so-called "German Christians" (*Deutsche Christen*), see the essay "Confession and Confessing." RF

entirely different dimensions, the Protestantism of other countries understands why we make the following assertion: *The Evangelical [Lutheran] pastor must, simply out of Christian love* (even if he does not completely understand it, and for the sake of the poor congregation, which he serves), *once again take upon himself the burden, and if need be, the distress, of an absolutely earnest doctrinal pledge.* If he does this then he himself will experience the greatest blessing from doing so. For only the absolutely earnest and seriously taken doctrinal pledge makes a pastor the *minister Verbi Divini,* the "servant of the divine Word." Otherwise he remains the mere official of a religious society.

2. An actual and serious doctrinal pledge can never consist in the pastor pledging himself to a confession *in so far as* this confession agrees with the Word of God. For it is self-evident that a confession in any church which stands upon the *sola scriptura* ["Scripture alone"] has authority only so far as it agrees with the Bible as the *norma normans* and correctly explicates the same. Here the Lutherans and Reformed are in complete agreement. Only crass ignorance or malevolent slander has, since the days of the Formula of Concord, been able to condemn our church for placing the confessions over the Bible. I am of course prepared to surrender any assertion of the confessions or the confessions in their entirety if it be shown to us that the doctrine contained therein is contrary to Scripture. If the *quatenus* is meant to say nothing more than this, then we find no difficulty with it. But the distinction must be made between the question of what we would have to do if our confession did not teach scriptural truth and the entirely different and for us essential question, namely, whether they in fact do teach truth or falsity. We reject the *quatenus* because it is used to avoid or minimize the seriousness of this question. I can only preach with conviction when I, with Luther, am convinced that what I preach is the pure doctrine of the Word.

What in our church's doctrine is false? Where does it contradict the Word of God? Where does it fail to rightly understand the Gospel? There are concrete answers to these concrete questions. Thus far Holy Scripture has not been shown to refute our confessions. The most significant attacks upon our dogma, Calvin's doctrines of the Lord's Supper and predestination, are, at most, based upon philosophical considerations and are not grounded in Holy Scripture. What our congregations ought and must expect from their pastors is a clear yes or no to the question with which we are dealing here. If we do not know what we teach as church and why we do so, if we leave the question open as to what of our doctrine is correct or perhaps false, then it is actually more correct to replace the pledge to Scripture and confession with the pledge to teach the Holy Scripture according to our best understanding and conscience. I can only ordain on the basis of the Augustana *because,* after the most serious study of the Scriptures, I am convinced that it is the correct explication of the Gospel. *Only the* quia *establishes a real pledge to the confessions. The* quatenus *is in reality only a polite and mild form of the disintegration of doctrinal confession.*

3. The destructive and thereby church-dissolving effect of the *quatenus* becomes clear in the conclusion which Pastor Höppl quite correctly draws. We can be nothing but thankful for the honorableness with which this has happened, and rightly thankful for it. He sees quite clearly what others do not wish to see: *that the* quatenus *over against the confessions necessarily leads to a* quatenus *over against the Holy Scriptures.* When the *norma normata* [the "norm" (confessions) which is "normed" (by the Bible)] of the confessions tumbles, the *norma normans* [the "norming norm," the ultimate authority] of the Holy Scriptures of necessity falls as well. Let whoever does not believe this study the destruction of scriptural authority in all the modern churches which have nullified the authority of the confessions of the Reformation and of the ancient church. What then becomes the *norma normans* in place of the Scriptures? "Christ!" comes the answer. But who is "the Christ," who is to be sought "through the Bible"? We know only of the Christ who is to be found in the Bible, because he speaks there, and there alone. Who is the judge who will tell me in a doubtful case where Christ and where only the Scriptures speak? Have I not then elevated my reason—which includes also my religious-moral feelings—to *norma normans?*

It was surely also the voice of reason which Pastor Höppl spoke when he said that "the *natus ex virgine* [is] no longer tenable," though he has to grant that it is literally taught in the Bible. Here my honored opponent now finds himself in the very best company of highly distinguished theologians, about whose orthodoxy no doubts have been publicly raised. Perhaps this is cause to direct the question to a wider circle. Is there clarity in our theology on what the denial of the virgin birth of the Lord means? It means that an article of faith of the Evangelical [Lutheran] Church—though it stands in all our confessions and is, without doubt, biblically grounded—is as little true as the Roman Catholic dogma of the immaculate conception of Mary. Its denial means further that we have surrendered a biblical article of the faith to the Catholic churches. It means finally the *abandonment of all scriptural evidence in dogmatics.* And it means this: *the end of the Reformation.*

Nothing other than concern for the maintenance of the Gospel and the church of the Gospel in Germany, so far as this concern is laid upon the office of the ministry by God as an obligation, moves us in our fight for the Lutheran confession. May this concern be understood also there, where the real situation our church faces today is not yet understood—before it is too late.

Dr. H. Sasse
Erlangen

The Presence of Christ and the Future of the Church[1]

Once again, Sasse speaks to our own day about a weakness of faith which cannot always hear the promise of God, the presence of Christ for and in his church. Today we often seem to lack faith in that promised presence through the means of grace. Sasse's words are confident in belief of that promise.

Huss number 205
Hopf number 132

—◦◦◦—

Today in Germany much is said about the future of the church, particularly the Lutheran Church. With fearful trepidation about the one and undisguised satisfaction about the other, it is said that the thousand-year day of Christendom in Germany is nearing its end. To both the fearful friends and the reveling opponents of the church we must hold up the biblical truth proven through so many centuries: that the future of the church nowhere and never has lain in the hands of people. And therefore it certainly can neither be foreseen nor prophesied by people. A favorite prophecy today predicts that in a generation or two Christianity in Germany will be a thing of the past because the youth will no longer know anything of the dogmas of the church which are rooted in the Orient. Such prophecies will appear as laughable to future generations as the following prophecy of a French revolutionary regarding the church in 1796:

> This old idol will come to nothing; it will be replaced by freedom and philosophy. But politics alone can determine when and how. It is too bad Pope Pius VI[2] did not live two more years so that philosophy would have had time to fulfill its work and leave this lama of Europe without a disciple. It is the

---

[1] This essay first appeared as "Die Gegenwart Christi und die Zukunft der Kirche" in *Lutherische Kirche* 20.10 (August 1, 1938): 129–36. It was reprinted in *ISC*, 2:13–18. MH

[2] Giovanni Angelo Braschi (1717–1799; pope from 1775) took part in the first European coalition against France (formed 1792/1793). Defeated by Napoleon I, he died a prisoner at Valence, France (*Lutheran Cyclopedia*, 628). His rule was marked by the struggle against the rising tide of secularism. MH

will of the Directory[3] that when the time comes the pope go under completely and be buried together with his religion.[4]

We could fill a thick volume with such predictions uttered over the course of the history of the church. They are prophecies spoken with complete seriousness and apparently with good cause, but real life and living history proceeded to prove them wrong. These predictions would show that certainly not only the foolish fantasizers such as the members of that French Directory, but precisely the most intelligent thinkers, the wisest and most influential politicians, the best historians, even the wisest church historians, such as Harnack and Holl,[5] have erred in a very fantastic way when they expressed their thoughts on the future development of the church. This fact must not only give those who, watch in hand, eagerly await the end of the church to take possession of their inheritance, cause to reconsider. Time and again it also makes theology conscious of the deep riddle presented by the earthly history of the church.

The existence of the church is the most profound riddle of history. No one can explain it. No one can say how the church finally continues to exist. Statesmen have been convinced, as the elector of Saxony once expressed it over against Luther with the most friendly intentions, that the protection of the state is what finally makes the existence of the church possible. But the church first experienced its great flowering in the centuries in which it was not acknowledged. And the great canon law of the first centuries, on which entire churches still depend today, came to exist in a church which as far as public law was concerned did not even exist. To this day how the church outlived the demise of the ancient world in the centuries of the great migrations is an inexplicable mystery of history. No one could have known that the sixteenth century would not result in the complete dissolution of the church. Nor could anyone have known that the apparent self-destruction of the church in that struggle, in which Luther expected and longed for the Last Day, was not the end of the church, but its Reformation. The age of Rationalism around 1800, when the preaching of the Gospel in broad areas of Lutheran Germany was almost completely extinguished, demonstrated that it is not the faith, hope, and love of people which sustains the life of the church. Even if today in Germany a "theology" should come to rule

---

[3]   The "Directory," a five-man executive, was formed during the French Revolution in November 1795. RF

[4]   "At [Pius VI's] death, many assumed that the destruction of the Holy See had at last been accomplished, and the fortunes of the papacy had indeed reached their nadir under him" (J. N. D. Kelly, *The Oxford Dictionary of Popes* [Oxford: Oxford University Press, 1986], 302). RF

[5]   Sasse once observed this about his time at the University of Berlin (1913–1917): "My main teachers in church history were Harnack and Holl" ("Reminiscences of an Elderly Student," *Tangara* 9 [1976]: 4–5). On Harnack (1851–1930), see "The Theologian of the Second Reich: Thoughts on the Biography of Adolf von Harnack" in this collection. Holl's famous lecture "What Did Luther Understand by Religion?" given on Reformation Day 1917, is said to have begun the rebirth of Luther studies in this century. RF

which was similar to the estrangement from Christ and the despising of the Holy Scriptures of the teachings of Rationalism, this would not in and of itself mean the end of the church. For the mystery of the church is the real and essential presence of Jesus Christ in the world.

Whether the church is present or not does not depend on the good or evil will of people, but only on his will. If he in his limitless mercy wills that his Gospel be preached also in the future among our people, and that generations of our people yet unborn should hear the saving message of the forgiveness of sins for the sake of Christ, then it will most certainly happen. No one knows how it happens. It may be that it will happen without the methods of modern "publicity" and without the technical means of the modern transmission of information. But there can be no doubt that the mandate shall be carried out: "What is whispered in your ear, proclaim from the rooftops!" [Matt 10:27]. "Go forth and preach the Gospel to all creatures!" [Mark 16:15]. What an unbelievable lack of faith it would be if we were to somehow believe today that the Gospel would be in danger if the freedom of the press of 1848 and 1871 no longer existed! He who believes in the mighty power of the divine Word with the strong, unshakable faith of Martin Luther knows that this Word does its punishing and saving, building and destroying work without respect to human help or earthly impediments. What was said to the prophets regarding the world-historical effects of the divine Word given to them to bear (e.g., Jer. 1:10) remains true today. What Luther said unflinchingly about this Word at the *Reichstag* ["diet"] at Worms [1521] to the governing authority of his people, when it was held up to him that his doctrine would necessarily lead to an "inhuman sundering" of the German nation, remains true also in the twentieth century. The Word which created the world and everything in it, visible and invisible, does not need the achievements of the French Revolution in order to be effective today. No matter what we think of the "rights" of the freedom of speech or of the press, which since the eighteenth century have been defined as "human rights" of democratic peoples, Almighty God does not need "human rights" when *he* wills to speak his Word. It is of the essence of this Word that it creates its own means. Therefore the church will remain among us in the future so long as Christ remains with us. "For thus he speaks, and so it happens; he commands and so it stands" [cf. Ps 148:5]. The church exists in our century as a miracle of God. To people it is an inconceivable riddle, to many a terrible offense. Its future is not determined by people, just as it cannot be foreseen by people. For the future of the church is the future of Christ.

How is it that this understanding of the church, which depends not on people, but only upon Christ, has perished throughout broad stretches of Evangelical Christianity? Once at the beginning of the second century a great church father said, "Where Christ is, there is the church."[6]

---

[6]   Sasse refers to Bishop Ignatius of Antioch, martyred under Trajan ca. A.D. 107. The passage cited is from the *Epistle to the Smyrnaeans* 8:2. On this same topic, see Sasse's essay "Where Christ Is, There Is the Church" in this collection. MH

How is it that this truth, which Luther still believed so firmly and which gave him so firm and peaceful a heart in the midst of all the struggles over the church, has been forgotten? We speak a good game about how the existence of the church depends alone on Jesus Christ being with us always until the end of the world. But we live and act as though the church were built upon bishops and synods, Councils of Brethren[7] and professors of theology, pastors and congregations, and not solely "on the foundation of the apostles and prophets, where Jesus Christ is the cornerstone" [Eph 2:20]. And because we have much too high a regard for our own thought and doing, our faith and our speaking, nothing comes of our nervous fastidiousness, our anxiety and grief over the future, and our self-inflicted and increasing pain brought on by ecclesiastical busyness. We do not note that with this we only pay our tribute to the world, which condemns itself to destruction in anxiety and grief because it knows nothing of the great "Fear not!" of the NT. Nor can it know anything of it. We do not mean that the Word of God is in any way sluggish. Luther was not slothful, and neither were the apostles, though they knew that of themselves they could not have maintained the church. Quite to the contrary! The experience of the history of the church teaches that generally in the church there is the most fervent and blessed labor where people really understand that "with might of ours can naught be done, Soon were our loss effected."[8] We do not see a foreboding sign for our ecclesiastical life in the fact that in the church today we work seriously and hard, harder than in previous times—indeed we have the negligence of entire generations to make up for! We see it rather in the fact that we, more often than not, do this work as though Jesus Christ were not really present in his church. That is the secret disbelief which has more deeply and adversely affected the Lutheran Church than any external influences of older or newer paganism. The effects of that hidden unbelief are a hundred times worse and more dangerous than everything which [movements] from a short-lived modern counter-movement of monism[9] down to the German Faith Movement,[10] or what ever other movements may be mentioned, have done to the church or are prepared to do to it. Indeed, we speak in our preaching as though the Lord Christ were present, but our hearers understand it as rhetorical language

---

7   A reference to the *Bruderräte* of the "Confessing Church" during the Third Reich. RF

8   From stanza 2 of "A Mighty Fortress Is Our God." The English translation is that found in *The Lutheran Hymnal* 262 and *Lutheran Worship* 298. RF

9   Monism is a "metaphysical theory that reduces all phenomena to one material or spiritual principle. It considers God and world, matter and spirit, body and soul to be modifications of one principle. Manifestations of monism include pantheism, which identifies God and the world; materialism, which regards matter as basic reality; and spiritualism or idealism, which regards spiritual beings or ideas as the only basis of reality. Metaphysical monism is opposed to Christianity. The Bible asserts essential difference bet[ween] Creator and creation" (*Lutheran Cyclopedia*, 554). MH

10 The neo-pagan "church" of the Third Reich. The movement consisted of sworn enemies of prior religions. An improvised offshoot of the Nazi movement in the spiritual sphere, the movement was designed to replace traditional Christianity. It banned nativity plays and carols from schools and called for an end to required daily prayers in the classroom (Louis L. Snyder, *Encyclopedia of the Third Reich* [New York: Paragon House, 1989], 64). RF

which we do not take seriously ourselves. Even our good churchly congregations often no longer grasp the full seriousness and comfort of the real presence of the Lord. Even so it must be said that in the experiences of recent years many a pastor and many a congregation has again had their eyes opened to this most profound comfort of our church. But by and large we all act in our church as though Jesus Christ were not really present, as though he were further removed from our time than any other age in the history of the church.

If we attempt to understand this development, this dwindling of faith in the presence of Christ, we will be prone first off to blame the modern Enlightenment for it. In the eighteenth century human reason placed itself on the judgment seat of God and curtailed and rejected the preaching of the apostles and prophets, the doctrine of the Scriptures and the church, because they are higher than any reason. Indeed all truths of the Christian faith have faded. This enlightened modern Christendom and its theology has smothered the fires of hell with mountains of paper and declared the devil a mere idea.[11] Claus Harms[12] already said it in thesis 21 of his Ninety-five Theses [1817]: "The forgiveness of sins still cost money in the sixteenth century; in the nineteenth it is completely free, and every man rewards himself with it." The Christians in the earliest church said, "Our God is a consuming fire" [Heb 12:29, quoting Deut 4:24]. The God of Kant,[13] Hegel,[14] Schleiermacher,[15] and Harnack[16] is no longer a consuming fire. It is self-evident that here also the countenance [*Gestalt*] of Christ pales. The crucified and risen Son of God, who was raised to the right hand of the Father and to whom all authority in heaven and on earth has been given, became a teacher of divine truth, the founder of the purest morality, a religious genius, a noble man, who lives on in the memory of man because his sublime, divine thoughts are undying.

But as consequential as the influence of the modern Enlightenment in the church has been for faith in Christ, this alone does not explain the dwindling of the belief in the presence of Christ. This faith has also certainly been crippled

---

[11] Sasse would often contrast the Enlightenment's "idea" or "concept" to the church's historic doctrine or faith. RF

[12] Claus Harms (1778–1855) had been a rationalist impressed by Schleiermacher but then turned to orthodox Lutheranism. In 1817 he issued his famous Ninety-five Theses against Rationalism and the proposed Prussian Union (*Lutheran Cyclopedia*, 361). MH

[13] Immanuel Kant (1724–1804) denied the metaphysical and considered morality to be the chief content of Christianity. MH

[14] Georg Wilhelm Friedrich Hegel (1770–1831). His thesis-antithesis-synthesis gave philosophical rationale to the consummation of the Prussian Union, hence he is known as the "philosopher of the Prussian Union." MH

[15] Friedrich Daniel Ernst Schleiermacher (1768–1834) is widely regarded as the founder of modern theology. He is also considered the "theologian" of the Prussian Union. MH

[16] Karl Gustav Adolf von Harnack (1851–1930) was Sasse's great teacher at the University of Berlin. His expertise lay in the history of dogma. He denied the metaphysical and creedal truths of Christianity as the effects of pagan philosophy on the "Gospel." Christianity was finally a matter of ethics, not dogma. Sasse thought it significant and telling that it was Rudolf Bultmann who later wrote a preface for an anniversary reissue of Harnack's *The Essence of Christendom*. MH

where Christ has been confessed as the crucified and risen Son of God without respect to the reigning philosophies of the day. Thus there must be still another reason for this phenomenon. We believe it is not a mistake to see a correspondence between the celebration of the Holy Supper and the correct understanding of this Sacrament on the one hand, and the belief in the real presence of Christ in the church on the other hand. Since the celebration of the first Supper, the church has been connected with the Supper in a very unique way. Where the Supper is celebrated, there is the church. When the church is described as the body of Christ in the NT it can only be understood on the basis of this Sacrament. "The participation in the body of Christ" (1 Cor 10:16) means at the same time the participation in the true body of the Lord, who is given to us in the Supper, and membership in the church as the body of Christ. The Evangelical Lutheran Church had always understood it this way, when it derived from 1 Cor 10:16 the principle that church fellowship is altar fellowship, and altar fellowship is church fellowship. It can still be historically demonstrated that the entire life of the early church was defined by the Supper: the liturgy, its charity, indeed even its constitution. The presbyters or elders were originally not office bearers, but they formed one estate in the congregation. They were to assume the foremost places at the Supper. "Bishops" were originally the men who were entitled to lead the celebration of the Supper. Therefore, even if the congregation had more than one bishop (Phil 1:1), it was always the case that only one could officiate at the Supper. And then he stood in the place of Christ. The deacons are those who during the Supper "wait at table" and who afterward go to the houses of the ill and provide for their need. This connection between diaconate and liturgy was later again seen when the diaconate was revived in the Evangelical Lutheran Church in the previous century. We only need to think of Löhe's work in Neuendettelsau in order to understand this, or of the general significance of the deaconess houses for the liturgical life of the church.[17]

Luther had still perceived in a very vibrant way the connection between the Supper and all other expressions of the life of the church. He had been raised in the great liturgical traditions of the late medieval church and never considered destroying the liturgy as it had been handed down. He only purified it from the paganism which had forced its way into it, especially the works-righteousness of the sacrifice of the Mass. In distinction from Zwingli and Calvin, he left the Lord's Supper in its position in the Sunday Divine Service (there was no Lord's day without the Supper in the early church). He would never have understood the objection that in the Evangelical Divine Service not the Sacrament, but the Word must form the center point, because for him as for the church of the NT, Word and Sacrament belonged inseparably together. Or was something preached in the Wittenberg City Church and in the old Lutheran churches in general which in

---

[17] Johann Konrad Wilhelm Löhe (1808–1872) established a deaconess society and mother house in Neuendettelsau in 1854, one of the first in modern Lutheranism. RF

the churches of our day has become quite inconceivable? But taking seriously the sermon does not exclude taking seriously the Sacrament! Both belong together and perhaps the preaching of the Gospel lives precisely from the celebration of the Sacrament of the Altar which accompanies it. For without the legitimate celebration of the Supper, the sermon becomes a subjective religious speech, whether or not we know it or intend it. This is what has happened in modern Christianity. And it has happened also in the Lutheran churches in the latter centuries since the Supper was forced out of its old position and became an occasional appendage to the Divine Service.

Next to onslaught of the Enlightenment there has not been an event which has so profoundly affected the inner life of the church as the destruction of the old Lutheran liturgy which began about 1700. This destruction however was not only a concurrent phenomenon of the Enlightenment—indeed, it began already in the age of Pietism—it rather signified the victory of the Reformed understanding of the Divine Service and the Supper. Since then also in our church the idea has increasingly prevailed that the Supper is properly only the seal, the confirmation of a fellowship with Christ, which we also possess otherwise.[18] Then we no longer understand the hunger and thirst for the Sacrament which animated earlier generations. We no longer know anything of the profound miracle of the real and essential presence of the entire Christ according to his divine and human natures, that the ascended Lord according to his true divinity and true humanity in the fullness of his might and love is really present in the Sacrament of the Altar, even though hidden from our eyes. He gives us in, with, and under the bread and wine his true body and his true blood to eat and to drink. This profound miracle of our Divine Service has been abandoned. In its place has come the view that the Lord, absent from the world, is made present by the mediation of the Holy Spirit and that the Christ is now present only according to his divine nature. But with this not only the doctrine of the Supper has changed, but also the entire understanding of the presence of Christ and the church as the place of this presence in the world.

We make this assertion even at the risk of once again becoming guilty of "confessionalistic baiting." It is really not a lack of brotherly love if we clearly present what separates the Lutheran Church from the Reformed in these great questions. We know that in very many questions of the faith we are in agreement with our Reformed brethren in Christ. And we view things as the great Lutheran Wilhelm Löhe, who could not conceive of heaven without his Reformed teacher Krafft.[19] But no Christian love can and shall prevent us from decisively rejecting

---

18 "In fact, what the Supper gives us we have every day in the sermon, as we read Scripture, as we pray. What other fellowship should there or could there be than that which is created through Word and Spirit!" Thus W. Niesel (*Calvins Lehre vom Abendmahl* [2d ed.], 97) describes the Reformed viewpoint. HS

19 Johann Christian Gottlieb Ludwig Krafft (1784–1845) was a Reformed clergyman, pastor at Erlangen (1817), and professor at Erlangen. He helped revive the Protestant church in Bavaria (*Lutheran Cyclopedia*, 451).

what according to our deepest conviction was a powerful and false exposition of the divine Word by Calvin. Therefore today we still stand at the side of Luther against the Sacramentarians. We stand on the side of Westphal,[20] the faithful head pastor of Hamburg, who defended Luther's doctrine against the great Calvin and his plan for worldwide union. We stand on the side of the Formula of Concord against all who murmur piously, shunning the necessity of confessing "with clear German words" what is received in the Lord's Supper. And we deplore nothing more painfully than the fact that in broad sections of Germany the "Confessing Church"[21] tolerates brazen deniers of the two natures in Christ in their ranks as confessors of the faith. Luther confessed this from his Great Confession of 1528[22] to his last confession regarding the Supper.[23] And he died with this confession and appeared before the judgment seat of his Lord Jesus Christ with it. But if Luther were to return to his church today, which in Germany still bears his name, he would evidently be rejected as an outsider not to be taken seriously.

And yet no one has understood more profoundly than Luther—and the Lutheran Church should honorably hold on to this knowledge as a holy legacy—how inseparably the Holy Supper and the church of Christ belong together and how necessary therefore the correct understanding of the Sacrament of the Altar is for understanding the church. Only in the context of the Supper can we understand the heated struggle of our Reformer and the struggle of the old Evangelical Lutheran Church to maintain the correct understanding of the biblical Supper. And perhaps the understanding of this indissoluble connection between church and Lord's Supper will open anew to our generation access to the truths of the Bible and the Reformation, which have been lost to modern Protestant Christianity. Every celebration of the Supper ought remind us that Jesus Christ in the time between his earthly days and the revelation of his glory at his "return"

November, 1826, saw Wilhelm Löhe enter the University of Erlangen and begin his actual theological studies. The most impressive teacher under whom he studied was Christian Krafft, professor of Reformed theology and pastor of the Reformed congregation in Erlangen. At Roth's recommendation Löhe, who was not obliged to hear any of Krafft's lectures, became an ardent student of this man who was the chief representative of the awakening in Erlangen and whose influence on Löhe and other students can hardly be overestimated. It was not only Krafft's academic ability but also the deep piety of the man which so impressed his students and led Löhe to say that Krafft gave his thirsting soul the water of life while in comparison all that the other professors had to offer was a burning sand. (James L. Schaaf, introduction to Three Books about the Church, by Wilhelm Löhe [trans. James L. Schaaf ; Philadelphia: Fortress, 1969; repr., Fort Wayne: Concordia Theological Seminary Press, 1989], 4) MH

[20] Joachim Westphal (1510–1574) was a student of Luther and Melanchthon. He lectured at Wittenberg and was superintendent in Hamburg beginning in 1571 (Lutheran Cyclopedia, 814). He is noted for his very vigorous debate with John Calvin. MH

[21] The so-called Bekennende Kirche was that movement within the German church during the Third Reich which was dominated by the theology of Karl Barth. RF

[22] This is a reference to Luther's Confession concerning Christ's Supper (LW 37:151–372). RF

[23] Brief Confession concerning the Holy Sacrament, 1544 (WA 54.141–67; LW 38:279–319). MH

is not distant from us, that he even now exercises his glory "hidden under the cross" through the means of Word and Sacrament in his church, that the present Christ is the greatest power and the most important fact of world history in our day. We should know this as we ponder the future of the church. The presence of Christ is the life of the church. The future of the church is the future of the Lord.

ARE WE STILL THE CHURCH OF THE REFORMATION?[1]

In this essay, Sasse addresses the growing pressure on the Lutheran churches in Germany to compromise their confessional foundation for the sake of the almost ubiquitous appeal for Prussian Union ecclesiology—that all Lutherans and Reformed churches unite in the so-called Union (*Uniert*) churches as the basis for a united "confession" against the threat of Nazism.

Sasse wrote the following as a footnote to the title: "The following statements were written at the end of October for the Reformation festival but had to be put aside for printing-technical reasons." This seems to indicate that this essay had been scheduled to be published in the November 1 issue of the bimonthly journal *Lutherische Kirche*. At this time Sasse was the editor. The journal, started in 1934 by Sasse's Erlangen colleague Friedrich Ulmer, appears to have had a poor rating with the Reich officials. Ulmer "often picked an argument with the National Socialists. And his journal *Lutherische Kirche* was perpetually forbidden."[2] One issue in 1938 published only its cover with this announcement: "By order of the Secret State's Police, State's Police Office Berlin, the bimonthly journal *Lutherische Kirche* in Erlangen was forbidden for the period of three months." The three-month period was February 15–May 15, 1938.

Huss number 211
Hopf number 137

———⌇∾∾∾⌇———

Among the great men in the history of the church, few have had to experience the *thanklessness* of men as did Martin Luther. Here we do not have in mind only the greater portion of Western Christianity which once rejected the pure doctrine of the Gospel in rejecting Luther's Reformation. Nor do we have in mind that

---

[1] The following statements were written at the end of October for the Reformation festival but had to be put aside for printing-technical reasons. HS

This article originally appeared as "Sind wir noch Kirche der Reformation?" in *Lutherische Kirche* 20.17 (November 15, 1938): 242–48. RF

[2] This remark was made by Sasse's student and friend Pastor Hans-Siegfried Huss, Würzburg, September 29, 1989. RF

thanklessness of which Luther prophetically spoke in the year 1524 in his well-known statement concerning the Word of God, which passes over peoples like an intermittent shower: "You Germans dare not think that you will always have it. For thanklessness and contempt will not allow it to remain." We are thinking only of the thanklessness which Luther has had to endure in the church which emphatically confesses his Reformation. We are thinking especially of the actual thanklessness and contempt which men in the broadest circles of the German Evangelical Lutheran Church hold against the heritage of the Reformation, while asserting before the world that they are preserving it. There are "Evangelical" churches in which pastors can no longer be theologians who believe, teach, and confess what Luther believed, taught, and confessed. We actually know of one "intact" territorial church in which the church government, which is not under the leadership of the German Christians, denies ordination to every young theologian who for the sake of his conscience, which is bound to the Word of God, declares that he can only be sworn to the Augsburg Confession and not simultaneously to the Heidelberg Catechism. No, we hardly need to look as far as the German Christians to see the complete collapse of Evangelical Lutheran doctrine in German Protestantism.

The members of the Prussian Council of Brethren[3] all passed their theological examinations. There is not one of them who could not have known that Luther, without surrendering his own doctrine, could have sanctioned neither the Barmen Declaration, with its completely un-Lutheran, Reformed concept of church and confession, nor the Halle resolutions,[4] which correspond completely with the views of Calvin regarding altar fellowship. But we act "as though" we walk in the paths of the Reformer when we do the opposite of what he did and taught. Indeed, he can no longer prevent the misuse of his name. To be sure, seeing this misuse coming he solemnly confessed his faith before the world:

> I am determined to abide by it until my death and (so help me God!) in this faith to depart from this world and to appear before the judgment seat of our Lord Jesus Christ. Hence if any one shall say after my death, "If Luther were living now, he would teach and hold this or that article differently, for he did not consider it sufficiently" etc., let me say once and for all that by the grace of God I have most diligently traced all these articles through the Scriptures, have examined them again and again in the light thereof, and have wanted to defend all of them as certainly as I have now defended the sacrament of the altar. I am not drunk or irresponsible. I know what I am saying, and I well realize what this will mean for me before the Last Judgment at the coming of the Lord Jesus Christ. Let no one make this out to be a joke or idle talk; I am in dead earnest, since by the grace of God I have learned to know a great

---

[3] The Councils of Brethren, administrative councils or consistories within the Confessing Church, were alternatives to the official church government. RF

[4] See the introduction to "Theses on the Question of Church and Altar Fellowship" in this collection. RF

deal about Satan. If he can twist and pervert the Word of God and the Scriptures, what will he not be able to do with my or someone else's words?[5]

Once more, a year before his death, he wrote down his confession again.[6] Should not merely human respect for a great person now deceased necessitate serious consideration of such a confession made before the judgment seat of God? No one is forced to make this confession his own.

It may be that someone comes to the conviction that Luther's doctrine of the Supper is, as the Halle theologian Loofs[7] put it, "one of the most magnificent aberrations of the conception of the Christian faith." We respect anyone who on the basis of his serious effort to understand the Bible comes to different conclusions than Luther and the Augsburg Confession. But what we must expect of him on the grounds of human decency and Christian truthfulness is this: that he honorably confess the fact that he teaches differently than Luther. We must demand of him that he not call upon Luther and proclaim himself Luther's legitimate heir precisely in [the area] where he teaches the very opposite of Luther, all with the substantiation "were Dr. Luther living today"—in view of the altered exegetical situation or because the Reformed today are different people than were the Reformed in 1545, or in view of the threat to all confessions—"he would teach and hold this or that article differently, for he did not consider it sufficiently." If human respect already forbids putting words in the mouth of someone living and making his words say the opposite of what he said, how much more does this apply to the fathers, who can no longer defend themselves, who cannot speak to us in any other way than in their written word! We may say this not only for Luther, but for the fathers of our church in general, from the much-maligned authors of the Formula of Concord to the "Neo-Lutherans"[8] of the nineteenth century (whom certain theologians of our time are accustom to bathe with scorn and derision after they have plundered their works for learned citations), and even down to the teachers and leaders of our church in our own day.

What do we say to the fact that Hermann *Bezzel*[9] is claimed as an advocate for the altar fellowship between Lutherans and Reformed which is demanded today only because he, like every believing Lutheran Christian, did not deny his Christian solidarity with Reformed believers and was of the very correct opinion

---

[5]   From Luther's *Confession concerning Christ's Supper* (the English translation is from *LW* 37:360–61; cf. WA 26.499–500). MH

[6]   This is perhaps a reference to Luther's *Brief Confession concerning the Holy Sacrament* of 1544 (two years before his death; *LW* 38:287–319; WA 54.141–67). RF

[7]   Friedrich Loofs (1858–1928), a church historian, was influenced by Ritschl and von Harnack. He taught at Leipzig (1882–1887) and Halle (1887–1926) (*Lutheran Cyclopedia*, 478). MH

[8]   In general terms, this was a movement of confessional renewal which can be divided into sub-movements. RF

[9]   Hermann Bezzel (1861–1917) was one of the most important leaders of Lutheranism in Sasse's day. He became a successor to Löhe at Neuendettelsau and was opposed to all unionizing. RF

that a signature under the Formula of Concord does not yet make anyone a Lutheran? This same Bezzel fought like no one else against the impending "German Evangelical Church" and had such strong views on altar fellowship that he, the very busy president of the Munich High Consistory, for a year made the several-hour trip to receive the Holy Supper in Ansbach until the Reformed Christians in Munich had their own church and no longer had to live in emergency altar fellowship [Notabendmahlsgemeinschaft] with the Lutherans. He could not have attended such a mixed altar without a distressed conscience. According to the Lutheran view, it is of the essence of the church that in it are united not only those presently living, but "those living even now and those who shall come after us" [FC SD XII 40]. The believing and those who have completed their course in faith are united. Is there a more evil denial of this unity, is there a more unmerciful offense of Christian love than if we so twist and reinterpret the confession which the fathers put their very lives on the line to confess, upon which they died and with which they appeared before the judgment seat of God, until finally it says the very opposite of what was originally intended? We leave this reinterpretation to those "Luther scholars" of our day, who present us with a Luther who finally in the depths of his soul did not at all believe what he proclaimed as teacher of the church. In the church, however, there should be no room for this renunciation of the Reformer.

The thanklessness for the work of the Reformation, the renunciation of the doctrine of Luther, is the deep *distress* of the Evangelical Lutheran Church of Germany. It is the real cause for the public apostasy happening within the church. It is meaningless for us to lament what the opponents of the church are doing to us. They execute a sentence which must come and which those who have a little deeper insight into the inner condition of our church have long seen coming. For those who were present, the words of Wilhelm Zoellner[10] directed at a circle of younger theologians in Berlin in the summer of 1930 are unforgettable. He had called them together as a result of the Nuremberg *Kirchentag* ["Church Congress"] which had been held in connection with the anniversary of the Augsburg Confession, in order to outline for them the enormous seriousness of the situation faced by the church. Then, the president of the Rhenish Provincial Synod, Walther *Wolff*, a celebrated Reformed churchman and a pillar of the German national movement in the Rhineland, delivered an address regarding "The Right and Authority of the German Reformation to Form the Church" [*Recht und Kraft der deutschen Reformation zur Kirchenbildung*]. The "Pronouncement

---

[10] Wilhelm Zoellner (1860–1937) was a pastor at Friedrichsdorf near Bielefeld and Barmen-Wupperfeld. He was director of the deaconess institution at Kaiserswerth (1897), general superintendent of the Church of Westphalia (1905), and chairman of the Committee of the German Federation of Churches in Kirchenkampf (1935) (*Lutheran Cyclopedia*, 843). Sasse praises Zoellner in "Wilhelm Zoellners Kampf um das Bekenntnis," *Lutherische Kirche* 19.10 (August 1, 1937): 129–34, but takes him to task for not finally opposing the Union with sufficient intensity (unlike Bezzel or Vilmar). MH

on the Church Question," which was adopted on the basis of this address, lighted the path for the German Evangelical Church Federation like lightning. Here was the "German Evangelical Church" with its marks: the *German* Bible, the *German* hymnal, the *German* catechism already there! Which catechism was meant was not stated. Not a word was said of the Augsburg Confession which had just been celebrated. Here already was article 1 of the constitution of July 11, 1933,[11] which called upon confessions of the Reformation which were intentionally no longer mentioned by name. They all applied as equally true and valid and therefore only have an authority as long as no one takes them seriously. This is the article of faith which one enlightened theologian of our day has designated the *articulus stantis et cadentis ecclesiae,* "the article by which the church stands or falls"—in this case it indeed "falls." Today the previous vice president of the Evangelical High Consistory, *Burghart,* seeks to assemble German Protestantism around this view of the confessions of the Reformation, arm in arm with the men of the earlier Dahlem "Temporary Leadership" of the DEK [German Evangelical Church]. Finally, the entire theology of the "German Christians," which indeed at base is nothing other than the theology of the entire official Prussian Church, was already present. For whatever the differences between Ludwig Müller[12] and George Burghart,[13] between Joachim Hossenfelder[14] and Otto Dibelius,[15] there was no fundamental theological difference between them when they switched places. We generally do a great injustice to the "German Christians" when we always only treat them as heretics. The proposition "I must under all circum-

---

11 This is a reference to the day when the (National Socialist) constitution for the German Evangelical Church (DEK) was passed. It was then confirmed by Reich law on July 14. "In conformity with his policy of *Gleichschaltung,* or coordination, Hitler wanted a Reich church that would bring all Protestants together in one easily ruled body" (Louis L. Snyder, *Encyclopedia of the Third Reich* [New York: Paragon House, 1989], 235). See further the essay "Church Government and Secular Authority according to Lutheran Doctrine" in this collection. MH/RF

12 Ludwig Müller (1883–1945), a fanatical supporter of the Nazi regime and a leader of the *Deutsche Christen* ["German Christians"], was elected Bishop of the Reich in September 1933. His attempt to unite the Protestant churches of Germany in harmony with Nazi party principles led to opposition by what became the "Confessing Church" movement (*Lutheran Cyclopedia,* 331), of which Sasse remained an active, albeit critical, participant. MH

13 George Burghart, clergy vice president of the Prussian *Oberkirchenrat* [Evangelical High Consistory], was deemed to be Prussia's leading clergyman, at least in the period before the Nazi party came to power. He raised some objections to the guidelines of the Faith Movement of German Christians when they were submitted by Hossenfelder in June 1932 (Klaus Scholder, *The Churches and the Third Reich* [London: SCM Press, 1987], 1:209–10). RF

14 Joachim Hossenfelder was the national leader of the German Christians. After 1932 he became "one of the most important figures in German Protestantism" (Scholder, *The Churches and the Third Reich,* 1:204). RF

15 Friedrich Karl Otto Dibelius (1880–1967) was general superintendent of the Kurmark (a section of the Prussian Union Church). Dismissed from all offices by the Nazis in 1933, he became a leader of the Confessing Church. He was evangelical bishop of Berlin (1945), president of the council of the Evangelische Kirche in Deutschland (1949), and president of the World Council of Churches (1954) (*Lutheran Cyclopedia,* 235). MH

stances be bishop!" is not yet heresy—though it always has played a devastating role in the church, as is well known. St. Augustine, who well understood the fight against heresy, once expressed the profound truth that only great men can really be heretics. A person must have a certain intellectual demeanor in order to mislead large numbers of people into heresy. But those church politicians who in 1933 inherited the old church-political parties do not possess this demeanor. The church which collapsed had merited its judgment. Therefore the terrible crisis into which it has fallen can certainly not be solved by blaming one particular church-political group. In the meantime the principle malefactors of 1933 indeed have converted to the "Confessing Church" in dense throngs. Nor can it be solved by now hoisting the Barmen Declaration or the fatal article 1 as the banner of the church, and separating the sheep from the goats on that basis. The sole salvation of the Evangelical Church in Germany consists much rather in this, that we finally have done with the awful untruthfulness in which German Protestantism has now lived for generations. It will no longer suffice for us to operate on the pretense that we are the church of the Reformation and yet take one step after another to deny the Reformation in word and deed. Either "through faith alone" is the "article by which the church stands or falls" (*articulus stantis et cadentis ecclesiae*) or it is not. And if not, then it is no other article, including any article regarding some kind of church constitution. In the final analysis, it is senseless to maintain the confessional division. We could then form one national church with the Catholics. Either Luther correctly explained the Supper in the Sixth Chief Part or he did not. If so, then we must and ought remain with his teaching, as we expressly or tacitly have sworn in our ordination vow "to speak or write nothing publicly or privately against it." If Luther's explication is false, then we must, as painful as it would be, for the sake of truthfulness, renounce our vow. But we can under no circumstances speak and act *as though* it were correct, but in truth interpret it otherwise.

Since Schleiermacher, theology has for many theologians consisted of *the art of using the words of the church's confessions to teach the very opposite of what these confessions state*. This untruthfulness, which arose out of a deep philosophical distress, lies like a curse upon theological scholarship, and since it forced its way from scholarship into the praxis of the church, it has poisoned ecclesiastical life. This is the sickness from which the Evangelical Lutheran Church suffers. It has so deeply corroded the church that people no longer have any idea of how diseased this situation is. The common pastor of today no longer has any sense that it is a violation of the truth to teach the Sixth Chief Part in Luther's Catechism, but to explain it in a Calvinistic fashion. Many church governments appear completely unconcerned that we cannot in the sight of God solemnly swear candidates to confessions when neither the one ordaining nor the ordinand really know what these confessions contain. Indeed, it even happens from time to time that they do not even know which confessions they are dealing with. In the "Confessing Church" itself it is not understood that a Lutheran cannot ordain someone who is Reformed nor a Reformed [pastor] a Lutheran without the most terrible untruthfulness creeping into the ordination.

In this deep distress of our church lies one of the most important causes of why the *proclamation* of the Evangelical churches is largely without credibility and thus has become so ineffective. We ought not believe that the vehement contradiction and the terrifying indifference which our preaching meets is explained only by the contradiction of the natural man against God's Word. This contradiction has always been present, and it was also present at the time of the Reformation. He who knows but a little of the present spiritual life of the German people recognizes the powerful desire for certainty, for a final, incontrovertible truth. And the church must give an answer to this desire. For the world with its dogmas cannot provide an answer which will suffice for the duration. Indeed, it appears as though the dogmatic claims which today are made everywhere by the various philosophical systems are explained by the fact that the church no longer satisfies that desire. It was the great error of Protestantism in the eighteenth and nineteenth centuries that it thought it could pave the way for the modern world to Christianity by surrendering the church's doctrine. The only thing that it accomplished was that no one any longer took its proclamation seriously. For who should take a church seriously which no longer knew itself what it believed, taught, and confessed? Do we really believe that such a church could have been prepared to stand its ground in the gigantic battles to maintain the substance of Christianity in the once Christian peoples of the West? Neither ought we believe that a contempt for the church's confessions could enhance the authority of the Holy Scriptures. It is a completely incontrovertible fact of church history that the authority of the Bible stands and falls with the authority of the confessions which interpret the Bible. The greatest example of this is the Reformation itself. Without the confession of the church with its "service to the Word," with its respect for the Word, the Bible becomes the plaything of arbitrary, sectarian exposition. Is there a deeper, more humble exposition of the Holy Scriptures, more obedient to the Word than the confessional writings of our church? No one asserts that they say everything there is to be said. No one contests that there are truths of the Scriptures which must be still more deeply and better understood. No one claims infallibility for their statements and formulizations. But we do believe that the church can only be granted a new recognition and a deeper understanding of the Scriptures if it does not forget or despise the truth which was granted it in Luther's Reformation once and for all time.

1939

THE HOLY SUPPER AND THE FUTURE OF OUR CHURCH

A REFORMATION FESTIVAL ADDRESS IN A NEWLY CONSTRUCTED CHURCH[1]

This sermon is rich in the language of the Sacraments and the liturgy, and properly in that order. The liturgy serves the Sacraments. Indeed, the Sacraments, along with the Word, define the church.

Huss number 217
Hopf number 144

⚋⚋⚋

The message of the Reformation is inexhaustibly rich, as inexhaustible as the Gospel. It is finally at its deepest foundation nothing other than the Gospel itself. Thus we venture to single out a theme from the rich treasure which the doctrine of the Reformation means for us, a theme which in our time appears to be gaining a very unique importance for the church and which therefore concerns us all, pastors and congregational members alike. We desire to ask what *significance the Holy Supper has for the life and future of our church*. Our church, that is, the church of the Lutheran Reformation, the church which has baptized and confirmed us, the church in whose catechism we have been instructed, the church which has led our dear German people through four centuries, the church without which Germany would never be what it is today and without which none of us could conceive of the future history of our people. The events of recent years have made it necessary for all of us to more deeply consider her essence. And in so doing we have gained a deeper understanding than that of former generations of the great concern of the Reformer for her future. We have learned once again who is the sole Lord Protector of this church. We have learned once again, or have begun to learn what he has entrusted to our church: the pure Gospel of the justification of the sinner by faith alone; Holy Baptism; the Holy Supper of Jesus Christ. We

---

[1] This essay originally appeared as "Das Heilige Abendmahl und die Zukunft unserer Kirche: Ein Reformationsfest-Vortrag in einer neuerbauten Kirche" in *Predigtbuch der Lutherischen Kirche: Abendmahlspredigten* (ed. Friedrich Wilhelm Hopf; Erlangen: Martin Luther-Verlag, 1939), 156–67. MH

have learned what an enormous responsibility has thus been placed upon us. And we have once again learned to implore the Lord of the church with the fathers of the Reformation:

> That we keep pure till life is spent
> Your holy Word and Sacrament.[2]

If we desire to understand Luther's concern and the concern of the old Evangelical [Lutheran] Church to maintain the Sacrament of the Altar and keep it pure, then we must realize a fact which the majority of people in our church generally no longer understand: the fact, namely, that there would be no church at all without the Holy Supper. Where the church is, there the Supper is also celebrated; where the Supper is celebrated, there is the church. Where it is no longer celebrated, there the church dies. Our fathers knew this when in the great confessions of the Reformation they placed the Lord's Supper together with Holy Baptism immediately alongside the Gospel as an essential mark of the church which could not be surrendered.

Many people, also many Evangelical [Lutheran] Christians, no longer understand this at all today. But it must indeed give [one] much cause to consider that the experiences of the history of the church simply prove the Reformers correct. Can we conceive of the church at the time of the apostles without the breaking of the bread of the early congregation of Jerusalem, without the Lord's Supper of the Pauline congregations? Anyone who is familiar with the NT must answer no! A Sunday without the Supper, a Lord's Day without the Lord's Supper is inconceivable in the church of the NT. For the celebration of the Supper was the heartbeat of this church. In ancient times it was held behind closed doors, and this was not merely for fear of persecution. For all the rest of the Divine Service was public, accessible even to Jews and pagans, and this is the basic principle of the church even down to today. The preaching of the Gospel, according to the will of Jesus himself, should be public: "What I say to you in the dark, speak in the light; and what is whispered in your ear, preach from the roof tops!" [Matt 10:27]. "Go forth into all the world and preach the Gospel to all creatures!" [Mark 16:15]. The church has always allowed all people to come to its Divine Service on the basis of these basic principles, upon which is based the right to the free, public proclamation of the Gospel, acknowledged by all peoples of Christianity. Even the civilized pagan states do not contest this.

But the Supper was never for all those present, rather for the baptized and later for the confirmed. Only one who believes in Christ can understand the Supper. For everyone else it is necessarily inconceivable, senseless, and offensive.

---

[2]   Sasse quotes a favorite hymn, "Lord Jesus Christ, Will You Not Stay" (*Ach Bleib Bei Uns*), by Nikolaus Selnecker. This translation is from *Lutheran Worship* 344, stanza 2. These words are cited again later. MH

"Take, eat; this is my body. . . . Take and drink all of it: this cup is the new testament in my blood" [Matt 26:26–28]. What should the world say to such words? "He who eats my flesh and drinks my blood has eternal life, and I will raise him up on the last day" [John 6:54]. "This is a hard saying. Who can hear it?" [John 6:60]. If many of the disciples spoke thus and left him forever, what shall the world say to these words? Are not the most foolish rumors which circulated in the ancient world understandable? According to these rumors the Christians in their secret Divine Services practiced cannibalism. In a similar way Frederick the Great,[3] one of the least Christian great men of our people, ridiculed the Supper because there a man "should eat his God"! The church of all ages, misunderstood by the world, has always celebrated its Supper as it were "behind closed doors." But it knew that at every celebration of the Supper what is written in the Revelation of St. John again became true: "Behold! I stand at the door and knock. If anyone hears my voice and opens the door, I will come dwell with him and sup with him and he with me" [Rev 3:20].

The church of the NT learned this by experience at every celebration of the Supper, or, as this Sacrament was also called, the Eucharist, the prayer of thanks. Eucharist! He "took the bread, gave thanks, and broke it" [Matt 26:26]—this thanksgiving [*Danken*] the church then took over from him, and how it has made use of it! It belongs to the essence of the church that it can give thanks. Imagine what it would be like if the church were to disappear from among our people. Then for all time the great hymns of praise and thanksgiving would be silenced in our language—as has indeed already broadly occurred. But what is a people which can no longer sing a Te Deum? And we can indeed only sing it to the God and Father of our Lord Jesus Christ. It can only be sung at the altar. But there we can do so, indeed for all time.

The church once sang its powerful Te Deum laudamus upon the ruins of the ancient world in the days of the migration of peoples: "Lord God, we praise you; Lord God, we thank you." In the midst of the distress of the Thirty Years' War the German Te Deum rang out in our church: "Now thank we all our God!" The church had learned this thanksgiving from her Lord: "He took bread, gave thanks, and broke it" [Matt 26:26]. "I praise you, Father and Lord of heaven and earth, that you have hidden these things from the wise and intelligent and have revealed them to infants" [Matt 11:25]. Indeed, the church learned to praise and give thanks in his thanksgiving and in his praise. With her thanksgiving she joins together in his, in the praise which the eternal Son brings to the Father. The church learned this in the Eucharist, in the Supper, just as she on the whole first

---

[3] This is a reference to Frederick II (1712–1786). He is not to be confused with Frederick William of Brandenburg (1620–1688), who was known as "the Great Elector." Frederick the Great was a religious skeptic whose religion was "duty." RF

learned there to pray correctly. For the *liturgy*, the prayer of the church, proceeds from the celebration of the Supper.

Our Bavarian Territorial Church is among those fortunate churches which, by God's mercy, without any merit or worthiness in us, and through the service of genuine men of God in the previous century, has maintained a rich treasure of the old liturgical heritage [*Gebetsgut*] of the church. Do we realize that our liturgy in large measure goes right back to the Supper of the ancient church? How thoughtlessly we so often hear the altar prayer which begins with "The Lord be with you—and with your spirit" and which ends with the words "through Jesus Christ, your beloved Son, our Lord." Do we realize what this "The Lord be with you—and with your spirit," which comes from the Supper liturgy of the second century, perhaps even from the time of the apostles, means? It is not only the pastor and the congregation who pray here. Another prays with them, the merciful High Priest who always is interceding before his heavenly Father for us. He makes our prayer his, and this "prayer in the name of Jesus" is received as the prayer of Jesus by the One who has promised to hear us—through Jesus Christ our Lord.

Thus we could proceed piece by piece through the liturgy and find therein the remnants of the early church's celebration of the Supper: in the Kyrie and in the Gloria, in the "Lift up your hearts—we lift them up unto the Lord" and in the "Holy, holy, holy is the Lord," which the church since the first century has sung at the celebration of the Supper. And we could proceed from the liturgy to the life of the congregation, to the work of love of the diaconate which proceeds from the celebration of the Supper, or even to such external matters as the manner in which the church is constituted. Everywhere we would find confirmation for the principle for the ancient church that *the Supper is the very heartbeat of the church*.

This also applies, and perhaps in a special way, to the churches of Christianity in which the Gospel has been forgotten or completely falsified. We know what a difficult struggle Luther fought against the destruction of the Gospel in the medieval Roman Church. We know how he found this destruction to be most dangerous in the *Mass* of the Papal Church. In the Smalcald Articles he posed with complete clarity the antithesis which obtained between him and Rome in this regard: Campegio,[4] the papal legate, had said at the Augsburg *Reichstag* ["Imperial Diet"] in 1530 that "he would be torn to pieces before he would relinquish the Mass, so by the help of God, I [Luther], too, would suffer myself to be reduced to ashes before I would allow a hireling of the Mass [be he good or bad] to be equal to Christ Jesus, my Lord and Savior, or to be exalted above him" [SA II II 10].[5] No one can criticize the doctrine of the Roman Church on the sacrifice

---

[4]   Lorenzo Campeggio (1472–1539) was nuncio at the imperial court (1513–1517) and papal legate to England (1518). He was made cardinal in 1517 and archbishop of Bologna in 1523. He was sent to Germany to contend on behalf of papal interests. He was at Augsburg with Charles V in 1530, where he tried to bribe Melanchthon (*ODCC*, 273–74; *Lutheran Cyclopedia*, 127). MH

[5]   Luther mentions this story several times (for example, *LW* 47:45; *LW* 54:215–16). RF

of the Mass as a human work more sharply than did Luther. No one had seen more clearly than Luther how the Supper of Christ had here been given a new interpretation by people.

But the very same Luther also acknowledged that under all the human reinterpretations, distortions, and additions, the institution of Christ was still present. Thus, as in the *Hagia Sophia*, the great church of Constantinople, which the Turks had made into a mosque, the glorious old mosaic of *Christus Pantocrator*[6] was still present under the layers of plaster and glimmered through. Therefore he [Luther] did not destroy the Mass, rather purified it. He once confessed

> before God and the whole world that . . . where according to Christ's order the Mass is held, be it among us Lutherans or in the papacy or in Greece or in India, even if it be under one form, which is indeed incorrect and a misuse, as happens in the papacy around Easter or other times of the year when they provide the Sacrament to the people, thus is same true body of Christ given for us on the cross [present] under the form of the bread and the true blood of Christ shed for us [present] under the form of the wine.[7]

If this were not so, where would the Holy Supper have been in the many centuries of the Middle Ages? But it was an inconceivable thought to our Reformers that all the millions of our people through the seven hundred years in which the church had already existed in Germany had in the Sacrament of the Altar perhaps not received what was given therein: the body and blood of the Lord and with it the forgiveness of sins, life, and salvation. Luther at least took the institution of Christ this seriously. He generally acknowledged [the real presence of the body and blood of Christ] where the command of the Lord "This do in remembrance of me" was still followed in accord with the Words of Institution. So we also make the validity of Baptism dependent not on the faith or life of the one baptizing, but only on it being carried out in accord with its institution. But if this is so, then we grasp the source of life of the Catholic churches at its most profound basis. The source of the life of the Roman Church today is not the fact that it has a pope and cardinals, or bishops and archbishops. Its life does not depend on the fact that it possesses powerful external means and great wealth. The theology of the Jesuits and Benedictines does not sustain its life, nor does the veneration of relics and the cult of Mary. Neither does it live from the sacrifice of the Mass—for there is no such thing, because the one, sole sacrifice through which we have been reconciled with God can in no way be repeated nor does it require completion. The Catholic Church lives only and alone from the remnant of the holy Gospel, which underneath everything is still alive—from the Gospel, the joyous message of the forgiveness of sins, which, though generally otherwise forgotten, still lives in the

---

[6] *Pantocrator* is Greek for "Almighty [Ruler]." Reference is here made to the mosaic of Christ on his throne. RF

[7] WA 38.264.26 ff.; cf. *LW* 38:224. RF

Words of Institution: "Given and shed for you for the forgiveness of sins." It lives from the fact that Jesus Christ, as he has promised, is really and personally present in this Sacrament. And it is exactly the same with the churches of the East and in the poor, weak remnants of the church which have been preserved in the Islamic countries, in Africa and the Near East. Externally nearly destroyed, internally fallen, they live through the centuries. From what do they live? What has saved them from complete ruin? The answer is found by reading her liturgy. There it is, often deeply hidden under the rubble which the centuries of human tradition have laid over it, the last treasure of the church, the remnant of the early Christian Supper.

Thus the experiences of the history of the church verify the truth which Luther found in the NT. There is an indissoluble connection between church and Supper, between the Supper and the Gospel. This also explains the passionate fight which Luther led to maintain the biblical Supper. Over against Rome he had to fight for the maintenance of the pure Sacrament. With the same passion, however, he fought against a *false Protestantism*, which no longer understood the Sacrament. This Protestantism in rejecting the heresy of Rome regarding the sacrifice of the Mass and transubstantiation rejected also the real presence of the body and blood of Christ under the forms of the bread and the wine. Luther truly knew what the church of the Word is. But he also knew why he placed the Sacrament next to the Word. And the entire old Evangelical [Lutheran] Church was completely clear about why it prayed with such passion:

> That we keep pure till life is spent
> Your holy Word and Sacrament.

It knew that the Gospel cannot be purely maintained if the Sacrament was allowed to decay. It knew that a church could not remain an evangelical church for the duration if it did not purely preserve the Sacraments of the Lord. Therefore the Lutheran Reformation protested against the Protestantism for which the Sacraments were only an appendage to the Word, comparable to a seal on an old parchment. Thus it passionately protested against the Protestantism which rejected the necessity of the Baptism of children, maintaining with Calvin that the children of Christians were already holy in and of themselves, without Baptism. Thus the old Evangelical [Lutheran] Church passionately protested against a Protestantism which made out of the celebration of the Supper a celebration of a merely spiritual fellowship with Christ, as though the Supper were nothing other than the fulfillment of this promise: "Where two or three are gathered in my name, there I am in their midst" [Matt 18:20]. This explains why in the Lutheranism of the sixteenth and seventeenth centuries the Supper maintained its position in the Divine Service. A Sunday Divine Service whose highpoint was not the Supper would have been inconceivable in Nuremberg of the seventeenth century. The objection that the *sermon* should be the chief thing would not have been at all understood. No one can maintain that when this was the case the sermon had become too short. Quite the opposite! The Evangelical [Lutheran] sermon, that is, the sermon in which Christ and his merit were actually proclaimed, had its great era in Protestant Germany when it preceded the celebration of the Supper. It was at the same time when the great churchly theology bloomed in Germany, the great hymnody and the great church music. Johann Sebastian Bach produced his powerful compositions in a church in which there still stood an altar about which Sunday after Sunday the congregation assembled for the celebration of the Supper.

But then came the great turn of events in the eighteenth century. There began that sinister event in the Evangelical [Lutheran] churches of Germany which we can call the dying of the Sacrament. We can clarify this by way of a few examples, from the statistics from Silesia, a country which in the eighteenth century had still proportionally least felt the effects of the Enlightenment. In the decade from 1701 to 1710, 196,526 guests had gone to the Supper per year in Görlitz. In the decade from 1791 to 1800, the average yearly attendance was 95,743 guests. That means that within 80 years there were suddenly 100,000 fewer each year, thus nearly 2,000 fewer people attended every Sunday! At one particular city church in Breslau, attendance at the Supper sank from 35,950 communicants in the year 1701, to 9,500 in the year 1800. That is an average [decrease] of from 700 to 180 every Sunday. The numbers for the other regions of Germany are not available to me—but they are similar for all of German Protestantism. These are the effects of a single century. It is necessary to note that the Divine Service had at that time already been completely changed. In spite of everything, the Supper numbers for the year 1800 are still amazingly high. The development seems to have continued in the same manner in the nineteenth century.

Since the previous century, we are accustomed to painstakingly reckoning the numbers according to the methods of modern statistics. The results of course are not always entirely unequivocally clear. In one and the same territorial church there are congregations with very high and others with very low communicant numbers. In the statistics this is not apparent. Furthermore, the statistics never say whether a small number of communicants attend the Table of the Lord often or a larger number once during the year. The numbers are always extraordinarily instructive. I'll mention only the most important areas of the church and indeed the statistics for the year 1931, thus before the church struggle: Of 100 Evangelicals (children also included in the statistics) in the territorial churches of Schaumburg-Lippe 59 [attended the Supper], Bavaria 58, Hessen-Kassel 55, Waldeck 52, Hessen 41, Hanover—Lutheran 40 (Reformed 9), Baden 38, Württemberg 36, Palatinate 34, Nassau 32, Lippe 30, Reuss 26, Saxony 22, Old Prussia 21 (Grenzmark 52, Silesia 33, Saxony 19, Rheinland 18, Berlin 8), Mecklenburg-Schwerin 20, Thüringia 19, Braunschweig 16, Anhalt 15, Mecklenburg-Strelitz 13, Schleswig-Holstein 11, Oldenburg 9, Lübeck 8, Hamburg 5, Bremen 5. The average for the entire sphere of the federation of churches at that time was 25 percent, that is, of 100 Evangelicals, 25 still went to the Supper. In 1920 it was still 30 per 100.

The numbers for the half century from 1880 to 1930 have been calculated, and it has been found that with slight variations they fell for the first time to 40 per hundred in 1904. They reached 39 in 1914 after climbing 7 percent, but otherwise have continued to fall uniformly. Since 1920 the number is under 30. Apparently we now have seen throughout Germany a participation in the Supper of just over 20 percent.

This is a very shocking picture, especially since the inexorable statistics show that hitherto this development has never been able to be halted. The numbers are all the more shocking when we compare them to the communicant statistics of Roman Catholic Germany. While of 100 Evangelicals 25 went to the Supper in 1931, among the Catholics the number of communicants in the same year came to 1,124 per 100 church members. The number for 1936 is 1,396, which means every German Catholic goes to the Supper nearly 14 times a year. To be sure the circumstances within the various confessions cannot be compared without further consideration (indeed, the number of times the sermon is heard also needs to be compared). Finally it can be said that the Supper, if this trend continues, is on the verge of becoming in Germany a privilege of the Catholic Church! In broad areas among us it is already generally at the very point of becoming extinct. For when of 100 church members only 5 (including confirmands) go to the Supper, then the Supper is practically as good as extinct. We are at the point of becoming a church without the Supper and leaving the Supper to the Catholic Church. What would Luther have to say to a church which has come to this? Would not a church without the Supper be for him a much greater abomination than a church with the sacrifice of the Mass? We must also consider that the loss of the Supper has consequences. Where the Supper has become extinct, there the Divine Service in general has become extinct. For ten years already now in Germany we have had villages where Sunday after Sunday the Divine Service has ceased because no one any longer came. Shall this really be the fate of the Evangelical [Lutheran] Church of Germany? NO! We will implore God that he open our eyes to this profound distress of the church, that he open our eyes to the glory of his gifts of grace, before it is too late.

We must hold these sobering facts before our eyes if we are to grasp *Luther's* great concern to *preserve the Sacrament*. One of the most profound theological perceptions which God had graciously given Luther, one of the greatest things which Luther had learned from the NT was that he understood how closely the Supper and the Gospel are connected. You can by no means preserve saving faith in the merit of your Lord Jesus Christ if you do not ever and again come to his Table, where he himself gives to you anew the profit of his bitter suffering and death: "Take and eat, this is my body which is given for you. Take, drink all of it. This cup is the new testament in my blood, which is poured out for you and for many for the forgiveness of sins." Where the Supper is no longer celebrated, experience shows that the concept of sacrifice is no longer understood. Where the Supper is no longer celebrated, there faith in the Son of God as the Lamb of God who consequently bore your sins dies. But where this faith dies, there the church also dies. There her profound, blessed mystery is no longer understood. Since the collapse of the Supper in German Protestantism of the eighteenth and nineteenth centuries, the church is understood among us Evangelicals [Lutherans] as a philosophical or religious society. People join it, so it is believed, in order to foster a philosophical worldview. This worldview is faith. They build their meeting places—these are church buildings. They have their solemn ceremonies—these are the Sacraments. According to this view, the church is finally nothing other than one fellowship with a philosophical worldview alongside others. It is a place where the religious man has his spiritual needs satisfied. And if he discovers that other fellowships can do this better, then he leaves the church.

But the church is in truth something completely different. The Supper tells us what it is. It was in the Supper that Paul once learned to understand that the church is the *body of Christ*. Because Jesus Christ, both High Priest and sacrificial Lamb, gives us his body and blood to eat and drink, we who were once incorporated into him in Holy Baptism will be preserved in fellowship with him. It is a miraculous eating and drinking, indeed, just as the fellowship with him is something for which there is no possible comparison. It is a *miracle*, like the eating of the manna and the drinking of the water from the rock in the OT, to which Paul compares it [see 1 Corinthians 10–11]. It is a miracle like that of the feeding of the five thousand. Marvelous is this presence of Christ, who is among us, not only spiritually, not only in remembrance and in hope, but in the divine mystery of the real and essential presence. It is the *entire* Christ who is present—true God, begotten of the Father from eternity, and also true man, born of the Virgin Mary, the crucified and risen one, who descended to hell and ascended into heaven. He is there, in the midst of his church: "Behold there the tabernacle of God is among men" [Rev 21:3]. What one day will be fulfilled in the kingdom of God is present already here. He who will one day come in glory is already present here hidden.

When you enter a Catholic Church in Upper Bavaria or in other regions where there is heavy tourist traffic, you can often read an inscription which is intended for the non-Catholic visitor. "This church," so it is stated, "is a true house of God, where the God-man, Jesus Christ, is present and adored in the tabernacle, under the forms the bread and wine." No matter what we as Evangelical [Lutheran] Christians always have to say against [reserving the elements in] the tabernacle and against the false conceptions which are attached to it, such an inscription presents us with a serious question and admonition. In which sense are *our* churches really and truly houses of God? In which sense are they places of the real and essential presence of Christ? We can desire nothing more beautiful and greater for our houses of God than that they be places where the Holy Supper is celebrated according to the institution of Christ, and a believing congregation is gathered about the altar to receive the true body and the true blood of our Lord. Only then will the church of the Gospel, the church of the pure doctrine remain among us. Only then will it remain, but it will truly remain, "and the gates of hell shall not overpower her" [Matt 16:18]. And everywhere a congregation is gathered about her altar in the deep faith in the one who is her Lord and her Head because he is her Redeemer, where she sings the Kyrie and the Gloria and lifts her heart to heaven and with all angels and archangels and the entire company of heaven sings, "Holy, holy, holy" to the Triune God—there will her church be a true house of God, a place of the real presence of Christ in the midst of a boisterous and unholy world. And this text will apply to her: "The LORD is in his temple! Let all the world be silent before him!" [Hab 2:20].

INDEX